The Military Revolution Debate

HISTORY AND WARFARE
Arther Ferrill, *Series Editor*

THE MILITARY REVOLUTION DEBATE

Readings on the Military
Transformation of Early Modern Europe

edited by

CLIFFORD J. ROGERS

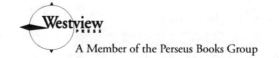

A Member of the Perseus Books Group

History and Warfare

Copyright © 1995 by Westview Press, Inc, A Member of the Perseus Books Group

Published in 1995 in the United States of America by Westview Press, Inc., 5500 Central Avenue, Boulder, Colorado 80301-2877, and in the United Kingdom by Westview Press, 12 Hid's Copse Road, Cumnor Hill, Oxford OX2 9JJ

Library of Congress Cataloging-in-Publication Data
The military revolution debate : Readings on the military transformation of early modern Europe /
    edited by Clifford J. Rogers.
        p.   cm. — (History and warfare)
    Includes bibliographical references and index.
    ISBN 0-8133-2053-4. — ISBN 0-8133-2054-2 (pbk.)
    1. Europe—History, Military.   2. Europe—History—1517–1648.
I. Rogers, Clifford J.   II. Series.
D231.M55   1995
355'.0094—dc20   94-45319
                                                                                                                      CIP

Printed and bound in the United States of America

 The paper used in this publication meets the requirements
of the American National Standard for Permanence of Paper
for Printed Library Materials Z39.48-1984.

Contents

Rejoinder

Preface

THE 1991 MEETING OF the American Military Institute, held in Durham, North Carolina, witnessed a truly extraordinary conference session. Four historians each gave a short presentation, then the discussion was thrown open. It seemed that everyone in the audience had something to say—a question to ask, a fact to offer, an interpretation to suggest. Ideas flew across the room until the last moment of the time allocated to the session, and afterwards two different historians commented to panel members that it had been the most remarkable conference discussion in their experience.

The topic that had evoked so much interest and debate was, of course, the "Military Revolution" in early modern Europe. The excitement generated by that roundtable discussion inspired me to begin the process of putting together this book—which includes, along with other key essays on the military revolution, article-length versions of each of the short presentations that began that session. Consequently, I wish to dedicate this anthology to my fellow panel members (and mentors)—John F. Guilmartin, Jr., John A. Lynn, and Geoffrey Parker—and to all those who participated in the debate and discussion that day.

Clifford J. Rogers

Credits

Chapter 1 is a revision of an inaugural lecture delivered before The Queen's University of Belfast on 21 January 1955; it was first published in its current form in Michael Roberts, *Essays in Swedish History* (Minneapolis, 1967), pp. 195–225. It is reprinted here by the kind permission of the author.

An earlier version of Chapter 2 was originally published in *Journal of Modern History* 48 (1976), pp. 195–214. The revised version, reprinted here with the gracious permission of the author, was originally published in Geoffrey Parker, *Spain and the Netherlands 1559–1659: Ten Studies* (London, 1979), pp. 86–103.

Chapter 3, which is printed here with some revisions, first appeared in *Journal of Military History* 57 (1993), pp. 241–278. It is republished with the generous permission of the Society for Military History.

Chapter 5 originally appeared in a somewhat shorter form in *French Historical Studies* 18 (1994), pp. 881–906; the author wishes to thank the editors of *French Historical Studies* (and its publisher, Duke University Press) for permission to reprint the article in this volume.

Chapter 6 first appeared in its current form in Michael Duffy (ed.), *The Military Revolution and the State, 1500–1800: Exeter Studies in History 1* (Exeter, 1980), pp. 29–48. It is reprinted with the gracious permission of the University of Exeter Press. Parts of this chapter have been extracted from the author's "The Welfare of the French Foot-Soldier from Richelieu to Napoleon," *History* (1980). They are reproduced here with the kind permission of the editor of *History*.

Chapter 7 first appeared in *Journal of Military History* 55 (1991). It is reprinted here with the generous permission of the Society for Military History.

Chapter 9 first appeared in *Militärgeschichtliche Mitteilungen* 18, no. 2 (1985). It is reprinted here with the generous permission of the editors.

Chapter 10 first appeared in John A. Lynn (ed.), *The Tools of War* (Champaign: University of Illinois Press, 1990). Copyright 1990 by the Board of Trustees of the University of Illinois. Used with the permission of the University of Illinois Press.

It should be noted that some typographical errors in the original versions of articles reprinted in this volume have been corrected.

The Military Revolution in History and Historiography

CLIFFORD J. ROGERS

"THE ORDINARY THEME and argument of history," wrote Sir Walter Raleigh early in the seventeenth century, "is war."[1] Few of his contemporaries would have disagreed with this assessment: as J. R. Hale has pointed out, "there was probably no single year throughout the period in which there was neither war nor occurrences which looked and felt remarkably like it."[2] Until recently, however, most academic historians have treated war and military affairs as subjects of tertiary interest at best, completely overshadowed in importance by social and economic structures and processes.

I am by no means one to disregard the importance of economic forces in history. There can be little doubt, for instance, that the development of civilization proper along the banks of the Nile, Indus, Yellow, and Tigris and Euphrates Rivers can be rivalled only by the Industrial Revolution as a key turning point in human history, or that both of these were, first and foremost, economic phenomena. But if the "carrot" of the production and allocation of wealth is one of the basic motive forces of history, the "stick" of the creation and application of coercive force is the other. The walls of Uruk, like the steam-powered European gunboats that coursed the Yangtze in the nineteenth century, symbolize how economic and military developments almost inevitably go hand in hand. Control over the means of violence, as sociologists from Aristotle to Weber and Andreski have argued, can have as much impact on social and political systems as does control over the means of production.[3]

Unfortunately, however, military history has been nowhere near as successful as economic history in integrating its material into the "big picture" presented in general histories. There are exceptions, of course—Heinrich Brunner and Lynn White, for example, enjoyed remarkable success in arguing that the rise of heavy cavalry to military predominance in Western Europe laid the foundation for the feudal system, and so for medieval society as a whole.[4] In general, though, mili-

1

tary historians have been much more effective in showing how revolutions in military technique and technology can transform the art of war than in showing how the resulting changes in warfare can alter entire *societies*.[5] As Michael Roberts put it, "the experts in military history have been mostly content to describe what happened, without being overmuch concerned to trace out broader effects; while social historians have not been very apt to believe that the new fashions in tactics, or improvements of weapon-design, were likely to prove of much significance."[6]

Yet it would be fair to say that at least one area of historical scholarship has done a good job of weaving the thread of military history into the overall picture it presents. Ever since the mid-1950s, the "Military Revolution," as Roberts dubbed it, has been thoroughly integrated into the canon of early modern European history—and, increasingly, into early modern world history as well. As described in Roberts' brilliant and seminal 1956 article on the subject, the Military Revolution centered on tactical reforms undertaken by Maurice of Nassau and Gustavus Adolphus, most notably a return to linear formations for shot-armed infantry and aggressive charges for cavalry. These tactical changes required more highly trained and disciplined soldiers; this led to the general adoption of drill, uniforms, and standing armies organized into smaller, more standardized units. These armies rapidly grew to unprecedented size as a "result of a revolution in strategy, made possible by the revolution in tactics, and made necessary by the circumstances of the Thirty Years' War."[7]

At this point, Roberts' analysis of military changes merges into a consideration of their constitutional and societal impact. Larger, more permanent armies and the more intensive marshaling of resources which they required "led inevitably to an increase in the authority of the state." Governments used that authority, backed by new-style armies, to impose far heavier burdens (taxes, *corvées*, and other impositions) than ever before on society at large, so that warfare on the vast new scale could be fought. In order to manage and direct these resources, governments had to employ a host of new officials. Thus, the centrally organized, bureaucratically governed nation-state—the paramount symbol of the modern era—ultimately grew from the tiny seed of late-sixteenth century tactical reforms. Military factors played a key, even a pre-eminent, role in shaping the modern world.

Over the nearly four decades since Roberts first presented his thoughts on the Military Revolution, a number of historians, Geoffrey Parker foremost among them, have studied, discussed, and debated nearly every aspect of his argument. Many elements of Roberts' conception have been convincingly challenged; new analytical components added; and different interpretations of its significance put forward. But the essential point is that these scholars never lost sight of the need to keep discussions of military matters closely tied to the impact they had on society as a whole.

That is why the Military Revolution in early modern Europe is as important historiographically as it was historically. In addition to helping us understand such diverse issues as bureaucratization, the nature of revolutions, state formation, and the rise of the West—as well as specific historical episodes from the Wars of Italy to the Thirty Years War to the British conquest of India—the active and wide-ranging debate over the Military Revolution has brought the explanatory value of military history to the attention of the historical community as a whole. Only four decades ago, academic military history in the United States was almost non-existent; today, even an economic/social historian like Princeton's Charles Tilly can comment that "military competition ... underlay both the creation and the ultimate predominance of the national state."[8] The ongoing Military Revolution debate is at least partially responsible for this historiographical revolution.

COURSE OF THE DEBATE

Roberts' article immediately found wide acceptance among early modern historians, partly because Sir George Clark incorporated the idea of the Military Revolution into his 1958 *War and Society in the Seventeenth Century*.[9] A somewhat revised version of "The Military Revolution, 1560–1660" appeared in Roberts' 1967 *Essays in Swedish History* (and is reprinted here), but the minimal scale of the alterations after ten years demonstrates how successfully the piece had avoided criticism. Indeed, it was only after *another* decade had passed that the first major revision of the Military Revolution thesis appeared, with Geoffrey Parker's "The 'Military Revolution', 1560–1660—a myth?"

As we might expect from a biographer of Gustavus Adolphus, Michael Roberts had made Sweden and the Thirty Years War the focus of his analysis. Parker, primarily a Spanish historian (and later a biographer of Philip II), expanded the Military Revolution theme both geographically and chronologically to embrace what some have termed the "Hapsburg hegemony." Although he pointed out that the roots of the Military Revolution extended back as far as the 1430s,[10] he concentrated on the period 1530–1710. The regression of the starting date by thirty years, though seemingly innocuous, had major conceptual repercussions. Parker accepted the key importance of the growth of armies over this period, but argued that since the first surge in military manpower came *before* the reforms even of Gustavus' predecessor, Maurice of Nassau, the tactical developments described by Roberts could not be the cause of the gargantuan armies which stalked the fields of early modern Europe.

To provide an alternative explanation for this phenomenon, Parker turned to the new style of artillery fortifications developed in Italy in the first decades of the sixteenth century, the *trace italienne*. The superb ability of this type of fortress to resist both bombardment and infantry assault tipped the strategic balance in favor of the defensive. Battles became "irrelevant—and therefore unusual"; war became primarily an affair of sieges. Siege warfare, with its vast entrenchments and numerous garrisons, demanded money and manpower on an unprecedented scale—at the same time as the growth of the population and wealth of Europe made it possible to meet that demand. By emphasizing the *trace italienne,* Parker added a key new ingredient to the Military Revolution debate: military technology as a causative factor.[11]

The publication of his article in 1976 in the prestigious *Journal of Modern History* already signalled a breadth of interest in this conception. Parker's ideas were soon incorporated into wide-ranging studies like William H. McNeill's *The Pursuit of Power.*[12] Though somewhat altered, the basic idea of the Military Revolution continued to hold the high ground both in early modern and in military historiography. Further work in the field began to appear, including Colin Jones' "The Military Revolution and the Professionalisation of the French Army under the Ancien Régime" and the other two articles in Michael Duffy's *The Military Revolution and the State, 1500–1800.*[13] These studies tended both to expand the dates of Military Revolution even further, and also to re-emphasize the connections between the Military Revolution and state formation, bureaucratization, and military professionalization. While Roberts and Parker had mentioned the greater impact of the new large armies on society, Jones' article spelled out the details of plundering, taxation, billeting, and *Kontributions.* It also pointed out the transition from the *ad hoc* mobilizing expedients of the early Military Revolution, "cobbled together with an almost prodigal delegation of powers," to the more systematized, professional (even "absolutist") methods of the later *ancien régime.*[14]

After what had been a gradual evolution of the debate,[15] there was an explosion of scholarship in the mid-1980s, which can be said to have revolutionized the study of the phenomenon. David Parrott published his "Strategy and tactics in the Thirty Years War: the 'military revolution,'" which offered what may be the most important critique of the entire Military Revolution thesis yet produced, in 1985.[16] Parrott pointed out that, before making arguments based on tactical reforms, historians should look carefully at how battles were actually fought. His conclusion—that the tactical reforms described by Roberts were in practice nearly irrelevant to the battles after the Swedish invasion of Germany[17]—is certainly open to debate; but the questions he asks, and the issues he raises, are important ones. Rather than emphasizing tactical or technological factors, Parrott turned to logistic and political influences when addressing the subject of army growth. This, too, has had a lasting impact on the historiography.

No fewer than four studies of the impact of the Military Revolution in Scandinavia appeared between 1983 and 1985.[18] J. R. Hale's masterly 1985 study, *War and Society in Renaissance Europe, 1450–1620,* devoted a chapter to what he termed the "Military Reformation."[19] In the same year, John Lynn contributed a study of French tactical developments, 1560–1660, arguing that the French evolved the small tactical units and linear infantry formations typical of the Military Revolution independently of Dutch and Swedish developments.[20] In 1986 Gunther Rothenberg published an excellent study on the Military Revolution in the seventeenth century, focussing on its intellectual component, while Pepper and Adams'

Firearms and Fortifications offered a valuable case-study of the impact of *trace italienne* fortifications.[21] The high point of this burst of scholarly effort came with the publication of Parker's 1984 Lee Knowles lectures as *The Military Revolution: Military innovation and the rise of the West, 1500–1800* in 1988.

The Military Revolution—which this anthology is intended to complement—attracted a great deal of attention, even before it won the Best Book Award of the American Military Institute (1989) and the Dexter Prize for the best book on the history of technology published between 1987 and 1990.[22] It offered a number of refinements to earlier work, including a survey of the military changes (or lack thereof) away from the "heartland" of the Revolution, in areas like Britain and Eastern Europe, where cavalry retained more of its old importance and the *trace italienne* remained rare. Logistics, recruitment, and military organization received more in-depth treatment, and the naval aspects of the Military Revolution, *per se,* were given their first real analysis. All of this material provided ammunition for Parker to make his main point: that "the key to the Westerners' success in creating the first truly global empires between 1500 and 1750 depended upon precisely those improvements in the ability to wage war which have been termed 'the military revolution.' "[23]

"Who is so thoughtless and lazy," asked the historian Polybius in the second century B.C., "that he does not want to know how ... the Romans, in less than 53 years, conquered nearly the entire inhabited world and brought it under their rule—an achievement previously unheard of?"[24] If the rise of Rome to imperial power continues to hold our interest today, it is easy to see why Europe's ascension to genuinely global predominance—so much more immediate—is a subject few students of history can resist. By harnessing the concept of the Military Revolution to this issue, Parker added substantially to its breadth and its importance. Henceforth it would be clear that the consequences of military innovation in early modern Europe belonged at least as much to World as to European History.

The pace of publications relating to the Military Revolution has continued unabated up to the present. Simon Adams, in his 1990 "Tactics or Politics? 'The Military Revolution' and the Hapsburg Hegemony, 1525–1648," follows David Parrott's lead in arguing against tactical or technological causes for army growth, which he sees as resulting more from changing political balances and strategic approaches. Adams also claims that the great increase in military manpower usually attributed to the Thirty Years War took place almost entirely on paper: "the number of effectives rose but little, and the scale of battles and campaigns was unchanged."[25]

John Lynn, one of the most important writers on the Military Revolution, is equally skeptical of the significance assigned by Parker to bastioned-trace fortifications. Lynn's "The *trace italienne* and the Growth of Armies: The French Case" offers a powerful critique of a technologically-based view of the Military Revolution, and stresses the growing population and wealth of Europe as the key factors behind the development of the massive armed forces of the sixteenth and seventeenth centuries.

In addition to Lynn's article, 1991 also saw the publication of Jeremy Black's short monograph, *A Military Revolution? Military Change and European Society,* which attacked the Military Revolution thesis by emphasizing continuity rather than change in early modern European warfare. Black's study also argued that the major changes in matters military which *did* take place belonged primarily to the period *after* 1660. This changed chronology implies that absolutism was more the cause than the result of the Military Revolution. He has taken up this later period again in his new article, "A Military Revolution? A 1660–1792 Perspective," which appears for the first time in this anthology. This piece helps to round out our view of the Military Revolution, which tends to focus too much on the first half of the 1500–1800 period. After all, it was only in the century after the failure of the siege of Vienna in 1683 that Western European arms showed a reasonably consistent ability to overcome their most advanced opponents—Ottomans, Mughals, and other civilizations with developed gunpowder technology.

Although Black deals mainly with changes in the art of war from 1660–1720, he also credits the years 1470–1530 and 1792–1815 with "revolutionary" status in military history.[26] This echoes the argument of my own 1993 article, "The Military Revolutions of the Hundred Years' War," which holds that the military innovations which underlay the rise of the West did not occur in a single revolution, but rather through a process of "punctuated equilibrium evolution"—that is, through a series of intense revolutionary episodes, each built on a more extended base of slow evolutionary change. This process began with the "Infantry Revolution" of the fourteenth century and the "Artillery Revolution" of the fifteenth, and has continued to the present day. Each revolutionary period in military affairs has had dramatic consequences for the history of Europe, and eventually for the world.[27]

Like my own article, John Lynn's recently published study, "Recalculating French Army Growth during the *Grand Siècle,* 1610–1715," is presented here with some revisions, consisting mainly of expanded documentation in the endnotes.[28] The importance of army growth in the Military Revolution has received universal agreement, though its causes have not. Lynn's article, taking France as a case study, subjects this key issue to the most rigorous analysis it has yet received. This provides relatively hard data with which historians can test the various paradigmatic approaches to the Military Revolution, on one of its analytical axes at least.

Another case-study which emphasizes the importance of army growth is I. A. A. Thompson's "'Money, money, and yet more money!' Finance, the Fiscal-State, and the Military Revolution: Spain 1500–1650." From the first, scholars have emphasized how the Military Revolution imposed unprecedented burdens on both state and society in early modern Europe, burdens reflected in higher taxation and more elaborate bureaucracies. In Spain, for example, royal expenditures (nine-tenths of which went to pay for wars present or past) roughly quadrupled in real terms between 1500 and 1650.[29] Thompson's article, written for *The Military Revolution Debate,* studies this phenomenon in detail, elucidating both its causes and its effects. One of his important conclusions is that the great bulk of the increase in military expenditure can be attributed directly to the growth of military manpower—not to tactical or technological changes related to the general adoption of gunpowder weapons or to the cost of the *trace italienne*. Perhaps even more significant is the article's argument that the fiscal pressures of hegemonic war would not necessarily drive a "coercion-extraction cycle"[30] leading to the increased power and capability of the bureaucratic central state.[31] Instead, the need to marshal ever-greater war resources could force the center to make political concessions in order to gain the cooperation of the periphery in raising the necessary finances.

Thomas Arnold's new contribution, "Fortifications and the Military Revolution: The Gonzaga Experience, 1530–1630," points out another way in which the Military Revolution could work *against* the centralizing tendencies of the emerging nation-states. Through a careful study of how the *trace italienne* molded the political and military strategy—and, ultimately, the fate—of the Duchies of Mantua and Monferrat, Arnold shows how the defensive power of fortifications *alla moderna* could place a stumbling block in front of the ambitions of expansionist or centralizing royal governments, much as medieval stone castles had done before the Artillery Revolution of the fifteenth century. Arnold's conclusions, like Thompson's, argue against the widely held belief that only the emerging Great Powers could afford the state-of-the-art military technology of the early modern period.

One of the growing "gunpowder empires" which stumbled over the *trace italienne* was the Ottoman state.[32] In another article published here for the first time, John F. Guilmartin, Jr., looks at how the military innovations arising from the Wars of Italy helped the Hapsburgs check the Porte's expansion in the Balkans. "The Military Revolution: Origins and First Tests Abroad" also looks at three other early 16th-century cases: the handful of Spanish conquistadors who overwhelmed the Inca and Aztec empires, the Portuguese soldier-merchants who so rapidly seized control over the Indian Ocean, and the various powers who struggled for control of the Mediterranean through the end of the century. By showing us how the European arms forged by the early Military Revolution fared against opponents of various levels of technological and military sophistication, Guilmartin's article helps us analyze which innovations in the craft of war were truly significant, and which were merely incidental.

The last word in this volume belongs to Geoffrey Parker, since it is primarily his conception of the Military Revolution which has served as a quintain for the pens of the other contributors. His new essay, "In Defense of *The Military Revolution*," responds to many of the critiques of his work contained in the other studies in this volume, and some others as well. But Parker does not merely attempt to parry every attack on his original thesis: he integrates some of the divergent perspectives provided by the other contributors to this book with new material of his own, pointing the way to a new synthesis. Of course, that new synthesis, in good dialectical fashion, will only be the basis for continued debate in the future.

THIS BOOK

The summary of the debate on the Military Revolution offered above is by no means exhaustive.[33] The volume of material on the subject has made it impossible to include every relevant article in this introduction, much less this anthology. Instead, this book aims to do three things:

First, by bringing together the most important previously published articles on the Military Revolution, to make them easily accessible both to scholars working in this area and to a wider audience of students of early modern and military history. The literature is, after all, too broad to be adequately addressed by reading Parker's book alone. This is particularly important because many of these studies were published in hard-to-get places: Parrott's in *Militärgeschichtliche Mitteilungen,* Jones' in a pamphlet published by the University of Exeter, and so on.

Second, to fill some gaps (chronological and thematic) which I perceived in the Military Revolution literature. The new articles by Thomas Arnold, Jeremy Black, John F. Guilmartin, Jr., and I. A. A. Thompson serve this purpose. In a way, Geoffrey Parker's defense of his view of the Military Revolution does so, too.

Third, to enable the reader to pull the diverse viewpoints represented by these articles into an overall framework which will both solidify his or her understanding of the Military Revolution and highlight questions which have been raised but not fully answered. My hope is that this collection will introduce a wider audience to the burgeoning research in this area, and also serve to spur further work on the Military Revolution.

Notes

1. Quoted in J. R. Hale, *War and Society in Renaissance Europe, 1450–1620* (London: Fontana, 1985), 39.

2. Hale, *War and Society in Renaissance Europe,* 21.

3. Stanislav Andreski, *Military Organization and Society* (London: Routledge & Kegan Paul, 1968 [First edition 1954]); Cf. Aristotle, *The Politics,* ed. Stephen Everson (Cambridge: Cambridge University Press, 1988), esp. IV.3, IV.13, VI.7; Max Weber, *General Economic History,* tr. Frank Knight. (Glencoe, Illinois: The Free Press, 1950 [reprint of 1927 ed.]), 324–5.

4. Heinrich Brunner, "Der Reiterdienst und die Anfänge des Lehnwesens," *Zeitshcrift der Savigny-Stiftung für Rechtsgeschichte, Germanistische Abteilung* VIII (1887) and Lynn White, Jr., "Stirrup, Mounted Shock Combat, Feudalism, and Chivalry" in his *Medieval Technology and Social Change* (Oxford: Oxford University Press, 1962). The criticism of Lynn White's version of the stirrup/shock combat/feudalism nexus is discussed in Kelly DeVries, *Medieval Military Technology* (Peterborough, Ontario: Broadview, 1992), 95–122.

5. Another exception to this proposition—and a very important one—is William H. McNeill's *The Pursuit of Power* (Chicago: University of Chicago Press, 1982).

6. Page 13, below.

7. Below, p. 18.

8. Charles Tilly, *Coercion, Capital, and the European States, AD 990–1990* (Oxford: Blackwell, 1990), 191. The significance of Tilly's remarks is underlined in John A. Lynn's excellent review essay, "Clio in Arms: The Role of the Military Variable in Shaping History," *Journal of Military History* 55 (1991), 83–95.

9. George N. Clark, *War and Society in the Seventeenth Century* (Cambridge: Cambridge University Press, 1958), 73–75.

10. Below, pp. 40, 42.

11. Technology had, of course, long been recognized as the motor of economic change. It is no surprise that technical and technological developments should have as much impact on society through the "means of violence" as through the "means of production." Parker's use of military technology as a key explanatory variable has been criticized (with reference to his 1988 book, *The Military Revolution: military innovation and society, 1500–1800*) as technological determinism, though not very convincingly. See Bert S. Hall and Kelly R. DeVries, "Essay Review—the 'Military Revolution' Revisited" *Technology and Culture*, 31 (1990), 500–507, rebutted by Harold Dorn in the following issue of the same journal, pp. 656–658. Cf. George Raudzens, "War-Winning Weapons: The Measurement of Technological Determinism in Military History," *Journal of Military History*, 54 (1990), 407–415.

12. McNeill, *The Pursuit of Power*. McNeill, interestingly, was the editor of the *Journal of Modern History* at the time when Parker's article was accepted for publication.

13. Also published in this period was John Lynn's "The Growth of the French Army during the Seventeenth Century," *Armed Forces and Society*, 6 (1980), the precursor of his related article in this volume (below, Ch. 5).

14. Below, Ch. 6, here at p. 150.

15. Roberts' article was published in 1956 and reissued in 1967; Parker's appeared in 1976; the Duffy pamphlet (*The Military Revolution and the State*) and John Lynn's article, "The Growth of French Army," were published in 1980.

16. David A. Parrott, "Strategy and Tactics in the Thirty Years' War: the 'Military Revolution,'" *Militärgeschichtliche Mitteilungen* 38/2 (1985), reprinted below, Ch. 9.

17. Below, pp. 227, 228, 234, 235, 236.

18. K. J. V. Jespersen, "Social Change and Military Revolution in Early Modern Europe: Some Danish Evidence," *Historical Journal*, XXVI (1983); three articles in *Scandinavian Journal of History*, X (1985).

19. J. R. Hale, *War and Society in Renaissance Europe, 1450–1620* (London: Fontana, 1985).

20. John A. Lynn, "Tactical Evolution in the French Army, 1560–1660," *French Historical Studies*, XIV (1985). In this article Lynn included the following memorable epigram: "Trying to understand seventeenth-century European history without weighing the influence of war and military institutions is like trying to dance without listening to the music" (p. 167).

21. Gunther E. Rothenberg, "Maurice of Nassau, Gustavus Adolphus, Raimondo Montecuccoli, and the 'Military Revolution' of the Seventeenth Century," in *Makers of Modern Strategy*, ed. Peter Paret, Gordon A. Craig, and Felix Gilbert (Oxford: Clarendon Press, 1986), 32–63. Simon Pepper and Nicholas Adams, *Firearms and Fortifications. Military Architecture and Siege Warfare in Sixteenth-Century Siena* (Chicago: University of Chicago Press, 1986).

22. The 1989 AMI Best Book Award was shared with James McPherson's *Battle Cry of Freedom.*

23. *The Military Revolution,* 4.

24. *Histories* 1.1.15.

25. Below, Ch. 10, here at p. 258.

26. Below, p. 110.

27. This article was awarded a Moncado Prize by the Society for Military History in 1994.

28. Originally published in *French Historical Studies* 18 (1994).

29. Below, p. 274.

30. A concept developed by S. E. Finer in "State and Nation-Building in Europe: The Role of the Military," *The Formation of National States in Western Europe,* ed. Charles Tilly (Princeton: Princeton University Press, 1975).

31. Compare Brian M. Downing, *The Military Revolution and Political Change: Origins of Democracy and Autocracy in Early Modern Europe* (Princeton: Princeton University Press, 1993).

32. For the idea of "gunpowder empires," see McNeill, *The Pursuit of Power,* 95–99.

33. Some of the noteworthy works dealing with the military revolution, other than those mentioned above, are: Weston F. Cook, *The Hundred Years War for Morocco. Gunpowder and the Military Revolution in the Early Modern Muslim World* (Boulder: Westview, 1994); Edward M. Furgol, "Scotland turned Sweden: the Scottish Covenanters and the Military Revolution, 1638–51" in J. Morrill, ed. *The Scottish National Covenant in its British Context* (Edinburgh: Edinburgh University Press, 1990); Mahinder S. Kingra, "The *Trace Italienne* and the Military Revolution during the Eighty Years' War, 1567–1648," *Journal of Military History,* 57 (1993); Bruce D. Porter, *War and the Rise of the State* (New York: The Free Press, 1994), ch. 3: "The Military Revolution and the Early Modern State"; David Ralston, *Importing the European Army: the Introduction of European Military Techniques and Institutions into the extra-European World, 1600–1914* (Chicago: University of Chicago Press, 1990); and Frank Tallett, *War and Society in Early-Modern Europe, 1495–1715* (London: Routledge, 1992).

Paradigms

The Military Revolution, 1560–1660

MICHAEL ROBERTS

IT IS A HISTORICAL commonplace that major revolutions in military techniques have usually been attended with widely ramifying consequences. The coming of the mounted warrior, and of the sword, in the middle of the second millennium BC; the triumph of the heavy cavalryman, consolidated by the adoption of the stirrup, in the sixth century of the Christian era; the scientific revolution in warfare in our own day—these are all recognized as major turning-points in the history of mankind. The period in the history of the art of war with which I shall try to deal in this lecture may seem from this point of view to be of inferior importance. But it brought changes which may not improperly be called a military revolution; and that revolution, when it was accomplished, exercised a profound influence upon the future course of European history. It stands like a great divide separating mediaeval society from the modern world. Yet it is a revolution which has been curiously neglected by historians. The experts in military history have mostly been content to describe what happened, without being overmuch concerned to trace out broader effects; while social historians have not been very apt to believe that the new fashions in tactics, or improvements in weapon-design, were likely to prove of much significance for their purposes. Some few sociologists, indeed, have realized the importance of the problem; but historians tend to find their expositions a trifle opaque, and their conclusions sometimes insecurely grounded. Yet it remains true that purely military developments, of a strictly technical kind, did exert a lasting influence upon society at large. They were the agents and auxiliaries of constitutional and social change; and they bore a main share of responsibility for the coming of that new world which was to be so very unlike the old.[1]

The military revolution which fills the century between 1560 and 1660 was in essence the result of just one more attempt to solve the perennial problem of tactics—the problem of how to combine missile weapons with close action; how to unite hitting power, mobility, and defensive strength. And the solution offered by the reforms of Maurice of Orange and Gustav Adolf was a return, under the inspiration of Vegetius, Aelian, and Leo the Isaurian, to linear formations.[2] In place of the massive, deep, unwieldy squares of the Spanish *tercio*, or the still larger but more irregular blocks of the Swiss column, they relied upon a multiplicity of small units ranged in two or three lines, and so disposed and armed as to permit the full exploitation of all types of weapon. Maurice used these new formations wholly for defence; but it was the great achievement of Gustav Adolf to apply them with brilliant success in offensive actions too. Moreover, he restored to cavalry its proper function, by forbidding the caracole; he made it charge home with the sword; and he insisted that it rely for its effect upon the impact of the weight of man and horse. And lastly, as a result of his experiments in gunfounding, he was able to arm his units with a light and transportable field-piece designed to supply close artillery support for infantry and cavalry alike.

These were fundamental changes; and they were essentially tactical in nature. But they entailed others of much larger implication. They entailed, for instance, a new standard in the training and discipline of the ordinary soldier. The soldier of the Middle Ages had been, on the whole, an individualist; and he (and his horse) had been highly trained over a prolonged period. The coming, first of firearms, then of the Swiss column, put an end to this state of affairs. The mercenary in the middle of a pike-square needed little training and less skill: if he inclined his pike in correct alignment and leaned heavily on the man in front of him, he had done almost all that could be required of him.[3] So too with the musketeer: a certain dexterity in loading—it could take as many as ninety-eight words of command to fire a musket—a certain steadiness in the ranks, sufficed to execute the counter-march, since no one could reasonably demand of a musket that it should be aimed with accuracy. The training of a bowman, schooled to be a dead shot at a distance, would be wasted on so imperfect an instrument as an arquebus or a wheel-lock pistol; and the pike, unlike the lance, was not an individual weapon at all. One reason why firearms drove out the bow and the lance was precisely this, that they economized on training.[4] Moreover, deep formations, whether of horse or foot, dispensed with the need for a large trained corps of officers, and required a less high morale, since it is difficult to run away with fifteen ranks behind you.

The reforms of Maurice inaugurated a real, and a lasting, revolution in these matters. Maurice's small units had to be highly trained in manoeuvre; they needed many more officers and NCOs to lead them. The tactics of Gustav Adolf postulated a vastly improved fire-discipline, and long practice in the combination of arms. The sergeant-major of the *tercio* had been well content if he mastered the art of 'embattling by the squareroot';[5] the sergeant-major of Maurice's army must be capable of executing a great number of intricate parade-ground evolutions, based on Roman models,[6] besides a number of battle movements of more strictly practical value. For Londoño drill and exercises had been designed primarily to promote physical fitness; for Lipsius they were a method of inculcating Stoic virtues in the soldier; for Maurice they were the fundamental postulates of tactics. From Aelian Maurice borrowed the whole vocabulary of military command, transmitting it almost unaltered to our own day.[7] Contemporaries found in the new drill which he introduced a strange and powerful fascination: it was an 'invention', a 'science',[8] indeed, a revelation; and a large literature appeared, designed to explain to the aspiring soldier, in two pages of close print, the precise significance of the order 'right turn'—a service the more necessary, since it sometimes meant, in fact, turn left.[9] And so officers became not merely leaders, but trainers, of men; diligent practice in peacetime, and in winter, became essential; and drill, for the first time in modern history, became the precondition of military success. The decline in the size of the basic infantry unit from about three thousand to about thirty meant that individual initiative was now expected at a far lower level of command than before. The slowly-increasing technical complexity of firearms was already beginning the process of forcing the soldier to be a primitive technician. If the revolution in drill implied a more absolute subordination of the soldier's will to the command of a superior, it implied also an intelligent subordination. Henceforth it might not be the soldier's business to think, but he would at least be expected to possess a certain minimal capacity for thinking. The army was no longer to be a brute mass, in the Swiss style, nor a collection of bellicose individuals, in the feudal style; it was to be an articulated organism of which each part responded to impulses from above. The demand for unanimity and precision of movement led naturally to the innovation of marching in step, which appears at some date impossible to establish about the middle of the seventeenth century.[10] And the principle of mass-subordination, of the solution of the individual will in the will of the commander, received a last reinforcement with the slow adoption of uniforms: 'without uniforms', said Frederick the Great, 'there can be no discipline.' The process was already observable in the 1620s; but it was scarcely complete by the end of the century. The long delay is easily explained. As long as body-armour remained general, uniforms were scarcely practical; and even when armour was abandoned, the common use of the sword-resisting buff-coat prevented for a time a general change.[11] Moreover, the habit of using mercenary armies, and the notorious readiness of mercenaries to change sides, induced men to prefer the 'token'—a kerchief round the arm, a green branch in the hat—which could be discarded easily as the occasion for it passed. Nevertheless, by the time Louvois was well in the saddle it was sufficiently plain that the general adoption of uniforms would not long be delayed.[12] Their mass-psychological effect will be readily appreciated by anyone who has ever worn one. The way was clear for the armies of the nineteenth century: it remained only for the twentieth to complete the process by replacing dolmans, busbies, eagle's wings, and all the flaunting *panache* of Cossack and Hussar, by the flat uniformity of field-grey and khaki.

The new emphasis on training and drill seemed to contemporaries to reinforce their already established convictions about the best way to recruit an army. The armies which carried through the military revolution—or upon which that revolution impinged—were nearly all mercenary armies. It has indeed been argued, with some plausibility, that the great military innovations throughout history have generally coincided with the predominance of mercenaries;[13] and it has been asserted, more specifically, that the reforms of Maurice were possible only in a mercenary force, since the prolonged drilling and high degree of professional skill which they demanded would have been impossible to obtain from a citizen militia.[14] But though this last contention (as we shall see in a moment) cannot be sustained, there is no doubt that the use of mercenaries was attended with certain obvious advantages. The mercenary had no local attachments, was indifferent to national sentiment; and this made him an invaluable agent in the suppression of popular disturbances. A mercenary army cared not at all if the war were prolonged, or fought far from home; it economized the state's own manpower, and hence its wealth; the system of recruiting through captains relieved the government of a good deal of administrative work. There were, of course, many countervailing disadvantages: the mercenary was undisciplined, unreliable, and averse to battle; his arms and equipment were unstandardized and often bad;[15] the employer was invariably swindled by the captains; and the whole system was ruinously expensive. So expensive, indeed, that the smaller and poorer states were forced to look for alternatives. Around the turn of the century many of the lesser German states—and even some quite big ones such as Saxony, Brandenburg and Bavaria—began to experiment with local militias.[16] Military writers such as Machiavelli and Lazarus von Schwendi had urged the superiority of the citizen army, with many a backward glance at the military virtues of republican Rome.[17] But it was forgotten that the classical authors whose military teachings formed the basis of the Maurician reforms all dated from times when the Roman forces were citizen-armies no longer. The event proved that the half-trained militias were incapable of mastering the modern art of war. Their failure in Germany was universal, ignominious and complete; and it seemed that those were right who contended that in the new conditions only mercenary armies could be effective. The Swedish victories, however, were a warning against too hasty a conclusion; for the Swedish army was a conscript national militia—the first truly national European army—and it proved capable of mastering military techniques much more complex than had been seen before. The second and more important stage of the military revolution, which Gustav Adolf carried through, was in fact launched, not by highly-skilled professionals, but by conscript peasants; and experienced mercenary soldiers such as Robert Monro had to go to school again to learn the new Swedish methods.[18] And not only were the Swedish armies better than any mercenaries; they were also incomparably cheaper. There was no peculation by captains; and payment could be made in land-grants, revenue-assignments, tax-remissions, or in kind.

But conditions in Sweden were exceptional, and other European countries felt unable to follow the Swedish example. The Spanish army under Philip II did indeed contain some conscripts, as well as international mercenaries and Spanish 'gentlemen-rankers', and the Prussian army of Frederick William I was a mixed

army too;[19] but on the whole the rulers found no feasible alternative to a mercenary force, drawn, often enough, from the more impoverished and mountainous
regions of Europe such as Scotland, Albania, or Switzerland.[20]

Few monarchs of the sixteenth and seventeenth centuries were prepared to establish national armies; for most of them agreed with Christian IV of Denmark
and John George of Saxony in being unwilling to put arms into the hands of the
lower orders:[21] only where the peasantry had been reduced to a real serfdom was
it esteemed safe to proceed upon the basis of conscription. This stage was not
reached in Prussia before the end of the century; nor even in Russia before the reforms of Peter the Great. Except in Sweden, therefore, and to some extent in
Spain, the armies continued to be mercenary armies throughout the century. The
difference was that they became standing armies too. And this change arose
mainly from the obvious need to make them less burdensome to the state. Already before the end of the sixteenth century it was realized that the practice of
disbanding and paying-off regiments at the end of each campaigning season, and
re-enlisting them in the following spring, was an expensive way of doing business.
Large sums were payable on enlistment and mustering, and (in theory at least) all
arrears were paid up on disbandment. But between mustering and disbandment
pay was irregular and never full, despite the so-called 'full-pays' which occurred
from time to time.[22] If then a mercenary force were not disbanded in the autumn,
but continued from year to year, the calls upon the exchequer were likely to be
considerably lessened, and the general nuisance of mutinous soldiery would be
abated. Moreover, if the army remained embodied throughout the winter, the
close season could be used for drilling and exercising, of which since the tactical
revolution there was much more need than ever before. There were, moreover,
special areas where winter was the best season for campaigning: it was so in the
marshy regions of Poland and north-west Russia; and it was so in Hungary, for
the Turkish camels could not stand the cold of the Hungarian plain, and their annual retirement provided the Habsburgs with the chance to recoup the losses of
the preceding summer.[23] Considerations such as these led one prince after another to retain his mercenaries on the strength throughout the winter months:
Rudolf II was perhaps the earliest to do so; but Maurice of Orange was not far behind. From this practice arose the modern standing army; and it is worth while
emphasizing the fact that it was the result of considerations of a military and financial, and not of a political or constitutional nature. Writers such as de la Noue,
Duplessis-Mornay, Wallhausen and Montecuccoli all advocated standing armies
on purely military grounds.[24] There seems little basis for the suggestion that
standing armies were called into being by artful princes in order to provide employment for their turbulent nobility;[25] or that they were a sign of the inherent
Drang nach Machtentfaltung of the monarchs;[26] or that they were designed to enable the rulers to establish a sovereignty unrestrained by law and custom and free
from constitutional limitations—though they did, no doubt, prove very serviceable instruments of despotism. Where absolutism triumphed in this century, it

did so because it provided the response to a genuine need; and though an army might be useful for curbing aristocratic licence, it was but an accessory factor in the general political situation which produced the eclipse of the Estates. Essentially the standing armies were the product of military logic rather than of political design. And the same is true of the permanent navies: greater obligations in the way of commerce-protection, increased need for making blockades effective, the demand for trained crews and officers constantly at call, economy of administration—these were some of the factors that produced permanent navies; and it was a constitutional accident that the first two attempts in this direction—the *Compagnie van Assurantie* of Frederick Henry, and the Shipmoney fleets of Charles I—should both have acquired a sinister significance in the minds of their opponents.[27]

But it was not only that armies were tending to become permanent; it was also that they were rapidly becoming much larger. And this I take to be the result of a revolution in strategy, made possible by the revolution in tactics, and made necessary by the circumstances of the Thirty Years' War. The sixteenth century had already seen a notable broadening of strategic horizons: in the long duel between Valois and Habsburg, simultaneous operations on two or more fronts had been the rule, and it would have been difficult at times to decide which was the encircler, and which the encircled. The same was true, on a vaster scale, of the struggle against the Turks: Portuguese attacks on Eritrea, Persian assaults upon Asia Minor, were balanced by Turkish alliances with France and England. At the same time the discovery of the New World, and the penetration of the East Indies, extended the possible area of European conflict until it covered most of the globe, and inaugurated a new age of amphibious warfare. But these developments were for long unsystematic, the realm of the project-maker and the armchair strategist: the day had not yet arrived when the military and naval administrations of Europe were equal to the coordination of effort over distances so formidable. The sterility of warfare in Europe, in the time of Prince Maurice, is the accurate measure of the strategic thinking of the age.

The Thirty Years' War brought a change. Battle came again into favour, perhaps under the influence of confessional ferocity, and with it a strategy aiming at battle; and as hostilities ranged back and forth over Germany, and along the borders of Germany from Poland and Transylvania to Italy, Lorraine and the Netherlands, commanders were driven to look at the whole of central Europe as one great theatre of war. When Gustav Adolf wrote that 'all the wars of Europe are now blended into one',[28] he was thinking in terms of politics; but the remark was equally true in regard to strategy. Wallenstein sends Arnim to fight on the Vistula; Pappenheim rushes to the relief of Maestricht; Olivares dreams of seizing Göteborg, and of a Spanish naval base at Wismar, to be made accessible by a Kiel canal:[29] Piccolomini makes a famous march from Flanders to Bohemia;[30] Savoy, Venice, Transylvania and even the Tatars of the Crimea become elements in everwider and more unified plans of operations. Above all, Gustav Adolf's strategic thinking seems a whole dimension bigger than any that had preceded it. He successfully combines two types of strategy: on the one hand a resolute offensive strategy designed to annihilate the enemy in battle—the product of confidence in the superiority of the new Swedish tactics; on the other a wholly new gradualist strategy, designed to conquer Germany by the occupation and methodical consolidation of successive base-areas. The two blend in his plan for the destruction of the Austrian Habsburgs by the simultaneous and effectively co-ordinated operations of five or seven armies moving under the king's direction on an enormous curving front extending from the middle Oder to the Alpine passes.[31] It was a strategic concept more complex, vaster, than any one commander had ever previously attempted. His death prevented its being carried out; but the closing years of the war saw other developments of interest. The strategy of devastation began to be employed with a new thoroughness and logic; and, as its consequence, the war became pre-eminently a war of movement, best exemplified in the campaigns of Baner, Torstensson and Gallas.[32] Not all of these developments were to be pursued in the years that followed: an age of reason and mathematical logic would try to bring war itself within the scope of its calculations, to the detriment of that offensive spirit without which wars cannot be won; but the effects of the strategic revolution of which Gustav Adolf was the most illustrious exponent were not to be effaced.

The most important of them was the great increase in the scope of warfare, reflected in a corresponding increase in the normal size of the armies of the major powers. Philip II had dominated Europe in his day with the aid of an army which probably did not exceed 40,000 men: a century later, 400,000 were esteemed necessary to maintain the ascendancy of Louis XIV.[33] In 1627, under the Elector George William, Brandenburg possessed a defence force totalling 900:[34] under Frederick William I, the normal establishment was about 80,000. The previous millennium could show nothing to compare with this sudden rise in the size of western European armies. Great agglomerations of troops for a particular occasion had indeed occurred in the past, and the Turks had brought vast hosts to bear upon their enemies; but in the West, at least, the seventeenth century saw the permanent establishment of some armies at levels which earlier ages had rarely, if ever, known. With Louvois, indeed, the passion for mere numbers had something of a megalomaniac quality: an aspect, perhaps, of that 'pursuit of the quantitative' which has been considered as an essential characteristic of the new industrialism.[35] It may perhaps be legitimately objected that the instances I have chosen to illustrate the growth of armies are hand-picked: the Spanish armies of 1690 were certainly no bigger than those of 1590; and the army with which Charles XII won the battle of Narva was slightly smaller than that with which Charles IX lost the battle of Kirkholm:[36] that Gustav Adolf had 175,000 men under arms in 1632 was for Sweden a quite exceptional circumstance, never repeated. But this does not alter the fact that the scale of European warfare was throughout the century prodigiously increasing: the great armies of Louis XIV had to be met by armies of comparable size; and if one state could not manage it, there must be a Grand Alliance. Moreover, in the seventeenth century numbers had acquired a precise meaning: when Charles V is credited with assembling an army of 120,000 men to repel the Turkish attack, we are perhaps entitled to decline to take the figure too literally; but when Louvois states the French army at 300,000, it is safe to assume that there was just that number on the muster-rolls, even though not all of them may have appeared in the ranks. And so it happened that (as Montecuccoli observed) men, no less than money, became in the seventeenth century the sinews of war:[37] hence the concern of the earliest demographical investigations to make sure that population was not declining; hence the insistence of the mercantilists, with their eyes ever upon the contingency of war, that a copious population is among the chief riches of the state.

The transformation in the scale of war led inevitably to an increase in the authority of the state. The days when war partook of the nature of feud were now for ever gone, and the change is reflected in (among other things) the development of international law, of which I shall speak in a moment. Only the state, now, could supply the administrative, technical and financial resources required for large-scale hostilities. And the state was concerned to make its military monopoly absolute. It declared its hostility to irregular and private armies, to ambiguous and semi-piratical naval ventures. Backward countries such as Scotland were the exceptions that proved the rule: the failure of Scottish parliaments to disarm Highland clans was a sign of weakness in the body politic. Navies become state navies, royal navies: the old compromise of the armed merchantman falls into disuse; the Dutch West India Company goes bankrupt. Effective control of the armed forces by a centralized authority becomes a sign of modernity: it is no accident that the destruction of the *streltsi* by Peter the Great preceded by a century and a quarter the destruction of the Janissaries by Mahmud II.

This development, and the new style of warfare itself, called for new administrative methods and standards; and the new administration was from the beginning centralized and royal. Secretaries of state for war are born; war offices proliferate. The Austrian Habsburgs had possessed a *Hofkriegsrat* since the mid-sixteenth century; but in the seventeenth the rising military powers—Sweden, France, Brandenburg, Russia—all equipped themselves with new and better machinery for the conduct of war. Inevitably these new officials spent a good deal of their time in grappling with problems of supply—supply of arms and armaments, supply of goods, clothing, transport and the rest. Experience showed that it was bad for discipline, as well as inefficient, to permit the mercenary armies to equip themselves:[38] it was better to have standardized weapons, a limited number of recognised calibres, an agreed maximum of windage, a consistently-compounded gunpowder, and, in the end, uniform clothing, and boots in three standard sizes. Hence the state was driven to attempt the supervision of supply; in many cases, to production on its own account; sometimes, to monopoly: the Spanish Netherlands had a state monopoly of the manufacture of gunpowder, the Swedish Trading Company was created to facilitate control of a strategic material—copper. Military needs drove the monarchs into ever-increasing interference in the lives of their subjects: in Sweden, as in England, there were bitter complaints at the grisly perquisitions of the saltpetre-collector. The developments in the science of fortification, of which Vauban was to be the most eminent exponent, meant new fortresses for the *pré carré,* and this in turn meant heavier *corvées,* the subversion of municipal liberties, and the increased power of the sovereign: 'fortresses', says Montecuccoli, 'are the buttresses of the crown'; and he added that the fact that 'licentious' nations such as the English disliked them merely proved their utility.[39] The stricter discipline, the elaborately mechanical drilling, required by the new linear tactics, matched the tendency of the age towards absolute government, and may well have reinforced it: it was tempting to think that the discipline which had succeeded so well in the field might yield equally satisfactory results if applied to civil society. The ruler was increasingly identified with the commander-in-chief, and from the new discipline and drill would be born not merely the autocrat, but that particular type of autocrat which delighted in the name of *Kriegsherr.* It was not the least of England's good luck, that for the whole of the critical century from 1547 to 1649 she was ruled by monarchs with neither interest nor capacity for military affairs. It was certainly no accident that Louis XIII should have been 'passionately fond' of drill;[40] nor was it a mere personal quirk that led Louis XIV to cause a medal to be struck, of which the reverse displays him in the act of taking a parade, and correcting, with a sharp poke of his cane, the imperfect dressing of a feckless private in the rear rank.[41] The newly-acquired symmetry and order of the parade-ground provided, for Louis XIV and his contemporaries, the model to which life and art must alike conform; and the *pas cadencé* of Martinet—whose name is in itself a programme—echoed again in the majestic monotony of interminable alexandrines.[42] By the close of the century there was already a tendency in monarchs of an absolutist cast to consider military uniform as their normal attire—as Charles XII did, for instance, and Frederick William I. It was not a fashion that would have commended itself to Henry VIII, or Gustav Vasa, or Philip II.

One very important effect of all these developments was in the sphere of finance. The ever-increasing cost of war—the result of larger armies and navies, more expensive armaments, longer periods of training, bigger administrative staffs, in an age when prices were still rising—embarrassed the finances of every state in Europe. Kings were presented with new problems of paying large and distant armies, which posed new difficulties of remittance; and the solutions they found to these difficulties contributed a good deal to the development of financial instruments and a structure of credit: Wallenstein's ties with the great German financiers were an essential element in his success.[43] Everywhere kings found that though they might still—with care—live of their own in peacetime, they plunged into debt in wartime. And in this period it was almost always wartime. They fell back on *affaires extraordinaires,* on *ad hoc* financial devices, some of them sufficiently remarkable: this is the age of Peter the Great's *pribylshtiki,* or tax-inven-

tors, and of the analogous officials employed after Colbert's death by Le Pelletier
at the *Contrôle Générale*.[44] They had recourse to currency debasement, sale of monopolies, sale of crown lands, inflation of honours, and above all to the sale of offices, which in this century for the first time becomes a general European phenomenon.[45] But sooner or later financial stringency, in country after country,
involved the authorities in constitutional crises: the monarchs found themselves
forced to parley with their Estates, or to violate the ancient constitutional liberties. Behind all the great insurrectionary movements of the age—the Thirty Years'
War, the English rebellion, the Fronde, the revolts in the Spanish realms—there
lay, as one major element in the situation (though of course not the only one) the
crown's need for money; and that need was usually produced by military commitments whose dimensions were in part the result of the military revolution. On the
whole, the monarchs prevailed; the income for maintaining standing armies was
taken out of the control of the Estates; sometimes military finance—as in Brandenburg—was wholly separated from the ordinary revenues. And in Germany
this issue of the conflict resulted, in part, from the fact that in the last resort the
Estates had rather sacrifice a constitutional principle, and retain the security afforded by a standing army, than risk the appalling sufferings and crushing financial exactions which, as the experience of the Thirty Years' War had shown,
awaited the militarily impotent or old-fashioned.[46] Nevertheless, though the
standing army thus came to be accepted as the lesser of two evils, it was a grievous
burden to the smaller and financially weaker states. They had discarded the alternative of a militia; a standing army seemed inescapable; but many of them could
scarcely finance it from their own resources. It was this situation which presented
such opportunities to that subsidy-diplomacy upon which the aggressive policies
of Louis XIV were to thrive.

If liberty, then, were thus to be sacrificed to the army, it ought at least to be an
army that was really the property of the king, and not a mere agglomeration of recruiting speculators. The free bargaining between recruiting captain and employing prince, the Articles of War which partook more of the nature of an industrial
agreement than of a code of military discipline,[47]—these things were repugnant
to the orderliness and efficiency of the new military ideal. The larger the army, the
greater the need for disciplining it from above.[48] The monarch must take over the
business of recruiting and paying men, as he was already beginning to take over
the business of supplying material and supervising war-industries. And the monarchs, in fact, did so. The Articles of War of Gustav Adolf set a new standard of
royal control, and were imitated even in countries which employed a predomi-
nantly mercenary army. Wallenstein made a start in curbing the independence of
the recruiting captains;[49] and a generation later Louvois and the Great Elector
were to profit from his example.[50] By the end of the century the monarchs had
mostly gained effective control of their armies. It was a significant development;
for once the armies became royal (as the navies already were) the way was open
for their eventually becoming national.

The social consequences of the military revolution were scarcely less important than the constitutional. In the Middle Ages war had been almost the privilege of a class; by the seventeenth century it had become almost the livelihood of the masses. The Military Participation Ratio (to borrow the language of the sociologists)[51] rose sharply. Men flocked to the swollen mercenary armies. In part they did so, no doubt, because in the Germany of the 1630s and 1640s the army was the safest place to be;[52] but also, and more generally, because the new warfare offered fresh prospects of a career. Never before had commanders required so many subalterns and NCOs. It was no wonder that impoverished Scots and Irish made all haste to the wars of Low Germanie: 'He who is down on his luck', ran the contemporary Gaelic proverb, 'can always earn a dollar of Mackay'.[53] Even the cavalry, which had once been the close preserve of the nobility, was now open to all who could sit a horse and fire a pistol; for with the abolition of the lance the European nobility tended to abandon heavy cavalry to the professionals, while light cavalry had long appeared to them almost as socially subversive, since it eliminated the difference, in mount, arms and equipment, between the noble and his esquire. The decline of expensive heavy armour, which was a consequence of the growing realization that no armour could stop a musket ball, and that in any case few musket balls hit their mark, had obvious social implications too. The obliteration of the old distinction between cavalry and foot, gentlemen and others, is a matter of common remark in the seventeenth century: as Sir James Turner put it, 'the ancient distinction between the Cavalry and Infantry, as to their birth and breeding, is wholly taken away, men's qualities and extractions being little or rather just nothing either regarded or enquired after; the most of the Horsemen, as well as of the Foot, being composed of the Scum of the Commons'.[54] The new armies, in fact, served as the social escalators of the age; the eternal wars favoured interstratic mobility; and for a young man with some capital behind him a regiment could be a brilliant investment: Wallhausen lamented that war was ceasing to be an honourable profession, and was becoming a mere traffic.[55] But even for the youth who had no other assets than a native pugnacity and the habit of survival, advancement was now probable, and the impecunious commoner whose wits were sharp might certainly hope for a commission. He could not, indeed, feel that he carried a baton in his knapsack. Very few of the leading commanders on the Continent were of humble origin: Aldringen had been a lackey, Derfflinger was a tailor's apprentice, Jean de Werth rose from absolute obscurity; but the great names are still noble names: even Catinat came from the *noblesse de robe*.[56] Nevertheless though the highest positions might in practice remain unattainable, the army had become an attractive career, and in France three generations of military service would enable a family to claim reception into the *noblesse de race*.[57] As the old custom of conferring knighthood on the battlefield declined, the new custom of ennoblement came to take its place. Nor were the possibilities of advancement restricted to the army in the field. A host of clerks and secretaries was now required to keep the muster- and pay-rolls, and conduct the correspondence of semi-literate commanders:[58] Grimmelshausen makes Herzbruder's father a muster-clerk in the Saxon army, and the merchant's son, Oliver, becomes secretary to a Swedish general. Administrators were in brisk demand for the new war offices;[59] business heads were needed to solve the ever-widening problems of logistics: such careers as those of Michel Le Tellier, Johan Adler Salvius, and Louis de Geer, tell their own tale. The importance of the civilian, bourgeois, administrators in bringing order and method into the management of the fighting services has often been re-marked, and Colbert and Louvois are the most famous representatives of this de-velopment. But it has less often been pointed out that it was the purely military changes of the late sixteenth and early seventeenth centuries that opened to the middle classes a quite new field of activity, and tempting prospects of social ad-vancement. How good those prospects could be may best be seen from a glance at the peerages conferred by successive Swedish monarchs upon persons of this sort.

It is true that the enhanced opportunities provided by the new style of army tended, before the century was out, to be somewhat restricted. The decay of heavy cavalry, the decline of individualist warfare, was accompanied by the gradual withering away of such remnant of the old noble obligation of military service as had survived from the middle ages. In France, in Sweden, in Brandenburg, knight-service had vanished for all practical purposes by the third quarter of the century.[60] It was outmoded and inefficient, disorderly and unreliable, and subver-sive of the new principle of concentrating military power under the absolute con-trol of the sovereign. But the nobility found, in the new standing armies, an open-ing which more than compensated them for the loss of their own special military organization; and the monarchs, indeed, took care that it should be so. The more impoverished of them—the *hoberaux,* Junkers, *knapar*—were delighted to be re-lieved of the burden of supplying the expensive equipment of the heavy cavalry-man, and glad to be able to find a full-time career in the king's service. It was not long before they attempted to claim, as a privilege of birth, an excessive share of the new opportunities. By the beginning of the eighteenth century, though the so-cial escalator was still on the move, there was a widespread tendency to label it 'Nobles Only', and this tendency was not wholly counteracted by the practice (prevalent in some countries) of ennobling non-noble officers who might attain to a certain grade.

Meanwhile, the arm which presented the aspiring soldier with the fewest social barriers was undoubtedly the artillery.[61] Empirical in method, generously approx-imate in effect, the artillery was nevertheless ceasing to be a 'mystery', and was on the way to becoming a regular arm of the services, with a normal military organi-zation: the first purely artillery regiment seems to have been that established by Gustav Adolf in 1629.[62] And behind the artillery lay a fringe of scientific laymen and minor mathematicians—those 'mathematical practitioners' whose part in educating the seamen, gunners and surveyors of the age has now been made clear.[63] Indeed, one main element in the military revolution was the harnessing, for the first time and on a large scale, of science to war: the invention of corned powder towards the end of the sixteenth century gave to firearms a new effectiveness, and would have been still more important if the techniques of metallurgy had been able to take full advantage of this advance.[64] A century of notable technical progress, nevertheless, lay behind the Swedish light artillery. Very soon after the invention of a satisfactory portable telescope it was being used in the field by Maurice and Gustav Adolf. The importance for military purposes of advances in cartography seems first to have been recognized by Stefan Batory, who caused military maps to be drawn for him in the 1580s.[65] Technicians and theoreticians vied with each other in devising new and more terrible weapons: multiple-barrelled guns were invented upon all hands; Napier, the father of logarithms, was more favourably known to his contemporaries as the man who built a submarine, suggested the use of gas-shells, and designed an armoured fighting vehicle; Gilius Packet invented the first hand-grenade for Erik XIV in 1567;[66] Jan Bouvy in his *Pyrotechnie militaire* (1591) described the first practicable torpedo.[67] Maurice of Orange dallied with *saucisses de guerre*, with saws fitted with silencer attachment (for nocturnal attacks upon fortresses), and with other contrivances more curious than effective.[68] In 1650 the Venetians resorted to biological warfare in the defence of Crete, despatching Dr Michael Angelo Salomon thither to infect the Turkish armies with 'the quintessence of the pest'.[69] It comes as no surprise that when Colbert founded his *Académie royale des Sciences,* one of its main objects should have been the application of science to war.

These developments brought to an end the period in which the art of war could still be learned by mere experience or the efflux of time. The commander of the new age must be something of a mathematician; he must be capable of using the tools with which the scientists were supplying him. Gustav Adolf consistently preached the importance of mathematics; Monro and Turner spoke slightingly of illiterate old soldiers.[70] And since war must be learned—even by nobles—institutions must be created to teach it: the first military academy of modern times was founded by Johan of Nassau at Siegen in 1617. The need for military education was especially felt by the nobility, whose former supremacy in arms was beginning to be challenged; and the century saw the foundation of noble academies or cadet-schools, which sought to combine the now gentlemanly acquirement of fortification with the Italian tradition of courtly education: such were Christian IV's Sorø, Louvois' short-lived cadet-school, and the similar Austrian establishment, founded in 1648 by the ominously-named Baron de Chaos.[71]

Side by side with the older stratification of society based upon birth or tenure, there now appeared a parallel and to some extent a rival stratification based on military and civil rank. The first half of the seventeenth century sees the real emergence of the concept of rank. In the armies of the *Landsknechts,* for instance, the distinction between officers and men had been faint, and their bands had at times something of the aspect of a self-governing democracy.[72] All that was now changed. After captains came colonels; then (in the Thirty Years' War) majors; then a regular hierarchy of generals and field-marshals. Soon after 1660 Louvois regulated precedence in the French army.[73] And this hierarchization was the more necessary, since very soon military ranks were drawn into that general sale of offices which was one of the characteristics of the age. On the whole, the parallel hierarchies of rank and birth avoided conflict; the nobility contrived to evade non-commissioned service, except in special regiments (such as Charles XII's guards) where it was recognized to be no derogation; and the locution 'an officer and a gentleman' became a pleonasm rather than a nice distinction. But in some countries at least (Russia and Sweden, in particular) the state found it expedient to promulgate Tables of Rank, in order to adjust delicate questions of precedence as between (for instance) a second lieutenant and a university professor, or an ensign and a college registrar. By the close of the century, the officer-corps had been born: a European, supranational entity, with its own ethos, its own international code of honour, its own corporate spirit. The *duellum* of a dying chivalry is transformed into the affair of honour of a military caste. And the military revolution is seen to have given birth, not only to modern warfare, but also to modern militarism.

The effect of war upon the economic development of Europe in this period is one of the classic battlefields of historians—a 'dark and bloody ground' whereon Professor Nef still grapples valiantly with the shade of Werner Sombart, much as Jacob wrestled with the Angel—and it would be rash for one who is not an economic historian to intrude upon this argument. But this at least may be said: that war was a fundamental presupposition of mercantilist thought, and by many mercantilists was considered to be necessary to the health of the state—and implicit in all their theories was the new concept of war-potential.[74] The mercantilists held that the economic activities of the state must be so directed as to ensure that it be not at the mercy of a foreign power for those commodities—whether men, money, or goods—without which wars cannot be waged: Thomas Mun, for instance, urged the stockpiling of strategic raw materials.[75] And when mercantilist writers in France and England and Austria—and even in Sweden—boasted that their respective countries excelled all others in fertility of soil and mineral wealth, they were in fact proclaiming their preparedness for war, and warning off an aggressor. But since few states could be truly autarkic, there arose, more clearly than ever before, the idea of economic warfare; the more so, since the needs of armies were now greater and more varied. There had, of course, been conscious economic warfare before: repeated attempts had been made to cut off the Turks from supplies of war-materials; similar attempts were made in the 1560s to deny them to Muscovy; Sweden had been hard hit in the Seven Years' War of the North by the Danes' stoppage of her imports of salt. But in the seventeenth century economic warfare became wider in range, sharper, and more effective than before. This increased efficacy is a consequence (but also a cause) of larger navies, and of the building of ships with a greater sea-endurance. It was a sign of the new scope of economic warfare that the Dutch in 1599 not only declared a total blockade of the entire coasts of Italy, Portugal and Spain, but also proceeded to a serious attempt to make that blockade effective.[76] At the same time, the notion of contraband of war underwent a considerable extension: by the mid-century it could be made to cover even such commodities as corn, specie, cloth and horses.[77] It was to meet this situation that the legists of Europe began the attempt to formulate an international law of contraband and blockade. Before the middle of the century the Dutch had already induced at least three nations to recognize the principle 'free ships make free goods';[78] and it was partly because of the serious military implications that there had arisen the classic controversy between the advocates of *mare liberum* and *mare clausum*. The military revolution, indeed, had important effects upon international relations and international law. There can be no doubt that the strengthening of the state's control of military matters did something to regularize international relations. The mediaeval concept of war as an extension of feud grows faint; military activities by irresponsible individuals are frowned on; the states embark on the suppression of piracy; the heyday of the Algerines and the Uscocchi is drawing to a close. The century witnessed a steady advance towards restriction of the old rights of looting and booty, and before the end of it cartels governing the exchange of prisoners had become usual. This was a necessary consequence of the decline of individual warfare; for looting and booty had been juridically based on the idea of feud, and the apportionment of booty had been generally linked to the amount of capital invested by the soldier in his arms and equipment, so that the cavalryman received more than the footsoldier: hence when the state provided the capital it reasonably claimed the disposition of the loot.[79] Nevertheless, before this stage had been arrived at, Europe had endured a period—the period of the Thirty Years' War—when war-making seems to have been only intermittently under the state's control, and when ordinary conduct was of exceptional savagery. The explanation of this state of affairs lies, it seems to me, in the technical changes which I have been considering. The increased size of armies, the new complexity of their needs, at first confronted the states with problems of supply which they were incapable of solving—hence the bland indifference of most generals during the Thirty Years' War to any threat to their line of communications. Armies must live off the country; looting and booty were necessary if the soldier were to survive.[80] The occupation of territory thus became a legitimate strategic object in itself; and conversely, the commander who could not deny to the enemy the territory he desired must take care so to devastate it that it became useless to him. Thus, as Piero Pieri observes, frightfulness became a logistical necessity,[81] a move in a struggle for supply which was itself the result of the increased size of armies and the low level of administrative techniques. Already, however, there were signs of better things. Gustav Adolf, despite his dictum that *bellum se ipsum alet*,[82] was not content to plunder Germany haphazard; and among other innovations he introduced a system of magazines, by which supplies and war material were concentrated at strategic points such as Erfurt, Nuremberg, Ulm, and Mainz:[83] it was a development that looked forward to the eighteenth century. Nevertheless, the menace of the self-supporting army, wandering at large over central Europe, lasted sufficiently long to induce in Germany's neighbours a sharpened consciousness of frontiers, and a new determination to make them defensive. Richelieu put the point clearly when he wrote in his *Testament politique* that a well-fortified frontier was necessary to prevent the raids of a marauding enemy. A generation later the idea of a frontier as one or more lines of fortified places was well developed, and from it there followed the rather new notion that frontiers must be 'rectified' to meet strategic requirements. The age of Vauban, of the *pré carré*, of the *Réunions*, is not far ahead.[84]

Before that stage was reached, the administrative nihilism which had been one of the early consequences of the military revolution made it urgent to draw up afresh some code for the conduct of war. This was the situation in which Hugo Grotius wrote his *De Jure Belli ac Pacis*. It bears on every page the impression of the military revolution; for it was the hopelessness of maintaining the old standards in the face of the new situation that forced Grotius to go so far in the condonation of evil. It seemed to Grotius that the old restraints—moral, conventional or religious—had ceased to be effective, and that man in his war-making had sunk to the level of the beasts. The last vestige of chivalry had perished in the French civil wars; and the antagonism of Catholic and Protestant had made religion the pretext for ferocity, rather than a check upon it. To these factors were now added the growing predominance of missile weapons, which were dehumanizing war into an affair of undiscriminating slaughter at a distance,[85] and also the new strategy of devastation. It was an age when the soldiery came near to asserting a prescriptive right to massacre a recalcitrant civilian population;[86] and the armies of the Thirty Years' War had latterly to contend, not only with their official enemies, but with the bloodthirsty vengeance of peasant guerillas: Simplicissimus might well comment on 'the enmity which there ever is between soldiers and peasants'.[87] In this situation, Grotius sought to set limits to what was legitimate in war. But the importance of his attempt has obscured the fact that the limits he did set were appallingly wide: wider, for instance, than in Suárez and Gentili; and far wider than in Vitoria.[88] Grotius taught that it is lawful to kill prisoners of war; that assassination is legitimate, if not accompanied by perfidy; that unrestricted devastation of the lands and cities of the enemy is permissible, even if they have surrendered; that the civilian has no right to special consideration; and that 'the slaughter of women and children is allowed to have impunity, as comprehended in the right of war'—a position which he buttressed, according to his habit, with an apposite quotation from the 137th Psalm: 'Blessed shall he be that taketh thy children and dasheth them against the stones.'[89] It is true that he proceeded to urge moral considerations which must deter the good man from making use of these rights; but they remain rights none the less. Grotius, in fact, reflects the logistical devastation of the age of the Thirty Years' War;[90] though it was to the same classical authorities which had given Maurice the inspiration for his disciplinary reforms, that he turned for his repertory of convenient instances. The absolute, feral warfare of the epoch, with which Grotius thus felt obliged to come to terms, gave a peculiar incisiveness to the logic of Leviathan.

The continued use of mercenary armies, with their professional codes and traditions, and the rise of an international officer-class, did indeed provide mitigations before many decades had passed: new military conventions grew up, to regulate the relations of armies to one another. But it was long before these restrictions were applied to civilians: not until the most civilized state in Europe, impelled by military logic, had twice devastated the Palatinate, did public opinion begin to turn against the type of warfare which Grotius had been compelled to legitimize. Grotius, indeed, represents a transitional stage at which the military revolution had not yet worked out its full effects. A completer control by the state of its armies, better administrative devices—and the fear of reprisals—were required before there could be any real alleviation. If the military revolution must be given the responsibility for the peculiar horrors of the Thirty Years' War, it did at last evolve the antidote to them. The eighteenth century would bring to Europe a long period in which a limitation of the scope of war was successfully maintained. But it is a long way still, in 1660, to the humane rationalism of Vattel.

Such were some of the effects of the military revolution: I have no doubt that others could be distinguished. I hope, at least, to have persuaded you that these tactical innovations were indeed the efficient causes of changes which were really revolutionary. Between 1560 and 1660 a great and permanent transformation came over the European world. The armies of Maximilian II, in tactics, strategy, constitution and spirit, belong to a world of ideas which would have seemed quite foreign to Benedek and Radetzky. The armies of the Great Elector are linked infrangibly with those of Moltke and Schlieffen. By 1660 the modern art of war had come to birth. Mass armies, strict discipline, the control of the state, the submergence of the individual, had already arrived; the conjoint ascendancy of financial power and applied science was already established in all its malignity; the use of propaganda, psychological warfare, and terrorism as military weapons was already familiar to theorists, as well as to commanders in the field. The last remaining qualms as to the religious and ethical legitimacy of war seemed to have been stilled. The road lay open, broad and straight, to the abyss of the twentieth century.

Notes

1. For a general treatment of the period Hans Delbrück, *Geschichte der Kriegskunst im Rahmen der politischen Geschichte,* Berlin, 1920. iv, is the best authority, though this volume is on a slighter scale than its predecessors. Paul Schmitthenner, *Krieg und Kriegführung im Wandel der Weltgeschichte,* Potsdam, 1930, is a stimulating and suggestive survey. Sir Charles Oman's *A History of the Art of War in the Sixteenth Century* (1937) necessarily ends with Maurice of Orange. The best discussions in English are the chapter in Sir George Clark, *The Seventeenth Century,* Oxford, 1929, and the same author's *War and Society in the Seventeenth Century,* Cambridge, 1958.

2. For a fuller consideration of the changes in the art of war in Europe, and the reforms of Maurice and Gustav Adolf, see chapter 3 of M. Roberts, *Essays in Swedish History* (Minneapolis, 1967).

3. 'Non bisogna credere che l'addestramento dei combattanti richieda tempo e spese: non ci sono esercizi d'armi nel senso moderno. Una sia pur rudimentale istruzione permette agli Svizzeri di formare dei corpi tattici ...': Piero Pieri, *Il Rinascimento e la Crisi militare italiano*, Turin, 1952, p. 236.

4. There were many reasons for the decline of the lance, but this was certainly one of them: see Raimondo Montecuccoli, *Memoires*, Strasbourg, 1735, p. 16; and *cf.* J. J. Wallhausen, *Art militaire à cheval*, Frankfurt, 1616, pp. 3–22.

5. I.e., the art of drawing up a given number of men into a perfect square. There is a description in Sir James Turner, *Pallas Armata* (1683), pp. 266–8.

6. E.g. 'The Quadrate or Square, the Wedg, the *Tenaille* or Tongs, the Saw, and the Globe': Turner, *op. cit.*, pp. 112–14.

7. Werner Hahlweg, *Die Heeresreform der Oranier und die Antike*, Berlin, 1941, pp. 25–93, 110–16; J. W. Wijn, *Het Krijgswezen in den Tijd van Prins Maurits*, Utrecht, 1934, pp. 74, 138–40, 430; H. Wertheim, *Der toller Halberstädter. Herzog Christian von Braunschweig im pfälzischen Kriege*, Berlin, 1929, i, 116. Jähns suggested that Maurice's reforms may have been forced on him by the great wastage of trained soldiers during protracted hostilities in a small area, and the consequent need to use untrained men. But the old style would have suited untrained men much better. Max Jähns, *Handbuch einer Geschichte des Kriegswesens von der Urzeit bis zur Renaissance*, Leipzig, 1880, p. 1207.

8. J. J. Wallhausen, *L'Art militaire pour l'Infanterie*, Oppenheim, 1615, p. 65.

9. Jähns, *op. cit.*, p. 1208.

10. The matter of marching in step needs investigation. The only discussion appears to be E. Sander, 'Zur Geschichte des Gleichschrittes', *Zeitschrift fur Heeres- und Uniformkunde* (1935), who as a result of a misreading of Francis Grose, *The Military Antiquities of Great Britain* (1812), i, 345, attributes the credit for the idea to the Earl of Essex, on the strength of a sentence which he believes to be contained in *A Worthy Speech spoken by his Excellence the Earl of Essex* (1642). But the quotation is in fact (as Grose plainly states) from the Regulations of 1686; and confidence in Sander's views is not much restored by his suggestion that marching in step was the 'gegebene Form' for armies of the Nordic Race. It has been said that it was Leopold of Dessau who made it the rule in the Prussian army (W. Sombart, *Der moderner Kapitalismus*, i, 345); but it seems probable that it was used much earlier. The Swiss columns and the *tercios*, though they marched to tap of drum, do not seem to have kept step; and such reproductions of Callot's etchings as I have seen suggest that the armies of the Thirty Years' War did not keep step either. Wallhausen says nothing of it in his chapter on marching (Wallhausen, *L'Art militaire pour l'Infanterie*, pp. 121–4); nor does Monro (*Monro his Expedition* [London, 1637], ii, 190). But whatever may have been the case on the march, it seems quite certain that the infantry of the early seventeenth century kept step for drill. Thus Wallhausen writes (*op. cit.*, p. 73): 'Tenez le pied gauche coy, conversez vous en reculant le pied droict'; and E. D. Davies, in *The Art of War and Englands Traynings* (1619), is even more explicit: 'The Captaine commands, *Files to the right hand Counter march*, and then the Leaders of the Files advancing with their right legge, turn to the right hand, and march downe towards the Reare ...' (p. 194). Indeed, it might be possible to argue from Davies that English soldiers already kept step on the march: 'Let him march then with a good grace, holding vp his head gallantly, his pace full of grauities and state ... and that

which most imports, is that they haue alwaies their eies vpon their companions which are in ranke with them, and before them going iust one with the other, and keeping perfit distance without committing error in the least pace *or step* [my italics]' (p. 76). This may be to attach too much importance to a mere flower of Davies' exuberant style; but it seems very likely that pikemen, at least, could not afford to be out of step when marching in close order, for the position of the pike when held at the trail, and its extreme length, would otherwise have been liable to imperil the haunches of the man in front: see Davies' description, *loc. cit.*

11. 'Il n'y a pas un Cavalier dans les trouppes de France, qui n'ait un habillement de Bufle, depuis que l'on s'est deffait de ceux de fer': Gaya, *Traité des Armes*, Paris, 1678, p. 56.

12. R. Knötel, H. Knötel, J. Sieg: *Handbuch der Uniformkunde. Die militärische Tracht in ihrer Entwicklung bis zur Gegenwart*, Hamburg, 1937, is a standard history. The authors consider that there were no true uniforms before about the middle of the century; but it is possible to dispute this view: see, e.g., Wertheim, *op. cit.*, i, 94; E. von Frauenholz, *Das Söldnertum in der Zeit des dreissigjährigen Krieges*, Munich, 1938, i, 41–2; K. C. Rockstroh, *Udviklingen af den nationale haer i Danmark i det 17. og 18. Aarhundrede*, Copenhagen, 1909, i, 18, 52–3.

13. Paul Schmitthenner, *Europäische Geschichte und Söldnertum*, Berlin, 1933.

14. *Ibid.*, p. 26; Piero Pieri, 'La formazione dottrinale di Raimondo Montecuccoli', *Revue internationale d'histoire militaire*, x, (1951), p. 94: 'le esigenze della nuova tattica esigono insomma degli eserciti mercenari permanenti'.

15. See on this Eugen Heischmann, *Die Anfänge des stehenden Heeres in Österreich*, Vienna, 1925, pp. 199–200.

16. For these attempts see E. von Frauenholz, *Die Landesdefension in der Zeit des dreissigjährigen Krieges*, Munich, 1939; H. Wertheim, *Der toller Halberstädter*, i, 68–75; Max Lenz, *Landgraf Moritz von Hessen*, in *Kleine historische Schriften*, Munich and Berlin, 1920, ii, 128–31; C. Jany, *Geschichte der Königlich Preussischen Armee*, Berlin, 1928, i, 26–9, 61; Otton Laskowski, 'Uwagi na marginesie nowego wydania Zarysu Historii Wojskowośce w Polsce Generata Mariana Kukiela', *Teki Historyczne*, v (1951–2), p. 39; Rockstroh, i, 4–38, 65; H. Kretzschmar, *Sächsische Geschichte*, Dresden, 1935, ii, 39.

17. For Lazarus von Schwendi, see E. von Frauenholz, *Lazarus von Schwendi. Der erste deutsche Verkünder der allgemeinen Wehrpflicht.*

18. As Gustav Adolf put it to Adolf Frederick of Mecklenburg; 'Es möchtte E. L. imandt einbilden wollen, als wen das lands volck nicht zum krige tauget, lasen sich solches ja von den grossprecheren nicht einbilden, glauben mihr (der ich tegelich die probe da von nehmen muss) das wen sihe wol gefürret vnd gecommendiret werden, mit ihnen mehr, dan mit der irregularen soldatesce, auss zu richtten': C. G. Styffe, *Konung Gustaf II Adolfs skrifter*, Stockholm, 1861, p. 414. Sweden did indeed employ mercenaries in time of war to supplement her standing army of conscripts; but the permanent force, as provided for in the Form of Government of 1634, was a militia.

19. R. Altamira y Crevea, *Historia de España y de la Civilizaciòn española*, Barcelona, 1927, iii, 289–93; P. Schmitthenner, *Krieg und Kriegführung im Wandel der Weltgeschichte*, p. 196.

20. V. K. Kiernan, 'Foreign Mercenaries and Absolute Monarchy', *Crisis in Europe 1560–1660*, ed. T. Aston (1965), pp. 122–3.

21. Rockstroh, i, 4, 6, 31, 65; G. Irmer, *Die Verhandlungen Schwedens und seiner Verbündeten mit Wallenstein und dem Kaiser von 1631 bis 1634*, Leipzig, 1899, i, 259: in August

1632 John George told Lars Nilsson Tungel, 'Ich will die bauren nicht bewehren, solte auch das land unter sich, über sich gehen'.

22. For all this E. von Frauenholz, *Das Söldnertum in der Zeit des dreissigjährigen Krieges* is now the best authority.

23. Heischmann, pp. 105–6.

24. Wallhausen also made the point that a standing army eased the burdens of the civil population, since it avoided the excesses which usually accompanied disbandment: Wallhausen, *L'Art militaire pour l'Infanterie,* pp. 19–20; Montecuccoli, p. 64. In the last months of his life, Gustav Adolf was driven to attempt to form a standing army for the whole of Protestant Germany, in the interests of *discipline.*

25. As suggested by A. Vagts, *A History of Militarism* (1938), p. 46.

26. As suggested by Werner Sombart, *Der moderne Kapitalismus,* i, 345, though he did add, 'Die Waffentechniek mag dabei mitgesprochen haben'.

27. J. E. Elias, *Het Voorspel van den eersten Engelschen Oorlog,*'s Gravenhage, 1920, i, 150–1, for a suggestive comparison of the two cases.

28. *Axel Oxenstiernas skrifter och brefvexling,* Stockholm, 1888-, II, i, 396.

29. The Kiel canal was Wallenstein's idea. It is noteworthy that the biggest canal enterprise of the century—the Canal des Deux Mers, linking Bordeaux with the Mediterranean—was essentially a strategic work.

30. In 1639: one of the great military feats of the war: see Birger Steckzén, *Johan Baner,* Stockholm, 1939, p. 330.

31. Lars Tingsten, 'Några data angående Gustaf II Adolfs basering och operationsplaner i Tyskland 1630–1632', *Historisk tidskrift,* I Series, xlviii (1938); *Sveriges krig 1611–1632,* v, 282–4, 314, 330–8; vi, 7, 33–4, 179, 259. For a fuller discussion of Gustav Adolf's strategy, see Roberts, *Essays in Swedish History,* pp. 71–3.

32. B. Steckzén, *Baner,* pp. 208, 332, 342; Piero Pieri, 'La formazione dottrinale di Raimondo Montecuccoli', pp. 100, 110: 'La guerra cessa per sfinimento, attraverso una strategica logoratrice sempre più crudele e implacabile'; and *cf.* Per Sörensson, 'Fältherrar, härorganisation och krigföring under trettioåriga krigets senare skede' *Scandia,* iii (1930), *passim.*

33. Altamira, iii, 295; J. Colin and J. Reboul, *Histoire militaire et navale* (=*Histoire de la nation française,* ed. G. Hanotaux, vii), Paris, 1925, i, 428, 432, 433; General Weygand, *Turenne,* Paris, 1934, p. 98.

34. C. Jany, *op. cit.,* i, 53.

35. J. U. Nef, *La Naissance de la civilisation industrielle,* Paris, 1955, *passim.*

36. The Swedes had 10,800 at Kirkholm; 'at most 10,000' at Narva: G. B. C:sson Barkman, *Svea Livgardets historia,* Stockholm, 1938–9, ii, 537; Rudolf Fåhraeus, *Karl XI och Karl XII,* Stockholm, 1932, p. 338.

37. Pieri, 'Formazione dottrinale di ... Montecuccoli', p. 114.

38. 'Self-equipment is conducive to the relaxation of discipline—that is, to the flattening of the pyramid of subordination': Stanislaw Andrzejewski, *Military Organization and Society* (1954), p. 99. But I cannot agree with his view that arms monopolies were 'the expression of [the rulers'] desire to assert their control, and not dictated by technical necessities': *ibid.,* p. 88.

39. Montecuccoli, pp. 110–11.

40. Colin and Reboul, p. 368.

41. Weygand, *Histoire de l'Armée française,* p. 144, reproduces this medal.

42. For a discussion of related problems, see James E. King, *Science and Rationalism in the Government of Louis XIV,* Baltimore, 1949.

43. A. Ernstberger, *Hans de Witte, Finanzmann Wallensteins,* Wiesbaden, 1954.

44. J. Saint-Germain, *Les financiers sous Louis XIV,* Paris, 1950, p. 17. V. Klutchevski, *Pierre le Grand et son oeuvre,* Paris, 1953, pp. 162–6.

45. K. R. Swart, *The Sale of Offices in the Seventeenth Century,* The Hague, 1949, *passim.*

46. The point is well made in M. Ritter, 'Das Kontributionssystem Wallensteins', *Historische Zeitschrift,* 90 [N.F. 54] (1930), pp. 248–9.

47. G. Droysen, *Beiträge zur Geschichte des Militärwesens in Deutschland während der Epoche des dreissigjährigen Krieges,* Hanover, 1875, pp. 28–31, for the resemblances between a mercenary company and a gild.

48. Andrzejewski, *op. cit.,* p. 96.

49. V. Loewe, *Die Organisation und Verwaltung der Wallensteinischen Heere,* Freiburg i.B., 1895, pp. 22–4.

50. L. André, *Michel Le Tellier et Louvois,* Paris, 1942, pp. 327–40; Gordon A. Craig, *The Politics of the Prussian Army 1640–1945,* Oxford, 1955, pp. 5–6.

51. The term is Andrzejewski's.

52. Especially for those who lived on a main traffic artery: one major cause of the decline in the population of Coburg during the period was enlistment. G. Franz, *Der dreissigjährige Krieg und das deutsche Volk,* Jena, 1943, p. 41.

53. T. A. Fischer, *The Scots in Germany: being a contribution towards the History of the Scots abroad,* Edinburgh, 1902, p. 74, gives the proverb in the original. *Cf.* the Scots ballad: "First they took my brethren twain, Then wiled my love from me, O, woe unto the cruel wars In Low Germanie!" See B. Hoenig, *Memoiren Englischer Officiere im Heere Gustaf Adolfs und ihr Fortleben in der Literatur,* in *Beitr. z. neueren Philologie J. Schipper dargebracht,* Leipzig, 1902, pp. 324–50.

54. Turner, *Pallas Armata,* p. 166. Or as Wallhausen put it, when lamenting the decline of the lance, 'on est contraint de se servir de gens basses et vils': *Art militaire à cheval,* p. 3; and *cf.* similar remarks in Richelieu, *Testament politique,* p. 476.

55. Wallhausen, *L'Art militaire pour l'Infanterie,* pp. 9–10.

56. There is a good discussion of the question in H. J. C. von Grimmelshausen, *Simplicissimus the Vagabond* [trans. A. T. S. Goodrick] (1912), in chapters xvi–xvii: 'Who was the Imperialist John de Werth? Who was the Swede Stalhans [i.e. Stålhandske]? Who were the Hessians, Little Jakob and St André? Of their kind there were many yet well known, whom ... I forbear to mention'. He argues that this is no new state of affairs; but when he comes to give a list of earlier examples he can think of no instance between Hugh Capet and Pizzaro except Tamerlane. Simplicissimus was mistaken about Stålhandske, moreover: his father had been *kammarjunkare* to Erik XIV.

57. Roland Mousnier, *La Vénalité des Offices sous Henri IV et Louis XIII,* Rouen, n.d., p. 506; *cf.* Frauenholz, *Söldnertum,* i, 27: 'vom Ritterschlag hört man nichts mehr, an denen Stelle tritt die Nobilitierung'. For conditions in Sweden, E. Ingers, *Bonden i svensk historia,* Stockholm, 1943, i, 234; B. Steckzén, *John Baner,* p. 57: 'Their [*sc.* Swedish infantry officers'] coats of arms are often of recent origin, and many of them are not easily distinguishable from the young peasant lads that serve as NCOs, or fill the ranks as privates'.

58. It was said of the *Feldschreiber* that 'er muss fast des Hauptmanns Meister sein, der selber oftmals nicht schreiben und rechnen kann': Loewe, *op. cit.,* p. 20.

59. As for instance in the Great Elector's *Generalkriegskommissariat:* 'From the beginning its civilian officials interfered with military affairs and acted very independently of the army command': F. L. Carsten, *The Origins of Prussia*, Oxford, 1954, p. 263.

60. Richelieu, *Testament*, pp. 393–4, condemns *ban* and *arrière-ban;* and see, for Sweden, P. Sörensson, 'Adelns rusttjänst och adelsfanans organisation', *Historisk tidskrift*, 42 (1922), 145–50, 221–3; and for Brandenburg, Jany, *op. cit.*, i, 10–12.

61. In the armies of the Great Elector, for instance, 'the officers of the artillery and the engineers were almost exclusively commoners': Carsten, *op. cit.*, p. 271.

62. *Sveriges krig 1611–1632*, supplementary vol. ii, 295.

63. E. G. R. Taylor, *The Mathematical Practitioners of Tudor and Stuart England*, Cambridge, 1954, *passim.*

64. A. R. Hall, *Ballistics in the Seventeenth Century*, Cambridge, 1952, p. 16: 'The standard of engineering technology was not merely insufficient to make scientific gunnery possible, it deprived ballistics of all experimental foundation, and almost of the status of an applied science, since there was no technique to which it could, in fact, be applied'.

65. M. Kukiel, *Zarys historji wojskowośce w Polsce*, London, 1949, p. 46. For Gustav Adolf's interest in cartography, see Försvarsstabens krigshistoriska avdelning, *Vägar och vägkunskap i Mellaneuropa under trettioåriga krigets sista skede*, Stockholm, 1948, pp. 41–2.

66. L. Hammarskiöld, 'Ur svenska artilleriets hävder', *Artilleri-Tidskrift*, 1941–4, p. 93.

67. *Krijgskundige Aantekening van Johan van Nassau*, ed. J. W. Wijn, p. xii.

68. *Saucisses de guerre* are described by Johan of Nassau as 'korbe welche langerlich und geflochten sint … mit eisernde schroten kugel oder kleinen steinen auffollet', and as 'wurste welche voll pulvers gefullet und in die rustlöcher [of a fortress] so viel man dun kan, gesteckt, und die mauer also gesprengt werden'. They are said to have been sacks an ell thick and ten to twelve feet long: *Krijgskundige Aantekening—van Johan van Nassau*, pp. 50, 94 and note 2. They are possibly to be distinguished from the *saucissons* described in a note to Montecuccoli (*Mémoires*, p. 137, note) as 'grosses fascines liées en trois endroits'.

69. Sir G. N. Clark, 'The History of the Medical Profession', *Medical History*, X, (1966), p. 218.

70. Styffe, *Gustaf Adolfs skrifter*, pp. 65, 67; *Monro His Expedition*, II, 175, 196; and in general for military education W. Sjöstrand, *Grunddragen av den militära undervisningens uppkomst- och utvecklingshistoria i Sverige till år 1792*, Uppsala, 1941. The concluding section of Wallhausen's *Art militaire à cheval* (pp. 97–134) is 'a discourse of two persons … on the excellence of the Military Art, maintaining that (except Theology) it excels all the other arts and sciences, as well liberal as mechanical', and insisting that 'the Military Art ought to be taught in Academies, as Letters are'. And Davies writes (*The Art of War and Englands Traynings*, p. 29) that the military profession 'being then more perfect and aboue all other Arts, consequently it is necessarie we vse in the same greater Studie, and more continuall exercise then is to be vsed in any other Art'.

71. Sjöstrand, pp. 177–83; Wijn, pp. 74–80; Heischmann, pp. 211–13.

72. Loewe, pp. 18–25.

73. André, *Le Tellier et Louvois*, pp. 317–21; and (on the emergence of rank) Wijn, pp. 62–73; Frauenholz, *Söldnertum*, i, 28–9; Sjöstrand, p. 71.

74. Edmond Silberner, *La Guerre dans la Pensée économique du XVIe au XVIIIe siècle*, Paris, 1939.

75. *Ibid.*, p. 99.

76. J. E. Elias, *Het Voorspel van den eersten Engelschen oorlog*, i, 141–2.

77. Bulstrode Whitelocke, *Memorials of the English Affairs* (1732), pp. 633 ff.

78. Elias, *op. cit.*, i, 134–177, especially pp. 157, 167–8; Charles E. Hill, *The Danish Sound Dues and the Command of the Baltic*, Chapel Hill, 1926, p. 155.

79. For all this see F. Redlich, *De praeda militari. Looting and Booty 1500–1815*, Wiesbaden, 1956.

80. See, e.g., M. Ritter, 'Das Kontributionssystem Wallensteins', *passim*.

81. Pieri, 'Formazione dottrinale', p. 100.

82. Styffe, *Gustaf II Adolfs skrifter*, p. 520.

83. *Axel Oxenstiernas skrifter och brefvexling*, I, vii, 126.

84. For Vauban and the notion of the *pré carré*, see *Makers of Modern Strategy*, ed. E. M. Earle, Princeton, 1944, pp. 40–6.

85. The best early example of this is perhaps the close-action broadside; but the new linear tactics were not far behind.

86. 'Les maisons n'étoient que de bois, comme dans la pluspart de l'Allemagne, et en moins de six heures tout fut reduit en cendre: exemple terrible mais nécessaire contre des bourgeois insolents qui ne sachent ce que c'est que de faire la guerre, osent insulter de braves gens et les défier d'entrer dans leurs murs, lors-qu'ils n'ont ni l'adresse ni le courage de s'y défendre': G. Gualdo-Priorato, *L'Historie des dernières campagnes et negociations de Gustave Adolphe en Allemagne. Avec des notes ... par M. l'Abbé de Francheville*, Berlin, 1772, p. 185. It is difficult to agree with Professor Nef (*War and Human Progress* [1950], pp. 138) that Spinola's courteous treatment of the enemy at the surrender of Breda (1625), as against the horrors of Magdeburg (1631), marks the beginning of a new chivalrousness and the age of limited warfare, though Oestrich (*op. cit.*, p. 31) endorses Nef's comment. Breda capitulated; Magdeburg was stormed: the two cases are not comparable.

87. Grimmelshausen, *Simplicissimus*, p. 32.

88. Francisco Suarez, *De Triplici virtute theologica, fide, spe, et charitate* (1621) (new edn, Oxford, 1944), especially vii, p. 13–16; Alberico Gentili, *De Jure Belli Libri Tres* (1612) (new edn, Oxford, 1933), II, iv, viii, xxi, xxiii; James Brown Scott, *The Spanish Origin of International Law: Francisco de Vitoria and his Law of Nations*, Oxford, 1934, especially p. 285.

89. *Hugonis Grotii De Jure Belli ac Pacis Libri Tres*, ed. W. Whewell, Cambridge, 1853, III, iv, 9 § 1, for this passage; and see *ibid.*, III, iv, 8–10, 15, 16; III, v, 1; III, viii, 1–4.

90. Bynkershoek is said to have remarked 'dat de Groot zich steeds aan de bestaande gewoonten en gebruiken houdt, zoodat hij bij gebreke daarvan nauwelijks eenigen regel van jus gentium durft te stellen': J. Kosters, 'Het Jus gentium van Hugo de Groot en diens voorgangers', *Mededeelingen der Koninklijke Akademie van Wetenschappen*, Afd. Letterkunde, 58 (1924). Series B., p. 13.

2

The 'Military Revolution, 1560–1660'—A Myth?

GEOFFREY PARKER

'THE SIXTEENTH CENTURY constitutes a most uninteresting period in European military history,' wrote Sir Charles Oman in 1937, and no one then dared to disagree with him. Today, however, few historians would endorse his verdict. The early modern period has come to be seen as a time of major change in warfare and military organization, as an era of 'military revolution'. This shift in historical perspective is mainly the work of one man: Michael Roberts, until recently Professor of History at the Queen's University of Belfast. His inaugural lecture, entitled 'The Military Revolution, 1560–1660' and delivered at Belfast in January 1955, was an undisguised manifesto proclaiming the originality, the importance, and the historical singularity of certain developments in the art of war in post-Renaissance Europe. Now most inaugural lectures, for better or worse, seem to fade into the seamless web of history, leaving little trace; yet Professor Roberts's inaugural is still quoted time after time in textbooks, monographs, and articles. His conclusions, as far as I know, have never been questioned or measured against the new evidence which has come to light in the twenty years or so which have elapsed since he wrote. Such an examination is the aim of this paper.[1]

Roberts's 'military revolution' took place between 1560 and 1660 in four distinct areas. First and foremost came a 'revolution in tactics': certain tactical innovations, although apparently minor, were 'the efficient cause of changes which were really revolutionary'.[2] The principal innovation in the infantry was (he claimed) the eclipse of the prevailing technique of hurling enormous squares of pikemen at each other in favour of linear formations composed of smaller, uniform units firing salvos at each other; likewise the cavalry, instead of trotting up to the enemy, firing, and trotting back again (the *caracole*), was required to charge, sabres in hand, ready for the kill. According to Roberts, these new battle procedures had far-reaching logistical consequences. They required troops who were highly trained and disciplined, men who would act as cogs in a machine; and the cogs had to learn how to march in step and how to perform their movements in perfect unison—they even had to dress the same.[3] Individual prodigies of valour and skill were no longer required. Of course all this training cost money; and, because the troops had acquired their expertise at the government's expense, Roberts claimed that it was no longer economical for armies to be demobilized when the campaigning ended: the trained men had to be retained on a permanent footing. The new tactics, he argued, thus gave rise inexorably to the emergence of the standing army, and the first to pioneer these tactical reforms—and therefore one of the first to create a standing army in Europe—was Maurice of Nassau, captain-general of the army of the Dutch Republic.[4]

A 'revolution in strategy' formed the second major strand of Roberts's thesis. With the new soldiers, it proved possible to attempt more ambitious strategies: to campaign with several armies simultaneously and to seek decisive battles without fear that the inexperienced troops would run away in terror. Gustavus Adolphus of Sweden, victor of the Breitenfeld and conqueror of Germany, certainly put these new strategic concepts into effect; according to Roberts, he was the first.

A third component of the military revolution theory was a 'prodigious increase in the scale of warfare in Europe' between 1560 and 1660. The new strategy, Roberts pointed out, required far more troops for its successful execution: an articulated force of five armies operating simultaneously according to a complex plan would need to be vastly more numerous than a single army under the old order. Fourth and finally, this prodigious numerical increase dramatically accentuated the impact of war on society. The greater destructiveness, the greater economic costs, and the greater administrative challenge of the augmented armies made war more of a burden and more of a problem for the civilian population and their rulers than ever before.

These four assertions form the kernel of the military revolution theory. There was, of course, a great deal more—the development of military education and military academies,[5] the articulation of positive 'laws of war',[6] the emergence of an enormous literature on war and war studies,[7] and so on—but the four essential ingredients of the theory were tactics, strategy, army size, and overall impact. Have these assertions been modified in any way by recent research?

In the first place, it has become clear that the choice of the year 1560 as the starting point of the military revolution was unfortunate. Many of the developments described by Roberts also characterized warfare in Renaissance Italy: professional standing armies, regularly mustered, organized into small units of standard size with uniform armament and sometimes uniform dress, quartered sometimes in specially constructed barracks, were maintained by many Italian states in the fifteenth century. Machiavelli's oft-quoted jibe about the campaigns of the *condottieri*—that they were 'commenced without fear, continued without danger, and concluded without loss'—was unfair and untrue. The armies of Renaissance Italy were efficient and effective; and the French, German, Swiss, and Spanish invaders had to adopt the methods of the *condottieri*, both in attack and defence, before they could make real headway against them. To a remarkable degree, as we shall see, the character of early modern European warfare, even down to its vocabulary, came direct from Renaissance Italy.[8]

There is no doubt, however, that Maurice of Nassau and his cousin William-Louis made some important tactical innovations in the army of the Dutch Republic. They reduced the size of the tactical units and increased significantly the number of officers and under-officers; they increased the number of musketeers and arquebusiers (the 'shot') in each unit; and they introduced the classical technique of the countermarch, whereby successive ranks of musketeers advanced, fired, and retired to reload in sequence. The latter was certainly new, but, until the introduction of a more accurate musket which could also be swiftly reloaded, the countermarch was of limited practical value.[9] Moreover, Maurice's other tactical innovations, described by Roberts, derived at least some of their 'revolutionary' character from a rather unfair portrayal of the 'prerevolutionary' warfare of the earlier sixteenth century. The Spanish army in particular, which Roberts used as a foil to the tactical reforms of Maurice of Nassau, was a force of impressive military efficiency. By the 1560s Spanish infantry on active service was normally made up of small, uniform companies of between 120 and 150 men, grouped into *tercios* (or regiments) of between 1200 and 1500 men.[10] The Spanish infantry normally contained a heavy concentration of shot—it was the Duke of Alva who pioneered the introduction of musketeers into every company in the 1550s—and in the 1570s there were at least two companies which consisted solely of shot in every *tercio* on active service.[11] Throughout the Spanish army, as elsewhere, the basic tactical and administrative unit was the company: men were raised, trained, and paid in companies, not in regiments and not as individuals. Although the Spanish army had no larger formal tactical units like the brigades or battalions of the Swedish army, it was Spanish practice to group a number of experienced companies together for special assignments to form a task force, known as an *escuadrón,* which might number anywhere between 600 and 3000 men, depending on the task to be performed.[12] This flexible, informal arrangement for the infantry proved highly satisfactory. The Spanish cavalry, too, was impressive in action. It comprised mainly companies of light horse, each numbering between 60 and 100 troopers, some of them lancers and some of them mounted gunmen (*arcabuceros a caballo*). In battle, as at Gembloux in 1578, their intervention was decisive; at other times they policed the countryside with ruthless efficiency. Dressed in turbans like the Turkish light horse, whose tactics were successfully emulated, the Spanish cavalry was as feared and as formidable as the *tercios*.

Spain's more permanent armies were also distinguished by a sophisticated panoply of military institutions and ancillary services. In the Netherlands and Lombardy, at least after 1570, there was a special military treasury, an elaborate and autonomous hierarchy of judicial courts, a well-developed system of medical care—with a permanent military teaching hospital, mobile field-surgery units, and resident doctors in every regiment—and a network of chaplains under a chaplain-general covering the entire army.[13] Some, if not all, of this administrative super-structure was also to be found attached to the permanent Spanish forces in Naples and Sicily. Sixteenth-century Spain also had a complex training scheme for its men. In the words of an envious English observer of 1590, 'Their order is, where the Warres are present, to supplie their Regiments being in Action with the Garrisons out of his dominions and provinces; before they dislodge, *besonios* supply their place; raw men as we tearme them. By these means he traines his *besonios* and furniseth his Armies with trained Souldiers.'[14] From at least the 1530s Spanish recruits were sent initially not to the front line but to the garrisons of Italy or North Africa, where they learned the rudiments of arms drill and combat discipline for a year or two before leaving for active service. Their places were then taken by another generation of recruits.[15] It was an extremely efficient system, and it helps to explain the remarkable military calibre, reputation, and track record of the *tercios*. It was they, after all, who routed the 'new model' Swedish army at Nördlingen in 1634.

Lest this should seem like special pleading from a starryeyed student of Spanish history, one could point equally effectively to the Austrian Habsburgs, who introduced much the same system for their permanent armies on the Croatian and Hungarian borders with the Ottoman empire during the 1570s.[16] And, if even that were not enough, there are the military organizations of France, England, and the Italian states during the fifteenth century: all developed permanent standing armies which were highly trained; seasoned in garrisons before they went to the front; capable of fighting in linear formations as well as in columns or squares; organized into small, self-contained tactical units; and controlled by a special military administration.[17] The simple fact is that, wherever a situation of permanent or semi-permanent war existed, whether the Hundred Years' War of the later Middle Ages or the Thirty Years' War of the seventeenth century, one finds, not surprisingly, standing armies, greater professionalism among the troops, improvements in military organization, and certain tactical innovations. Gustavus Adolphus in the 1620s and Maurice of Nassau in the 1590s were forced to overhaul their armies dramatically because of the disastrous defeats which their predecessors had suffered in the preceding years. For inspiration, it is true, they turned in part to classical writers like Frontinus, Vegetius, and Aelian; but, like other rulers, they also turned to other more successful military practitioners, especially to the generals of Spain. Three of the best English military writers of the reign of Elizabeth—William Garrard, Humphrey Barwick, and Sir Roger Williams—had all served in the Spanish Army of Flanders for several years and held up its practices as examples to others.[18] The war in the Low Countries was a seminary in which many of the great commanders of the German Thirty Years' War and the English Civil War were formed.[19] It is no accident that a large part of the military vocabulary of northern Europe should have come from Spanish.[20]

The Dutch, however, did make a distinctive contribution of their own. Maurice of Nassau and his cousin were convinced of the need for standardization and uniformity in their forces. In 1599 they secured funds from the States-General to equip the entire field army of the Republic with weapons of the same size and calibre. At about the same time, Count John II of Nassau began work on a new method of military training: the illustrated manual. He analysed each of the different movements required to manipulate the principal infantry weapons, gave each of them a number, and prepared a series of corresponding drawings to show what was required. There were fifteen drawings for the pike, twenty-five for the arquebus, and thirty-two for the musket. In 1606–7 the whole scheme was recast—now there were thirty-two positions for the pike and forty-two for each of the firearms—and a sequence of numbered pictures was engraved and published under Count John's supervision: Jacob de Gheyn's *Wapenhandelingen van roers, musquetten ende spiessen* [Arms drill with arquebus, musket and pike] (Amsterdam, 1607). The book went rapidly through numerous editions in Dutch, French, German, English, even Danish; there were pirated and plagiarized versions; there were many subsequent attempts to produce rival manuals (of which the best were Johan Jakob von Wallhausen's *Kriegskunst zu Fusz* of 1615, Henry Hexham's *Principles of the Art Militarie* of 1637, and Jean de Lostelneau's *Mareschal de bataille* of 1647). The sudden popularity of the new genre of military textbook is explained by the tactical changes of the sixteenth century. The evolution from monolithic, massed pike formations to articulated combinations of pike and shot, which made a more elaborate hierarchy of ranks necessary, placed an increasing burden on the junior officers and underofficers. They became the crucial links between the army commanders and the small tactical units; they had to control, discipline and drill their men. It was to answer their needs that de Gheyn and the rest produced their drill books. The situation depicted in a picture of a company of the Amsterdam militia in 1625, painted by W. van den Valckert, must have been fairly typical: the captain is shown standing with de Gheyn's *Wapenhandelingen* actually open in front of him, trying to work out what to do next! The Dutch may not have invented the 'revolution' in tactics, but they certainly invented the best way of coping with some of its effects.[21]

There is thus room for doubt concerning the novelty of the tactics and the standing ..mies introduced by Prince Maurice and King Gustavus. There is also some question about the originality of Gustavus's strategy. Again, Roberts starts with a damaging critique of the practice of sixteenth-century generals: 'The sterility of warfare in Europe, in the time of Prince Maurice, is the accurate measure of the strategic thinking of the age.' And in another passage, 'Strategic thinking withered away; war eternalized itself.'[22] Now the crucial influence on the evolution of strategic thinking in the sixteenth century was the appearance of an entirely new type of defensive fortification: the *trace italienne*, a circuit of low, thick walls punctuated by quadrilateral bastions. In the course of the fifteenth century it became obvious that the improvements in gun founding and artillery had rendered the high, thin walls of the Middle Ages quite indefensible. A brief cannonade from the 'bombards' brought them crashing down. The reason why the kingdom of Granada fell to the Christians so easily in the 1480s, when it had resisted successfully for seven centuries, lay in the fact that Ferdinand and Isabella were able to bring a train of almost one hundred and eighty siege guns against the Moorish strongholds.[23] The English possessions in France were likewise reconquered in the 1430s and 1440s largely by Charles VII's artillery; at Castillon in 1453, the big guns even won a battle. The initiative in warfare now lay with the aggressor, and, not surprisingly, by 1500 every major European state possessed a powerful artillery park for use against its neighbours or against its dissident subjects. Military architects in Italy, where siege warfare was most common, were the first to experiment with new techniques of fortification which might withstand shelling; and Professor John Hale has traced the evolution of the bastion defence in Italy from about 1450, when it made its first appearance, until the 1520s, when it was fully fledged. It was a development which 'revolutionized the defensive-offensive pattern of warfare', because it soon became clear that a town protected by the *trace italienne* could not be captured by the traditional methods of battery and assault. It had to be encircled and starved into surrender.[24] The French military writer Fourquevaux declared in 1548 that towns whose fortifications were more than thirty years old, that is, which were built before the age of bastions, hardly deserved to be called fortifications at all. 'We must confesse,' echoed Sir Roger Williams, 'Alexander, Caeser, Scipio, and Haniball, to be the worthiest and famoust warriors that euer were; notwithstanding, assure your selfe, ... they would neuer haue ... conquered Countries so easilie, had they been fortified as Germanie, France, and the Low Countries, with others, haue been since their daies.'[25] There was therefore a scramble among the great powers to build the new 'miracle' defences wherever there existed a risk of attack: in Lombardy, in Hungary, in the Low Countries, along the south coast of England, and elsewhere. As it happened, these areas were all large plains—'continental islands', to use the language of Fernand Braudel—where a few great towns dominated the countryside. Whoever controlled the towns controlled the countryside; and therefore in all these areas war became a struggle for strongholds, a series of protracted sieges. Battles were often irrelevant in these areas unless they helped to determine the outcome of a siege. Even total victory in the field did not necessarily compel the well-defended towns to surrender: they could continue to resist, as did St Quentin after the famous battle in 1557, or as the towns of Holland and Zealand were to do after 1572, either until they were starved into submission or until the enemy gave up through exhaustion.[26] Naturally, since the *trace italienne* was introduced in those areas most likely to be fought over, and since most of the fighting of the sixteenth century did in fact take place there, it is true to say with Roberts that most generals, like Maurice of Nassau, 'had no ambition whatever to fight battles'. This proves only that they had a sound grasp of strategic realities. But whenever wars happened to occur in areas where the *trace italienne* was absent—in Italy before 1529, in central France during the religious wars, in the British Isles, or in Germany—then battles were both frequent and important: Pavia in 1525, Mühlberg in

1547, Ivry in 1590, and so on. It was even possible in such areas to operate a conscious *Vernichtungsstrategie*.[27] It was also true that, where bastions were absent and battles more frequent, cavalry was more prominent: on Europe's steppe frontier, for example, with the cossacks and stradiots, or during the civil wars in Germany and England, with the furious charges of Pappenheim, Prince Rupert, and Cromwell's Ironsides. But even in these theatres of conflict, battles were seldom 'decisive', in the sense that they brought the wars to an immediate end. Neither the Breitenfeld, nor Lützen, nor Wittstock, nor Jankow—four resounding victories for the 'new-model' Swedish army—terminated the Thirty Years' War. The two battles of the war which came nearest to achieving 'total' victory were, as it happened, won by Spanish 'old-style' forces: the White Mountain in 1620 and Nördlingen in 1634.

The generals of the seventeenth century, like their predecessors, were compelled to respect the dictates of military geography. When in 1632 the imperial army under Wallenstein retreated into the Alte Veste, a specially prepared stronghold near Nuremburg, Gustavus Adolphus was compelled to expend a great deal of time, men, and money in trying to starve them out. And in the end he failed. In France, Vauban diligently erected a chain of modern defences all around the sensitive and exposed frontiers of the country. Coehoorn did the same in the United Provinces. These fortifications of the later seventeenth century, vast star-shaped complexes which kept the besieging artillery out of range of its prey, continued to be of strategic importance until the 1860s. Wherever they existed, they made battles irrelevant—and therefore unusual. Throughout modern times, as in the Middle Ages, military geography shaped strategy.[28]

There is thus some doubt about the significance of both the tactical and the strategic aspects of Roberts's military revolution. But there is absolutely no doubt about its third constituent: the growth in army size. Between 1530 and 1710 there was a ten-fold increase both in the total numbers of armed forces paid by the major European states and in the total numbers involved in the major European battles. Table 2.1 demonstrates the inflation in armies—which was paralleled in navies—and the rise in combatants is obvious when one compares battles like Pavia (1525) and Nieuwpoort (1600), with 10,000 combatants on either side, and a battle like Malplaquet (1709), with 200,000 men involved.

If, however, we can accept Roberts's assertion about military manpower growth, we cannot *a priori* accept his explanation of it. It cannot stem, as he thought, from the tactical and strategic innovations of Maurice of Nassau and Gustavus Adolphus: first, because these modifications were not so new; second, and more important, because the rapid and sustained growth in army size predated them. The Emperor Charles V had 55,000 men at the siege of Metz in 1552, long before Maurice was born, and the Spanish Army of Flanders already numbered 86,000 men in 1574, when the prince was only six years old. There were, in fact, certain other tactical changes which cleared the way for the 'prodigious increase' in army size.

Table 2.1: Increase in Military Manpower, 1470-1710

Date	Spanish Monarchy	Dutch Republic	France	England	Sweden	Russia
1470s	20,000		40,000	25,000		
1550s	150,000		50,000	20,000		
1590s	200,000	20,000	80,000	30,000	15,000	
1630s	300,000	50,000	150,000		45,000	35,000
1650s	100,000		100,000	70,000	70,000	
1670s	70,000	110,000	120,000		63,000	130,000
1700s	50,000	100,000	400,000	87,000	100,000	170,000

Sources: For figures on Spain, *Castilla y la conquista del reino de Granada* (Valladolid, 1967), p. 159; G. Parker, *The Army of Flanders*, p. 6; and H. Kamen, *The War of Succession in Spain 1700-1715* (London, 1969), pp. 59-60 (for metropolitan Spain only). For the Dutch Republic, F. J. G. Ten Raa and F. de Bas, *Het Staatsche leger, 1568-1795*, 6 vols. (Breda, 1911-18), vol. I, passim. For France, Contamine, *Guerre, état et société*, pp. 313-18; F. Lot, *Recherches sur les effectifs des armées françaises des guerres d'Italie aux guerres de religion (1494-1562)* (Paris, 1962), pp. 135-88; L. André, *Michel le Tellier* (Paris, 1906), pp. 271-328; and H. Methivier, *Le Siècle de Louis XIV* (Paris, 1962), p. 68. For England, C. G. Cruikshank, *Elizabeth's Army* (Oxford, 1966), passim; C. Firth, *Cromwell's Army* (London, 1962), pp. 34-5; and R. E. Scouller, *The Armies of Queen Anne* (Oxford, 1966), Ch. 3. For Sweden, M. Roberts, *The Early Vasas: A History of Sweden, 1523-1611* (Cambridge, 1968), pp. 399-404; and C. Nordmann, 'L'armée suédoise au XVIIe siècle', *Revue du Nord*, LIV (1972), pp. 133-47. For Russia, *New Cambridge Modern History*, V (Cambridge, 1964), p. 577.

For most of the Middle Ages, the principal arm in any military force was the heavy cavalry, made up of fully armed knights on horseback, three hundred-weight of mounted metal apiece, moving at speed. The knights were clumsy, expensive, and scarce; but they were capable of winning great victories: Antioch (1098), Bouvines (1214), and Roosbeke (1382), for example. There were also, however, disastrous defeats, especially in the fourteenth and fifteenth centuries, when it was discovered that a heavy cavalry charge could regularly be stopped either by volleys of arrows or by a forest of pikes. Later it was found that pikemen could be used offensively to charge other groups of pikemen, once the mounted knights had been impaled and disposed of. The victories of the Swiss infantry against Charles the Rash of Burgundy in the 1470s wrote the lesson large, and in the Italian wars the infantry component in every army became steadily more numerous and more decisive. Charles VIII's army in 1494 comprised about 18,000 men, half of them cavalry; Francis I's army in 1525 comprised some 30,000 men, one-fifth of them cavalry. The number of horsemen had decreased both absolutely and relatively.[29] This shift in emphasis from horse to foot was crucial for army size. Whereas there was a limit to the number of knights who could manage to equip themselves and their horses ready for a charge, there was none to the number of ordinary men who could be enlisted and issued a pike, sword, and helmet. A pikeman's basic equipment cost little more than his wages for a week, and in some cases even this paltry sum could be deducted from the soldier's pay.

Thanks to the triumph of the pikemen, therefore, it became possible for governments to recruit, arm, and train an unlimited number of men. The road to unrestrained military increase lay wide open. But it only lay open. There was nothing in all this which actively *compelled* an army to augment its numbers. Indeed, over fifty years were to pass between the final defeat of Charles the Rash in 1477 and the first major increase in army size in the 1530s, an increase necessitated by the vast number of men required to starve out a town defended by the *trace italienne*. After this period of growth came four decades of stagnation: there was no further increase in army size until the 1580s. No government could dream of bringing larger concentrations of troops into action, for the simple reason that none possessed the organization necessary to mobilize, pay, and supply such a force. By the middle of the sixteenth century, there were only ten cities in all of Europe with a population in excess of 60,000. Before the promise of the Swiss achievement could be fully realized, before the threshold of medieval army size could be crossed, there had to be important changes in the financial and administrative resources of the European states.[30]

The growth of military manpower depended not only on internal factors like tactics but also on a number of extrinsic factors, totally unrelated to the art of war itself. Perhaps four can be identified as critical. In the first place, there clearly had to be governments capable of organizing and controlling large forces. It is interesting to note that the major waves of administrative reform in western Europe in the 1530s and 1580s and at the end of the seventeenth century coincided with major phases of increase in army size.[31] On the one hand, the growth of a bureaucracy was necessary to create larger armies; on the other, it was necessary to control them. The rapid numerical expansion of the early seventeenth century forced some decentralization: governments used entrepreneurs to raise their soldiers, sailors, and (in the case of the Mediterranean states) their galley fleets. It has been estimated that between 1631 and 1634 there were some 300 military enterprisers raising troops in Germany alone, ranging from Albrecht von Wallenstein, Duke of Friedland and imperial commander-in-chief (who raised entire armies under contract) to minor gentry from Switzerland and the Tyrol (who raised single companies or even single squadrons). It was the same story in most areas of Europe, even in countries like Spain, where troop raising had been a jealously guarded royal monopoly in the sixteenth century.[32] However, it is important to note that, in all Europe, only Oliver Cromwell managed to emulate the generals of Rome or the *condottieri* of Italy and wrest political power from his civilian employers. Elsewhere, if we except the Ottoman empire with its janissaries, governments always maintained a close rein on their commanders and kept their armies under constant surveillance. War departments proliferated in every country, squeezing out military entrepreneurs and other middlemen and establishing a direct link with every soldier in the army. Detailed records of the troops began to be kept, so that the only surviving historical trace for hundreds of thousands of men in early modern times is their army paysheets.[33]

The numerical expansion of armies was also dependent on certain elementary technological improvements. In order to supply 50,000 men (and camp followers) on the march, it had to be possible to concentrate enough ovens to produce 50,000 loaves of bread a day; enough water, wine, and beer had to be concentrated for them all to drink; and there had to be enough carts and horses to carry their baggage (which might amount to half a ton per man!) and enough tents, beds, or shelters to accommodate at least the officers.[34] Only in the later sixteenth century did it become possible to meet these basic human needs on a grand scale. Another elementary technological frontier to be crossed concerned roads. It was not possible to move large concentrations of troops at speed before the seventeenth century because there were no roads outside Italy which were capable of carrying a large army, its supply train, and its artillery. In the sixteenth century, even on a route used regularly by troops, like the 'Spanish Road' from Lombardy to Luxemburg, it was necessary to build new causeways in the mountains and across marshes and to construct special bridges over rivers and streams for every military expedition—once every two years on average because, after the troops had passed, everything was allowed to revert to its former state.[35] Only in the later seventeenth century did governments see the need, and possess the means, to construct and maintain permanent military highways: Charles XI of Sweden and Louis XIV of France led the way during the 1680s. In the eighteenth century roads even began to be used as an instrument of imperialism, as they had once been by the Roman, Chinese and Inca empires, with General Wade's network of military roads, laid out mainly between 1726 and 1767, to tame the Scottish highlands.

However, for all this one needed money, and here we come to two other, and perhaps more important, extrinsic limits to military growth. First, there had to be a certain level of wealth in society before heavy and prolonged military expenditure could be supported; second, there had to be ways of mobilizing that wealth. It would seem that between 1450 and 1600 the population of Europe almost doubled, and in some areas it more than doubled; and there is little doubt that, over the same period, there was a notable increase in the total wealth of Europe. After about 1660 both population and wealth began to increase again. This new prosperity was tapped everywhere by taxation, either indirectly through excise duties upon consumer goods or directly by a variety of levies on land, capital, and (very rarely) income. Government revenues increased everywhere in the sixteenth century, delving ever deeper into the pockets and purses of the taxpayers. However, no government could pay for a prolonged war out of current taxation: the income which sufficed for a peacetime establishment could in no way prove equal to the unpredictable but inevitably heavy expenses of a major campaign. The state therefore had to spread the costs of each war over a number of peaceful years, either by saving up in anticipation (as Queen Elizabeth did before she decided to make war on Spain in 1585) or by spending in advance the income of future years with the aid of loans from bankers and merchants. With a small army this might not be such a great problem—France appears to have financed her Italian wars from 1494 until 1529 with few ill effects[36]—but in the sixteenth century the problem was very different because, apart from the growth in numbers and the greater

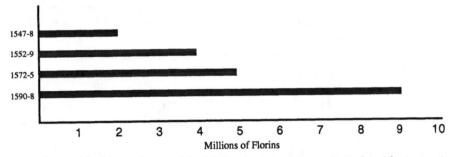

Figure 2.1   Average Annual Cost of Spain's Foreign Wars. *Source:* G. Parker, *The Army of Flanders*, pp. 134, n. 2; 287.

duration of wars (which of course increased the overall cost), there was also the 'price revolution', which meant that it cost far more to put a soldier into the field in 1600 than it had in 1500. This fact naturally did not escape the notice of contemporaries: 'If comparison were made between the present cost to His Majesty [Philip II] of the troops who serve in his armies and navies and the cost of those of the Emperor Charles [his father], it will be found that, for an equal number of men, three times as much money is necessary today as used to be spent then.'[37] Written in 1596, this was, if anything, an underestimate; but it was indisputable that each war cost more than the preceding one and that for Spain, involved in so many long-enduring conflicts, the progression was particularly alarming (see Figure 2.1). Fortunately for Habsburg imperialism, the Spanish crown was able to draw on a relatively efficient financial system which enabled it to borrow (or 'anticipate') the revenues of up to ten years in advance and, by brutal treatment of its lenders, to keep the interest rate down to 7 per cent or less. But even this did not produce all the money required for wars and many of the troops were left unpaid, sometimes for months and sometimes even for years. As a result, Spain's soldiers regularly mutinied for their pay; and mutiny became almost an institution of military life. However, it was an institution shared with other armies. The Dutch army was periodically paralysed by mutinies in the 1580s, as was the Parliamentary army during the English Civil War (especially in 1644 and 1647). Many units of the Swedish army in Germany mutinied in 1633, dissipating the prestige won by the victories of the Breitenfeld and Lützen, and again in 1635, encouraging many German Protestants to make peace with the Habsburgs.

The fact that the second mutiny was called an 'alteration', the term invariably used by the Spanish mutineers to describe their activities, betrayed the parentage of the practice. The perennial problem for the Swedish, the Spanish, and indeed every government in wartime was money. In the words of an English adviser to the Dutch Republic during their war with Spain: 'The matter of greatest difficulty [in war] ... is in proportioning the charge of the warres and the nombers of the souldiers to be maynteyned with the contribucions and meanes of the countreys.'[38] It was, above all else, the financial resources of a state which held down the size of its armed forces. If too many troops were engaged, or if they were engaged for too long, mutiny and bankruptcy resulted.

It was the Dutch who first perfected techniques of war finance capable of sustaining an enormous army almost indefinitely. The cost of the war with Spain from 1621 until 1648 steadily increased (from an average of 13 million florins in the 1620s to an average of 19 million in the 1640s), but there was not a single mutiny or financial crisis. On the contrary, in an emergency, the Dutch Republic could raise a loan of 1 million florins at only 3 per cent in two days. The key to this effortless financial power was, in part, the enormous wealth of Amsterdam, which by 1650 was the undisputed commercial and financial capital of Europe; but it was equally the good faith of the Dutch government, which always paid interest and repaid capital on time. This combination enabled the Dutch to raise an army and go on fighting, whatever the cost, until they got their own way: something no previous government had been able to do. It was not long before others followed. Soon after the accession of William of Orange in 1689, 'Dutch finance' was adopted in England. The foundation of the Bank of England, Parliament's guarantee of all government loans, and the organization of a sophisticated money market in London made it possible for a British army of unprecedented size—90,000 men—to fight overseas for years; while in France the credit network of Samual Bernard and other Swiss bankers financed Louis XIV's later wars.[39]

Thanks to all these improvements, by the first decade of the eighteenth century the major wars of Europe involved some 400,000 men on each side, and major battles involved up to 100,000.[40] It therefore comes as something of a surprise to find that the major conflicts of the 1760s and 1780s involved no more—that there was no further growth in army size until the French Revolutionary wars. In the eighteenth century, as in the fifteenth, it seems that the military power of the various European states had reached a threshold. Further economic, political, technological, and financial advances would be required before this new threshold could be crossed in the 1790s.

However, the revolution in military manpower between 1530 and 1710 was extremely important. It certainly had all the significant consequences which Roberts attributed to it: it made war impinge more upon society; it increased the authority of the state (partly at the expense of the citizen); it accentuated social mobility; and it undoubtedly retarded the economic development of most participants (although it stimulated that of many neutrals).[41] In addition, it certainly helped to precipitate the numerous confrontations between governments and the governed which are commonly referred to as the 'general crisis' of the seventeenth century. The 'prodigious increase in the scale of warfare' alone merits the title of 'military revolution' which Roberts bestowed upon it twenty years ago.

It has been suggested that the half-life of major historical theories is roughly ten years; and the fates of Trevor-Roper's 'general crisis', Elton's 'Tudor revolution', and Porshnev's 'popular uprisings' seem to bear this out. By this standard,

Roberts's 'military revolution' has lasted well. Hitherto unchallenged, even this extended examination has failed to dent the basic thesis: the scale of warfare in early modern Europe was revolutionized, and this had important and wide-ranging consequences. One can only conclude by wishing the theory and its author many more years of undiminished historical life.

Notes

1. Michael Roberts, *The Military Revolution, 1560–1660* (Belfast, 1956); reprinted in a slightly amended form in M. Roberts, *Essays in Swedish History* (London, 1967), pp. 195–225 (and above, Ch. 1), with some additional material on pp. 56–81. For examples of how the 'military revolution' has been accepted by other scholars *cf.* G. N. Clark, *War and Society in the Seventeenth Century* (Cambridge, 1958), and again in *New Cambridge Modern History,* V (Cambridge, 1964), ch. 8. Compare the approach of C. W. C. Oman, *A History of the Art of War in the Sixteenth Century* (London, 1937). I am grateful to the following for their helpful suggestions concerning the preparation of this chapter: Mr Brian Bond, Dr Peter Burke, Professor John Hale, Professor H. G. Koenigsberger, Mrs Angela Parker, Dr Ian Roy and Professor John Shy. I would also like to thank the 'subject' of this paper, Professor Michael Roberts, for his help over many years and for his encouragement to publish.

2. Roberts, *Military Revolution*, p. 29, above.

3. On the whole, troops did not dress alike in most armies until the later seventeenth century. It was the 1650s before the English and Swedish armies adopted uniform; the French did not do so until the 1660s. Before that, the troops dressed as they (or their commander) wished, carrying only distinguishing marks such as a feather, a scarf or a sash of the same colour to mark them out from the enemy. Not surprisingly there were a fair number of cases of units from the same army attacking each other in the confusion of battle. *Cf.*, for the introduction of uniforms, C. Nordmann, 'L'armée suédoise au XVIIe siècle', *Revue du Nord,* LIV (1972), pp. 133–47 (at p. 137); L. André, *Michel le Tellier et l'organization de l'armée monarchique* (Paris, 1906), pp. 339–42; and Geoffrey Parker, *The Army of Flanders and the Spanish Road, 1567–1659. The logistics of Spanish victory and defeat in the Low Countries' Wars* (Cambridge, 1972), pp. 164–5.

4. On the reorganization of the Dutch army by Prince Maurice and his cousin, William-Louis, *cf.* W. Hahlweg, 'Aspekte und Probleme der Reform des niederländischen Kriegswesen unter Prinz Moritz von Oranien', *Bijdragen en Mededelingen betreffende de Geschiedenis der Nederlanden,* LXXXVI (1971), pp. 161–77; and M. D. Feld, 'Middle-class society and the rise of military professionalism. The Dutch Army, 1589–1609', *Armed Forces and Society,* I (Aug. 1975), pp. 419–42. Both authors stress that, although classical precedents were closely studied by the Nassau cousins (especially outstanding successes like the battle of Cannae in 216 BC), their relevance to military conditions in the Netherlands was also carefully evaluated.

5. There were a few centres of instruction like the 'academia militaris' of John of Nassau at Siegen (1617–23), and courses of obvious military utility such as mathematics and fencing were added to the curricula of a number of colleges and schools; but when one remembers the central place of war in seventeenth century society the lack of more formal education in military matters is somewhat surprising.

6. Professor Roberts commented on the proliferation of studies on the 'law of war' in the seventeenth century (*Military Revolution,* pp. 28–29); the basic principles, however, already affected the conduct of wars in the Middle Ages; *cf.* M. H. Keen, *The Laws of War in the Late Middle Ages* (London and Toronto, 1965).

7. In England alone, between 1470 and 1642 a total of at least 164 English and 460 foreign books were published. *Cf.* M. J. D. Cockle, *A Bibliography of Military Books up to 1642* (London, 1900; reprinted 1957), and H. J. Webb, *Elizabethan Military Science: the Books and the Practice* (Wisconsin, 1965). For many years, Venice appears to have been the centre of printed military culture: between 1492 and 1570, some 67 new titles on military matters were published in the city, compared with about 64 in the whole of the rest of Europe (J. R. Hale, 'Printing and the military culture of Renaissance Venice', *Mediaevalia et Humanistica,* N. S. VIII [1977], 21–62). It is interesting to note that scarcely any work dealt with naval warfare (*ibid.,* p. 49).

8. On the influence of the Italian wars upon Europe's military history *cf.* P. Pieri, *Il Rinascimiento e la crisi militare italiana,* 2nd ed. (Turin, 1952) and M. E. Mallett, *Mercenaries and their Masters. Warfare in Renaissance Italy* (London, 1974), especially chs. 7 and 9. The points at which the European 'military revolution' tended to follow Italian precedents are indicated *seriatim* in the notes below; *cf.* note 20 for the linguistic inheritance.

9. The 'countermarch' was devised by William-Louis of Nassau, and a diagram showing what was involved was sent to Count Maurice on 8 Dec. 1594: *cf.* a facsimile of this on p. 6 of J. B. Kist's *Commentary* to J. de Gheyn, *The Exercise of Armes* (New York, facsimile edition, 1974). Professor Maury Feld has claimed that the countermarch turned an army into 'a unit of continuous production' and the soldiers into some sort of assembly-line workers, and that this constituted a major tactical improvement. In theory, this is true; but, as noted above, there were, in practice, serious technical limitations. (*Cf.* M. D. Feld, 'Middle-class society', *art. cit.* in note 4. This important and interesting article was kindly brought to my attention by Professor P. David Lagomarsino of Dartmouth College.)

10. It is incorrect to say that 'a Spanish army of 12,000 men would have four units' (Roberts, *Military Revolution* [1956], p. 7); although Professor Roberts omitted this passage from the second edition of his paper, he still overestimated the size of the Spanish units on active service (*Essays,* pp. 59–60 and 62). It now appears that the Swedish army, also, did not have regiments of uniform size (Nordmann, 'L'armée suédoise', p. 137 n. 23), and that there was no fixed ratio of pike to 'shot' in the army of Gustavus Adolphus—it all depended on the availability of weapons at the time of recruitment.

11. Take, for example, the peacetime muster of the four Spanish *tercios* in the Netherlands, held on 12 May 1571. There were 50 companies (an average of 12 per *tercio*) and 7509 men (an average of 150 men—9 of them officers—per company). Of the 7509 men, 596 (9 per cent) were musketeers and 1577 arquebus-men, a total of 30 per cent 'shot'. (Archivo General de Simancas, *Estado,* leg. 547 fo. 99 *bis,* 'Relación sumaria de los soldados que se pagaron'.)

12. The *escuadrón* was also a common tactical unit in the Dutch army, *eo nomine; cf.* J. W. Wijn, *Het krijgswezen in den tijd van prins Maurits* (Utrecht, 1934), p. 424. For the Swedish equivalent *cf.* A. Åberg. 'The Swedish Army, from Lützen to Narva', in M. Roberts (ed.), *Sweden's Age of Greatness, 1632–1718* (London, 1972), pp. 265–87, at p. 282.

13. G. Parker, *The Army of Flanders,* pp. 167–72, and the sources there quoted. It seems that Spain and Sweden were far ahead of the field in the provision of religious care for their troops. There were even Jesuit priests aboard the Dunkirk privateers after 1623 (*cf.* E.

Hambye, *L'aumônerie de la flotte de Flandre au XVIIe siècle,* Louvain, 1967) and every soldier aboard the Spanish Armada of 1588 received a leaden medallion with the Virgin on it (and several of these have been found by nautical archaeologists excavating the Armada wrecks off Ireland). The Swedish Army in Germany had an 'ecclesiastical consistory' under an Almoner-General and every soldier was issued with a Lutheran prayer-book (Nordmann, *art. cit.,* p. 136).

14. J. X. Evans, *The Works of Sir Roger Williams* (Oxford, 1972), p. 15. *Cf.* the confirmation of Sir Francis Bacon in 1624 that 'the great Secret of the Power of Spaine ... will be found, rather to consist in a Veterane Army (such as vpon several Occasions and Pretensions, they haue euer had on foot, in one part or other of Christendom, now by the space of [almost] sixscore yeares) than in the strength of the Dominions and Prouinces.' (Quoted *apud* Evans, *op. cit.,* p. cxli.)

15. Parker, *op. cit.,* pp. 32–5.

16. G. E. Rothenburg, *The Austrian Military Border in Croatia, 1522–1747* (Urbana, Ill., 1960), chs. 3–5; E. Heischmann, *Die Anfänge des Stehenden Heeres in Oesterreich* (Vienna, 1925), *passim.*

17. R. A. Newhall, *Muster and Review: a Problem of English Military Administration, 1420–1440* (Cambridge, Mass., 1940); P. Contamine, *Guerre, état et société à la fin du moyen âge. Etudes sur les armées du roi de France, 1337–1494* (Paris, the Hague, 1972); C. T. Allmand, *Society at War. The Experience of England and France during the Hundred Years' War* (Edinburgh, 1973); M. E. Mallett, *Mercenaries and their Masters: Warfare in Renaissance Italy* (London, 1974).

18. Garrard served in the Burgundian regiment of the baron de Chevreux in the Netherlands for fourteen years; Williams served in the Spanish *tercio* of Julian Romero from 1574 until 1578; Barwick mentions his Spanish service but does not indicate how long it lasted. All three put their experience to good use in their writings: *cf.* H. J. Webb, *Elizabethan Military Science,* pp. 44–50. There was, of course, a vigorous debate throughout most of the sixteenth century between the 'Ancients' (who believed that Greece and Rome had provided exemplars to be copied in all spheres save religion) and 'Moderns' (their opponents, of whom the three writers above are examples). *Cf.* also Hahlweg, 'Aspekte und Probleme', *art. cit.* in note 4.

19. F. Redlich, *The German Military Enterpriser and his Workforce,* I (Wiesbaden, 1964), pp. 157–62 for examples.

20. Sir Roger Williams stressed the point to readers of his *Discourse of Warre* (1590): 'Some will condemnde mee for my strange names of fortifications, they ought to pardon me: for my part, I knowe no other names than are given by the strangers, because there are fewe or none at all in our language.' (*Works,* ed. Evans, p. 41). In the Netherlands, Simon Stevin's manual of fortification—*Stercktebouwing* (1594)—carried foreign military terms in the margin with an explanation in the text; while a popular account of the Dutch Revolt, Emanuel van Meteren's *History of the Low Countries* (the Hague, 1612), contained a special glossary of foreign military words (*'Vreemde Krijghsvocabulen'*). In every modern army, many of the current officers' titles (captain, sergeant etc.) and some of those now obsolete (e.g. 'reformado', an officer who is temporarily without a unit to command) appear to have come from Spanish or Italian to France, the Netherlands, and England. *Cf.* J. Herbillon, *Eléments espagnols en Wallon et dans le Français des anciens Pays-Bas* (Liège, 1961). It seems likely, however, that many of these military terms came to Spanish from Italian first: J. Terlingen, *Los Italianismos en español desde la formación del idioma hasta principios del siglo*

XVII (Amsterdam, 1943). There is no full analysis of the Spanish words loaned to Flemish and Dutch although there is a sketchy introduction by C. F. A. van Dam, 'De Spaanse woorden in het Nederlandsche', in *Bundel ... aangeboden aan Prof. Dr C. G. N. de Vooys* (Groningen, 1940), pp. 86–103.

21. Van den Valckert's painting of Captain Burgh's militia company hangs—like Rembrandt's more famous picture of the company of Captain Hans Banning Cocq, done in 1642—in the Rijksmuseum, Amsterdam. There is a reproduction of the portion which clearly shows de Gheyn's book on p. 37 of Kist's *Commentary* to the facsimile edition of de Gheyn cited in note 9. Dr Kist establishes beyond all doubt the influence of Johan II of Nassau on the composition of the *Wapenhandelingen* (pp. 14–15) and he describes the measures taken in 1599 to standardize armament in the Dutch army. For a little more information on the first English edition of de Gheyn, *cf.* Anna E. C. Simoni, 'A present for a prince', in *Ten Studies in Anglo-Dutch Relations*, ed. J. A. van Dorsten (Leiden and London, 1974), pp. 51–71.

22. Roberts, *Military Revolution* (1956), p. 7, and *Military Revolution*, above p. 18.

23. M. A. Ladero Quesada, *Castilla y la conquista del reino de Granada* (Valladolid, 1967), p. 127. For a general assessment of the importance of artillery to Europe, *cf.* C. M. Cipolla, *Guns and Sails in the Early Phase of European Expansion, 1400–1700* (London, 1965). However the demise of the old-style castles did not occur overnight. In many areas where artillery could not easily be brought in, medieval fortifications retained their value. *Cf.* H. M. Colvin, 'Castles and government in Tudor England', *English Historical Review*, LXXXIII (1968), pp. 225–34.

24. J. R. Hale, 'The early development of the bastion: an Italian chronology, *c.* 1450–*c.* 1534', in *Europe in the Later Middle Ages*, ed. J. R. Hale, J. R. L. Highfield and B. Smalley (London, 1965), pp. 466–94.

25. G. Dickinson (ed.), *The 'Instructions sur le Faict de la Guerre' of Raymond de Beccarie de Pavie, sieur de Fourquevaux* (London, 1954), p. 58; *The Works of Sir Roger Williams*, p. 33.

26. G. Parker, *The Army of Flanders*, pp. 7–11 and notes. The same was true for many of the wars of the Middle Ages. The Hundred Years' War was, according to a recent study, 'characterized more by sieges than by any other form of martial exercise' (C. T. Allmand, *Society at War*, p. 7; *cf.* also pp. 6–9 and 10–22).

27. *Cf.* the policy of Sir Humphrey Gilbert, commander of Queen Elizabeth's forces in Ireland in 1579 and a veteran of the Low Countries Wars: 'He further tooke this order infringeable, that when soever he made any ostyng, or inrode, into the enemies Countrey, he killed manne, woman, and child, and spoiled, wasted, and burned, by the grounde all that he might: leavying nothing of the enemies in saffetie, which he could possiblie waste, or consume ... The killing of them by the sworde, was the waie to kill the menne of warre by famine, who by flight oftentymes saved them selves from the dinte of the sworde.' (Quoted from Thomas Churchyard's *Generall Rehearsall of Warres* of 1579 by J. T. Johnson, *Ideology, Reason, and the Limitation of War. Religious and secular concepts, 1200–1740* [Princeton, N. J., 1975], pp. 141–2. Dr Johnson points out that this is an early application of the counter-revolutionary doctrine that 'if revolutionaries live among the people like fish in water, the way to kill the fish is to dry up the water'.)

28. Military geography also affected military theory. It is true that Londoño, Valdes, Escalante and the other Spanish writers of the period who dealt with war said very little about battles; but this was because after 1559 Spain fought very few wars in which battles were necessary. At least two of the wars in which she was engaged were little more than ex-

tended guerilla actions: in New Galicia and in Chile. It is therefore no surprise to find that the first European manual of guerilla warfare was written by a Spaniard, Bernardo de Vargas Machuca, who had fought long years in Chile. His *Milicia de las Indias* of 1599 described jungle warfare with operational units of 20 or 30 men under a *caudillo* (leader) who knew not only how to lead and how to fight but also how to cure sores and wounds inflicted deep in the forest (most of his remedies involved the use of tobacco as a pain-killer), which vegetable seeds to take on the march to sow over the winter and harvest in the spring, and so on. The Indians of Chile never fought battles, Vargas Machuca observed, because they had learned from bitter experience that they always lost them! (For an account of the similar guerilla war on the northern frontier of Spanish America *cf.* P. W. Powell, *Soldiers, Indians and Silver: the Northward Advance of New Spain, 1550–1600* [Berkeley, 1969].)

29. F. Lot, *Recherches*, pp. 21 and 56. Even where cavalry continued to play a decisive role in battles, as in the French religious wars, its character and composition (as well as its tactics) were entirely different from those of the fifteenth-century *gendarmerie. Cf.* R. Puddu, *Eserciti e monarchie nazionali nei secoli XV–XVI* (Florence, 1975), pp. 35–6.

30. R. Bean, in an article of 1973, advanced a similar argument but failed to provide convincing evidence. *Cf.* the telling criticisms of Professors David Ringrose and Richard Roehl in *Journal of Economic History,* XXXIII (1973), pp. 203–31.

31. J. Vicens Vives, 'Estructura administrativa estatal en los siglos XVI y XVII', *in XIe congrès internationale des sciences historiques. Rapports,* IV (Stockholm, 1960), pp. 1–24; I. A. A. Thompson, 'The Armada and administrative reform', *English Historical Review,* LXXXII (1967), pp. 698–725; G. N. Clark, *The Seventeenth Century,* chs. 6 and 7; J. A. Maravall, *Estado moderna y mentalidad social,* 2 vols. (Madrid, 1972), *passim,* and especially 513–85.

32. The classic account of the organization of war by military middlemen is F. Redlich, *The German Military Enterpriser and his Workforce,* 2 vols. (Wiesbaden, 1964). For military contracting in early modern Spain, see I. A. A. Thompson, *War and Government in Habsburg Spain, 1560–1620* (London, 1976).

33. For some uses to which these copious military records can be put, *cf.* for the sixteenth century G. Parker, *The Army of Flanders and the Spanish Road;* for the eighteenth century A. Corvisier, *L'armée française de la fin du XVIIe siècle au ministère de Choiseul. Le Soldat,* 2 vols. (Paris, 1964); and for the nineteenth century E. Le Roy Ladurie and P. Dumont, 'Quantitative and cartographical exploitation of French military archives, 1819–1826', *Daedalus* (spring, 1971), pp. 397–441.

34. For some examples from the Army of Flanders *cf.* G. Parker, *op. cit.,* chs. 2 and 3.

35. *Cf.* Parker, *op. cit.,* ch. 3. However for a reminder that roads were not the only brake on military mobility *cf.* J. Milot, 'Un problème opérationnel du XVIIe siècle illustré par un cas regional', *Revue du Nord,* LIII (1971), pp. 269–90, which argues that until 1700, at least, tactics dictated that armies on active service had to march as a single formation (which might be 50,000 strong). No existing road network could cope with a horde like that, and most of the troops had to plough their way through trees and scrub just like their predecessors in earlier centuries.

36. P. Contamine, 'Consommation et demande militaire en France et en Angleterre, XIIIe–XVe siècles' (paper given at the *Sesta settimana di studia* at the *Istituto internazionale di storia economica,* Prato, 3 May 1974), pp. 26–7.

37. Esteban de Ibarra, Spanish secretary of war; quoted Parker, *op. cit.,* p. 134.

38. For 'alterations', see G. Parker, *Spain and the Netherlands*, 242, n. 23. For the quotation: 'Declaration' of Thomas Wilkes, 22 July 1587, printed in H. Brugmans (ed.) *Correspondentie van Robert Dudley, graaf van Leycester,* II (Utrecht, 1931), p. 402. For further information on mutinies, see chapter 5 of *Spain and the Netherlands*.

39. For a brief survey of the financial organization of the European states during this period see G. Parker, 'The emergence of modern finance in Europe', in C. M. Cipolla (ed.) *The Fontana Economic History of Europe,* II (London, 1974), pp. 560–82.

40. In France, A. Corvisier has suggested that one man in six was called up during the war of the Spanish succession (*L'armée française,* I, p. 65). The calculation of 'military participation ratios' before 1700 is extremely hazardous since we cannot be sure of the exact size either of the army or of the total population which it defended; and there is also the problem of 'foreign' troops serving in 'national' armies. But there are some interesting calculations in A. Corvisier, *Armées et sociétés en Europe de 1494 à 1789* (Paris, 1976), p. 127, but these almost all come from the eighteenth century.

41. See the attempt to establish the costs of the Low Countries Wars in chapter 10 of G. Parker, *Spain and the Netherlands.*

The Military Revolutions of the Hundred Years War[1]

CLIFFORD J. ROGERS

THE MILITARY REVOLUTION

The concept of the "military revolution" first[2] entered the historical literature with Michael Roberts's famous inaugural lecture, "The Military Revolution, 1560–1660," at the Queen's University of Belfast some forty years ago. Roberts proposed that the art of war in early modern Europe was radically transformed over that space of a century. A tactical revolution based on the use of linear formations of drilled musketeers had led to a massive increase in the size of armies, which in turn had dramatically heightened the impact of war on society. The new armies of Maurice of Nassau and Gustavus Adolphus, larger and more disciplined than any seen before, had made it possible to execute more complex strategic plans.[3]

The idea of the military revolution rapidly became the "new orthodoxy" in early modern military history, passing almost unchallenged until 1976,[4] when Geoffrey Parker's article, "The 'Military Revolution,' 1560–1660—a myth?" appeared. Parker argued that Roberts had overemphasized the importance of Gustavus Adolphus at the expense of French, Dutch, and Hapsburg developments; underemphasized the importance of siege warfare; and put the starting-date of the revolution perhaps half a century too far forward. Still, Parker concluded that he had "failed to dent the basic thesis" propounded by Roberts.[5] Subsequent studies stretched the parameters of the Military Revolution even further, and argued that its key significance lay in the development of state governmental bureaucracies which the revolution made necessary.[6]

The next major step in the development of Military Revolution historiography came with the 1988 publication of Parker's *The Military Revolution: Military innovation and the rise of the West, 1500–1800*. In that work, Parker posed the question which has come to define the significance of the Military Revolution as an historical phenomenon: "Just how did the West, initially so small and deficient in most natural resources, become able to compensate for what it lacked through superior military and naval power" and thus to conquer global empires covering over a third of the world's surface by 1800?[7] To answer that question, scholars of the subject have looked primarily at the period after Charles VIII's invasion of Italy in 1494, when the French demonstrated so dramatically the power of the new siege artillery. Thus, these historians have made the advent of the Military Revolution more or less synchronous with the early modern period, and tied it even more closely to the development of the *trace italienne* and earthwork artillery fortifications.[8]

Without doubt, the rapid development of fortifications against artillery during the Wars of Italy, the concomitant improvements in siege and field artillery, and the subsequent growth of army sizes all play important roles in answering Parker's question. So, too, do the reforms of Maurice of Nassau and Gustavus Adolphus. All of these aspects of the Military Revolution have been considered at some length by the works cited above.

I believe, however, that the focus on the centuries after 1500 obscures the importance of the period in which the most dramatic, most truly revolutionary changes in European military affairs took place: the period, roughly, of the Hundred Years War (1337–1453). The armies that dominated the battlefields of Europe from the mid-eleventh century through the early fourteenth were composed primarily of feudal warrior-aristocrats, who owed military service for lands held in fief.[9] They served as heavily armored cavalry, shock combatants, relying on the muscle power of man and steed, applied directly to the point of a lance or the edge of a sword.[10] They fought more often to capture than to kill. The armies which conquered Europe's first global empires, on the other hand, differed from this description on *every single count*. They were drawn from the common population (albeit often led by aristocrats); they served for pay; they fought primarily on foot, in close-order linear formations which relied more on missile fire than shock action; and they fought to kill.[11] The tremendous revolution in warfare represented by these changes was well underway by the middle of the Hundred Years War, and solidly in place by the end of that conflict.

This paper will argue that twice over the course of the Hundred Years War new developments revolutionized the conduct of war in Europe, in each case with consequences as significant for the history of the world as those which took place during Parker's Military Revolution (1500–1800). The first was the transition outlined in the paragraph above, which I shall refer to as the "Infantry Revolution."[12] The second, the "Artillery Revolution," occurred when gunpowder weapons reversed the long-standing superiority of the defensive in siege warfare. Each of these transformations fundamentally altered the paradigm of war in Europe, with far-reaching consequences for the structures of social and political life, and thus truly deserves to be termed a "military revolution" in itself.

When we consider that these two "revolutions" were followed in the succeeding centuries by a revolution in fortification (which once again reversed the balance between offense and defense) and then another in the administration of war (Roberts's original "Military Revolution"), we are led to reconsider whether the answer to Parker's question can possibly be a single "Military Revolution." In the last section of this paper, I will address that issue, and propose an alternative paradigm based on the biological concept of "punctuated equilibrium evolution." In essence, I will argue that Western military dominance derived from a *series* of sequential military revolutions, each an attempt to reverse a disequilibrium introduced by the previous one, rather than from a single "Military Revolution."[13] First, though, we must consider the warfare of the earlier Middle Ages, and the two revolutions which so dramatically altered its character over the course of the fourteenth and fifteenth centuries.

WAR IN THE "AGE OF THE HORSE"

In 1898, C.W.C. Oman described the period from 1066–1346 as the age of "the supremacy of feudal cavalry."[14] Recently, some scholars have attempted to dispute this conception, arguing that "cavalry was never militarily superior to foot soldiers" and that infantry played an equal or greater role on the medieval battlefield.[15] It is true that Oman, Delbrück, and other earlier authors failed to acknowledge the significant role of infantry in the High Middle Ages, but the fact remains that "medieval warfare was characterized by the dominant role of the heavy cavalry."[16] At Tinchebray in 1106, Bouvines in 1214, Dunbar in 1296, and Falkirk in 1298 (to consider only battles cited by authors who emphasize the role of the infantry), it was a cavalry charge that decided the battle.

Throughout this period, infantry on the battlefield generally acted in a purely defensive role, using a tight formation "like a great wall" of pole-arms and crossbowmen to protect the cavalry while it formed up for a charge. The importance of this "wall" derived in part from the men-at-arms' practice of riding from place to place on palfreys and mounting their chargers only immediately before battle, making it critically important for them to be protected while changing horses and forming up. To use the metaphor of single combat, the infantry served as a shield to the cavalry's sword.[17] Infantry could be very important, but it could not defeat an enemy unless he bashed his head against it.

The effectiveness of the cavalry is not hard to explain. The medieval knight, supported as he was by the labor of others, had plenty of time to train for combat.[18] His better diet made him larger and stronger than most of the commoners who formed the infantry.[19] Most importantly, the capital he had invested in horses, arms, and armor magnified his capabilities. Mail armor, reinforced by a leather cuirass or a padded gambeson, made him nearly invulnerable on the battlefield. The mobility afforded by his horses, in addition to its obvious strategic value, enabled him to pursue a defeated enemy effectively, to flee rapidly if himself defeated, and to avoid unwanted battles with slow-moving infantry forces. The combination of armor and mobility made the man-at-arms particularly effective as a forager, giving him a critically important role in extended sieges, which were more likely to be broken by lack of food than by enemy action.[20] Of course, the extremely high cost of a knight's equipment, which in the mid-thirteenth century cost about £32 (over ten years' wages for a foot archer),[21] strictly limited the number of knights and men-at-arms in medieval armies. By contrast, a well-equipped bowman of the early fifteenth century could buy all his arms and armor—a bow, sheaf of arrows, sword, bascinet, and brigantine—for £1 6s 8d. A crossbowman could potentially pay as little as 15s 4d for a crossbow, sword, bascinet, and jack—about one-fortieth the cost of the knight's equipment.[22]

The huge population and vast agricultural wealth of France, however, meant that the French could muster large numbers of men-at-arms despite their cost. Furthermore, French men-at-arms were widely regarded as the finest in the world.[23] Within the feudal military "ecosystem," the royal army of France dominated;[24] thus, it is no surprise that the Infantry Revolution first developed among the neighbors and opponents of France: the English, the Flemings, and the Swiss.[25]

THE INFANTRY REVOLUTION

In the thirteenth century, infantry played an important role on the battlefield, but it did not win battles. In the opening decades of the fourteenth, however, we can observe the first glimmerings of the revolution which was to overtake European warfare a generation later. At Courtrai in 1302, Bannockburn in 1314, and Morgarten in 1315, infantry armed with pole-arms triumphed over feudal cavalry.[26]

The importance of these early victories, however, should not be overemphasized. In each case, the infantry were able to achieve victory only because of peculiarities of the terrain, and the mistakes of their enemies. The Flemings at Courtrai chose a position which prevented the French from forming up properly before charging; and when the men-at-arms began their assault, their horses were severely hampered by the swampy ground—"caught by the net as bird is in snare," as a contemporary song had it. Unable to break through the serried ranks of the Flemish pikemen, they were equally unable to retreat. The burghers "made the glory of France into dung and worms."[27] The Scots put the English in a very similar situation at Bannockburn (1314), and the battle ended in much the same way. At Morgarten, the Swiss ambushed the Austrians in a narrow mountain pass and gave them no chance to form up or to flee.[28] On different terrain, though, the French chivalry remained quite capable of defeating even the staunch Flemish communal levies, as the battles of Mons-en-Pével (1304) and Cassel (1328) showed.[29]

The battle of Laupen (1339), where Swiss halberdiers and pikemen resoundingly defeated the cavalry and infantry of the Burgundian nobility, was something different. "For the first time almost since the days of the Romans," as Oman

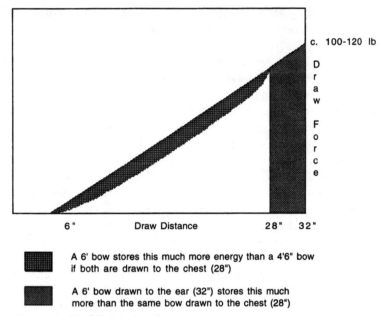

Figure 3.1   Total Energy in a Drawn Arrow

rightly points out, "infantry, entirely unsupported by horsemen, ranged on a fair field in the plains, withstood an army complete in all arms and superior in numbers."[30] Something new was afoot in European warfare, as the battle of Crécy confirmed seven years later.[31] Using the "pike-and-shot" combination of dismounted men-at-arms and archers which they had developed in the 1330s in Scotland, the English at Crécy devastated a French force (primarily men-at-arms fighting on horseback) approximately three times as numerous as themselves. Over the succeeding decades, major cavalry actions on the field of battle became rare, with even the French usually choosing to fight on foot.[32]

The new success of infantry forces in Western Europe rested on a number of developments. In the case of the English, the development of the six-foot yew longbow, substantially more powerful than the approximately four-foot Welsh elm bows of the early thirteenth century, played an important role. According to P. H. Blyth,[33] for a given draw strength and distance a six-foot longbow stores 25 percent more energy than a four-foot-eight-inch bow. The longbow, however, is drawn to the ear rather than to the chest (as the Welsh bow was[34]), increasing draw distance by several inches. Since the draw force of a longbow plotted against draw distance shows a nearly linear relationship, and the total energy stored is equal to the area under that line, each extra inch of draw adds more stored energy than the previous one. Those extra few inches are, therefore, of critical importance (Figure 3.1).

Thus, a six-foot longbow which at a twenty-eight-inch draw had the same draw weight as a four-foot-eight-inch bow, would have a substantially higher draw weight at its full thirty-two-inch draw, and would in total store about half again more energy than the shorter bow at the shorter draw. It seems reasonable to hypothesize that this increase could make the difference between ineffectiveness and lethality when attempting to penetrate an enemy's armor. Even arrows fired from the strong shortbows of the Moslems in the Crusades of the late twelfth century proved rather ineffective against European armor.[35] In contrast, a later medieval writer held that "the most important thing in the world, for battles, is the archers."[36] Of course, the draw weight increased with draw distance, so the longbow required a very strong archer to use it effectively.[37] Archaeological evidence shows that some medieval archers used longbows with draw weights up to 180 lbs., and the average was probably around 100.[38] England developed a pool of strong yeomen archers over decades of more-or-less constant warfare against the Scots and the Welsh—it is no coincidence that Cheshire archers, considered the best in England, came from the Welsh marches.[39] The French, despite numerous attempts, never succeeded in producing a comparable body of skilled archers.[40] Indeed, one could argue that France failed to join in on the Infantry Revolution until the late fifteenth century, and that many of her military failures prior to the advent of the Artillery Revolution in the mid-fifteenth century could be ascribed to that fact.

The growing importance in the English tactical system of dismounted men-at-arms, who used lances like pikes in a close-order formation designed to stop an enemy's cavalry charge, was, of itself, a less dramatic break with the past. What made these horsemen on foot so effective was their integration with the archers. Because the English formations had missile superiority, their dismounted men-at-arms could not be dispersed by enemy archers, in the way that the English themselves dispersed the pike formations of the Scots.[41] Even so, we must assume that the English victories, combined with the partial success of Flemish pikemen, encouraged others—including but not limited to the Swiss—to develop effective infantry armies, even though not provided with missile troops the equivalent of the English archers. For, once the possibility of victory through common infantry[42] was demonstrated, further experimentation became inevitable. Infantry possessed important advantages over cavalry. A common infantryman could be equipped for much less than a man-at-arms; he was paid less;[43] he could be trained more quickly;[44] and the ranks of the infantry could be filled from a much broader section of the population.[45] Nothing demonstrates the importance of these factors better than the fact that the lone county of Flanders could muster a larger army at Courtrai than could the entire kingdom of France. Because of its broader recruitment pool and lower costs of equipment and training, a military system based on common infantry—and *only* such a system—could turn surplus agricultural population into large numbers of soldiers for export to the world at large.[46] Thus, the Infantry Revolution was a necessary precondition for the European conquests of the sixteenth through eighteenth centuries.

SOCIAL IMPACT OF THE INFANTRY REVOLUTION

The significance of the Infantry Revolution, which reached fruition in the 1330s and 1340s, extends far beyond its immediate impact on the conduct of war. That there is a relationship between military power and political power is self-evident; thus, it should come as no surprise that the growing importance of common infantry on the battlefield was reflected in the political influence of the commons, especially in those nations such as England and Switzerland where the Infantry Revolution was the most completely embraced.[47] It is true that this growing importance of the commons derived as much from governments' need to secure the financial support of the people to sustain long-term war efforts as from the need to secure their military services,[48] but part of the reason why the great nobles needed the consent of the commons before appropriating their wealth lay in the increased ability of the people to resist oppression by military means, an ability due in large part to the Infantry Revolution. In 1340, for example, the English administration did not dare gather the tax money Edward III needed for his war on the Continent "for fear of [civil] war, and that the people would rise against them before they would give any more."[49] The commoners who joined the Great Revolt in England in 1381, which was sparked by the regressive poll taxes of 1377–80, were generally armed with longbows, and their leader, Wat Tyler, had seen service in France.[50] They did not accomplish all their goals, but they did succeed in abolishing the poll tax. Contemporary rulers well understood this connection between the military and the political power of the commoners: Charles VI of France gave up his attempt to impose universal training with the bow when he realized that the common archers "if they had been gathered together, would have been more powerful than the princes and nobles."[51]

It is little more than a striking coincidence that the French Estates-General met for the first time in the year of the battle of Courtrai.[52] The connection between the Infantry Revolution and the increasing importance of the Commons (who were elected by, and to a significant extent represented, the common freemen of the boroughs and shires,[53] though the MPs themselves were usually drawn from the gentry and urban elites) in the English Parliament, however, cannot be so easily dismissed. In wars against the Scots and Welsh, the English borough and shire levies had proved increasingly important since the late thirteenth century. Tactics based on the use of the longbow developed almost simultaneously with the regularization of Parliament under Edward I, and earned for that monarch a reputation as the "father" of both innovations.[54] Not until the reign of Edward III, however, did the importance of the Commons in Parliament come to equal that of the Lords—just as the importance of the archers drew even with that of the men-at-arms on the battlefield.[55]

The first record of the Commons meeting separately from the Lords in Parliament occurs in 1332, just after the battle of Dupplin Muir, the first of the great victories won by English archers during the reign of Edward III. By the 1340s, after the archers had further proved their worth at Halidon Hill (1333), Cadzand (1337), and Sluys (1340), the Commons had reached political maturity. At about the same time, the Commons began to take the initiative in legislation on a regular basis, acceding to new taxes only in return for political concessions.[56] In 1351, midway between the battles of Crécy and Poitiers, the Commons added control over indirect taxation (mainly the wool customs duties) to its established right to grant direct taxation. "By 1369," writes the Parliamentary historian G. L. Harriss, "the Commons ... had secured all the powers they were to enjoy for the next 200 years."[57] I do not mean to suggest that the connection between these two series of events is a simple and direct one. Still, there can be little doubt that a connection *does* exist, and that the military enfranchisement of the non-aristocratic population contributed to its increased political influence.[58] After all, in the medieval mind the profession of arms was inextricably related to *franchise* and *noblesse*.[59] Thus it should come as no surprise that the minimum property qualification which gave a man the right to vote in Parliamentary elections was set at the low level of 40 shillings of land income per year—the same amount which legally obliged him to own a bow, and put him in the class from which most foot archers were drawn.[60] In at least one other case, indeed, the connection between growing military and political power *was* quite simple and direct: as J. F. Verbruggen has pointed out, the Flemish guilds, which provided the framework for their communal levies, "acquired political power, made their own legal systems, and controlled their own finances" from the battle of Courtrai on.[61]

On a less elevated plane, the social impact of the Infantry Revolution made itself felt on the battlefield, with remarkable consequences for the European conception of war. War under the feudal regimes of Western Europe in the twelfth and thirteenth centuries often seemed more like sport than serious business. In the Flanders War of 1127, which involved about a thousand knights fighting for over a year, only one died by the hand of an enemy; an equal proportion of the total losses of the war resulted from excessive horn-blowing.[62] At Bouvines, which Ferdinand Lot described as "un Austerlitz médiéval," the victorious French are said to have lost only two men-at-arms (out of about 3,000); perhaps 70–100 of the 1500 defeated German knights were killed. At Lincoln in 1217, three knights were killed and four hundred captured.[63] Orderic Vitalis tells us that at Brémule (1119), where 900 knights of two royal armies came head-to-head, only three were killed.[64] Such low casualty figures characterized European warfare before the onset of the Infantry Revolution. The French at Courtrai, in contrast, lost a thousand knights; in return, they slew some six thousand Flemings at Cassel in 1328.[65] Agincourt brought an end to the lives of over 1,600 French knights, and perhaps 8,000 other men. Over 8,000 died at Verneuil (1424).[66] Without question, the Infantry Revolution made the European battlefield a much more sanguinary place.

How are we to explain this contrast? Orderic Vitalis explains the low casualties at Brémule by saying "they were all clad in mail and spared each other on both sides, out of fear of God and fellowship in arms; they were more concerned to capture than to kill the fugitives."[67] He tactfully leaves out what may well have been the primary motive which led them to "spare each other on both sides": ransom. The phrase "worth a king's ransom" remains in common use today to indicate a huge sum of money, and with good reason: the ransom of Jean II of France was set at 3,000,000 crowns (£500,000) in 1360. This figure was truly exceptional—equal to some 20 years worth of English ordinary royal revenue[68]—but even lesser captives could bring tremendous sums. Henry of Grosmont apparently received over £80,000 for his share of the ransoms of the prisoners taken at Auberoche and Bergerac; the Duke of Alençon brought £26,666; and Bertrand du Guesclin, the low-born soldier who became Constable of France, brought 100,000 francs (about £11,000).[69] Lesser knights brought lesser sums, but still enough to make capturing them far preferable to killing them.

When common infantry became a major force on the battlefield, much changed. The commoners, in general, did not command large enough ransoms to make their capture worthwhile. Nor did they share in the "fellowship in arms" which bonded chevaliers even of different nationalities. Quite the opposite: the class differences between knight and bourgeois or peasant often encouraged extreme bloodthirstiness. From Morgarten onward, the Swiss were famous for neither asking nor giving quarter. The Flemings at Courtrai took no prisoners. The victorious French at Roosebeke, having defeated the Flemish infantry, "had no mercy on them, no more than if they had been dogs."[70]

Simple technical factors also contributed to the increase in casualties evident during the Infantry Revolution. Pikes and longbows, by their very nature, are intended to kill an opponent before he can come in striking distance of the wielder, and it is difficult to offer or accept a personal surrender at a distance.[71] The value of the pike, furthermore, rested entirely on its use in a tight formation, and, again, it would have been impossible to take prisoners without breaking formation.[72] Halberds, goedendags, and bills, it is true, do not keep the enemy at such a distance. They are, however, slow and unwieldy weapons. Thus, a halberdier must strive to down his enemy with his first blow, for he is unlikely to get a second; and a full-arm swing from a halberd will rarely leave the person struck in much shape to surrender.[73]

Considering these social and technical factors, it is easy to see why the battlefields of the Infantry Revolution became such bloody places. It is hard to overemphasize the consequences of this development. Ever since, Europeans have had an unusually lethal approach to warfare. Geoffrey Parker has outlined the importance of this European conception of war in the European conquests of the early modern period, but he does not identify its origin. He contrasts the "bloody and devouring" warfare of the Europeans with that of the Narragansett Indians, who "might fight seven years and not kill seven men."[74] As we have seen, the same was true of Western Europeans in the twelfth and thirteenth centuries, but not after the advent of the Infantry Revolution.

The Infantry Revolution, however, was only the first of a series of periods of rapid change in European warfare which bring into question the concept of a single, overarching Military Revolution. Even as the Infantry Revolution reached its full maturity, early signs of the next "military revolution"—the Artillery Revolution—began to appear.

THE ARTILLERY REVOLUTION

Gunpowder artillery first appeared in Europe almost exactly a century before it revolutionized warfare in the 1420s–1440s. Roger Bacon's recipe for gunpowder dates back to 1267, but gunpowder seems not to have been used for war in Europe until the third decade of the fourteenth century. The earliest depictions of cannon in action, which are no later than the earliest documentary reference, appear in the manuscript of Walter de Milemete's *De Officiis Regnum,* completed in 1326.[75] According to the Scottish chronicler John Barbour, the English used some type of gunpowder weapon ("crakkis of wer") during the Weardale campaign of the following year. Guns, probably much like the Milemete weapons, were employed by German knights at the siege of Cividale in 1331.[76] Already by 1333, cannon had taken their place alongside catapults, springalds, and trebuchets as important siege engines. In that year, the English besieged Berwick and

> made meny assaute with gonnes and with othere engynes to the toune, wherwith thai destroide meny a fair hous; and cherches also weren bete adoune vnto the erthe, with gret stones, that spytously comen out of gonnes and of othere gynnes. And notheles the Scottes kepte wel the toune, that tho ij knyghtes [Edward III and Edward Balliol] might nought come therin long tyme. and notheles the Kynges abiden there so longe, til tho that were in the toune faillede vitailes; and also thai were so wery of wakyng that thai wiste nought what to Done.[77]

This account is worth quoting at some length because it concisely sums up the way in which gunpowder artillery was used throughout the fourteenth century. The gunstones were fired *into* the town, where they knocked down houses and churches, not against the walls.[78] The gunpowder artillery was used in conjunction with older forms of siege engines. And, most important, the use of guns did not appreciably lessen the duration of the siege; the defenders still had to be starved out.

The cannon of the early fourteenth century were both small and inexpensive. A gun, probably weighing 40 pounds, was purchased for just 13s 4d in 1353, when a springald cost 66s 8d.[79] At this point, gunpowder artillery had no more power than traditional siege engines (and, indeed, far less than some), but this cost advantage, combined with the psychological impact of a new and frighteningly loud weapon, ensured that its use would grow rapidly. Edward III had at his disposal for the siege of Calais in 1346 at least 10 cannon (including two "grossa") and materials for over 5,000 lb worth of gunpowder.[80] The French had 24 iron cannon made in 1345 at Cahors for the siege of Aiguillon, and at least 36 cannon were provided for the siege of Saint-Sauveur-le-Vicomte in 1374–5.[81] Froissart claimed that the English had 400 guns at the siege of St. Malo in 1378, though most were probably handguns.[82] Over the seven years from 1382–1388, the English Privy Wardrobe purchased 87 cannon.[83] By 1409, Christine de Pisan could argue that no less than 248 guns were needed to take a strong place, including 32 firing shot of 200 lb. or more.[84]

Even as the number of cannon employed increased, so too did their size. The early guns were very small, and shot pellets of lead or iron, or sometimes iron "lances" feathered with bronze. A much larger cannon prepared for the siege of Saint-Sauveur-le-Vicomte in 1375 fired stone shot of a hundredweight, and Froissart records the use of a gun firing 200-pound stones two years later. The Count of Holland purchased 400-pound stones for his "grooten donrebusse" in 1378.[85] Two bombards purchased by the Duke of Burgundy in 1409 hurled stones of 700–750 and 800–950 pounds.[86] *Faule Mette,* cast circa 1411, fired stones of over half a ton. The massive *Pumhart von Steyr,* forged c. 1420, fired an 80cm stone weighing over *fifteen hundred* pounds.[87]

How did this increase in the size and quantity of gunpowder artillery affect actual campaigns? At first, not much. The English managed to destroy the strongpoint of Romorantin in 1356 by using cannon to send "Greek fire" into the courtyard, but gunpowder artillery could prove equally useful to the defense. At Breteuil in the same year, for instance, the besieged English used cannon to destroy a French assault tower.[88] Furthermore, the guns were simply not powerful enough to do much damage to castle walls. Even at the end of the fourteenth century, siege guns could do little more than knock in the roofs of towers.[89] The balance between offense and defense remained firmly tilted towards the latter; as late as c. 1420, a German author held that the defender of a well-equipped castle, provided with artillery and good gunners, "whatever his enemy may attempt, will be able to hold off the enemy ... until he is relieved or the enemy is given a good thrashing and departs the siege."[90]

The siege of Harfleur by Henry V in 1415, for which we have several contemporary accounts, provides us with a clear picture of the use of gunpowder artillery in the early fifteenth century. As at Berwick almost a century earlier, the main role of the cannon was to wreak devastation within the town in order to encourage the besieged to surrender. With his twelve great guns, Henry "plaid at tenys with them that were in the toune" so that "really fine buildings, almost as far as the middle of the town, were either totally demolished or threatened with inevitable collapse."[91] In this case, the devastation succeeded in bringing the defenders out to treat with the king, praying him that "he schuld make his gunneres to sese, for it was to [t]hem intollerabil."[92]

Gunpowder artillery also had a new part to play at Harfleur, one not seen at the 1333 siege of Berwick. At Harfleur, the guns were fired not only into the town, but also against the walls and wooden bulwarks defending it. Although certain passages suggest that Henry hoped to knock assailable breaches in the walls,[93] as was to become common practice a generation later, it seems more likely that his intention was, rather, to silence the guns and catapults with which the defenders harassed his army.[94]

The many long sieges of the 1410s and early 1420s show that artillery was not yet then capable of rapidly battering its way into a strong fortress garrisoned by determined defenders.[95] The siege of Rouen lasted nearly six months, from 31 July of 1418 to 19 January of 1419, even though the town "was battered severely, within and without, because the English had there so many large bombards."[96] At the end, it was starvation, not the bombards, which brought the inhabitants to terms.[97] The town of Cherbourg was starved out after seven months in 1418; Melun after eighteen weeks in 1420; Meaux after seven months in 1421; Montaguillon after six months in 1423. The strong castle of Château Gaillard in Normandy held out for six months, until the cords the garrison used to draw up drinking water wore out. The English began besieging Guise in January of 1424, but did not enter the town until February of 1425.[98]

In all the cases cited above, the chroniclers give lack of supplies as the primary reason for the eventual surrender of the besieged.[99] Around the middle of the 1420s, however, we begin to hear of garrisons surrendering, not because of hunger, but because the besiegers' guns have rendered their position indefensible.[100] According to the French chroniclers, this was the case at Le Mans, Sainte-Suzanne, Mayenne-la-Juhez, Montmiral, and Gallardon, all in 1423.[101] At Sainte-Suzanne, then the second largest town of Maine, "the Earl of Salisbury had nine large bombards and many large cannon and fowlers [lighter cannon] sited and set up. These bombards and cannons, after eight or ten days, began to fire incessantly, day and night, so that they beat down the walls of the said town from more than a bow-shot away."[102] The following year the Duke of Bedford besieged Gaillon, "a very strong place," and "it was battered so effectively, that the garrison surrendered on having their lives spared."[103] In Bohemia, too, we first hear in the early 1420s of "large cannon, with which one might knock down strong walls."[104]

These events did not yet demonstrate the complete triumph of gunpowder artillery over medieval fortifications. As mentioned above, the siege of Guise in 1424 lasted over a year, and Ferté-Bernard managed to hold out against Salisbury for several months in the same year. In 1429 the English had to spend six months starving out the castle of Torcy; the French garrison of Château Gaillard had once again to be starved out that year; the siege of Laigny-sur-Marne took over five months in 1432; and as late as 1440 Harfleur was able to resist an English siege for over three months.[105] Each of these places, however, was exceptionally strong, and each was attacked by a relatively weak English siege train.

The powerful Burgundian artillery of the 1430s, on the other hand, could de-molish the walls of most fortifications. In 1430, the Burgundian siege train was able to "do so much damage to the walls of the castle [of Choisy] that the garrison capitulated" in a mere few days. Similarly, at Avalon in 1433, the Burgundian artillery was "pointed against the gates and walls, and damaged them greatly, breaches being made in divers parts."[106] By 1437, even the English artillery was capable of leaving a stronghold with "a great part of the walls ... thrown to the ground, so that it was in no way defensible."[107]

By the late 1440s the Franco-Burgundian artillery could destroy even the most powerfully defended places. Mighty Harfleur, which had held out so long against the English in 1440, made terms after a seventeen-day bombardment in 1449.[108] After a sixteen-day siege in 1450, almost the entire wall of Bayeux was "pierced and brought down." The story was much the same at Dax and Acx: "their walls were so battered in many places that by diverse breaches they could be taken by assault." At Blaye, in 1451, it took only five days before "the town walls were com-pletely thrown down in many places."[109] A contemporary English document lists one-hundred strongpoints taken by the French in 1450, including Chateau Gaillard, St.-Sauveur-le-Vicomte, Cherbourg, Roche-Guyon, and Rouen, all of which had earlier required long sieges to capture.[110] In 1451, all of Guienne fell rapidly to the French despite the deeply ingrained pro-English sympathies of the inhabitants of the duchy.

Based on the above accounts, it seems fair to say that a revolution occurred in the art of war around the 1420–30s, as gunpowder artillery overturned the centu-ries-old dominance of the defensive in siege warfare. What was the nature of this revolution?

At first glance, contemporary descriptions of the 1450 campaign might lead the historian to attribute the incredible French successes to the Vaubanesque system of siegecraft so carefully described by Leseur and Chartier. The former author's passage on the siege of Dax is worth quoting at length:

> The watch ordered and set, our prince sent for a force of pioneers and miners, who, all night long, he had make broad approaches and deep ditches and trenches, [and] set up his large artillery, and put the protective mantles there; and he was so diligent that the said artillery was ready to fire at dawn. And in the same way my lord the prince made huts by filling wickerwork and faggots with earth, in the manner of a broad mound, to shelter the watch from the artillery of the town; and the trenches were so advanced the next day that one could go safely under cover from one quarter of the siege to another, and in the same way one could come by the said approaches to the artillery, and even up to their fosses. And always, day and night, the said pioneers worked on them. ... Furthermore, the large artillery was fired assiduously day and night. Inside of a few days it had done great damage, so that the defenses of the tow-ers ... and a great part of the forward walls were thrown down to the ground; and our said artillery made large and wide breaches there, over which watch was held; and we fired the large culverines at these, so that, when the enemy wished to make shelters or

otherwise repair them, our culverines often killed and wounded their men and knocked them down to the ground, them and their shelters.[111]

Jean Chartier, in his *Chronique de Charles VII*, also emphasized the "marvelous ... approaches, fosses, entrenchments and mines which the aforesaid [Bureau brothers] had made before all the towns and castles which were besieged" during the reconquest of Normandy in 1450.[112] Decades later, Jean de Bueil's *Le Jouvencel* continued to advocate the same method of siegecraft.[113]

There is no doubt that the Bureau brothers' methods were admirable, impressive, and contributed significantly to the success of the French artillery in the middle of the fifteenth century. However, an account of the siege of Harfleur, written in 1416–7, already describes much the same method of approach and bombardment from covered positions.[114] Thus, we must look elsewhere for the developments which enabled the artillery of the 1450s to tumble down the walls of the strongest fortresses.

It has been argued that gun design remained essentially stagnant until well into the fifteenth century, and that the most important advances were made after the artillery pioneers, Jean and Gaspard Bureau, became Treasurer and Master of Artillery of France, respectively, around 1440.[115] In fact, however, cannon developed steadily throughout the fourteenth century, and very rapidly in the early fifteenth. Indeed, the developments in cannon design most critical for the Artillery Revolution appeared in the years 1400–1430. These developments included changes in the design and manufacture of the guns themselves, in loading methods, and in powder formulation.

Probably the most important of these involved the lengthening of gun barrels. In 1400 most large bombards seem to have had barrel-lengths about equal to 1–1.5 times the diameter of the balls they shot (Figure 3.2). By 1430 at the latest, the ratio of barrel length to ball diameter had grown to 3:1 or more.[116] In addition to increasing the accuracy of the shot (making it possible to concentrate the force of a large number of shots on a smaller area), this increased the amount of time over which the pressure of the exploding gunpowder accelerated the ball, and thus significantly increased the muzzle velocity of the shot. Since the kinetic energy of the ball is a function of the *square* of the velocity, this meant a major increase in the effectiveness of the newer guns. As contemporary gunners realized, it also meant an increase in range.[117]

The lengthening of bombard barrels had an equally important indirect effect. In the early years of the fifteenth century, with the shorter-barreled bombards, a rather complex loading process had to be employed.[118] The gun crew filled the chamber with gunpowder for the rear three-fifths of its length. The next fifth was left empty, and the last fifth filled by a soft wood plug cut to fit the chamber bore exactly. Then the cannonball was fixed in place in the barrel with soft wood wedges. Finally, to get the tightest possible seal (thus minimizing pressure loss to windage), wet mud mixed with straw was put in place and allowed to dry (Figure

Figure 3.2   Small early bombard, in the collection of the Army History Museum in Vienna. The long section on the wooden base is the powder chamber; the wider section forward of that is the barrel. Note the shortness of the barrel, which has an internal length only about 1.5 times its diameter. Photo by Clifford J. Rogers.

3.3). After the bombard had been fired, it had to be allowed to cool before more powder could be packed in.[119] This elaborate procedure so slowed down the firing process that one master gunner, who achieved the remarkable feat of firing his bombard three times in a single day and hitting different targets each time, was forced to make a pilgrimage from Metz to Rome, because it was thought that "he could only have been in league with the devil."[120]

Guns with longer barrels, however, ameliorated this problem. Since the ball was under pressure from the expanding gas for a longer period of time, somewhat more gas loss due to windage could be allowed, and the wet loam seal dispensed with. This, in turn, permitted more rapid firing.[121]

As guns of this sort became more common, there was an important change in the process used to manufacture them. In the late fourteenth century, the barrels of large iron bombards were made either by forging a large iron plate into a cylinder, or by spiraling out a broad iron band, forming a cylinder in the same way that the coils of a spring do. These methods, however, could not be scaled up past a certain point.[122] Sometime in the early fifteenth century, probably shortly before 1420, gunsmiths developed a new technique which made possible large guns with long barrels: they built up large iron guns out of long staves.[123] The staves were set

Figure 3.3 Illuminations from a "master-gunner's handbook" (*Büchsenmeisterbuch*) in the Austrian National Library. Illustration on left shows how to wedge the cannon ball in place. Illustration on right shows how to load the powder chamber correctly. Accompanying text explains the procedures. (Cpv 3069, fos. 8v, 9v.) Photos courtesy of Austrian National Library.

ilt du ein püchßen meyſtlich vñ recht ladñ ſo ſich
du der erſt dz dz pulñ gůt ſ̃ ſ̃ nÿ .j. maß vñ
teilt ſ̃ jn die pñeiſch̃ vñ teil die maß glich in fünf teil
als du dñ d' figur wol ſicheſt vnd lad die drÿ teil mit pulñ
als die maß ſagt ſo iſt ſ̃ mit pulñ recht geladñ wõ d'
blotz bedarf ſ̃ñer airts ſo ſol zwiſchent de blotzkñw de
pulñ ſich ein airts ſÿ dz dz für zů recht pñnaiſt vñ zů
recht kraft magk kome ſ̃ d' nach mache du dñ
ainn blotz vñ ainn ſteñ deſt' paß ſchieſſen

Figure 3.4   The editor at the Army History Museum, Vienna, examining the *Pumhart von Steyr*, which fired an 80-cm. stone ball weighing over 1,500 pounds. Note the hoops on the outer surface of the gun and the ends of the staves protruding from the barrel. Photo courtesy Dr. Erich Gabriel.

in place around a cylindrical mandrel, then reinforced with bands of white-hot iron, which were hammered down the cylinder like the hoops of a barrel.[124] The hoops shrank as they cooled, binding the staves tightly together.[125] (Figure 3.4).

At about the same time, a metallurgical innovation made the prodigious quantities of iron used in this process[126] less expensive: the addition of limestone to the flux during the ore refinement process. This increased the temperature necessary to make the slag free-running, so that it could only be used with developed blast furnaces,[127] but it changed the structure of the slag from $2FeOSiO_2$ to $CaOSiO_2$. The two atoms of iron thus removed from each molecule of slag were no longer wasted, increasing the iron output from a given quantity of ore and making iron cheaper.[128] Meanwhile, as the manufacture of large iron cannon became more routine, the services of cannon-smiths grew more affordable. The cost of cannon—which were priced in direct proportion to their weight—fell significantly (about a third) as a result of these changes.[129]

More or less simultaneously with these developments, an important change took place in a related area: the manufacture of gunpowder.[130] Around 1400, recipes for gunpowder began to appear which came quite close to the ideal proportions of saltpeter, sulphur, and charcoal.[131] But then, in the second decade of the century, it appears that the science of powdermaking took a retrograde step, moving significantly farther away from the "ideal" proportions.[132] Considering the high cost of gunpowder,[133] it seems strange that gunners would adopt a less effective form of it. The explanation of this seeming paradox lies in yet another new technique: the engraining or "corning" of powder. Although there is evidence that the English may have employed this process as early as 1372, it seems that it did not come into use on the Continent until around 1410; it was in almost universal use by 1420.[134] Corned powder, which was mixed together wet and then dried into kernels, had a number of advantages over the earlier "serpentine" powder, which was sifted together dry. Sifted powder tended to separate into its component elements when transported, but corned powder was immune to this deterioration. Most importantly, the structure of corned powder allowed the burning to progress mainly *between*, rather than *within* powder grains, resulting in a much more rapid evolution of the solid into gas.[135] Some contemporary master gunners claimed that engrained powder was three times as powerful as the sifted form.[136]

This posed a problem, however: the commensurate increase of the pressure in the chamber of the gun was more likely to burst the cannon than improve its effectiveness.[137] This, it seems reasonable to assume, explains the shift away from the "ideal" proportions in the mixing of gunpowder: engrained powder with less saltpeter would be both cheaper and more powerful than sifted powder with the "perfect" proportions, but not so much more powerful that it would be likely to burst the gun.

Thus, between 1400 and 1430, a whole series of interconnected innovations synergistically improved the power and efficiency of gunpowder artillery. The development of the hooped-staves method made it possible for even the largest iron cannon to have longer barrels, the adoption of which increased accuracy, power, and rate of fire. The new iron refining process, and the increasing skills of the gunsmiths, made guns cheaper to buy; and corned powder made them both more powerful and cheaper to use. The number and size of guns in use increased rapidly. Put together, these developments were enough to reverse the centuries-old superiority of the defensive in siege warfare, and bring the walls of medieval castles crashing down.[138]

Further important improvements were made in the 1450s–1470s, including the general adoption of the modern two-wheeled carriage, trunnions, and iron cannonballs. Large bombards increasingly gave way to smaller, cheaper, more easily transportable guns, particularly cast bronze muzzle-loaders.[139] However important these latter changes may have been from a technical point of view, though, it was the earlier changes which held the greatest importance for the actual conduct of operations, as the above analysis of the sieges of the 1410s–1430s shows.

IMPACT OF THE ARTILLERY REVOLUTION

The idea that the introduction of gunpowder led to sweeping changes in the political structure of Europe has been a familiar one from the days of Adam Smith, David Hume, Carlyle, and Macaulay. More recently, J.F.C. Fuller, Ferdinand Lot, and William H. McNeill have made similar arguments.[140] Others have tried to refute their case,[141] but the logic of the argument is as powerful as it is simple.

Artillery was expensive. As early as 1442, the French government was spending more than twice as much on its artillery train as it spent on more traditional war materiel—arrows, lances, bows, etc.[142] The central governments of large states could afford to acquire and maintain large siege trains: their subjects and smaller neighbors, in general, could not. The the imbalance between offensive and defensive in siege warfare led to a corresponding inequity in strategy: the offensive gained, the defensive suffered.

In the early 14th century, Pierre Dubois observed in his military treatise that

> A castle can hardly be taken within a year, and even if it does fall, it means more expenses for the king's purse and for his subjects than the conquest is worth. Because of these lengthy, dangerous and arduous sieges, and because battle and assaults can be avoided, leaders are apt to come to agreements which are unfavorable to the stronger party. ...[143]

Under such circumstances, local powers could effectively keep the interference of the central government to a minimum. The Artillery Revolution altered the situation dramatically. Regional interests lost their ability to defy central authorities; small states and semi-independent regions were gobbled up by their larger neighbors.

There were many exceptions, of course, but the process by which France and Spain became unified nation-states owed much to the Artillery Revolution. In France, the central government rapidly reconquered Normandy and Aquitaine, then established control over Burgundy and Brittany. In Spain, to quote Geoffrey Parker, "thanks to their command of a siege-train of some 180 guns, the 'Catholic Kings' Ferdinand and Isabella were able to reduce within ten years (1482–1492) the Moorish strongholds in the kingdom of Granada that had defied their forbears for centuries."[144] When the French marched into Italy in 1494, their artillery "could do in a few hours what in Italy used to take days," and the patterns of warfare on the peninsula were "turned upside down, as if by a sudden wind."[145]

The Florentine historian Guicciardini accurately perceived the impact which the Artillery Revolution had on warfare. Before, when the "slow and uncertain" methods for besieging towns led to long wars, "the ruler of a state could hardly be dispossessed." Effective siege cannon, however, "infused so much liveliness into our wars that ... whenever the open country was lost, the state was lost with it."[146] Before, a power on the defensive could hole up in its fortifications and wait for the enemy to run out of energy, money, or food. After the Artillery Revolution, defense had to be defense in the field—a truth which had already been clearly demonstrated by the French reconquest of Guienne in 1453.[147] This appears to have led to a significant increase in the frequency of battle.[148] After 1520, as the impact of the sunken-profile *trace italienne* earthwork fortress made itself felt, (in what could be dubbed an "Artillery Fortress Revolution") the frequency of battle again declined.[149]

The increased importance of battle after the Artillery Revolution tipped the scales of war even further in favor of large states and centralized governments, for only they had the resources to maintain sizable standing armies like the *compagnies d'ordonnance* established by Charles VII of France in 1445 and by Charles the Bold of Burgundy in 1471–3. In addition, by the 1450s, artillery was beginning to be as much a help in battles as in sieges—witness the battles of Formigny and Castillon.[150]

The great cost of artillery, and the larger armies engendered by the growing importance of open battle, put a premium on the ability to produce and manage large amounts of cash. This created a self-reinforcing cycle, which continued to spiral upwards at least until the advent of the Artillery Fortress Revolution of the early sixteenth century. It went something like this: central governments of large states could afford artillery trains and large armies. The artillery trains counteracted centrifugal forces and enabled the central governments to increase their control over outlying areas of their realms, or to expand at the expense of their weaker neighbors. This increased their tax revenues, enabling them to support bigger artillery trains and armies, enabling them to increase their centralization of control and their tax revenues still further, and so on.[151] One scholar has estimated that the tax revenues of central governments in Western Europe doubled in real, per capita terms between 1450 and 1500;[152] this feedback loop between military capability and economic mobilization ability helps account for that phenomenon.

Looking backward from the period of the Artillery Fortress Revolution, more than one scholar has tried to argue that "the view that the advent of cannon changed the balance between the attackers and the fortified defense is simply not supported by the evidence."[153] The contemporaries of the Artillery Revolution, from Chartier and Leseur to Guicciardini and Machiavelli, did not agree. Indeed, the fifteenth-century Italian architect Francesco di Giorgio Martini wrote that "the man who would be able to balance defense against attack, would be more a god than a human being."[154] Their accounts, and the other evidence presented in this article, makes it clear that gunpowder *did* reverse the balance between offense and defense around 1430 as the result of a rapid series of technical innovations built onto a century of gradual development. True, this superiority of the offensive itself eventually succumbed to another military revolution—but in the century between the initial triumphs of gunpowder artillery in the 1420s–40s and the flowering of the sunken-profile, bastioned-trace earthwork fortress in the 1520s–

40s, gunpowder artillery wrought a true revolution in European warfare, with great consequences for the continent and the world.

PARADIGMS: REVOLUTION VERSUS PUNCTUATED
EQUILIBRIUM EVOLUTION

Let us return to the question which launched our examination of the military revolutions of the Hundred Years War: "just how did the West, initially so small and so deficient in natural resources, become able to compensate for what it lacked through superior military and naval power?" I have argued that in order to answer that question we must turn our gaze back to the early years of the fourteenth century, when the Infantry Revolution reached maturity and cannon first appeared. It is clear that between that time and the end of the eighteenth century, the European military "macroparasite"[155] became far more effective than any the world had known before, and that this advancement of the craft of war played a crucial role in the rise of the West to global dominance. But that covers a span of a full half a millennium.

The concept of "revolution" in history is a flexible one, flexible enough to encompass phenomena as diverse as the Glorious, French, Copernican, and Industrial Revolutions. In each case, though, "revolution" refers to a rapid reversal in the state of affairs. The length of time involved can range from a year to a century, depending on the scope of the revolution—depending on whether it is a government, a social structure, an idea, or an economy which is overturned—but in none of these cases does the time-frame during which the reversal takes place exceed a single (maximum) human life span.

Furthermore, a revolution—however extended—must be in essence a single change, from state X to state Y, from front to back or top to bottom. Over the five centuries between 1300 and 1800, however, Europe experienced not one but several military revolutions, even considering land forces alone, each of which dramatically altered the nature of warfare over a short span of time. First, in the fourteenth century, the "Infantry Revolution," when common Swiss pikemen and halberdiers and English archers overturned the centuries-long dominance of aristocratic shock cavalry. Second, the "Artillery Revolution," which reversed the equally long-standing superiority of the defensive in siege warfare and provided a major impetus for the unification of France and Spain under central authorities. Third—getting into the period of the traditionally defined Military Revolution, and away from the period analyzed in the body of this paper—the "Artillery Fortress Revolution," based on the *trace italienne* and sunken-profile earthwork walls, which reinstated the superiority of the strategic defensive. Fourth, the "Military Revolution" which Michael Roberts outlined in his seminal paper—drill, military bureaucratization, and the growth of army size.[156] We are, thus, dealing not with one revolutionary change, but with a whole *series* of revolutions which synergistically combined to create the Western military superiority of the eighteenth century.

Is the answer to our question, then, a matter of *evolution?* Evolution normally implies advancement through a near-infinite number of infinitesimal changes, and that, clearly, is not the conceptualization we want. Each of the component revolutions mentioned above, it is true, involved a certain amount of slow, steady evolution both before and after the "revolutionary" period. Cannon evolved for a full century before they were able to dramatically change the European way of war, and they continued to improve steadily (if slowly) for centuries afterward.[157] But the concept of evolution, as commonly conceived, does not adequately address the critical period of rapid innovation from 1410–1430.

There is a paradigm, however, which may be able to provide a conceptual framework broad enough and sturdy enough to support analysis of the diverse events which must go into an explanation of the growth of Western military superiority. In 1972, Stephen Jay Gould and Niles Eldredge proposed a new model for the evolutionary formation of species, which they dubbed "punctuated equilibrium." They argued that evolution proceeded by short bursts of rapid change interspersed with long periods of near stasis rather than constant, slow alteration. Their theory aroused much controversy, and over the intervening years it has become clear that their initial formulation did not give sufficient play to gradual, incremental change.[158] But many scientists have accepted Gould and Eldredge's basic point—that much, though not all, evolutionary change occurs during short periods of rapid development. This newer conception of punctuated equilibrium evolution, combining both incremental and "revolutionary" change, seems to describe the process of military innovation extraordinarily well. After a long period of near-stasis, infantry began to evolve very rapidly around the beginning of the fourteenth century. Cannon appeared at about that time, evolved incrementally for a century, then in a burst of rapid advancement revolutionized war in Europe. Artillery fortifications began to develop at about the same time as artillery reached its height;[159] evolved gradually over the course of a century; then in their turn effected a military revolution. A similar process of punctuated equilibrium evolution in military technology continues even today.

It might be argued that, so long as we all know what we are talking about when we say "Military Revolution," my objections are mere quibbling, only a question of semantics. But, as George Orwell showed so effectively in *1984*, words shape ideas, and ideas shape the world. By attempting to subsume the innovations of five centuries into a single phenomenon, we may be imposing an artificial teleological unity onto a series of inherently distinct, separate developments. And, in doing so, we may be clouding our understanding of a critically important area of history, an area which fully deserves to be studied through the clearest possible lens.

Notes

1. A number of scholars have been kind enough to read drafts of this article and offer me their corrections and comments: thanks are especially due to my dissertation advisor, John F. Guilmartin, Jr.; to Andrew Ayton; Russell Hart; Geoffrey Parker; John Lynn; Williamson Murray; Anne Curry; Robert D. Smith; and the students in the Ohio State University seminar on "Technologically Oriented Military History," (Winter–Spring 1991), particularly Capt. Peter Mansoor. Thanks are also due to the Ohio State University for the Research and Graduate Council Fellowship which supported me while I researched and wrote this article, and the U.S.-U.K. Fulbright Commission for the grant which enabled me to put the finishing touches on it.

2. Stephen Glick has pointed out, however, that Sir Charles Oman may have prior claim to the concept: Oman's 1898 essay, *The Art of War in the Middle Ages,* refers to the time when pike-and-shot infantry took the premier part in withstanding the Ottomans as "the military revolution of the sixteenth century." C. W. C. Oman, *The Art of War in the Middle Ages,* revised and edited by John H. Beeler (Ithaca: Cornell University Press, 1953), 162.

3. Michael Roberts, "The Military Revolution, 1560–1660," reprinted in his *Essays in Swedish History* (Minneapolis: University of Minnesota Press, 1967), and above, Ch. 1.

4. Geoffrey Parker, "The 'Military Revolution,' 1560–1660—a myth?," *Journal of Modern History* 48 (1976) (above, Ch. 2); Geoffrey Parker, *The Military Revolution: Military innovation and the rise of the West* (Cambridge: Cambridge U.P., 1988), 2.

5. Parker, "The 'Military Revolution,'" 214 (above, p. 49), et passim.

6. E.g. Michael Duffy (ed.), *The Military Revolution and the State, 1500–1800,* Exeter Studies in History 1 (Exeter: University of Exeter, 1980), 3; John A. Lynn, "The Growth of the French Army during the seventeenth century" *Armed Forces and Society* VI (1980). Cf. William H. McNeill, *The Pursuit of Power* (Chicago: University of Chicago Press, 1982), chs. 3 & 4, and John Lynn's review article, "Clio in Arms" *Journal of Military History* 55 (January 1991).

7. Parker, *Military Revolution,* 4. All the participants on the Military Revolution Roundtable at the 1991 American Military Institute conference in Durham, North Carolina—i.e., myself, John F. Guilmartin, John A. Lynn, and Geoffrey Parker—agreed on the centrality of this question.

8. Previously cited works by Roberts, Parker, Duffy. Roberts, "Military Revolution," p. 195 (above, p. 13), specifically states that the Military Revolution "stands like a great divide separating mediaeval society from the modern world." Others include: John A. Lynn, "The *trace italienne* and the Growth of Armies: The French Case," *Journal of Military History* 55 (July 1991); Simon Adams, "Tactics or Politics? 'The Military Revolution' and the Hapsburg Hegemony, 1525–1648," in *The Tools of War* ed. J. A. Lynn. (Champaign, Illinois: U. of I. Press, 1990); David A. Parrott, "Strategy and tactics in the Thirty Years War: the 'military revolution.'" *Militärgeschichtliche Mitteilungen* XVIII, 2 (1985) (below, Chs. 7, 9, 10); and Jeremy Black's new book, *A Military Revolution? Military Change and European Society 1550–1800* (Atlantic Highlands, NJ: Humanities Press, 1990), which emphasizes the military changes which took place in the century *after* 1660. His work, though it seriously underestimates the military changes of the sixteenth century, does have important contributions to make for the seventeenth and eighteenth century phases of the process of Western military innovation which fit nicely with the "punctuated equilibrium evolution" model which I will develop later in this article.

9. They held primacy in importance, though often not in numbers. This statement will be developed further below. For the area between the Loire and the Rhine, feudal armies exercised their dominance from even farther back—arguably from Carolingian times—but by mid-eleventh century (i.e. after 1066) feudal warfare was well established in England, Italy, and Germany as well.

10. In the twelfth century many battles were fought by dismounted cavalry, but there is a great difference between dismounted cavalry and infantry, especially "common" (i.e. non-aristocratic) infantry. See below.

11. Parker, *Military Revolution*, 118, points out that this last was an important difference between the Europeans and many of those whom they sought to subdue.

12. This term has been used by John F. Guilmartin in his article "War, Technology of" in the 1991 *Encyclopaedia Britannica*, 539. He uses it, however, to refer to the progress of infantry over the entire period c. 1200–1500, whereas I limit it to the rapid and revolutionary rise to prominence of infantry in the years c. 1302–1346.

13. I will not make any attempt to produce a developed explanation of why this process of punctuated equilibrium military evolution "took off" in the West and not elsewhere in the world. I suspect that the answer has something to do with the combination of two factors: 1. the fragmented and competitive political structure of Europe; and 2. the technological orientation towards problem solving which appeared in Europe in the High Middle Ages. The former provided the need for military innovation; the latter helped provide the means.

14. Oman, *Art of War*, 47.

15. The quote is from B. Lyon, "The Role of Cavalry in Medieval Warfare: Horses, Horses All Around and Not a One to Use," *Mededelingen van de Koninklijke Academie voor Wetenschappen, Letteren en Schone Kunsten van België* 49 (1987), Nr. 2, 90. Jim Bradbury makes a stronger case in the same direction (albeit taking a less extreme position) in his *The Medieval Archer* (Woodbridge, Suffolk: The Boydell Press, 1985).

16. J. F. Verbruggen, *The Art of Warfare in Western Europe During the Middle Ages. From the Eighth Century to 1340* (Amsterdam: North Holland Publishing Co., 1977), 23; cf. Philippe Contamine, *War in the Middle Ages*, tr. Michael Jones (London: Basil Blackwell, 1984), 31. For a particularly well-balanced case study of the role of infantry in high medieval warfare, see R. C. Smail, *Crusading Warfare (1097–1193)* (Cambridge: Cambridge University Press, 1956), especially 116–130.

17. Smail, *Crusading Warfare*, 128–130, says this tactic was in common use during the Crusades. Perhaps the most vivid descriptions of it are found in Guillaume le Breton's account of the battle of Bouvines (1214); Beha al-Din's description of Richard I's forces at Arsuf (in Verbruggen, *Art of Warfare*, 215, 218), and especially Al-Heweri's description of the "Franks" in his military treatise of 1211 (in H. Ritter, "La Parure des Cavaliers und die Literatur über die ritterlichen Künste," *Der Islam*, 18 (1929), 147).

18. See R. Allen Brown, "The Status of the Norman Knight" in *War and Government in the Middle Ages*, ed. John Gillingham and J. C. Holt (Woodbridge: Boydell Press, 1984), 29, and Verbruggen, *Art of Warfare*, 28–39.

19. The *Chanson de Guillaume* implicitly recognized the connection between diet and military prowess: "By God, fair sire, he's of your line indeed,/Who thus devours a mighty haunch of boar/And drinks of wine a gallon at two gulps;/pity the man on whom he wages war." Although it deals with a different period, Geoffrey and Angela Parker's *European Sol-

diers 1550–1650 (Cambridge: Cambridge University Press, 1977), 22, gives some interesting statistics on this point. It seems that in that period, fewer than one common recruit in thirty was over five feet tall.

20. Richelieu was by no means the first to observe that "history knows far more armies destroyed through disorder and lack of bread than through the effort of enemy arms" (quoted in Parrott, "Strategy and Tactics," p. 93, p. 250, above); the same principle is emphasized in the military treatise of Vegetius, which was very popular in the middle ages. Geoffrey Lester (ed.), *The Earliest English Translation of Vegetius' De Re Militari* (Heidelberg: Carl Winter Universitätsverlag, 1988), 156, 158. For an outstanding discussion of strategy in the High Middle Ages, which will help make clear the importance of this capacity, see John Gillingham, "Richard I and the Science of War in the Middle Ages," in Gillingham and Holt, *War and Government in the Middle Ages.*

21. The "equipment" included a warhorse, palfrey, packhorse, armor, weapons, etc. The high cost of his equipment was reflected in the high wages he received when serving at his lord's expense. See note 43, below. Note that by the end of the thirteenth century, a knight was often expected to have not three but *five* horses, which would obviously be more expensive. See M. G. A. Vale, "The Anglo-French Wars, 1294–1340: Allies and Alliances" in Philippe Contamine, et al. (eds.) *Guerre et société en France, en Angleterre et en Bourgogne. XIVe–XVe Siècle* (Lille: Centre d'histoire de la region du nord et de l'Europe du nord-ouest, 1991), 23.

22. See the *Calendar of Inquisitions, Miscellaneous. VII (1399–1422)* (London: 1968), 29, 61, 313; 32, 276, 188. Compare Public Record Office, London: PRO/E101/392/13. Even a mounted archer's equipment, including his riding horse, could cost as little as £2 10s.: Philip Morgan, *War and Society in Medieval Cheshire, 1277–1403* (Manchester: Chetham Society, 1987), 154–5.

23. In this context it is worth quoting Petrarch (b. 1304), who wrote "In my youth, the Britons, who are called Angles or English, were taken to be the meekest of the barbarians. Today they are a fiercely bellicose nation. They have overturned the ancient military glory of the French by victories so numerous that they, who once were inferior to the wretched Scots, have reduced the entire kingdom of France by fire and sword." Quoted in R. Boutruche, "The Devastation of Rural Areas During the Hundred Years war and the Agricultural Recovery of France" in *The Recovery of France in the Fifteenth Century*, ed. P. S. Lewis (New York: Macmillan, 1972). Note that the reason the English were once inferior to the Scots is that the latter perceived the potential of the infantry revolution before their southern neighbors, just as the English appreciated it before the French. Cf. Jean le Bel's similar comment: *Chronique de Jean le Bel*, ed. J. Viard & E. Deprez (Paris: SHF, 1904), 1:155–6.

24. Cf. Pierre Dubois's treatise, quoted in Verbruggen, *Art of Warfare*, 273.

25. The Scots, too, had an important role to play in the Infantry Revolution. Although not enemies of the French, the Scots suffered an equivalent inferiority in heavy cavalry vis-à-vis their traditional opponents, the English.

26. For Courtrai, see Verbruggen, *Art of Warfare*, 166–173. For Bannockburn, see J. E. Morris, *Bannockburn* (Cambridge: 1914) and G. W. S. Barrow, *Robert Bruce & the Community of the Realm of Scotland* (Edinburgh: Edinburgh University Press), ch. 12. The account in Thomas Gray's *Scalacronica*, ed. J. Stevenson (Edinburgh: Maitland Club, 1836) is not very detailed, but it does note that the Scots at Bannockburn were specifically following the

example of the Flemings at Courtrai, who had defeated the French forces by fighting on foot (p. 142).

27. Thomas Wright, *The Political Songs of England, vol. III* (Edinburgh: Privately printed, 1884), 43, for the first quotation. For the second, see M. G. A. Vale, "The Anglo-French Wars, 1294–1340: Allies and Alliances," 21.

28. The battle of Bannockburn took place on "an evil, deep morass" on a very narrow front. *Scalacronica*, 142; John Barbour, *The Bruce*, ed. W. W. Skeat (Early English Text Society, 1889), 299. The battle of the Cephissus in 1311, when the infantry of the Catalan Company played the main role in defeating the heavy cavalry of Gautier de Brienne, the French duke of Athens, belongs to the same category. See K. M. Setton, *Catalan Domination of Athens, 1311–1388*, 9–12. These four battles, all fought within the brief span of thirteen years, show a remarkable similarity. Taking into account Thomas Gray's comment (see note 26), I suspect that the later three battles were conscious attempts to replicate the success of the Flemings in 1302. (Cf. Setton, *Catalan Domination*, 9, n35.) Furthermore, the Scots at least believed (and almost certainly correctly) that the English had learned the advantages of fighting on foot from their defeat at Bannockburn. The French experiments with infantry tactics, in turn, were undertaken in imitation of the successful English. See Geoffrey le Baker, *Chronicon*, ed. E. M. Thompson (Oxford: Clarendon, 1889), 143.

29. For Cassel, see le Bel, *Chroniques*, 1: 93–4, and Ferdinand Lot, *L'Art Militaire et les Armées au Moyen Age* (Paris: Payot, 1946), 274–8. For Mons-en-Pévèl, see Verbruggen, *Art of Warfare*, 176–183; although the battle was a draw overall, the annihilation of William of Jülich's Flemings demonstrates that the balance between infantry and cavalry had not entirely turned in favor of the former.

30. Oman, *Art*, 89.

31. Pun quite intended. For Crécy, see le Bel, *Chronique* 2:99 et seq., and le Baker, *Chronicon*, 82–85. Froissart, *Oeuvres*, 5: 37–78. Alfred H. Burne, *The Crecy War* (Westport, CT: Greenwood Press, 1976), Chapter 7.

32. Although a cavalry reserve was often kept for pursuits or special tasks, such as attempting to ride down the English archers, as at Poitiers in 1356.

33. "The Design and Materials of the Bow," in Robert Hardy, *Longbow: A Social and Military History* (Cambridge: Patrick Stephens, 1976), 195.

34. See the illustrations reproduced in Bradbury, *Medieval Archer*. The Norman archers at Hastings, if we can trust the depictions of the Bayeux Tapestry, also used short bows drawn to the chest (Bradbury, 32–34).

35. See Jean de Joinville, *Chronicle*, in Sir Frank Marzials, ed., *Memoirs of the Crusades*, (London: Everyman's Library, 1964), 195, and Beha-al Din's account of Arsuf, quoted in Verbruggen, *Art of Warfare*, 215. Of course, these were composite recurved shortbows, but since they were more powerful than the Welsh selfbows, the point stands. The effects of the English archers' arrows at Crécy, Poitiers, Verneuil, or Agincourt were much more serious. E.g. see *Chronographia Regum Francorum*, ed. Moranvillé, (Paris: SHF, 1891), 2:232, and the sources in note 71, below.

36. Philippe de Commynes, *Mémoires*, ed. R. Chantelauze (Paris: Firmin-Didot, 1881), 23–24. He goes on to describe the archers in the Burgundian army at Montlhéry (1465) as "the flower and hope of their army."

37. A failure to take into account the great strength needed to use a medieval longbow effectively has led many authors into the mistaken conclusion that a soldier could be

trained to its use with relative ease. E.g. see Richard Barber, *The Knight and Chivalry*, (Ipswich: The Boydell Press, 1974), 199.

38. Bradbury's estimate of 50 lbs. as a typical medieval draw weight is far too low, and would not have produced the high pressures which caused the skeletal deformation of the archers on the wreck of the Tudor warship, the *Mary Rose*—compressed left forearms, twisted spines, and flattened draw-fingers. Guilmartin, "War, Technology of," 541; Bradbury, *Medieval Archer*, 148, 157. Cf. Hardy, *Longbow*, 53. Robert Hardy revealed in a paper presented at the Hundred Years War conference held at Oxford University, 8–10 November, 1991, that the 138 longbows recovered from the *Mary Rose* ranged in power from 100–180 (!) pounds draw weight.

39. "In this arte [archery] englishmen are lerned from theire yong age/ wherefor contynuingly they passe al othre archers." Christine di Pisan, *The Book of Fayttes of Armes and of Chyvalrye* tr. William Caxton, ed. A.T.P. Byles. (London: EETS, 1937), 34. For a good discussion of the human element of archery, see John F. Guilmartin, *Gunpowder and Galleys* (Cambridge: Cambridge University Press, 1974), 151.

40. In 1384, for example, Charles VI of France prohibited any games except those involving the longbow or crossbow. Contamine, *War*, 217. Cf. note 51, below.

41. The beauty of the English archer and man-at-arms combination was that it could convert either into an offensively powerful cavalry-and-missile combination when used against infantry fighting on the defensive (e.g. vs. the Scottish schiltrons at Falkirk), or into an equally effective defensive "pike-and-shot" combination to destroy attacking cavalry and infantry forces (e.g. at Crécy, Agincourt). In the latter case, the archers' fire served to disorder and demoralize the attacking forces (when it did not wound or kill) before they smashed into the steady, tightly-formed men-at-arms.

42. Here, and throughout this paper, "common infantry" refers to infantry drawn from non-aristocratic classes. I also consider troops like the English mounted archers, who rode from place to place but invariably fought on foot, as they had neither the training nor the mounts to fight on horseback, to be essentially infantry rather than cavalry. A mounted archer's horse could be had for £2 (E101/397/5), while a knight would likely spend at least ten times that amount for a courser, palfrey, and rouncy (E101/19/36).

43. A very important consideration when victory in war often went to the side with the last reserves of money. In 1326, for example, an English knight bachelor was paid twelve times as much as a footman (2s/ day vs. 2d/ day).

44. Although this advantage was less pronounced for longbowmen, who required years of training to build up the strength to use their bows.

45. The broader social base from which infantry forces were drawn became crucial later in the "military revolution" of the sixteenth–seventeenth centuries. From the mid-sixteenth to the end of the seventeenth century, the French army grew from a maximum wartime strength of about 50,000 to one of about 400,000 (Parker, *The Military Revolution*, 24). Virtually every man of the 350,000 added came from the common population: as late as 1775, the total number of *gentilshommes* employed by the French military, including the navy and retired officers, was only 20–25,000 (Duffy, *Military Revolution and the State*, 4). To borrow Michael Roberts' nicely turned phrase, "In the Middle Ages war had been almost the privilege of a class; by the seventeenth century it had become almost the livelihood of the masses." "Military Revolution," p. 208 (above, p. 23).

46. By the end of the Hundred Years War, the Berry Herald precociously described the English as follows: they "are all good archers and soldiers ... They also make war on all na-

tions of the world by sea and land and all that they gain in the foreign parts to which they have gone they send back to their realm and through this it is rich." Quoted in Contamine, *War in the Middle Ages*, 125. The Swiss, of course, also exported large numbers of mercenary infantrymen.

47. Stanislav Andreski provides an outstanding theoretical treatment of the relationship between military and political enfranchisement in his *Military Organization and Society* (London: Routledge & Kegan Paul, 1968).

48. See the poem in John Barnie, *War in Medieval English Society* (Ithaca: Cornell University Press, 1974), 21. Edward Miller has noted that in the early fourteenth century "there is, in fact, a close correlation between periods of war taxation and 'constitutional movements' "—he might have made it "periods of war taxation *and recruitment*." Edward Miller, "War, Taxation, and the English Economy in the late 13th and early 14th centuries," in J. M. Winter, ed., *War and Economic Development* (Cambridge: Cambridge University Press, 1975). Note that in areas where the Infantry Revolution was not fully experienced during the fourteenth century, such as France, the political influence of the commons was much less than in places like England, Switzerland or Flanders, even though the French commons were rich enough. This supports the argument that commons' military enfranchisement, as well as their growing wealth, contributed to their increasing political role.

49. See G. J. Aungier, ed., *French Chronicle of London*, Camden Series, 28 (1844), 83: "ils n'oserent plus reddour faire pur doute de guerre, et qe le poeple einz vodroyent lever encountre eux avant q'ils vodroient plus doner."

50. Froissart, *Chronicles*, 5 vols., tr. Thomas Johnes (Haford: Haford Press, 1803), 2:469, 477, 479; Cf. *Anonimalle Chronicle*, 148. That there was a similar connection between military service and the infamous *Jacquerie* of 1358 is suggested by the fact that the name given to the rebels—*Jacques Bonhommes*—had previously been used to describe urban militia contingents sent to participate in royal campaigns. See Françoise Autrand, "La déconfiture. La bataille de Poitiers (1356) à travers quelques textes français des XIVe et XVe siècles," in Philippe Contamine, et al. (eds.) *Guerre et société en France, en Angleterre et en Bourgogne. XIVe–XVe Siècle.* (Lille: Centre d'histoire de la region du nord et de l'Europe du nord-ouest, 1991), 99. Cf. Richard Kaeuper, *War, Justice and Public Order. England and France in the Later Middle Ages* (Oxford: Clarendon, 1988), 360.

51. Jean Juvenal des Ursins, *Histoire de Charles VI*, in *Choix de chroniques et mémoires sur l'histoire de France. XIVe siècle* (Paris: Panthéon Littéraire, 1838), 385. See Rymer, *Foedera*, vol. III, pars 2, 704, for the very different English royal attitude.

52. But cf. Thomas N. Bisson, "The Military Origins of Medieval Representation," *American Historical Review* 71 (1966), 1207.

53. One fifteenth-century list of participants in a Parliamentary election, for example, includes 1 knight, 8 esquires, 10 "gentilmen" and 105 common freemen. See J. G. Edwards, "The Huntingdonshire Parliamentary Election of 1450," in *Essays in Medieval History Presented to Bertie Wilkinson*, ed. T. A. Sandquist and M. R. Powicke (Toronto: University of Toronto Press, 1969), 385. *Mum and the Sothsegger*, a poem written around 1400, emphasizes the role of good "schire-knyghtis" as mere representatives of the electorate: "We are servants taking a salary and sent from the shires to show their grievances and to speak for their profit ... and if we are false to those who send us here, then little are we worthy of our hire." *Mum and the Sothsegger*, ed. Mabel Day and Robert Steele (London: Early English Text Society, 1936) 24–25. For the "free" nature of elections, see A. Luders, et al. *Statutes of the Realm* (London: Record Commission, 1810–20) 2:156.

54. For a good survey of the early development of the English Parliament, see G. L. Harris, "The Formation of Parliament, 1272–1377," in R. G. Davies, ed., *The English Parliament in the Middle Ages* (Manchester: Manchester University Press, 1981). For the early development of the longbow and tactics based on its use, see Hardy, *Longbow,* 36–49.

55. Sir Goronwy Edwards, *The Second Century of English Parliament* (Oxford: Clarendon Press, 1979), 38, and G. L. Harriss, *King, Parliament, and Public Finance in Medieval England to 1369* (Oxford: Clarendon Press, 1975), 271, 513, for the Parliamentary side. For the military side, see the Lanercost Chronicle's description of Dupplin Muir and Halidon Hill, and Froissart's descriptions of Cadzand, Hennebon, Quimperlé, Bergerac, Auberoche, and Crécy, all in the first two decades of Edward's long rule. Froissart already has the French at Hennebont in 1342 refer to "les arciers qui tous les desconfisoient," (*Oeuvres,* 4:51), while the Lanercost chronicle says of Dupplin Muir (1332) that "victi sunt Scotti maxime per sagittarios Anglicorum." J. Stevenson, ed. *Chronicon de Lanercost* (Edinburgh: Maitland Club, 1839), 268.

56. *Rotuli Parliamentorum,* 2:67; Goronwy Edwards, *The Second Century of English Parliament,* 49. Harriss, *King, Parliament, and Public Finance,* 259, 320, 359. Note also the statute cited in Michael Prestwich, *The Three Edwards: War and the State in England 1272–1377* (London: Weidenfeld and Nicholson, 1980), 235.

57. Indirect taxation: Goronwy Edwards, *The Second Century of English Parliament,* 19–21. This was of great importance, as indirect taxation was then replacing direct subsidies as the largest source of royal income, as the research of Mark Ormrod is showing. 1369 powers: Harriss, *King, Parliament, and Public Finance,* 513.

58. The increasing economic importance of the towns also played a part in their gain in political power, but wealth can only be exchanged for power if the transaction is protected by force: otherwise, he who holds the power is likely to take the wealth without making political concessions.

59. See Morgan, *War and Society in Medieval Cheshire, 1277–1403,* 4–5, 52–3, and Maurice H. Keen, *The Laws of War in the Late Middle Ages* (London, 1965), 130, 150, 163, 229.

60. For the 40s. voting qualification, see *Rotuli Parliamentorum,* 4:350. Cf. S. J. Payling, "The Widening Franchise—Parliamentary Elections in Lancastrian Nottinghamshire," in *England in the Fifteenth Century* ed. Daniel Williams (Woodbridge, Suffolk: The Boydell Press, 1987), and J. G. Edwards, "Election," 386. For the 40s. "archer class," see Michael Powicke, *Military Obligation in Medieval England* (Oxford University Press, 1962), 193, 182, 190; cf. Rymer, *Foedera,* II.ii.900, 901. During the same period, a horse archer's annual wage was nearly five times that amount, which shows that it was indeed a very moderate property qualification.

61. Verbruggen, *Art of Warfare,* 132.

62. Contamine, *War in the Middle Ages,* 256.

63. Ibid. Lot, *L'art Militaire,* 1:223–235; Joseph Dahmus, *Seven Decisive Battles of the Middle Ages* (Chicago: Nelson-Hall, 1983), 167.

64. Orderic Vitalis, *Ecclesiastical History,* tr. Marjorie Chibnall (Oxford: Clarendon Press, 1969), 6:241. Cf. Guillaume le Breton's *Philippiad,* Song 11, verses 120–132.

65. Verbruggen, *Art of Warfare,* 173. Lot, *L'art Militaire,* 1:277. Froissart (*Oeuvres,* 2:225) reports that "there was a great slaughter of the Flemings, because none was given mercy."

66. Alfred H. Burne, *The Agincourt War* (London: Eyre & Spottiswoode, 1956), 87, 210. The French casualties at Crécy were similar: 1,542 men-at-arms and an uncertain number

of commoners. Burne, *The Crecy War*, 184. At Poitiers, over 2,000 knights and men-at-arms lost their lives. Ibid., 307.

67. Orderic Vitalis, *Ecclesiastical History*, 6:241.

68. Excluding customs revenue. Hariss, *King, Parliament and Public Finance*, 523–6. "Ordinary" revenue does not include the direct taxes on movable wealth granted intermittently by Parliament.

69. Jonathan Sumption, *The Hundred Years War*, v. 1: *Trial by Battle* (London: Faber and Faber, 1990), 470. Philippe Contamine, "Rançons et butins dans la Normandie anglaise (1424–1444)," in his *La France aux XIVe et XVe siècles. Hommes, mentalités, guerre et paix* (London: Valorium Reprints, 1981), 260.

70. Froissart, *Oeuvres*, 10:171. In the same battle, the Flemish leader commanded his troops under pain of death to take no prisoners, but "Kill all, kill all," ibid., 158. See also 4:406, 2:221–2; *Chronicles*, 1:306, 325, 2:356–7, 432, 448, 599, 609, etc.; Jean le Bel, *Chronique* ed. J. Viard and E. Déprez (Paris: SHF, 1905), 2:82 ("archiers qui tuoient gens sans deffense et sans pitié"); *Chronicon de Lanercost*, 350–6; and Verbruggen, *Art of Warfare*, 170. Similarly, the Scottish men-at-arms who rode down the English archers at Bannockburn "slayand thamme without ransounne." Such a slaughter had been seen "neuir quhar, in na cuntre." Barbour, *The Bruce*, 308 (cf. 319). Another good example, by coincidence from the same year as the battle of Crécy, is the battle of Vottem, where the Liegeois militia, fighting on foot with axes and warhammers, "tuoient et assommoient ces chevaulx et ces chevalliers sans nulle pité et sans point de renchon," killing, according to one chronicler, 1,600 men-at-arms. Kervyn de Lettenhove (ed) *Récits d'un bourgeois de Valenciennes* (Louvain, 1877), 212–213.

Concerning the disinclination of the Swiss to take prisoners, Contamine (*War in the Middle Ages*, 291) points out that the 1444 *Kriegsordnung* "thought it necessary to prohibit combatants from tearing out the hearts of their dead enemies and cutting up their bodies."

71. For the lethality of the arrow, see the *Chronographia Regum Francorum*, 2:232 ("plures autem ex eis ceciderunt ex sagitis Anglicorum" etc., re. Crécy); Froissart, *Oeuvres*, 4:75, 406, 5:49, 52; *Chronicles* 2:196; William Stewart, *The Buik of the Cronicles of Scotland* (London: Rolls Series, 1858), 3:367; Jean de Hocsem *La Chronique de Jean de Hocsem* ed. Godefroid Kurth. (Brussels: Commission Royale d'Histoire, 1927), 345 ("saggittarios infinitos qui telis suis majorem numerum occiderunt.") For iconographic evidence, see the depiction of the battle of Poitiers (from BN MS fr. 2643, fo. 207) reproduced in David R. Cook, *The Black Prince* (Canterbury: Cathedral Gifts, 1990), 16–17. Pikes were also considered "but too mortal": Froissart, *Chronicles*, 2:496; cf. Jehan de Wavrin *Anchiennes Cronicques d'Engleterre* (Paris: SHF, 1858), 3:74.

72. Commanders often made ordinances to prevent this from happening. An Anglo-Burgundian ordinance of 1423, for instance, stated that "no person, whatever might be his rank, should dare attempt making any prisoners on the day of the battle until the field should be fairly won. Should any such be made, the prisoner was to be instantly put to death, and with him the person who had taken him, should he refuse to obey." Enguerrand de Monstrelet, *Chronicles*, tr. Thomas Johnes (London: William Smith, 1840), 500. Similar ordinances were made in many other instances, e.g. by the English at Crécy and Neville's Cross and the Flemings at Roosebeke.

73. When the graves of those killed by the Swiss at the battle of Sempach were opened at the end of the nineteenth century, it was found that "the skulls were nearly all dreadfully split by halberd-strokes." C. W. C. Oman, *A History of the Art of War in the Middle Ages*

(London: Meuthen, 1924), 251n. Cf. Froissart on Roosebeke: *Oeuvres*, 10:170. See Matthew Bennett, "*La Règle du Temple* as a Military Manual *or* How to Deliver a Cavalry Charge," in *Studies in Medieval History Presented to R. Allen Brown* (Woodbridge, Suffolk: The Boydell Press, 1989), 17, for some interesting observations on the very different mechanics of cavalry vs. cavalry fights. Part of the reason casualties were higher after the Infantry Revolution is simply that men on foot cannot escape from battle as easily as men on horseback, and a large proportion of those killed in a medieval battle were struck down while seeking to flee.

74. Parker, *Military Revolution*, 118, quoting two American colonials.

75. There is a good color reproduction of one of the Milemete guns in Richard Humble, *Warfare in the Middle Ages* (Leicester: Magna Books, 1989), 147. J. R. Partington, *A History of Greek Fire and Gunpowder* (Cambridge: W. Heffer & Sons, 1960), 105, gives what purports to be a Florentine *provisione*, also of 1326, for the acquisition of cannon and iron balls for the defense of the Republic. The document is somewhat questionable, however: according to Bernhard Rathgen (*Das Aufkommen der Pulverwaffe* [Munich: Verlag Die Schwere Artillerie, 1925], 15), its "discoverer" was later sentenced to ten years in prison for stealing documents, altering them to make them seem more valuable, and then reselling them. On the other hand, J. F. Finó has published a photograph of the document in "L'artillerie en France à la fin du moyen âge," *Gladius* 12 (1974), 14, and it certainly appears to be written in a hand of the early fourteenth century. Finó also reproduces the other Milemete illumination.

76. Called "vasa" and a "scolpo." Rathgen, *Aufkommen der Pulverwaffe*, 14.

77. *The Brut, or the Chronicles of England*, ed. F. W. Brie (London: Early English Text Society, 1960), 282, version "O."

78. The same was generally true of the use of other stone-throwing siege engines of the day (mainly trebuchets), as innumerable examples from Froissart show. At the siege of Mortagne in 1340, for example, the besiegers from Valenciennes had "ung très-bel enghien et bien jetant, qui portoit grosses pierres jusques dedens le ville et jusques au castiel, et ce travailloit et cuvrioit forment chiaux de Mortaigne." *Oeuvres*, 3:265.

79. T. F. Tout, "Firearms in England in the Fourteenth Century," *EHR* 26 (1911): 682–3; Cf. Rathgen, *Aufkommen der Pulverwaffe*, 36. Of course, guns were much more expensive than older forms of artillery to operate, if not to purchase, because of the very high cost of gunpowder.

80. Tout, "Firearms in England," 689–691.

81. For Cahors: Napoleon III and I. Favé, *Études sur le passé et l'avenir de l'Artillerie* (Paris: J. Dumaine, 1846–1871) 3:82n. For St.-Sauveur: ibid., 4: pièces justicatives, xviii–xlii. The largest of these guns required 2,385 lb. of iron and steel to manufacture, but most were much smaller guns of cast bronze. A recent master's thesis by Peter J. Burkholder, "The Manufacture and Use of Cannons at the Siege of St-Sauveur-le-Vicomte, 1375" (U. of Toronto, 1992) gives extensive details and shows that most of these guns arrived too late to affect the course of the siege.

82. Froissart, *Chronicles*, 2:246. Perugia, similarly, had 500 "cannoni" made in 1364, "da spararsi a mano," but each was only a few inches long. Angelo Angelucci, *Delle Artiglierie da Fuoco Italiane. Memorie storiche con documenti inediti* (Torino, 1862), 16.

83. Tout, "Firearms in England," 677–8.

84. Christine de Pisan, *The Book of Fayttes of Armes and of Chyvalrye*, tr. William Caxton, ed. A.T.P Byles (London: Early English Text Society, 1937), 153–4. The largest of the guns

was to throw five-hundred-pound shot. Although she claimed to have based her list on the advice of "wyse knyghtes that be expert in the sayde thynges of armes," this seems to be a rather extreme number. By comparison, the large and well-provided Bohemian armies besieging Carlstein in 1422 had only 52 guns, of which 6 were very large (Wenceslai Hagecii, *Böhmische Chronica* [Cadan: J. S. Zluticensem, 1596] fo. 114v); and the artillery train purchased for the Earl of Salisbury in 1428 comprised just 72 guns, of which only seven fired 100+ lb. shot (P.R.O.: Exchequer, Accounts Various [E101]/51/27, 30)

85. M. Lantier, ed. *Cent cinquante textes sur la guerre de Cent Ans dans le bailliage de Cotentin* (St.-Lô, 1978), 140; Froissart, *Oeuvres*, 8:411; Karl Jacobs, *Das Aufkommen der Feuerwaffen am Niederrhein bis zum Jahre 1400* (Bonn: Peter Hanstein, 1910), 56, 86.

86. Joseph Garnier, *L'Artillerie des Ducs de Bourgogne, d'après les documents conservés aux archives de la Côte-d'Or* (Paris: Honoré Champion, 1895), 26–7, 265. I am indebted to Kelly DeVries for advising me of this valuable source.

87. W. Hassenstein (ed.), *Das Feuerwerkbuch von 1420* (Munich: Verlag der Deutschen Technik, 1941), 145. Schmidtchen, B*ombarden, Befestigungen*, 32. Note that 80cm is nearly twice the diameter of the shells fired by the 16-inch main guns of twentieth-century battleships!

88. Froissart, *Oeuvres*, 5:389, 376. In both cases the guns shot both fire and large bolts. Cannon were also used to drive the French besiegers away from Quesnoy in 1340, according to the same author.

89. Froissart, *Chronicles*, 2:246, 250. *Chronique de Du Guesclin*, ed. M. Fr. Michel. (Paris: Bibliothèque Choisie, 1830), 121. Jacobs, *Das Aufkommen der Feuerwaffen*, 129–30.

90. Hassenstein, *Feuerwerkbuch von 1420*, 31. Cf. the *Royal Armouries Firework Manuscript*, Royal Armouries Library (Tower of London), MS I-34, fo. 36v–37v. For a concrete example, see the siege of Bourges in 1411, where an assault was driven off by fierce cannonfire. Pierre de Fenin, *Mémoires* ed. Dupont (Paris: SHF, 1837), 27.

91. The quotes are from the *English Chronicle of the Reigns of Richard II, Henry IV, Henry V, and Henry VI* (Camden Soc., 1868), 40, and the Pseudo-Elmham, *Gesta Henrici Quinti: The Deeds of Henry V,* ed. and tr. Frank Taylor and John S. Roskell (Oxford: Oxford University Press, 1975), 39. The number of Henry's guns is given in a contemporary letter; see Burne, *Agincourt*, 36. The reference to tennis alludes to the story of the tennis balls mockingly sent to Henry V by the French Dauphin.

92. John Capgrave, *The Chronicle of England* ed. F. C. Hingeston (London: Rolls Series, 1858), 310; *Chronique Normande*, in *Henrici Quinti, Angliae Regis, Gesta*, ed. Benjamin Williams (London: English Historical Society, 1850), 168.

93. *Gesta Henrici Quinti*, 37; *English Chronicle of the Reigns of Richard II, Henry IV, Henry V, and Henry VI*, op. cit.; Sir Harris Nicolas, *History of the Battle of Agincourt* (London: Johnson & Co., 1832), 310.

94. *Gesta Henrici Quinti*, 39.

95. *Contra* the argument of B. H. St. J. O'Neil that "in the years 1369 to 1375, the French were able to batter down walls of fortresses both successfully and quickly." *Castles and Cannon* (Oxford: Clarendon, 1960), 33; cf. a similar statement in Rathgen, *Aufkommen der Pulverwaffe*, 4.

96. *Chronique Normande*, 188.

97. A poem written by an eyewitness to the siege, John Page, eloquently expresses the supply problems of the townsmen: "They etete doggys, they ete cattys;/They ete mysse,

horse and rattys/ ... /For xxxd. went a ratte/For ij noblys went a catte./For vj d. went a mous;/They lefte but fewe in any house." *Poem on the Siege of Rouen* in *The Historical Collections of a Citizen of London in the Fifteenth Century,* 18 (Cf. 38). See also Monstrelet, *Chronicles,* 1:404, and the *Chronique Normande,* 191.

98. *Chronique Normande,* 191, 202; John Holinshed, *Holinshed's Chronicles: Richard II 1398–1400, Henry IV and Henry V,* ed. R. S. Wallace and A. Hansen (Oxford: Clarendon, 1928), 64–5, 109, 123–7; J. H. Wylie & W. T. Waugh, *The Reign of Henry the Fifth* (Cambridge: Cambridge University Press, 1929), 3:107–9, 210–15, 351. Louis Bellaguet (ed.), *Chronique du religieux de St. Denys (1380–1422)* (Paris: Crapelet, 1839), 6:446–8; Monstrelet, *Chronicles,* 421, 468–76, 498, 508–522; Thomas Gregory, *Gregory's Chronicle* in *Historical Collections of a London Citizen,* ed. J. Gairdner (London: Camden Society, 1876), 148; John de Wavrin *A Collection of the Chronicles and Ancient Histories of Great Britain, Now Called England* ed. W. and E. Hardy. (London: RS, 1887), 3:32; R. A. Newhall, *The English Conquest of Normandy, 1416–24* (New Haven: Yale University Press, 1924), 131.

99. Although Waurin, *Recueil des Croniques,* 2:394, 401, and Fenin, *Mémoires,* 174, emphasize the role of the artillery at Meaux.

100. There are several earlier examples of significant artillery successes, but these, in terms of the Artillery Revolution, are analogous to the harbinger infantry victories of Courtrai, Bannockburn, and Morgarten, in that they were only possible because of special circumstances. In 1405, Henry IV's bombards flattened a substantial portion of the walls of Berwick (British Library, MS Vespasian FVII, f. 71), but from the south side where the fortifications were so low and so thin "that a man may stand within the wall and take another by the hand without the wall." James Wylie, *History of England under Henry the Fourth* (London: Longmans, Green & Co., 1884–1898), 2:271. The walls were in any case falling down for "verray feblesse." S. B. Chrimes, "Some Letters of John of Lancaster as Warden of the East Marches towards Scotland" *Speculum* 14 (1939), 20.

Two years after that, Spanish "lombardas" were "demolishing a great part of the wall" of Zahara when the garrison surrendered ... but the Moors had only recently begun to repair the fortifications of the town. Fernan Perez de Guzman, *Crónica del serenissimo rey don Juan el segundo deste nombre* (1517), cap. xxxv–vi.

101. Le Mans, Sainte-Suzanne, Mayenne-la-Juhez: Jean Chartier, *Chronique de Charles VII* ed. Vallet de Viriville (Paris: P. Jannet, 1858), 1:45–47. See also Guillaume Cousinot, *Chronique de la Pucelle,* ed. V. de Viriville (Paris: Garnier Frères, 1892), 199–200. For Montmiral and Gallardon: *Chronique du religieux de Saint-Denys,* 6:463. Artillery was equally effective at Quesnoy in 1421, but the place was only poorly fortified. See Waurin, *Recueil des Croniques,* 2:395–6.

102. Chartier, *Chronique de Charles VII* 1:45–47. The meaning of the last part of the sentence is unclear: it may mean that the guns made a breach in the wall more than a bow-shot wide.

103. Monstrelet, *Chronicles,* 509.

104. Franz Palacky, *Urkundliche Beiträge zur Geschichte des Hussitenkrieges vom Jahre 1419 an* (Prague: E. Tempsky, 1873), 151.

105. Monstrelet, *Chronicles,* 1:566; Waurin, *Recueil des Croniques,* 3:346, 348; Chartier, *Chronique de Charles VII,* 1:47, 143–146; A. J. Pollard, *John Talbot and the War in France, 1427–1453* (London: Royal Historical Society, 1983), 53. Burne (*The Agincourt War,* 291) has the siege of Harfleur opening in August rather than July, which would make it just under

three months, and the chroniclers (e.g. Chartier, 1:259) generally have the siege beginning in April, which would make it six months.

106. Monstrelet, *Chronicles*, 1:570, 619.

107. Description of the newly recaptured castle of Castelnau-de-Cernès in a grant by Henry VI. Malcolm Vale, *War and Chivalry* (London: Ducksworth, 1981), 132.

108. Charles VII made use of 16 large bombards for the siege. Chartier, *Chronique de Charles VII*, 2:178–179.

109. Chartier, *Chronique de Charles VII*, 2:205; Guillaume Leseur, *Histoire de Gaston IV, comte de Foix* ed. H. Courteault (Paris: SHF, 1893–6), 119–21; Chartier, *Chronique de Charles VII*, 2:254–256.

110. J. Stevenson, ed. *Letters and Papers illustrative of the Wars of the English in France during the Reign of Henry the Sixth, King of England* (London: Rolls Series, 1861–4), 2:619 et seq. Most of the 100 strongpoints referred to were actually never assaulted; they surrendered before then. Yet this does not mean that artillery did not play a key role, for it was the threat of assaults through breaches made by cannon which caused the defenders to surrender so readily. At Harcourt, for example, "The Frenchmen who were before the town set up their cannon; and at the first shot they pierced right through the walls of the lower court. Then the said English [of the garrison] were filled with doubt, and agreed to surrender the said castle ..." Gilles le Bouvier, *Le Recouvrement de Normendie, par Berry, Herault du Roy* in J. Stevenson, ed. *Narratives of the Expulsion of the English from Normandy* (London: Rolls Series, 1863), 274; cf. 321, 327, 339, 341, 366. "Never," writes le Bouvier, "was so large a country conquered in such a short time." In explaining this "moult grant marveille," he emphasizes the role of the artillery. "There was such a great number of large bombards, large cannon, fowlers, of serpentines, of capadeaux, of ribaudequines and of culverins, that not in the memory of man has anyone ever seen a Christian king with such great artillery." (Ibid, 368, 373–4). See also Anne Curry, "Towns at War: Relations between the Towns of Normandy and their English rulers, 1417–1450" in J. A. F. Thomson, ed., *Towns and Townspeople in the Fifteenth Century* (Gloucester: Alan Sutton, 1988), 149–50, 155–6.

111. Leseur, *Histoire de Gaston IV*, 119–20.

112. Chartier, *Chronique de Charles VII*, 2:235–238, after le Bouvier, *Recouvrement de Normendie*, 373–4. He adds that the French could have taken by assault any of the places which surrendered, if they had wanted to.

113. Jean de Bueil, *Le Jouvencel*, ed. Léon Lecestre (Paris: SHF, 1887), 37.

114. *Gesta Henrici Quinti*, 37.

115. For the first, see O'Neil, *Castles and Cannon*, 24, and H. Dubled, "L'artillerie royale française à l'époque de Charles VII et au début du règne de Louis XI (1437–69); les frères Bureau" *Memorial de l'Artillerie Française* 50 (1976), 563. For the second, see Dubled, passim, and Napoleon and Favé, *Études sur le passé et l'avenir de l'Artillerie*, 2:99.

116. Schmidtchen, *Bombarden, Befestigungen*, 17–18, 49. The master-gunner's book of 1411 in the Austrian National Library (Handschriftsammlung, Codex 3069, ff. 9v, 19v, cf. fo. 31) shows similarly-proportioned guns. For bombards from the late 1430s on, in contrast, a barrel:ball ratio of 5:1, as recommended in the *Feuerwerkbuch*, seems to have been typical.

117. Hassenstein, *Feuerwerkbuch von 1420*, 71; Schmidtchen, *Bombarden, Befestigungen*, 50–51.

118. It is described in detail in Codex 3069 of the Austrian National Library (written 1411), fos. 8v–9v. Cf. the nearly identical text (taken from Munich CGM 600) in Gustav

Köhler, *Die Entwicklung des Kriegswesens und der Kriegführung in der Ritterzeit* (Breslau: W. Koebner, 1887), 231.

119. Fowlers and other smaller guns, however, usually had longer barrels with removable powder chambers shaped like beer steins, of which each gun was supplied with two or more. These could be loaded from the breech; the balls did not need to be wedged or sealed in place; and the chambers could be kept pre-prepared and replaced without waiting for the gun to cool fully. Thus, they could fire much faster.

120. Schmidtchen, *Bombarden, Befestigungen*, 44 (re. 1437). It seems from a few pieces of evidence, however, that a maximum of six to eight shots per day could be fired from large bombards of the shorter-barrelled type (*contra* Schmidtchen, 44). Perez de Guzman, *Crónica*, cap. xli–xliii; Partington, *History of Greek Fire and Gunpowder*, 114; Hagecii, *Böhmische Chronica*, fo. 114v et seq. Bellaguet, Louis (ed.) *Chronique du religeux de St. Denys (1380–1422)* (Paris, 1839) 5:652, has a big gun being fired 12 times a day.

121. Schmidtchen, *Bombarden, Befestigungen*, 49–50, *contra* Dubled's assertion that "the manner of loading artillery pieces hardly changed after the beginning of the [fifteenth] century" (p. 580).

122. The Amsterdam Bombard, probably one of the largest made by the spiral method, has a barrel length of 53 cm and a caliber just slightly less. Thus, it would have fired a stone of about 400 lbs. Jacobs, *Aufkommen der Feuerwaffen*, 68–71.

123. The best description of this process is in Robert D. Smith and Ruth Rhynas Brown, *Bombards: Mons Meg and Her Sisters* (London: Royal Armouries, 1989), 20.

124. Thus the "barrel" of a gun.

125. From the very first, smaller guns and some large ones were also cast of bronze (or other copper alloys). From 1422, cast iron guns also begin to appear in inventories occasionally, including some of substantial size. Garnier, *L'Artillerie des Ducs de Bourgogne*, 267.

126. For example, see the 17,700 lbs. of iron used for making guns for Henry IV (P.R.O., Foreign Accounts, E364/43/6), or the 35,150 lbs. of iron used to make seven large guns for the Earl of Salisbury's artillery train in 1428 (Accounts Various, E101/51/27).

127. Blast furnaces were in use in Belgium by 1340; by 1420 these were designed with separate hearths for fining and reheating. The Low Countries, in addition to being the center for the development of the blast furnace, were also the most important cannon-manufacturing area in Europe. See Alex den Ouden, "The Introduction and early spread of the blast furnace in Europe," *Wealden Iron Research Group Bulletin*, No. 5, 2nd ser., 1985. Thanks to Robert D. Smith of the Tower Armouries for bringing this article to my attention.

128. A. R. Williams, "Medieval Metalworking," *Chartered Mechanical Engineer* (September 1978), passim.

129. T. F. Tout has shown that guns were generally priced by weight at 4d/lb in the fourteenth century (Tout, "Firearms in England," 682–3), but by the 1430s the price had fallen to about 3d/lb. The bombard "Bedford," weighing 8,000 lb, was appraised at 1,000 l.t. in 1434, which works out to 2.5 s. t. (= 3.3 d. sterling) per pound (Stevenson, *Letters and Papers*, 566) Another great bombard, Mons Meg, was purchased in the 1450s by weight at 2 s. t. (2.66 d. sterling) per pound (Contamine, *War*, 49). The rate of 2 s. t. per pound also appears for a 4,000 lb cannon in 1447 and a 12,000 lb. bombard in 1446 (Garnier, *L'Artillerie des Ducs de Bourgogne*, 57, 112). In England in 1428, the large iron guns purchased by John Parker, Master of the King's Ordinance, went for 2.2 or 2.4 d. per pound (PRO E101/51/27, 30). Smaller guns generally went at even lower rates: by the end of the Hundred Years War, as low as 12–18 d. t. per pound. Garnier, *L'Artillerie des Ducs de Bourgogne*, 111, 115.

130. The paragraphs which follow offer a somewhat simplified history of the development of gunpowder after its introduction in Europe. As I intend to present the matter more fully in another article, I have kept the notes here to a minimum.

131. The ideal mix is about 75% saltpetre, 12% sulphur and 13% charcoal. A widely-used formula of c. 1400 called for 71%/13%/16%. See Napoleon and Favé, *Études sur le passé et l'avenir de l'Artillerie,* 3:107; Partingdon, *History of Greek Fire and Gunpowder,* 324.

132. E.g. the formulae in Hassenstein, *Feuerwerkbuch von 1420,* 61 et seq. (Cf. the *Royal Armouries MS I–35,* fo. xxxxvi et seq.); Garnier, *L'Artillerie des Ducs de Bourgogne,* 60; and Napoleon and Favé, *Études sur le passé et l'avenir de l'Artillerie,* 3:145–6. For a more extreme example, see ibid., 124.

133. For example, Jean Bureau expected to spend 2,200 l.t. to purchase powder in preparation for the 1443 campaigning season. Contamine, *Guerre,* 666.

134. *Contra* the universal claim (Hassenstein, *Feuerwerkbuch von 1420,* 84, 61; Schmidtchen, *Bombarden, Befestigungen,* 46; Contamine, *War,* 197; Dubled, "L'artillerie royal française," 571) that it was invented only c. 1420. See PRO, E101 (Exchequer: Accounts Various)/31/4, and Codex 3069 of the Austrian National Library, fo. 2, for (somewhat ambiguous) evidence of corned powder in England in 1372 and (fairly clear) in Germany in 1411. Napoleon and Favé, *Études sur le passé et l'avenir de l'Artillerie,* 3:124, show that the use of the new type of powder was still not universal by 1417, however.

135. John F. Guilmartin, Jr. "Ballistics in the Black Powder Era," in R. D. Smith, ed. *British Naval Armaments* (London: Royal Armouries, 1989), 87. The more rapid evolution into gas meant that more of the force of the explosion was produced *before* the shot left the barrel of the gun, and therefore applied to the ball. Tightly loaded serpentine powder burned like a single giant "corn" of powder, relatively slowly.

136. Austrian National Library, Handschriftsammlung, Codex 3069, fo. 2; Contamine, *War,* 197; Napoleon and Favé, *Études sur le passé et l'avenir de l'Artillerie,* 3:146. The author of the *Feuerwerkbuch,* which Hassenstein dates at c. 1420, more modestly claims that corned powder was half again as strong as sifted powder. Hassenstein, *Feuerwerkbuch von 1420,* 17; cf. *Royal Armouries MS I-34,* fo. 4v.

137. The bursting of cannon was fairly common in any case. At the siege of Aberistwyth in 1408, for example, the English lost their great guns "Neelpot" and "Messager" as well as two smaller cannon, shortly after bursting "Kyngesdoghter" at Harlech. PRO E364 (Foreign Accounts)/49/3.

138. *Contra* the assertion of J. R. Hale that firearms "had little effect on the fortunes of campaigns as a whole or on the balance of political power." J. R. Hale, "Gunpowder and the Renaissance: An Essay in the History of Ideas," in his *Renaissance War Studies* (London: The Hambledon Press, 1983), 390.

139. For example, see the unconvincing arguments of Gary M. Anderson, "Cannons, Castles and Capitalism: The Invention of Gunpowder and the Rise of the West," *Defence Economics* 3 (1992), and of J. R. Hale, who asserts that "The case for the suggestion that artillery was an instrument centralizing power is … feeble." *War and Society in Renaissance Europe* (London: Fontana, 1985), 248; cf. 251.

140. For these devlopments, see Dubled, "L'artillerie royal française," passim. The idea that effective siege artillery was introduced only around 1494 is widespread. For recent examples, see George Raudzens, "War-Winning Weapons: The Measurement of Technological Determinism in Military History" *Journal of Military History,* 54 (Oct. 1990), 407, and Marguerita Z. Herman, *Ramparts,* (Garden City Park, NY: Avery, 1992), 9.

141. Hale, *Renaissance War Studies*, 389–90; McNeill, *Pursuit of Power*, 89; Lot, *L'art Militaire*, 2:466. Much of the following section of this article follows the trail blazed by McNeill.

142. Contamine, *Guerre*, 666. As a result, a royal *ordonnance* of the following year required the Master of Artillery to present an account of his expenses to the king on a monthly basis. Dubled, "L'artillerie royal française," 558.

143. Quoted in Verbruggen, *Art of Warfare*, 273; Cf. Froissart, *Oeuvres*, 3:358. DuBois exaggerated the difficulties of siege warfare somewhat—castles could rarely withstand a full year's siege, and often fell within a few months or even weeks due to treachery or mines—but his essential point is valid. A similar situation obtained after the development of the *trace italienne* fortress in the sixteenth century: see the statement by Don Luis de Requesens, quoted in Geoffrey Parker, *The Dutch Revolt*, (Revised edition. London: Peregrine, 1988), 165.

144. *The Military Revolution*, 8. The knowledge of artillery developed by the Spanish and Portuguese in fighting the Moors transferred easily to Iberian conquests in the New World, Africa, and Asia: it was a short step from *Reconquista* to *Conquista*. See also Weston Cook's important study, "The Cannon Conquest of Nāṣrid Spain and the End of the Reconquista," *Journal of Military History* 57 (1993), 44, 51.

145. Guicciardini, *History of Italy*, ed. J. R. Hale, tr. Grayson (New York: Washington Square Press, 1964), 153, and *History of Florence* in ibid., 20. Cf. Cook, "Cannon Conquest," 51.

146. From his *Counsels and Reflections*. Quoted in Parker, *The Military Revolution*, 10. Comparison of these quotes from Guicciardini with the remarks of Pierre Dubois (see quotation in the text at footnote 142) will do much to answer the "critical" question John Keegan poses in the introduction to his *The Mask of Command* (New York: Elizabeth Sifton Books - Viking, 1987), 8: "whether there is an alternative style of … strategy not of conquest but of security, and if so, how and why it came to be supplanted." Strategy based on conquest generally flourishes only when the balance in siege warfare lies with the offensive, as in c. 1420–c. 1520.

147. Cf. Guicciardini, *History of Florence*, in *History of Italy*, 20; and Felix Gilbert, "Machiavelli" in Peter Paret, ed., *Makers of Modern Strategy from Machiavelli to the Nuclear Age* (Oxford: Clarendon Press, 1986), 23.

148. Though it is, of course, impossible to isolate out the effects of the Artillery Revolution from other factors.

149. For the "artillery fortress," see John Lynn, "The *trace italienne*." For the decline in battle, see McNeill, *Pursuit of Power*, 91. The frequency of battle seems to be a good barometer of military revolutions. There was a certain surge in frequency c. 1300–45 as the Infantry Revolution hit the stage, then another, greater one after the advent of the Artillery Revolution. Battle went out of favor with the Artillery Fortress Revolution of the early sixteenth century, but came back into favor with the "Gustavian" revolution a century later. This dialectic could perhaps be extended to the periods of Vauban, Napoleon, the First and Second World Wars. …

150. See Burne, *Agincourt War*, 319, and "Lettre sur la Bataille de Castillon en Périgord, 19 juillet 1453" in *BEC* 8 (1846): 246.

151. Cf. the closely related "coercion-extraction cycle" proposed by S. E. Finer in "State and Nation-Building in Europe: The Role of the Military" in *The Formation of National States in Western Europe*, ed. C. Tilly (Princeton: Princeton University Press, 1975), 96.

152. McNeill, *Pursuit of Power,* 105n, citing Richard Bean, "War and the Birth of the Nation State," *Journal of Economic History,* (1973), 33.

153. The quote is from Martin van Creveld, *Technology and War from 2000 B.C. to the Present* (New York: The Free Press, 1989), 106. For similar statements, see J. R. Hale, *Renaissance War Studies,* 390–391, and the citations in note 139, above.

154. Quoted in Gilbert, "Machiavelli," 15. Giorgio's *Trattato di architettura civile e militare* is believed to have been written around 1495, just after the Artillery Revolution hit Italy.

155. To use William H. McNeill's valuable concept.

156. One might continue this list with the changes in European military systems of the seventeenth century described in Jeremy Black's book; the changes of the French Revolutionary period; of industrialized war; and of the nuclear revolution. Once the process of punctuated equilibrium evolution in the European craft of war got started, it never stopped.

157. With bursts of more rapid development in the early seventeenth and late nineteenth centuries.

158. For a concise but informative recent summary of the course of the punctuated equilibrium debate, see Tim Beardsly's overview, "Punctuated Equilibrium: Darwin Survives as the Debate Evolves" in *Scientific American* (March 1990). See also Niles Eldredge and S. J. Gould, "Punctuated Equilibria: An Alternative to Phyletic Gradualism" in T. J. Schopf (ed.), *Models in Paleobiology* (San Francisco: Freeman, Cooper, 1972); and the articles in Albert Somit and S. A. Peterson, *The Dynamics of Evolution: The Punctuated Equilibrium Debate in the Natural and Social Sciences* (Ithaca: Cornell U.P., 1992).

159. Vale, *War and Chivalry,* 141–2; J. R. Hale, "The Early Development of the Bastion," in *Europe in the Late Middle Ages* ed. J. R. Hale (Evanston, Ill., 1965); Contamine, *War,* 203–4.

◀ 4 ▶

A Military Revolution?
A 1660–1792 Perspective

JEREMY BLACK

THE NOTION OF A MILITARY revolution in the period 1560–1660 has been useful in offering a conceptual framework within which early-modern warfare can be discussed. It offered an alternative to a narrative account, one that at once addresses the central questions of change and, or as opposed to, continuity, and the causes and consequences of change. The concept was also fundamental in that it addressed narrowly military questions, particularly tactics and training, in a fashion that, apparently, directly brought out their wider implications for broader issues of governmental and political development. This was crucial because the relationship between military innovation and 'state formation', or at least domestic political history, is one that has to be put alongside the more conventional account of the military aspects of inter-state competition.

Furthermore, the thesis of a military revolution was well suited to the approach towards 'state formation' that was dominant in the 1950s, 1960s and 1970s. This approach emphasised coercion and force and thus focused on qualitative and quantitative developments in the armed forces at the disposal of central governments and the consequent ability of these governments to establish absolutist regimes. In the 1980s, however, both absolutism and early-modern European state formation have been redefined, for example in William Beik's *Absolutism and Society in Seventeenth-Century France* (Cambridge, 1985), away from an emphasis on coercion and, instead, towards one on a greater measure of consensus, at least within the elite. This has important implications for the study of early-modern military history, not only because the purpose of military change requires re-examination, but also as its *process* needs re-consideration. The extent to which more effective military forces reflected not more autocratic states but rather crown-elite co-operation is more apparent.

The use of the concept of a military revolution in the early-modern period was greatly advanced by Geoffrey Parker in his *The Military Revolution. Military inno-*

vation and the rise of the West, 1500–1800 (Cambridge, 1988), for, with valuable insights based upon incredibly wide-ranging knowledge, Parker located European developments in the wider global context of 'the rise of the West'; although, as he made clear, the latter was far from a smooth process in military terms. Parker's work was even more valuable because most of the work on the rise of the West, not least Wallerstein's thesis in his *Modern World System* (1974, 1980) of relationships based on zones of exploitation, adopted a somewhat crude economic causation that neglected military factors or treated them as a necessary consequence of other power relationships.

In focussing, in my *A Military Revolution? Military Change and European Society 1550–1800* (London, 1991), on the period after 1660, I was motivated by a sense that this had been neglected in terms not only of what happened then, in both a qualitative and quantitative sense, but also of the significance of these developments. An examination of this period, most commonly known as the *ancien régime,* throws light both on the previous century and on the subsequent period of the Revolutionary and Napoleonic Wars, 1792–1815. If themes of change and continuity are to be addressed in studying 1560–1660 and 1792–1815, then it is crucially necessary to consider *ancien régime* warfare, as claims of change are often made for 1560–1660 and 1792–1815 in the context of misleading assumptions about the stagnation, indecisiveness and conservatism of *ancien régime* warfare.

These assumptions are but part of a more general historiographical neglect of change in the *ancien régime* that rest in part on the very conceptualisation of that period, and indeed on the connotations of its linguistic description.[1] In crude terms, the general model is of a resolution of the mid-seventeenth century crisis in the shape of absolutist states and societies, the subsequent stability of which was a crucial component of the *ancien régime,* but one that was faced in the late eighteenth century by a new general crisis.[2]

Thus the chronology of military change is apparently matched by a more general political chronology, although there has been no attempt to relate the two. This analysis is, however, problematic. If too static an interpretation, in both political and military terms, is adopted for the *ancien régime,* then major change must be sought and explained in the late-eighteenth century. Conversely, if the emphasis is rather on a more dynamic, fluid or plastic *ancien régime* or early modern period, then it is less necessary to focus on change or the causes of change in the late-eighteenth century.[3]

This dynamism can indeed be demonstrated by arguing that the early modern military revolution requires reconceptualisation. Rather than adopting the notion of a single revolution (the Roberts thesis) it is more accurate to suggest that, if early-modern changes can be described in terms of revolution, there were two 'revolutions', one in the late fifteenth and early sixteenth centuries, the other in c.1660–c.1720. The first has been ably described by Parker, with his emphasis on firearms and the *trace italienne,* but because he both failed to break free from Roberts' model and neglected to consider the post-1660 period, he gave the misleading impression that the Roberts thesis could be sustained and amplified by his own emphasis on the preceding period. Instead, it is apparent from a consideration of seventeenth-century warfare that the major changes took place *after* 1660, and, indeed, it can be argued that Roberts' century was in relative terms one of limited change between two periods of greater importance.

The principal changes in *c.*1660–*c.*1720 were both qualitative and quantitative. The replacement of the pike by the newly-developed socket bayonet, the pre-packaged cartridge, the substitution of the matchlock musket by the flintlock and the replacement of the pike increased infantry firepower and manoeuvrability. It led also to a decline in the relative importance of cavalry in most European armies.

Navies provide some of the best indicators of change in the period 1660–1720. The development of line-ahead tactics greatly altered naval warfare, not only tactically but also by increasing the importance of heavily gunned ships of the line, and thus of the states able to deploy and maintain substantial numbers of such ships. In 1639 at the Downs, the attack in line-ahead was first executed in European waters. The English fleet was ordered in 1653 to use the line-ahead formation pioneered by the Dutch. The new fighting instructions for the Dutch fleet issued in 1665 laid down that fighting be done in a single line of battle. In 1666 the signal for forming line of battle was added to the general signal book, thereby completing the adoption of line-ahead tactics by the Dutch navy.

Qualitative changes, i.e. line-ahead tactics, were accompanied by, indeed required due to the stronger emphasis on gunnery, greater specialisation in warships, so that, with the exception of the heavily-armed East Indiamen, merchantmen were no longer used as warships. Furthermore, there were significant developments in the size of navies. The Dutch, English and, from the 1660s, the French substantially increased the size of their fleets in the 1650s–80s and the power of their gunnery also rose appreciably. New bases were created, for example by the French at Lorient, Rochefort and Brest, while Dunkirk and Toulon were enlarged. Advanced shipbuilding techniques were followed and in about 1680 the French developed the bomb-ketch, a very useful warship for attacking positions on land. A professional naval officer corps was developed.[4]

Accounts of the English navy make it clear that, although there had been appreciable developments in the sixteenth century, they were dwarfed in terms of numbers of warships, tactics and naval organisation by those in the second half of the seventeenth century.[5] In the early-eighteenth century these developments were followed by the launching of Russia as a naval power under Peter the Great and the dramatic revival of Spanish naval strength and organisation under Philip V.[6] Thus larger 'standing navies' were a feature of the late-seventeenth century, although there are major problems in producing aggregate totals of European warships—the lists in George Modelski and William Thompson's *Seapower in Global Politics, 1494–1993* exclude several important second-rank naval powers, most obviously Denmark and Sweden, and revise upwards the number of guns required for a ship to be counted—it is nevertheless clear that aggregate numbers rose appreciably in the late-seventeenth century, and then again in the eighteenth.[7] These large permanent naval forces were a critical factor in enabling European powers to secure their overseas empires.

Similarly, larger standing armies developed in the century after the Roberts period. The bulk of the growth occurred in the later period and it was of such an order that it cannot be described simply in terms of the continuation of already established patterns of growth. Again there are problems with counting numbers and, in particular, effectives,[8] and it is necessary to exercise considerable caution even when using oft-cited figures. One of the most useful, and necessarily collective, projects that military historians could engage in would be the production of an authoritative data-bank on army strengths in the early-modern period. Contemporaries had no doubt that the rise of armies was exaggerated and that many units were incomplete. Thus, the theoretical size of the Portuguese army in 1761 was 31,000; the actual numbers, 16,500.[9]

Accepting these caveats, it is nevertheless clear that the army sizes of the major powers rose dramatically in the period 1660–1720. This was certainly true of Austria, France and Russia, and was also true of second-rank powers, particularly Britain, Prussia and Savoy-Piedmont. The French army was cut after the War of the Spanish Succession finished in 1714, but in the period 1720–80 the size of the Austrian, Prussian and Russian armies continued to grow appreciably. There were also important improvements in 1660–1720 in military and naval administration, especially in the ways in which armies and navies were trained, equipped, paid and controlled by their governments. The French[10] and Prussian armies were obvious examples. This administrative dimension was the one in which many of the most important changes occurred. Better administration allowed the recruitment and maintenance of larger armies.

Thus, on both land and sea, and in both qualitative and quantitative terms, there were major changes in the period after 1660. Whether they deserve description in terms of a revolution is of course subjective: there are no agreed-upon criteria by which military change, especially qualitative development, can be measured or, more significantly, revolution discerned. If simply quantitative criteria are to be addressed then it is difficult to compare aggregate and percentage increases. Again different aggregate figures can point to different results. With ships, for example, tonnage, number of guns and weight of guns can provide different results. Eighteenth-century British warships were less impressive than their Bourbon counterparts. French and Spanish ships were better designed and generally faster. In 1744 Admiral Mathews complained about the British warships under his command and provided an indication of the danger of judging naval effectiveness in terms of the number of guns per warship:

> Nor can ships which cannot make use of their lower tiers of guns, though they mount ninety and eighty guns, do the duty expected (by the ignorant) against the 74 and 64

gun ships of France who can fire theirs … there is no proportion of metal, our lightly gunned ships having but twelve and six pounders, whereas some of the enemy's seventy-four gun ships carry forty, eighteen and nine pounders … the rest of them, thirty two, eighteen and nine; their ships of sixty four guns have twenty four, eighteen and nine pounders, which makes even them better men of war than our eighty gun ships that cannot make use of their lower tiers which they will ever seldom be able to do … I have now but two ships of ninety and three of eighty guns, that can make use of their lower tiers of guns, if it blows a cap full of wind … not in [my] power to engage the enemy, when he is superior to them, nor to escape when he is inferior.[11]

In counting numbers of guns it is also necessary to note that the ability to use them varied: the regular gun-drills of the British navy enabled their ships to maintain a heavier and more accurate fire for longer.

Clearly numbers, therefore, were not the sole factor. This was also the case on land, most spectacularly during the Spanish defeat of the empires in the New World. The Aztec and Inca empires were overthrown by tiny forces, as discussed by John Guilmartin in this volume. Indeed it is at the level of global significance, so ably discussed by Parker, that the importance of the changes in the post-1660 period can best be considered. There are problems in considering European and extra-European warfare as parts of a single whole. The physical conditions, the size of the forces involved and the problems of central control of them were all very different in the two areas. Yet an assessment of revolutionary impact requires such a perspective. In terms of the global reach of seapower, the balance had swung towards the European powers long before 1660, but that was not true on land.

The post-1660 period was unfortunately neglected by Parker; indeed his book carries misleading dates, for it principally deals with 1500–1650 and not the following century and a half. This is especially unfortunate because it is related to a stress on the clash between trans-oceanic European forces and non-European powers, and a consequent lack of emphasis on Europe's land frontier: the border with the Turks and, farther east, with Persia. Indeed, whereas Parker mentions the siege of Vienna,[12] it is disappointing, in light of the valuable attention he focuses on relations between European and non-European powers, that he subsequently neglects Austro-Turkish warfare.[13] The same is also true of its Polish-Turkish and Russo-Turkish counterparts, and of Russian warfare with Persia and in Central Asia.[14]

Yet it is in this sphere that change can most obviously be noted. For centuries European powers had been under pressure from the east; essentially settled societies resisting the inroads of partly nomadic peoples. Such an assessment can be taken back to the last centuries of Imperial Rome (Persian attacks on Classical Greece were somewhat different), and then the successive attacks made by Arabs, Magyars, Seljuk Turks, Mongols, Ottoman Turks and Timur (Tamerlane), although the pressure from the east was not continuous and the Crusades were an important example of European powers applying pressure in the opposite direction. It was the Ottoman Turks who finally conquered the Balkans and in 1453 overthrew Byzantium. In the sixteenth century, thanks in part to the effective use of firearms and cannons, Turkish power expanded even further. Selim I defeated the Safavids of Persia at Caldiran (1515) and pushed Turkish frontiers eastwards. Victories at Marj Dabik (1516) and Cairo (1517) led to the conquest of the Mameluke Empire. The frontiers of Christendom were pushed back. In the Mediterranean, Rhodes fell in 1522 and Cyprus in 1570–1 and all of North Africa bar Morocco acknowledged Turkish lordship. Belgrade fell in 1521 and the decisive victory of Mohacs (1526) was followed by the conquest of most of Hungary by Suleiman I (the Magnificent).

The Turkish advance was held—a series of unsuccessful sieges (Vienna 1529, Corfu 1537, Reggio 1543 and Malta 1565) marking the limit of advance—but that did not end the Turkish threat to Christian Europe. The Turkish state was one of the most populous in Europe, its military system the most sophisticated in sixteenth-century Europe. The Austro-Turkish war of 1593–1606 revealed the logistical strength of the Turkish army.[15] It was fortunate for the European powers that the Turks devoted so much energy to their long wars against Safavid Persia: that of 1578–90 led to a welcome reduction in the threat to Habsburg Europe.[16] In the mid-seventeenth century Turkish power suffered a decline, but there was then a revival of strength and energy under the first two grand viziers of the Köprülü dynasty. They benefited from the end of war with Persia in order to revitalise the Turkish state and this enabled them to take a more active role in Europe: the long conflict with Venice over Crete (1645–69) was brought to an end successfully with the fall of Candia. Turkish authority in Transylvania was made more effective as a result of a war in 1658–61, and the Turks were left in complete control there after a brief war with Austria in 1663–4. A war with Poland, 1671–6, led to the acquisition of Podolia, a large territory stretching from the Dniester to the Dnieper which increased their ability to intervene in Poland and the Ukraine. The disturbed state of the latter encouraged the Turks to attack Russia in 1677–81, although war brought them no gains. In 1682 Imre Thököly, the leader of the anti-Habsburg rebels in the section of Hungary ruled by Austria, agreed, in return for Turkish help, to become a vassal of the sultan, and in 1683 the Turks advanced on Vienna.

Thus, the Turks were still very much a dynamic force in the late–seventeenth century. Indeed, in so far as there was a military revolution either in the Roberts period or earlier, it had not hitherto led to a decisive shift in the military balance or movement in the frontier between Christendom and Islam, a point that was further underlined by the peripheral nature of the Christian military impact on North Africa.[17] This situation was to change radically by 1718, so that in 1730 there was no doubt that Henry Fielding was being satrical in his play *The Coffee-House Politician* when he had Politic repeatedly express his concern about Turkish intentions, culminating in his fear that we should see Turkish galleys in the [English] Channel ... it is possible for the Grand Signior to find an ingress into Europe. — Suppose, Sir, this spot I stand on to be Turkey—then here is Hungary—very well—here is France, and here is England— granted—then we will suppose he had possession of Hungary—what then remains but to conquer France, before we find him at our own coast ... this is not all the danger ... he can come by sea to us.[18]

There had been a dramatic reversal, a true military revolution. The Turkish defeat at Vienna (1683) was followed by substantial Austrian advances. Buda fell in 1686, 1687 brought a decisive victory at Berg Harsan (Nagyharsany) and the deposition of Sultan Mehmed IV, and 1688 saw the fall of Belgrade. The collapse of the Turkish position in the Balkans and an Austrian advance into the world of the Orthodox appeared imminent. The Austrians developed links with rebellious elements among the Bulgarians and Serbs and began negotiations with the prince of Wallachia, a Turkish client-ruler. In 1689 they seized Nish and Skopje and reached Bucharest. The Serbian patriarch of Pec was persuaded to take an oath of loyalty to Leopold I, who on 6 April 1690 issued an appeal for the support of all Balkan peoples against the Turks and promised liberty under their lawful ruler, himself as King of Hungary.

Austrian victories reflected the improvements introduced by Montecuccoli, Commander-in-Chief and President of the War Council 1668–80. The Austrian army became larger and more mobile and this was subsequently furthered by the introduction of flintlocks. Flintlocks and bayonets gave the Austrian infantry an important tactical advantage over the Turks who had neither. Logistics, rather than the Turkish armies, became the principal problem facing the Austrians.

The late 1680s may have represented the best opportunity for driving the Turks out of all or most of the Balkans until the nineteenth century, but Turkish resilience should not be underrated, while from 1688 the Austrians were distracted by the outbreak of war in Western Europe (the Nine Years War or War of the League of Augsburg, 1688–97). The chaos that greeted Suleyman II (1687–91) was quashed, and a new grand vizier from the Köprülü family, Fazil Mustafa (1689–91) restored order to army and government. In 1690 he took Nish and Belgrade, but in the following year Fazil and the Turkish hopes of recapturing Hungary were both killed at the major defeat at Zalánkemén.

Conflict over the next few years was indecisive and difficult, due to Austrian commitments against Louis XIV, and, in the battle-zone, improved fortifications, the depletion of local sources of supply and the problems of fighting in undrained marshy lowlands. Matters moved to a climax as a result of the accession of the energetic Mustafa II (1695–1703) and the end of the war in Italy in 1696 which enabled Leopold to transfer more troops and his rising general, Eugene of Savoy, to Hungary. Euguene routed Mustafa at Zenta in 1697, the latter suffering possibly 30,000 casualties. The eventual peace settlement at Karlowitz (January 1699) saw

Austria gain Transylvania and all of Hungary except the Banat of Temesvár (Timisoara), while her allies Poland and Venice acquired Podolia and the Morea.

Conflict was resumed in 1716, the Austrians winning crushing victories at Petrovaradin (1716) and Belgrade (1717) and capturing Temesvár (1716) and Belgrade (1717). The Peace of Passarowitz (1718) left Austria with the Banat of Temesvár, Little (Western) Wallachia and northern Serbia. These victories indicated the increasing vulnerability of Turkish mass formations to the firepower of disciplined Austrian units. The shift in the balance of military advantage between Austria and Turkey was also significant, as the best way to put a definite temporal boundary on the Military Revolution (in Parker's valuable globalist sense of the term) is to isolate the period when Europeans became militarily superior to people who in the past had been their equals or superiors, most pointedly the Turks. In contrast to the receding frontier of Europe in the sixteenth century, there was expansion in the late seventeenth and early eighteenth: the military balance between 'West and East' had reversed. This clearly qualifies as a 'revolution' of the wheel of military fortune, to restore the word to its original metaphor.

Austrian victories were part of a more general shift in European warfare away from speed, mobility and primal shock-power and towards defensive tactics based on infantry firepower, a shift that was already apparent among the major European powers during the first half of the sixteenth century. It was this shift that also led to the defeat of 'Gaelic' forces in Britain, culminating at the killing field at Culloden in 1746.[19]

More generally, the period from 1660 on until the outbreak of the French Revolutionary Wars saw the victory of armies emphasising the concentrated firepower of disciplined infantry and their supporting artillery over more mobile forces that stressed the use of shock-power in attack. This theme links both a number of otherwise disparate campaigns and, more generally, the struggle between established governments and rebellious 'marginal' forces, for example the Cossacks and Jacobites, and that between European Christian states and their Islamic neighbours.

As with all theses, this one must not be pushed too far: the Turks were essentially a settled people, and the western Europeans had been so long before the 'military revolution' but without enjoying military superiority over their more-mobile opponents. A similar contrast between the more specialised and organised forces of essentially settled peoples and their more mobile, often nomadic opponents was scarcely new and can be seen elsewhere in the period 1660–1792, for example in the struggles between the Turks and the Bedouin, Mughal India and invaders from Afghanistan, and Manchu China and the peoples of lands conquered between 1691 and 1760, such as the Khalkhas of Eastern Mongolia and the Dzungarians of Western Mongolia.[20]

Nevertheless in the period 1660–1792 the success of the major European states in creating effective forces able to use concentrated and disciplined firepower in order to defeat opponents was very important in global terms. The success of these forces against opponents armed with guns was particularly significant. In short, it can be argued that the qualitative European military changes already noted—the bayonet, the flintlock musket, accurate and mobile grape- and canister-firing field artillery, and warships firing a greater weight of metal—were crucial in that they opened up a major gap in capability among armies and navies armed with firearms. In addition, while earlier European conquests (America, Philippines, Portuguese coastal gains in Africa and Asia) could rely on superior technology (gunpowder, fortifications, steel), those of the period 1660–1792 reflected not only superior technology but also a superiority in military technique (broadly conceived to include drill, cartography, logistic and financial institutions, as well as tactics) which was more difficult to transfer or replicate than technology, resting as it did on the foundations of centuries of European social and institutional change.

It would be misleading to imply that European forces were invariably successful. There were a number of prominent failures, including Golitsyn's campaigns in the Crimea in 1687 and 1689, the Russian siege of Azov of 1695, Peter I's campaign against the Turks in 1711 and Austrian campaigns against the Turks in 1739 and 1788. A less well-known failure was the encirclement and annihilation of a Russian force on the bank of the river Sunja in 1785 by North Caucasian Muslims taking part in the holy war launched by Sheikh Mansur.[21] The Russians also found it difficult to impose control in north-east Siberia.[22] The Aleuts destroyed the recently founded Russian base of Mikhailovsk in 1802.

There were also setbacks for European powers in North Africa. The English abandoned Tangier in 1683, the Spaniards lost Oran in 1708, recaptured it in 1732 and evacuated it in 1792, the Portuguese lost Mazagam in 1765 and major Spanish attacks on Algiers in 1775, 1783 and 1784 were repelled. Some 6,000 Spaniards died in the 1775 attack. In 1741 the Bey of Tunis seized the offshore island of Tabarca which the French had purchased from the Lomellino family, defeated a French counterattack and sacked the French Africa Company's base at Cape Negre.

Elsewhere in Africa the attempt by the Portuguese to expand their influence up the Zambesi was defeated by a widespread tribal rising in 1693–5. In 1698 their leading base in East Africa, Mombasa, fell to the Omani Arabs, who had captured Muscat from the Portuguese in 1650, developed a formidable navy with well-gunned warships, and sacked Diu in 1668. Retaken in 1728, Mombasa and the attendant suzerainty over the Swahili islands and states of East Africa—Pate, Pemba, Zanzibar and Malindi—were lost again in 1729. The French did not control Madagascar from the coastal bases they established.

In South Asia Louis XIV's intervention in Siam (Thailand) was unsuccessful, as was the attempt by both the British and the French to benefit from the Burmese civil war in the 1750s. An alliance of the British of Bombay and the Portuguese of Goa was unable in 1721 to capture Culabo (Colabo) the principal base of the Angria family of corsairs. In 1737–40 Goa was involved in a disastrous war with the Maratha confederation, which led to the loss of the Portuguese 'Province of the North'. The British settlement of Balambangan on Borneo was destroyed in

1775 by a local uprising. In 1792 the British prudently refused a request from the Rajah of Nepal for assistance against Chinese military pressure although the Ch'ing intervention cut off Tibet-Bengal trade and closed Bhutan to the British. Similarly, the decision was taken not to offer the Rajah of Kedah assistance against Siam even though the British had obtained Penang in 1786 by offering the prospect of such assistance.[23]

It is therefore possible to suggest the marginality of European military pressure in Africa and Asia. Many of the non-European states were powerful and aggressive. Even when the Europeans made gains they were not always preserved. In 1689 Russia ceded the Amur valley to China by the Treaty of Nerchinsk. In 1722 Peter the Great advanced along the Caspian. Darband and Resht were occupied in 1722, Baku in 1723 and in 1723 Shah Tahmasp of Persia was persuaded to yield the provinces along the southern and western shores of the Caspian. A Persian revival and the loss of many soldiers to disease, however, led the Russians to abandon their gains by the Treaties of Reht (1729, 1732) and Gence (1735).

Yet if the global territorial position in 1792 is compared with that in 1660 the gains of territory between European and non-European powers are overwhelmingly to the benefit of the former, and the land frontier between Christian and non-Christian Europe had changed dramatically. This was of crucial importance for Christian Europe. Up to 1683 the tide had flowed in the opposite direction. The Austrian conquest of Hungary was the precondition of Austrian strength in the eighteenth century; indeed the Austrian successes in the 1680s marked a major shift in the European balance of power against Louis XIV. Similarly, Russia was able to act effectively in part because its southern question had been radically altered: the issue was now how far it would be possible to advance.

The successes against the Turks were crucial triumphs for the European 'land powers' and as major contests between land powers they were a fair test of military capability. The failures listed earlier were overwhelmingly those of amphibious power. Small settlements with only limited maritime connections with distant home bases were only infrequently the basis of imperial expansion in the eighteenth century, but the rationale of many of these bases was commercial rather than territorial, and indeed they were frequently controlled directly by trading companies.

The Europeans faced serious difficulties when they sought trans-oceanic territorial expansion, but their military power should not be underrated. In part their very difficulties, as in North America, came from the borrowing of European weaponry and, although to a lesser extent, tactics by their opponents.[24] Indeed John Macpherson, a senior official of the British East India Company, who in 1771 had noted that the French had 'disciplined some Regiments of Madegascar Cafres', wrote twelve years later that British forces had taken all the ports belonging to France's ally, Hyder Ali of Mysore, 'in some of which we have found the materials and great advancement of a very considerable naval power'. Nadir Shah only succeeded at the siege of Ganja with the help of Russian engineers disguised as Iranians. In 1787 the dynamic Bo-daw-hpaya, King of Burma, negotiated with the French at their Bengal base of Chandernagore in his search for Western arms. In the early 1790s Jezzar Pasa of Palestine was reported to have obtained British arms, including field artillery, from the British Consul in Alexandria, for his effective army.[25]

Nevertheless, despite the borrowing of European techniques by non-Western peoples, the European colonial powers still had considerable success. The Indians and others who adopted European military methods did not do so with full success: there was a major difference between technology which was relatively easy to acquire though less so to copy proficiently, and technique, which was culturally based and therefore very difficult to adopt. This was particularly so in the case of tactical developments. In India at least, when the Europeans ran into trouble, it was usually with local forces that had adopted technique as well as technology. In his *Importing the European Army. The Introduction of European Military Techniques and Institutions into the Extra-European World, 1600–1914* (Chicago, 1990), David Ralston emphasises the degree to which the full Europeanization of armed forces entailed social and cultural changes and was therefore very difficult.

The Dutch East India Company was not invariably successful, but it did succeed in considerably extending its territorial power in Java.[26] Elsewhere in Indonesia, despite the financial problems of the Company, it was still able to hold its own. If in 1759 Rajah Muhammad of Siak destroyed the Dutch post at Pulau Gontong, in 1761 a Dutch punitive expedition avenged the massacre and placed the Rajah's brother on the throne. In 1784 the Bugis' siege of Malacca was unsuccessful: the Dutch relieved their post, captured Riau and forced the Sultan of Riau-Johor to become in effect their vassal.

In southeast Asia as a whole the use of firearms was very extensive, but the volley technique was not adopted; the war elephant, pikes, swords and spears were still the dominant weaponry; firearms made little impact on tactics; and by the eighteenth century the southeast Asians had abandoned the attempt to keep pace with new developments in the production of both firearms and gunpowder. Thus wheel lock and flintlock mechanisms were not reproduced in southeast Asian foundries.[27]

Developments in India were more dramatic. The British succeeded in becoming the dominant power in both Bengal and South India, regions where the combined population far exceeded that of Britain. Small British forces defeated vastly larger numbers of Indians at Plassey (1757) and Buscar (1764). British military power led to a clear sense of superiority as in 1788 when the Commander in Chief and Governor General, Charles, 2nd Earl Cornwallis, proposed to pursue Britain's claim to the Circar of Guntur (Guntoor) against the Nizam of Hyderabad by force using diplomacy simply to secure the settlement:

> it will be most expedient that our troops should march into the Circar on Captain Kennaway's arrival at Masulipatam; and that our present Resident Meer Hussein

should about ten days before inform the Nizam of our intention, giving the most positive assurances that our design was entirely limited to the taking possession of the Circar as our undoubted right by treaty.[28]

This was very much the language of a general confident of his power, and the result justified Cornwallis' optimism. The value of the European model of warfare was shortly afterwards to be demonstrated again in both Indo-China and southern India.

The problems of France, already in political and serious financial difficulties, prevented her government in 1788 from fulfilling treaty commitments to send forces to the assistance of N'guyen Anh, son of one of the claimants to Cochin China (the area around the Mekong). N'guyen Anh, who was initially dependent on Chinese pirates and Cambodian mercenaries, captured Saigon in 1788. In place of royal forces, he received only French arms and a small number of advisers, hired thanks to the help of French merchants. Nevertheless, in 1789–92 the advisers trained his troops in European methods of war and helped N'guyen Anh conquer Cochin-China. Olivier du Puymanel was responsible for the army, Jean Marie Dayot for the navy. The Tayson capital at Hué was captured in 1801. By 1802 all of Vietnam had been conquered and N'guyen Anh proclaimed himself Emperor Gia-long of Vietnam.[29]

In southern India, another dynamic power, Mysore, was crushed by the British in 1791–2 and 1799. The ability of Britain to do so was an indication, not only of the global reach of its power, but also of the flexibility of European forces in the period. The British army succeeded in combining the firepower that was so effective against Mysore's fortresses with a reasonable degree of mobility. Cornwallis had stressed the value of mobility from the outset. In January 1787 he wrote, 'no man in India can be more convinced than I am of the importance of cavalry to our armies', and later that year he added,

> I found, in the extensive field in which I acted during my command in the southern provinces of America, very great advantage from mounting about eighty or an hundred men on ordinary horses, to act with the cavalry; By this means I could venture to detach my cavalry and strike an unexpected blow at a very considerable distance from my army. It occurs to me, that in case of an invasion of the Carnatic, you might find a corps of this sort picked from your European infantry ... very useful. It would not only protect the cavalry when detached in their camp or quarters, and assist them when harassed by swarms of irregular horse in the field, but it would enable you frequently either by surprise at night, or ambuscade, to punish considerable parties of plunderers, who are employed in laying waste the country.[30]

Once war had broken out with Tipu Sultan of Mysore, Cornwallis stressed the importance both of cavalry and of bullocks to move the artillery.[31] He was also well aware of the logistical problems, writing to the Prime Minister, William Pitt, 'it is no easy task to provide for the subsistence of vast multitudes in a distant desert'.[32] The Marathas and the Nizam of Hyderabad provided important assistance, especially in cavalry and supplies, but their forces were less valuable than had been anticipated. Cornwallis was not able to rely on their support and there was criticism of the quality of the cavalry and artillery.[33]

Cornwallis' success can be compared with that of the Russians in the Russo-Turkish wars of 1768–74 and 1787–92. In both conflicts the Russians were able to overrun the Turkish possessions north of the Danube and to cross the river. In 1791 Russian victories over the Turks in advances across the Danube at Babadag and Machin revealed the vulnerability of Selim III: his army was largely destroyed and he accepted Russian peace preliminaries. The following year Captain Sidney Smith was sent by the British government to Constantinople on a secret mission in order to report on the Turkish military position and 'to consider the means which the Russians may appear to him to have of making an impression upon Constantinople, or any other part of the Turkish Empire, by any attack made from the Black Sea, either by their naval force, or by an army landed near to Constantinople, and acting in concert with their fleet'.[34] The 'Eastern Question' had certainly begun.

The extent of the Russian military achievement has been challenged. Gunther Rothenberg argued that 'Suvorov's reputation rested on his victories over the poorly disciplined and rather backward forces of the Ottoman Empire and Poland ... His strategy was primitive, calling for an attack on the enemy wherever he was found, and his tactics, based on the cult of the bayonet, were outdated and wasteful when delivered against troops relying on fire'. This analysis, however, underrates the problems of campaigning in eastern Europe and mistakenly implies that there is a clear continuum of achievement in military method in the light of which it is readily possible to assess what was 'primitive'. Detailed studies of Russian warfare have been more positive. Russian military success has been attributed to grasping the necessary interrelationship of 'tactics, operations, and logistics', in order to pursue a 'strategy of annihilation' furthered by the use of compact mobile forces drawing on advanced bases and supply magazines, by reliance on storming fortresses rather than conventional sieges, and by a 'credible offensive formation': the battlefield use of mutually-supporting squares, attacking in an articulated fashion and benefiting from crossfire. Similarly, it was 'gun-power that decided the issue' between Russian and Turkish naval forces near Ochakov in 1788: larger Turkish fleets were defeated by more heavily-gunned Russian ships.[35]

The combination of mobility and firepower was crucial: the distances to be covered to the north and west of the Black Sea or in India were immense and certainly different from those covered by most European armies campaigning in Germany, Italy and the Low Countries between 1660 and 1779. The focus on European warfare in that period has always been on those countries, and it is not surprising that this has led to a less than full appreciation of warfare in the period. In particular, there has been a neglect of the more mobile warfare that was characteristic of eastern Europe and of extra-European offensive operations. This is possibly a reflection of a historiographical bias in favour not only of western and cen-

tral European warfare, but more markedly, in both German works and those of
Anglo-American scholars heavily influenced by German suppositions, in favour
of the notion that Frederick II represented the highest point of *ancien régime* warfare. This is arguably misleading in terms of the European forces competing in
western and central Europe in the Frederician period, not least through leading to
a relative neglect of the French under Saxe and the Austrians under Daun. It also
underrates the potential diversity of warfare in western and central Europe, a diversity that was to be underlined from 1792 as Frederician linear tactics were
shown to be at a disadvantage in the face of troops fighting in open order in the
enclosed and wooded country of the Austrian Netherlands and eastern France.
Furthermore, such a notion also leads to a treatment of warfare outside this region as largely peripheral.

This essay, on the contrary, argues that if the global and military significance of
the second stage of the early-modern 'military revolution' is to be grasped, it is
necessary to look at that warfare. It has to be considered both on land and on sea,
for scholars mostly concerned with Frederician warfare and more generally with
that of the eighteenth century have tended to neglect the naval side—and yet it is
clear that the concept of a military revolution must address it.

As yet much of the work necessary for a general re-evaluation of extra-European warfare in the period 1660–1792 has not been carried out, but a number of
points emerge from a preliminary consideration. First, it is necessary not to assume that success is simply measured through the conquest of territory: as ever, it
is necessary to consider the purposes of military force(s), not least their cost-ef-
fectiveness. Secondly, military effectiveness could also be demonstrated in defence, a point that is often overlooked. Thus, rather than concentrating solely on
the struggles between European and non-European (including Turkish) forces, it
is also important to direct attention to extra-oceanic struggles between European
powers; and, in the case of the Thirteen Colonies, peoples. It is readily apparent,
for example, that the strength and flexibility of the Spanish system in the New
World has been underrated. This is demonstrated in part by the advance of New
Spain—in Chile and the modern southwest of America, while in the 1690s the
Mayans were brought under Spanish control—and more so by the ability of Spain
to resist the pressure of other states, not least Britain. In the New World, Spain
had created a generally successful defensive system based on fortifications supported by militia.[36] This was a system well adapted to the environmental and eco-
logical problems of warfare in the tropics. Havana was also the site of an important naval dockyard. The navios and frigates built there out of the durable local
cedar and mahogany woods proved strong and long-lasting ships.[37] Furthermore,
the Spanish military system in the New World was also effective in attack, as was
demonstrated during the American War of Independence.[38]

Consideration of the Spaniards in the New World is valuable because it underlines the flexibility of European military models. The same point also emerges
from consideration of warfare in North America, before, during and after the War

of American Independence.[39] The flexibility of the Americans in using their colonial experience of warfare is the point commonly underlined, but it is also the case that the British varied their tactics. A more-open, less packed, two-deep line was adopted in the middle colonies because of the relative unimportance of cavalry. In the South the British under Cornwallis sought to make their forces more mobile. Tarleton's infantry advanced to the Waxhaws on horseback and attacked 'cavalry and infantry blended'.[40] The eventual failure at Yorktown in 1781 has distorted the analysis of the campaigns in the South. Archibald Campbell's rapid capture of Savannah in 1778, Prevost's success in routing a North Carolina force at Briar Creek in 1779 by attacking it from the rear and his advance on Charleston in 1779, Clinton's encirclement and successful siege of Charleston in 1780, and Cornwallis' success at Camden that year and his march across North Carolina in early 1781, were evidence of British flexibility and mobility, as was Clinton's flanking manoeuvre at Brandywine in 1778. In the West Indies in 1794–5 the British used specially-raised units of slaves, with European commanders, capable of moving rapidly and acting as light infantry.

The notion that mobility on campaign and the value of the attack in battle were not rediscovered until the Revolutionary Wars is therefore misleading. It does not describe adequately campaigning in western and central Europe where there were striking examples of mobility. Marlborough's march to the Rhine in 1704 is the best known, but there were other instances of rapid movement over considerable distances, for example some of the movements of Frederick II and Prince Henry of Prussia during the Seven Years War. The improvement of European roads during the century further aided mobility. As already implied, the ability of European forces to solve the tactical and strategic problems of warfare a world away from the parade-ground conventions of western and central Europe was instrumental in the decisive driving back of the Turks and in the establishment of Britain as a territorial power in India. It is therefore pertinent to stress innovation, change and impact when considering warfare in the period 1660–1792.

The destruction of Cossack independence by the Russians was symptomatic of this process. What was until then, in effect, an independent warrior people was brought under control by the 'westernised' military units of Peter I's army. In 1709 the Cossack headquarters at Stara Sich was destroyed.[41] The Cossacks were permitted to establish a new centre at Nova Sich, but that also was destroyed in 1775 and all of Zaporozhia was made part of an imperial province known as New Russia. Military strength was linked to centralization and state expansion, a crucial theme in the early-modern 'Military Revolution'.

Change and impact must also be stressed in the case of naval power. In 1788 Cornwallis wrote with reference to a proposed attack on the French in India, 'unless we have a fleet capable of looking the enemy in the face, we must not hazard a considerable body of troops.' Naval power was crucial to imperial expansion and consolidation, and in military terms there was a significant expansion in amphibious capability, the basis of imperial expansion in the nineteenth century. Amphibious operations faced serious problems,[42] many of which were not resolved, but, nevertheless, substantial forces were sent considerable distances, as when the British captured Manila in 1762 or New York in 1776.[43] The crucial nature of army-naval cooperation was demonstrated in the Yorktown campaign of 1781, the reach of naval power by the establishment of the first European settlement in Australia in 1788. Two years later, during the Nootka Sound controversy, as earlier during the War of American Independence, the British considered far-flung attacks on the Spanish empire. They established a base on the Andaman Islands in 1789. The French were also active, charting the coast of Asia in the 1780s and sending naval expeditions into the Indian and Pacific oceans, while this was also a period of Spanish activity in the Pacific and of the expansion of Russian power on North America's Pacific littoral.[44]

The potential gap between European military capability and that of non-European peoples was demonstrated most clearly in the Pacific, not only in Australia but also in eastern Indonesia. Captain John Blankett sailed through the Moluccas in December 1790 and found 'the natives ... were all armed with spears and shields, and all on horseback'. He was, however, unimpressed by the Dutch fort on Timor that he visited: 'a miserable band, composed of a few German deserters and Malays compose a sort of garrison'. Blankett noted that the Dutch preserved their position by exploiting the rivalries of the rulers of Timor.[45] This was scarcely a picture of unrivalled European supremacy, but Blankett's very voyage demonstrated that the European powers were taking the initiative. Similarly, in central Amazonia in the 1760s and 1770s, the Portuguese were unable to defeat the guerrilla attacks of the mobile Mura with their ambushes of Portuguese canoes and their attacks on isolated settlements. The Muras did not learn the use of firearms, but were very effective with their bows and arrows. Nevertheless, the Muras could not defeat the Portuguese and the peace they sought in 1784 appears to have reflected the need to reach an accommodation with colonial power.[46]

To conclude, the 'revolutionary' periods were c. 1470–c. 1530, c. 1660–c. 1720 and (primarily because of the levée on masse rather than tactics) 1792–1815. Roberts' emphasis on 1560–1660 is incorrect. Equally, though 1660–1720 and 1792–1815 might be periods of fairly dramatic change, the intervening era was not static and unchanging. Historians, with the obvious exception of Parker, have tended to neglect the significance of European conflict in the wider world. The significance of the lessons of colonial warfare, however, were often lost on contemporaries in Europe. Leaving aside the wider historical significance of European overseas expansion in the eighteenth century, the military impact on the way European wars were fought was often slight. The British, for example, failed to develop light infantry despite the lessons of the American War of Independence. Nevertheless, it is perhaps significant that the European powers engaged in land conflict with non-European states in the 1720–92 era (Russia, Austria and Britain) proved more resilient than Prussia (and other states) in standing up to revolutionary France; although other factors were also pertinent.

The nature of the 'military revolution' thesis also poses a problem. Parker, and especially Roberts, link broad military and societal change to changes in tactics and military technology and argue that these were both revolutionary and innovative. The problem is, as ever, one of terms. Not only is revolution a tricky concept, but clearly many tactical developments were hardly innovative in the sense of being truly original. The use of dragoons in the Thirty Years War, for example, was little different from the use of mounted infantry in India and elsewhere in the late-eighteenth century. Equally, the Spanish system of colonial defence based on fortresses and local militia mirrors the efforts of many European states to organize for defence at the beginning of the seventeenth century, for example German states such as Nassau. What was really going on in large part was the clever adaptation of existing ideas to suit local circumstances. While at the micro level these changes in tactics could bring revolutionary results, in the sense of decisive local victories, it is difficult to link these together at the macro level into some all-embracing theory of revolutionary change. These changes have to be distinguished from truly original innovations, such as the flintlock and the socket bayonet, which altered the parameters of conflict.

On sea as on land the military capability of the European powers was far from static in the period 1660–1792. There is still much work required on the age, but it is already clear that, in order to assess both the 'Roberts century' and the Revolutionary/Napoleonic period it is essential to consider the intervening years. Doing so on the global scale underlines their importance.

Notes

I would like to thank Matthew Anderson, Michael Hill, Geoffrey Parker, John Plowright, Cliff Rogers and Peter Wilson for their comments on earlier drafts of this chapter.

1. H. E. Bodeker and E. Hinrichs (eds.), *Alteuropa-Ancien Régime-Frühe Neuzeit. Probleme und Methoden der Forschung* (Stuttgart, 1991), pp. 11–50.

2. A good recent summary is offered by W. Doyle, *The Old European Order 1660–1800* (Oxford, 1978), pp. 295–6.

3. J. M. Black, 'Ancien Régime and Enlightenment', *European History Quarterly* 22, (1992), pp. 247–55.

4. On tactical changes, B. Nosworthy, *The Anatomy of Victory. Battle Tactics 1689–1763* (New York, 1990). On the French navy see most recently, G. Symcox, 'The Navy of Louis XIV', in P. Sonnino (ed.), *The Reign of Louis XIV* (Atlantic Highlands, New Jersey, 1990), pp. 127–42 and Philippe de Villette-Mursay, *Mes Campagnes de Mer sous Louis XIV avec Un Dictionnaire des personnages et des batailles* edited by M. Verge-Franceschi (Paris, 1991).

5. D. Loades, *The Tudor Navy* (Aldershot, 1992); K. R. Andrews, *Ships, Money and Politics. Seafaring and naval enterprise in the reign of Charles I* (Cambridge, 1991); M. Duffy, 'The Foundations of British Naval Power', in Duffy (ed.), *The Military Revolution and the State 1500–1800* (Exeter, 1980), pp. 49–85; B. Capp, *Cromwell's Navy. The Fleet and the English Revolution, 1648–1660* (Oxford, 1992); D. Davies, *Gentlemen and Tarpaulins: The Offi-*

cers and Men of the Restoration Navy (Oxford, 1991); J. Ehrman, *The Navy in the War of William III 1689–1697* (Cambridge, 1953).

6. J. P. Merino Navarro, *La Armada Espanola en el Siglo XVIII* (Madrid, 1981).

7. Modelski and Thompson, *Seapower in Global Politics, 1494–1993* (London, 1988), pp. 27–61 and esp. 62–70.

8. For some useful comparisons for the Austrian army in 1740–75, P. G. M. Dickson, *Finance and Government under Maria Theresia 1740–1780* (2 vols., Oxford, 1987), II, 355.

9. State of the Portuguese army enclosed in Mello, Portuguese envoy in London, to Earl of Egremont, Secretary of State for the Southern Department, 15 Dec. 1761, London, Public Record Office (hereafter PRO) 30/47/2. On the Spanish army, Benjamin Keene, envoy in Spain, to the Duke of Newcastle, Secretary of State for the Southern Department, 7 Ap. 1734, PRO. State Papers 94/119. On the Russians, Frederick II to Klinggraeffen, 28 May, 8 June 1754, *Politische Correspondenz Friedrichs des Grossen* (46 vols., Berlin, 1879–1939) X, 342, 346; Charles Fraser, Secretary of Legation in St. Petersburg, to Sir Robert Murray Keith, 31 May 1788, London, British Library, Department of Manuscripts, Additional Manuscripts 35540 f.249.

10. J. Chagniot, 'La Rationalisation de l'Armée Française après 1660', in *Armées et Diplomatie dans l'Europe du XVIIᵉ Siècle* (Paris, 1992), pp. 97–108.

11. Mathews to Newcastle, 17 Feb. 1744, Mill St. House, Iden Green, papers of Edward Weston. I should like to thank John Weston-Underwood for permission to consult these papers.

12. Parker, *Military Revolution,* p. 126. Aside from the works he cites, it is also useful to consult T. M. Barker, *Double Eagle and Crescent: Vienna's Second Turkish Siege and Its Historical Setting* (Albany, New York, 1967); J. Berenger (ed.), *Les Relations Franco-Autrichiennes sous Louis XIV. Siege de Vienne (1683),* (proceedings of Saint-Cyr colloque 1983); Barker, 'New Perspectives on the Historical Significance of the "Year of the Turk"', *Austrian History Yearbook,* 19–20 (1983–4) pt. 1, pp. 3–14.

13. See most recently, A. Balisch, 'Infantry Battlefield Tactics in the Seventeenth and Eighteenth Centuries on the European and Turkish Theatres of War: the Austrian Response to Different Conditions', *Studies in History and Politics,* 3 (1983–4), pp. 43–60.

14. See recently, B. Menning, 'G. A. Potemkin and A. I. Chernyshev: Two Dimensions of Reform and the Military Frontier in Imperial Russia', in *The Consortium on Revolutionary Europe, Proceedings, 1980;* C. Duffy, *Russia's Military Way to the West. Origins and Nature of Russian Military Power 1700–1800* (London, 1981), pp. 27, 49–53, 168–78, 185–9; L. Hughes, *Sophia. Regent of Russia 1657–1704* (New Haven, 1990), pp. 197–203, 206, 211–17; A. S. Donnelly, *The Russian Conquest of Bashkiria, 1552–1740; A Case Study in Imperialism* (New Haven, 1968).

15. C. Finkel, *The Administration of Warfare: the Ottoman Military Campaigns in Hungary, 1593–1606* (1988).

16. W. E. D. Allen, *Problems of Turkish power in the sixteenth century* (London, 1963).

17. A. C. Hess, *The forgotten frontier: a history of the sixteenth-century Ibero-African frontier* (Chicago, 1978).

18. Fielding, *Coffee-House Politician* (London, 1730) I, iii, iv, II, xi.

19. I owe to Cliff Rogers the reference to the original metaphor of revolution. J. M. Hill, 'The Distinctiveness of Gaelic Warfare, 1400–1750', *European History Quarterly,* 22 (1992), pp. 323–45. See, more generally, his *Celtic Warfare 1595–1763* (Edinburgh, 1986), and Black, *Culloden and the '45* (Gloucester, 1990).

20. A. Cohen, *Palestine in the Eighteenth Century. Patterns of Government and Administration* (Jerusalem, 1973), pp. 104–11; R. Tapper, 'The Tribes in Eighteenth and Nineteenth Century Iran', in *The Cambridge History of Iran VII* (Cambridge, 1991), pp. 513–18.

21. A. Bennigsen, 'Un mouvement populaire au Caucase au XVIIIe siècle', *Cahiers du monde russe et soviétique*, 5 (1964), pp. 159–97; M. B. Broxup (ed.), *The North Caucasus Barrier. The Russian Advance towards the Muslim World* (London, 1992), pp. 3, 75.

22. J. Forsyth, *A History of the Peoples of Siberia. Russia's North Asian Colony 1581–1990* (Cambridge, 1992), pp. 81–2, 144–6, 149.

23. K. C. Chaudhuri, *Anglo-Nepalese Relations from the Earliest Times of the British Rule in India till the Gurkha War* (Calcutta, 1960), pp. 68–70; J. K. Fairbank (ed.), *The Cambridge History of China*, X (Cambridge, 1978), p. 103; V. T. Harlow, *The Founding of the Second British Empire 1763–1793 II* (1964), pp. 355–6.

24. B. P. Lenman, 'The Transition to European Military Ascendancy in India, 1600–1800', in J. A. Lynn (ed.), *Tools of War. Instruments, Ideas, and Institutions in Warfare, 1445–1871* (Urbana, 1990), pp. 119–20; P. M. Malone, *The Skulking Way of War. Technology and Tactics among the Indians of New England* (1991); Forsyth, *Siberia*, p. 144; S. Subrahmanyam, *The Portuguese Empire in Asia 1500–1700* (Harlow, 1993), pp. 256–60.

25. Macpherson to 2nd Earl of Shelburne, 16 July 1771, 17 Ap. 1783, Bowood, papers of 2nd Earl, Box 56; P. Avery, 'Nadir Shah and the Afsharid Legacy', in *The Cambridge History of Iran VII* (Cambridge, 1991), p. 38; W. J. Koenig, *The Burmese Polity, 1752–1819* (Ann Arbor, 1990), pp. 22–5; Cohen, *Palestine in the Eighteenth Century*, p. 291.

26. M. C. Ricklef, *War, Culture and Economy in Java, 1677–1726* (The Hague, 1990).

27. L. Y. Andaya, 'Interactions with the Outside World and Adaptation in Southeast Asian Society, 1500–1800', in N. Tarling (ed.), *The Cambridge History of Southeast Asia*, I (Cambridge, 1992), pp. 380–95.

28. Cornwallis to Sir Archibald Campbell, 12 Ap. 1788, London, PRO, 30/11/159 f.123–4.

29. A. Faure, *Les Français en Cochinchine au XVIIIe siècle. Mgr. Pigneau de Behaine* (Paris, 1891); G. Taboulet, *La Geste française en Indochine* (2 vols., Paris, 1955–6), I, 161–279; P. Pluchon, *Historie de la Colonisation Française. I. Le Premier Empire Colonial* (Paris, 1991), pp. 760–4.

30. Cornwallis to Campbell, 7 Jan., 11 Oct. 1787, PRO. 30/11/159 f.23, 83–4.

31. Cornwallis to Henry Dundas, Commissioner of the Board of Control for India, 5 Aug., 12 Nov. 1790, PRO. 30/11/151 f.54, 64.

32. Cornwallis to Pitt, 3 Dec. 1791, PRO. 30/11/175 f.19.

33. F. and M. Wickwire, *Cornwallis. The Imperial Years* (Chapel Hill, 1980), pp. 147, 152, 162–3.

34. William, Lord Grenville, Foreign Secretary, to Smith, 19 June 1792, Oxford, Bodleian Library, Bland Burges papers 41 f.6.

35. G. E. Rothenberg, *Napoleon's Great Adversaries. The Archduke Charles and the Austrian Army 1792–1814* (London, 1982), p. 58 (quote), and *The Art of Warfare in the Age of Napoleon* (London, 1977), pp. 21–2; B. Menning, 'Russian military innovation in the second half of the eighteenth century', *War and Society*, 2, 1 (1984), pp. 23–41; I. R. Christie, 'Samuel Bentham and the Russian Dnieper Flotilla', *Slavonic and East European Review*, 50 (1972), pp. 187–96.

36. G. E. Sanders, *The Spanish Defence of America 1700–63* (unpublished Ph.D., Southern California, 1974); R. Harding, *Amphibious Warfare in the Eighteenth Century. The British*

Expedition to the West Indies 1740–1742 (Woodbridge, 1991), pp. 154–60. See also J. C. M. Oglesby, 'England versus Spain in America, 1739–48; the Spanish side of the hill', *Canadian Hist. Assoc., Historical Papers* (1970), pp. 147–57; C. I. Archer, *The Army in Bourbon Mexico 1760–1810* (Albuquerque, 1977); J. R. McNeill, *Atlantic Empires of France and Spain. Louisbourg and Havanna, 1700–1763* (Chapel Hill, 1986).

37. J. D. Harbron, *Trafalgar and the Spanish Navy* (London, 1988), pp. 51–75. This work is chronologically more wide-ranging than the title might suggest; C. Fernandez-Shaw, 'Participation de la Armada Española en la Guerra de la Independencia de Los Estados Unidos', *Revista de Historia Naval,* 3 (1985), pp. 75–80.

38. N. O. Rush, *The Battle of Pensacola* (Tallahassee, 1966); W. S. Coker and R. Rea (eds.), *Anglo-Spanish Confrontation on the Gulf Coast during the American Revolution* (Pensacola, 1982).

39. J. M. Dederer, *War in America to 1775. Before Yankee Doodle* (New York, 1990); J. M. Black, *War for America. The Fight for Independence* (Stroud, 1991).

40. Black, *War for America,* p. 189.

41. O. Subtelny, *Domination of Eastern Europe. Native Nobilities and Foreign Absolutism, 1500–1715* (Kingston, 1986), p. 136. This wide-ranging and interesting study largely ignores the military dimension.

42. P. Mackesy, 'Problems of an Amphibious Power: Britain against France, 1793–1815', *Naval War College Review* (1978).

43. The New York force operated from Halifax, the Manila force from India.

44. C. Gaziello, *L'Expédition de Laperouse 1785–1788* (Paris, 1984); M. E. Thurman, *The Naval Department of San Blas: New Spain's Bastion for Alta California and Nootka 1767 to 1798* (Glendale, California, 1967); W. L. Cook, *Flood Tide of Empire: Spain and the Pacific Northwest, 1543–1819* (New Haven, 1973), pp. 65–396.

45. Blankett to Lord Hawkesbury, 1 Mar. 1791, BL. Add. 38226 f. 114, 116.

46. D. Sweet, 'Native Resistance in Eighteenth-Century Amazonia: The "Abominable Muras" in War and Peace', *Radical History Review,* 53 (1992), pp. 49–80.

Aspects

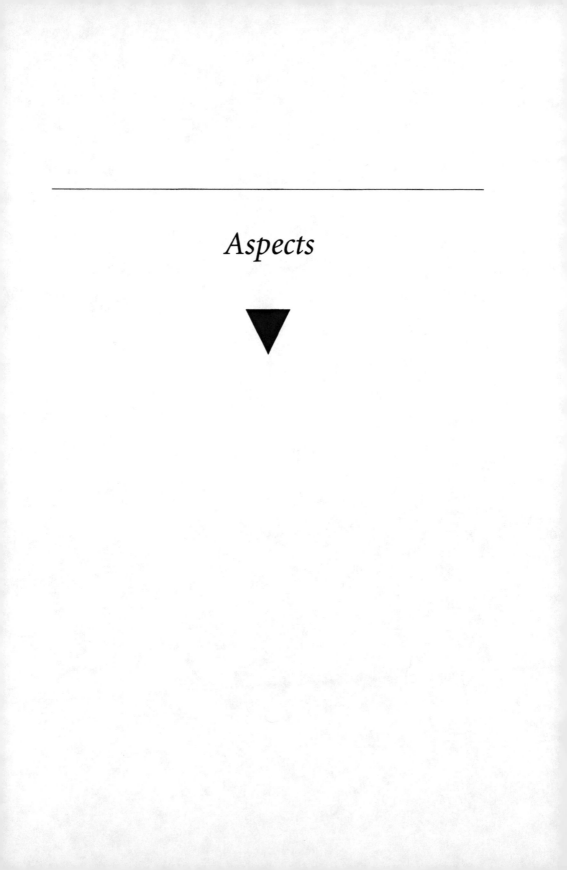

◄ 5 ►

Recalculating French Army Growth During the *Grand Siècle,* 1610–1715

JOHN A. LYNN

BY THE END OF THE SEVENTEENTH century, European warfare had become an affair of giants, as colossal armies battled against one another. France boasted the greatest of these Goliaths, a force which totaled as many as 400,000 soldiers, at least on paper. It was the largest and hungriest institution maintained by the state. That this Titan existed by 1700, no one denies; but the pattern and timing of its growth and its final dimensions remain matters of debate. This article presents a new and more rigorous calculation of French army expansion 1610–1715.

For over a century, historians divided French military expansion into two stages. First, in order to challenge Spain, Richelieu and Louis XIII assembled an army of unprecedented size in 1635. Totaling 150,000 or more, this force was at least twice as large as any previous wartime military maintained by the French monarchy. A second phase of growth followed the military and administrative reform associated with the first decades of the personal reign of Louis XIV. Troop strength reached 280,000 during the Dutch War (1672–78) and hit 400,000 in the War of the League of Augsburg (1688–97), continuing at that level for the War of the Spanish Succession (1701–14).

Since the mid-1950s, proponents of a Military Revolution in early modern Europe, most notably Michael Roberts and Geoffrey Parker, have insisted that the need to raise and support armies larger than ever before called for administrative, fiscal, and governmental reforms.[1] This side of the Military Revolution has attracted historians and social scientists concerned with state formation, most notably Charles Tilly, who writes, "As they fashioned an organization for making war, the king's servants inadvertently created a centralized state. First the framework of an army, then a government built around that framework—and in its shape."[2] Of course, reason dictates that in order for military necessity to have brought on government reform, the growth of the army must have predated that reform, not the other way around.

Recently published revisionist scholarship jettisons this long-standing portrayal. The most serious attack denies military growth prior to 1659, while asserting that growth after that date came as a by-product of social stability under Louis XIV. David Parrott, a young English scholar, has played a key role in questioning substantial military expansion before the Peace of the Pyrenees.[3] While not the first, he has been the most effective in arguing that very little actual reform occurred during the war years of the Richelieu era.[4] Concerning army growth, Parrott states that the historical thesis that Richelieu instituted a virtual administrative revolution is, "underpinned by an assumption that the size of the army increased massively from 1635. But this assumption proves ... untenable."[5] His research has already influenced others, including Jeremy Black, who praises it as "a fundamental work of revisionism."[6] In his recent *A Military Revolution?*, Black embraces Parrott's arguments, putting them in even stronger terms than Parrott intended. Black disputes the concept of a Military Revolution, particularly as originally proposed by Michael Roberts, who assigned it to the century 1560–1660. Crucially, Black ascribes all French military growth to Louis XIV's personal reign. The fact that he shifts the time period away from Roberts's original dates is of little consequence in itself, since others, including Parker, had done that before. However, much more essential, Black insists that the military expansion occurring after 1660 came only as the consequence of increased government capacity made possible by social and political compromises hammered out under Louis XIV. Therefore, Black reads out the army and war as *causes* of political change, and instead reduces them to mere *effects*.

While controversy over the Military Revolution draws attention to military expansion during the mid-seventeenth century, André Corvisier requires historians to look again at the army that fought the last war of the Sun King. For years Corvisier has argued that the forces mobilized to fight the War of the Spanish Succession approached in size those raised by revolutionary France nearly a century later. Recently he restated this thesis in the first volume of the new *Histoire militaire de la France*.[7] He constructs his argument by attaching additional contingents, such as the navy and provincial militias, to the 300,000 French troops he claims for the regular army. Corvisier's controversial mathematics seems to flow from his resolution to demonstrate both that a high percentage of the French male population was involved in the profession of arms and that a patriotic wave *à la* 1792 engulfed the France of the Sun King. In this last concern he follows the lead of Émile G. Léonard, who posited this view in the 1950s.[8]

Revisionist challenges to traditional conceptions of army growth as they relate to the Military Revolution, state formation, and a "patriotic" effort under Louis XIV make a recalculation of military expansion necessary. Until the last few years, it was acceptable to speak of army size by appealing to official financial and military statements, *états,* but today an evaluation of army size demands a new methodology employing a wider range of source material.

METHODOLOGY: DISTINCTIONS AND SOURCES

An effort to set the record straight must be very careful concerning exactly what is to be counted and the kinds of sources to be employed. Trying to fix army size involves a good number of technical points, but many of them come down to not comparing apples with oranges. The first and the most basic difference to bear in mind is that between a field force and a state's entire army. A single field force, usually assembled in one location under one commander, only constitutes part of the total armed might of the state, which may have more than one army on campaign at the same time, while committing still other troops to garrison duty. As strange as it may seem, historians are forever muddying the distinction between the troops marshaled for a single battle and the army as whole.

This leads to the question of who should be counted as part of an army. Obviously, field armies and garrison forces composed of regular troops must be included, but who else? Local and provincial units who stayed at home to guard their towns and man their walls but were not supported by the monarchy and did not necessarily serve full time ought not to be tallied as royal troops. However, militiamen who after 1688 served the king at the front in their own or regular battalions belong in the totals presented here. Non-combatants traveling with the army pose another problem. Often discussions of early modern armies calculate the numbers of traders, women, and children who accompanied the troops; however, such camp followers will not be considered in this article. Neither do valets, pages, grooms, or other personal servants qualify.

In counting troop numbers, it is also important to differentiate when units are tallied. Above all, one must differentiate peacetime from wartime forces, because they differed in size and composition. Obviously, peacetime figures were much smaller than wartime numbers, with few exceptions. By 1670, wartime tallies generally stood three times higher than the number of troops maintained between conflicts. At the end of each war the government demobilized, or "reformed," individual soldiers, surplus companies, and entire regiments. The fact that armies were much smaller during peacetime years under Louis XIV meant that when conflicts began these forces had to expand, and, understandably, this took some time. Beyond these dramatic shifts, more subtle rhythms determined army size during times of conflict. The combat strength of military units normally fluctuated over the course of the year. Established regiments enjoyed their most complete complement just as they entered the campaign season in May or June, but battle casualties and losses from disease and desertion eroded numbers over the summer months. Winter quarters provided time for rest, refitting, and recruitment. New levies arrived in late winter or early spring to flesh out units, so that they grew until they went off on campaign to repeat the cycle.

Not only does a careful accounting of army size need to bear in mind the nature of forces to be compared and the times when those forces are to be examined, but it must also take into account the different types of sources which provide the basis for such a study. In general this includes four varieties of records: 1) military ordonnances; 2) financial *contrôles* and *états;* 3) review reports and *routes;* and 4) miscellaneous correspondence. A minute study of the first, military ordonnances, promises to reveal the decrees altering army size. In the nineteenth century, Victor Belhomme made the most thorough attempt to undertake this laborious feat. He charted the number of French regiments year by year, sometimes month by month, for the entire seventeenth century.[9] However, the problem with employing military ordonnances is that, as in other aspects of government as well, official ordonnances may bear little relation to reality. In fact, Belhomme's figures are suspect, because they much exceed the levels generated by other sources until he deals with the period after 1670, by which time Louis and Louvois had imposed greater regularity on the system.

Administrators also left behind a number of contemporary *états* that supply numbers of troops for the army as a whole. Such *états* come in several forms. A small collection known as the "Tiroirs de Louis XIV" were reports and planning documents in the king's own possession.[10] In the majority of cases, however, official records stating the size of the entire army are financial documents generated as aids in estimating the cost of supporting the army in the present or coming year. Such financial *contrôles* provide a consistent, and convenient, source for the study of army size; therefore, generations of historians have uncritically appealed to them when judging army size. Yet the *contrôles* have recently come under attack. David Parrott questions their value, making the important and valid point that they were only financial documents designed to predict the amount of money that would be paid out by the monarchy for salaries and sustenance. Troop sizes drawn from them are entirely theoretical, so Parrott would completely discard them.[11] But this goes too far. True, *contrôles* were statements of anticipated expenditures rather than head counts; however, the expenditures in question were figured as a given number of payments to a given number of troops, and therefore they were related to a projection of army size.

Financial *contrôles* retain important value as theoretical maximums that can then be discounted to approximate real numbers. A basic method used to set army size in financial documents and other estimates of total army size involved calculating the number of companies or battalions and squadrons present, and then multiplying that number by the regulation complement of men set for that unit by ordonnance. While this method of calculation is not always explicitly employed, it is so common that it can be assumed as underlying virtually all gross statements of army size and cost. Working within the parameters of this seventeenth-century technique, other documents, review reports and *étapes routes,* allow the raw data supplied in *états* and *contrôles* to be refashioned into more realistic estimates of actual army size.

Review reports and *étapes routes* provide actual head counts of troops. Review reports were prepared by military bureaucrats for administrative reasons, as when distributing pay and rations to soldiers. Troops on the road traveling from place to place carried *routes,* documents that stipulated their route and the stops they were allowed to make along the way. At each stop they were entitled to rations and lodging, so the *routes* stated exactly how many men of what ranks were to be fed and housed. By their nature, review reports and *routes* dealt only with individual units or small groups of units, rather than with an entire army, but they will be put to a broader use here. Because the actual sizes of units can be calculated from reviews and *routes,* these numbers can be used to estimate the percentage of regulation strength actually present under arms. Gross statements of army size can then be discounted by this percentage to yield a reasonable estimate of real troop numbers.

The last category of sources covers a varied range of documents that, while not systematic, can be very useful. In particular, when government officials discuss the king's forces in their letters and memoranda, they provide valuable corroboration of other sorts of documents, notably those financial *contrôles* that have come under attack. The use of sources in this manner underlines the fact that the best estimates of army size emerge from combining different sources and cross-checking whenever possible.

A NECESSARY BASELINE: ARMY FIGURES, 1300–1610

No matter how careful the selection and calculation of figures, a study of military expansion can still go awry should it fail to establish a proper baseline against which to measure growth after 1610.[12] In the interest of creating a reasonable grounds for comparison, a careful study must go back before the start of the century, even extending the search to the medieval era.

Philippe Contamine supplies a series of estimates for the size of royal forces during the late middle ages. He believes that the medieval French monarchy mustered its largest force in 1340, when it assembled 60,000 troops in two theaters at the start of the Hundred Years' War, although this number included feudal levies.[13] Over the course of the next century, the ravages of the Black Death precluded putting as many men in the field again.[14] Under Louis XI (1461–83), wartime highs began to approach the proportions of the pre-plague past. Taking the entire second half of the fifteenth century into consideration, Contamine pegs wartime forces as generally reaching between 40,000 and 45,000 combatants.[15]

During the fifteenth century, peacetime forces also grew. Charles V (1364–80) kept garrison forces that reached only 5,200.[16] Charles VII (1422–61) created the first permanent standard units, the *compagnies d'ordonnance,* in 1445. These 15 companies each contained 100 lances, at a time when a lance included six mounted men, of whom only four qualified as combatants. Therefore, 1,500 lances produced 6,000 combatants, not the 9,000 often cited. Adding in garrison infantry, the *mortes payes,* Contamine estimates the average peacetime level of the army, 1445–1475, as about 14,000.[17] During the last three years of his reign, Louis XI maintained a huge force of 47,500—24,000 of which assembled in his "camp de guerre."[18] This costly military establishment did not survive Louis's death, and by 1490 the army contained only about 12,800 cavalry, 3,500 *mortes payes,* and 800 household guards.[19]

As the focus changes to the sixteenth century, Ferdinand Lot, *Recherches sur les effectifs des armées françaises des Guerres d'Italie aux Guerres de Religion, 1494–1562,* provides the best guide to the study of French army size. However, two caveats must be borne in mind when using Lot's work. First, it is not always clear whether his figures should be taken as theoretical or real totals. Second, he emphasizes field forces for particular campaigns, rather than estimates of total army size; therefore, his figures often need to be supplemented by the research of other historians.

Lot deflates traditional, overblown statements of French army size. He rejects exaggerated notions of the army that Charles VIII led on his first invasion of Italy. Excluding Italian units not in the pay of France, Lot arrives at a figure of 22,000–27,200.[20] The French staged the invasion of 1499 in much the same proportions, with 23,000–29,000 troops.[21] He argues that this second figure represented the entire force of the French army, since Louis XII left only "a simple escort" back in France. Lot estimates that 41,000 troops served Francis I at the time of Marignano, 1515, including troops left north of the Alps to protect the provinces.[22] Putting his faith in the Bourgeois de Paris, a source Lot rejects, Henry Lemonnier gives the number of troops at 57,750 in 1523, which again includes 10,200 left to garrison France.[23] Lot speculates that the field army size during the first half of the century may have reached an apogee of 50,000–60,000 late in 1536, but even Lot regards his sources here as "naturally doubtful."[24]

In fact, 1544 seems a better candidate for peak total army size. In April, French forces won the Battle of Ceresoles in Piedmont, but summer brought invasions by both Henry VIII and Charles V in the north of France. Francis scurried to assemble forces to meet them, withdrawing as many as 12,000 troops from Italy and hiring thousands of Swiss and Germans. Counting Francis's main army around Jalons, Brissac's force that confronted the Imperials at St. Dizier, Biez's army that threw itself into Montreuil, the garrison of Boulogne, Vendôme's army around Hesdin, and troops remaining in Italy, as well as providing for miscellaneous garrisons, the total of French forces probably added up to 69–77,000 troops.[25] This was an extraordinary and short-lived strain on French resources, since the army only existed at this level briefly during the late summer. It is worth noting that Francis I wrote that at best, his subjects could support 50,000 troops.[26]

There is little reason to believe that the French topped this figure during 1552, the year which witnessed both the "voyage d'Allemagne" and the siege of Metz by Charles V. Lot's analysis reveals that Henri II conducted only 36,650 paid troops on his "voyage," while another 11,450 remained to defend France.[27] Even if an additional 10,000 troops garrisoned Piedmont and certain French outposts, the total still only reached 60,000. Henri again led field forces of similar proportions in 1558, when he assembled 40,150–40,550 at Pierrepont.[28] Winding up his discussion of the Italian Wars, Lot credits Charles IX with an army of 36,720 in 1562, after the Peace of Câteau-Cambrésis, but it seems best to reject this exaggerated estimate, because it rests on very questionable sources.[29]

Unfortunately, Lot did not devote his considerable skills to the study of the Wars of Religion (1562–98). To be sure, the confusion of the Wars of Religion daunts the boldest of scholars. In his treatment of them, Corvisier provides only a few generalizations for the second half of the sixteenth century. He concludes that owing to demographic, fiscal, and military limitations, the kings of France could support no more than 50,000 men at any one time.[30]

Recently, James B. Wood has presented more impressive estimates for the maximum size of the royal army during the months of December 1567 and January 1568. He calculates that the monarchy claimed a paper force of 72,388 troops in the theater of combat.[31] To this substantial force he would add 12,000 troops stationed elsewhere in France and Italy as well as an unknown number of small garrisons, raising the theoretical total to at least 84,000, the largest force mustered by the French monarchy during the Wars of Religion.[32] However, the manner in which Wood calculated his estimate requires that it be shaved down to an absolute paper maximum of no more than 80,000.[33] Even allowing for this, Wood demonstrates that the government intended to maintain wartime forces that equaled those marshaled by Francis I and Henri II. Of course, the rebel armies arrayed against the king are not counted, even though they too were French forces maintained by French resources. Royal peacetime forces were understandably much smaller. Wood documents the average peacetime strength of the gendarmerie at 6,500 horsemen between 1559 and 1576.[34] Adding this to the 6,229 infantry garrison troops listed for January 1572, generates a total of approximately 12,700 standing troops that year.[35]

In the final stage of the Wars of Religion, after Henri IV ascended to the throne in 1589, the best estimates put his army in the neighborhood of 50–60,000 based on multiplying the number of companies by their theoretical strengths.[36] The return of peace at the close of the sixteenth century brought a thorough demobilization of French forces under the thrifty and efficient direction of Sully. Soon after Treaty of Vervins, 1598, the army shrank to a strength of 7,200–8,500.[37] After the brief Savoyard War (1600), the figure seems to have hovered about 10,000 during the first decade of the seventeenth century.[38] When Henri IV decided to challenge Spain in 1610, he and Sully drew up plans for wartime forces on the scale of the previous century, totaling about 55,000 men in two major armies, a mobile reserve, and garrison troops.[39] Assassination put an end to both the monarch and his plans.

This examination of the period from the late middle ages through 1610 reveals less military growth than might be expected. Wartime highs ranged from 40,000 to 45,000 in the late fifteenth century and reached 50,000 to 80,000 in the sixteenth. Peacetime levels varied more, but considering the period as a whole, peacetime highs of 10,000–20,000 were common; Louis XI's attempt to maintain permanent forces far in excess of that figure was simply a brief aberration.

THEORETICAL MAXIMUM TROOP FIGURES, 1610–1715

Bearing this benchmark in mind, consider the theoretical paper totals raised and maintained by the French after 1610. [Figure 5.1] The minor wars of the 1620s sent the size of the French army above the 10,000 peacetime level of the previous decade.[40] At the Assembly of Notables held in 1626, marshal Schomberg announced the monarchy's intention to maintain an army of 30,000.[41] However, a "Projet de dépense" for 1627 indicates a strength of only about 18,000 men.[42] Renewed war with the Huguenots made such a force inadequate; the siege of La Rochelle, 1627–28, alone required 28,000 troops.[43] David Parrott believes that by 1630 the official strength of the army, with forces in Champagne and Italy, stood at 39,000.[44]

Full scale war would send these figures soaring in the next five years. Direct French participation in the Thirty Years' War began in 1635, and the struggle continued long after the Treaties of Westphalia were signed in 1648; not until the Treaty of the Pyrenees in 1659 would peace return. This war with Spain created armies of unprecedented size, according to official documents. Since so much of the current historiographical debate rests on the timing and level of increases 1635–59, they demand special attention.

Several sources point to important increases in 1634 as the French mobilized to enter the war with Spain. An "Estat des gens de guerre qui sont sur pied à la fin d'Aoust 1634," shows 100,368 soldiers in service at that time.[45] A letter from Richelieu to the King in September supports this figure, mentioning 89,000 men in French service, out of an intended 95,000, with more on the way.[46] In October, an additional "Estat des troupes faict en octobre 1634," boosts the number to 124,500.[47] Building from such an expanding base, the financial documents for 1635 seem reasonable. A projection for 1635 drafted in November 1634 set the number of troops slightly higher at 125,000.[48] Again correspondence confirms this financial document as more than merely a statement of funds to be spent. Servien, the Secretary of State for war, outlined the use of 115,000 men for 1635 in a document written in January of that year; even in Parrott's opinion this letter is "an indication of actual intentions."[49] Servien's total falls short of 125,000 by a mere 8 percent. It seems reasonable to surmise that as war approached and tensions grew, so did the desire for more troops, and this may explain the higher projections made by mid-1635. A contrôle from April sets troop size at 142,000–144,000.[50] The well-known and much misused contrôle for May 1635 prominently reprinted in Avenel's collection is usually employed to justify claims that the French planned to mobilize 150,000 troops; however, if its numbers are calculated with care, they actually project a force of as many as 168,100.[51] With such documentation as a basis, it seems entirely reasonable, even modest, to adopt the tradi-

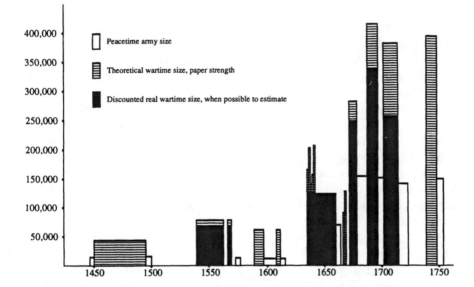

Time Period or War	Theoretical Peace High	Theoretical War High	Discounted War High
1445-1475	14,000		
Second half of the 15th Century		40-45,000	
1490	17,100		
1540s & 1550s		70-80,000	60-70,000?
1567-68		80,000	70,000?
Early 1670s	12,700		
Wars of Religion, 1589-98		50-60,000	
1600-10	10,000		
1610, as Planned		55,000	
1610-15	10,000		
Thirty Years' War, 1635-48		200,000	125,000
1660-1666	72,000		
War of Devolution, 1667-68		134,000	
Dutch War, 1672-78		279,600	253,000
1678-88	165,000		
War of the League of Augsburg, 1688-97		420,000	340,000
1698-1700	140-145,000		
War of the Spanish Succession, 1701-14		380,000	255,000
1715-25	130-160,000		
War of the Austrian Succession, 1740-48		390,000	
1749-56	160,000		

Figure 5.1   The Growth of the French Army, 1445–175c

tional estimate of French intentions: 150,000 troops for the campaign season of 1635.[52]

1636 brought even higher projections. A "Contrôle général des armées du Roy pour l'année 1636" dated December 1635 and contained in the collection of military ordonnances at the Archives de Guerre, breaks the year into three periods with the following troop strengths: 157,979 to 15 April, 179,900 from 15 April to the end of July, and 164,260 from the end of July to the point when the troops would enter winter quarters.[53] Since this particularly interesting document takes into account the natural growth and decline in numbers over the course of the year, it seems to reflect military reality more than simply to serve as a financial convenience. Other *contrôles,* apparently put together later, gave markedly higher estimates. Both David Parrott and Richard Bonney cite *contrôles* that projected 172,000 infantry, 21,400 cavalry, and 12,000 additional cavalry, for a total of 205,000 troops, which included the small army under Bernard of Saxe Weimar, which received French pay.[54]

Numbers dropped in 1637—a *contrôle* for that year reduced the troop total to 134,720—however, numbers mounted again 1638–39.[55] An "État des troupes devant servir en 1638," which dealt with forces in the spring, listed 160,010 troops.[56] Another "État des troupes pour 1639," describing winter quarters 1638–39, brought the number down to 148,180.[57] However, a July 1639 *état* presents a much higher total, perhaps the highest for the war, 211,950.[58] This again includes troops under Bernard. One last source worth mentioning provides the basis for an estimate of troop strength in 1642. This "Estat des armées du roy en 1642" lists only the numbers of infantry and cavalry companies, but figuring these at their full strengths produces a total of at least 164,000 troops.[59] So the Richelieu ministry recorded paper numbers that varied from 135,000 to 211,000, and commonly hovered around 150,000–160,000. Lest these grand sums seem entirely out of line, it is worth noting that Richelieu reconciled Louis XIII to the expense of the war by reminding him that by sustaining 180,000 troops the king had provided "posterity an immortal argument of the power of this crown."[60]

It seems that *contrôles* and *états* listing the entire army are rare or non-existent during the Mazarin regime. Still, Belhomme's study of the ordonnances may aid in tracing the pattern of army size after 1642. While his numbers are not acceptable as literal reality, their rise and fall probably reflect official intentions to alter army size by changing company strengths and adding or subtracting entire regiments. His calculations indicate two high points in the curve of army size, one in 1636 and a second somewhat higher level from 1644 until the partial demobilization that followed the Treaties of Westphalia.[61] After 1649 the army never again matched the levels it had hit 1635–48.[62]

At the victorious conclusion of the long and exhausting struggle with Spain, the French "reformed" the army, by cutting the number of companies drastically, and the number of troops decidedly less. Belhomme's purely speculative figures for infantry alone show a drop from 156,000 infantry in 1658 to a post demobilization figure of 67,000 in 1659, rising to 75,000 in 1660.[63] Given his methods, he really only demonstrates an abolition of units after the war. In fact, Louis apparently kept a large percentage of the actual troops. Mazarin informed Turenne late in 1659, "It is therefore necessary to eliminate [*reformer*] a good number of companies ... [but] it is the King's intention not to discharge a single cavalryman or infantryman, but to fortify well the companies that remain, by incorporating into them the soldiers from those [companies] that are eliminated."[64] Review reports collected by Kroener reveal the practical effect of the pruning and filling that followed the war. Companies that presented only 15 men in 1659, or 50 percent of their regulation strength of 30, mustered fully 50 men or more, 100 percent of their new increased official complement, in 1660.[65]

Louis XIV himself boasted of having nearly 72,000 troops in 1660, after demobilization, clearly the largest peacetime force the French had ever supported.[66] The army continued to shrink for the next several years, declining sometime before early 1665, when a tally of units pegs the army at about 50,000 just before the build up for the War of Devolution (1667–68) sent totals upwards again.[67] The number of troops began to increase late in 1665, probably passing 60,000.[68] Referring to a letter of March 1666, Rousset concludes that the King's troops reached 72,000 then, whereas Louis André, citing other documents, argues that the army topped 97,515 later in the year, a figure that seems high.[69] During the first year of the War of Devolution, Louis's personal information set the strength at about 82,000, but this may not include all garrisons.[70] The careful historian Paul Sonnino estimates the size of Louis army at 85,000 by the end of the 1667 campaign.[71] 1668 brought even larger armies totaling 134,000.[72] The return to peace again caused the French to demobilize to only 70,000.[73]

Louis next began to gear up for the Dutch War. In 1670 he expanded his army once again by raising 20,000 new men to bring his forces up to 90,000.[74] In 1671 additional soldiers were hired, so that in early 1672 the army reached about 120,000.[75] This figure grew over the course of the year, as Louis issued orders to recruit enough troops to raise the number to 144,000.[76] The Dutch War high hit 279,610, as indicated by a key document from January 1678.[77] This included 219,250 infantry and 60,360 cavalry, while 116,370 of the total served in garrisons. The inevitable "reform" of the army after the Treaty of Nijmegen reduced forces to 146,980 men, officers not included, in 1679.[78] This seems to have fallen to about 125,000 in 1681.[79] Numbers increased again for the brief contest with Spain (1683–84), with demobilization back to 165,000 after the Truce of Ratisbon.[80]

During the War of the League of Augsburg, the French army topped 400,000 for the first time, at least on paper. At the start of the conflict, Louvois believed that he could field about 207,000 by late 1688, with the levies he anticipated.[81] In his *L'Armée française en 1690*, Belhomme argues that forces reached 381,819 men and 23,138 officers, for a total of 404,957 that year.[82] It should be remembered that in 1688 Louvois instituted the royal *milice* which allowed the monarchy to conscript men to serve at the front in new provincial battalions. Here Belhomme's figures do not appear to be high, since other sources ascribe even greater numbers to the French army. No less an authority than Louis's great engineer, Sébastien le Prestre de Vauban, a man quite given to calculations and statistics, estimated royal forces in 1693 at the generous figure of 438,000.[83] A financial *état* dating from the 1690s gives a detailed accounting of 343,323 infantry and 67,334 cavalry, a total of 410,657 troops, not including officers, for the year 1696.[84] Adding officers to the numbers in the *état* would produce a total equal to that supplied by Vauban. These sources, then, exceed the traditional figure of 400,000 French troops for the War of the League of Augsburg; in fact an estimate of 420,000 officers and men would not be out of place.[85] According to the above-mentioned *état*, by early 1699 the army had fallen to about 185,716 enlisted men, after regiments had been disbanded.[86] With a reduction of company strength in December 1699, the size of the army fell by about 40,000, contracting it further to 140,000–145,000.[87]

The return of fighting in 1701 sent army size spiraling upward again. In 1702 it reached 220,502.[88] Servan's study set the wartime high at 392,223.[89] However, original sources set the number as smaller than Servan's figures. A detailed financial *état* listing troops to be employed in 1707 supports an estimate of army size at 318,000 infantry, 39,000 cavalry, and 16,000 dragoons, for a total of 373,000 officers and men.[90] This document, which does not appear to have been used by military historians before now, corroborates another much-used *état* dating from 1710 enumerating 323,665 infantry, including detached companies, 41,073 cavalry, and 16,491 dragoons, adding up to a total of only 377,105 troops, of whom 21,062 were officers.[91] Once again, the monarchy called upon the *milice*, although its conscripts no longer stayed in their own battalions at the front, but simply filled the gaps in regular regiments. These numbers fall short of justifying the traditionally-accepted paper figure of 400,000 soldiers engaged as full time troops in garrison or with the field armies; in fact, 380,000 would seem more in line with archival sources. After peace returned, the army fell back to a peacetime strength of about 133,000.[92] Over the remaining decades of the *ancien régime*, the army typically echoed the figures it had reached under Louis XIV in war and peace.[93]

Such is the tally of theoretical numbers; however, revisionist scholarship rightly demands that historians probe for the firmer core of reality within the inflated paper totals.

DISCOUNTING THE PAPER FIGURES

By establishing the difference between the official dimensions and the actual size of units, review reports and *routes* provide the data necessary to discount official statements of army size. Bernard Kroener supplies the foundation of this effort by compiling review reports that establish the average number of men actually present under arms in French infantry and cavalry companies, 1635–60.[94] A second data set compiled from archival sources for this article covers the remainder of the *grand siècle.*

Since the most crucial figures for the first half of the seventeenth century, and those best documented in the *contrôles,* come from the period 1635–39, these five years deserve the most attention. Unfortunately, Kroener's treatments of 1635 and 1636 are in error to some degree. On average, the infantry companies he studied for 1635 claimed 43 men present; however, he mistakenly assumes that regulation company strength for French foot in both 1635 and 1636 was 50 men when it was, in fact, 100.[95] Thus, while he put the infantry at a suspiciously high 86 percent of regulation strength, they actually stood at only 43 percent.. This lower figure tallies much better with the percentage for cavalry companies, which only reached to 46 percent of official strength. Pursuing this line even further, in 1636, usually accepted as a high point for the army as it massed to repel a Spanish invasion, Kroener's sample suggests an infantry company strength of only 35 percent with cavalry at 38 percent.

Combining the corrected version of Kroener's numbers with theoretical highs taken from financial *contrôles* results in some unexpected findings. The discounted size of the army in 1635 falls to about 72,000 troops. This seems a small figure, particularly in light of the fact that Richelieu already believed that 89,000 men had been massed before the end of 1634.[96] However, if Kroener's sample can be trusted, not only was the army of 1635 small, but it was not exceeded by the forces assembled in 1636. However, the situation changed greatly 1638–39, years for which Kroener's methods seem both clear and correct. For these two years, the infantry complement rose to 64 percent and 72 percent, and cavalry stood at 45 percent and 70 percent. Such full ranks make 1639 the year of highest troop strength, with a very substantial 152,000 men.[97] It should be noted that André Corvisier also employed Kroener's work to calculate actual numbers, but Corvisier erred by accepting Belhomme's inflated estimates as the raw data to be discounted. As a result, Corvisier credits infantry alone with a discounted size of 166,320 soldiers for 1639; the addition of similarly elevated cavalry figures would drive the estimate for the total army above 200,000.[98]

Given the great variety between the lows and highs generated by Kroener's percentages, perhaps it is a safer course not to accept his exact estimates year by year, but to take them as a basis to arrive at a general discount rate to cover the first critical five years of the war. A straight mathematical average of Kroener's corrected estimates results in a discount rate of 57 percent. At one point in his own work, David Parrott proposes an estimate built upon Kroener's original figures and his own examination of reports from field armies: "The forces maintained by France were probably 50 percent smaller than the sweeping estimates of 130–150,000 soldiers that have been proposed."[99] Here, Parrott echoes Richelieu who commented, "[I]f one wants to have fifty thousand effectives, it is necessary to levy one hundred, counting a regiment of twenty companies that ought to have 2,000 men as only 1,000."[100] Parrott then further reduces the actual number by assuming a 25 percent error caused by officers padding their companies with phony soldiers, *passe volants*, to make their companies look bigger at reviews. With all these deductions, Parrott pulls down the traditional figure of 150,000 for 1635 to 50–55,000.[101] But Parrott cites varying figures in somewhat different contexts in such a way that they can be read, and cited, to support conflicting theses. At another point, he credits the real force with about 70,000 troops, at least for the first half of the campaign.[102] And both figures need to be put in the context of his overall estimate that, "Aside from the exceptional, by definition, temporary, peaks in troop strength, such as that of summer 1636, the French army was rarely of more than 60–70,000 infantry and 15–20,000 cavalry during the 1630s."[103] Accepting this last, and most authoritative, set of figures produces a total of 75,000–90,000 troops, which he would peg even higher in 1636.[104]

While there is no simple mechanical method to manufacture a discount rate from the above findings and claims, an overview of the best research suggests that a rate of 60 percent provides the most reasonable guide. This is the discount rate that Corvisier accepts, and even Parrott gives it credence as the contemporary principle of "*douze pour vingt.*" [105] Multiplying official tallies for 1636 and 1639 by this discount yields a high point for the war of about 125,000 men. Such an estimate falls between the extremes generated by Kroener's modified numbers. Moreover, it even approaches Parrott's second estimate of 75,000–90,000, when one adjusts for extreme wartime peaks, such as occurred in 1636 and 1639. Adopting 125,000 as a wartime peak for the war with Spain might even be credited as an act of moderation, since a case could be made for a top figure of 152,000 in 1639.

Turning to the data collected for this article, the next discounted wartime high dates from the Dutch War, since data for the War of Devolution is very thin.[106] According to a sample of 155 companies, in 1676–77, when a French infantry company was supposed to number 50 men, actual companies mustered a surprisingly high average of 44.4 men, or 89 percent of full strength. As strange as this may seem, it accords with Louis's own evaluation, since he argued in 1667 for a discount to 85 percent.[107] Cavalry companies were even more likely to fill up, mounting 96 percent of a full complement. This very high percentage of cavaliers in a unit was typical of the personal reign of Louis XIV. Three factors explain this phenomenon: 1) the much greater prestige of service in the cavalry, 2) the larger recruitment bounties paid to cavalrymen, and 3) the higher salaries they earned. Owing to all three factors, cavalry regiments had their pick of men, meeting their goals before infantry units did.

Using these percentages in conjunction with paper figures for peak size during the Dutch War leads to an estimate of 253,000 actual troops. This figure certainly seems high; it may result from the fact that the sample dates from the end of winter quarters, when recruits had just been added and units enjoyed their maximum strength of the year. In any case, the numbers show units far closer to their theoretical strength than they had been before 1659. With the return of peace, reviews of 171 companies in garrison in Italy in 1682 suggest that companies approached full strength during the period of half war/half peace that was the 1680s.[108] With such high percentages, the official figure of about 150,000 men in the peacetime army need be pared down only to roughly 120,000 in real terms.

The War of the League of Augsburg provides some of the most interesting discoveries. Early in the war, 1689–92, company strengths ran fairly high once again. A sample of 226 companies, all of which passed through Amiens and left *routes* in their wake, reveals an average infantry company of 42.2 men and sergeants, or 84 percent of the official full strength of 50.[109] A small sample from Burgundy and a much larger one from Alsace, 1691–92, correspond with the Amiens numbers. The 40 companies from Burgundy stood at an average of only 33.5, but this low figure results from the inclusion of one particularly understrength regiment; without it, the average rises to 39.0.[110] The massive sample of units receiving *étapes* in Alsace must be handled with great care, since the accountants listed several regiments as full that were not. However, using only the most solid listings, the Alsace sample still consists of 416 companies, and these records suggest an average of about 41 men per company, or 82 percent.[111] The 57 cavalry companies from six different regiments listed on Amiens *routes* averaged 34.9 men, or 87 percent of official strength of 40; dragoons had essentially full complements of 40.[112] A sample of 90 cavalry companies which rode through Alsace during the first half of 1691 numbered 36.3 men per company, or 90.1 percent of full strength; 47 dragoon companies averaged out at 37.4, or 93.5 percent.[113]

Later, 1695–96, the percentages had not changed much, according to a sample of 523 companies all from Amiens *routes*. French infantry companies, supposed to contain 55 men by then, had 43.8, or 80 percent of capacity. *Milice* companies, theoretically at 60, had 50.2, or 83.7 percent[114]; cavalry and dragoons claimed 35.5 and 35.3 respectively, or 88.8 and 88.3 percent of a full complement each.

The *étapes* documents employed for the War of the League of Augsburg do not simply date from the spring, when regiments had just incorporated recruits, but from the fall as well, when regiments would be at a relatively weak point. The balance seems reasonable. Therefore, if one accepts that theoretical size stood as high as 420,000 in 1696, a sixth of which would have been cavalry, the real count could have reached 340,000.[115]

During the few years between the War of the League of Augsburg and the War of the Spanish Succession, the official number of men in French companies fell somewhat, but the percentage at full strength rose. In 1700, French line infantry companies, which were then set at 35 by regulation, averaged out at 35.1 men per company in the 39 companies of the sample.[116] Cavalry companies, which in December 1699 were officially reduced to only 20 troopers each, showed 20.3 men present, so their numbers topped 100 percent of full strength.[117] Putting all this together fully justifies the estimate of total troop strength at about 140,000 men.

With the return of war, an exhausted France mobilized once again, but it did not reach the level of forces it had hit in the previous contest. A sample of 240 infantry companies that passed through Amiens and Lille puts the size of the average company at only 32.3 in 1702–1704.[118] This, at a time when regulation size was 45, meant real companies were only 72 percent of full size.[119] A much smaller sample of only 16 cavalry companies again shows them at very near their regulation strength of 35. With 34.1 men per company, they mounted 97 percent of theoretical size.

By late in the war, 1709–11, both infantry and cavalry companies had declined somewhat. The large and varied sample of companies used here includes 1,284 French companies listed in *routes* from Amiens, review reports from Dijon, and tallies of front-line units reported in military correspondence.[120] French infantry companies changed in size during the war; until 1710 they stood at 45 men, but a regulation of that year raised their size to 50 soldiers.[121] The average company strength of 31.2 means that infantry units were 62–69 percent complete. Cavalry and dragoons were again organized in companies of 35 men; but in reality cavalry companies stood at 30.5, or 87 percent, and dragoons at 31.1, or 89 percent. The sources that generate these estimates deserve some discussion, since they lead to important conclusions.

Documents from Amiens, Dijon, and the front showed roughly similar company sizes. The average number of men in infantry companies moving through Amiens stood at 29.9, whereas it rose to 34.0 in Dijon reports. This is a significant difference, to be sure, but it only amounts to 8 percent in a company of 50 men.[122] Another key document is the "Etat de la force de quarante-deux battalions et de ce qu'on leur donne de recrues," dated 17 September 1709, but it requires some interpretation, since the battalions listed had just suffered casualties at the bloody battle of Malplaquet. Approximate battalion size before the battle can be reconstructed by allowing for the casualty rates of these battalions. This method yields an average company of 31.9 men.[123] Interpreting the document in another fashion, one can add in the number of replacements assigned to each battalion to arrive at a new company strength of 30.9. A second battlefield report listing units to be sent to Douai in April 1710, shows company strength down to 28.2.[124]

Using the sample collected for this study to discount army size as in 1707 and 1710 yields a figure of about 255,000 troops.[125] This is much smaller than the 340,000 estimated for the War of the League of Augsburg. Remember, both figures are only estimates, and since they discount the army on the basis of percentages for only French regiments, they may understate the totals somewhat, since foreign regiments in French service tended to be closer to their full complements than were native units.

COMPARING RESULTS: REVISIONISM REVISED

With the discounted figures in hand, it is possible to make certain judgments concerning the pattern of military expansion during the *grand siècle*. [See Figure 5.1.] Most importantly, the data presented in this article demonstrate that with the onset of war in 1635, royal forces increased significantly over previous levels. Their expansion ought to be measured against a baseline of wartime highs, 1495–1610, which repeatedly reached 50,000 and peaked at 80,000 on occasion before 1570. If such levels are compared with theoretical maximums of 205,000–211,000 soldiers during the period 1635–48, the increase ranges from 250 percent to 400 percent. But this would not be a fair comparison, since the key figures for the earlier period collected in this article are closer to actual than theoretical maximums. The discounted totals for 1635–42 arrived at above reduce the peak size of the army to 125,000. Consequently, even if the 50,000–80,000 total for the period before 1610 is taken without discount, the army raised under Richelieu was still at least 60 percent larger than anything that preceded it, and if the earlier tallies are discounted by as little as 10 percent, which seems reasonable, even modest, then one has to conclude that the army of 1635–42 exceeded sixteenth-century highs by at least 75 percent. In addition, the army created in 1635 doubled the size of any royal French force mobilized since 1570. Such increases may not equal the extreme estimates of some historians, but they still constitute a quantum leap upward. The contrast between the 55,000 troops Henri IV intended to raise for his struggle with Spain in 1610 and the 150,000 Louis XIII tried to mobilize against the same enemy in 1635 highlights the military expansion of the first half of the seventeenth century.

In his dissertation, David Parrott makes a strong case that the Richelieu ministry bungled its way through the daunting task of supporting its army without engaging in substantial reform. Parrott believes that the army did not grow enough to impose reform upon the government; moreover, he seems to assume that if the army existed at a given size it had to be supported by the government at that size. Yet the French monarchy fielded armies larger than it could maintain from its own resources. These armies made ends meet by two methods. First, the monarchy called upon the personal financial resources of the officers, who contributed to the maintenance of their own commands.[126] Second, despite official protests, soldiers took for themselves what the state failed to supply; in short, they pillaged.[127] The chaos and horrors typical of the war between France and Spain, 1635–59, came precisely because the army grew substantially, not because it did not grow enough to precipitate reform. Jeremy Black would uncouple the reforms that occurred after 1659 from the strains exerted by army growth before that date, but they were as important to the process of institutional change in France as was the abuse of Brandenburg during the Thirty Years' War to the creation of the state and army of the Great Elector after 1648.

While military expansion before 1659 rates as substantial, that occurring after 1659 was staggering. Theoretical maximums topped 400,000 during the War of the League of Augsburg, while discounted figures for the same war set the number of troops under arms as about 340,000. Measured by either scale, this was unparalleled. By the end of the century theoretical wartime levels had increased 500 to 800 percent over the peaks of the sixteenth century. Discounted tallies rose 400 to 700 percent. Peacetime levels rose by even greater percentages; if theoretical peacetime figures before 1610 were normally between 10,000 and 20,000, the peacetime strength after 1679 hovered between 130,000 and 150,000, an increase of 650 percent to 1500 percent!

However, the expansion of the army during the War of the Spanish Succession, when discounted regular army strength only reached 255,000, did not match that attained during the War of the League of Augsburg. This happened despite the fact that the paper figures for both wars hovered in the range of 400,000. On reflection, this makes sense. The number of troops that the state could support depended directly upon the amount of wealth that the monarchy could mobilize for its army, and Louis XIV had run out of resources. First, the War of the League of Augsburg had exhausted government finance. Second, the potential to raise "contributions," or war taxes, on occupied territory decreased as repeated defeats drove French forces back to their own borders in the northeast. And third, the traditional recourse of relying upon aristocratic officers to maintain their units out of pocket had already overtaxed noble fortunes in the previous war, so that particular well was going dry.

The numbers do not support Corvisier's thesis that the forces raised under Louis XIV matched those levied in 1794, the height of Republican defense. To his count of 300,000 troops in regular French regiments, Corvisier adds naval forces, bourgeois militias, and coast guards to yield a grand total of 600,000. If the point that Corvisier wishes to make is that far more men bore arms than a simple tally of soldiers would indicate, he makes his point admirably. However, it is another matter to compare this to the national defense mounted by the Revolutionary regime. If one adds together numbers in this fashion for Louis XIV, one must do it for the Revolution, and the sum of the army, navy, National Guard, and *armées révolutionaires* in 1793–94 would greatly surpass anything under Louis XIV.[128] Returning the focus to front line troops only, once the *levée en masse* had raked in its bounty of recruits, the French had mobilized 1,169,000 men by the late summer of 1794, and it has become almost traditional to discount this to 750,000 men actually under arms.[129] This far exceeds the 255,000 army troops credited here to Louis XIV, 1709–11.[130]

A CAVEAT: BEYOND THE NUMBERS

All the attention given here to figures should not obscure the point that the contrast between the army of the seventeenth century and that which preceded it was more than just a matter of how many more soldiers served Louis XIV than fought for Francis I. Beyond the simple question of size, the army changed in character over time, and it could be argued that this difference in character mattered as much or more than did numbers alone.

Consider, for example, the way in which armies were assembled, the time they remained together, and the rapidity with which they were dismissed. During the Italian Wars, French kings built their armies, particularly their infantry, from mercenary units which could be purchased "off the shelf." Thus in 1544, Francis I only concluded his contract with the Swiss in July, but this still gave them time to arrive and constitute the core of the Valois infantry at the camp de Jalons in late August and early September. Hiring Swiss or Landsknecht bands was more expensive than paying native French units on a day-to-day basis, but the mercenaries arrived fully armed and fully trained, ready to put in the line. When the threat ended, Francis put them back on the shelf just as easily as he had taken them off it in the first place; thus, a sixteenth-century army could be created for a particular campaign and then dismissed.

In the seventeenth century all this changed. While the Bourbons still recruited foreign troops, the great majority of the army was now made up of French regiments maintained permanently or for the duration of a particular war. In 1544, the foreign infantry contingents in Francis's main force amounted to over half the foot soldiers present; one source puts them at 80 percent of the total.[131] Yet by 1710 the number of foreign infantrymen in French service had sunk to 14 percent, and certain of these "foreign" units were from areas which, in fact, lay within the domains of Louis XIV.[132] When war came, new recruits fleshed out established French regiments or stood to colors in entirely new units. In such a system, the government equipped the common soldier, fed him, and paid him while he learned and practiced his profession. Characteristically, it took many months for a seventeenth-century French army to be ready to go into action at full force, and regiments now served summer and winter, as long as the war lasted. In fact, much of our knowledge of the size of army after 1635 comes from *winter quarters* reports, which is a significant fact in itself. Thus, the Bourbon state created and maintained an army in being, as opposed to assembling an army from "spare parts" for a particular campaign. And such an army in being put a consequently greater burden on finance and administration. Over and above the great increase in numbers, saying that Francis I mustered 80,000 troops in the fall of 1544 means something very different from saying that Louis XIV commanded 400,000 in 1696.

CONCLUSION

This article has charted the dimensions and development of one of those giants that dominated warfare by 1700: the army of France. On the whole, earlier, traditional notions of French army growth have fared well in these pages, even though particular figures have been questioned or redefined. The two-step concept of French military expansion, first substantial under Richelieu and later spectacular under Louis XIV, emerges in a modified form, but still intact. Louis XIII nearly doubled previous troop levels when he and his able first minister entered the lists against Spain. Later, the Sun King commanded wartime forces five to eight times greater than those which had fought for his Valois predecessors, and perhaps even more impressive was the standing army that remained in peacetime to support the monarchy. Yet this recognition of dramatic army expansion under Louis XIV is qualified by the knowledge that the aging monarch's forces during the War of the Spanish Succession did not reach the proportions of those he had marshaled for the War of the League of Augsburg.

Most readers are, understandably, more interested in the implications of this army growth than in the mounting numbers themselves, yet time and space prohibit a discussion of their great political and social impact on these pages. But certainly any argument based on cause and effect must begin with knowledge of the timing and extent of that expansion. So here it is enough just to get the numbers and timing right, or as right as the current state of research permits.

Notes

Research for this project was made possible by an NEH Summer Stipend, a Hewlett Summer Research Stipend, and a grant from the College of Liberal Arts and Sciences at the University of Illinois at Urbana-Champaign.

1. For the earliest elaborations of the theory of the Military Revolution, see Michael Roberts, *The Military Revolution, 1560–1660* (Belfast: 1956) and George Clark, *War and Society in the Seventeenth Century* (Cambridge: 1958). Geoffrey Parker's discussion of the theory include his "The 'Military Revolution' 1560–1660—a Myth?" *Journal of Modern History* 48 (June 1976) and his prize-winning *The Military Revolution: Military Innovation and the Rise of the West, 1500–1800* (Cambridge: 1988). The most recent discussions of the theory are the critical essay, Jeremy Black, *A Military Revolution? Military Change and European Society, 1550–1800* (Atlantic Highlands, NJ: 1991) and John A. Lynn, "The *trace italienne* and the Growth of Armies: the French Case," *Journal of Military History*, July 1991 (reprinted below, Ch. 7).

2. Charles Tilly, *The Contentious French* (Cambridge, MA: 1986), 128. More to the point of state formation, see his *Coercion, Capital, and European States, AD 990–1990* (Oxford: 1990). There he wrote that European "state structure appeared chiefly as a by-product of rulers' efforts to acquire the means of war." (p. 14). For other recent works with an historical view of state formation that highlights military pressures in the process, see Brian M. Downing, *The Military Revolution and Political Change in Early Modern Europe* (Princeton: 1992); David Kaiser, *Politics & War: European Conflict from Phillip II to Hitler* (Cambridge, MA: 1990); and David Ralston, *Importing the European Army: The Introduction of European Military Techniques and Institutions into the Extra-European World, 1600–1914* (Chicago: 1990).

3. His most important work is David Parrott, "The Administration of the French Army During the Ministry of Cardinal Richelieu," diss., Oxford University, 1985, which has yet to appear in hard covers. Seldom has a dissertation exerted such an immediate effect. He has also authored "Strategy and Tactics in the Thirty Years War: The 'Military Revolution,'" *Militärgeschichtliche Mitteilungen*, XVIII, 2 (1985), pp. 7–25; reprinted below, Ch. 9.

4. For examples of other works which detail the ineffectiveness of reform before 1659 and/or argue that military growth was limited before the personal reign of Louis XIV, see the following: Patrick Landier, "Guerre, Violences, et Société en France, 1635–1659," doctorat de troisième cycle, Université de Paris IV, 1978; Jonathan Berger, "Military and Fi-

nancial Government in France, 1648–1661," diss., University of Chicago, 1979; and Bernard Kroener, *Les routes et les étapes. Die Versorgung der französchichen Armeen in Nordostfrankreich (1635–1661)*, 2 vols. (Münster: 1980). Parrott employed both Landier and Kroener. Ronald Martin, "The Army of Louis XIV," in Paul Sonnino, ed., *The Reign of Louis XIV* (Atlantic Highlands, NJ: 1990), 111–26, also stresses the lack of fundamental administrative change before the personal reign of Louis XIV.

5. Parrott, "The Administration of the French Army," iv.

6. Black, *A Military Revolution?*, 98.

7. Corvisier section in Philippe Contamine, ed., *Histoire militaire de la France*, vol. 1, (Paris: 1992), 531. He also argues in this manner in André Corvisier, *Louvois* (Paris: 1983), 345, for the War of the League of Augsburg.

8. Émile G. Léonard, *L'armée et ses problèmes au XVIIIe siècle* (Paris: 1958).

9. Victor Belhomme, *Histoire de l'infanterie en France*, 5 vols. (Paris: 1893–1902). Actually, his lack of theoretical discussion and footnotes hide his exact sources, but it seems virtually certain that he based his work on the military ordonnances collected at the ministry of war and the Bibliothèque Nationale.

10. Louis was probably referring to these when he confidently stated, "What makes me more certain of my enterprises is that I have an accurate *état* of my troops, their quartering, and their number." Louis's journal for April 1667, Louis XIV, *Mémoires de Louis XIV*, Charles Dreyss, ed., 2 vols. (Paris: 1860), 2:167.

11. He chides historians for making "the mistaken assumption that the *contrôles* represent intended troop strengths." Parrott, "The Administration of the French Army," 135.

12. A common fallacy committed by those who turn their attention to the study of the seventeenth-century army is to argue that the army increased or decreased in size without any reference to the dimensions of the army before 1610. David Parrott, for example, argues that no major military growth occurred 1635–42, simply by saying that the real figures for the French army did not match the theoretical numbers previously accepted. But that is not the point; to argue for growth one must compare figures for the 1630s with those of previous periods, not simply discount the accepted numbers. Parrott, "The Administration of the French Army," iv.

13. He bases his calculations on financial accounts. Contamine, *Histoire militaire*, 137–38. The feat is even more impressive when the non-combatants are added in, raising the total to 100,000.

14. After 1340, numbers fell off rapidly; in 1342, the king could claim only 9,500, and in 1383 he sent off but 16,000 to the relief of Ypres, although this was only a single field army. Contamine, *Histoire militaire*, 137, 172.

15. Philippe Contamine, *Guerre, état et société à la fin du moyen âge. Études sur les armées des rois de France, 1337–1494* (Paris: 1972), 316–17.

16. On average, Charles kept about 5,200 troops during the four months of the best weather and 3,400 during the other eight months. Contamine, *Histoire militaire*, 145.

17. Contamine, *Guerre, état et société*, 278–83, 286.

18. According to Philippe de Commynes in Contamine, *Histoire militaire*, 229–30, 232. Philippe Contamine refers to it as "plus de 45,000 combatants" in his *Guerre, état et société*, 298–301.

19. 3,200 lances figured at 4 combatants each. Contamine, *Histoire militaire*, 219–21. See total figure of 18,400 in Contamine, *Guerre, état et société*, 317.

20. Ferdinand Lot, *Recherches sur les effectifs des armées françaises des Guerres d'Italie aux Guerres de Religion, 1494–1562* (Paris: 1962), 21. He devotes his entire first chapter to conflicting claims. Compare this conclusion with the 30,500 estimated by Henry Lemonnier, *Histoire de France*, ed. Ernest Lavisse, vol. 5, part 1, *Les guerres d'Italie, 1492–1547* (Paris: 1903), 28 fn. Lemonnier counts the French lance as a full 6 and adds in the Italian lances. On the very high end, see E. Boutaric, *Institutions militaires de la France avant les armées permanentes* (Paris: 1863), 369–70, who stated the size of the force as 66,500.

21. Lot, *Recherches sur les effectifs*, 27. This represents something of a discounted figure, since on page 26 Lot also presents a less critical figure of 26–38,000 as presented by Léon Pellisier, *Louis XII et Ludovic Sforza*, 1:384–86.

22. Lot, *Recherches sur les effectifs*, 41.

23. Lemonnier's figures for cavalry are bound to exceed Lot's, since the former counts the entire lance and the latter counts only the combatants within it. Henry Lemonnier, *Histoire de France*, ed. Ernest Lavisse, vol. 5, part 2, *La lutte contre la maison d'Autriche, 1519–1559* (Paris: 1904), 84fn. Lot, *Recherches sur les effectifs*, 50, finds the Bourgeois potentially suspect; however, this source matches up well with finance accounts.

24. Lot, *Recherches sur les effectifs*, 65.

25. Lot, *Recherches sur les effectifs*, 95, 104; Charles Oman, *History of the Art of War in the Sixteenth Century* (London: 1937), 340, 343; Lemonnier, *La lutte contre la maison d'Autriche*, 114; Contamine, *Histoire militaire*, 242.

26. Contamine, *Histoire militaire*, 305.

27. "Estat de l'armée," Bibliothèque Nationale, hereafter cited as BN, f. fr. 2965, fol. 2–4, in Lot, *Recherches sur les effectifs*, 129–30, 133, with corrections and additions for garrison troops. Lot makes a mistake in his addition, sending the figure 1,000 men higher than shown here. These figures are clearly not discounted as literal head counts, they are simply the usual maximum figures based on units present and round numbers. In contrast to Lot, Reboul in Gabriel Hanoteau, ed. *Histoire de la nation française*, vol. 7, *Histoire militaire et navale*, vol. 1 (Paris: 1925), 252 and 260, supplies one of the more typically inflated estimates of 68,320–70,320 just for the "voyage."

28. Review of Pierrepont and Rambutin in Lot, *Recherches sur les effectifs*, 179–86, gives 40,150–40,550 at review, plus reinforcements of 8,400 and surviving cavalry from Gravelines, p. 186.

29. "Abrégé de l'État militaire de la France," a financial document, in Lot, *Recherches sur les effectifs*, 190–192. James Wood dismisses this estimate. "His documentation for this (unlike other estimates he makes) is very poor. By that time there were only substantial numbers of French troops abroad in what was left of French Piedmont, the gendarmerie had been reduced, the infantry reformed by Guise and company strengths cut to an unknown level, most probably 50 men. If that many soldiers had remained on strength in 1562 there is absolutely no way the crown could have paid them nor would you have had the universal lament of soldiers at being forcibly demobilized after the Italian Wars." Personal letter of 3 September 1992.

30. Contamine, *Histoire militaire*, 305. He also presents figures that could lead one to believe that the maximum strength of royal forces during the Wars of Religion did not exceed 40,000. Contamine, *Histoire militaire*, 310–314.

31. These figures are based on a series of manuscript *états* presented in table form by James B. Wood, "The Royal Army During the Early Wars of Religion, 1559–1576," in Mack

P. Holt, ed. *Society & Institutions in Early Modern France* (Athens, GA: 1991), 10–11. Upon my request, he kindly sent me copies of his archival sources so that I could verify his calculations. I thank him for his assistance.

32. In a letter of 3 September 1992, Wood states that the 72,000 was only a theater estimate and that elsewhere: "there were another 40 infantry co's in the SW, more than 30 gendarme co's elsewhere, 11 co's of Italians in Piedmont, plus the remaining customary garrisons at places to guard them against Huguenot surprises. So if we are counting all the troops raised during this period, I would argue that 72,000 is probably a bit low." He goes on to state: "I have now finished by analysis of all of the first 5 wars (through 1576) and I will have to revise my statement that the forces raised in the 3rd war (1568–70) may have been larger than in the 2nd war. In fact I think the 2nd war represents a maximum for the royal forces."

33. To form his estimate, Wood combined the maximum sizes for all units mentioned in the documents he collected, even if particular units might be cited as smaller in another document.

34. Wood claims that during peacetime lulls, 1559–76, the monarchy supported on average 64–69 companies of gendarmes, totaling about 6,500 horsemen. His table on page 3 indicates that in 1671 there were 69 companies of gendarmes. Wood, "The Royal Army During the Early Wars of Religion," 3.

35. Ibid., 5–6.

36. For 1588–89, see BN, Chatre de Cangé, vol. 18, #393, "Estat des compagnies de gens de guerre à pied." See as well, Édouard La Barre Duparcq, *L'art militaire pendant les guerres de religion, 1562–1598* (Paris: 1863), 24. He supplies a figure for infantry only in 1589 which implies an army of about 50,000. For 1597 see BN, Chatre de Cangé, vol. 20, #33, "État des regiments et des capitaines ayant charge de compagnies de gens de pied pour le service du Roy tant en son armée que aux garnisons de Picardie, Champagne, Bourgoyne et Brisse en janvier 1597."

37. Sully, *Mémoires de Maximillien de Béthune duc de Sully*, 3 vols. (London: 1747), 2:26. Joseph Servan, *Recherches sur la force de l'armée française, depuis Henri IV jusqu'à la fin de 1806* (Paris: 1806), 2, uses the same figures. This book, which combines the work of both Grimoard and Servan, is a much cited work; however, its value is limited by the fact that it does not cite its archival sources.

38. Infantry regiments stood at 4,100, cavalry at 2,637, and garrison infantry at 3,000 for a total of 9,737, according to Servan, *Recherches*, 2–4.

39. Sully, *Mémoires des sages et royales oeconomies d'estat de Henry le grand*, vols. 8 and 9 in Petitot, ed., *Collection des Mémoires relatifs à l'histoire de France*, 2nd ser.(Paris: 1821), 8:351, 9:65–68. Different editions and translations of Sully's *Mémoires* give different figures; see 55,600 in Sully, *Memoirs*, trans. Charlotte Lennox, 5 vols. (Philadelphia: 1817), 5:108, and 54,600 according to Sully, *Mémoires* (London: 1747), 3:360.

40. Belhomme would have us believe the French mustered 97,000 infantry in 1622 and 64,000 in 1624, figures which go right through the roof. Belhomme, *Infanterie*, 1:331, 337.

41. Figures in Édouard La Barre Duparcq, *Histoire de l'art de la guerre*, vol. 2 (Paris: 1864), 159, and detailed in Belhomme, *Infanterie*, 1:337.

42. BN, Chatre de Cangé, vol. 22, #64, "Projet de dépense de l'extraordinaire des guerres pour l'année 1627." Actually counts 12,572 men, but it gives the financial upkeep for "garnisons ordinaires," and figured at the same rate as line infantry, this would yield an-

other 5,500 troops. See as well, BN, Chatre de Cangé, vol. 22, #63, which gives a count of 11,810 without garrisons.

43. F. de Vaux de Folletier, *Le siège de la Rochelle* (Paris: 1931), 237–38.

44. Table of projected and real troop strength in Parrott, "The Administration of the French Army," 142.

45. BN, f. fr. 6385.

46. Armand du Plesis, duc de Richelieu, *Lettres, instructions diplomatiques et papiers d'état du cardinal de Richelieu,* ed. Avenel, 8 vols., (Paris: 1853–77), 4:601, 13 September 1634, Richelieu to the King. It reads in part "but all this is uncertain; and, besides the levies that it would be necessary to carry out for a new army destined for Germany, six thousand men are lacking from the count of 95,000 of M. de Bouillon." Literally this would mean that 89,000 actual men were on foot. Discussing this letter, even Parrott is willing to accept a figure of 45,000 infantry, 8,000 cavalry, and an additional 30,000 garrison troops, a total of 83,000 troops in service at the time. Parrott, "The Administration of the French Army," 106.

47. BN, f. fr. 6385.

48. Archives des Affaires Étrangères, hereafter cited as AAE, 811, fol. 120, 7 November 1634 plans for 1635, in Parrott, "The Administration of the French Army," 19. AAE, France 811, fol. 129, 7 November 1634 in Richard Bonney, *The King's Debts* (Oxford: 1981), 173, arrives at 124,500.

49. AAE, France, 813, fol. 15, letter of 10 January 1635, Servien to Richelieu, in Parrott, "The Administration of the French Army," 107.

50. AAE, France 813, fol. 301, 23 April 1635, in Bonney, *The King's Debts,* 173.

51. AAE, 70, fol. 37, *Contrôle* for 1635, in Avenel, ed., *Lettres,* 5:3–6. The confusion arises from the complicated way that totals are shown. First there are two different columns for infantry with a difference of 1,500 between them, 134,000 or 135,500. Cavalry is then shown as 16,680, though it would appear that it should have been 16,480. Some take this as the full count, giving a total of 150,680. However, it misses three points. Sandwiched in the cavalry is a notation for 6,000 "chevaux" not counted as cavalry because they might have been some other form of "horse." Next to the cavalry is a column for 4,200 "dragons;" these should be counted too, giving a corrected total for all mounted arms of 26,680 (with corrected addition), not 16,680. Moreover, a notation on the infantry says "Garrisons, 36,000, who at the most will be paid only as 30,000," and since the document is fundamentally a financial one, garrisons are counted only at the lower figure; however, the infantry total with the larger garrison figure should be 140,000–141,500. This plus the corrected cavalry total gives 166,680–168,180.

52. Such up-to-date scholars as Contamine and Parker both accept this as a projection, at least. Contamine, *Histoire militaire,* 354, 412. Parker, *The Military Revolution,* 58.

53. Archives de Guerre, hereafter cited as AG, Collection des ordonnances militaires, vol. 14, #87, "Contrôle general des armées du Roy pour l'année 1636," dated December 1635.

54. AAE, France 820, fol. 200, Contrôle générale, 15 April 1636, in Parrott, "The Administration of the French Army," 91, 99. Bonney, *The King's Debts,* 173fn employs the same piece to reach a lower total of 199,400. Bonney omits mention of the additional cavalry and states the first cavalry as 27,400 rather than 21,400, consequently the difference. Bonney gives an additional citation to AAE, France 823, fol. 255.

55. AAE, France 828, fols. 311–23, 330–51, 1637, in Parrott, "The Administration of the French Army," 115.

56. AAE, France 832, fol. 1, in Bernard Kroener, "Die Entwicklung der Truppenstärken in den französischen Armeen zwischen 1635 und 1661," in Konrad Repgen, ed. *Forschungen und Quellen zur Geschichte des Dreissigjährigen Krieges* (Münster: 1981), 201. Using other documents in the same carton, AAE, France 832, fols. 1–19, 1638, Parrott, "The Administration of the French Army," 117, calculated a total of 164,000.

57. AAE, France 832, fols. 288–293, in Kroener, "Die Entwicklung der Truppenstärken," 201. This is apparently the "État au vrais des effectifs et de la solde" for 1639 cited by Ernest Lavisse, *Histoire de France*, ed. Ernest Lavisse, vol. 6, part 2, (Paris: 1911), 318, since it lists the same total.

58. BN, f. fr. 17555, fol. 1, "État des troupes tant d'infanterie que de cavalerie dont seront composées les armees du roy durant l'année 1639," in Kroener, "Die Entwicklung der Truppenstärken," 203.

59. BN, Collection Dupuy, #590, #244.

60. Richelieu, "Succincte narration des grandes actions du roi," in Petitot, ed., *Collection des mémoires relatifs à l'histoire de France*, 2nd ser. (Paris: 1821), 11:317. He sets the size as 150,000 infantry and 30,000 cavalry for each of the first five years of the war.

61. See Belhomme, *Infanterie*, vols. 1 and 2.

62. Corvisier's statement that the paper strength of the French army stood at 250,000 in 1658 simply cannot be accepted. Corvisier, *Louvois*, 83. This comes from accepting Belhomme's figure for infantry in 1658.

63. Belhomme, *Infanterie*, 2:88, 92.

64. Jules Mazarin, *Lettres du cardinal Mazarin pendant son Ministère*, Chéruel and Avenel, eds., vols. 6–9 (Paris: 1890–1906), 9:378, letter of 19 October 1659.

65. Bernard Kroener, *Les routes et les étapes*, 177.

66. Louis XIV, *Oeuvres de Louis XIV*, Grimoard and Grouvelle, eds., 6 vols. (Paris: 1806), 3:32. An editorial comment criticizes *Recherches* as giving an estimate based on a public document designed to exaggerate size of force; that volume stated that Louis still had 125,000 men after discharging 15–20,000 right after the Peace of the Pyrenees. Servan, *Recherches*, 53–54.

67. AG, Arch. hist. 78, feuille 165.

68. AG, Arch. hist. 78, feuille 165, states that early 1665 size was 805 companies of infantry, totaling 45,216 men, and 103 companies of cavalry, totaling 5,850; the army expanded over 1665 by 270 companies of infantry at 50 men each, or 13,500, making a grand total of 64,566.

69. AG, A1198, 5 March 1666, letter from Louvois to Pradel in Camille Rousset, *Histoire de Louvois*, 4 vols. (Paris: 1862–64), 1:97. Louis André, *Michel Le Tellier et l'organisation de l'armée monarchique* (Paris: 1906), 294, and Louis André, *Michel Le Tellier et Louvois* (Paris: 1942), 314n. Based on BN 4255 folios 5–8, 9–13, 177, he arrives at the figure of 97,515. However, this is not so high as Belhomme, who once again leaves reality behind, arguing for 155,000 infantry alone. Belhomme, *Infanterie*, 2:130.

70. AG, Bibliothèque du Ministère de Guerre, hereafter cited as BMG, Tiroirs de Louis XIV, page 36, "États des regiments de cavalerie en 1667"; page 37, "États des troupes destinées pour la garde de S. M. et pour servir dans les armées"; and pages 39–40, "État des troupes d'infanterie estants sur pied en l'année 1667."

71. Paul Sonnino, *Louis XIV and the Origins of the Dutch War* (Cambridge: 1988), 17. Again, Belhomme's figure of 178,500 infantry alone in December 1667 cannot be taken seriously. Belhomme, *Infanterie*, 2:134.

72. AG, BMG, Tiroirs de Louis XIV, pages 46–48, "Estat des trouppes d'infanterie que le Roy a sur pied en mars 1668"; pages 50–64, "Estat des trouppes de cavalerie que le Roy a sur pied en mars 1668". It shows 1865 companies of infantry and 477 companies of cavalry. Sonnino repeats this figure, *Origins of the Dutch War*, 17, 28.

73. Sonnino, *Origins of the Dutch War*, 127–28fn.

74. Sonnino, *Origins of the Dutch War*, 127. This accords with Corvisier's statement that the peacetime strength of the army between the wars was 95,000. Corvisier, *Louvois*, 325. Servan, *Recherches*, 54, putting it at 131,265, allows for virtually no demobilization at all.

75. For 1671 levies see Sonnino, *Origins of the Dutch War*, 155. AG, BMG, Tiroirs de Louis XIV, pages 76–77, 4 February 1672, puts the French infantry in 1,287 companies with 446 companies of cavalry, and 2,950 additional troops in the royal household, but it may not take garrisons into account. Rousset, *Louvois*, 1:346–47, refers to this document and figures the total at 120,000. Ernest Lavisse, *Histoire de France*, ed. Ernest Lavisse, vol. 7, part 2, *Louis XIV, 1643–85* (Paris: 1906), 238, refers to a control of 2 February 1672 setting the number at 120,000, but he too must be referring to the document in the Tiroirs.

76. Orders issued January–March 1672 to raise another 400 companies of infantry and 120 companies of cavalry, 26,000 men, that would make the total size of army 144,000. Louis wanted to start the war with 144,000. Sonnino, *Origins of the Dutch War*, 177, 162. Servan, Recherches, 54, put the invading army at 176,087; clearly this is too high.

77. AG, BMG, Tiroirs de Louis XIV, page 110, "Troupes que le Roy auvis sur pied le premier janvier 1678." Interestingly, it is at this point that Belhomme's figures and archival sources begin to coincide. Belhomme gives the infantry figure for May 1667 as 229,970 (Belhomme, *Infanterie*, 2:206–7), while the Tiroir document puts it at 219,250 in January 1668. Perhaps by this point, the world of the ordonnances had come to represent reality in a way it had never done before. If so, it is a credit to the administrative abilities of Louvois and his master.

78. Archives Nationales, hereafter cited as AN, G⁷1774, #52, "État des troupes que le Roy a eu sur pied," this interesting financial document details troop strength for 1679, 1684, 1696, and 1699. More conservative estimates put the figure some 10,000 lower, including officers—138,432 in Servan, *Recherches*, 54, and 140,000 according to Corvisier in Contamine, *Histoire militaire*, 531.

79. AG, A¹687, 20 September 1681, letter from Le Pelletier to Louvois, in *Rousset, Louvois*, 3:216.

80. AN,G⁷1774, #52, sets the number at 165,807 troops, without including officers. AG, A¹772, #267, in Rousset, *Louvois*, 3:287, puts it at 161,995. Servan, *Recherches*, 57, states the 1684 size at 158,005.

81. AG, A¹808, 8 September 1688, letter from *Louvois* to Asfeld, in Rousset, Louvois, 4:88.

82. Victor Belhomme, *L'armée française en 1690* (Paris: 1895). With Belhomme, it depends on what you count. He figures the royal army at 363,154 (p. 104), the provincial militia at 24,930 (p. 119), and the local Protestant militia of Languedoc and Dauphiné as 14,600 (p.119). Since these various forces are all tallied in AN, G⁷1774, #52, referred to below, they are also counted here. Belhomme would add to this 52,927 of the local militias (p. 119) which played a military role to be sure, but were not full time soldiers. Since AN, G⁷1774 does not include these local militias, neither will I; if I did the total would rise to 455,884.

83. Sébastien le Prestre de Vauban, *Oisivetés de M. de Vauban*, 3 vols. (Paris: 1842–46), 2:237, 252–60. He complained that the king's troops stood at 438,000, and he wanted them reduced to 355,000.

84. AN,G⁷1774, #52. This gives the "total of the troops, the officers not included" as 415,237, but this figure includes 1,500 for the Hotel des invalides and 3,080 for the arrière ban, which I have subtracted. After the total for troops, it also wants to add in 31,374 men for those reformed from mounted companies and for the milice discharged in 1693 and 1694 to give a total for all men at the height of the war of 446,612.

85. Servan, *Recherches*, 58, credits Louis with 395,865.

86. AN,G⁷1774, #52. See Georges Girard, *Le service militaire en France à la fin du règne de Louis XIV: Racolage et milice (1701–1715)* (Paris: 1915), 4, concerning the cut in company size, as cavalry companies were reduced to 20 men and infantry to 35.

87. For reduction of 40,000, see Girard, *Racolage et milice,* 4. Belhomme gives a figure for French infantry as that supplied by the 1 February état above, 156,676. However his figure for infantry in December 1699 fell to 120,566, but remember, this excludes cavalry, which would have numbered about 20,000. Belhomme, *Infanterie,* 2:342–43. This gives a good indication of declining numbers. Servan, *Recherches,* 58, gives the interwar low as 140,216, which seems reasonable as it is roughly 45,000 below the early 1699 levels.

88. AG, A¹1579, "Mémoire des trouppes que le roy a sur pied, janvier, 1702" in Girard, *Racolage et milice,* pp. 5–7.

89. Servan, *Recherches,* 58–59.

90. AN, G⁷1780, #212, État des régiments d'infanterie, cavalerie et dragons, companies d'infanteries separées, companies de fusilliers des officers majors des places et des partisans et autres troupes qui seront au service du Roy pendant la campagne 1707." This valuable document lists companies and regiments, not men. The figure of 373,000 resulted from: 1) multiplying listed units by their official size; 2) using AG, MR 1701, #13, to supply figures for certain regiments that were not included, most notably the Swiss line infantry and the regiments of guards; and 3) also using AG, MR 1701, #13, to provide a basis for calculating the number of officers. According to Belhomme, who counted regiments, 1706 marked the high point for the French army during the War of the Spanish Succession, so the projected figures for 1707 would seem to represent a reasonable high for total army size.

91. AG, MR 1701, #13, "Estat contenant le nombre des officers, des soldats, des cavaliers, et des dragons dont les regimens etoient sur pied en 1710." It lists 336,918 men and 21,062 officers, plus 425 detached companies of 45 men each, totaling 19,125 men. Since the officers are not listed for the detached companies, and a normal infantry company would require three (captain, lieutenant, and sous-lieutenant), there would probably have also been an additional 1,275 officers, driving the total up to 378,380. This is a much used document. See, for example, André Corvisier, *L'armée française de la fin du XVIIe siècle au ministère du Choiseul: Le soldat,* 2 vols. (Paris: 1964), 1:55. The similar size of the army in 1707 and 1710 will come as a surprise to readers of Belhomme, because he saw the two years as high and low points. The count of regiments in Belhomme, *Infanterie,* vol. 2, puts the high of 335 infantry regiments in 1706 and the low of 290 in 1710.

92. Servan, *Recherches,* 60.

93. See the discussion of army size 1715–1789 in John A. Lynn, "The Pattern of Army Growth, 1445–1945," in John A. Lynn, ed., *The Tools of War: Ideas, Instruments, and Institutions of Warfare, 1445–1871* (Urbana, IL: 1990), 3–4.

94. Kroener, *Les routes et les étapes,* 177–78.

95. He seems to arrive at this incorrect official size by reading backwards from winter quarters regulations for 1637. Kroener, "Die Entwicklung der Truppenstärken," 169. But a

variety of sources make clear that the official company size stood at 100. Richelieu spoke of 100 man companies as well, stating that by regulations a battalion of 20 companies should contain 2000 men. Richelieu, *Testament politique*, ed. Louis André (Paris: 1947), 478. See as well AG, $A^1 32$, #250, 1636 commission to Pontchartrain to raise 4,000 troops in companies of 100, and AG, $A^1 29$, fol. 219, 13 September 1636, order for La Tremouille to raise two regiments of 20 companies, totaling 2,000 men each. I must thank David Parrott for supplying these last two archival references.

96. Avenel, *Lettres*, 4:601, 13 September 1634, Richelieu to the King.

97. Figured on the basis of "État des troupes tant d'infanterie que de cavalerie dont seron composées les armees du roy durant l'année 1636," BN, f. fr. 17555, fol. 1, in Kroener, "Die Entwicklung der Truppenstärken," 203.

98. For Corvisier's graph of full and discounted figures for infantry, 1635–1660, see Contamine, *Histoire militaire*, 364.

99. Parrott, "The Administration of the French Army," 135.

100. Richelieu, *Testament politique*, 478.

101. Parrott, "The Administration of the French Army," 135. Here he states that this is the possible maximum maintained "consistently" through 1635.

102. "In the first half of the campaign [of 1635] it is probable that Richelieu's armies in the field numbered some 60,000 infantry and 9–9,500 cavalry." Parrott, "The Administration of the French Army," 110–111.

103. Ibid., iv.

104. There is reason to accept the largest estimate as being Parrott's primary thesis. In a letter of 2 August 1992 he stated that his 70,000 estimate for 1635 was "well on the way to the 80–100,000 that I suggest is the size of force which the government is striving to maintain from 1636."

105. Corvisier, *Louvois*, 82. Contemporaries recognized that to add twelve real men to the ranks it was necessary to issue commissions to recruit twenty. AAE, France, 814, fol. 262, 14 July 1635, in Parrott, "The Administration of the French Army," 111. He argues that this level of wastage was so commonly assumed that in documents estimating army size for 1637, regiments of 20 companies were counted not as 2000 men but as 1200. AAE, France, 828, fols. 265–862.

106. See the numerous *routes* preserved in the Archives municipales d'Amiens, hereafter cited as Amiens, EE 392, March 1676, plus the following documents: Archives du Département du Nord, hereafter cited as Nord, C 2321, 6 October 1672; AG, Bibl., $A^{1b} 1628$, vol. 2, 5–7, 9–10, 13–15, 17–19, 21–23, 25–27, 33–35, 65–67, 69–71; AG, $A^1 295$, #86; and AN, $G^7 1774$, #10, #11.

107. "I counted always on a real strength [*pied*] much less than the declared one [*effectif*], because I knew how a fall in numbers always occurs when troops have been on campaign a while. So that in place of the 40,000 men that I can comfortably send [faire marcher] [on campaign], I count only on 35,000." Louis XIV, *Mémoires*, 2:306. Supplement for 1667.

108. In 1682 the infantry companies in question boasted at least 84 percent of a full complement, while mounted companies reached 77 percent for regular cavalry and 98 percent for dragoons. AN, $Z^{1c} 414$, August 1682, December 1682. The fact that all the mounted units were reviewed in December, the depths of winter quarters, may explain their weaker numbers. Infantry companies contained 42.2 men at a time when they were to hold 45 or 50

men. Cavalry companies had 34.6 men when a full company held 40 or 45, and dragoon companies mounted 39.2 horsemen, just a bit shy of their regulation strength of 40.

109. Amiens, EE 394, EE 395, EE 396.

110. Archives municipales de Dijon, hereafter cited as Dijon, H 228, 8 February 1692; Dijon, H 228, 8 February 1692; and Archives du Département de Côte d'Or, C 3675, 23 January 1693. The Manlenvine(?) regiment passing through Dijon had a company strength of only 22.1.

111. BN, f. fr. 4565–4567, three "estat et compte ... de la fourniture des estappes faites aux troupees" presented to la Grange, conseiller du roi, covering the months from April 1691–March 1692. For reasons as yet unknown, these very impressive formal accounts listing over 1200 companies seem to follow an administrative convenience of listing as completely full, battalions that almost certainly were not. This is unmistakably the case in some instances that listed a regiment at partial strength on one day and full on the next, at a time when replacements would not have been arriving at the front. Consider, for example, the first battalion of the Normandy infantry regiment with 567 privates on 17 May, but a full complement of 768 on 19 May. My guess is that allowances were awarded at full strength to compensate officers for building up their companies. It is clear also that in Amiens, small batches of *recrues* were sometimes counted at 15 men even if they were clearly fewer in number according to the route itself. The reason for this strange accounting method escapes me, but it bears witness to the fact that sometimes units might be counted as full (the ideal *recrue* was 15) when they were not. So to make use of the Alsace account books without skewing the sample to imply that the average company was much larger than it really was, I have excluded from my count any infantry companies listed as 48–50. This reduces the sample from 1239 infantry companies to only 416, but it saves the sample from producing absurd results. This much smaller, but safer, sample shows an average size of 40.9 men. I must thank two graduate students whom I employed to chase down the figures in these volumes of accounts, Mr. Richard Lundell of the University of Illinois and, especially, Dr. David Stewart of Hillsdale College, a gentleman who did a splendid job.

112. Belhomme, *L'armée française en 1690*, 88, 93–96, states that the size of both cavalry and dragoon companies in 1690 was 40 men; the maréchal de logis is counted as an officer. AN, $G^7 1774$, # 52, seems to count cavalry and dragoon companies at 35 men in 1696.

113. BN, f. fr. 4566. These mounted units had to be treated much as had the accounts of infantry. If a unit was shown as absolutely full, it was not used in the sample. The percentages stated here were arrived at only by using accounts of the 137 companies shown as being less than complete, and thus trustworthy. Since it is not beyond the realm of possibility that some regiments were at full strength, the averages may somewhat understate the full size of the army, but this is a lesser risk than that of mistaking administrative procedure for real head counts.

114. An ordonnance of 12 December 1691 raised the size of milice companies from 50 to 60. Léon Hennet, *Les milices et les troupes provinciales* (Paris: 1884), 32.

115. AN, $G^7 71774$, # 52, credits the army with 343,323 infantry and 67,334 cavalry in 1696, exclusive of officers. However, this estimate includes 15,000 of local militia but excludes officers, who would have numbered more than 20,000 in an army of this size. If these two figures influence the calculations, 335,000 remains a modest estimate of discounted size.

116. Archives municipales de Lille, hereafter cited as Lille, 11,113, 10 & 24 October, 7 & 8 November, and 2, 12 & 26 December 1700.

117. For changes in company size in 1699 see Girard, *Racolage et milice,* 4.

118. Amiens, EE 411, EE 412; Lille 11,113, 5 & 26 March, 4 April 1702; See as well, Girard, Georges, ed., "Un soldat de Malplaquet: Lettres du capitaine de Saint-Mayme," *Carnet de Sabretache* (1922), 515.

119. Infantry company size stood at 45 until the regulation of 20 September 1710 raised it to 50. Girard, *Racolage et milice,* 11.

120. Amiens, EE 421, EE 423, EE 424, EE 427, EE 432; Dijon, H 243, H 244; AG, A^{1}2152, #208, 17 September 1709, "État de la force de quarante-deux battalions et de ce qu'on leur donne de recrues," in Vault and Pelet, ed., *Mémoires militaires relatifs à la succession d'Espagne sous Louis XIV,* vol. 9 (Paris: 1855), 383; AG, A^{1}2214, 10 April 1710, letter from d'Alborgessy, review of troops being sent to Douai.

121. This was the regulation of 20 September 1710. See Girard, *Racolage et milice,* 10–11 for a discussion of this increase.

122. The larger Dijon figure is explained by the passage through Dijon of one large and probably brand new regiment enjoying a nearly full complement. Dijon, H244, 6–7 May 1710.

123. In early August, the army of Flanders claimed 128 battalions of infantry. See AG, A^{1}2152, #31, "Disposition de l'infanterie," in Vault and Pelet, *Mémoires militaires,* 333–34. Detailed casualty reports for officers at Malplaquet suggest that the battalions of the 17 September review suffered average casualties on the same level as the other battalions in the army. (There was no detailed accounting of casualties among enlisted ranks.) See AG, A^{1}2152, #225, "État des officiers tués, blessés et prisonniers à la bataille de Malplaquet," in Vault and Pelet, *Mémoires militaires,* 378–81. The average battalion in the army suffered 9.8 officers killed and wounded, while these 37 suffered 10.3. Consequently, it is reasonable to argue that the battalions suffered no more than an average number of casualties in the ranks. If 11,000 is a reasonable estimate for French casualties at Malplaquet, the infantry alone would perhaps have lost 2/3 of these men. Gaston Bodart, *Militär-historisches Kriegs-Lexikon, 1618–1905* (Vienna and Leipzig: 1908), 160; Claude G. Sturgill, *Marshal Villars and the War of the Spanish Succession* (Lexington, KY: 1965), 98. (It should be remembered that there was very heavy cavalry fighting and great losses at Malplaquet.) So infantry losses can be roughly estimated at 7,330; and each battalion lost on average about 57 men (7,330/120). This would mean that the sample which claimed an average company strength of 27.2 after Malplaquet probably was up to 31.9 before the action.

124. AG, A^{1}2214, #107, 10 April 1710, letter from d'Alborgessy, review of troops being sent to Douai. Claude Sturgill correctly insists that the French army never reached the proportions it was supposed to have attained. However, he overstates his case. He argues that in the spring of 1710, the average strength of the 156 battalions under Villars was only 250, yielding a company size of 19.2 men. It is difficult to discover how he arrived at this figure, since the documents he cites in the military correspondence do not in any way justify it. Sturgill, *Marshal Villars,* 101–2. A footnote on page 102 reads "AG 2214, 86–107, gives strength reports for the various French units." However, a careful check of these sources in this carton by my graduate student, George Satterfield, turned up only a single document reporting specific unit sizes: AG, A^{1}2214, #107, 10 April 1710, "Estat de la force des bataillons destinez pour la garnison de la ville de Douai donnée par les majors des regimens du 14 Avril 1710" attached to a letter from d'Alborgessy dated 10 April. It gave the strengths of 14 battalions destined for the garrison of Douai, but their average strength was 372 men, not 250. In his letter from Douai, AG A^{1}2214, #92, 13 April 1710, d'Abergon complained that

"the strongest battalions have not 400 men to perform duty [pour faire le service]" accords with the d'Alborgessy's review more than with Sturgill's statement. In addition, d'Abergon's words may imply that the battalions had other men present but not fit. A battalion of 400 men, by the way, had companies numbering 30.8 men.

125. According to AG, MR 1701, #13, the total number of infantry, both in French and foreign mercenary regiments, fighting for Louis XIV totaled 319,541, including detached companies, while the cavalry numbered 41,073 and the dragoons 16,491, producing a grand total of 377,105. The 1710 document seems to represent a transition from a company strength of 45 to one of 50, since 27 percent of the French companies are specifically listed as containing 45 men each and 73 percent had 50. This would average out to a company size of 48.7; I will use this as a basis for computing the percentage of full size reached by all infantry units.

126. This is a point made by Parrott in his dissertation. See as well Louis Tuetey, *Les officiers de l'ancien régime. Nobles et roturiers* (Paris: 1908). In addition John A. Lynn, "The Pattern of French Military Reform, 1750–1795," at the February 1974 Consortium on Revolutionary Europe, 1750–1850 and published in the *Proceedings of the Consortium on Revolutionary Europe* (Gainesville, FL: 1978), discusses this practice for the eighteenth century.

127. On the tax of violence, see John A. Lynn, "How War Fed War: The Tax of Violence and Contributions During the *grand siècle*," *Journal of Modern History* 65 (June 1993), 286–310.

128. The National Guard alone was supposed to provide a reserve of 1,200,000 men in 1789. Jacques Godechot, *Institutions de la France sous la Révolution et l'Empire* (Paris: 1968), 133.

129. Godechot, *Institutions de la France*, 362. For example both Godechot and Jean-Paul Bertaud, *La Révolution armée* (Paris: 1979), 137–39, work with the 750,000 man figure. However, this is not the same thing as discounting official estimates of Louis XIV's army, since the revolutionary figures were based on actual head counts, not on multiplying the number of battalions on the army list by the wishful thinking of the regulation sizes for units. The reason that historians have traditionally cut down the figure of 1,169,000 is to make allowance for the wounded, the sick, those on leave, etc.. I would argue the 1,169,000 figure makes a fairer comparison.

130. The forces marshaled by the Republic are also far more impressive than those that served Louis XIV if we calculate their numbers as percentages of French population. If the population of France stood at 21,500,000 in 1700—J. Dupaquier, ed. *Histoire de la population française*, vol. 2 (Paris: 1988), 64–65—then the amount of troops maintained for each 1,000 of population was 15.8 in 1696 and 13.4 in 1710. (However, Dupaquier's figures somewhat overstate the French population in 1700, since they are based on the modern borders of France, meaning Lorraine, Corsica, and Savoy are counted.) Since the French population rose to about 28,600,000 by 1790, an army of 750,000 meant the French fielded 26.2 soldiers per thousand of population. And if one wanted to take into account only *Frenchmen* mobilized to fight for their king during the *ancien régime*, the disparity would be even greater, since Louis XIV recruited many soldiers from outside France.

131. Lot, *Recherches sur les effectifs*, 103–104.

132. Based on AG, MR 1701, #13, "Estat contenant le nombre des officers, des soldats, des cavaliers, et des dragons dont les regimens etoient sur pied en 1710."

6

The Military Revolution and the Professionalisation of the French Army Under the Ancien Régime

COLIN JONES

THE MIDDLE DECADES of the seventeenth century saw a shift in the centre of gravity of European dynastic politics from the Habsburgs to the Bourbons. The grandiose schemes of European dominance held by the combined Spanish and Imperial Habsburg power in the sixteenth century had foundered on the opposition of the Turks on one hand and the Dutch and their allies on the other. Even so, in the closing years of the century, Habsburg Spain had still been indisputably the greatest power in Europe, while France had been in eclipse, submerged in a welter of internal dissension which would last down to the Fronde (1648–1653). Nevertheless, in the Treaty of Westphalia in 1648 with the Imperial power and in the Treaty of the Pyrenees in 1659 with Spain, France was to assert its primacy in Europe. The resultant change in international ranking order derived above all from feats of arms. Spain had, it is true, developed grave internal problems which weakened its international standing; but its defeat was ultimately military and the French victory over the legendary Spanish *tercios* at Rocroi in 1643 had symbolically tolled the knell of Habsburg dominance in Europe.

It was France's army which lay at the nub of her newfound primacy of place in Europe: her navy in the 1640s and 1650s was still inconsiderable and was never to be ascribed more than a subaltern role in grand strategy. Successive Bourbon rulers and their principal ministers—Richelieu (1624–1642) and Mazarin (1642–1661) not least—managed to create an original and cogent blend of state power and military strength which, from the middle of the seventeenth century down to the end of the Ancien Régime in 1789, would enable France to aspire to European hegemony. This was an achievement which was intricately associated with profound changes which had been taking place since the late sixteenth century in the conduct of war. These changes, dubbed by Michael Roberts as a 'Military Revolution', significantly intensified the impact of warfare on the rest of society.[1] They also pointed logically towards the professionalisation of European armies. It is upon the pioneering role of the emergent absolutist monarchy in France in this process that this article will focus.

1. THE INITIAL EXPANSION OF THE ARMY:
RECRUITMENT AND SUPPLIES

The growth in the size of armies was perhaps the most obvious aspect of Europe's Military Revolution.[2] The Spanish army, for example, which had numbered 150,000 men in the 1550s had doubled in size by the 1630s; the Dutch Republic more than quintupled the size of its forces between the late sixteenth and late seventeenth centuries; and Sweden's army mushroomed from a mere 15,000 men in the 1590s to 100,000 men by the close of the seventeenth century. In France, the expansion was arguably even more sudden and abrupt than elsewhere. In the sixteenth century, the crown's army had rarely, and even then by little, exceeded 50,000 men. Indeed, on the death of Henri IV in 1610, numbers stood at less than 20,000 men and this figure was more or less maintained during the next couple of decades. Once Richelieu and Louis XIII had in 1635 thrown in France's lot against the Habsburgs in the Thirty Years War, however, the strength of the army grew rapidly to over 150,000 men. The rise in numbers continued after Richelieu's death in 1642 and from the last decades of the seventeenth century to the end of the Ancien Régime, the state had at least a quarter of a million soldiers on its books—and sometimes double that number in time of war. This sharp rise in numbers was all the more remarkable in that whereas hitherto most armies had been extensively dismantled at the end of each campaigning season, the new armies were primarily standing forces maintained on a quasi-permanent basis.

This quantum leap in the size of the French army was only made with the greatest difficulty especially in the early years. The administrative infrastructure of the armed forces which Richelieu and Louis XIII had inherited was unimpressive in the extreme and the sheer speed of the build-up in forces left no time for traditions of military administration to develop. Although the French army's later prestige was to be based upon centralised state control, it is important to recognize that, in the early stages, the fighting forces pitted against Spain had to be cobbled together with an almost prodigal delegation of powers. This was particularly apparent in the field of recruitment. The new army was a mixture of the most diverse elements. A great number of the troops—perhaps more than a third—were foreign mercenaries, for the most part brought over to the French side by their commanders. In 1636, for example, Richelieu had secured the support of some 20,000 foreign troops under the great military enterpriser Bernard of Saxe-Weimar. The ancient provincial militias of the frontier regions and the bourgeois militias of the towns were pressurised into providing contingents of men to fight alongside such mercenaries in the war emergency of the late 1630s. The feudal levy—repeated periodically down to the 1690s—also brought some men to the standards. The bulk of foot-soldiers, however, were recruited through a system of more or less voluntary enlistment. What normally happened was that the crown granted a commission to a regimental commander—a colonel—who in return undertook to supply an agreed number of men. To make up the required numbers, colonels sold the posts of company-commanders—captains—to the highest bidders. Captains, the colonels themselves, or on occasion special recruiting officers (*racoleurs*) appointed by the commanders, set about raising the numbers by whatever means seemed most effective. Commanders who were seigneurs—and most were—could count on enlisting peasants from their estates during the winter months; otherwise any method of obtaining recruits was fair enough, even if it meant raiding prisons and hospitals. If the men who were enlisted were, in their different ways, 'serving the king', their prime allegiance was likely to be to their captains and colonels. Even royal muster rolls referred to the men as 'soldat du sieur (X), capitaine au régiment de (Y)'. Not until 1745 was this formula changed to a more impersonal form.

The colonels and captains who played such a notable part in recruitment procedures in the early seventeenth century were also responsible for many of their troops' supplies and provisions. Each new recruit was entitled to a bounty from the royal treasury. This, along with the men's wages, was normally paid to their commanders who were permitted to deduct various sums which represented the cost of food, equipment and other ancillary services. Many commanders, for example, provided their men with a suit of clothing—scarcely a uniform as yet— and any arms and ammunition they were to have. Commanders were also responsible for establishing the military hospitals and chaplaincies which a royal edict of 1629 had introduced. For many of the supplies, commanders relied on contracts which either they or the central government made with civilian entrepreneurs. Given the only very rudimentary supervision which the government could exercise over armies in the field, these arrangements strongly favoured corruption and peculation on the part of commanders and contractors. Both stood to make considerable profits at the expense of the troops on one hand and the state on the other.

There was a variety of ways in which commanders and contractors could turn warfare into a profitable entrepreneurial exercise. They could, firstly, economise on the services they were theoretically bound to supply. Clothing and food often arrived late or not at all, or was of poor quality. The regimental hospitals, theoretically introduced in 1629, were in practice rarities well into the 1640s and 1650s. Secondly, commanders could charge excessively for those services they did supply—bills for expenses would be met out of the wages fund, for example, rather than out of the pockets of commanders. Thirdly, commanders were prone to withhold part or even all of the men's wages. Finally, commanders could defraud the government by putting in requests for payment for a fictitious number of troops. The government fixed the wage-bill of each regiment after a periodic muster at which it was notoriously easy to swell numbers with soldiers borrowed from other regiments, camp-followers, servants on the retinue of the officers and the local inhabitants. So numerous were 'paper recruits' (*passe-volants*) that one historian has calculated that the effective strength of the seventeenth-century army may well have been as much as a third inferior to the numbers on paper.[3]

The virtual absence of solidly-based state-controlled military institutions allowed such fraudulent practices to flourish as never before. Networks of financial, commercial and familial relations linked commanders, contractors and personages close to the centre of government in business cartels which made the fortunes of their members through cheating the state. There were, moreover, no keener enthusiasts of this form of activity than Richelieu and Mazarin who both flagrantly utilised their key position in the king's counsels as a means of personal enrichment. In addition, the notorious parsimony of the government in regard to its army also encouraged corruption. The huge standing army with which the state was waging war from the 1630s was immensely expensive and governments were obliged to have recourse to a plethora of extreme financial policies—tax-rises, creations of venal offices, the floating of huge loans, devaluations, revaluations, and the like—in order to ensure that their armed forces remained in the field. In such fevered financial circumstances, the state often looked on the pay of the men as more of a luxury than a necessity. Moreover, in order to save money the government periodically disbanded some of the newer regiments—which formed the majority—before their commanders had had sufficient time to amortize the investment they had made in purchasing a commission. This governmental stratagem inevitably had the effect of whetting commanders' appetites for a fast return on outlay by whatever means lay at hand.

2. THE INITIAL EXPANSION OF
THE ARMY: INCENTIVES

The most frequent victim of the whirligig of corruption and the cut-throat competition for fast profits and big savings which characterised the military machine created in the second quarter of the seventeenth century was the well-being of the soldiers. The increased size of the army presented unparalleled problems of control—not least of sanitary control. With regimental infirmaries still little more than a pipe-dream, for example, medical aid tended to be forthcoming either from charitably-disposed barber-surgeons on the retinue of the officers; from local quacks or charlatans; or from the prostitutes and camp-followers who were called on to justify their existence from time to time by acting as unpaid nurses. Health conditions were primitive in the extreme, especially in military camps, deaths in which always far exceeded deaths in battle: 'A body of troops which camps cannot remain for long in the same place', stated one government report in the early seventeenth century, 'without an extreme infection occurring as a consequence of the dirtiness of the soldiers, the horses which die there and the beasts slaughtered'.[4]

Disease was thus a frequent visitor to the camps of the army, and there combined with the effects of exposure to climatic extremes and the hunger which might arise when supplies or wages failed to materialise. It was little wonder that armies were important vectors of disease: most critically of plague, most frequently perhaps of syphilis, as well as of the dreaded 'camp fever'—the generic name given to a wide variety of infectious diseases including typhus, typhoid fever and dysentery. Scurvy also caused much damage—testimony to the poor diet of the troops. Pulmonary and respiratory diseases, skin ailments and sores, rheumatism, gout, hernias and premature senility also took their toll.

Given this litany of misery and woe—as well as the fact that wages were low or non-existent and that chances of promotion were probably slim—it may seem somewhat surprising that the state was able to increase the size of its armed forces as rapidly as it did in the 1630s. It is true that a large number of *passe-volants* and an exceptionally high desertion rate may distort the extent of the build-up. It is also true that civilian life in this period was stark and miserable and might offer fewer employment opportunities than the army—particularly now it was a standing army. Nevertheless, it would appear that by far the greatest incentive to recruitment was the opportunity for plunder which warfare then permitted.

Pillage—'Mademoiselle Picorée' in army slang—constituted, along with women and drink, the unofficial wages of war. It was a form of activity at which the authorities connived or even shared. For Richelieu, for example, plunder by the troops was to be tolerated if only because it comprised 'an encouragement for the soldiers to do better'.[5] It formed a sort of military cement which kept armies together especially during the long sieges with which the wars of the period were replete. It was, significantly, when the prospect of plunder disappeared that desertion rates were liable to rise. Theft and violent crime in the towns, banditry and highway-robbery in the hills might offer alternative forms of subsistence and enrichment in which both officers and men could deploy their martial arts.

The perpetual financial embarrassment of the government in the early-seventeenth century helped to generalise the practice of plunder. A single delay in state income from taxes or the borrowing process—a tax-revolt, for example, or an unexpected piece of financial jiggerypokery—could trigger off a failure of supply which left the armies in the field little option but to live off their wits. Louis XIV's great military engineer Vauban, for example, could remember going three weeks in the field in his younger days without a single food convoy reaching his detachment. In such circumstances, plunder was an unavoidable necessity. It mattered little whether the indigenous population was friend or foe. Although it was desirable that the troops should, in the current military jargon, 'maintain themselves at the expense of the enemy', hungry soldiers were likely to pillage French peasants as cruelly and mercilessly as they might German, Italian or Spanish ones.

Open looting was only the least organised of a whole spectrum of techniques by which the army extracted its means of subsistence from the civilian population. Although no one—even their officers—could count themselves immune from the troops' penchant for pillage, it was usually the least privileged and therefore most defenceless part of the civilian population who suffered most from military depredations. It was they who, in the first place, paid the lion's share of the taxes which went to support the newly-expanded army. They also bore the brunt of troop billeting. In the absence of centrally-administered barracks or garrisons, troops were billeted on private households which were obliged by law to provide shelter, bedding, food, cooking utensils, heating, lighting and salt. This was an extremely heavy burden—more than one authority accounted it as even heavier than the conventional tax burden. It could drag on for months, moreover, when a detachment was 'wintering' in a region awaiting the opening of the campaigning season in spring. Besides the statutory obligations of the civilian hosts, the latter also had to bear with the whims and petty violence of their uninvited armed guests. Immediate gratification did not exhaust the appetite of the troops for pillage. Camp-followers and military suppliers acted as middle-men in the creation of markets for booty. Treasures, foodstuffs, livestock, farm equipment, even prisoners and civilians held to ransom—all was grist to the booty mill. Transmuted into cash, such spoils allowed the formation of private capital which, provided the soldier was provident and that he survived his war days, might do something to compensate for the rigours of military life. Helpful in this respect too was the so-called 'Contribution System' from which the men benefited. This glorified system of 'protection money', already exploited by Portuguese commanders in the Indian Ocean in the sixteenth century, had been popularised in Europe in the 1620s and 1630s by the great German mercenary commander Wallenstein. Under its provisions a town or village agreed to levy a sum with which to purchase from passing troops an exemption from direct plunder.

The prevalence of plunder was not of course new. Its precepts and practices had long been codified: there was little that the Italian Renaissance *condottiere* or his overseas equivalent, the Portuguese or Spanish conquistador, had not devised before the French line regiment of the Thirty Years War. What was new, however, was the scale of the impact which the sprawling and decentralised new armies could make on civilian populations. The strain was all the greater where the men sought enrichment as well as subsistence. In addition, the beleaguered, over-taxed and ill-treated agricultural producer had to contend with the often desperate violence and criminality of huge numbers of camp-followers in the train of any army. Ex-soldiers and deserters in particular formed a marginal and rootless element in war zones whose lawlessness repressive government legislation vainly attempted to curb. The cumulated sum of war damage could thus be considerable. Population losses—in a labour-intensive agricultural system, a rough and ready quantitative index of minimum damage—were often sizeable. The presence of royal armies in the Paris region during the Fronde caused the reduction of the indigenous population by about a fifth. Lorraine was even worse affected: Jacques Callot, the artist of horrors of early seventeenth century warfare, was a Lorrainer and Saint Vincent de Paul used the area as a laboratory for his charitable experiments in the 1630s and early 1640s. Certain areas there and in neighbouring Franche-Comté lost between two-thirds and three-quarters of their population during the course of the Thirty Years War, and the traumatic war experiences marked a profound caesura in the social and economic development of both provinces.

It was thus little wonder that the mere arrival of troops in an area could trigger off a mass exodus of frightened peasants. The numerous popular revolts of the period also bear witness to a less resigned form of resentment against the military and the state that it underpinned. Whatever the determination of rebels, however, the huge and undisciplined army made a very effective policing agency. Indeed, the very threat of the appearance of troops was on occasion enough to induce spontaneous docility in populations angry with tax innovations.

3. THE RATIONALE OF STATE CENTRALISATION

In spite of the evident advantages of having the army, through widespread plundering and through its more licit tax-extractive activities, pay for its own upkeep, there eventually came a point at which the operations of the ill-disciplined military seemed self-defeating. Governments increasingly receptive to mercantilistic arguments, for example, began to realise that the army, by crippling the subsistence-oriented economy of the majority of Frenchmen, was killing the goose that laid the golden eggs. If the fighting strength of the state really did depend, as the mercantilists suggested, upon the solidity of its financial and economic institutions, then it was crucial that these institutions be properly protected and nurtured. This was particularly true after the signing of peace with the Spanish in 1659. Peace put an end to the continued possibility of living at the expense of the enemy and highlighted the need for the development of more rational forms of exploitation of the nation's resources.

There were moreover powerful military arguments in favour of closer state controls over the kind of wildcat private enterprise which had dominated military institutions in the early seventeenth century. Failures of discipline and supply had on occasion reduced the effectiveness of the army in the field. As Richelieu learned to his cost,

'History knows more armies ruined by want and disorder than by the efforts of their enemies'.[6]

In the late 1630s, the young Turenne had kept the French army intact on the German front only by selling off his family pewter and placing his personal credit at the disposal of his army's suppliers. When the state's cheques bounced, the military machine could falter. The collapse of France's expedition in the Valtelline in

1637, for example, was directly linked to a delay in levying a forced loan on French towns. A question-mark also came to hang over the customary toleration of indiscriminate plundering. On frequent occasions—most notoriously in the indiscipline which French troops were to display in the invasion of the Palatinate in 1689—plunder revealed itself less as a cohesive element among the troops than as a military solvent. The growth in the size of armies also placed too heavy a load on many areas where it proved simply impossible to extract sufficient to feed the troops. This in turn necessitated sending men further and further afield on foraging expeditions. When times were hard, this was tantamount to encouraging desertion. High desertion rates could not be tolerated in a period in which discipline and training on the field of battle seemed the passport to military success. The growing facility which generals after Gustavus Adolphus displayed in handling large numbers of men on the battlefield, the intensification of fire-power as a result of improvements in firearm technology and the growing prevalence of linear tactical formations on the battlefield all placed a premium on having an army which was not only large but was also sufficiently well-drilled to obey orders swiftly and unflinchingly. Trained and battle-hardened troops became a much sought-after item of military hardware. The master-tactician of eighteenth-century warfare, the Marshal de Saxe, was indeed to maintain, as a logical consequence of this, that the sign of truly intelligent generalship was to go through one's entire military career without fighting a single battle. As he advised on another occasion:

> 'It is better to put off the attack for several days than to expose oneself to losing rashly a single grenadier: he has been twenty years in the making'.[7]

Increasingly, therefore, military requirements were for a better trained and more well-disciplined soldier—of a type which only the state had the resources or indeed the incentive to create.

From about the middle of the seventeenth century, other factors were favouring the limitation of private enterprise within the army and the increase of state intervention in all spheres of military administration. Any state—and *a fortiori* a supposedly absolutist one—requires its orders to be obeyed. To the extent therefore that many of the reforms aimed merely to correct abuses, there was an inbuilt bias towards centralisation once the over-arching authority of the state was better established—as was the case from the personal reign of Louis XIV onwards. Military reform could also have salutary political consequences. Closer controls over the noble officer corps, for example, helped defuse the constitutional and political threat which, as the Fronde demonstrated, independently-minded and discontented grandees still posed the state. Questions of finance also lay close to the heart of the government's thinking on the issue of military reform. It could scarcely escape attention that under the old scheme of things, the pockets of colonels, captains and contractors were being lined at the direct expense of the state treasury. It was symptomatic of the general drift of reform that the so-called

'Contribution System' was not done away with but was now run by the government bureaucracy rather than by commanders in the field. The state was not against fleecing enemy populations; but it wished to end arbitrary plundering done on home soil, and to ensure that the state took the biggest cut of any proceeds.

4. THE FORMATION OF THE STATE BUREAUCRACY

The tightening of state control over the military establishment would have been unthinkable without the formation of the parallel institutions characteristic of the absolutist state. The colossal sums of money required for the state to prosecute warfare on a regular basis and on a new and massive scale had been organised, initially at least, by a formidable array of emergency measures, whose general effect had been the delegation of powers. In much the same way that the new army had been recruited and supplied largely by private enterprise, so, for example, direct taxes were placed in the hands of *officiers*, officials who purchased their posts and even, on payment of an annual sum known as the *paulette*, could dispose of them as pieces of private property; while indirect taxes were farmed out to similarly independent *traitants* and *partisans*. That the ranks of the new bureaucracy were frequently called upon to place their personal credit at the disposal of the state merely typified the amalgam of ingenuity and desperation which constituted French financial policy in this critical period. It could not, however, obscure the problems of central control which the sprawling new bureaucracy posed.

Much of the administrative machinery introduced in the early seventeenth century remained more or less intact down to the end of the Ancien Régime. With only very limited financial resources at its disposal, for example, the state simply could not have afforded to have bought itself out of its dependence on the prodigious numbers of venal officials in the new bureaucracy—any more, indeed, than it dared risk alienating the nobility by drumming them out of the officer corps in the new army. In order to check and counteract the centrifugal forces which the state had unleashed within its own administration, however, the monarchy began to develop the system of *commissaires*. These were royal officials appointed by the crown for specific tasks and their commissions were revocable at will. The *Intendant*, the best-known of all the types of *commissaires*, came to represent the very quintessence of strong central control. In particular, the *Intendants de police, justice et finances* appointed eventually to every *généralité* acted as the 'administrative factotum'[8] of the crown, supervising, controlling and where necessary duplicating the activities of the other layers of the bureaucracy and acting virtually as royal viceroy to each province.

It was eloquent of the blend of military and civilian functions which the absolutist monarchy achieved that the *Intendants* played an important role too in supervising and facilitating the expansion of the army. Down to 1789, for example, they assisted in recruitment, organised the militia, supervised troop accommodation, controlled a number of other ancillary services and generally oversaw relations between soldiers and civilians. From the late 1630s too, a number of *Intendants aux armées*—like the *Intendants* assigned to the provinces, directly responsible to the crown—were created to supervise the munitions, logistics and financing of the armies to which they were attached. They checked on all financial transactions, arbitrated in disputes, investigated the dealings of military suppliers and generally attended to the needs of the army. It was very much as a result of the activities of the *Intendants aux armées* that the most flagrant abuses of the military suppliers and contractors—'those colossal cheats', in Richelieu's acerbic phrase[9]—were stopped. The *Intendants* also had a strategic role vis-à-vis the military high command, for they were briefed to ensure that orders emanating from Paris were properly observed. Aristocratic commanders regarded it almost as a derogation of noble status to defer to orders which proceeded from a civilian bureaucracy in the capital: 'Allez vous faire f.....', one commander told a hapless official brutally, 'avec vos f..... ordres'.[10] Curbing the aristocratic *morgue* of the generals was not an easy task and disputes were frequent.

That the bureaucracy was ultimately able to impose its will upon obstreperous field commanders owed much to the character and abilities of successive heads of the war department which had sprung up to organise the war effort in the early seventeenth century. First Sublet de Noyers (from 1637 to 1643), one of Richelieu's favoured *créatures*, then Michel Le Tellier (1643 to 1666) followed by his son Louvois (1666 to 1691) were bureaucrats of exceptional administrative gifts. They were not slow to invoke the authority of ministers and even of the king himself in order to establish their dominance over the high command. In this struggle, they were considerably aided by the crown's suppression of a number of high military posts each of whose incumbents could use his power, in the words of Louis XIV, to make himself 'more master than the king himself of the principal strength of the state'.[11] In 1626 Richelieu, acutely aware of the imposing power-base which high military dignitaries could establish through their control over place and patronage had abolished the post of *Connétable*, formerly supreme commander of the land forces. At about the same time he also neutralised the *Connétable's* naval equivalents, the *Amiral* and the *Grand Général des Galères*. Early in his personal reign, Louis XIV went on to abolish the similarly prestigious posts of *Colonel-général de l'Infanterie* and *Colonel-général de la Cavalerie*, in 1661 and 1675 respectively.

By the time of Louis XIV's last campaigns, the anarchic, bloodyminded and entrepreneurial army officer of the time of Richelieu and Mazarin had given way to an altogether more docile and obedient character. The officer now accounted himself less an autonomous agent and more—though never entirely—a delegate of royal authority. This transformation was evidently part of the more general process by which the absolutist state subdued the nobility and defused the threat which they embodied to political stability. The bureaucracy contributed to the taming of the noble officer corps. After 1664, for example, the creation of non-venal posts of high command had the effect of encouraging promotion by merit. The corps might be as thoroughly noble in its social composition as ever—after all, the monarchy wanted to domesticate the nobility, not to liquidate them—but a hierarchy of talent now existed alongside the hierarchy of cash and prestige; and the patronage machines of regimental commanders had been seriously weakened. Cadet schools instituted by Louvois encouraged the idea that the status of officer necessitated a degree of instruction. The in-service training in which certain regiments, especially those of the royal household, specialised, made them seedbeds of officers for the rest of the army. By the early eighteenth century too, arrangements were being made for the more technical military professions such as artillery officers and engineers. The art of war was on its way to becoming, for the officers, a branch of a body of learning dispensed by state-controlled agencies. The officer corps thus illustrated particularly well the absolutist precept that the nobility could retain their primacy within society at the cost of the repression of their instincts and an acceptance of the framework of social and political power erected by the state.

5. THE BUREAUCRATISATION OF THE ARMY: SUPPLIES, RECRUITMENT, MILITARY 'WELFARE'

By exerting more rigorous and exacting supervision over the activities of its military subordinates, the state greatly circumscribed the extent and the effects of decentralisation inherent in the army of Richelieu's time. It acted further in this direction, moreover, by seeking to extend control over areas of administration formerly in the hands of colonels, captains and contractors. Not content, in other words, with overseeing the activities of its servants, the state set out to supplant them and to build up a less mediated, more direct relationship with the common soldier. Arms and ammunition, for example, which had previously been charged for out of wages or on the accounts of commanders, were gradually standardised and became a state concern. After 1718, government-sponsored arms factories were producing to order; and after 1727 arms were provided *gratis* by the state. Uniforms, which strictly speaking had not existed prior to Louis XIV's personal rule, were now generalised at the state's expense. Furthermore, the War Department came to run a proficient system of magazines from which supplies could be drawn. This system, tried out by Le Tellier in the 1640s and perfected by Louvois, did not altogether put an end to armies living off the land. The troops still aimed to live 'at the expense of the enemy'. But the state now supervised and encouraged the 'Contribution System' in preference to indiscriminate plundering; while the magazines supplemented resources appropriated in this way and, during sieges and while the army was on home territory, made the recourse to plunder unnecessary.[12]

Recruitment was a further sphere of military administration in which the central government expanded its role at the expense of troop commanders. Foreign mercenaries, drawn from the poorer regions of Europe such as parts of Ireland, Scotland, Switzerland and Germany, continued to be drawn on; indeed in the eighteenth century they probably comprised a quarter of the army's strength in peace-time and up to a third in time of war. The continuing soundness in the logic behind their use was underlined by Marshal de Saxe:

> 'A German in the army serves us as three soldiers: he spares France one, he deprives our enemies of one and he serves us as one.'[13]

The practice was now, however, for these mercenaries to serve under French or French-trained officers rather than under their native commanders. By mid eighteenth century, the age of the old mercenary captain was long past; and mercenary troops were subject to the same bureaucratic controls as French troops.

There were other ways too in which the state stimulated recruitment. Indeed it was obliged to make moves in this direction: the old practice of seigneurs recruiting the peasants on their estates proved increasingly unreliable, while the imposition of restraints on plunder effectively dissolved the most potent incentive to recruitment of the early seventeenth-century soldier. A combination of all available methods was necessary to provide the two million men who entered the army in the first two-thirds of the eighteenth century. The enlistment bounty rose faster in this time than the cost of living—a sure sign of the state's difficulties in this sphere. In 1688, a national conscript militia had been formed, members of which were incorporated into the regular forces in time of war. Administrative arrangements were periodically made to facilitate entry into the army of all sorts of social outcasts such as beggars, vagrants, prisoners and orphans. After 1763, moreover, in the interests of greater efficiency and standardisation, the state declared recruitment a royal monopoly and placed the whole system under close bureaucratic scrutiny for the first time.

The government also intervened more and more in the sphere of military hygiene and welfare which had in the past been almost exclusively the province of unit commanders. From the time of Richelieu onwards and particularly from the last decades of the seventeenth century, governments spent increasingly large sums on the provision of regimental medical staff, field hospitals, garrison infirmaries and chaplaincies. Copious military welfare legislation in the eighteenth century attested the government's continuing concern in this sphere. In 1708, for example, 50 royal military hospitals were created and their number was added to over the course of the century. A hospital inspectorate was established and more constructive policies towards hospital and regimental hygiene were adopted. Doctors and surgeons attached to the army proliferated and were, in the medical profession as a whole, among the most practically orientated and theoretically advanced. After 1775, for example, clinical teaching methods—unknown in the majority of civilian hospitals—were introduced in a number of military hospitals.

Government military welfare measures were often adduced as evidence of the benevolent paternalism allegedly characteristic of Bourbon absolutism. Yet they had a pragmatic edge. The greater importance of discipline and training in warfare had made the hardened man-of-war a valuable commodity for which the state was willing to pay dearly. It thus behoved the government to nurture the object of its investment. As Richelieu, architect of many of the later welfare policies, had perceived, 'Two thousand soldiers leaving a hospital cured and in a certain sense broken into their profession' were infinitely preferable to 'six thousand new recruits'.[14] Moreover, a show of concern for the welfare of the rank and file bolstered morale as well as strengthening effectives. Mazarin grasped this point particularly well in one of his administrative letters:

'I believe we must give priority to everything which is necessary for hospitals. Besides the fact that charity requires it, there is nothing which produces a better effect in armies than that the sick and wounded are looked after.'[15]

There was a similarly sternly practical intent in the creation in 1670 of the *Hôtel des Invalides*, a retreat for retired soldiers. Although the organisers and historians of this institution presented it as an example of bountiful royal grace and favour, the *Invalides* was repressive as well as charitable in design. It not only rewarded the meritorious veteran; it also aimed to keep off the street the impoverished and desperate ex-soldier whose activities threatened property and social stability. Such an idea typified the government's social policy in the second half of the seventeenth century, which aimed to place social problem groups within special institutions where they could not harm society at large. In the same way as, after 1656, the pauper and beggar would be confined in the *hôpital général*, or the gypsy (after 1682), the prostitute (after 1684) or the Protestant (after 1685) could find themselves shut away in penal and workhouse-like institutions, so from the last decades of the seventeenth century the ex-soldier, whether disabled or able-bodied, would be likely on completion of his service to find himself placed within the *Invalides*.

While the *Invalides* served to insulate the retired soldier from civilian society, the barracks came to perform a similar function for the serving soldier. Barracks rendered largely redundant the violently extractive relationship between soldiers and civilians under the old system of billeting. Within them, the needs of the men could be met by bureaucratic arrangement and not left to private initiative. Significantly, it was a report in 1691 which stated that pillaging by billeted troops in the Maine and Orléanais regions was rendering the local population incapable of paying their taxes which led the government to place its crack troops in barracks. The movement towards barracks which got under way in the next decades was facilitated by the emergence of repressive agencies which rendered the policing function of the regular army less crucial. In the 1690s, police bodies were created in most major towns with powers modelled on those enjoyed since 1667 by the *Lieutenant général de police* in Paris; and in 1720, the *maréchaussée*, the para-military mounted police force responsible for the maintenance of law and order in the countryside, was extensively reformed. A royal decree in 1719 stipulated that barracks were to be constructed in towns on all major roads along which troops would be likely to pass. By 1742, over 300 towns contained barracks and by 1775 some 200,000 men were housed in them.

The concentration of troops in barracks also facilitated the instilling of the discipline and self-control which tactical changes had rendered so important on the field of battle. The barrack was a kind of discipline factory. At its most efficient, as with industrial production, greater concentration allowed a much higher degree of control and coordination and an inbuilt bias towards technical improvements; at very least the barracks helped keep in check the desertion which was still the running sore of every Ancien Régime army. It encouraged too a regimental *esprit de corps.* The state poured forth an enormous volume of military regulations in the late seventeenth and eighteenth centuries with the aim of producing, as one manual put it, 'the perfections of the cloister'.[16] Military discipline became in this period not merely a structured and all-encompassing way of life but even a particular mode of bodily comportment: the pace was to be brisk, the head held high, the chest out, the moustache trimmed and shaped, and so on.

The generalisation of disciplinary values among the troops was a development which was popular with the civilian population. Whereas in the early seventeenth century the very mention of troops passing had been enough to provoke a rush for the protection of the woods or of the local château, with much locking up of wives and daughters, by the late eighteenth century, in contrast, civilians were as likely to turn up and cheer as the gallant soldiery marched by with their bright uniforms to the regular beat of the drum and the sound of military music. This greater acceptance of—even fondness for—the common soldier owed much also to the fact that, unlike the previous century, the eighteenth century saw very little fighting or civil strife on French soil. This, along with barracks, the *Invalides,* the imposition of discipline and the growth of state controls over military subsistence distanced the army physically from the rest of society.

6. THE LOT OF THE COMMON SOLDIER

If, as a result of this constellation of changes, the army was infinitely more professional than before, and much less feared and hated by the civilian population, the soldiers themselves did not necessarily approve of the resultant changes in their life-style. The reforms aimed to achieve efficiency, not well-being; they treated the men as unreasoning objects of administration rather than as human beings with flesh and blood under their military uniforms.

One of military life's traditional compensations upon which military regulations now frowned, for example, was sex. Camp-following prostitutes had been an accepted part of the baggage-train of every European army in the early seventeenth century, when military theorists calculated that they should be allowed to flourish at the rate of four to every hundred men. By the end of the century, however, in France as elsewhere in Europe, 'we find' (to use the clipped Germanic English of the historian Fritz Redlich) 'a policy of restricting soldiers' copulations'.[17] A series of laws passed between 1684 and 1687, aimed apparently both to arrest the spread of syphilis among the troops and to make them more willing to risk death in battle by giving them less to live for, stipulated that any prostitute found within two leagues of a military camp was to have her nose and ears split. Military regulations at about the same time actively discouraged the marriage of troops. More populationist military policies towards the end of the eighteenth century caused a relaxation of the ban on marriage. Prostitutes were still frowned on however—by the authorities at least. If the laws of 1684 and 1687 were no longer applied in all their grisly detail, new regulations in 1768 stated that any prostitute found consorting with the troops should be imprisoned. In 1781, any soldier who caught venereal disease more than three (!) times was obliged to spend an extra two years service within the army.

The example of sex is a good illustration of the fact that the professionalisation of the army did not necessarily improve the perceived well-being of the common soldier. True, soldiers were now relatively protected from being swindled by their commanders, and the worst excesses of the military suppliers had also been checked. True, too, wages were now paid with greater regularity and exactitude. Nevertheless, all was far from rosy. The state's financial position never permitted it to do without private contractors, and inefficiency and corruption could still reappear in the supply services, especially when the system was strained by wartime conditions. If wages rose over the course of the century, prices rose faster. With the higher echelons of command fiercely competed for by nobles and bourgeois, chances of promotion must have remained slim. Moreover, although more officers were found urging humane treatment of their men, the aura of success attaching to Frederick the Great's Prussian army meant that the imported codes of discipline were Spartan at best, Draconian at worst.

Despite the state's elaboration of wide-ranging ancillary and welfare services, therefore, the soldier's lot was still a far from happy one. His living conditions were often little short of abysmal. If uniforms were now issued free of charge, it was widely acknowledged that they were more suited to the parade-ground than the battlefield or military camp. Moreover, in war-time they were frequently in short supply. The old military diseases—apart from plague—were still rife. Indeed, there is a strong case for arguing that the move into barracks made the troops more susceptible than before to 'crowd diseases' such as typhus, typhoid fever and dysentery. Certainly, conditions in barracks could be most insanitary. The constructions were often jerry-built and were insufficiently heated or ventilated; overcrowding was always a problem; and even at the best of times the men slept two to a bed. Life on campaign continued to be brimful of miseries and privations. 'Once the rainy season has arrived', commented Marshal de Saxe of the general conditions of the common soldier, 'his head is seldom dry. As for his feet, it cannot be doubted that his stockings, shoes and feet all rot together.'[18] Hospital care for the ailing was unimpressive, especially in time of war. Health care was often hardest hit by cash shortages and the corruption of military suppliers. The Marquis de Feuquières commented following the War of Austrian Succession, for example, that

> 'The roguery committed in the hospitals is limitless. Greed for profit induces the entrepreneurs to act beyond all consideration of humanity.'[19]

So deep-dyed were corruption and abuse in the military hospitals, indeed, that regulations on the eve of the Revolution envisaged the total closure of the vast majority and their replacement by regimental infirmaries which would, it was hoped, prove less of a health risk than the old hospitals.

The now accepted restrictions on plunder also severely reduced a component of the soldier's income which had allowed his seventeenth century forebear a chance of emerging from his army days with money in his pocket. From the ranks, greater state control over the 'Contribution System', for example, must have seemed tantamount to forcible expropriation. Denied the opportunity of engaging in the petty entrepreneurial activities of appropriation and disposal of loot, and more dependent than before on his wage, the soldier had become proletarianised. He was more likely to end his soldiering days destitute. The economy found it difficult to absorb soldiers especially in the mass demobilisations following the end of a war when up to 100,000 men might suddenly be thrown onto the labour market. It was symptomatic of the problem for social order which the ex-soldier comprised that the main bouts of government legislation against criminal vagrancy occurred in the years following the end of major wars: 1719, 1720 and 1724 after the demobilisations of 1717 and 1718; 1750, after the War of Austrian Succession (1740–1748); and 1764 and 1767 after the Seven Years' War (1756–1763). Aware of the social threat that the demobilised soldier represented, conscious of welfare provisions as a possible incentive to recruitment and somewhat influenced too by the voguish philanthropy current towards the end of the Ancien Régime, the state turned its mind to the care of the retiring soldier. The Order of Saint Louis, established in 1693, provided pensions for valorous retired officers; the *Invalides* was expanded so that by the end of the Ancien Régime its numbers exceeded 30,000 men; and soldiers with very long terms of service were, from the 1760s onwards, awarded a pension as of right. As the prelude to the French Revolution was to reveal, however, all this was to a certain extent only papering over widening cracks.

7. THE AFTERMATH OF THE SEVEN YEARS' WAR:
REFORMS AND TENSIONS

Military welfare measures illustrate the wish of the monarchy to use every means at hand to build and maintain a large army of well disciplined career professionals. Yet the proof of the pudding lies in the eating: the miseries of the everyday life of the common soldier highlighted the insufficiences of the state's commitment in this sphere. Such failings remained relatively masked as long as the French kept their reputation as having the most formidable army in Europe. The stunning military defeats which they endured at the hands of Prussia in the Seven Years' War, however, provided a rude and unwelcome shock to a complacent military establishment. Besides contributing to the ruination of the state's finances under the pressure of colossal military expenditure, the war thus called into question if not the rationale at least the effectiveness of the state's measures to achieve the full professionalisation of its army. There followed a spate of reforms aimed at rectifying matters by increased state control. In the darkening social and political atmosphere of the final decades of the Ancien Régime, however, with state bankruptcy threatening on the horizon, attempts to ensure the further professionalisation of the army only brought to the surface of military life a host of complexes, strains and resentments whose consequences were to transcend the inner workings of the military machine.

Much of the state's attention was now focussed on streamlining the officer corps. Though far more ready to accept the structures of discipline and training imposed by the state than their pre-Fronde ancestors, most nobles still aspired to maintain their corps—which the Seven Years' War had nevertheless revealed as riddled with privilege, private fiefs and petty vanities—as a preeminently noble preserve. Over-zealous reform in this sphere touched many raw nerves. The phasing out of the evidently unprofessional practice of purchase of commissions after 1776, for example, aroused the hostility of potential buyers. Preference now given to nobles who had been presented at court profoundly irritated ambitious commoners and country gentry who aspired to posts of high command. Commoners and the newly-ennobled were also upset by the notorious Ségur ordinance of 1781. This regulation which attempted to restrict entry to the officer corps to individuals with four generations of nobility in their families typified the thinking behind much of the reform movement which was that, although the occasional gifted commoner might make a good officer, it was above all noble stock which produced the required military virtues. All officers, whether nobles or not, were, however, likely to be dismayed by government measures which, in the interests of economy, abolished many posts and even disbanded companies. The state was evidently finding it increasingly difficult to afford a large standing army. From the point of view of the officers, however, cheeseparing of this sort reduced career prospects. Finally, many officers were to feel that the government's attack in the late 1780s on the fiscal privileges of the class from which most derived was unconstitutional and placed them outside their oath of loyalty. The common front which many made, between 1786 and 1788, with their noble *confrères* in the Assembly of Notables, the *Parlements* and the Assembly of the Clergy revealed the failure of the apparent professionalisation of the army officer corps over the course of the seventeenth and eighteenth centuries to expunge basic class solidarities.

The picture was much the same at the other end of the social spectrum. For the army rank and file, the reforms of the last decade of the Ancien Régime consisted in a further attempt to improve efficiency rather than living conditions. The new Prussian-style disciplinary code was particularly deeply hated. The deterioration of morale among officers may also, in turn, have affected the common soldiers. In addition, the troops came to resent the way in which, at the height of the social and economic crisis of the late 1780s, they were used as a policing agency to quell grain riots and other disturbances. This policy in fact probably intensified the sympathy which the soldiers felt for the peasantry and the urban labouring classes, from whose ranks they were themselves drawn. Certainly by early 1789 there were substantial portions of the army on whose obedience the king could no longer count. It was highly appropriate that, on 14 July 1789, the fall of the Bastille, supreme symbol of the naked coercive power of French absolutism, should be engineered by dissident soldiers.

By the end of the Ancien Régime, the structural limits of the policies of centralised state control over military institutions and the insulation of the army from the rest of society were seemingly being reached. The standing army forged in the wake of the Military Revolution had, it is true, permitted successive Bourbon rulers to sustain a permanent challenge to European hegemony. This was only achieved, however, at the cost of financial strains which tore the state asunder in the 1780s. Moreover, dependence on the nobility—one, if not *the,* major bulwark of absolutist rule—for the staffing of the officer corps imposed certain limitations on the professionalisation and centralisation which were the state's constant aim. The perceived need to revitalise the officer corps after the disasters of the Seven Years' War meant the monarchy overstepping the long-drawn and tacitly-agreed line dividing state interest from noble privilege. The involvement of the officer corps—and, in a different but no less important way, the rank and file—in the outbreak of the Revolution showed that, despite the instilling of disciplinary and professional values, soldiers were not the mindless automata which the military machine required but self-interested and reasoning members of a wider community. The events of the Revolutionary decade were to underline this fact even more spectacularly. In wider perspective too, the secure position of military institutions at the heart of the absolutist state helped produce a fatal unevenness in the development of the French armed forces. In particular the failure to build up a strong navy cost the French dear. Just as the unimpressive performances of the regular troops in the Seven Years' War revealed deficiencies in the army's vaunted 'professionalism', so too overseas losses in the same war showed the inability of an army alone to achieve a sound basis for international dominance in the expanding mercantile economy. By the late eighteenth century, the French recipe for military strength and state power which, since the mid seventeenth century, other states had found so attractive, was made to seem outmoded by another, more naval, more mercantile power: England.

Notes

1. For the historiographical debate on the Military Revolution, see the introduction to M. Duffy, (ed.) *The Military Revolution and the State: Exeter Studies in History 1* (Exeter University, 1980).

2. For a table of increases in army size, G. Parker, 'The "Military Revolution", 1560–1660—a myth?', *Journal of Modern History* (1976), p. 206 (above, Table 2.1). For France, cf. the additional materials in G. d'Avenel, *Richelieu et la monarchie absolue* (4 vols., Paris, 1884–1890), pp. 42–43; and A. Babeau, *La Vie militaire sous l'Ancien Régime* (2 vols., 1889–1890), i, p. 14 n.

3. R. Mandrou, *Louis XIV en son temps, 1661–1715* (Paris, 1973), p. 229.

4. Cited in G. d'Avenel, *op. cit.*, iii, p. 148.

5. D'Avenel, *op. cit.*, iii, p. 99.

6. Richelieu, *Testament politique*, critical edition edited by L. André (Paris, 1947), p. 480.

7. Cited by X. Auduoin, *Histoire de l'administration de la guerre*, (Paris, 1811), p. 232.

8. W. O. Doyle, *The Old European Order, 1660–1800* (Oxford, 1978), p. 253.

9. D'Avenel, *op. cit.*, p. 133.

10. *Ibid.*, p. 56.

11. Cited in M. Marion, *Dictionnaire des institutions de la France aux XVIIe. siècle* (Paris, reprint, 1968), p. 111.

12. See the discussion of this important aspect of military administration in M. van Creveld, *Supplying War: logistics from Wallenstein to Patton* (Cambridge, 1977), pp. 23–26.

13. Cited in A. Corvisier, *L'Armée française de la fin du XVIIe. siècle au ministère de Choiseul. Le soldat* (2 vols., Paris, 1964), i, p. 260.

14. Cited in A. Cabanès, *Chirurgiens et blessés à travers l'histoire: des origines à la Croix-rouge* (Paris, 1912), p. 167 n.

15. Cited in J. Des Cilleuls, 'Le Service de santé en campagne aux armées de l'Ancien Régime', *Revue historique de l'Armée* (1950), p. 7.

16. Boussanelle, cited in M. Foucault, *Discipline and Punish. The Birth of the Prison*, English translation (Harmondsworth, 1979), p. 150.

17. F. Redlich, *The German Military Enterpriser and his Work-force. A study in European economic and social history* (2 vols., Wiesbaden, 1964), p. 208.

18. *Ibid.*, p. 226.

19. Cited in A. Cabanès, *op. cit.*, p. 256.

7

The *trace italienne* and the Growth of Armies: The French Case[1]

JOHN A. LYNN

STALWART STONE SENTINELS guarded the borders of seventeenth-century France. An interlocking system of strongholds barred her frontiers, particularly to the northeast, where the great engineer Vauban designed a double line of fortresses and fortified cities across traditional invasion routes. French fortifications proved their value in the wars of Louis XIV and saved revolutionary Paris a century later. But did these grim giants simply shelter France, or did they also shape her? The noted historian Geoffrey Parker argues that because the attack and defense of the new style of bastioned fortress demanded huge numbers of troops, European states increased the size of their armies to immense proportions. To take Parker's assertion one step further, military expansion then compelled states to claim the authority and develop the institutions to marshal the vast resources demanded by gargantuan forces—*voilà* Absolutism. This article tests the theory that fortifications drove up army size in France, with all the attendant consequences.

Over the past decade and a half, Geoffrey Parker has repeatedly accounted for the growth of European armies in the early modern period by reference to the creation and spread of a style of fortress created in Italy during the late fifteenth and early sixteenth centuries. This *trace italienne* employed the bastion to render fortifications far less vulnerable to armies equipped with the more plentiful and much improved artillery of the age. He first stated his thesis in a 1976 article, "The 'Military Revolution' 1560–1660—a Myth?," and recently up-dated it in his prize-winning volume, *The Military Revolution.*[2]

Parker defines the "military revolution" as a series of fundamental developments in weaponry, tactics, and institutions. "First, the improvements in artillery in the fifteenth century, both qualitative and quantitative, eventually transformed fortress design. Second, the increasing reliance on firepower in battle ... led not only to the eclipse of cavalry but to tactical arrangements that maximized the opportunities of giving fire. Moreover these new ways in warfare were accompanied by a dramatic increase in army size."[3] This is not the place to examine the tactical side of his theory, or, for that matter, the sticky questions of dating the transformation or of defining it as a revolution or merely as an evolution.

For Parker, the primacy of siege warfare practically defines the fully developed military revolution. When he asks the rhetorical question why did the military revolution come to different parts of Europe at different times, he replies: "The key variable appears to have been the presence or absence of the *trace italienne* in a given area, for where no bastions existed, wars of manoeuvre with smaller armies were still feasible."[4] And so he chases the *trace italienne* throughout Europe, and eventually throughout the world.

Fortresses drove up army size in two ways. In his earlier article, Parker stresses the huge numbers of troops required to besiege a fortress. Speaking of the Spanish in the 1530s, he argues that military expansion was "necessitated by the vast number of men required to starve out a town defended by the *trace italienne*."[5] In his later book, he emphasizes the need to garrison great lines of fortresses more than the need to starve out or storm individual works. Garrisons, by his account, consumed large numbers of men, indeed, roughly half the strength of armies.[6] In his words, "the greater part of military expenditure and military resources in every early modern state went not on offence but on defence."[7] Both of these arguments deserve consideration here.

Parker paints on a very broad canvas. Some critics have been equally ambitious; Bert Hall and Kelly DeVries globally reject the notion that fortresses compelled army expansion in their recent review of *The Military Revolution*.[8] However, the critique of Parker's thesis probably best functions on a state-by-state basis. Simon Adams has already disputed Parker's notions about military expansion and fortresses for sixteenth-century Spanish holdings.[9] Here I will examine the French case.

The immediate question at hand is to determine the degree to which the adoption of the *trace italienne* influenced the particular pattern of French military growth. From 1445 through the early seventeenth century, the manpower mobilized by the French monarchy for war remained surprisingly static. In wartime, the French put 30,000–60,000 men in the field. The long war with Spain that began in 1635 ushered in rapid expansion. Wartime highs approached 150,000 in the late 1630s, dipped to 134,000 during the brief and minor War of Devolution, soared once again to 279,000 for the Dutch War, and hit 400,000 for the last phase of the Nine Years' War and the War of the Spanish Succession.[10] During intervals of peace, 1445–1635, the French state maintained roughly 10,000 troops, at times keeping less and once jacking it up to 25,000 for a few years. Peacetime levels climbed to just over 70,000 in the 1660s, hitting 130–150,000 from the 1670s to the end of Louis XIV's rule. These are all paper figures, but if official figures are discounted to estimate the number of men actually present under arms, the increase over the course of the *grand siècle* is even more striking, since real troop strength corresponded more closely to regulation unit size under the Sun King than it had under his father.[11]

Behind a concern with the technical issues of defensive architecture and man-power stand fundamental questions about the influences that shaped French Absolutism. The seventeenth century stands out as the critical period of state formation in France. To be sure, the French began construction of their centralized, bureaucratic government before 1600. The work made notable progress, particularly from the mid-fifteenth through the mid-sixteenth centuries, but decades of religious warfare undermined much of what had been built. Under the direction of the Bourbons, old foundations had to be repaired and extended before their edifice of Absolutism could rise to define and confine an age.

War compelled the state to grow in power if it was not to perish. France's seventeenth-century conflicts became wars of attrition, during which the Bourbons fielded ever larger forces. In such contests, when victory depended on the ability to maintain huge armies in the field for years on end, resource mobilization held the key. A greater army demanded greater quantities of funds, food, and fodder, so the existing state apparatus scrambled to mobilize them. Despite its efforts, the state fell short of satisfying the army's appetite, and was forced into a turbulent but necessary transformation in order to muster and maintain its troops. The process brought into being the centralized, bureaucratic monarchy. Recent scholarship on state formation in early modern Europe recognizes this link between war and emerging Absolutism.[12]

Therefore to examine the expansion of the French army is to study one of the fundamental facts of the *grand siècle.* If Parker is correct, the implications of his assertions boggle the mind. If technological innovations in military architecture imposed greater armies on European states, and the challenge of maintaining those expanded forces compelled the adoption of Absolutism, then the *trace italienne* constituted the most important piece of military technology in modern European history, measured by its impact on society.

However, while I agree that army growth played a crucial role in state formation, I cannot wholly subscribe to Parker's thesis. To be specific, I reject Parker's earlier emphasis on the attack of fortresses in the *trace italienne,* although I find his later emphasis on garrison forces more convincing, at least in setting peacetime army strength.

THE GEOMETRY OF THE *TRACE ITALIENNE*

The relationship between the attack and defense of fortifications and the tremendous expansion of French military forces can best be addressed by examining the influence of seven variables in the formula of siege warfare: (1) the geometry of the *trace italienne;* (2) the length of lines of circumvallation; (3) the size of attacking and defending forces; (4) the cost of sieges in time and casualties; (5) the number of sieges undertaken; (6) the proportions of covering or relieving forces; and (7) the quantity of troops assigned to garrison duty.

Let us begin with a technical examination of geometry in the new style of fortifications. Parker insists that the spread of the *trace italienne* revolutionized warfare, rendering positional defense possible against the new cannon. Remember, a trace is a ground plan or outline—an aerial view of the fortification, as it were—which stresses the bastion. Fascinatingly intricate, indeed beautiful, the *trace italienne* as brought to its zenith by Vauban would seem to be a dominant piece of military technology.

Yet the trace possessed no special invulnerability, since a determined siege almost always resulted in the fall of the fortress. The great advantage of the new fortresses lay in the fact that they inflicted a great cost in time, materiel, and manpower on an enemy determined to take one in a formal siege. Reviewing the pattern of a siege, it began by investing the fortress and digging massive entrenched lines circling the entire fortress at a considerable distance from its walls. From these lines a series of zigzag approach trenches, parallels, and batteries moved closer and closer until the attacker breached the fortress wall and stormed the works.

During the last decades of the fifteenth century and the first of the sixteenth, Italians engineered defensive works that could both withstand bombardment by artillery and use gunfire effectively in their own defense—permit me to create my own term for their product, the "artillery fortress." One key to the new design was the bastion. While medieval square and round towers provided flanking positions from which to fire down on attackers before the main walls, they left "dead zones" in which attacking forces could shelter from defending fire at the base of such towers. The bastion, an arrowhead-shaped artillery tower, eliminated dead zones and allowed cannon and hand guns to sweep the ground in front of the walls (see Figure 7.1). While the first bastion design dates from the 1480s, it was the French invasion of Italy in 1494 and the wars that it precipitated that drove the adoption and improvement of the bastion.[13] The bastioned trace, or fortress plan, was so rooted in Italy, that it became known as the *trace italienne*. The first bastions, offspring of medieval towers, were rather small and built entirely of masonry. They projected at intervals from the walls, rather in the fashion of their ancestors. By the seventeenth century bastions had evolved into large, flattened structures built entirely of earth or of earth faced with stone or brick.

While the bastion was unquestionably a crucial development in fortress architecture, most historians have become seduced by it. More fundamental than the bastion were the walls themselves and the cannon that stood atop them. To be effective in the gunpowder environment of early modern warfare, defensive works had to: (1) protect the fortress from storm by infantry; (2) absorb bombardment without toppling or crumbling; (3) shelter the defenders from attacking fire, and (4) subject the attackers to effective artillery fire. The bastioned trace was abso-

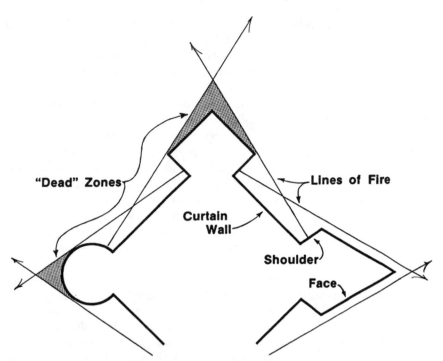

Figure 7.1 Advantages of the Bastion over Round and Square Towers.

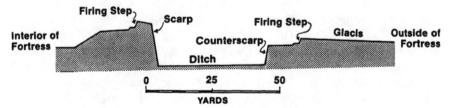

Figure 7.2 Cross-section of a Fortress Wall and Ditch, ca. 1700.

lutely essential only to the first of these requirements, resisting close-in attack by enemy infantry.

To prevent infantry from storming the fortress, either in a sudden coup de main or in a final coup de grâce of a formal siege, engineers designed a new style of wall, surrounded by ditches, unless the terrain provided better obstacles. (See Figure 7.2.) Height remained the best barrier, but the height of a medieval wall simply made it vulnerable, since it was usually too thin to resist the battering of artillery. By greatly thickening the wall and making it protrude less above ground level, military architects rendered it artillery resistant. Its function as a high barrier to infantrymen was preserved by surrounding it with a ditch. Thus in a sense, architects preserved the high wall by simply sinking it into the ground. The defenders atop the wall sheltered behind thick earthen ramparts, stout enough to protect them from musket and cannon balls. Just over the outside wall of the ditch, the counterscarp, further firing positions for infantry defended the fortress, and beyond these the ground sloped away in a glacis that provided infantry and artillery on the wall with the best possible fields of fire against attacking infantry.

The fact that defenders now fired from behind as much as twenty feet of earth and stone meant that they were masked from the ditch directly below them, and they could not shoot down into it without exposing themselves to enemy fire. Consequently, some firing platform had to project from the walls to flank the ditch. This brings us back to the bastion. By the seventeenth century it was a direct geometric necessity of the thicker walls of the now artillery-resistant walls. Bastions allowed defenders to sweep the ditch between them with flanking fire from cannon and musket. The arrowhead design of these structures themselves allowed gunfire from neighboring bastions to sweep the ditches before the faces of threatened bastions. Thus, the essential function of the seventeenth-century bastion was close-in defense of the ditch.

The massive earth-backed walls of the modern fortress provided excellent, stable positions for defensive artillery to answer the attacker's guns and drive off his infantry. The most effective defense of the artillery fortress was the fire of its own cannon. Far more than the bastion, the characteristics of artillery determined the patterns of siege warfare. Most importantly, siege operations began at such great distances from fortresses because of the range of artillery, not because of the projections of bastions. In a sense, as long as the modern wall cross-section was applied, a fortress could have been a simple square and it would have been just as effective at resisting and dueling with the enemy guns at a distance. So even if you accept the notion that the artillery fortress drove up army size, it was not simply the bastion, the *trace italienne,* that gave the fortress its power to resist attack and thus to call into existence greater armies to besiege it.

Perhaps bastions have seduced historians because in addition to sweeping the ditch, bastions also bristled with a fortress's main guns. Therefore, these structures encompassed all vital aspects of the artillery fortress. But functions must be separated. Ditch defense relied upon cannon firing from the shoulders of the bastion, probably the worst place for guns meant to force a besieging army to keep its distance. However, the batteries atop the walls of bastion faces effectively threatened besieging armies at long range. Such guns were not tied to close-in defense, and could almost as effectively have been stationed on the curtain walls between bastions.

THE LENGTH OF LINES OF CIRCUMVALLATION

When arguing that the attack of fortresses drove up army size, the determining factor is the fact that it took so many troops to hold the lines encircling a besieged town. Certainly this argument demands respect. At mid-century a formal siege called for lines of contravallation to confine and isolate the garrison, and several hundred yards further from the town, lines of circumvallation designed to shelter the besieging army from any relieving force. In the second half of the seventeenth century the use of lines of contravallation declined, but lines of circumvallation, the longer of the two, were still required. Such entrenchments commonly stretched for fifteen or twenty miles. The need to hold these lines with an adequate number of troops per mile of entrenchment determined the size of besieging armies. What was the relationship between the adoption of the *trace italienne* and the massive siege lines of early modern positional warfare?

The addition of bastions to older walls did render fortresses somewhat larger, and piling on additional embellishments, such as ravelins, hornworks, and crownworks, increased the effective circumference of fortifications even more. Did bigger, or more intricate, piles of masonry and earth themselves demand longer siege lines? No. A little geometry dispels this notion. The great Vauban insisted that lines must be dug no closer than fourteen or fifteen hundred toises from cannon of the enemy fortress.[14] A toise equals 2.14 yards, so Vauban believed that artillery could do some damage at a range of over a mile and a half. This range, not size of the fortress, exerted the greatest influence on the extent of lines.

Consider as an ideal case a completely symmetrical fortress of minimum size; a circle some 300 toises in diameter could encompass all its defensive works.[15] (See Figure 7.3.) To surround this small example of military architecture with lines of circumvallation at 1,500 toises distance would generate a circular trench line 3,300 toises in diameter, or nearly thirteen miles in circumference. Expand the fortress to cover a surface area ten times greater and maintain the textbook regularity of the walls. A circle 950 toises in diameter would now enclose all the bastions of this much greater fortress. Besiegers would have to maintain lines with a diameter of 3,950 toises to maintain proper distance. Such new siege lines would run fifteen miles, but that would amount to an increase of only 15 percent. Therefore, multiplying the size of the fortress tenfold only lengthened the line by a small fraction.

By this geometric logic, enlarging fortresses by the addition of bastions, or even the dramatic growth of cities and their encircling walls did not drive up army size. Lille provides an interesting case of considerable expansion. Louis XIV took Lille by siege in 1667, after which Vauban nearly doubled the size of its defenses. In addition, he buttressed the existing sections of wall with sophisticated outworks and a clever system of wet ditches and inundations. A generation later, in 1708, the allies besieged it again. The 1667 siege involved lines of over fifteen miles, and the 1708 siege lines of nearly twenty miles.[16] This was a real increase but one far less than the expansion of the city itself or, for that matter, of the French army in the same period. In fact the number of troops employed in the siege was only slightly larger than that which surrounded Lille in 1667, 35,000 in the later siege as opposed to 30,000 in the earlier.[17]

John A. Lynn

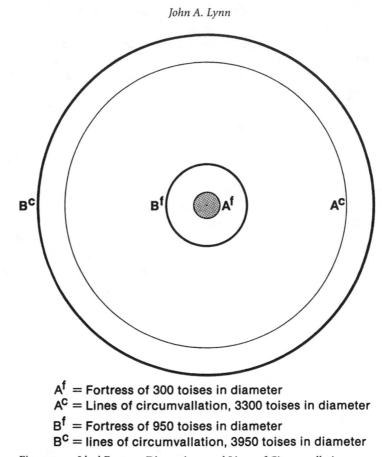

A^f = Fortress of 300 toises in diameter
A^c = Lines of circumvallation, 3300 toises in diameter
B^f = Fortress of 950 toises in diameter
B^c = lines of circumvallation, 3950 toises in diameter

Figure 7.3   Ideal Fortress Dimensions and Lines of Circumvallation.

THE SIZE OF ATTACKING AND DEFENDING FORCES

This brings us to the central concern, not the siege lines themselves but the number of men who occupied them. Vauban argued that the minimum reasonable force required to hold even short lines of circumvallation was about twenty thousand men.[18] To do so with less spread the men too thin. The attacking forces in the two sieges of Lille fell within parameters he could accept. But Lille is only one case, and to carry the argument further requires some historical data on the size of attacking and defending forces in actual sieges. The sample of 135 sieges dating from 1445 to 1714, collected in the appended Table of French Sieges, provides the basis for some judgments. Granting that pegging numbers in early modern history presents many risks and pitfalls, here the pattern of numbers matters more than any individual case.

The figures presented in the Table of French Sieges represent a reasonable sampling of available scholarship.[19] It relies on currently available military handbooks, supplemented and corrected by other sources. While the resulting sample might invite the criticism that it is not based on first-hand archival research, that is not a fatal flaw. For one thing, those claiming to see a strong relationship between army size and fortification have not, to my knowledge, presented any such sample, archival or otherwise, in defense of their claims—and this includes Parker, whose published arguments concerning the *trace italienne* use numbers more for illustration than for statistical analysis. But more to the point, while a more substantial data base may be necessary to establish a theory, a systematic and fair reference to available scholarship is enough to demonstrate that these sources do not support a proposed thesis. They suffice to win a verdict of not proved. Since the Table constitutes the ammunition for criticism rather than assertion, it will hit its mark.

According to the assembled figures, from the middle of the fifteenth century, the attacking armies in sieges involving French troops most commonly numbered 20,000–40,000. Surprisingly, this figure is essentially stable. Besieging armies during the 1500s averaged 26,000, with 21 percent of them over 35,000. In the long war with Spain, 1635–59, attacking armies averaged 17,000. This figure climbed dramatically for 1672–97, when they hit an average of 41,700, but that trend did not continue. During the numerous sieges of the War of the Spanish Succession, the size of besieging forces essentially equalled those of the sixteenth century in the sample. Attackers averaged 26,500 men with 21 percent of besieging armies topping 35,000. In reality, most of the time Vauban's dictum on the minimum force required by a formal siege held true; there was no clear trend toward greater and greater armies stuffed into siege lines.

While all the figures in the Table date from the gunpowder era, they do not necessarily concern fortresses built in the *trace italienne*. Many of the towns attacked in France or on her frontiers could hardly be called "state of the art" before the mid-seventeenth century. But with a reasonable investment, medieval walls could be made serviceable in modern warfare if they were surrounded by a moat, buttressed by piled earth to withstand artillery, and garnished by temporary earthworks of a more modern pattern. The formal *trace italienne* was not absolutely essential. When 28,000 troops in English pay besieged Thérouanne in 1513, the town walls remained essentially medieval, yet it still held out for over two months.[20] Boulogne still had old walls in 1544.[21] The troops that Charles V and his allies led against Metz in 1552, variously numbered from 60,000 to 80,000, constituted a mighty force, even allowing for a degree of inaccuracy and exaggeration. But they failed in a siege of two and a half months against a town blessed with about 10,000 stout French defenders and surrounded by walls of medieval design.[22] Certain fortresses did not even receive modern walls until well into the seventeenth century.[23] Spanish and Imperial troops in Saint-Omer in 1638 kept at bay some 30,000 French troops for two months behind medieval walls.[24] Even late in the century, a fortress with only medieval walls could be turned into an effective defensive work with rather minor effort. When Turenne decided to hold Lauingen, which had only old-style defenses, in two weeks 2,300 men dug ravelins and put the town in a state of defense, so that only 800 men were required for its garrison.[25] So, while modern fortifications claimed very real advantages over updated medieval walls, the effect on army size seems to have been much the same.

Fortress improvements on a grand scale did not necessarily call forth grand-scale armies, as the case of Lille demonstrates. For whatever reasons, and we could go round the bush a long time in this debate, the techniques of siege warfare, as far as it involved the French, tolerated armies of roughly the same size between 1445 and 1715. Vauban appears to have been correct in setting the minimum size of an attacking force in the late seventeenth century at 20,000 men, but it had already hit that figure in the late fifteenth century. Since there was no trend toward larger siege armies, the figures simply do not support the notion that they explain French military expansion.

The next matter may come under the category of flogging a dead horse, since the data base contained in the Table of French Sieges already establishes the average size of siege armies. However, since a plausible explanation might peg the size of besieging armies to the size of the defending garrisons, rather than to the length of siege lines, this matter deserves at least a brief treatment.

Vauban boasted that before his improvements in the art of siege warfare, an attacking force required a numerical advantage of ten to one in order to succeed, but that his system brought success with only a six or seven to one advantage.[26] He also made the size of the garrison seem a matter of exact calculation, setting the number of men as a function of the number of bastions in the walls. He fixed the number of men necessary per bastion at 600 infantry and 60 cavalry, and then produced a neat chart for fortresses protected by anywhere from four to eighteen bastions.[27] Thus the typical citadel with five bastions should contain a garrison of 3,000 infantry and 300 cavalry. To attack it, the besieging force should number 19,800–23,100. All quite orderly.

But Vauban made it seem too scientific. In fact, the relationship between attackers and defenders never followed his rules so closely. During the War of the Spanish Succession, the average ratio of besieging forces to garrisons was 7.3:1; however, this is a trick of numbers. In fact only 30 percent of the cases fell into the range 5:1 to 8:1. Normally, besieging forces towered over garrisons by much greater margins or attempted to undertake sieges with odds as slight as 2:1. At the 1708 siege of Lille, Prince Eugene took the town with an advantage of no more than 2.5:1.

The limited sample provided in the Table of French Sieges suggests that Vauban reported an important trend, even if his definition of the ratio was not quite as hard and fast as he would have had his readers believe. Sieges required less of an advantage for the attacking force as time went on. Another way to express the same facts would be to say that garrisons exerted more leverage in boosting besieging numbers in earlier eras than they did later on. Based on the admittedly small sample contained in the Table of French Sieges, during the sixteenth century, attackers possessed a greater advantage over defenders, 15.9:1, than was the case in the seventeenth century, when the ratio stood at 8.6:1. Its decline to 7.3:1 after 1700 seems once again to represent a pattern. The curious thing about this pattern is that it would seem to run counter to the argument that improvements in fortification drove up army size. In fact, as time passed, and both fortresses and siege techniques improved, the forces required by a besieging army decreased, when measured in relation to the garrisons they overcame.

THE COST OF SIEGES IN TIME AND CASUALTIES

Should the cost of sieges in time or casualties have increased, this might also have consumed larger armies; however, the sample here does not suggest that this occurred. If anything, the length of sieges may have declined over the period 1500–1714. The average length of sixteenth-century sieges in the Table was sixty-five days, with a median siege length of sixty-one days. This increased somewhat in the period 1635–59, when the average climbed to seventy-six days, though the median fell to thirty-four days. The eras 1672–84 and 1688–97 produced nearly identical statistics, with average lengths of thirty-two and thirty-six with medians at twenty-five and twenty-six days. With the very large sample of sieges from the War of the Spanish Succession the average mounted to forty-three days with a median of thirty-seven. Such variations do not account for army growth in the seventeenth century, when, if anything, the length of sieges declined.

While the sample collected is too incomplete to provide the basis for very firm conclusions regarding casualties suffered during sieges, what information it does contain provides no evidence that such losses explain army growth. The sample yields the following averages for casualties suffered by an attacking army in sieges: 1635–59, 5,750; 1672–84, 7,500; 1688–97, 7,840; and 1702–14, 4,617. These averages are not to be taken too seriously, since only the sample from the War of the Spanish Succession provides enough examples for solid judgments. Nonetheless, the sample suggests a rise in casualties 1672–97, followed by a marked decline after 1702—a pattern that in no way accounts for the extraordinary growth of the French army, 1635–1714.

THE NUMBER OF SIEGES UNDERTAKEN

Even though the absolute size of besieging forces remained relatively the same, at roughly 27,300, through most of the era 1445–1715, and even if sieges remained constant in cost, there may still be a way to salvage a causal link between the spread of new fortress designs and growing armies. That link might still exist if the French undertook a number of sieges at the same time. After all, if 20–30,000 men composed an adequate force for a single siege, 100–150,000 would be necessary if five places were to be attacked simultaneously. Did the spread of fortresses greatly intensify the frequency of formal sieges?

Again, take the War of the Spanish Succession, since it presents a fairly complete series of fifty-eight sieges involving French troops. For the French, the land war in Europe broke down into four fronts: the Low Countries and certain areas of the lower Rhine that were strategically tied to the Low Countries; the Alsace-Lorraine frontier and that part of Germany and Luxembourg that faced it; the land south of Switzerland extending to the Mediterranean, that is Provence, the frontier with Italy, and northern Italy; and Spain. While forces from one theater occasionally acted in another, most importantly in 1704, it is still important to respect the separate theaters of the war when discussing campaigns and sieges.

Only twice did French forces in a theater undertake two sieges at the same time. In 1704, a small French army of 12,000 under La Feuillade besieged Susa, 31 May to 8 June.[28] The main French force of 26,000 under Vendôme began its attack on Vercelli, which proved a much tougher nut to crack, on 5 June.[29] In 1712, Villars's victory at Denain set the tide of success firmly in a French direction. Villars detached 28,000 men under Saint-Frémont to besiege Le Quesnoy, 8 September–4 October, but before that siege had run its full course, Villars began the siege of Bouchain on 1 October with 20,000.[30] In both cases, the new siege only began during the final three days of an ongoing attack.

More common were sequential sieges by the same army. In fact, both of the brief overlaps cited above made up part of a series of French successes. In the first case, Vendôme, after taking Vercelli (5 June–24 July 1704), went on to take Ivrée (30 August–30 September 1704), and Verrua (14 October 1704–9 April 1705). In the second, French forces under Villars in the Low Countries took Marchiennes (25–30 July 1712), then Douai (14 August–8 September), then Le Quesnoy (9 August–4 October), and finally Bouchain (1–19 October).

If the reality was that, with minor exceptions, the French and their enemies only undertook one siege at a time in a given theater of war, it was equally true that only rarely did the French take part in sieges that went on simultaneously in different theaters of war. For example, of the sieges on the Table initiated by the French during the War of the Spanish Succession, only in one instance, involving a total of three sieges, did the French pursue different sieges in different theaters of war at the same time. In 1704–5, the siege of Gibraltar (21 October 1704–30 April 1705) overlapped the sieges of Verrua (14 October 1704–9 April 1705) and Mirandola (19 April–10 May 1705). Therefore, a multiplicity of coincident sieges did not drive up army size.

THE PROPORTIONS OF COVERING

OR RELIEVING FORCES

Another aspect of the military equation that changed over the seventeenth century was the size of relief and observation forces. These forces grew dramatically. Relief armies tried to raise sieges by defeating or drawing off attacking forces, and armies of observation covered the troops engaged in siege works to fend off relief forces. During the sixteenth and early seventeenth centuries, relief and observation forces were not the constant companions of sieges. But later in the seventeenth century, particularly at its end, great numbers of troops were devoted to these purposes. At Mons in 1691, while 46,000 French troops occupied the siege lines, an equal amount covered the siege, while 38,000 tried to relieve the garrison.[31] A later siege of Mons in 1709 turned the tables, and while 20,000 allied troops surrounded the town, a covering force of 90,000 fought at Malplaquet against Villars with a relief force of 90,000.[32]

The great size of relief and observation forces might be seized by advocates of Parker's theses as proof. After all, these armies were accessories to sieges—part of the practice of positional warfare. Since these forces unquestionably grew so much, and since their activities related to the taking or defending of fortresses, can we not ascribe their growth to the technology of the *trace italienne* fortresses that so concerned them? Or, at the very least, can we not credit their growth to the techniques of siege warfare? The answer to both these questions is no. Relief and observation forces were not involved in the actual defense or attack of fortresses. By definition, they stood off miles, often tens of miles, from the actual siege. Since they occupied neither the besieged fortress nor the trenches that threatened it, such armies could not have been dictated either by the narrowly technical characteristics of the *trace italienne* or by the Vaubanesque style of attack.

Greater relief and observation forces were more a result of army expansion than its cause. To argue otherwise puts the cart before the horse. Consider the logic behind armies of observation. At a time when armies on campaign hovered around 20,000, roughly the number also required for a successful siege, an army attacking a fortress could depend upon its own numbers to deal with a relief force. Thus, Turenne, when engaged in the siege of Dunkirk in 1658 with 21,000 men, turned to face a Spanish relief army of 14,000. Leaving troops to hold the siege lines, Turenne mustered 15–16,000 for battle, and triumphed.[33] He needed no army of observation. But as entire armies grew and field forces mushroomed, mainly in the Nine Years' War and the War of the Spanish Succession, a siege force required an army of observation to protect it. Thus when the allies besieged Landrecies in 1712, 20,000 men sufficed to hold the lines and pursue the siege against the French garrison of 5,000. But because Villars could march to the relief of Landrecies with 90,000, Prince Eugene braced to resist him with 60,000 troops.[34] Siege forces required armies of observation because great field forces had been mobilized.

Usually an army in the field had little choice but to become involved in an on-going siege. As objects of value, important enough to be worth the considerable expense and effort of formal sieges, fortresses were also worth the time of field forces. In addition, an army besieging a fortress posed a threat not only to the fortress, but to the enemy's field forces as well, since it could turn away from the siege at any time, and certainly would once the siege was over. Thus, a relief army was not only laboring to save a fortress but also to confront the enemy's forces. Lastly, siege armies could be vulnerable since they were often smaller than field armies from the 1690s on; therefore, the siege army as a thing of value itself had to be protected by an army of observation. So sieges attracted conflicting field armies, drew them close, and made battle between them likely.

With relief armies maneuvering against armies of observation, many, if not most, of the great battles of Louis XIV's later wars were associated with the attack of fortified towns and fortresses. The Battle of Schellenberg allowed the taking of Donauworth by Marlborough in 1704. The French risked the Battle of Ramilles to prevent Marlborough from seizing Namur in 1706, and in the same year, the Battle of Turin lifted the long and fruitless siege of that city by the French. Marlborough and Eugene attacked the French at the Battle of Oudenarde to rescue that town from siege in 1708. And the greatest battle of the period, Malplaquet, resulted from Villars's attempt to forestall an allied siege of Mons in 1709.

In a greater Clausewitzian sense, armies are instruments intended to force the enemy to do your will, but in the narrower context of seventeenth-century strategy, armies were instruments to seize and protect territory. Territory was the object of, and the key to, the ruler's will. But perhaps even more fundamental was the fact that command over territory brought with it the ability to tap that area's resources. Since the ultimate challenge of seventeenth-century warfare was simply to sustain an army, and since local funds, food, and fodder were essential to this task, logistics absolutely demanded territorial control. The larger the field army, the more it needed the resources that only territorial possession and control insured. Holding towns and fortresses was the sine qua non of tapping enemy lands, and, for that matter, of defending your own.

There is no contradiction in denying that siege warfare created larger armies while maintaining that larger armies became harnessed to siege warfare in the late seventeenth century. The fact that great battles were generally associated with great sieges was not a product of the technology of defensive artillery or the *trace italienne,* but instead, stemmed from a strategic and logistical fixation on land. And it was not the necessities of positional warfare that called great armies into existence, but the creation of greater armies that influenced positional warfare. As states were willing to raise the stakes of war and put more chips on the table, this act alone changed the rules of the game.

QUANTITY OF TROOPS ASSIGNED TO GARRISON DUTY

If the preceding assertions are true, then the increasing wartime strength of the French army during the *grand siècle* did not result from the intricacies of the *trace italienne* and the demands of siege warfare. However, this leaves open the possibility that army size might still have been driven up by the need to garrison France's fortified frontier. Here we are on far more solid ground.

The number of troops committed to garrison duty multiplied during the reign of the Sun King. In the mid-1630s, frontier garrisons consumed only about 30,000 soldiers.[35] Figures from the era of the War of Devolution echo this level. Louvois reported in 1666 that 25,000 men garrisoned the frontier fortresses at a time when he counted total troop strength at 72,000.[36] Yet, at the height of the Dutch War, garrisons consumed nearly half of French forces. An état dated 1 January 1678 lists 279,610 troops under arms, of which 116,370 stood behind walls.[37]

Vauban authored the key documents concerning the growth of garrisons after the Dutch War. In a highly detailed memoir drawn up early in the Nine Years' War, he presented a table listing 221 fortresses and fortified posts throughout France that swallowed up 166,000 troops.[38] A second report drafted in 1705 increased the number of cities, fortresses, and fortified posts in the tables to 297 requiring garrisons totalling 173,000 infantry and cavalry.[39]

By the 1670s, seventeenth-century military opinion insisted that it was unacceptable to maintain a fortress without a garrison. Not to staff a fortress on the frontier was to offer a defensive position to the enemy, who could take the works with a small force that, once ensconced there, could do infinitely more damage than its modest numbers might imply. They could interdict communications and subject the surrounding area to extortion and requisition from the relative safety of the fortifications. Unmanned or weakly held forts located in the interior might be seized by rebels, giving them a bastion to resist royal authorities. Therefore, if a fortress existed, it demanded a garrison, and the character and size of the fortification set the number of troops it required.

To cut the number of troops consumed by this duty, required the abandonment and dismantling of unnecessary strongholds. This explains Vauban's obsession with cutting down the number of fortresses. As early as 1675 Vauban urged elimination of forts to save manpower: "It seems to me that the King has only too many advanced places; if he had fewer, five or six that I know well, he would be stronger by 12–14,000 men and the enemy weaker by at least 6–7,000."[40] In 1678 he calculated that "ten fortresses less ought to be worth 30,000 men more to the King."[41] He would later address the memoirs cited above to Louis. His figures carry weight not only because of his unquestioned expertise in fortifications and his unrivalled knowledge of French works, but because he had no vested interest in the argument. His influence rested upon the importance of fortifications. One would think that such a man would want to emphasize their value and multiply their number. Yet those memoirs argued that the French already had too many forts and that they demanded garrisons entirely out of line with the state's capacity to mobilize men and materiel.

The numbers presented by Vauban do not account for the 400,000-man forces of the Nine Years' War and the War of the Spanish Succession, although they do explain about 40 percent of army strength during wartime. More importantly, the need for garrison forces explains the peacetime size of the army. Vauban's two memoirs accord well with a third piece he wrote concerning French infantry. In it he asserted that about 132,000 French foot, assisted by 30,000 foreign and household troops, could effectively garrison French fortresses "in time of peace and war." Should war break out, 30–40,000 men could be siphoned off this force for immediate action while the numbers of French and Swiss troops were doubled or tripled.[42]

The usual assertion that peacetime armies were garrison armies can be a bit of a tautology. Where else were they to go? Except for the act of changing stations, which put units on the road, or the occasional instruction camp or civic works project, troops in peacetime occupied towns, which became garrison towns by definition simply because soldiers were there. What Vauban's memoirs demonstrate is that this was not simply a matter of convenience, of using fortresses and fortified towns as handy containers for the army between wars. With authority, he argued that the numbers of men maintained in peacetime were the minimum needed to provide garrisons at sufficient strength when war made its inevitable return. Any less, and fortresses would become prey to enemy action at the outset of the next conflict. Therefore, the French peacetime army, which in reality hovered around 150,000 troops, was defined by garrison duty.

To a large degree, this justifies Parker's later claims that the need to garrison fortresses propelled military expansion. Yet Parker seems to have been talking about wartime levels, whereas the greatest influence of garrison forces was on peacetime strengths, at least for the French army during the *grand siècle*. In addition, the mere physical existence of fortresses did not in itself determine the number of troops told off to hold them. As late as mid-century, fortresses might stand unguarded. In 1653 Turenne reported that there was "no infantry at all in the fortresses" in the war zone, because the King was so short of troops.[43]

In fact, decisions made by the Bourbons gave fortresses their leverage over military institutions. Ironically, France probably bristled with more fortresses early in the *grand siècle* than existed by its close, but many had no appreciable garrisons. Alternatively, they might be held by the personal retainers of great lords or by urban militias. Of course, strongholds not firmly in a king's grasp could turn against him. Louis XIII and Louis XIV acted from political as well as military motives when they destroyed some fortifications and garrisoned the remainder with royal troops. Strategic conceptions also played a role. The maintenance of large garrison forces resulted from the Sun King's resolve to secure his territory with a great fortress line. Louis XIV chose to build barriers, whereas earlier and later military men, Turenne and Napoleon for example, preferred mobile forces. Once these fundamental choices had been made, judgments as to the size and composition of garrisons rested on the state of the art in fortress design and siege warfare, which had grown considerably more demanding by the late seventeenth century.[44]

Thus, the rise in peacetime army size, with all its political and strategic implications, would seem to have been an unintended consequence, one might even say an accidental result, of another strategic decision, that to rely on fortresses held by the king's troops. As Williamson Murray reminds us, the formation of strategy often is not a rational process. Earlier decisions imprison reluctant statesmen within the logic of their own choices, finally imposing policies and actions that these leaders would have preferred to avoid.[45]

This being said, Parker has done notable service by drawing our attention to the way in which fortresses influenced the size of standing armies in a given political, strategic, and tactical environment. One of Parker's more provocative assertions, that "the greater part of military expenditure" in early modern Europe was lavished on the defense, does seem to hold, at least in the main.[46] The amount of the French budget set aside for fortress construction itself never dominated military expenses, peaking at 17 percent of total military outlays during the peacetime years, 1682–83.[47] Once war began, the money spent on fortresses fell, because funds went to maintain the higher number of troops. But to calculate the real cost of fortress construction, one would have to include all the money contributed by fortified towns to the maintenance of their own walls plus the forced labor exacted from peasants living in the surrounding countryside. This would be sure to drive up the total a great deal. In addition to construction costs, the pay and maintenance of garrisons should be put into the balance. During peacetime, virtually all troops garrisoned forts, so their maintenance costs could be considered as defensive. During wartime, no less than 40 percent of the total army was needed to occupy garrisons, according to Vauban, so even then defensive costs stayed high.

THE SEARCH FOR AN ALTERNATE EXPLANATION:
POPULATION AND WEALTH

This rejection of much of the *trace italienne* thesis implies at least some outline of an alternative explanation. There is a need both to establish the potential for military expansion and then to identify the trigger that set it off. The former must lie in demographic and economic development.

The proportions to which the Bourbons expanded their armies could not exceed the capacity of French population and economy, although the Bourbons also recruited troops outside their borders. It is interesting to note that the French army stayed at roughly the same size from 1445 to 1635. During these two centuries, Europe restored the population lost to the plague in the late middle ages. Demographic growth supplied the raw materials for military expansion. The potential had been accumulated, like a great wound spring awaiting a release to set the machine in motion. Of course, this does not mean that expansion was easy. Certainly by the Nine Years' War, the supply of affordable mercenaries began to dry up. Consequently, Louvois resorted to the device of conscripting soldiers through the milice system. Still, the bodies could be found to shoulder the pikes and muskets.

There was no magical source of food and forage to sustain larger armies; it was a product of the land and those who farmed it. Population growth implied a rise in agricultural output. Without peasants in the fields, the land did not grow the crops that armies required. In the direct, unvarnished words of Villars to his troops when they marched onto German lands in 1707: "My friends ... if you make the people run away, you will die of hunger."[48] And whether the marginal productivity rose or declined, the surplus that could be pulled off in taxes, requisition, or pillage increased. Armies could take what they wanted only if it was there to take.

Lastly the mercantile wealth of Europe expanded, both through fulfilling the needs of a greater European population and by exploiting the riches of world trade and imperialism. This produced wealth, credit institutions that mobilized that wealth, and urban development. Parker seems to have hit upon these connections, at least obliquely. He included "the lands of the Hapsburgs or of their neighbors: ... Spain, Italy, the Netherlands, and France" as the core of the military revolution.[49] To be sure, he sees this more in terms of the prevalence of fortification than I am happy with. But his broad net reels in that part of Continental Europe blessed with the greatest wealth and most advanced urban economies.

I would suggest that Parker's assertion that large armies and fortresses occurred in the same places at the same time could be explained by insisting that the two were results of a similar economic-political-strategic complex. For fortifications to multiply, the area in question must be populated by the cities, or at least large towns, that required fortifications. And the walled cities had to be rich enough to contribute substantially to the construction of their modern defenses. Even then, it would be foolish to invest in fortifications were the area not strategically open to repeated attack. Now an area that was urbanized, wealthy, and in danger might well spawn both fortifications and large armies.

THE SEARCH FOR AN ALTERNATE EXPLANATION:
THE DIPLOMATIC ISOLATION OF FRANCE

The search for the trigger that activated the potential created by demography and economics leads to French international ambition. First, Richelieu's desire to establish French preeminence in place of Spanish dominance stretched French military capacity. Second, Louis XIV's quest for *gloire* isolated France and forced her to match the forces united by great coalitions.

To be sure, the Bourbons were not the first French monarchs to challenge all of Europe, and thus fight multiple foes. The great Hapsburg-Valois wars, 1495–1559, found France equally isolated and surrounded. When Francis I faced off against Charles V, he struggled against the same kind of great alliance that faced Louis XIV. The French repeatedly fought in Italy, along the Rhine, and in the Low Countries all at once. Therefore ambition and isolation cannot alone explain military expansion in the seventeenth century, since they did not lead to it in the sixteenth. But in the seventeenth century these factors could activate a potential that did not exist before.

Richelieu and his successor, Mazarin, adopted international goals designed first to forestall Spain, and later to bring her down. This involved taking on the greatest power in Europe on battlefields from Italy to the Netherlands. To do so required the mobilization of armies and resources on a far greater level than ever before. The work of David Parrott demonstrates just how grand were the schemes and how they exceeded French capacity.[50] Estimates of the forces required stood as high as 200,000, although this was a spike that did not stand long, even in the world of wishful thinking.[51] Real force levels surely never reached this goal, and probably never exceeded 100,000. The paper figure of 150,000 used as a wartime high in this article makes sense only as an index against which to measure earlier and later theoretical sizes.

Military expansion after 1659 was more substantial and more lasting. Louis XIV pursued a foreign policy that marked a very real break with those of the strong first ministers who manipulated the international scene before 1661. Richelieu and Mazarin had succeeded to some degree in isolating their enemies and gaining allies. The strategic lesson that Mazarin imparted to Louis had more to do with diplomatic finesse than naked force. Later, when Louis's brutal methods and obsession with the absolute security of France united the Grand Alliance against him, this seemed a new and catastrophic development. Gone was the standing of France as the guarantor of German liberties, the natural ally of the Dutch, and the occasional friend of England. Louis's foreign policy doomed France to isolation in a hostile Europe.

As early as the Dutch War, Louis confronted a combination of enemies greater than he had anticipated, and this meant that the forces that he had committed to the war at first proved to be insufficient. At the close of 1672, Condé urged Louvois to put more troops in the field, because the French had to contend with not only the Dutch, but the German states and the Spanish as well.[52] Condé did not define fortresses as the culprit, but rather the fact that Louis had to keep forces along the Pyrenees, in the Dutch and Spanish Netherlands, and along the Rhine.

The pressures only became worse. In his final two conflicts, Louis XIV pursued military operations in four separate theaters in order to fight off his many enemies, who now included the English as well. It is a simple but fundamental truth that fighting on several fronts required several armies. Louis in 1704 commanded one field army in the Low Countries, one in Spain, one in Italy, and three in Germany. As Tallard's shattered army made its way back to France after Blenheim, Vendôme besieged and took Verrua coincidentally with Tessé's unsuccessful bid for Gibraltar.

On this point, Vauban makes a good witness. His technical memoirs deserve more attention, since they provide one of the rare documents that discuss army size and the demands of positional warfare between the same covers, and relate the one to the other. Vauban did not directly discuss the question of whether or not the *trace italienne* design drove up army size; one doubts that the notion ever occurred to him. While he saw the need to garrison fortresses as a powerful factor increasing the base size of the army, he did not see it as responsible for driving up the wartime size to 400,000. Instead, he ascribes military expansion to the need to fight the united forces of Europe. His concern to cut fortresses and garrisons arises from the fact that, in his words, "however great the forces of the kingdom, one ought not to imagine that it alone can furnish troops to guard and maintain so many fortresses and at the same time put armies in the field as great as those of Spain, Italy, England, Holland and the Empire joined together."[53] Vauban worried that the field armies of France would be overwhelmed by the forces mustered by a great coalition, which could threaten the full extent of France's land border and undertake descents on her coasts as well.

In a sense, Louis took heed of Vauban's logic, if not of his conclusions. The Sun King did not sacrifice his fortresses and their garrisons as Vauban proposed, but instead created the 400,000-man army to insure his *gloire*.

CONCLUSION

The adoption and spread of the *trace italienne* does not in itself explain the growth of the French army during the *grand siècle*, nor was it the most fundamental variable in the equation. Military architecture was at best only one factor urging army growth.

A more plausible argument would take a broader view. French economic and demographic development made military expansion possible. Dynastic ambition and eventual diplomatic isolation forced the Bourbons to multiply the number of their battalions. Only later did fortresses exert an influence, as a territorial conception of strategy led Louis XIV to rely on massive fortress lines. Once fortifications became the centerpiece of French military policy, contemporary techniques of siege warfare dictated the forces sufficient to garrison them. This contributed to wartime force levels and set the size of the peacetime army.

Parker's theory survives this critique, but not intact. To say that the Sun King's reliance on fortifications contributed to French military expansion by setting a dramatically higher level for the standing army is to say a great deal. Large standing armies exerted considerable influence on political and social institutions. But this conclusion does not go as far as Parker's assertions in his 1988 volume and, especially, in his 1976 article.

My goal here has not been to elaborate a theory in competition to that proposed by Parker, but rather to demonstrate that such a great and influential phenomenon as army growth did not arise from a single technological innovation, such as the *trace italienne*. Despite Benjamin Franklin's tale of the lacking nail, horseshoe, et al., I remained convinced that great effects do not result from small causes.

Table of French Sieges, 1445–1715

Date	Fortress or town	Attacking force*	Garrison	Relief/ Observ.	Casualties attacker	Casualties defender	Attacker:Garrison ratio Comments
1445–1500 (15,500 — average size of attacking force)							
1451 (fell 6/30)[1]	Bordeaux	6,000(F)					
1476 (lifted 6/22)[2]	Morat	20,000(Bur)		r25,000(Sw)			
1478 (fell 5/1)[3]	Condé	20,000(F)					
1492[4]	Boulogne	20,000(E)	1,800(F)				Strong art. in Boulogne
1500s (26,600 — average size of attacking force, 21% over 35,000; average days 65, median 61)							
1512 (3–4)[5]	Ravenna	23,000(F)	5,000(S)	r16,000			4.6:1
1513 (6/-8/22)[6]	Thérouanne	31,000(E)	(F)	r15,000			Still medieval walls 1553
1524 (8/27–9/28)[7]	Marseille	20,000(I)	3–4,000(F)	r19,000			5:1
1524 (10/28)–1525(2/24)[8]	Pavia	25,000(F)	6,000(I)	r20,000			4.3:1
1543 (6–9/8)[9]	Nice	14,000(T) 19,000(F)					
1543 (9)[10]	Landrecies	40–45,000(I)	2,500(F)	r35,000			18:1
1544 (4–6/4)[11]	Carignano	17,000(F)	1,500(I)	r13,800			11.3:1
1544 (5/25–8/17)[12]	Luxembourg	26,000(I)	1,500(F)				17.3:1
1544 (6/7–8/17)[13]	Saint-Dizier	42,000(I)	2,100(F)				20.4:1
1544 (began 7/14)[14]	Montreuil	30,000(E)	6,000(F)				5:1
1544 (7/14–9/13)[15]	Boulogne	29,000(E)	1,800(F)				16.1:1; walls medieval
1552 (19/10–1/1)[16]	Metz	60,000(I)	10,000(F)		30–48,000		6:1
1554 (8)[17]	Renty	50,000(F)					
1557 (8/8–8/27)[18]	Saint-Quentin	50,000(S)	1,000(F)	r23,000			50:1; back-filled medieval walls
1558 (fell 6/30)[19]	Dunkirk	10,500(F)					50:1: not modern
1558 (1/2–7)[20]	Calais	25,000(F)	500(E)				12.7:1; only modernized in 1590
1558 (fell 6/22)[21]	Thionville	17–19,000(F)	1,500(S)				
1590 (2–3)[22]	Dreux	11,000(Fp)	(Fc)	r16,000(Fc)			
1590 (5–8)[23]	Paris	25,000(Fp)	(Fc)	r26,000(S)			
1591 (11/11)–1592(4/20)[24]	Rouen	9,000(Fp)	(Fc)	r23,000(S)			11.7:1; no lines, med. walls
1592 (5)[25]	Craon	7,000(E)	5–600(F)	r4,800(S)			
1595 (6–7)[26]	Doullens	16,000(S)					
1596 (9/4–25)[27]	Calais	17,000(S)	(F)				modern walls
1597 (6–9)[28]	Amiens	25–30,000(F)	5,000(I)	r30,000			6:1; only partially modernized

1600-1634

1627 (8/15)-1628(10/28)[29]	La Rochelle	23,000(F)	4-5,000(Fp)			5.8:1	
1633 (8/31-23/9)[30]	Nancy	30,000(F)	4,300			7:1	

1635-1659 (17,000 — average size of attacking force, 0% over 35,000; average days 76, median 34)

1637 (7)[31]	Landrecies	20,000(F)					
1638 (2/6-12/17)[32]	Breisach	18,000(F/Swe)					
1638 (5/24-7/16)[33]	Saint-Omer	30,000(F)	20,000(S/1)		4,000	1.5:1; still medieval in 1668	
1640 (5/14-9/24)[34]	Turin	15,000(F)	4,000(S)	r16-18,000	4,000	3.8:1; Harcourt undertook initial circumvallation with only 9,500.	
1641 (3/15-6/25)[35]	Ivrée	7,400(F)	1,800(Sa)			4.1:1	
1643 (5/19-9/8)[36]	Thionville	21,000(F)	3,000(S)			7:1; lines of cir. 18 km	
1644 (5-7/28)[37]	Fribourg	17,000(Bv)	600(F)			25:1; lines stop relief	
1644 (8/23-9/17)[38]	Philippsburg	5,000(F)	6-700(Bv)			7.1:1	
1644 (9)[39]	Landau	3-4,000(F)	2-300(L)			13.3:1	
1646 (5/10-11/21)[40]	Lerida	12,000(F)	5,000(S)	r18,000		2.4:1	
1646 (9/7-10/11)[41]	Dunkirk	30,000(F)	3,000(S)			10:1	
1647 (5/14-6/17)[42]	Lerida	16,000(F)	4,000(S)		8,000	4:1	
1647 (6/27-7/17)[43]	Landrecies	16,000(S)	1,600(F)	r16,000		10:1	
1649[44]	Cambrai		2,000(S)	r22,000	2,000		
1650 (ca.9/18-11/6)[45]	Mouzon	14,000(S) at end		r17,000ca. o3,000		No circumvalation	
1654 (7/14-8/24)[46]	Arras	25-30,000(S) (F)	2,600(F)	r14,000	7,000	11.5:1	
1655 (fell in 3 days)[47]	Condé	(F)	1,700(S)				
1655 (6/19-7/14)[48]	Landrecies	22,000(F)	2,100(S)			10.5:1	
1656 (6/20-8/17)[49]	Valenciennes	20,000(F)	1,500(S)	r20,000		13.3:1	
1657[50]	Cambrai	(F)	(S)	r4,000			
1657 (6/12-8/6)[51]	Montmédy	10,000(F)	700(S)			14.3:1	
1658 (5/25-6/23)[52]	Dunkirk	21,000(F)	3,000(S)	r16,000	3,300	7:1	

1667-1668

1667 (6/30-7/6)[53]	Douai	21 reg inf(F) 23 of cav	970(S)			Walls a bit above medieval back-filled walls, 1630	
1667 (7/8-8/28)[54]	Lille	30,000(F)	5,000(S)			6:1	

1672-1684 (41,000 — average size of attacking force, 64% over 35,000; average days 32, median 25)

1673 (6/5-30)[55]	Maestricht	44,000(F)	6,000(S)				
1673 (9/6-12)[56]	Naarden	25,000(D)				2.3:1	

Table of French Sieges, 1445–1715

Date	Fortress or town	Attacking force*	Garrison	Relief/ Observ.	Casualties attacker	Casualties defender	Attacker:Garrison ratio Comments
1674 (7/29–10/25)[57]	Grave	(D)	4,000(F)			500	
1675 (8/13–9/1)[58]	Trier	15,000(I)	4,000(F)				3.8:1
1676 (4/17–26)[59]	Condé	50,000(F)					Cir. done 23 April; fell in 3 days
1676 (6/23–9/11)[60]	Philippsburg	60,000(I)	5,000(F)		10,000		12:1
1676 (7/7–8/29)[61]	Maestricht	40,000(D/S)	7,000(F)		5,000		5.7:1
1677 (2/28–3/17)[62]	Valenciennes	40,000(F)	3,000(S)				13.3:1
1677 (3/22–4/20)[63]	Saint-Omer	(F)		r35,000			
1677 (3/23–4/19)[64]	Cambrai	30,000(S)	4,000(S)				7.5:1; 7,000 peasant workers dug siege lines
1678 (3/1–10)[65]	Ghent	60,000(F)					
1678 (3/13–26)[66]	Ypres	50,000(F)	3,000(S)				16.7:1
1684 (4/28–6/4)[67]	Luxembourg	32,000(F)	6,000(S)				5.3:1

1688–1697 (42,400 — average size of attacking force, 50% over 35,000; average days, 36, median 26)

Date	Fortress or town	Attacking force*	Garrison	Relief/ Observ.	Casualties attacker	Casualties defender	Attacker:Garrison ratio Comments
1688 (10/5–29)[68]	Philippsburg	30,000(F)	2,000(I)				15:1
1689 (7/16–9/8)[69]	Mainz	60,000(I)	8,000(F)				7.5:1
1689 (9/16–10/12)[70]	Bonn	30,000(I/B)	3,000(F)		4,000		10:1
1691 (3/15–4/10)[71]	Mons	46,000(F)	4,800(S)	r38,000 o46,000			9.6:1; 20,000 pioneers dug siege lines
1692 (5/26–7/1)[72]	Namur	60,000(F)	9,280(S/D)	o60,000	7,000	4,000	7.2:1; 20,000 pioneers from conquered provinces dug siege lines
1693 (9/10–10/11)[73]	Charleroi	38 bats., 38 esq., est. 30–35,000(F)	3,500(S)			2,200	8.6:1
1694 (6/17–29)[74]	Gerona	18,000(F)	5,000(S)				3.6:1
1695 (7/1–9/6)[75]	Namur	80,000(E/D/S)	13,000(F)		18,000	5,000	6.2:1
1697 (5/15–6/5)[76]	Ath	40,000(F)	3,850(S)		53	500	
1697 (6/6–8/10)[77]	Barcelona	30,000(F)	12,000(S)		10,000	7,000	2.5:1

1702–1714 (26,500 — average size of attacking force, 21% over 35,000; average days 43, median 37)

Date	Fortress or town	Attacking force*	Garrison	Relief/ Observ.	Casualties attacker	Casualties defender	Attacker:Garrison ratio Comments
1702 (4/18–6/15)[78]	Kaiserworth	22,000(D/P)	5,000(F)		2,900	1,000	4.4:1
1702 (6/18–9/9)[79]	Landau	46,000(I)	4,400(F)		3,000	1,700	10.5:1
1702 (8/29–9/9)[80]	Guastalla	33,000(F/S)	2,200(I)				15:1

1702 (9/11–23)[81]	Venlo	30,000(D/P)	1,100(F)		1,100	840	27.3:1
1702 (9/25–10/20)[82]	Stevenswaert	30,000(E/D)	1,500(F)				20:1
1702 (9/26–10/6)[83]	Ruremonde	25,000(E/D)	2,400(F)		60	40–50	10.4:1
1702 (10/13–29)[84]	Liège	40,000(E/D)	8,000(F)		1,000	3,000	3.47:1
1703 (2/25–3/9)[85]	Kehl	28,000(F)	2,200(I)				12.7:1
1703 (4/27–5/15)[86]	Bonn	40,000(E/D/P)	3,600(F)		600	860	11.1:1
1703 (8/15–25)[87]	Huy	42,000(E/D)	7,500(F)		60	1,200	5.6:1
1703 (8/15–9/7)[88]	Breisach	24,000(F)	3,500(I)		900	300	6.9:1
1703 (9/10–27)[89]	Limburg	16,000(E/D)	1,400(F)		100	60	11.4:1
1703 (10/13–11/17)[90]	Landau	26,000(F)	3,800(I)		5,000	1,800	6.8:1
1703 (12/3–16)[91]	Augsburg	23,000(F/Bv)	6,000(I)				3.8:1
1704 (5/31–6/8)[92]	Susa	12,000(F)	2,300(Sa)				5.2:1
1704 (6/5–7/24)[93]	Vercelli	26,000(F)	7,000(Sa/I)		1,100	900	3.7:1
1704 (8/23–9/11)[94]	Ulm	11,000(I)	2,600(F/Bv)				4.2:1
1704 (8/30–9/30)[95]	Ivrée	10,000(F/S)	2,000(I)				5:1
1704 (9/9–11/11)[96]	Landau	30,000(I)	5,000(F)		5,000	3,000	6:1
1704(10/14)–1705(4/9)[97]	Verrua	30,000(F/S)	6,000(Sa/I)	r14,000	12,000		5:1
1704(10/21)–1705(4/30)[98]	Gibraltar	20,000(E/I)	4,000(E)		12,000		5:1
1704(11/4–12/20)[99]	Trarbach	20,000(E/1)	600(F)		1,000	350	33.3:1
1705 (4/10–10/17)[100]	Badajoz	25,000(E/Po)	1,000(S)	r14,000			25:1
1705 (7/16–9/8)[101]	Mirandola	5,000(F)	1,500(I)				3.3:1
1705 (9/18–10/6)[102]	Barcelona	11,000(E/D/I)	5,800(S)				1.9:1
1705(10/31)–1706(1/7)[103]	Nice	7,000(F)	1,400(Sa)				5:1
1706 (4/3–5/12)[104]	Barcelona	24,000(F)	8,000 + 8,000		200	600	3 or 1.5:1
1706 (5/1–12)[105]	Hagenau	5,000(F)	2,000(I)				2.5:1
1706 (6/2–9/7)[106]	Turin	40,000(F)	14,700(Sa/I)	r30,000 o48,000	14,000	3,000	3.42:1
1706 (6/29–7/6)[107]	Ostende	20,000(E/D)	5,000(F/S)				4:1
1706 (8/9–18)[108]	Menin	30,000(E/D)	5,500(F/S)		2,620	1,101	5.5:1
1706 (8/27–9/5)[109]	Dendermonde	6,000(E/D)	2,000(F/S)				3:1
1706 (9/16–10/2)[110]	Ath	21,000(E/D)	2,000(F)		800		10.5:1
1707 (6/12–7/11)[111]	Lerida	32,000(F/S)	2,500(E/D)			1,000	12.8:1
1707 (7/14–8/22)[112]	Toulon	38,000(Po/I/E)	9,000(F)	r40,000	10,000		4.2:1
1707 (9/18–10/4)[113]	Ci. Rodrigo	9,500(S/F)	1,400(E/Po)				7.8:1
1708 (6/12–7/11)[114]	Tortosa	30,000(F/S)	3,800(I/D)		1,800	1,800	7.9:1
1708 (8/13––12/9)[115]	Lille	35,000(E/D/I)	16,000(F)	o55,000 r90,000	14,000	7,000	2.5:1

Table of French Sieges, 1445–1715

Date	Fortress or town	Attacking force*	Garrison	Relief/ Observ.	Casualties attacker	Casualties defender	Attacker:Garrison ratio Comments
1708(12/25)–1709(1/2)[116]	Ghent	40,000(E/I)	15,000(F)		4,800	4,000	2.18:1
1709 (6/26–9/3)[117]	Tournai	40,000(E/D/I)	7,000(F)		5,400	3,200	5.7:1
1709 (9/24–10/20)[118]	Mons	20,000(E/D/I)	4,300(F/S)	r90,000 o90,000	2,300	980	4.7:1
1710 (4/23–6/27)[119]	Douai	60,000(E/D/I)	8,000(F)		8,000	3,000	7.5:1
1710 (7/14–8/28)[120]	Béthune	31,000(E/D/I)	4,000(F)		3,000	1,800	7.75:1
1710 (9/6–29)[121]	Saint-Venant	9,000(E/D/I)	3,000(F)		960	400	3:1
1710 (9/12–11/8)[122]	Aire	28,000(E/D/I)	7,000(F)		7,000	3,400	4:1
1710(12/12)–1711(1/24)[123]	Gerona	30,000(F/S)	2,400(I)				12.5:1
1711 (8/7–9/13)[124]	Bouchain	30,000(E/D/I)	5,000(F)		3,000	1,800	6:1
1711 (11/12–12/22)[125]	Cardona	8,000(F/S)	2,500(I)	r3,000			3.2:1
1712 (6/8–7/3)[126]	Le Quesnoy	18,000(D/I)	5,500(F)		3,000	2,000	3.2:1
1712 (7/17–8/2)[127]	Landrecies	20,000(D/I)	5,000(F)	o60,000 r90,000			4:1
1712 (7/25–30)[128]	Marchiennes	22,000(F)	7,000(D/P)		400	200	3.1:1
1712 (8/14–9/8)[129]	Douai	25,000(F)	3,300(D/I)		5,000	1,000	7.6:1; 20,000 pioneers dug siege lines[130]
1712 (9/8–10/4)[131]	Le Quesnoy	28,000(F)	2,200(D/I)		1,000	700	12.7:1
1712 (10/1–19)[132]	Bouchain	20,000(F)	2,000(D/I)		400		10:1
1712(11/1)–1713(1/3)[133]	Gerona	9,000(I)	4,000(S)	r24,000(F) o12,000			2.3:1
1713 (6/11–8/20)[134]	Landau	40,000(F)	7,000(I)	o70,000	10,000	2,000	5.7:1
1713 (9/22–11/16)[135]	Fribourg	80,000(F)	9,300(I)		10,000	3,600	8.6:1
1714 (7/7–9/12)[136]	Barcelona	70,000(F/S)	16,000(S)		20,000	6,000	4.4:1

* Forces are coded as follows: F = French, Fc = French Catholic, Fp = French Protestant, Bur = Burgundian, Bv = Bavarian, D = Dutch, E = English, I = Imperial, Po = Portuguese, S = Spanish, Sa = Savoyard, Sw = Swiss, Swe = Swedish, T = Turkish, r = relief army, o = army of observation.

1. R. Ernest Dupuy and Trevor N. Dupuy, *Encyclopedia of Military History* (New York, 1970), 418.

2. Dupuy and Dupuy, 428-29.

3. Guy Capelle, *Histoire de Condé et ses fortifications* (Beuvrage, 1978), 27.

4. André Verley, *Boulogne-sur-mer à travers les ages*, vols. 2-3 (Paris, 1978), 2: 87.

5. Dupuy and Dupuy , 471.

6. Christopher Duffy, *Siege Warfare: The Fortress in the Early Modern World, 1494-1660* (London, 1979), 46; Dupuy and Dupuy, 472.

7. Dupuy and Dupuy, 474.

8. Ibid.

9. Vezio Melegari, *The Great Military Sieges* (New York: 1972), 130-33; see as well Ferdinand Lot, *Recherches sur les effectifs des armées françaises des Guerres d'Italie aux Guerres de Religion, 1494-1562* (Paris, 1962), 69-70, for total effectives of the attacking French army.

10. A. Rozet, *L'invasion de la France et le siège de Saint Diger, 1544* (Paris, 1910), 6; Pauline Giloteaux, *Histoire de Landrecies des origines à nos jours* (Le Quesnoy, 1962), 57; Lot 70-71.

11. Charles Oman, *The Art of War in the Sixteenth Century* (London, 1937), 229-33; Lot, 81-84.

12. Rozet, 39, 66, 155; Oman, 338, puts the besieging force at only 12,000 and states that Luxembourg fell June 6.

13. Rozet, 39.

14. Oman, (London, 1937), 340.

15. Alain Lottin, *Histoire de Boulogne-sur-mer* (Lille, 1983), 106-10.

16. H. Noel Williams, *Henri II* (New York, 1910), 282, credits the three forces besieging Metz at 70-80,000 and the French garrison at 10,000. Herny Lemonnier, *La lutte contre la maison d'Autriche: La France sous Henri II, Histoire de France*, ed. E. Lavisse, vol. 5, pt. 2 (Paris, 1904), 154, gives Guise's estimate of 60,000.

17. Lemonnier, 156.

18. Dupuy and Dupuy, 477.

19. Ibid.

20. Oman, 264; Dupuy and Dupuy, 477.

21. Lot, 174-75.

22. Dupuy and Dupuy, 481.

23. Ibid.

24. Jean Pierre Babelm, *Henri IV* (1982), 519-21.

25. Gaston de Canne, ed., *Documents sur la ligue en Bretagne: Correspondence du duc de Mercoeur et des Ligueurs breton avec l'Espagne*, vol. 1 (Vannes, 1899), 125, letter from Mercoeur to Philip II.

26. M. Pernot, *Les guerres de réligion, 1559-1598* (Paris, 1987), 170.

27. Nelly Mulard, *Calais au temps des Lys* (Calais, 1961), 34-38.

28. Jeanne Estienne, *Le bel Amiens* (Amiens, 1967), 114.

29. Gaston Bodart, *Militär-historisches Kriegs-Lexikon, 1618-1905* (Vienna and Leipzig, 1908), 53. Bodart has been used quite extensively as a statistical source in this table. Bodart concerned himself with the statistics of war, even writing a study of casualties. His work seems very much a work of serious scholarship, commanding the respect of such a historian as David Chandler, who also relies on his figures in his studies.

30. *L'armée à Nancy, 1633-1966* (Nancy, 1967), 11.

31. Giloteaux, 65-67.

32. Bodart, 64.

33. Ibid., 62.

34. Ibid., 66; *Turenne et l'art militaire* (Paris, 1975), 174-76; Duffy, *Siege Warfare*, 125; Jean Bérenger, *Turenne* (Paris, 1987), 159.

35. *Turenne et l'art militaire*, 195.

36. *Histoire de la Fortification dans le pays de Thionville* (Thionville, 1970), 11.

37. Turenne, *Mémoires de Turenne* (Paris, 1872), 4-5; Dupuy and Dupuy, 544.

38. Turenne, 21-24.

39. Ibid., 25.

40. Bodart, 75.

41. Ibid.

42. Ibid., 76; Marc Blancpain, *Monsieur le prince* (Paris, 1986), 99-100.

43. Giloteaux, 69-71.

44. Louis Trenard, *Histoire de Cambrai* (Lille, 1982), 146.

45. Turenne, 111, 116.

46. Ibid., 198-99; *Turenne et l'art militaire*, 143-44.

47. Capelle, 28.

48. Bérenger, 325-27; Giloteaux, 74; *Turenne et l'art militaire*, 146, states the French attackers had 21,000.

49. Bérenger, 329-31; *Turenne et l'art militaire*, 147-48; Eveline Godly, *The Great Condé* (London, 1915), 463-73.

50. Trenard, 146.

51. P. Lazard, *Vauban, 1633-1707* (Paris, 1934), 112, Vauban's figures.

52. Dupuy and Dupuy, 561-62.

53. Michel Roche, *Histoire de Douai* (Westhoek, 1985), 125-26.

54. Bodart, 90.

55. Ibid., 93; André Corvisier, *Louvois* (Paris, 1983), 281, letter from Colbert stated that Louis had only 20,000 men and that the garrison was 6,000.

56. Stephen Baxter, *William III* (London, 1966), 105.

57. Ibid., 121-22.

58. Bodart, 97.

59. Capelle, 29.

60. Bodart, 100.

61. Ibid.

62. Ibid.; Jean-Michel Lambin, *Quand le Nord devenait français* (Paris, 1980), 73.

63. Lottin, 114; Dupuy and Dupuy, 566.
64. Bodart, 101; Lottin, 114; Trenard, 150.
65. John B. Wolf, *Louis XIV* (New York, 1968), 262.
66. Bodart, 103.
67. Ibid., 105; Jacques Dollar, *Vauban à Luxembourg* (Luxembourg, 1983), 57, gives the French besiegers only 20-21,000 infantry and 7,000 cavalry.
68. Bodart, 109; Georges Michel, *Histoire de Vauban* (Paris, 1879), 211-18; Henri Martin, *The Age of Louis XIV*, vol. 2 (Boston: 1865), 82.
69. Bodart, 110; Martin, 96-97.
70. Bodart, 111.
71. Ibid., 114; Lazard, 225-26; Corvisier, 468.
72. Bodart, 116; Chistopher Duffy, *Fire and Stone* (London, 1975), 163-74; Lazard, 230-31; Louis XIV, *Oeuvres*, eds. Grimoard and Grouvelle, 6 vols. (Paris, 1806), 4:357-59, gives garrison size as 9,280 and states that 20,000 pioneers were raised from conquered provinces to dig the five leagues of lines.
73. Lazard, 257-58; Reginald Blomfield, *Sébastien le Prestre de Vauban* (London, 1938), 134.
74. Bodart, 120.
75. Ibid.; Michel, 283-309; Martin, 142-46.
76. Bodart, 121, gives size of besieging army as 52,000; Lazard, 274, states that the 40,000 included three corps of which only one, under Catinat, was actually engaged in the trenches, while the other two covered; Christopher Duffy, *The Fortress in the Age of Vauban and Frederick the Great, 1660-1789* (Lonton, 1985), 30, concerning Ath, he sets garrison as 3,850 and French losses as 53 dead and 106 wounded.
77. Bodart, 122; Michel, 178; Martin, 198-200.
78. David Chandler, *Marlborough as a Military Commander* (London, 1973), 336-37; Bodart, 125.
79. Bodart, 128.
80. Ibid., 127.
81. Ibid., 128; Chandler, 336-377.
82. Chandler, 336-37.
83. Ibid.
84. Bodart, 129; Chandler, 336-37.
85. Bodart, 130.
86. Ibid., 131; Chandler, 336-37.
87. Bodart, 132; Chandler, 336-37.
88. Bodart, 132.
89. Ibid., 133; Chandler, 336-37.
90. Bodart, 134.
91. Ibid., 135.
92. Ibid., 136.
93. Ibid., 137.
94. Ibid., 139.
95. Ibid.
96. Ibid., 140.
97. Ibid., 141.
98. Ibid., 142.
99. Chandler, 336-37.
100. Bodart, 144.
101. Ibid., 142.
102. Ibid., 143.
103. Ibid., 145.
104. Ibid., 146.
105. Ibid.
106. Ibid., 149, differs in listing besiegers as 36,000 and garrison as 10,500; Duffy, *Fortress in the Age of Vauban and Frederick the Great*, 50.
107. Bodart, 148; Chandler, 336-37.
108. Bodart, 148; Chandler, 336-37.
109. Bodart, 148; Chandler, 336-37.
110. Bodart, 150; Chandler, 336-37, differs in giving French casualties as 60.
111. Bodart, 153.
112. Ibid., 152.
113. Ibid., 153.
114. Ibid.
115. Ibid., 158; Dupuy and Dupuy, 623; Chandler, 338-39, presents allied losses as 15,000; Duffy, *Fortress in the Age of Vauban and Frederick the Great*, 38-39.
116. Bodart, 161; Dupuy and Dupuy, 623; Chandler, 338-39.
117. Bodart, 160; Chandler, 338-39, gives casualty figures as 3,800 for the French.
118. Bodart, 161; Dupuy and Dupuy, 623; Chandler, 338-39.
119. Bodart, 162; Chandler, 338-39, sets the French garrison at 7,500, French casualties at 2,860 and allied losses at 8,009.
120. Bodart, 163; Chandler, 338-39, gives casualty figures for the allies of 3,365 and 1,200 for the French.
121. Bodart, 163; Chandler, 339.
122. Bodart, 163; Chandler, 338-39, assigns 7,200 casualties to the allies and 1,400 to the French.
123. Bodart, 164.
124. Ibid., 166; Chandler, 338-39, assigns 4,080 casualties to the allies and 2,500 to the French.
125. Bodart, 166.
126. Ibid., 167.
127. Ibid., 168.
128. Ibid.; Pierre Paul, *Denain* (Paris: 1963), 172, gives the garrison as only 4,500.
129. Bodart, 168.
130. Roche, 138.
131. Bodart, 169.
132. Ibid.
133. Ibid., 170.
134. Ibid.; Claude C. Sturgill, *Marshal Villars and the War of the Spanish Succession* (Lexington, Ky., 1965), 130, gives the garrison's size as 10,000 and its casualties as 4,550 and French casualties as 4,800 dead; Paul, 187-91, credits the French with 45-50,000 and the allied garrison with 9,700.
135. Bodart, 171; Sturgill, 133, gives garrison size as 13,000 and its casualties as 7,000.
136. Bodart, 171.

Notes

1. I would like to thank the following for research support: the National Endowment for the Humanities, summer stipend for 1989; the Research Board, University of Illinois at Ur-bana-Champaign (UIUC); the Program in Arms Control, Disarmament, and International Security, UIUC; the College of Liberal Arts and Sciences, UIUC; and the Department of History, UIUC. I also owe many a debt to my research assistants Jeffrey McKeage and Edward Tenace, and to my colleague, Geoffrey Parker, who has been so supportive throughout this project.

2. Geoffrey Parker, "The 'Military Revolution' 1560–1660—a Myth?" *Journal of Modern History* 48 (June 1976) reprinted above, Ch. 2, and *The Military Revolution: Military Innovation and the Rise of the West, 1500–1800* (Cambridge, 1988). The original publication of this article ("The *trace italienne* and the Growth of Armies") in the *Journal of Military History* erroneously read "late fourteenth and early fifteenth centuries" for "late fifteenth and early sixteenth centuries."

3. Parker, *Military Revolution*, 24.

4. Ibid.

5. Parker, "The 'Military Revolution,'" 208 (above, p. 45). In the initial publication of this article (i.e., "The *trace italienne* and the Growth of Armies"), "1630s" was incorrectly printed in place of "1530s."

6. Parker, *Military Revolution*, 40.

7. Ibid., 39.

8. Bert S. Hall and Kelly R. DeVries, "The 'Military Revolution' Revisited," *Technology and Culture*, July, 1990, 500–7.

9. Simon Adams, "Tactics or Politics? 'The Military Revolution' and the Hapsburg Hegemony, 1525–1648," in *Tools of War*, ed. John A. Lynn (Champaign, Illinois, 1990), 28–52, reprinted below, Ch. 10.

10. John A. Lynn, "The Growth of the French Army during the Seventeenth Century," *Armed Forces and Society* 6 (Summer 1980): 568–85; and John A. Lynn, "The Pattern of Army Growth, 1445–1945," in *Tools of War*, 1–27.

11. David Parrott, "The Administration of the French Army During the Ministry of Cardinal Richelieu," diss., Oxford University, 1985, 142, estimates that the numbers of men actually present in units stood at only 50 percent of full strength for the years 1630–38. In contrast, *Etapes* records at Amiens, 1695–96, reveal that regular infantry units stood at 80 percent of official strength, and cavalry at 97 percent. Archives municipales d'Amiens, EE 403 and 405.

12. See Charles Tilly, *Coercion, Capital, and European States, AD 990–1990* (Oxford, 1990); David Kaiser, *Politics & War: European Conflict from Philip II to Hitler* (Cambridge, Mass., 1990); and Brian M. Downing, *The Military Revolution and Political Change in Early Modern Europe* (Princeton, forthcoming 1991). According to Charles Tilly, European "state structure appeared chiefly as a by-product of rulers' efforts to acquire the means of war." (*Coercion, Capital, and European States*, 14.)

13. On Italian Renaissance fortifications see: J. R. Hale, "The Early Development of the Bastion: an Italian Chronology, c. 1450–c. 1534", in J. R. Hale, J. R. L. Highfield, and B. Smalley, eds., *Europe in the Late Middle Ages* (London, 1965), 644–94; J. R. Hale, *Renaissance Fortification: Art or Engineering* (London, 1977); and Simon Pepper and Nicholas Adams, *Firearms and Fortifications* (Chicago, 1986).

14. Sébastien le Prestre de Vauban, *Oeuvres de M. de Vauban*, 3 vols. (Amsterdam and Liepzig, 1771), 1:33.

15. Ibid. Vauban stated that the smallest fortresses were 200–300 toises in diameter.

16. V. Derode, *Histoire de Lille* (Lille, 1848), 118; Alain Lottin, *Les grandes batailles du nord* (Paris, 1984), 125.

17. Gaston Bodart, *Militär-historisches Kriegs-Lexikon, 1618–1905* (Vienna and Leipzig, 1908), 90, 158.

18. Vauban, *Oeuvres*, 1:33.

19. The table has been drawn from a number of sources. The most important among them is Bodart's *Kriegs-Lexikon*. I have also made use of R. Ernest Dupuy and Trevor N. Dupuy, *The Encyclopedia of Military History* (New York, 1970), for the past twenty years the standard reference work in military history. The other volumes cited will be found in the footnotes to the table itself.

20. Dupuy and Dupuy, *Encyclopedia of Military History*, 472. See wall diagram in *Délices des Pays-Bas*, vol. 2 (Liège, 1769), reproduced in Lottin, *Les grandes batailles*, 95.

21. Alain Lottin, *Histoire de Boulogne-sur-mer* (Lille, 1983), 106–10. See several plates of the city walls in André Verley, *Boulogne-sur-mer à travers les ages*, 3 vols., (Paris, 1978).

22. H. Noel Williams, *Henri II* (New York, 1910), 282; Henry Lemonnier, *La lutte contre la maison d'Autriche: La France sous Henri II, Histoire de France*, ed. E. Lavisse, vol. 5, pt. 2, (Paris, 1904), 154. See the plans of Metz walls in 1550 in François-Yves Le Moigne, *Histoire de Metz* (Toulouse, 1986), 223.

23. Abbeville's walls look essentially medieval until transformed 1634–1741. Lucien Lecat, *Deux siècles d'histoire en Picardie* (Amiens, 1982), 135; *Histoire d'Abbeville* (Abbeville, 1972), 15–16; Ronald Hubscher, *Histoire d'Amiens* (Toulouse, 1906), 140–41.

24. Bodart, *Kriegs-Lexicon*, 62. Saint-Omer's walls were still medieval in 1668. Alain Derville, *Histoire de Saint-Omer* (Lille, 1981), 151.

25. Jean Bérenger, *Turenne* (Paris, 1987), 237.

26. Vauban, *Oeuvres*, 1:32–33.

27. Ibid., 2:78.

28. Bodart, *Kriegs-Lexikon*, 136.

29. Ibid., 137.

30. Ibid., 169.

31. Ibid., 114; P. Lazard, *Vauban* (Paris, 1934), 225–26; and André Corvisier, *Louvois* (Paris, 1983), 468.

32. David Chandler, *Marlborough as a Military Commander* (London, 1973), 338–39; Bodart, *Kriegs-Lexikon*, 161; and Dupuy and Dupuy, *Encyclopedia of Military History*, 623.

33. Bérenger, *Turenne*, 335; Dupuy and Dupuy, *Encyclopedia of Military History*, 561; and Bodart, *Kriegs-Lexikon*, 84, who gives the size of the Spanish relief force as 12,000.

34. Bodart, *Kriegs-Lexikon*, 168.

35. Documents cited in Parrott, "The Administration of the French Army," 94.

36. Service Historique de l'Armée de Terre, Archives de Guerre (AG), A[1]198, 5 March 1666, letter from Louvois to Pradel.

37. Service Historique de l'Armée de Terre, Bibliothéque (SHAT, Bib.) Tiroirs de Louis XIV, état of 1 January 1678.

38. SHAT, Bib., Génie 11 (fol.), Vauban, "Les places fortifiées du Royaume avec les garnisons necessaires à leur garde ordinaire en temps de guerre." This document is without

date, but marginal notes, apparently by an archivist, analyze the date of the document by the fortresses mentioned.

39. SHAT, Bib., Gén. 11 (fol.), Vauban memoirs, "Etat général des places forts du royaume," dated November 1705.

40. Vauban to Louvois, 4 October 1675, Rochas d'Aiglun, *Vauban, sa famille et ses écrits,* 2 vols. (Paris, 1910), 2:131–32.

41. Vauban, "Mémoire des places frontières de Flandres," November 1678, in d'Aiglun, *Vauban,* 1:190.

42. Memoir on infantry, undated, ibid., 1:287.

43. Turenne, *Mémoires de Turenne* (Paris, 1872), 187.

44. At the March 1991 meeting of the American Military Institute, Christopher Duffy stressed the greater manpower demands created by multiplying the outworks of fortresses.

45. My thanks to Murray for applying his argument to the relationship between fortresses and garrisons when I presented this article as a paper at Ohio State University in October 1990.

46. Parker, *Military Revolution,* 39.

47. Based on figures from AN, KK 355, "Etat par abrégé des recettes et dépenses, 1662–1700."

48. Claude Villars, *Mémoires du maréchal de Villars,* ed. marquis de Vogüé, vol. 2 (Paris, 1887), 229–30.

49. Parker, *Military Revolution,* 24.

50. See his David Parrott "The Administration of the French Army During the Ministry of Cardinal Richelieu," and his "Strategy and Tactics in the Thirty Years War: The 'Military Revolution'," *Militärgeschichtliche Mitteilungen,* XVIII, 2 (1985), reprinted below, Ch. 9.

51. Lynn, "Pattern of Army Growth," 21, fn15.

52. 12 December 1672 letter from Condé to Louvois in Griffet, *Recueil des lettres pour servir d'eclaircissement à l'histoire militaire du règne de Louis XIV,* vol. 2 (Paris, 1760), 143–50. I thank George Satterfield for this reference.

53. SHAT, Bib., Gen. 11 (fol.), Vauban, "Les places fortifiées du Royaume," fol. 12 ver.

8

Fortifications and the Military Revolution: The Gonzaga Experience, 1530–1630

THOMAS F. ARNOLD

ALMOST FORGOTTEN TODAY, in the sixteenth and seventeenth centuries the Gonzaga lords of Mantua and Montferrat in North Italy were among the most notable princes of Europe (Figure 8.1). They could legitimately claim descent from the last emperors of the Eastern Roman Empire, and two Gonzaga women married Habsburg Holy Roman Emperors. The justifiably famous Gonzaga court at Mantua supported artists and musicians of European reputation. And at that court the Gonzaga regularly entertained royalty: Charles V of Spain in 1530, his son Philip in 1549, and Henry III of France in 1574. Though Mantua and Montferrat were not large territories in comparison with principalities outside Italy, they were populous and rich, and the Gonzaga capital of Mantua was famous for its gardens, churches, stately palaces—and formidable defenses. For the Gonzaga could not depend on ruling Mantua and Montferrat simply by right and reputation; other princes, inside Italy and without, could be expected to challenge Gonzaga rule at the slightest opportunity. Such were the facts of political life in dynastic Europe. To hold their lands in the turbulent sixteenth and seventeenth centuries, the Gonzaga turned to fortifications. The city of Mantua in the marquisate (later duchy) of Mantua and the city of Casale in Montferrat became two of the best-fortified cities in all of Europe. Belted with bastions and guarded by citadels, fortified Mantua and Casale ensured the continuity of Gonzaga rule; fortifications were the bedrock of the family's determination to survive as lords of Mantua and Montferrat.

The Gonzaga experience with fortifications at Mantua and Casale illustrates a celebrated larger pattern: the spread of angle-bastion fortifications throughout first Italy, and then the other regions of Europe most threatened by war (the Habsburg-Valois/Bourbon frontiers, the Netherlands, the Danube valley, Ger-

202

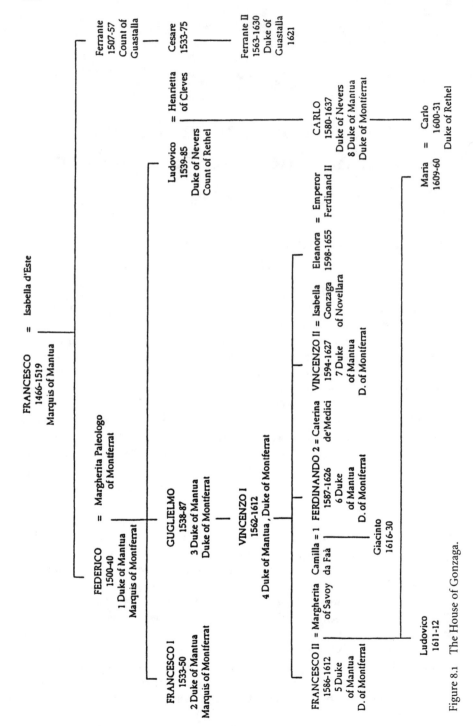

Figure 8.1   The House of Gonzaga.

many). But the Gonzaga experience was exceptional in three regards. First, the Gonzaga were among the very first princes in Italy—or Europe—to embrace the new-style fortifications, based on the angle bastion, that revolutionized military engineering after 1500. Second, the Gonzaga repeatedly embarked on projects at the cutting edge of fortification design: at Mantua in the 1530s, with the Porto Fortezza citadel, and then more dramatically in the 1590s, with the construction of a massive citadel at Casale. Third, the Gonzaga fortification strategy—reliance on Mantua and Casale as the fortified linchpins of the two Gonzaga principalities—was directly tested in war, during the War of the Mantuan Succession in 1628–1630. In that conflict Mantua and Casale suffered two sieges each by Imperial and Spanish forces, respectively. Mantua, fatally weakened by plague, fell and was sacked in July of 1630, but Casale held out against the king of Spain until a negotiated settlement ended the conflict. Even though Mantua fell, the survival of Casale vindicated the Gonzaga duke's political position—and his temerity in risking war with Spain and the emperor. Without the fortifications at Mantua and Casale, the Gonzaga duchies would have been virtually defenseless. The history of Gonzaga fortifications—their construction in the sixteenth century, their wartime record in the early seventeenth—makes them an ideal case study for a discussion of how fortifications helped make an early modern military revolution.

Geoffrey Parker, in *The Military Revolution* (1988), firmly identifies the angle bastion as one of the three critical innovations impelling a revolution in early modern land warfare: "a new use of firepower, a new type of fortifications, and an increase in army size."[1] Parker emphasizes the link between angle-bastion fortifications and a consequent growth in army size. According to Parker, the proliferation of the *trace italienne*—as the new Italianate fortification system was known north of the Alps—forced states to recruit and maintain larger armies both to take enemy fortressess and to garrison their own fortification works. In time of war, the new military architecture placed enormous demands on the warring parties. The culmination of many a campaign was the massive siege, where the attacker matched the defender's angle bastions with extensive earthwork lines, miles long and studded with fortified camps, infantry sconces, and angled ravelins. These lines sometimes faced out to fend off an army of relief as well as inward to enclose the city or citadel under siege; there could even be two separate lines, an inner and an outer belt of earthworks. The greatest sieges became simply monstrous, swallowing whole campaigns to become virtual wars unto themselves.[2] Where geography was most constraining, particularly in the Netherlands, earthwork lines following rivers defended whole frontiers. Armies often dug more than they marched, and a soldier needed to be as "willing to fight with the Spade as with the sword."[3] The need for massive fortifications required the mass mobilization of laborer auxiliaries, in peace and in war. And men were not the only resource needed in ever-greater quantities: cannon, gunpowder, shot, oxen, horses, grain, fodder, wood and a whole catalog of other siege requisites, from matchcord to shoes to shovels, chewed up the enormous sums devoted to war. The new scale of war, in geographic, human, and monetary terms, demanded the organization of (relatively) efficient commissariats and encouraged the growth of state and military bureaucracies to raise taxes, extort contributions, and cajole bankers. For Parker, these momentous changes in the scale and practice of warfare, especially the growth in army size, all flowed from the spread of the angle bastion after the year 1500. Though logically attractive, the essential link between army size and the angle bastion has been challenged as unproven, at least in the French case.[4] It may in fact be impossible to prove, with numbers, that the angle bastion was the root cause of the dramatic increases in army size across the sixteenth, seventeenth, and eighteenth centuries.

But the relationship between the angle bastion and army size is not the only issue. For Parker, the angle bastion had important political consequences. The new architecture was extremely expensive, a fact that suggests that the costs of the new warfare pushed smaller and poorer states out of the balance of power. To support this position Parker turns to the excellent, indeed model, analysis of the military architecture and warfare of the period: Simon Pepper and Nicholas Adams, *Firearms and Fortifications, Military Architecture and Siege Warfare in Sixteenth-Century Siena* (Chicago 1986).[5] This meticulous case study is one of too few monographs examining in detail the theoretical and technical issues of the military revolution in a particular political context. The Sienese experience with modern fortifications seems cautionary: despite much expenditure and effort, the walls of Siena were only partially modernized with angle bastions, and the city failed to hold off a Hispano-Florentine invasion at mid-century. Parker seizes upon this example:

> The Republic of Siena ... lost its independence ... largely because its leaders embarked upon a programme of fortification that they could not afford. In 1553, faced with the threat of imminent attack by its enemies, it was decided that seventeen towns, including Siena, would be equipped with new bastions and ramparts. But labour, funds and building materials were all so hard to come by that, when the invasion occurred in 1554, few of the projected defence works were complete; and yet the Republic had spent so much on fortification that it had no resources left either to raise a relief army or even hire and man a fleet to succour its coastal fortresses. So in April 1555, after a grueling ten-month siege, Siena surrendered unconditionally and was, after a short period of occupation, annexed by her neighbour, Florence. The military revolution had led directly to extinction.[6]

This conclusion, that "the military revolution ... led directly to extinction," suggests that the angle bastion assisted the emergence of wealthy and populous great powers, as the only states who could afford the new fortifications. Parker is not the only scholar to note this connection. In a review of Parker's *Military Revolution* an Italian historian, also citing Pepper and Adams' *Firearms and Fortifications,* concluded that "Italian liberty was certainly the first victim of the military revolution."[7] In this view, the new military architecture was an innovation that weakened the sovereignty of the Italian states, placing them at the mercy of the wealthier proto-national kingdoms of northern Europe and Iberia, leading directly to the so-called Spanish hegemony in Italy. The Sienese example has also led to a more general discounting of the *trace italienne* as an "ambiguous" innovation because "its spread throughout Europe in the century after 1500 was patchy, for the expense involved could bankrupt a small principality or a city-state (as it did Siena in the 1550s and Geneva in the 1580s), and no major city could afford a complete enceinte."[8] This line of argument charges that the overall importance of the angle bastion has been generally exaggerated.

But there is a different opinion as well, that the true political effect of the *trace italienne* was to stymie Habsburg imperialism:

> By checking the sovereignty of siege cannon so quickly, the *trace italienne* played a critical role in European history. By the 1530s ... high technology once again favored local defenses, at least in those regions where governments could afford the cost of the new fortifications and the large number of cannon they required. This put a very effective obstacle in the way of the political consolidation of Europe into a single imperial unity at almost the same time that such a possibility became conceivable, thanks to the extraordinary collection of territories [inherited by Charles V]. ... [In Italy] imperial consolidation halted halfway, with Spanish garrisons in Naples and Milan supporting an unstable Habsburg hegemony in Italy.[9]

In this view the angle bastion was indeed a revolutionary military innovation with significant political consequences—and not bad ones for the middling and smaller states of Europe. The coming of the *trace italienne* has also been identified as part of a larger European pattern of military innovation preserving political plurality:

> [The new military architecture] restored the security of the Italian city-states, or at least of those which had not fallen to a foreign conqueror and which possessed the vast amounts of manpower needed to build and garrison such complex fortifications. ... Above all, it hindered the easy conquest of rebels and rivals by one overweening power in Europe, as the protracted siege warfare which accompanied the Revolt of the Netherlands attested. ... The authority acquired through gunpowder [in Japan and India] was not replicated in the West, which continued to be characterized by political pluralism and its deadly concomitant, the arms race.[10]

Here the angle bastion is firmly identified as the weapon of the smaller power resisting a larger, but a caveat remains: states had to possess the "vast amounts of manpower" necessary to take advantage of the revolutionary new military architecture. That caveat would explain the failure of Siena's fortification policy in the mid-sixteenth century.

This survey of the literature reveals that there are, in general, two opinions regarding the larger political consequences of the *trace italienne*. One point of view maintains that the expense of angle-bastion fortifications limited their effective use to the larger, wealthier states. A second, contrary perspective argues that the new military architecture was widely available to the weaker powers, and effectively obstructed the ambitions of the larger. Because to date the only detailed examination of a smaller state's fortification policy is the case of Siena, the best published evidence supports the idea that the *trace italienne* helped push the smaller states of Europe into political oblivion.

But an examination of the Gonzaga experience proves that the coming of the angle bastion did not necessarily weaken the lesser powers of Italy or Europe. The angle bastion was not, by nature, solely a tool of empire. In Italy—and in Europe—smaller states were not universal victims of the military revolution, and the angle bastion did not usher in any mass political extinction. Contra the case of Siena, in Italy the new military architecture became the basis of a new strategic system in which the smaller and medium powers, though often the allies of the Habsburgs, preserved and even increased their independence. Embracing the new military architecture, the Italian states built furiously. For them, as for most states at most times, whether of the sixteenth or the twentieth century, massive expense and even the prospect of bankruptcy hardly impeded investment in military might. The Gonzaga participated in a trend that also included the Farnese, Este, Savoia, and Medici, as well as the Habsburgs and the popes.[11] The oligarchic merchant republics of Genoa and Venice (the first a firm ally, and the second an even firmer enemy of the Habsburgs) built as well.[12] Even tiny city-states, such as Lucca and Geneva, could successfully modernize their fortifications and rest secure behind massive bastion defenses.[13] At Geneva, the expensive new walls kept out the rapacious duke of Savoy in 1588 and again in 1602; though these new walls were costly, a decision not to build new fortifications would have been far more dear. As Geneva and Lucca show, with dedication almost any state could avail itself of the new military architecture. The example of Lucca in particular exposes the case of Siena as exceptional; with more prudent political policies—in particular, not harboring anti-Medici Florentine exiles—perhaps the Sienese Republic too could have survived and in time constructed a comprehensive circuit of modern defenses.

In the larger pattern, the case of Siena stands out as an exception, not the rule. The new military architecture ultimately imperiled the Spanish position in Italy, not the security of the independent Italian states, and in the end it was Spain, and not the lesser powers, that failed politically and militarily in the face of the angle bastion. Thus Charles V's legacy, Spanish hegemony in Italy, eroded at the same time and for the same reason that the Habsburg position in the Netherlands collapsed: angle-bastion fortifications.[14] Though in Italy in the second half of the sixteenth century there was no great political cataclysm to match the Dutch Revolt, a sixteenth-century Italian arms race in fortification construction just as decisively replaced Habsburg dominance with local independence.

In the 1520s a prince such as Federigo Gonzaga, the fifth marquis of Mantua, would be almost helpless before a Spanish or Imperial army; a century later Federigo's grandson, duke Carlo of Mantua and Montferrat, successfully defied both the king of Spain and the emperor, thanks to the security provided by angle-bastion fortifications. In 1500 any city in Italy was relatively defenseless before the siege cannon and gunpowder mines of an investing army. By 1600, after some seventy years of intense fortification construction, almost every major Italian city bristled with stout angle bastions. Even where there was no complete circuit of permanent fortifications, the maturing engineering science of earthworks could rapidly provide the necessary defensive horn- and crownworks. In the early campaigns of the Italian Wars—the 1494–95 *chevauchée* of Charles VIII of France being the famous example—an army could defiantly march hither and yon, with as much ease as the freebooting bands of the great fourteenth- and fifteenth-century mercenary captains: the Company of the Star, the Catalan Grand Company, the White Company. But by the seventeenth century fortified strong points—citadels, bastioned towns, earthwork lines—blocked free passage along the highways, navigable rivers, and mountain passes of Italy, and any campaign necessarily involved the systematic subjugation of many prickly fortresses. The sixteenth century encompassed a military and political revolution; a revolution wrought by the proliferation of the *trace italienne*. And no case better exemplifies this revolution—or better identifies how smaller states could benefit from it—than the Gonzaga fortification experience.

The 1520s were perilous years for Federigo Gonzaga, fifth marquis of Mantua (ruled 1519–1540). The danger came from the seemingly interminable fighting of the Italian Wars. These campaigns, after thirty years of war or the rumor of war, climaxed in the second decade of the sixteenth century as king Francis I of France and the emperor Charles V disputed their precedence in Europe—and their title to Milan and Naples. The armies of both monarchs, swelled by the forces of Italian allies, marched and countermarched across central and northern Italy, threatening neutrals as well as belligerents. These armies (of up to twenty thousand men or more) were as populous as good-sized cities, and they moved across the countryside like locusts, burning, pillaging, and demanding provisions from the villages and towns within their grasp. In 1527 one of the largest of these armies, a vagabond Imperial host of ill-paid Germans, Spaniards, and Italians, swept down on an ill-prepared and weakly defended Rome, the political base of the Medici pope Clement VII, the emperor's last rival for temporal supremacy in Italy. In a world where cruelties were commonplace and unremarkable, the sack of Rome which followed shocked all Italy.[15] The Florentine humanist Luigi Guicciardini, the elder brother of the historian Francesco, memorialized the fury of the sack in an essay written soon after events unfolded:

> In the streets you saw nothing but thugs and rogues [the Imperial soldiery] carrying great bundles of the richest vestments and ecclesiastical ornaments and huge sacks full of all kinds of vessels of gold and silver. ... Great numbers of captives of all sorts were to be seen, groaning and screaming, being swiftly led to makeshift prisons. In the streets there were many corpses. Many nobles lay there cut to pieces, covered with mud and their own blood, and many people only half dead lay miserably on the

ground. ... After the Spanish and Germans had rested and recuperated somewhat from the incredible fatigue they incurred while scouring the city for booty, they began with many painful and cruel tortures to interrogate their prisoners. Their aim was to discover both hidden riches and the quantity of money their prisoners were able to pay for their liberation. ... Many were suspended by their arms for hours at a time; others were led around by ropes tied to their testicles. Many were suspended by one foot above the streets or over the water, with the threat that the cord suspending them would be cut. Many were beaten and wounded severely. Many were branded with hot irons in various parts of their bodies. Some endured great thirst; others were prevented from sleeping. A very cruel and effective torture was to pull out their back teeth. Some were made to eat their own ears, or nose, or testicles roasted; and others were subjected to bizarre and unheard of torments that affect me too strongly even to think of them.[16]

The brutal sack of Rome in 1527 was only the most dramatic event of a decade heavy with terrifying military calamities. Several major Italian cities suffered sieges, including Parma in 1521, Genoa in 1522, Milan in 1522 and 1526, Cremona in 1523, Pavia in 1525 and again in 1527, Naples in 1527–28, and Florence in 1529–30.[17] Smaller towns and villages unlucky enough to lie along an army's line of march often survived only as smoking milestones marking the soldiers' passage. Field encounters took place as well, the battle of Pavia in 1525 being the most decisive, but that battle, like most others of the period, was the consequence of an on-going siege. For contemporaries the most fearsome aspect of the current wars was the vulnerability of towns and cities to murderous assault by willful, headstrong armies. Wise rulers accordingly turned their attention to the fortifications defending their chief cities.[18]

As a prudent prince, Federigo Gonzaga did everything he could to protect his principality from war, and especially its capital, the city of Mantua, from the twin disasters of siege and sack. He avoided open participation in the Italian wars, instead following the political middle road as long as he could without frustrating and thus angering any prince who seemed strong enough to win. Thus, in the campaign that preceded the 1527 sack of Rome, Federigo deliberately refused to honor a military contract obligating him to aid pope Clement. Instead of obstructing the advance of Imperial troops, he allowed the emperor's German mercenaries to cross the marquisate of Mantua and the river Po without hindrance, essentially wishing them godspeed on their way south towards Rome and Florence. In this way Federigo firmly, if not publicly, shifted his loyalty to the rising star of Charles V, a shift of allegiance that stood him and his family in good stead for the remainder of the century: in 1530 Charles V rewarded Federigo by elevating Mantua to a duchy.[19] Such duplicity should come as no surprise, considering that this was the world where Machiavelli learned and practiced the art of statecraft. But Federigo could not depend on political craft alone.

The safety of Mantua ultimately depended on the state of her defenses, and before the 1520s the city's only fortifications (Figure 8.2) were a medieval circuit of

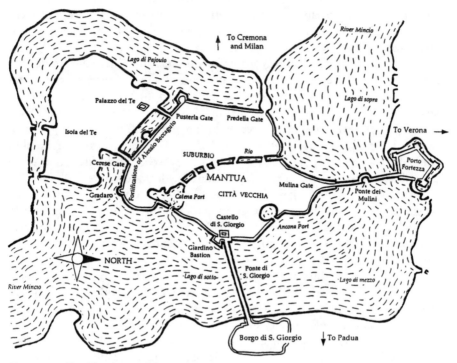

Figure 8.2 Fortifications at Mantua.

curtain walls and narrow towers erected in the opening years of the fifteenth century.[20] Tall and thin, these walls and towers were incapable of withstanding a modern sixteenth-century artillery bombardment and infantry assault. There was also the Castello di San Giorgio, a picturesque late medieval castle, but by the sixteenth century the Castello, as obsolete as the city walls, served only as an armory and as an annex to the surrounding Reggia palace complex. Mantua could still depend on her magnificent natural site, a large island surrounded by the broad waters of the Mincio river, but though formidable, this moat was no guarantee of invulnerability; the city still badly needed new fortifications able to resist the latest techniques of siege warfare. The only attempt to modernize the city's defenses had been made during the 1509 campaign against Venice, but the hasty works erected at that date, almost certainly of earth construction, apparently subsided in the following years.[21] Should a hostile—or merely uncontrollable—army fix on his capital, Federigo faced military and political disaster. Considering the uncertain swirl of power politics in Italy, no fears were groundless. Federigo, of course, was not alone in this insecurity: every Italian prince and government respected the power of the modern gunpowder assault, be it artillery or the mine, and all over Italy cities and towns belted by medieval walls were now relatively defenseless—or, more importantly, seemed relatively defenseless—before an invader's army. The full, horrible consequence of such vulnerability became terribly clear after the sack of Rome.

However, necessity had already sparked architects and military men to develop new methods and new materials of fortification, and by the early sixteenth century the resulting new styles of fortification offered the hope of real protection against attacking armies, even those well supplied with heavy siege cannon.[22] First of all, given the expertise, manpower, and time to prepare them properly, earthwork ditches and ramparts, effective and cheap if not glamorous or durable, could resist artillery fire and infantry escalade very well.[23] Such earthworks could also admirably mount defensive artillery, allowing defenders to reply to their besiegers in kind. By the Italian Wars the tradition of earthwork anti-artillery defenses was a century old, and experimentation with the form of earthworks certainly aided in the development of effective permanent anti-artillery fortifications. In the early sixteenth century there were essentially two schools of thought regarding permanent anti-artillery fortifications. One favored a brute bolstering of the medieval tradition of high masonry defenses: walls and massive artillery towers became extremely thick, fitted with internal casemates chambering defensive cannon.[24] More ingenious, and ultimately more successful, was the development of an entirely new theory of fortification, based on an angled defensive perimeter maximizing the enfilading fire of cannon and small arms to create a dense zone of cross-fire capable of decimating any enemy assault. The distinctive architectural form of this new defensive system was the angle bastion: a low, broad, thick artillery platform, spade- or arrow-shaped in plan. Usually an earth core faced with a masonry retaining wall, the massive bulk of such bastions could safely withstand a considerable pummeling by siege artillery before collapsing and breaching. A sole angle bastion was a negligible improvement to a city's or fortress's perimeter: the cross-fire that was the heart of the angle-bastion system depended on the paired flanks and faces of opposite bastions. For this reason early modern angle-bastion fortresses and fortified cities assumed their hallmark star or snowflake plan, with the flanks of each bastion providing the enfilading fire that protected its neighbor. Early examples of the angle bastion can be found from the last decades of the fifteenth century, from even before the opening of the Italian Wars with Charles VIII's invasion of Italy in 1494, and the idea of an angled defensive perimeter providing enfilading fire, the essential theory behind the angle bastion form, can be traced back even earlier.[25] But in the 1520s the advantages of the angle bastion were not yet conclusively proven. Only in the 1530s did the angle bastion become the unquestioned form of all military architecture in Italy: before that decade's end princes, architects, and engineers had to choose between various defensive options and strategies. Was it best to rely on ad hoc earthworks supplementing existing medieval walls? Or should the expense and effort of massive masonry artillery towers and walls be borne? Or were angle bastions (which must at first have looked queer to the uninformed or unconvinced) the best solution?

For the much-needed modernization of Mantua's defenses the young prince Federigo (born in 1500, he was an exact contemporary of Charles V) at first depended on the counsel of the more experienced military men at his court, men who had proven themselves in the many campaigns of Federigo's father, the marquis Francesco, who had led an allied Italian army against Charles VIII at the famous battle of the Taro, or Fornovo, in 1495. One of these men was Alessio Beccaguto, a veteran of 1495 and several other campaigns, who in the 1520s designed a bold new scheme of fortifications for Mantua.[26] Beccaguto originally hoped to ring the entire island city with fortifications built to his pattern, but financial constraints and other difficulties limited actual construction to the southern side of the city, where the newer Suburbio faced the marshy Te island. In the mid-1520s the Isola del Te was the site of another major architectural project: Federigo's new pleasure palace, the Palazzo del Te, where he could disport with his married mistress Isabella Boschetti, away from the disapproving eyes of the court (especially those of his mother, Isabella d'Este.)[27] Both projects, the Palazzo del Te and Beccaguto's new fortifications, were important for the projection of princely power; such civic landmarks won the approval and respect of the rare royal visitor, and meanwhile they awed the locals and impressed foreign ambassadors and passing tourists. The political purpose behind the new fortifications was very clear: to protect the city of Mantua, and thus the person of the prince and the prestige of the Gonzaga family, from the vicissitudes of politics and the threat of invasion. Hoping to convince Federigo to invest in his program for the complete refortification of Mantua, Beccaguto gushed the advantages of his plan to his master:

> When Your Excellency will have your city completely fortified, you will be able to reply to those who ask, "who is your friend?"—"[I am the] friend of God and the enemy of everyone else."[28]

Beccaguto was promising his master near immunity from the threat of siege and sack, and was therefore offering military security and the guarantee of political independence. For Beccaguto, and presumably for Federigo as well, walls were better than allies. In the war-stricken world of the 1520s, where powerful monarchs such as Charles V or Francis I could threaten invasion almost at a whim—and with those monarchs' mercenary armies often barely at the command of their generals, and sometimes only tenuously controlled by the policies of their cash-poor paymasters—there was compelling need for military and political security. Fortifications provided that security. Though newer and better designs soon eclipsed Beccaguto's efforts, the idea behind his work—that fortifications should provide military security and so ensure the prince's independence—remained the political theme behind all subsequent fortification construction at Mantua and at other Gonzaga cities.

Despite his assurances of their excellence, Alessio Beccaguto's new fortifications for Mantua, conceived by the early 1520s, were flawed in design, and it was just as well that the money or political will was never found for the complete implementation of his program. Beccaguto's design did not depend on angle bastions: rather, his fortifications as built on the southern side of the city consisted of two round artillery towers separated by long stretches of massive new walls (a third tower at the southwest corner of the city remained unfinished). The towers themselves were too far apart to rely on the protecting fire of their neighbors. Instead, it is clear that Beccaguto intended each tower to be a self-defending strong point, radiating artillery fire. Work on Beccaguto's fortifications, never steady, ended in 1528 with the onset of the plague—and Beccaguto died in the same year, perhaps himself a victim of the pest. When the tower he left unfinished was completed in 1531, it was completed as an angle bastion with a pointed salient and deep protected flanks. This tower, known as the Torre Alessio, was the first angle bastion at Mantua, and its construction marks the rise to influence of a new generation of engineers and military men. The two completed towers of Beccaguto's design were not rebuilt as angle bastions, suggesting some ambivalence regarding their design deficiencies. Significantly, when an Imperial army threatened the southern side of Mantua a century after Beccaguto's death, in the fall of 1629, new earthworks were built across the Te island for the defense of the city: the presiding engineer did not rely on Beccaguto's walls and towers, relics of the experimental age preceding the unquestioned acceptance of the angle bastion. After 1530 the root principle of the angle bastion—enfilading fire from protected flanks—determined the design of every fortification at Mantua.

The first great Gonzaga fortification program of the new era was the construction of a pentagonal angle-bastion fortress to the north of the city, on the far side of the Mincio. This fortress was known as the Cittadella or Porto Fortezza, and it remained, with modernizations, the heart of the city's defenses into the nineteenth century. The four massive bastions of this citadel (the fifth corner of the fortress was a gatehouse facing the Mincio) were only completed with difficulty, after much expenditure and time. Duke Federigo's government (Mantua was a duchy from 1530) needed a special duty, the *maccaluffo*, levied at the mills and gates of the city, to meet the costs of constructing the citadel. In 1542 cardinal Ercole Gonzaga, chief regent for the young duke Francesco, instituted a salt tax to finance the fortifications at Porto; this tax stayed in effect until at least 1559.[29] Other obstructions, including the legal procedures needed to evict landowners from the site, delayed progress as well.[30] The masonry facing of the Madonna bastion was only completed in 1570, thirty years after duke Federigo's death: construction of the citadel therefore took over a generation. Yet well before that date the site was defensible, and as early as 1540 the fortifications of Mantua as a whole were considered quite formidable. In that year a Venetian ambassador reported to the Senate the state of Mantua's defenses, including a thumbnail sketch of the city's strategic position and importance to Venice:

[Mantua is] a city very strong both by nature and by art: by nature, most of it is defended by the lake; by art, [it is defended] by a thick wall with heavy bastions where they are needed. [The city] is situated in a place so that, as our friend, it could support all of Lombardy and all the State of Your Serenity, and as an enemy it could endanger it in many ways, because it is 20 miles from Verona; from Legnago 25 miles; from Brescia, Parma, Reggio, and Modena 40; from Cremona, Milan, Padua 60; from Vicenza and Ferrara 50.[31]

From the perspective of Venice, Mantua was the fortified hub of a wider region strategically wedged between Habsburg Milan and the Venetian presence in Lombardy and the Veronese. A Venetian ambassador in 1564 remarked again that the city was "strongly and heavily bastioned," and by that date the Porto citadel would have been very impressive.[32] Fortifications, as well as a large population (some 40,000 inhabitants) and a vigorous economy (silk manufacture, a fertile countryside, and a prosperous Jewish community), made Mantua a city of the first class.

Gonzaga fortifications were not limited to the city or duchy of Mantua. In 1531 duke Federigo acquired title to the marquisate—later the duchy—of Montferrat through marriage to the heiress Margherita Paleologo. The Gonzaga succession to Montferrat was not an easy one. The local elites, both the feudal nobility and the privileged citizens of the principal towns, were unhappy at the prospect of passing from weak Paleologo to strong Gonzaga rule. The marquis of Saluzzo and the duke of Savoy as well had their own claims to Montferrat, and both disputed the Gonzaga inheritance. The Gonzaga acquisition of Montferrat ultimately depended on Habsburg support: for complex dynastic reasons, the original marriage between Federigo and Margherita depended on the grace of the emperor; the legality of the Gonzaga claim to Montferrat was upheld by Charles V in 1536; and Spanish troops from the Milan garrison were needed to help enforce the Gonzaga claim in 1533, 1536, and on several different occasions between 1560 and 1565. French intervention also complicated matters. In 1536 French soldiers pillaged the homes of Gonzaga supporters in the city of Casale. Most of Montferrat was occupied by France between 1555 and 1559, and was only given up as a condition of the 1559 Peace of Cateau-Cambrésis. Finally, in 1565, the citizens of Casale, the most important city in Montferrat, rose in open rebellion. Through a typically Gonzaga combination of guile and force, the rebellion was suppressed and its ringleaders executed or imprisoned in the duchy of Mantua. The first thirty-odd years of Gonzaga rule in Montferrat were therefore hardly settled or secure; in fact, Gonzaga rule could hardly be said to exist. The Gonzaga needed some bridle to curb the restive citizens and nobility of Montferrat, and to support Gonzaga rule against outside interference, especially from Savoy and even France. Perhaps as worrisome was a demonstrated dependency on Habsburg political support and the Spanish garrison in Milan. Revolt, intervention, and dependence on Spain all severely limited Gonzaga sovereignty in Montferrat.

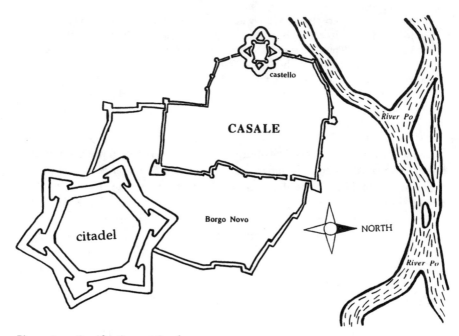

Figure 8.3   Fortifications at Casale.

After the suppression of the 1565 revolt the Gonzaga made fortifications the cornerstone of their Montferrat policy. Casale, formerly the center of opposition to the Gonzaga and the ancient capital of the region, now became the base for Gonzaga control of Montferrat, thanks to a massive fortification program[33] (Figure 8.3). The French, during their occupation, had perhaps first attempted the modernization of Casale's medieval walls with the addition of a single great angle bastion; they certainly considered building a pentagonal citadel. But the first significant fortification project to reach completion was the Gonzaga modernization of the existing medieval Castello, probably in the 1570s.[34] This modernization is a fascinating example of the angle-bastion system; an example in fact without true or classic angle bastions. Instead, four new ravelins—flankless pointed artillery platforms—were ingeniously built along the walls between the existing four towers of the castle. Casemates with steeply-angled firing ports in both the medieval towers and in the sides of the ravelins created the necessary defensive cross-fire. Surrounding the whole was a wet ditch conforming to the star pattern of a typical angle-bastion fortress. Though eccentric, and based on a medieval core, this was indeed a functionally modern fortification.

But a modernized Castello was not enough. Plans for the further, dramatic modernization of the city's defenses went forward. A 1585 plan proposed adding two new large angle bastions to the city's existing medieval walls.[35] After 1587, with the accession of duke Vincenzo I, an even bolder plan won out. Duke Vincenzo abandoned the idea of modernizing the city walls, and instead resuscitated the old idea of a citadel dominating the city, but on a much grander scale: the plan was for an enormous new six-bastioned citadel, thirty-five hectares in area and perfectly polygonal, the largest and most technically advanced angle-bastion fortification in Italy. This proposal was the work of Germanico Savorgnano, scion of a great military engineering family with a considerable reputation won in Venetian service.[36] An army of laborers began work on this superfortress in 1590, and massive earth-moving operations soon created the outlines of ditch, ramparts, and bastions. The more exacting work of facing the walls and bastions with brick and stone was not completed until 1595. Meanwhile, new support buildings—a governor's quarters, a granary, mill, bread oven, and powderhouses (one for each bastion)—went up inside the ample citadel. Integrating the new citadel with the old city took longer, but by around 1605 new ramparts connected both. One of these ramparts, angling between the city, the river Po, and the citadel, opened up space for a new extension of the city, the Borgo Novo. By the early seventeenth century Casale was one of the best fortified cities in Europe, and in size and for technical sophistication the citadel at Casale was unsurpassed in Italy. Duke Vincenzo explained the political purpose of this new fortress in a letter written to his duchess in Mantua on the occasion of the citadel's dedication in 1590. This was to be a fortress so strong "that there will not be another like it in Italy, ... a fortress so unassailable that it will be the key to this state."[37] Vincenzo clearly intended his citadel at Casale to be the main sinew of his family's hold on Montferrat.

Outside observers recognized the success of Vincenzo's intention. In his 1614 report to the Venetian Senate, Alvise Donato, general of the artillery for duke Ferdinando, identified fortified Casale as the "foundation of everything" in Montferrat, because "the citadel, the chief work—and I can say with truth—the glorious work of marquis Germanico Savorgnano, is in the universal judgement of well-informed men held to be one of the most perfect, one of the best planned and strongest places constructed in modern times."[38] Donato went on to explain that this great fortress held the necessary equipment for its defense: strong, modern cannon; weapons (pikes, muskets, arquebuses, corselets and helmets) for 6,000 men; and a continually replenished stockpile of 75,000 bags of grain (50,000 for the city of Casale, 25,000 for the citadel). Casale was the anchor of Gonzaga rule in Montferrat.

There was no lack of challenges to that rule, and events rewarded the sixteenth-century Gonzaga dukes' investment in fortifications at Mantua and Casale. The dukes of Savoy never accepted the Gonzaga acquisition of Montferrat, and a shortage of male heirs kept the house of Gonzaga perilously close to a succession crisis. Between 1613 and 1618 the duke of Savoy twice tried to annex Montferrat by force, causing the Montferrat War, a conflict also known as the first and second wars of the Mantuan Succession.[39] Venice and Spain supported the Gonzaga through the limited campaigning of these wars, but in late 1627 the governor in Milan, Don Gonzalo Fernández de Córdoba, switched Spanish support to the ambitious schemes of the duke of Savoy.[40] The reason for this change was the accession of Carlo Gonzaga in late December, 1627. Better known as Charles Gonzague, the duke of Nevers, Carlo headed the French branch of the Gonzaga family.[41] The Spanish court at Madrid was initially prepared to accept the duke of Nevers as duke of Mantua, but the precipitate military action of the governor of Milan involved Philip IV, and then his cousin the emperor Ferdinand II, in a war with disastrous and far-reaching consequences.[42] Duke Carlo Emanuele of Savoy and the governor of Milan agreed to separately invade and quickly divide the Gonzaga duchy of Montferrat: the duke of Savoy would get what his family had always claimed, and Don Gonzalo would be able to present his king with a nice piece of territory and the fortress of Casale. This neat plan of operations quickly unraveled.

Though planned in December of 1627, the Spanish invasion of Montferrat only went forward on the last day of March 1628. The duke of Savoy had begun his invasion the day before; through the spring and early summer Carlo Emanuele's army methodically occupied those parts of Montferrat allocated to the duke. Don Gonzalo found his campaign more difficult. His small army showed up before the walls of Casale in the first week of April, and the governor of Milan clearly expected the citadel to fall to bluster and the mere appearance of a Spanish force. A parley party from Don Gonzalo approached the citadel and announced— falsely—that they carried a letter from the emperor demanding that the city give itself up. The Gonzaga governor of Casale promptly asked to see the letter, and this simple request exploded Don Gonzalo's *ruse de guerre*.[43] Don Gonzalo then settled down to attempt a formal siege, but his army lacked the manpower to encircle and mask the city, the cannon to bombard it, and even the necesary experts to direct the siege: Don Gonzalo had to write to Genoa requesting the loan of the city's military engineer.[44] The governor of Milan had completely underestimated Casale's powers of resistance. As the spring turned to summer Don Gonzalo's force was finally reinforced enough to mount a proper siege, but the city showed no signs of weakness as the days shortened again and the rains of autumn approached.[45]

Meanwhile, the duke of Nevers directed the relief of Casale from the Gonzaga court in Mantua. At first he hoped to lift the siege of Casale with an army of mercenaries and vassals raised from his French estates, but this scratch force disintegrated as it tried to enter Savoy in the first week of August. With this failure, the duke of Nevers turned to the king of France. In April he had written to Louis XIII and the queen mother, Maria de' Medici, suggesting that an invasion of Italy and the rescue of Casale would be the continuation of Henry IV's unfinished anti-Spanish foreign policy.[46] Richelieu even considered exactly how much it would take to raise the Spanish siege: he estimated a force of 12,000 infantry, 2,000 cavalry, and a train of ten guns.[47] But a French expedition of relief was impossible, at least for now; the king's army was locked in its own siege, before La Rochelle, and Richelieu was determined to prosecute the siege without respite or compromise. The fall of La Rochelle in late October, 1628 made French intervention in Italy possible. On March 5, 1629, an army under the personal command of Louis XIII routed a Savoyard force at the Pass of Susa. The duke of Savoy immediately switched allegiances and agreed to assist the French army in a march on Casale. Don Gonzalo, with no prospect of taking Casale and facing a Franco-Savoyard invasion of Lombardy, had no choice but to abandon his siege on March 19, 1629.[48] Its mission completed, the French army went no farther into Italy, but instead returned to France for a last campaign against the Huguenots.[49] The first siege of Casale ended as a Spanish disgrace.

The war in Italy now became the priority of Spanish policy in Europe. Don Gonzalo's replacement was Ambrogio Spinola, a Genoese with long experience of serious siege warfare in the Netherlands and Germany.[50] He was given the full resources to take Casale. The government of the king of Spain also finally prevailed on the emperor Ferdinand II to intervene against the duke of Nevers, and so 1629 saw two Habsburg armies prepare for a renewed war in Italy. The Imperial army gathered in the Valtelline and then the Milanese over the summer of 1629; as well as reinforcing the Habsburg cause, the Imperial soldiers brought the plague into Italy. By the end of September this army was poised on the border between Spanish Lombardy and the duchy of Mantua.

The duchy of Mantua's first line of defense was the river Oglio, a north-south tributary of the Po.[51] A series of earthwork strong points, built under the direction of the military engineer Francesco Tensini, an expert in such works on loan from the duke of Nevers' lukewarm ally, Venice, reinforced this natural frontier. Despite intense preparation, these frontier defenses hardly withstood Imperial attack. On October 19 Imperial troops assaulted several points along the Oglio. Simultaneously, Imperial cavalry crossed the Oglio on a pontoon bridge at the far north end of the river line and swept down the east bank of the river, scattering what little opposition it met. The veteran Imperial army had expertly turned the flank of the Oglio line, trapping most of the Mantuan and Venetian defenders; only a few escaped the general collapse to find refuge in the city of Mantua.[52]

The city was already prepared for a siege. In late September the duke of Nevers issued a proclamation ordering the citizens of the city, including the religious and the Jews, to appear *en masse* with picks, shovels, baskets and whatever other tools they could muster to work on new earthworks (again designed by Tensini) for the defense of the city.[53] Workers clearing the suburbs of buildings to prevent their use as cover by the Imperial army used gunpowder to demolish several churches. Tensini's impressive new earthworks supplemented the existing fortifications of the city, especially on the Isola del Te and on the western side of the city, the Predella gate.

The siege began in earnest in the first week of November. The Imperial army forced a crossing onto the Te island (the explosion of a magazine holding several barrels of powder routed the defenders) and began to drive trenches toward the southern side of the city, defended by earth ravelins and hornworks in front of Beccaguto's century-old walls and towers. The low water table here made offensive siege operations impossible; the Imperial assault trenches only filled with water. Cannon were no more effective. The Imperial siege guns, mounted on the eastern bank of the Mincio, attempted a bombardment of the city, but the range across the lakes was so great that only three or four unfortunates were killed.[54] Perhaps overestimating the success of this cannonade, the Imperial army prepared an assault on the city by way of the long S. Giorgio bridge. With flags flying and drums beating, a deep column of German soldiers rushed along the causeway. On the city side of the bridge, in the Giardino bastion, a French lieutenant with a few Venetian soldiers had prepared a pair of cannon loaded with musket balls, aimed in a perfect enfilade down the causeway. The discharge of these pieces at point-blank range instantly decimated the Imperial attack; the Mantuan chronicler of the siege morbidly noted that the Imperials, now respectful of the city's defenses, left their dead and dying to rot on the bridge.[55] With the failure of this assault the Imperial army turned to slower methods. A dam on the Mincio downstream of the city backed up the water of the river, drowning the water wheels of the city's mills. Though well supplied with grain, the city faced starvation because grain could not be ground for meal to make bread. The defenders eliminated this threat in a daring night raid in which forty soldiers in small boats destroyed the dam and released the backed-up waters of the Mincio.[56] After these failures the Imperial army sat back to wait the city out. Conditions in the city— the population swelled by refugees from the countryside—soon became dire. Forage was especially scarce, and animals were slaughtered rather than allowed to starve. This created an odd abundance in a city of want: at one point meat sold for two pennies a pound, while a cartload of hay went for forty or fifty silver coins.[57] But as winter intensified the suffering of the Imperial soldiers, in the open and with the plague raging in their ranks, was worse than that of the citizens and garrison of Mantua. In the week before Christmas the Imperial army evacuated its siege lines for winter quarters along the Oglio and south of the Po.

Imperial retreat was a reprieve, not salvation. The defenders destroyed the Imperial earthworks, reinforced and extended their own, and sent cavalry patrols deep into the surrounding countryside. But the raising of the siege sowed the seeds of disaster; the Imperial lines had in effect enforced a quarantine on Mantua, and with the siege lifted the plague bacillus entered the city. In May the Imperial army resumed a close siege of Mantua, and through the early summer the Imperial soldiers watched the defense of the city disintegrate as the defenders died like flies: by mid-June there were only 16,634 sickly inhabitants left.[58] Disease, not any weakness in the city's fortifications, doomed Mantua. Sensing that the plague had worked its worst, the Imperial army assaulted the city from three sides on July 16, 1630. Resistance was brief and the Imperial soldiers soon began their plundering. The duke of Nevers at first retreated to the Porto Fortezza citadel, but on July

18 he surrendered himself and his family on generous terms. With his capital ravaged by war and disease, his cause seemed extinguished. But the duke of Nevers remained unbowed, and he well understood how his fight connected to the larger politics of Europe: after surrendering he airily discussed the wider wars coursing across Europe, especially the situations of Holland and Albania.[59] He then took horse for exile in the Papal States. Though Mantua had fallen, the fortress-city of Casale remained untaken, and as long as Casale held out the duke of Nevers' claims to Montferrat and Mantua remained very much alive.

The second siege of Casale was a much more scientific effort than the first. Unlike Don Gonzalo, Spinola did not underestimate his target, but Spinola's prudence and deliberation gave the duke of Nevers and the defenders of Casale what they needed most: time. Spinola's cautious invasion of Montferrat only reached Casale in the first week of May, 1630; he had already outlined his timetable for the reduction of Casale in a council of war on April 30: the siege lines would go up in mid-June, and Spinola estimated the city would fall by the end of September.[60] Casale failed to abide by these sanguine predictions; its governor, garrison, and citizenry proved tenacious. New defensive earthworks reinforced the city's already strong fortifications, and the defenders melted down a broken cannon to mint brass siege money (tokens that could be redeemed for specie after the war) stamped with defiant slogans such as "no retreat, no surrender."[61] While Casale held out, the plague destroyed Spinola's army. Spinola himself died of the sickness on September 25—ironically, at about the time he had expected the fall of Casale.

The continued resistance of Casale, past even the fall of Mantua in July, allowed a French army to fight a second campaign of relief. This French army crossed the French frontier with Savoy on March 19, even before Spinola opened his siege. The Savoyard citadel of Pinerolo, blocking the French advance, fell on March 29; between June 30 and July 6 the French army crossed the Mt. Cenis pass; and on July 6 the French scattered an army under prince Thomas of Savoy at the battle of Avigliano.[62] A reinforced French force, under marshal Schomberg, moved on toward Montferrat in late August. At this point diplomacy took over. France and Spain were technically at peace, and yet military operations in Italy pointed towards an armed confrontation at Casale. Any such encounter would mean open war. Delaying truces came and went, but in the end (by October 26 marshal Schomberg's army was within a few miles of Casale) Spain backed down. Casale was saved, and the diplomatic conclusions to the war (the two Peaces of Cherasco of April 6 and June 19, 1631) restored Mantua and most of Montferrat, including Casale, to the duke of Nevers, who also received the emperor's investiture.[63] The king of Spain and the emperor gained nothing and lost much; the war was a Habsburg catastrophe.[64]

The Spanish war effort failed because Richelieu and Louis XIII seconded the duke of Nevers, but the two French campaigns to relieve Casale would have been impossible had that city fallen. The primary cause of Spanish and Habsburg failure was therefore the independent strength of the Gonzaga fortress complexes at

Casale and Mantua. Mobilizing the resources to besiege these cities proved well within the powers of the king of Spain and the emperor; taking them proved vastly more difficult. And the taking of one city was not enough; the fall of Mantua—more the work of plague than military action—did not sink the duke of Nevers' cause. For a Habsburg victory Spain had to take Casale. Don Gonzalo expected Casale to fall easily to a *coup de main;* instead, the hasty action of the governor of Milan involved Philip IV in a politically unnecessary and perhaps militarily unwinnable war. Once committed, the Spanish government directed all available resources to taking Casale, but Spinola's siege also failed and the mountain of men, money, and materiel heaped together to crush Casale went to waste. The bastions of Casale, duke Vincenzo Gonzaga's pet project, did not bankrupt the Gonzaga state with their construction; instead those bastions defied Spain's very best effort to take them—an effort that absorbed the full resources of the Spanish empire. According to one historian:

> Spain gained nothing from the War of Mantua, and her responsibility for it was a departure from the doctrine of defence on which her foreign policy was professedly based. On both counts her prestige suffered. So did her resources: by this miscalculation Olivares sabotaged any hopes his administration may have entertained of financial recovery. *The Italian front swallowed up all the crown's returns from the Indies and a good portion of private returns.* [italics added] Of the 3 million ducats of private revenue brought on the Tierra firme fleet in 1629 the crown laid its hands on 1 million and added it to its own 800,000 for immediate dispatch to Italy. ... The War of Mantua was a distraction from, not a contribution towards, the central issue of Spanish policy, the war against the Dutch. Coinciding as it did with the financial stringency caused by the loss of the New Spain fleet in 1628 [seized in the Caribbean by the Dutch], it brought the campaign in the Low Countries virtually to a halt.[65]

In the age of the angle bastion, the cost of taking a sophisticated fortress eclipsed the considerable expense of constructing one. The daunting costs of fortifying *alla moderna* with angle bastions could be spread over decades, and often were, while the money for a siege had to be raised and spent in one campaigning season. The finances of fortress warfare could therefore work to the benefit of the small state. The Gonzaga proved they could afford to build Casale; Spain proved it could not afford to successfully besiege it. That is the tactical perspective. On the strategic level, the *trace italienne* took a weakly held, barely sovereign state— Gonzaga Montferrat—and made it politically viable and nearly invulnerable militarily. That is a revolution indeed.

The Gonzaga fortification experience was not an aberration, and the Spanish and Imperial invasions of Montferrat and Mantua between 1628 and 1630 were not the only campaigns to bog down in siege warfare. The events of several other conflicts in early seventeenth-century Italy reveal the friction fortifications exerted on the pace and effectiveness of offensive operations. The 1613–1618 Montferrat War between Savoy and a Spanish-Gonzaga-Venetian alliance was one of minor sieges of minor places: Casale, the fortified heart of Montferrat, was never even approached. The contemporaneous 1615–1617 Uzkok War between Venice and the archduke Ferdinand of Styria (the future emperor Ferdinand II) consisted almost entirely of a long-drawn Venetian siege of Gradisca. A decade later, in 1625, a quick Savoyard thrust at Genoa easily crossed the frontier, but then collapsed into a lackluster campaign of small sieges. As mentioned above, the duke of Savoy's similar attempts on Geneva (in 1588 and again in 1602) failed miserably before the walls of that city. Finally, the French relief expedition of 1630 had to fight its way to Casale past strong Savoyard fortifications: Richelieu retained one of these, Pinerolo, as France's permanent gate to the Po Valley. The sixteenth-century Italian arms race in fortifications, by bolstering the defensive strengths of all states that availed themselves of the new military architecture, had narrowed the power gaps between city-states and princely states, and between princely states and the great European kingdoms: thus the duke of Savoy could not take Genoa or Geneva, and the king of Spain could not swallow Montferrat.

The same dynamic existed outside of Italy. In the Netherlands the bastioned cities of the Union of Utrecht resisted Spanish reconquest and transformed the Dutch Revolt into an Eighty Years' War—a war that ended with the recognized independence of the United Provinces. In France the Huguenot cities of the southwest pursued a strategy identical to that of their Calvinist co-religionists in the Netherlands. These cities formed what has been titled the "United Provinces of the Midi," and their bastions held off the forces of the French crown for sixty years.[66] The two greatest Huguenot *places de sûreté* (fastnesses authorized by the Edict of Nantes and in earlier Valois concessions) were Montauban and La Rochelle; the second city defied a royal siege in 1573–74 and nearly survived Richelieu's truly massive effort of 1628. Its walls were as modern and as comprehensive as any in Europe. In late sixteenth-century Germany the Free Cities and princes of the Empire exhibited an enthusiasm for fortification construction equal to that of their peers in Italy. There were several northern Casales—fortress cities anchoring small states—in and around western Germany, including Hanau-Neustadt in Hanau, Karlshaven in Hesse, Jülich in the duchy of the same name, Nancy in Lorraine, and Philippsburg in the tiny bishopric of Speyer.[67] The electors Palatine—a family as ambitious in their own sphere as were the Gonzaga in Italy—remade the defenses of their Rhineland principality by constructing a major fortress-city at Mannheim, where from 1606 the Dutch engineer Bartel Jonson supervised the construction of the seven-sided Fredericksburg citadel and an equally heavily bastioned city proper.[68] Fortified Mannheim supplemented new walls at Frankenthal and Heidelberg; all three places held out against Imperial and Spanish armies long after the collapse of the elector Frederick V's Bohemian adventure in 1620, Frankenthal only giving up in March of 1623. In France, Germany, and the Low Countries, as well as in Italy, independent and quasi-independent cities and princes made fortifications the foundation of their military preparedness. No fortification was invulnerable, and in wartime a successful fortification strategy depended on more than strong bastions: allies, disease, generalship, and a thousand other variables affected the course of every siege. But in the broad analysis the *trace italienne,* unquestionably a tactical revolution in military architecture, accomplished a political revolution as well: restoring to the smaller states of Europe a military defensibility otherwise lost in the fifteenth century with the development of effective siege cannon.

Notes

I would like to thank Derek Croxton, Paul Kennedy, Geoffrey Parker, David Parrott, Clifford Rogers, and Geoffrey Symcox for their many helpful comments and suggestions. I am also grateful for the financial support of a John M. Olin Postdoctoral Fellowship at the International Security Program at Yale University.

1. Geoffrey Parker, *The Military Revolution* (Cambridge 1988) 43.

2. Salient examples of epic sieges are the Imperial siege of Metz in 1552, the Spanish siege of Antwerp in 1584–1585, the Spanish siege of Breda in 1624–1625, the royal French siege of La Rochelle in 1627–1628, and the Dutch siege of s'Hertogenbosch in 1629. For capsule surveys of significant siege campaigns see Christopher Duffy, *Siege Warfare, The Fortress in the Early Modern World 1494–1660* (London 1979).

3. The words of a 1643 pamphleteer quoted in Charles Carlton, *Going to the Wars, the Experience of the British Civil Wars 1638–1651* (London 1992) 158.

4. John A. Lynn, "The *trace italienne* and the Growth of Armies: The French Case," *The Journal of Military History* 55 (1991). Reprinted above, Ch. 7.

5. The thesis that fortification costs bankrupted Siena was first voiced in Judith Hook, "Fortifications and the End of the Sienese State," *History* 62 (1977).

6. Geoffrey Parker, *The Military Revolution* (Cambridge 1988) 12.

7. Piero Del Negro, review of Geoffrey Parker, *The Military Revolution* (Cambridge 1988), *Rivista Storica Italiana* 102 (1991) 258.

8. Simon Adams, "Tactics or Politics? 'The Military Revolution' and the Hapsburg Hegemony, 1525–1648," in John Lynn, ed. *Tools of War* (Urbana, Illinois 1990) 36. Reprinted below, Ch. 10, here at p. 259.

9. William H. McNeill, *The Pursuit of Power. Technology, Armed Force, and Society since* A.D. *1000* (Chicago 1982) 91. My thanks to Clifford Rogers for bringing this passage to my attention.

10. Paul Kennedy, *The Rise and Fall of the Great Powers, Economic Change and Military Conflict from 1500 to 2000* (New York 1987) 23–24.

11. For the Medici see J. R. Hale, "The End of Florentine Liberty: the Fortezza da Basso," *Renaissance War Studies* (London 1983) 38; Daniela Lamberini, "Le mura dei bastioni di Pistoia: una fortificazione reale del '500," *Pistoia Programma* 7 (1980); Andrea Andanti, "L'Evoluzione del sistema difensivo di Arezzo: 1502–1560" in Carlo Cresti, Amelio Fara, and Daniela Lamberini, eds. *Architettura militare nell'Europa del XVI secolo* (Siena 1988) especially fig. 1; and Daniela Lamberini, "Giovanni Battista Belluzzi ingegnere militare e la fondazione di Portoferraio," in Giuseppe M. Battaglini, ed. *Cosmopolis: Portoferraio Medicea secoli XVI–XVII* (Pisa 1981). For the Este see Umberto Malagù, *Le mura di Ferrara* (Ferrara 1960) and Paolo Ravenna, ed., *Le mura di Ferrara* (Ferrara 1983) especially the diagrams on 31–36. For the Savoia see Martha D. Pollak, *Turin 1564–1680; Urban Design, Mili-*

tary Culture, and the Creation of the Absolutist Capital (Chicago 1991). For Rome see Giulio Schmiedt, "Città e fortificazioni nei rilievi aereofotografici; II. Le fortificazioni dalla metà del secolo XVI all'Unità d'Italia," *Storia d'Italia* 5:1 (Turin 1973) 220–221.

12. For Venice see M. E. Mallett and J. R. Hale, *The Military Organization of a Renaissance State: Venice c. 1400 to 1617* (Cambridge 1984) 409–447; André Chastel and Antonio Corazzin, *L'architettura militare veneta del Cinquecento* (Milan 1988) and "Il Rinnovamento difensivo nei territori della Repubblica di Venezia nella prima metà del Cinquecento: modelli, dibattiti, scelte," in Carlo Cresti, Amelio Fara, and Daniela Lamberini, eds. *Architettura militare nell'Europa del XVI secolo* (Siena 1988).

13. For Lucca see Giulio Schmiedt, "Città e fortificazioni," 217–219. For Geneva see Jean Pierre Gaberel, *L'escalade de 1602* (Geneva 1855) and the plan in Giulio D. Argan, *The Renaissance City* (New York 1969) plate 89.

14. More than any other factor, the fortifications of the rebellious Dutch cities made Spanish reconquest impossible, despite the great wealth of Spain, the courage of her soldiers, and the competent professionalism of such men as Don Luis de Requesens, who in 1574 remarked: "There would not be time or money enough in the world to reduce by force the twenty-four towns which have rebelled in Holland," quoted in Geoffrey Parker, *The Dutch Revolt* (London 1977) 165.

15. For a political and military discussion of the sack see Judith Hook, *The Sack of Rome* (London 1972). For a discussion emphasizing the literary and especially artistic consequences of the sack see André Chastel, *The Sack of Rome* (Princeton 1983).

16. Luigi Guicciardini, *The Sack of Rome,* tr. James H. McGregor (New York 1993) 98, 108, and 109.

17. The best discussion of the Italian Wars remains Piero Pieri, *Il Rinascimento e la crisi militare italiana* (Turin 1952), especially volume 2 parts 4–6.

18. Again, Luigi Guicciardini: "The terrible events that have occurred from 1494 up to the present day [c. 1528] have brought all of Italy to the brink of ruin. Their example should make not only the wise governors of republics and principalities but even the ignorant multitude realize that no organization and no preparation offers greater security than to be inside your own fortified walls protected by your own army," *The Sack of Rome*, 61.

19. It should be noted that Charles V was Federigo's feudal superior, as technically Mantua was a fief of the Empire.

20. For the fortifications of Mantua under the Gonzaga see the articles in Maria Rosa Palvarini and Carlo Perogalli, *Castelli dei Gonzaga* (Milan 1983). Also important is Daniela Ferrari, "Ingegneri militari al servizio dei Gonzaga nel Cinque e Seicento," *Guerre stati e città. Mantova e l'Italia padana dal secolo XIII al XIX* (Mantua 1988).

21. The one record of the 1509 works is in the Archivio di Stato di Mantova (ASMn), Archivio Gonzaga (AG), 2475, May 2, 1509.

22. Writing in the 1530s, Francesco Guicciardini noted how the balance between offense and defense had swung to the advantage of the latter, in marked contrast to the early years of the Italian Wars. See his *History of Italy,* tr. Sidney Alexander (Princeton 1969) 340–342.

23. For a good discussion of fifteenth-century artillery and fortifications see Malcolm Vale, *War and Chivalry* (London 1981) 129–146. For a discussion of sophisticated fifteenth-century Venetian earthworks see M. E. Mallett and J. R. Hale, *The Military Organization of a Renaissance State, Venice c. 1400 to 1617* (Cambridge 1984) 92–94.

24. The culmination of the artillery tower, the elephantiasis of the medieval fortification tradition, came in Albrecht Dürer's treatise on fortifications, *Etliche Underricht zur*

Befestigung der Stett, Schloss und Flecken—published in 1527, the same year as the sack of Rome. Artillery towers were built in Italy as late as 1525 (at Verona) and 1535, at Assisi. These Italian examples are from Simon Pepper and Nicholas Adams, *Firearms and Fortifications* (Chicago 1986) 22–23.

25. J. R. Hale, "The Early Development of the Bastion: an Italian Chronology c. 1450–c. 1534," in *Europe in the Late Middle Ages* (London 1965). Leonbattista Alberti expressed the essence of the angle bastion system in his *De re aedificatoria*, written in the 1440s and first published in 1486: "There are others who contend that the best defense against a battery of missiles is for the line of the wall to follow the profile of the sawteeth. ... The wall should be flanked by towers acting as buttresses every fifty cubits. These should be round, standing out from the wall, and somewhat taller, so that anyone venturing too close would expose his flank to missiles and be hit; thus the wall is protected by the towers and the towers by each other." Alberti, *On the Art of Building in Ten Books*, tr. Joseph Rykwert, Neil Leach, and Robert Tavernor (Cambridge, MA 1988) 100–101.

26. Evidence for the form of Beccaguto's fortifications come principally from the early plans of Mantua, notably the 1596 engraved view map of the city by Gabriele Bertazzolo and the undated plan in ASMn, AG, 764. Besides scattered archival records of actual construction, the best intimation of Beccaguto's intentions for the form and function of his fortifications comes from a 1522 letter to the marquis proposing new fortifications to front the obsolete S. Giorgio Castello: ASMn, AG, 2503, March 23, 1522.

27. For an excellent analysis of the Palazzo del Te as a political object memorializing Federigo's military position see Egon Verheyen, *The Palazzo del Te in Mantua: Images of Love and Politics* (Baltimore 1977) 24–38.

28. Quoted in Stefano Davari, *Cenni Storici ad Opere di Fortificazione della città di Mantova del secolo XVI* (Mantua 1875) 8.

29. ASMn, AG, 2195, April 17, 1542 and ASMn, AG, 3613, 176.

30. Several documents testifying to the problems of evicting and compensating landowners survive in ASMn, MCA, O-I, including papers dated 1547, 1550, 1553, 1555, 1562, 1563, and 1567. The span of these documents reveals the extremely slow pace of construction.

31. Report of the ambassador Bernardo Navagero in 1540 on the occasion of the succession of Duke Francesco. In Arnaldo Segarizzi, ed., *Relazioni di ambasciatori Veneti al Senato* (Bari 1912) 1: 53. The report also noted that Mantua's defenses included 118 pieces of artillery, a considerable arsenal (though many of these pieces may have been small or antique).

32. Report of the ambassador Vincenzo Tron in 1564 on the occasion of the succession of Duke Guglielmo. In Arnaldo Segarizzi, ed., *Relazioni di ambasciatori Veneti al Senato* (Bari 1912) 1: 66.

33. For the fortifications at Casale see Anna Marotta, ed. *La cittadella di Casale da fortezza del Monferrato a baluardo d'Italia 1590–1859* (Casale 1990) and Anna M. Serralunga Bardazza, *Ricerche documentarie sulla Cittadella di Casale Monferrato* (Turin 1985).

34. The plan for this reconstruction survives: Archivio di Stato di Torino (AST), Corte, Carte topografiche per A et B, 1.

35. Plan dated 1585 by Giorgio Francesco Baronino, engineer of the ducal council of Montferrat: AST, Corte, Carte topografiche serie V Casale Monferrato, 8.

36. For Germanico's service to the Gonzaga see Savorgnano d'Osoppo F. Bonati, *Germanico Savorgnan* [sic], *architetto militare a Mantova* (Mantua 1965).

37. ASMn, AG, 2151, May 26, 1590.

38. Report to the Senate of February 3, 1614. In Arnaldo Segarizzi, ed., *Relazioni di ambasciatori Veneti al Senato* (Bari 1912) 1: 233–234. At this time Venice was allied to the duke of Mantua.

39. For this war see Antonio Bombín-Perez, *La cuestión de Monferrato (1613–1618)* (Valladolid 1975).

40. For an exhaustive account of the events behind the 1628–30 war see Romolo Quazza, *Mantova e Monferrato nella politica europea alla vigilia della guerra per la successione (1624–1627)* (Mantua 1922). For Don Gonzalo in Italy see Manuel Fernández Alvarez, *Don Gonzalo Fernández de Córdoba y la Guerra de Sucesión de Mantua y del Monferrato (1627–1629)* (Madrid 1955).

41. For the duke of Nevers see Émile Baudson, *Charles de Gonzague, Duc de Nevers de Rethel et de Mantoue 1580–1637* (Paris 1947).

42. The situation at the Spanish court is masterfully revealed in R. A. Stradling, "Prelude to Disaster: the Precipitation of the War of the Mantuan Succession, 1627–1629," in *The Historical Journal* 33 (1990).

43. Letter from Sannazaro in Milan to the duke of Nevers in Mantua, April 5, 1628. ASMn, AG, 1759.

44. Romolo Quazza, *La guerra per la successione di Mantova e del Monferrato (1628–1631)* (Mantua 1926) 1:117.

45. Only in early August did the Spanish government in Madrid realize that Casale was not about to fall at any moment, and that Don Gonzalo would need sizeable reinforcements. R. A. Stradling, "Prelude to Disaster: the Precipitation of the War of the Mantuan Succession, 1627–1629," in *The Historical Journal* 33 (1990) 783.

46. Chancellery minutes, April 26, 1628. ASMn, AG, 2309.

47. "Advis que le Cardinal donna au Roy à son retour de Paris à La Rochelle" on about April 20, 1628. In Pierre Grillon, *Les Papiers de Richelieu* vol. III 1628 (Paris 1979) 207.

48. Quazza, *La guerra* 1:337.

49. A small French force continued on to reinforce the garrison at Casale.

50. For Spinola see A. Rodríguez Villa, *Ambrosio Spínola, primer marqués de los Balbases* (Madrid 1905).

51. The strategy for the defense of the duchy of Mantua was prepared in the council meeting of January 5, 1628; ASMn, AG, 2309. A map of the Oglio defenses including troop strengths gives the situation in early September, 1629; ASMn, AG, 3590, 159.

52. Scipione Capilupi, "Memorie di molte miserie," *Raccolta di cronisti e documenti storici lombardi* (Milan 1857) 2: 513–514.

53. ASMn, AG, 2047 bis, 134–135, September 22, 1629.

54. Capilupi, "Memorie di motte miserie," 517.

55. Ibid., 519–520.

56. Ibid., 521 and 525.

57. Ibid., 528.

58. 13,500 secular Christians, 1,434 religious, and 1,700 Jews. ASMn, AG, 2786, June 12, 1630.

59. The duke of Nevers suggested that Dutch or Albanian help would aid his ally, Venice—and thus himself. This according to the eyewitness Giovanni Mambrino, "Vera relatione del modo col quale l'armata imperiale alloggiata nel Mantovano," *Raccolta di cronisti e documenti storici lombardi* (Milan 1857) 2:549.

60. Reported in a letter from Cornaro, the Venetian representative at Turin, to Busanello, the Venetian ambassador to Mantua. ASMn, AG, 737, May 4, 1630.

61. Siege money authorized by the proclamation dated June 18, 1630 in ASMn, AG, Gridario 1568–1650. Examples of these coins are illustrated in Mathew Merian, *Theatrum Europeaum* (Frankfurt 1662) 2: 282.

62. The French campaign is the subject of Jacques Humbert, *Une grand entreprise oubliée; Les Français en Savoie sous Louis XIII* (Paris 1960), for the cited events 170–177.

63. For the diplomacy see Quazza, *La guerra* 2:202, 273–278, and 303–306.

64. "For Spain the results were an unrelieved disaster. Its intervention in Mantua had antagonized European public opinion, driven the papacy into the arms of the French, strained Madrid's relations with Vienna almost to the breaking-point, and wrecked Olivares' grand design for securing peace with the Dutch on terms better than those of 1609." J. H. Elliott, *Richelieu and Olivares* (Cambridge 1984) 112.

65. John Lynch, *The Hispanic World in Crisis and Change* (Oxford 1992) 106–107.

66. For the "United Provinces of the Midi" see Janine Garrisson, *Protestants du Midi 1559–1598* (Paris 1991) 177–224.

67. Contemporaries north of the Alps recognized Casale as a model fortress. After taking Philippsburg in 1644, and improving its fortifications, a French official described it as now being the Casale of Germany. Letter of October 2, 1644, in Archives du Ministère des affaires étrangères, Correspondance politique, Allemagne, f. 376-8. My thanks to Derek Croxton for this reference.

68. Pierre Charpentrat, "Les villes, le mécénat princier et l'image de la ville idéale dans l'Allemagne de la fin du XVIe et du XVIIe siècles. Heidelberge et Mannheim," in Pierre Francastel, *L'urbanisme de Paris et L'Europe 1600–1680* (Paris 1969) 267–274.

Strategy and Tactics in the Thirty Years' War: The 'Military Revolution'

DAVID A. PARROTT

FOR TWENTY YEARS Professor Michael Roberts' work on the 'Military Revolution' of the period 1560–1660 enjoyed undisputed pre-eminence as the accepted interpretation of military developments in early modern Europe.[1] In 1976, an article by Geoffrey Parker made the first—and to my knowledge, only—general criticisms of Roberts' thesis that a series of tactical changes had a revolutionary impact upon European warfare.[2] Professor Parker expressed reasoned doubts about whether these changes could be described as revolutionary, since serious inconsistencies emerge in any attempt to assess their practical impact. Why, in 1634, did the tactically conservative Spanish army wipe out the 'new model' Swedish at Nördlingen?[3] Why were the developments in tactics and strategy unable to bring the European conflict to any decisive conclusion? Parker's suggestion is that Roberts greatly over-emphasized inflexibility and traditionalism in the 'conservative' armies, particularly the Spanish. He proposes that it is possible to trace a receptiveness to similar tactical developments back at least to the *condottiere* of the fifteenth century, and that a willingness to approach common military problems was not confined to the Dutch and the Swedes. In matters of developing firepower, the quality of cavalry, the deployment of small units and in effective training, the Spanish army was quite as progressive as its rivals.[4]

Yet the effect of this is to confirm by implication the importance of the tactical changes commonly ascribed to the Nassau and to Gustavus Adolphus. The value and relevance of these developments in explaining military success in the first half of the seventeenth century are not questioned; neither is the assumption of the importance of tactical change explored in any general way. Some further re-evaluation of the way in which battles were won and lost during the period may therefore be possible and valuable even though, in the absence of entirely accurate accounts of the conduct of specific engagements, some of the proposals must remain conjectural.

Professor Roberts moves from the tactical changes which were the essential element in the 'Military Revolution', towards their main consequence, the development of a new concept of strategy, which envisaged war upon a much broader scale, fought by incomparably larger armies.[5] This, once again, is supported largely by reference to Sweden. Professor Parker's modification—that strategy had always been determined by geography, and above all by the presence or absence of modern fortresses—is equally clearly a reflection of his concentration upon the Low Countries and the territories of the Spanish Crown.[6] My research into the administration and organisation of the French army in the second quarter of the seventeenth century leads me to propose an alternative argument; while it would not be reasonable to maintain that military art actually regressed after 1560, a case will be made that the characteristic of the period was not revolution, but an almost complete failure to meet the challenges posed by the administration and deployment of contemporary armies. Battles were won and lost largely incidentally of the tactical changes of the period. Moreover, battles themselves were rendered almost irrelevant by the failure of a broader concept of strategy to come to terms with the real determinants of warfare in this period.

I

Professor Roberts argues for tactical developments in two general respects: changes in the size and shape of formations deployed on the battlefield, and a more effective co-ordination of infantry, cavalry and artillery.

A) A central contention is that the average size of infantry units was very substantially reduced in the century after 1560, and that this reflected a conscious tactical choice on the part of the 'progressives'.[7] Yet as Parker suggests, the phenomenon of a decline in unit size was equally evident in the case of the Spanish *tercios*.[8] In France, the 1534 and 1558 plans for legions of 6,000 men gave way to the reality of regiments of 1,500–2,000 men by the later sixteenth century.[9] It seems more appropriate to regard the first stage of the reduction in unit size as a simple response to improvements in the firepower of hand guns. The primary aim of a general reduction was to make better use of the shot, which had hitherto been regarded as a secondary weapon, incapable of winning a battle in its own right.

The redoubtable Swiss phalanx of the later fifteenth century had been composed of two groups of soldiers, those carrying the *Langspiess*, the eighteen foot ancestor of the shorter, more manoeuvrable pike,[10] and those armed with close-range weapons, principally the halberd. The weight and awkwardness of the *Langspiess* rendered it far less attractive to the Swiss soldier, and the imbalance between the two weapons was causing concern by the early sixteenth century.[11] In fact, however, the increasing deployment of a third weapon—firearms under the generic term of *arquebuses*—completely changed this situation. While every attempt was made to preserve the proportion of *Langspiesse*/pike in the infantry unit, the halberd was sacrificed to the *arquebuse*, and the number of troops armed with these was permitted to rise.[12] The contributory factor in this may have been the development of more effective firearms, though whether this can be identified with a clearly recognised single innovation—the introduction of the musket—seems open to question.[13] The crucial decade for the emergence of firepower could well be the 1520's. Within three years both the Swiss phalanx and the French *gendarmerie* suffered crushing defeats at the hands of Spanish *arquebusiers* operating in conjunction with artillery from prepared positions.[14] From these events it is possible to trace a steady upward growth in the proportions of firearms within the infantry unit, through the Spanish developments of the 1550's/60's,[15] up to the high point of the concern to maximise firepower, evidenced in the reformed Dutch army of the late sixteenth century.[16]

In this situation, the reduction of the overall size of the infantry unit appears as a logical consequence. The shift from halberdiers to *arquebusiers*/musketeers is only comprehensible if it is assumed that the commanders actually wished to employ their enhanced firepower. There is necessarily a limit to the number of rows in a formation which can be equipped with firearms; beyond this depth the soldiers will obstruct one another, or the time taken for successive discharges by each row will exceed the time required for the first row to reload. The obvious means to ensure that all the firearms could be used was simply to decrease the depth of the entire unit, spreading the shot outwards in lines or shallow blocks. If, however, a large unit of c. 3,000 troops were to be disposed in this shallower formation, it would either be dangerously over-extended, or large numbers of shot would be excessively distanced from the protective body of pike. The reduction of the overall size of the unit to a typical 1,500–2,000 appears to have solved these problems.

The further reduction, undertaken by Maurice of Nassau, from 1,500 to 550 men, seems less clearly advantageous. Yet on the supposition that this was also integral to 'progressive' armies, considerable ingenuity has been devoted to showing the superiority of the Dutch battalion. One proposal is that as the proportion of officers in this smaller unit was much higher, the troops could be better drilled and supervised in the execution of complex commands. Yet Jacobi of Wallhausen, one of the strongest exponents of the Dutch reforms, criticises this as simple extravagance, increasing the wage bill for each unit to no practical purpose.[17] The implication of the proposal is that the existing regiments were passive monsters, incapable of adjustment to changed circumstances on the battlefield and impervious to the commands of their officers. In fact, the number of officers in a typical regiment appears to have been perfectly adequate. Manoeuvres and drill exercises depended less upon the officers than upon the experience of veterans, soldiers who were placed in the three important positions in each line: *chef de file, chef de demi-file* and *chef de serre-file*. These key men, the *appointés* in each company, would be expected to take up marker positions at the front, middle and rear of each line to ensure that the inexperienced recruits executed orders and held their positions.[18] It might be suggested that only states which lacked the nucleus of a 'standing' army would require the very elaborate drill instructions and small formations characteristic of the Dutch reforms.[19] Roberts himself speaks of the drill sense of the *tercios*,[20] while the ability of the Spanish infantry at Rocroi to transform themselves from a line into a massive hollow square is evidence of this capacity in action.[21]

The other argument advanced in favour of the Maurician battalion is the supposedly greater flexibility that it gave the commander of the army, who possessed two or three times the number of units as his traditional opponent. Professor Parker points out that the Spanish had employed *escuadrons* of between 600 and 3,000 men whenever these were required for a particular task.[22] The French readiness to form *bataillons* indicates a similar willingness to break up the regiment when it proved necessary.[23] Yet these smaller units were not systematised; pitched battles of the period had little to do with infantry flexibility; military survival and success required the highest levels of cohesion—both within individual units and across the entire front of the army. It is impossible to see how the Maurician battalions could provide this better than the larger units, and the evidence suggests that contemporaries remained in all significant cases unconvinced. The newly levied forces of the German protestants adopted these smaller units—probably to compensate for a shortage of experienced veterans. Their armies suffered an uninterrupted series of major defeats down to 1631. Indeed, even at Breitenfeld, the Saxon army, drawn up on the Dutch model and shattered by the impact of Tilly's regiments, nearly lost the battle for Gustavus Adolphus.[24] Although Gustavus himself was originally persuaded of the apparent advantages of the small unit,[25] his experiences in Poland led him to a recognition of the fragility of an army deployed in such formations. In consequence, he joined three or four squadrons together to form the brigade, whose cohesion and striking power was demonstrated so clearly at Breitenfeld and Lützen.[26] Though the squadron retained an administrative existence and could be called upon for special assignments, Swedish success in battle consisted in the greater and greater integration of squadrons into brigades.

By the 1630's it was evident that the formation of 1,500–2,000 men had sustained its position against the reformers. Yet despite this vindication, the strength of units continued to decline. This phenomenon indicates the limitations of any purely tactical explanation of military developments in this period; the decline owes nothing to conscious choice, everything to the vagaries and corruption of the systems for troop recruitment in a situation of protracted warfare.

In France, financial and supply difficulties, fraud, death, sickness and desertion, combined to ensure that unit strengths fluctuated wildly throughout the campaign, and were in all cases a small fraction of their theoretical 'paper' strengths. Although a prestige French regiment was supposedly composed of twenty companies of 100 men, even official calculations took the companies at 60, so that the unit was assumed to be 1,200 strong.[27] In reality the strength could be anything from 1,000 down to 200 effectives, with a typical strength of 500–650.[28]

Not surprisingly the French came increasingly to abandon the regiment as a tactical entity, and to amalgamate them into fighting *bataillons* of 800–900 men[29]— ironically these now proved, in general, to be the larger unit. The practice of separating the administrative and tactical unit, far from being an anachronism, was in fact the only practical approach to the organisation of armies whose effective strength fluctuated wildly. It seems possible that Gustavus Adolphus' decision to combine the two in the squadron, a step whose utility is considered to be self-evident,[30] may well have precipitated the same type of uncertainty about real unit strengths and provided an additional motive for the creation of the brigades. Certainly Professor Roberts' contention that the average size of units fell from 3,000 to about 30 men[31] draws attention to a circumstance that was far from generally welcomed. The latter figure reflected not a tactical decision, but the inability of governments to coerce their entrepreneurs into the recruitment and maintenance of full-strength companies. Jacobi of Wallhausen's complaints about the disproportionate cost of officers' salaries in small units find a practical echo in the French administrative correspondence of this period, deeply preoccupied with the financial burden and military inefficiency of supporting low-strength units with a full complement of officers.[32]

B) The assumption made about changes in tactical formations, and in particular about the respective deployment of pikes and firearms in the infantry unit, also seem open to question. Characteristic of the descriptions of these tactical developments appears to be an implicit convention that the enemy forces remained static, frozen in a formation that would best illustrate the improved tactics of the army under particular study. It is difficult to discover how, precisely, the *tercios* fought, but circumstantial evidence suggests that they were not prepared to maintain the illogical formations habitually ascribed to them.[33]

It is usually proposed that *tercios* and other 'large' units were always deployed in a square, deep formation, with a central block of pikemen surrounded on three or four sides by shot, with some additional firearms disposed in wings or separate platoons.[34] The overwhelming disadvantage of such a formation is held to be the restriction upon the firepower that could be brought to bear against an attack upon one side. Yet if the desire to increase the effectiveness of firepower is to be given due weight as the explanation for the reduction in unit size characteristic of *all* armies during the later sixteenth century, then its implications for the deployment of units must also be allowed. For the 'Military Revolution' thesis leads to the improbable conclusion that although the 'conservative' commanders reduced the size of their units, they persisted in a deep formation that deprived them of the enhanced firepower which had apparently justified the initial reduction.

Underlying this misconception is a persistent confusion between the tactics of the Swiss 'steam-roller' of the early sixteenth century, and the characteristic use of infantry as it developed through the century. The Spanish or Swedish pikeman was not part of a solid mass of troops depending upon weight of impact for effect, nor of some inanimate palisade relying upon mutual support and the weight of the ranks behind to meet an enemy assault. Tactical manuals suggest that 'close order' between pikes entailed a space of one and a half paces between each soldier to allow freedom to use the weapon. The order for an advancing formation was three paces between each pike.[35] Pikemen did not depend, as the Swiss spearmen had done, upon the support of their fellows; as early seventeenth-century manuals indicate, the use of the pike had become a skill quite as elaborate as swordsmanship.[36] Thus, there was no merit in depth of pike for its own sake; only the first six rows would be presenting arms to the enemy, while the other rows up to a generally accepted total of ten were a reserve to fill out gaps in the front lines.[37] The pikes would be deployed in a central, rectangular block, while the shot was arranged in groups of similar depth on either flank.[38] When these latter were to fire, they would move forward and take up positions in front of the pike, forming either long, well-separated rows or combining these with detached, slightly deeper, units.[39] Their fire was entirely unaffected by the pikes, and only when the enemy drew close would the shot fall back through the rows of pike, or resume their positions on either side of them. If the pikemen are assumed to be tightly packed in a square, the first of these manoeuvres would be dangerous, if not impossible. But this was not the case; the shot could easily pass through the well-spaced pikes, moving forward again when the enemy had retired. Moreover, the commander, if deciding upon an advance himself, could choose between his shot or his pikemen, for they were not locked together in any fixed order. At Nieuport, the Archduke Albert ordered a first assault upon the Dutch positions by 500 shot alone, and only when this failed did he send forward a mixed formation of infantry.[40]

It seems evident that from a comparatively early stage infantry units were no longer envisaged as independent moving fortresses; infantry were drawn up in lines and the central concern became the maintenance of a continuous front. What this required, however—and this did represent a seventeenth-century development—was a system of one or more lines of reserves. The Imperial disaster at Breitenfeld was largely a consequence of Tilly's decision, overconfident of the superiority of his troops, to place his entire army in a single line. Although this allowed him to concentrate a formidable shock against the Swedish/Saxon army, the principal lesson of the battle was that this gain did not justify the single-line deployment.[41] The contrast with Lützen is obvious; Wallenstein could contain and throw back successive Swedish breakthroughs by deployment of his reserves. Although possessing very limited numbers of troops, he created three lines so that his main positions were supported by two sets of reserves. There is in fact some dispute about the Imperial battle order. Most of the reliable sources attest to the three lines, with five regiments in the front and two each in the second and third, the cavalry being concentrated upon the wings.[42] Yet there is an alternative, frequently cited, account of an order centred upon four great infantry squares drawn up in a diamond formation, with one further square on the right flank amongst the cavalry.[43] The proposal is not inconceivable; this deployment in squares would be appropriate to a battle in which considerable Swedish superiority might lead to outflanking and attacks against the rear of the army. As it happens, the evidence for the line defence seems more convincing; while Wallenstein was pessimistic and did not envisage any possibility of assuming the offensive, he was sufficiently confident of his position and his entrenchments to draw up his troops in line. He considered, correctly, that the Swedes would concentrate the attack against his centre while his cavalry proved strong enough to hold the flanks. He chose therefore to maximise firepower along the front line.

However, at Rocroi, eleven years later, the Spanish infantry provide a rare example of troops who adopted a square formation. The hollow rectangle, formed after the French cavalry had shattered the Spanish second and third lines, included not merely the *tercios viejos* but also eighteen cannon which had originally been positioned just in front of the first line. The concentration of firepower and the formation's immense stability enabled the Spanish to beat off three attacks made on all sides by the entire French army. The battle was protracted from 8–10 a.m., and while this defence led to the wholesale massacre of the Spanish infantry, it also cost the French very heavily—some 4,000 dead and wounded in an army of 23,000. Most importantly, the defence might have permitted the arrival of Beck and the other Spanish corps, some seven kilometers away from the battle at 6:30 a.m.—an appearance which would have tipped a far from predictable engagement in Spain's favour.[44]

Lützen and Rocroi serve as practical evidence of the general attitude to this deployment. The square was not an archaic formation close to extinction, still less the fixed order for the *tercio* or other 'large' units. It had a place in tactical theory and, occasionally, practice, as an ingenious and skilful deployment of troops to meet one particular circumstance—a numerically superior enemy who might prove able to surround the units. Even works influenced by the Dutch reforms provide numerous prescriptions for assembling these formations. Jacobi of Wallhausen, in his *L'Art Militaire pour l'Infanterie*, illustrates a bewildering variety of rectangles, crosses, circles and other geometric devices for between 100 and 6,000 troops.[45] Indeed, it might be suggested that the concern with elaborate drill rituals and geometric precision was far more characteristic of the neo-classical reforms of the Dutch—the belief that geometry and mathematics could provide preconceived solutions to any likely military contingency.[46] Sir James Turner's criticism of 'embattling by the square-root' implies that such practices were still part of military theory in the second half of the century.[47] Elaborate prescriptions for square formations appear in Gaya's 1689 *L'Art de la Guerre*, where the specific context of their use is emphasized.[48]

Such deployment in the face of an enemy who might succeed in an outflanking or surrounding manoeuvre had an inherent logic which ensured its survival into the nineteenth century, and its most celebrated use on the Napoleonic battlefields. Yet this survival should not be allowed to conceal the essentially untypical nature of the 360° formation. Its abandonment in most circumstances was a general feature of the 'military revolution' period.

C) The argument for tactical change also rests upon assertions about improvements in weaponry and the coordination of the various arms in battle. Here it seems necessary to consider how, in fact, battles were fought in the first half of the seventeenth century. For it seems at least a reasonable hypothesis that the salient feature of battles—the increasing effectiveness of infantry acting in defence—renders most of the assumptions about tactical change irrelevant. Indeed, in so far as tactical innovations had any effect, it was to consolidate this supremacy of the defensive.

This opinion requires some qualification. When armies of obviously unequal capacities were set against each other, the defensive potential of the lesser force could not save it from annihilating defeat. This was the pattern of all the major engagements between the White Mountain and Breitenfeld. It is naive to seek explanations for the protestant—German, Dutch and Danish—defeats in terms of tactical theory: the overcomplexity and passivity of 'pure' Maurician tactics. The simpler explanation is that of Clausewitz's 'Military Spirit'; an army of veterans, habituated to a long series of wars and victories, possesses an inherent superiority over its contemporary rivals that no amount of tactical readjustment can offset.[49]

Clausewitz himself cites the Spanish under Farnese and the Swedes under Gustavus Adolphus as possessing this spirit in the highest degree. The same could be said of Tilly's Bavarian/Imperial army during the 1620's. In the last resort, the Spanish, Imperial and Swedish armies won battles, not because of their tactical practices or innovations, but because they perceived themselves as elite forces, embodying a national military reputation for which they were prepared to make a far greater personal commitment and sacrifice than their opponents. When such elite forces clashed with each other, the result would tend to be bloody and indecisive. The Imperialist/Bavarian forces greatly underestimated this Swedish spirit at Breitenfeld; subsequent battles at the Alte Veste, Lützen, Nördlingen and into the 1640's reveal opponents implacably committed to a *guerre à outrance,* characterised by an apparently incomprehensible spirit of mass and individual sacrifice. This 'Military Spirit' is thrown into sharp relief by contrast with the French involvement in the war after 1635; inexperienced armies, largely uncommitted to the foreign policy, were successively annihilated by Spanish and Imperial armies down to 1643. French forces proved consistently unable to sustain the offensive, despite numerical superiority. Even after this period, French military fortunes fluctuated, and forces always tended towards disaster when drawn into battle. Only after 1660 did growing national awareness and military reform produce an army comparably possessed of a 'Military Spirit'.

The 'committed' troops of the 1630's were operating in a situation where developments in firearms and their coordination with pikes, immensely strong cohesion within units, earthwork defences and the effective deployment of reserves, rendered the infantry centre of an army practically invulnerable to a frontal assault. Professor Roberts asserts that the improvements in firing drill, new combinations of musket and pike, developments in cavalry tactics and the emergence of a new light artillery, allowed the Swedes to resume the offensive on European battlefields. Great emphasis is placed upon the use of the salvo by the Swedish shot— the discharge of several rows simultaneously rather than in sequence or at will. It is claimed that this both improved the effectiveness of the defence, and permitted successful assaults against prepared positions.[50] The first claim seems open to question; why is 'one long and continuated crack of thunder' more intimidating than a continuous hail of fire? Though Professor Roberts asserts that Wallenstein's musketeers had adopted the salvo by the time of the Alte Veste,[51] eyewitness accounts suggest quite the contrary. The Swedish Intelligencer makes the more typical comment that: 'the cannons and muskets went off all day long incessantly: so that nothing was to be seen upon the mountain, but flame and smoke ...'[52]

When the practical impact of firepower from defensive positions was so clear, its superficial coordination was probably unnecessary. It may be suspected that salvos were simply the logical product of a specific drill for reloading and firing weapons—itself required as a means to ensure a reasonable rate of fire from units of inexperienced recruits.

The more important claim for the salvo is its supposed ability to 'shatter' the enemy's ranks and allow the pikemen to 'push into the ruins' in a successful offensive.[53] That a salvo will somehow blow a hole in an enemy unit is a classic piece of tactical theory divorced from battlefield reality. Even if a large number of shots did hit their mark, the effect would not be to break up the unit, but to create a barrier of dead and wounded, further impeding any subsequent advance.[54] In fact, however, the effects of firepower were never as overwhelming as the number of weapons and the close range would suggest.[55] As long as the defending unit was prepared to hold its ground, return fire and could draw upon a typical ten ranks to make good losses at the front, it would be capable of blocking and probably repulsing the post-salvo assault. The apparently improved coordination of pike and firearms was insignificant in comparison with the 'will to combat' of the forces involved.

This tactical development was virtually irrelevant to the battles after the Swedish invasion of Germany. Only at Breitenfeld did an assault preceded by heavy fire achieve the expected result—the rout of the Saxon army by Tilly's regiments. But again this is a typical case of a massively confident, 'professional' army pitted against a force that was demoralised and inexperienced. Brought up against the Swedish second line, the Imperial assault faltered and disintegrated. Equally, no amount of resolution in their assaults could gain the Alte Veste for the Swedes.[56] At Nördlingen, Saxe-Weimar's troops launched fifteen separate assaults against the Spanish positions on the Allbach without breaking through.[57] When, at Lützen, the Swedish assaults forced through Wallenstein's first line, they were thrown back by counter attacks made by cavalry and infantry reserves.[58] Faced by confident Dutch or French resistance, even the Spanish infantry proved unable to overcome well-prepared defensive positions—as Nieuport and Rocroi demonstrated.[59] Only one example appears to exist of a battle won by a successful, direct assault upon a prepared centre. At Rheinfelden in February 1638, Saxe-Weimar's troops routed the Imperial forces drawn up outside the town. The circumstances were somewhat exceptional, however, in that the Imperial commanders were totally unprepared for a further attack by Saxe-Weimar only three days after the apparent defeat of his forces. The units were scarcely deployed before the Weimarians made contact with them. There is little reason to suppose that such a direct assault would have succeeded against well-prepared positions.[60]

So how were battles won and lost in this period, given the dead-weight of the infantry's defensive supremacy? Essentially by operations on the wings of the armies, usually involving exclusively cavalry, which permitted the victor to outflank the main body of the enemy and to launch a simultaneous assault on the flank or rear. This, in conjunction with the continuous pressure of a frontal assault against the infantry centre, would stand a good chance of shattering the capacity for resistance, and precipitating a rout by those elements of the enemy army less committed to a suicidal defence of reputation.

Breitenfeld, again, is the exception which supports the rule. Had Tilly possessed more troops to fling into the assault upon the Swedish centre, his flanking advantage might have proved decisive. At Lützen, the collapse of the Imperial cavalry on the left flank after the death of Pappenheim almost gave the Swedes an outright victory in this typical fashion,[61] while at Nördlingen the Spanish/Imperial counter-offensive was successful precisely because the Spanish were able to break in between the forces of Saxe-Weimar and Horne, outflanking both and undermining their weakening defence.[62]

Baner's initial assaults against the front of the Imperial positions at Wittstock were repulsed with heavy loss; the victory was gained, not without considerable risk, by the lengthy manoeuvre which permitted a simultaneous assault on the rear of the Imperial positions.[63] Rocroi serves as the classic model of this type of victory; an initially weak French infantry defence in the centre just held against Spanish pressure. The situation was completely changed by the overwhelming victory of the French cavalry on the right wing, their ability to regroup and to move down against the flank of the second and third lines of Spanish infantry. These non-Spanish auxiliaries were routed, exposing the Spanish front line to simultaneous attack by the French cavalry, and by a considerably revived French infantry centre. Finding themselves in an untenable situation as an extended line, the *tercios* formed themselves into the great hollow square in an attempt to stave off disaster.[64] Further examples seem unnecessary;[65] the pattern by which battles between well-motivated, 'professional' armies were won and lost on the flanks, hence usually by the cavalry, was evident from Lützen onwards.

Given this circumstance, it may be suggested that Gustavus Adolphus' formal attempts to adjust the cavalry's role by a modification of the caracole, were of the most limited practical benefit. After their initial success in the mid-sixteenth century, particularly at Mühlberg, the adoption of firearms by cavalry proceeded everywhere in Europe.[66] The fact that in any engagement with cavalry who were prepared to resort to the *arme blanche,* the pistoleer force would be worsted, was overlooked.[67] The underlying rationale of cavalry equipped with firearms, and their elaborate employment in the caracole,[68] was the same orthodoxy that it would be possible to blow holes in ten-deep infantry formations as a prelude to charging to contact, or to break the order of an opposing cavalry force preparatory to a clash with swords. The inability to accept that this would simply not occur against well-disciplined and motivated troops had a predictable effect both upon 'progressive' tactical developments, and upon the efforts of their subsequent apologists.

The prescriptions for the deployment of Swedish cavalry, and their coordination with detached platoons of musketeers,[69] were based upon the assumption that pistoleer tactics could be made to work if only the weight of shot were sufficiently increased—the same misapprehension which informed tactical changes for the infantry. It is extremely difficult to see how the new system worked in practice; Professor Roberts himself considers that it may simply have been a trading of disadvantages. To make the musketeers' salvos successful—in terms of the theory—it would be necessary for both the cavalry and the platoons of shot to approach to a distance at which they would be subjected to equally heavy counterfire from the defenders. The cavalry themselves would then be so close that they would find it difficult to build up even the momentum of a rapid trot in the intervening distance, and would leave the defenders time to prepare themselves for the impact. In fact, as horses are not prepared to run straight into obstructions, the cavalry assault would disintegrate some yards away from the reassembled formation. Yet if the advance began out of range of the defenders, the musketeers' salvo would prove (even more) ineffective, and the subsequent cavalry charge stand no chance of success.

The real answer to this battlefield impasse was to encourage the cavalry to seek means of getting around the front of infantry units in order to attack on the flank or from behind. But by attaching groups of shot to the cavalry, and permitting the survival of the caracole, Gustavus Adolphus' reform may have made this type of manoeuvre more difficult by discouraging an essential mobility. It seems that the deployment of musketeers amongst the cavalry quickly lost its original character. At Lützen, Wallenstein made use of small groups of shot with the intention, not that they should assist a cavalry offensive, but simply to stabilise the Imperial front line up to Lützen itself.[70] In reality, even as tactical theory affirmed a direct reliance upon firearms, cavalry engagements on the flanks of the armies had become far too important to be fought in such a limited fashion. The typical cavalry conflict from Lützen onwards was a close quarter engagement in which both swords and firearms were used at point-blank range. Here again, the crucial factor was not 'new' tactics but the resolution of the combatants. The cavalry who defeated their opponents would then have an opportunity to break into the flank or rear of the enemy centre, making outright victory a possibility. At Lützen, the death of Pappenheim and the rout of the Imperial cavalry was, in tactical terms, almost as great a setback as the death of Gustavus Adolphus to the Swedes.[71] Even if the cavalry engagement began with an exchange of shot, or with the discharges of some supporting infantry, this would serve only as a prelude to the all-important hand-to-hand engagement on which the outcome of battles after 1632 almost invariably depended. The Swedish cavalry was no different from its enemies in its rapid *de facto* resumption of a fighting style which owed more to individual commitment and training than tactical reforms.

The developments in artillery in this period should not be isolated from these problems. What would have revolutionized the battlefield stalemate was the development of a light and highly mobile field artillery, the horse artillery of a later age, capable of the same degree of mobility as cavalry. The vaunted reforms of Gustavus Adolphus produced nothing capable of approaching this requirement. The Swedish king devised a three pound cannon, with an effective range of 300 yards, which required a crew of only two gunners and could be manoeuvred with the aid of one horse. The guns were produced in very substantial numbers, and attached to individual infantry squadrons. At Breitenfeld, the Swedes had at least 75 cannon, mainly of this three pound type, against 26 on the Imperial side.[72] Yet to all practical purposes, the guns were still stationary during a battle—or rather they were not mobile as a matter of course. The teams of good-quality horses and individual, portable supplies of ammunition did not exist to make mobility straightforward; it remained possible only as the result of specific, large-scale operations. This was the case at Jankow, where a large part of the Swedish military effort consisted in getting cannon up to a position, overlooking the flank of the Imperial army, that had earlier been taken by the cavalry.[73]

In contrast to this, Gustavus Adolphus considered it too difficult and dangerous to despatch infantry and artillery support to Saxe-Weimar, who had captured a vantage point overlooking Wallenstein's camp on the Alte Veste.[74] Professor Roberts' contention that it was artillery of the Swedish type, in conjunction with cavalry, that accounted for the destruction of the Spanish *tercios* at Rocroi, is misleading. It was the arrival of a couple of French field pieces which, in conjunction with massed infantry fire, made it possible finally to break open the Spanish square at the fourth assault. However, this success was in marked contrast to the failure of previous assaults without artillery support, during which time the French cannon were being moved painstakingly across a few hundred yards of battlefield.[75] Unable to move with the cavalry to exploit an advantageous flanking attack, the effect of light artillery was to strengthen the already weighty preeminence of defensive tactics, raising the levels of casualties and ensuring the costly failure of any direct assault upon prepared positions.

In the course of this discussion it becomes evident that an unbridgeable gap lies between tactical theory—the supposed resumption of the offensive with the aid of enhanced and redeployed firepower—and the perceived reality of battles characterised by a growing defensive capability and decided by 'traditional', close-quarter cavalry engagements. Whether or not this revision is accepted completely, it must indicate the dangers of relying upon justifications of self-conscious innovators and, in general, of attaching too much importance in any explanation of military success to the effects of tactical changes.

I I

Given this overwhelming superiority of the defensive, it might reasonably be asked why pitched battles occurred at all? The post-1621 phase of the war in the Netherlands was marked by the almost total disappearance of set-piece battles in favour of protracted sieges and elaborate manoeuvrings.[76] Yet elsewhere in Europe battles were still sought and waged with a commitment which suggests that they were considered to be of crucial importance. Paradoxically, the explanation for this readiness to commit armies to potentially decisive engagements lies not in a positive conception of the role of battle in an overall strategy, but in the failure of such strategy to provide any escape from the constraints of finance and logistics. Because of this failure, army commanders, even after victorious battles, were more likely to be prisoners of circumstances than masters of states.

Professors Roberts and Parker agree in regarding an immense increase in the size of armies over the period 1500–1700 as clear evidence of some type of revolution. It is perhaps necessary to draw a distinction between military and, broadly speaking, political factors in accounting for this expansion. In aggregate, armies increased at least ten-fold, from the forces of 25–30,000 men employed by the powers involved in the Italian Wars of the early sixteenth century,[77] to the 387,520 troops theoretically maintained in the armies and garrisons of France in 1690.[78] Yet such figures suggest a steady increase in the size of armies which is misleading. The forces involved in specific battles in the 1640's/50's were individually no larger than those of the previous century.[79] Even in the more prosperous 1630's, battles involving substantially more than 20,000 troops were rare. Breitenfeld, with 41,000 Swedes and Saxons set against Tilly's 31,000 troops, was unique down to the 1660's.[80] Indeed, the wars of Louis XIV were the first occasion of a real increase in the forces involved in battles.

This disparity between the overall size of the forces raised by the European powers, and those actually involved on the battlefield, deserves some attention. Professor Parker argues that the increase in the size of armies was due, in the first instance, to the development of fortification techniques—above all to the *trace italienne*—which required many more troops, especially relatively cheap infantry, to enforce an effective blockade.[81] However, overlapping with this, and increasingly taking over from it at the beginning of the seventeenth century, was a more obviously political conception of the role of military force.

Charles V does not appear to have thought beyond individual victories in the field towards a permanent military solution to the political challenge of the German protestant princes; Mühlberg was not followed by any systematic employment of military coercion. The contrast with the use of the Imperial and Bavarian armies in the 1620's is striking. The threat or reality of military pressure was here being used to enforce substantial political and religious change. From the expansion of the Army of Flanders in the 1570's, it seems clear that armies were perceived as a means to place pressure upon entire states and populations by their simple presence, as much as instruments for winning a specific military advantage. The imposition of the Edict of Restitution in a situation where the Catholic armies were unchallenged in Germany provides the clearest example of this conception of the use of military force.

To this political intention must be added the incontestable fact that the inflationary process was both cumulative and irreversible. Given that substantial numerical inferiority was a handicap that no strategic or tactical innovations could overcome, it became incumbent upon major states to raise the largest armies possible. Even if Gustavus Adolphus and Richelieu accepted neither the political nor technical justifications for military expansion, the established size of the Habsburg war machine by the 1630's made a comparable effort to raise unprecedented armies inevitable.

None of this seems particularly contentious; what does require more substantial modification is the assumption made by both Roberts and Parker that the expansion of armies was dependent upon the fulfilment of certain administrative and financial preconditions in the state. Both consider that 'there had to be governments capable of organising and controlling large forces', and capable of mobilising and expanding the financial resources of society.[82] While this was undoubtedly the case in the later seventeenth century—evidenced in Brandenburg-Prussia, Sweden, the Cromwellian Protectorate and, above all, France,[83] it was certainly not the case amongst the protagonists of the Thirty Years' War.

The period of substantial military expansion, above all, the 1620's/30's, coincided with the apogee of the military enterpriser, the colonel or 'General Contractor' who offered to undertake the administrative and (immediate) financial burdens of raising a regiment or an entire army for their overlords.[84] It seems paradoxical that monarchs, increasingly concerned to assert the theory of absolute sovereignty, should have had to rely upon armies raised and maintained by private contractors. Yet this is less contradictory than it appears, since the greatly inflated armies of this period were forced by external political circumstances upon states whose administrative structures were not able to cope with this expansion. Indeed, without the administrative and above all, credit facilities of the enterpriser, even the great powers of the early seventeenth century would have proved unable to raise the armies of 50,000–100,000 characteristic of this period. Even where, as in Holland, the capacity to fund the army through state channels existed, the enterprise system was still adopted to avoid the administrative burden and 'opportunity cost' of recruiting a directly levied militia in the Provinces.[85]

In most cases, however, the principal reason was financial incapacity—the broadening gulf between the revenues available to the state and the cost of the armies that it felt obliged to maintain. Not merely were the revenues inadequate overall, but the primitive mechanisms of tax extraction rendered it impossible to collect large sums at the crucial points in the military year: spring recruitment, initial campaign expenses, autumn disbandment or winter quarters. The entrepreneur could make good these inadequacies through his (comparatively stronger) credit facilities—the ability to mobilise a host of avaricious subcontractors, and his relationship with pure financiers who had access to the international money market.[86]

Yet all of this was ultimately sleight of hand; at some point the state had to pay for the army mobilised through the efforts of its entrepreneur-subjects. Merely to keep the credit-system running, Wallenstein stipulated that he required 'ein par Million alle Jahr'.[87] Beyond this, however, any substantial payment of the entrepreneurs' expenses would be outside the resources of the government. The 'solution' was the notorious *Kontributionssystem*—licence to exact cash payments from enemy, neutral and ultimately, friendly territory at well above the rates required for the basic subsistence of the army.[88] The difference would be employed to reimburse the colonels, captains and other subcontractors for a portion of their initial outlay, and to satisfy the most pressing demands of the financiers and suppliers.

The inherent problem of such a system was that, especially when combined with the general, illegal depredations of the soldiery, it would rapidly exhaust the economic potential of whole areas of the campaign theatre. This process was accelerated by the reluctance of the civilian populations to submit willingly to repeated, crippling exactions in money and kind. Contributions therefore had to be extracted under continuous military pressure. Wallenstein suggested that he could support an army of 50,000 men in Germany, but not one of 20,000.[89] The armies expanded for yet another non-military reason: to facilitate the levy of Contributions which, by their very scale, inevitably rendered this method of supporting the forces increasingly unreliable.

What were the alternatives? In this period it seems clear that there were none. France provides an illuminating example of a state which rejected a purely entrepreneurial model for its army. The experience of civil war and weak, regency government characteristic of most of the period 1560–1629, rendered the French crown implacably opposed to the principle of delegating military authority under any form of overt entrepreneurship.[90] Yet the resources available to the French crown were no more capable of supporting its military commitment. Officers and overall commanders were informally expected to contribute to the costs of their units or armies, but under various formulae which ruled out any claim to reciprocal entrepreneurial rights. The officer had no control over the disbandment or reformation of his unit, and could expect no compensation for any costs incurred during the command. Even if killed on active service, he had no guarantee that the unit would subsequently be transferred to one of his relatives, rather than to a fresh petitioner. The crown, attempting to sustain a military effort beyond its accessible resources, played upon the enthusiasm for military office amongst the wealthy groups of French society, and the subsequent threat to disband their units, as a means to obtain the additional credit that elsewhere was mobilised by an acknowledged, contracted entrepreneurial system. The price paid in terms of the absenteeism, insubordination and corruption of the French officer-corps was entirely disproportionate. Had an effective military administration existed as it was to do in the 1660s/70s, it might have proved possible to minimize the worst effects of this system. In fact, the financial inadequacy which pushed the government towards such dangerous expedients was matched by a complete failure of the existing administration to meet the challenge of controlling the army, or of disciplining and restraining the corruption of the officer-corps. Far from leading to rationalisation and development, large-scale warfare pushed this administration into an increasingly all-pervasive inadequacy. Together with the related inability to develop a permanent, professional officer-corps, this failure does much to explain the outstandingly poor performance of the French army during Richelieu's ministry.

Both entrepreneurship and this inadequate blend of central direction and unreciprocated credit-exploitation, imposed constraints upon army commanders. The general of an army made up of entrepreneur colonels and their regiments had to deploy his forces primarily to facilitate the extraction of Contributions, and had to maintain a sufficient number of troops under arms to coerce the payment of these by reluctant civil populations. Equally, the French commander was constantly faced by the realities of inherently inadequate central funding. A Contribution system was not (at least legally) authorised, and the compensatory mobilisation of the officers' resources confirmed their view of themselves as privileged volunteers, serving at personal convenience rather than under enforceable contracts.

It is the presence of these constraints which renders discussion of developments, or a revolution, in strategy largely unconvincing. The overriding need to pay and supply armies inflated beyond the capacities of their states, reduced strategy to a crude concern with territorial occupation or its denial to the enemy. Inadequate administration, or the limited Contribution-potential of the main campaign theatres sharply constrained the commanders' freedom of action. Large-scale transport of supplies—despite the establishment of rudimentary frontier magazines—was beyond the capacities of the early modern state, which could raise troops but not the horses, waggons and food supplies required to support them on an extended campaign. The constant penalty for failure to exact finance and supplies, or for the non-cooperation of *trésoriers,* financiers or *munitionnaires,*[91] was the dissolution of the army. Troops who had not received a basic subsistence in money or kind would desert. (Mutiny, although equally destructive, was the prerogative of elite forces, confident of their central importance to the war-effort.[92]) Mass desertion, facilitated by the corruption or absenteeism of the unit officers, could destroy the military capacity of the state far more effectively than enemy action.[93] The French army which attempted to invade Flanders in 1635 was fairly reliably calculated at 22,000 infantry and 4,500 cavalry.[94] By mid-June, supply problems had reduced this to 13,000 foot and 4,000 horse, while by the end of the campaign the army numbered fewer than 8,000 infantry and 2,000 cavalry, despite having received reinforcements from Picardy in July.[95] This wastage rate of between 50 and 75% was typical, striking only in that the French obligations to the Dutch ensured that the army began the campaign with an exceptionally high effective strength. In most cases the armies entered the campaigns significantly under strength. Large-scale desertion before and during the campaigns rendered calculations of army size meaningless, and suggests that the forces of 150–200,000 troops customarily ascribed to Richelieu's war effort overestimates the reality by at least 50%.[96] While the uniquely unsatisfactory relationship between the administration and the officer corps may have aggravated the problem of mass desertion in the French case, there can be no doubt that it was the common experience of all the armies of the period. Gustavus Adolphus' army in Bavaria was reduced by at least 50% during the fruitless three-month siege of Wallenstein's camp outside Nuremberg.[97]

How could a collapse of army strength be avoided? For the French, or any other army unable to draw upon Contributions, by not outrunning the supply facilities (however inadequate) established in the frontier provinces, and by imposing the most rigorous constraints upon military action. Attempts to move beyond limited policies simply revealed the extent to which logistical practice lagged behind the scale of armies—with invariably disastrous consequences.[98] Moving across the Rhine and living from a *de facto* Contribution system in competition with enemy forces might appear a solution. In reality the extent of the devastation in these areas, and the tenacity of the Imperial forces, rendered the systematic extraction of support almost impossible. Desertion in the French 'armies of Germany' was catastrophic; the simple news that a unit was to move into Germany could reduce it by 50% overnight, according to Richelieu.[99] Where the Contribution system *had* to be made to operate, it was unrealistic to envisage any type of strategy that did not accept this as the fundamental priority. The main issue was whether the Contributions could be gathered from enemy territory—thus imposing additional pressure upon the opponent—or whether the army would be forced to live off neutral or home territory. Campaigns reflected this simple logistical imperative: battles were about the control of territory with supply potential, not the culmination of any overall strategy clearly and directly related to the state's war-aims. In that fatal sense warned of by Clausewitz, warfare had become completely divorced from its political object.[100] Breitenfeld occured, not because Gustavus Adolphus was confident of his capacity to defeat Tilly's veterans and

anxious to seek out battle as quickly as possible,[101] but because of the need to expand the Contribution-base of his own army and to deny Tilly the opportunity of
using Saxony for the same purpose. After Breitenfeld, Gustavus did not use his
enhanced army in a direct advance against the Hereditary Lands to try to end the
war decisively, but moved into the Rhineland, subjecting the various principalities to systematic Contributions. Given the diplomatic difficulties that this provoked with France, angling as ever to create a Catholic, anti-Habsburg power-
bloc in Germany, and the essential strategic pointlessness of the move in terms of
Sweden's declared war aims, it must be taken as a clear instance of the influence of
logistics upon strategy.[102]

In 1632, the duel between Wallenstein and Gustavus Adolphus reflected the
same preoccupation. The destruction of half of the Swedish army before Nuremberg owed little to the specific failure to capture Wallenstein's positions, far more
to the confinement of 45,000 troops in an area whose supply-potential was
quickly exhausted and where the yield from more extended zones of Contribution
began to dry up. Having exploited this logistical circumstance to his advantage,
Wallenstein, dispersing his army rather than suffering its dissolution through
growing supply difficulties, was himself caught by Gustavus at Lützen.[103]

This explains the disparity between the size of armies overall and of the forces
involved on a specific battlefield. The limitations of the supply system severely restricted the number of troops who could be concentrated in one particular theatre. Gustavus Adolphus' 'Great Arc' of seven separate forces advancing across
Germany seems less the product of strategic genius,[104] more a response to the
common knowledge that 175,000 men (or whatever force Sweden *actually* had under arms at this stage) concentrated upon a single front would simply starve. Garrisoning, largely to supervise the extraction of Contributions, and the dispersion
of blocks of troops over broad areas of territory, were the unavoidable consequence of sustaining an army of this scale in the absence of effective centralised
administration and supply.

I have deliberately chosen examples of strategy determined by logistics from
the early 1630's, perhaps the halcyon period of military entrepreneurship. The situation for both *Kontributionssystem* and direct administration had deteriorated
significantly by the 1640's. The exhaustion of numerous campaign theatres was
compounded by the most notorious aspect of the Thirty Years' War—the systematic ravaging and destruction of whole areas of territory in a bid to deprive the enemy of logistical support after the 'friendly' army had withdrawn. Far from being
a product of confessional barbarism, the policy reflected a clear-sighted awareness
that the movements of the enemy could be severely restricted by the efficient destruction of local resources. So, however, were the subsequent strategic choices
available to the commander who ordered the destruction. The size of the individual armies involved in operations or battles fell drastically: 10–15,000 troops
seems to have been the typical size, outside of Franco-Spanish campaigns on the
Flanders frontier. Attempts are made to dignify what had degenerated into a

struggle almost exclusively concerned with control of territory which might provide temporary relief from the all-pervasive problem of supply and finance. The 'new style' of warfare—small armies containing at least 50% cavalry—abandoned systematic Contributions in favour of direct extortion and a *guerre des courses* devoid of strategic significance. The war became one of survival: the series of defeats suffered by the Imperial armies after 1645 did not bring a military solution within sight. They did, however, confirm that the Swedish and French armies controlled the exiguous supply potential of Germany. As long as the war continued the Emperor would be forced to support his shrinking armies from the resources of the Hereditary Lands. Even had he been prepared to accept such an expedient, it is probable that his military entrepreneurs would not. The Peace of Westphalia, with its concern for Swedish indemnities and the consolidation of the Emperor's power within his own territories, is a significant indication of the nature of warfare in the 1640's; victories could consolidate a military advantage but could not precipitate any overall defeat of the enemy state. The continuation of the Franco/Spanish conflict down to 1659 merely emphasised the same situation.

Peace, the return of relative prosperity, and the development of a far more effective military administration, permitted the further expansion of armies from the 1660's—an inflationary process fuelled on this occasion by Louis XIV's France. Yet the vice of logistical constraints was scarcely loosened in its grip upon the formulation and execution of strategy. As G. Perjes proposes:

> If the efficiency of strategy was impaired by the initial trouble, difficulties arising from the low standards of food supply and agrarian techniques, low population density and the backwardness of transportation methods, how much greater was the gulf between the political aims of the war and the strategy destined to realise them, since the inadequacy of state administration and financial difficulties themselves were instrumental in widening this gap.[105]

The central feature of seventeenth-century warfare was the relative ease with which states could raise large numbers of troops, but in circumstances where it proved impossible to match these forces with adequate or reliable administrative mechanisms. In the first half of the century the problem was above all of inadequate financial resources to pay or supply the armies. The 'administrative revolution' of the second half, and the full emergence of the 'coercion/extraction' cycle, may have gone some distance towards solving the immediate problem, but this served only to reveal the inherent technological and bureaucratic weaknesses of early modern states confronted with the burden of supporting armies 200–300,000 strong. Throughout the century the penalty for neglecting logistical imperatives—in effect, for pursuing a strategy reflecting political war-aims—remained the collapse of the army through mass-desertion or complete supply failure.

Thus on counts of both tactics and strategy, I have reservations about the concept of a 'military revolution' in the period 1560–1660. In the field of tactics there is little evidence to support a division into 'progressives' and 'conservatives' in matters of unit size and formations. Improvements in weaponry and the methods of combining the three arms merely consolidated the already imposing preeminence of the army drawn up on the defensive. The partial solution to the problem of reestablishing a balance between offensive and defensive came from a systematic resumption of close-quarter cavalry engagements.

While it might be too sweeping to suggest that commanders in the Thirty Years' War were entirely uninfluenced by strategic considerations, their freedom to act in accordance with any overall strategy was almost completely curtailed. The growing size of armies initially reflected political considerations and ambitions; subsequently it became a necessary response to the commitment of other powers. Forced to increase beyond the resources available to the state, the insoluble problems of pay and supply became progressively all-embracing as the war moved into its final crisis. Tactics and strategy in the Thirty Years' War are perhaps best characterised as being undermined by two persistent failures: in the one case, to break the dominance of the defensive; in the other, to cope with logistical inadequacy.

Notes

1. M. Roberts: 'The Military Revolution, 1560–1660.' Belfast 1955, reprinted above, chapter 1; id.: 'Gustav Adolf and the Art of War.' Belfast 1955, see also in id.: *Essays in Swedish History.* London 1967, pp. 56–81. Roberts: *Gustavus Adolphus. A History of Sweden 1611–32.* Vol.1.2. London 1953–58, here vol. 2, pp. 169–271.

2. G. Parker: 'The "Military Revolution", 1560–1660—a Myth?' In: *Journal of Modern History* 48 (1976) 195–214, reprinted above, chapter 2.

3. G. Parker: *Spain and the Netherlands, 1559–1659.* London, 1979, 85.

4. Parker, 'Military Revolution' (see Fn. 2), pp. 38–40.

5. Roberts: 'Military Revolution' (see Fn. 1), pp. 18–20.

6. Parker: 'Military Revolution' (see Fn. 2), pp. 41–43.

7. Roberts: *Essays in Swedish History* (see Fn. 1), pp. 60–62, 65–67; 'Military Revolution', 13 f.

8. Parker: 'Military Revolution' (see Fn. 2), p. 39.

9. R. J. Knecht: *Francis I.* Cambridge 1982, pp. 246–248; P. G. Daniel: *Histoire de la Milice Française.* Vol. 1.2. Paris 1721, here vol. 2, pp. 331–333.

10. H. Schneider: *Der Langspiess.* Wien 1976 (= *Schriften des Heeresgeschichtlichen Museums in Wien. Militärwissenschaftliches Institut.* Bd 7.), pp. 7–24, p. 14.

11. W. Schaufelberger: *Der Alte Schweizer und sein Krieg.* Zürich ²1966, pp. 7–24, p. 18.

12. By the second half of the sixteenth century the proportion of halberds had stabilized at around 10% of an infantry unit (J. R. Hale: *War and Society in Renaissance Europe, 1450–1620.* London 1985, p. 52).

13. Jacobi of Wallhausen stresses that 'presque tous les pais ont leur façon de mousquet', and suggests that although the 'musket' shot was meant to weigh 2 ounces, this was rarely the case since it required a weapon too heavy for most soldiers (id.: *L'Art Militaire pour l'Infanterie.* Paris 1615, p. 35). Jacob de Gheyn's distinction between the musket and the spe-

cific, small-calibre 'caliver', fired without a fork, seems more convincing. See the illustrations in *The Exercise of Armes for Calivers, Muskettes and Pikes*. London (?) 1608. In general I am sceptical of whether the 'innovation' of the musket consists in anything more than the adoption of a more fashionable name.

14. Battles of La Bicocca and Pavia (Knecht: *Francis I*—see Fn. 9—, pp. 114 f., 169).

15. Parker: 'Military Revolution' (see Fn. 2), p. 39.

16. Roberts: *Gustavus Adolphus* (see Fn. 1), vol. 2, p. 184, gives proportions of 300 shot to 250 hand weapons in a Dutch battalion. M. D. Feld: 'Middle Class Society and the Rise of Military Professionalism: the Dutch Army 1589–1609.' In: *Armed Forces and Society* 1 (1975) 419–442, here p. 426, suggests that a Dutch infantry company of 135 men consisted of 74 men with firearms and 45 with pikes.

17. Jacobi of Wallhausen: *L'Art Militaire pour l'Infanterie* (see Fn. 13), p. 102.

18. Clear descriptions of this system in J. de Billon: *Principes de l'Art Militaire*. Paris 1622, pp. 177–179; L. de la Fontaine: *Les Devoirs Militaires des Officiers de l'Infanterie et de la Cavalerie*. Paris 1675; John Keegan draws attention to the general thesis that the small group of soldiers, existing independently of the formal military structure, is far more important in explaining the success and motivation of troops in combat (id.: *Face of Battle*. London 1976, pp. 51 f.).

19. J. Chr. Allmayer-Beck, E. Lessing: *Die kaiserlichen Kriegsvölker. Von Maximilian I. bis Prinz Eugen 1479–1718*. München 1978, p. 116: 'Für die angeworbenen kaiserlichen Truppen schien ein besonderes Exerzitium wiederum nicht vonnöten, da diese ja, aus kriegsgeübten Söldnern bestehend, in der Lage sein sollten, unerfahrenen Rekruten das Notwendigste beizubringen.'

20. Roberts: *Essays in Swedish History* (see Fn. 1), p. 62.

21. D. H. d'Aumale: *Histoire des Princes de Condé pendant les XVIe et XVIIe siècles*. Vol. 1– 8. Paris 1863–96, here vol. 4, p. 114.

22. Parker: 'Military Revolution' (see Fn. 2), p. 39.

23. De Billon: *L'Art Militaire* (see Fn. 18), p. 181, implies that *bataillons* were established from the early seventeenth century.

24. Roberts: *Gustavus Adolphus* (see Fn. 1), vol. 2, p. 251.

25. Ibid., vol. 2, pp. 219 f.

26. Ibid., vol. 2, pp. 250–253.

27. See for example the *Archives des Affaires Etrangères, Mémoires et Documents, France*. Vol. 828, fos. 265–286: *états* of army strengths for 1637–projected.

28. Exact *revues* of units in the French army have not survived in large numbers, though the *Archives des Affaires Etrangères* (see Fn. 27) do contain a representative selection: for e.g. *Mémoires et Documents, France*. Vol. 819, fos. 1–5—*revues* of units under de La Force and the Cardinal de La Valette, 1635. See also B. Kroener: *Die Entwicklung der Truppenstärken in den französischen Armeen zwischen 1635 und 1661*. In: *Forschungen und Quellen zur Geschichte des Dreissigjährigen Krieges*. Münster 1981 (= *Schriftenreihe der Vereinigung zur Erforschung der Neueren Geschichte* e. V. Bd 12.), pp. 149–220.

29. H. de Besse: *Relation des Campagnes de Rocroi et de Fribourg*. Paris 1673, new ed. 1826, p. 98. Numerous other references.

30. Roberts: *Essays in Swedish History* (see Fn. 1), p. 65.

31. Ibid., p. 197.

32. For example, a letter of Le Tellier, then intendant of the army in Italy, from the early 1640's: printed in N. L. Caron: *Michel Le Tellier: son administration comme intendant*

d'armée en Piémont, 1640–43. Paris 1880, p. 75, 10th June 1641. Also *Archives de la Guerre.* Vol. A129, fo. 399, 27th September 1636: Typical order for the reformation of all units in the army of Italy under 30 strong.

33. Roberts: *Gustavus Adolphus* (see Fn. 1), vol. 2, pp. 175 f.

34. Ibid., vol. 2, pp. 173 f.

35. De Billon: *L'Art Militaire* (see Fn. 18), pp. 181, 209; Aurignac: *Livre de la Guerre.* Paris 1663, ed. Azan. Paris 1904, p. 48. Sir James Turner, inexplicably, reverses the prescriptions, suggesting three paces between defensive pikes, one and a half between those charging: *Pallas Armata.* London 1670/71, p. 268.

36. De Gheyn: *Exercise of Armes* (see Fn. 13); J. of Wallhausen: *Künstliche Piquen-Handlung, darinnen schriftlich und mit Figuren dieses Exercitium angewiesen und gelehret wird.* Hanau 1617.

37. Turner: *Pallas Armata* (see Fn. 35), p. 179.

38. This deployment seems to have been ignored by historians, though it is clearly indicated in tactical manuals: de Billon: *L'Art Militaire* (see Fn. 18), p. 168; de la Fontaine: *Devoirs Militaires* (see Fn. 18), p. 282 et seq. In artists' depictions of the battles—for example, those of Snaeyers—this order of battle is clear. See the sequence in Allmayer-Beck/Lessing: *Die kaiserlichen Kriegsvölker* (see Fn. 19), pp. 89–104. More accessible is Snaeyers' painting of Imperial infantry at Nördlingen, reproduced on the dust-jacket of Professor Parker's *Thirty Years' War.* London 1984. It is easy to see how assumptions might be made that these formations were 'typical' squares, but careful examination shows this not to have been the case.

39. The procedure is described by de Billon: *L'Art Militaire* (see Fn. 18), pp. 196–199, who combines it with the widely established countermarch: 'Tout aussi-tot que le premier rang (of shot) fera advancer pour tirer, il faut que le second rang prenne sa place et se remettre a l'esgal du premier rang et front des picquiers.'

40. Sir Ch. Oman: *A History of the Art of War in the Sixteenth Century.* London 1937, p. 596.

41. Aurignac: *Livre de la Guerre* (see Fn. 35), p. 105, considers that this was the principal reason for Tilly's defeat.

42. J. Seidler: *Untersuchungen über die Schlacht bei Lützen.* Memmingen 1954, emphasizes that the two accounts by officers present in the Imperial army—Holk and Diodati—agree upon this as the battle order. This verdict is accepted by Golo Mann in his biography of Wallenstein. Frankfurt a. M., pp. 877–880.

43. Most fiercely asserted by H. Diemar: *Untersuchungen über die Schlacht bei Lützen.* Marburg a. d. L. 1890, though this is convincingly attacked by Seidler (see Fn. 42). It has had many exponents, partly, it may be suggested, under the influence of the Merian engraving of the battle, prepared for the *Theatrum Europaeum.* (Reproduced as the endpiece of Parker's *Thirty Years' War*—see Fn. 38—). Yet there seems little reason to take this engraving as a reliable depiction of the battle order; even at the very simplest level, the number of infantry drawn up in the five squares does not approach Wallenstein's force of 8–9,000.

44. D'Aumale: *Histoire des Princes de Condé* (see Fn. 21), vol. 4, pp. 82–133; de Besse: *Relation des Campagnes de Rocroi et de Fribourg* (see Fn. 29), pp. 18–87.

45. J. of Wallhausen: *L'Art Militaire pour l'Infanterie* (see Fn. 13), p. 85 et seq.

46. See H. Eichberg: 'Geometrie als barocke Verhaltensnorm. Fortifikation und Exerzitien.' In: *Zeitschrift für Historische Forschung* 4 (1977) 17–50.

47. Turner: *Pallas Armata* (see Fn. 35), p. 268.

48. L. de Gaya: *L'Art de la Guerre*. Paris 1689, p. 171; de la Fontaine: *Devoirs Militaires* (see Fn. 18), pp. 245–261.

49. C. von Clausewitz: *On War*. (Ed. Paret, Howard, Brodie. Princeton, N.J. 1976), pp. 187–189.

50. Roberts: *Essays in Swedish History* (see Fn. 1), pp. 66 f.

51. Id.: *Gustavus Adolphus* (see Fn. 1), vol. 2, pp. 264 n. 3.

52. *The Swedish Intelligencer*. Vol. 3. London 1634, p. 42. Accounts of Fronmüller: *Geschichte Altenberg's und der Alten Veste b. Fürth*. Fürth 1860, and H. Mahr: *Wallenstein vor Nürnberg 1632: sein Lager bei Zirndorf und die Schlacht an der Alten Veste*. Neustadt/Aisch 1982.

53. Roberts: *Essays in Swedish History* (see Fn. 1), p. 67.

54. See John Keegan's account of the French advance at Agincourt: *Face of Battle* (see Fn. 18), pp. 98–101.

55. Again, Keegan's account of the substantially more effective British muskets at Waterloo, and the limited effects of their fire even at almost point-blank range (id.: *Face of Battle*—see Fn. 18—pp. 172 f.).

56. Mahr: *Wallenstein vor Nürnberg* (see Fn. 52), p. 80 et seq.

57. E. van der Essen: *Le Cardinal-Infant et la politique européenne de l'Espagne, 1609–41*. Louvain 1944, p. 419.

58. G. Priorato: *An History of the late Warres and other State Affaires of the best Part of Christendom, beginning with the King of Swethlands Entrance into Germany, and Continuing until 1640* trans. by Earl of Monmouth. London 1648, pp. 131–134.

59. Oman: *Art of War in the Sixteenth Century* (see Fn. 40), pp. 592–603; d'Aumale: *Histoire des Princes de Condé* (see Fn. 21).

60. I. M. vicomte de Noailles: *Bernhard de Saxe-Weimar*. Paris 1906.

61. Priorato (see Fn. 58); Mann: *Wallenstein* (see Fn. 42), pp. 883–891.

62. Van der Essen (see Fn. 57), p. 420.

63. C. V. Wedgewood: *The Thirty Years' War*. London 1938, pp. 366 f.

64. D'Aumale: *Histoire des Princes de Condé* (see Fn. 21), vol. 4, pp. 114–116.

65. Though see ibid., vol. 4, pp. 424–440, on Nördlingen II (Allerheim), and K. Ruppert: *Die kaiserliche Politik auf dem Westfälischen Friedenskongress, 1643–1648*. In: *Forschungen und Quellen zur Geschichte des Dreissigjährigen Krieges*. Münster 1979 (= *Schriftenreihe der Vereinigung zur Erforschung der Neueren Geschichte e. V.* Bd 10.), p. 81, on Jankow.

66. E. v. Frauenholz: *Das Heerwesen in der Zeit des freien Söldnertums*. München 1936 (= *Entwicklungsgeschichte des deutschen Heerwesens*. Bd 2, 1.), pp. 104–115.

67. Oman: *Art of War in the Sixteenth Century* (see Fn. 40), pp. 562 f., on the battle of Mookheide, where Spanish lancers routed Dutch pistoleers after their first ineffectual discharge.

68. Roberts: *Essays in Swedish History* (see Fn. 1), pp. 57 f.

69. Ibid., pp. 68 f.

70. Priorato (see Fn. 58), p. 131.

71. Ibid., p. 134; Mann: *Wallenstein* (see Fn. 42), pp. 883 f.

72. Parker: *The Thirty Years' War* (see Fn. 38), p. 126.

73. Ruppert: *Kaiserliche Politik* (see Fn. 65), p. 81.

74. Fronmüller (see Fn. 52).

75. Roberts: *Essays in Swedish History* (see Fn. 1), p. 60 and note 56. Roberts draws upon Weygand and Colin/Reboul, neither of whose accounts of Rocroi are satisfactory.

76. J. Israel: *The Dutch Republic and the Hispanic World*. London 1982, pp. 96 f. The one exception was at Kallo in June 1638, when the Army of Flanders inflicted a severe defeat upon the Dutch—ibid., p. 259.

77. Hale: *War and Society in Renaissance Europe* (see Fn. 12), p. 62; these are probably 'paper' strengths, considerably overestimating the real forces maintained during the campaigns.

78. A. Corvisier: *Louvois*. Paris 1983, p. 325.

79. Freiburg, in 1644, was fought between armies of about 17,000 (d'Aumale: *Histoire des Princes de Condé* (see Fn. 21), vol. 4, pp. 316–323), while Jankow involved Swedish and Imperial forces of only 15,000 (Ruppert: *Kaiserliche Politik*—see Fn. 65—, p. 80). Both of these appear to compare unfavourably with the battles of a hundred years earlier.

80. Parker: *The Thirty Years' War* (see Fn. 38), p. 126.

81. Id.: 'Military Revolution' (see Fn. 2), p. 45.

82. Roberts: 'Military Revolution' (see Fn. 1), pp. 20–22; Parker: 'Military Revolution' (see Fn. 2), pp. 45–48.

83. Professor Roberts' remark about the 'possibly overrated military reformers, Le Tellier and Louvois' (id.: *Essays in Swedish History*—see Fn. 1—, p. 65), dubious in itself, could only be sustained by ignoring simultaneous changes in the state which had a far more drastic influence upon the effectiveness of armies than any tactical redefinition could achieve. A comparison of the French armies of the 1660's/70's with those of preceding decades illustrates this clearly.

84. See particularly F. Redlich: *The German Military Enterpriser and his Work Force*. Vol. 1.2. Wiesbaden 1964/65 (= *Vierteljahrschrift für Sozial- und Wirtschaftsgeschichte*. Beihefte 47. 48.)

85. Feld: 'Middle Class Society and the Rise of Military Professionalism' (see Fn. 16); G. Oestreich: *Neostoicism and the Early Modern State*. Cambridge 1982, pp. 76–83.

86. The supreme example of this being Wallenstein's relationship with his foremost financier—see A. Ernstberger: *Hans de Witte—Finanzmann Wallensteins*. Wiesbaden 1954 (= *Vierteljahrschrift für Sozial- und Wirtschaftsgeschichte*. Beih. 38.)

87. Ibid., p. 166.

88. M. Ritter: *Das Kontributionssystem Wallensteins*. In: *HZ* 90. N. F. 54 (1903) 193–249; F. Redlich: 'Contributions in the Thirty Years' War.' In: *Economic History Review*. 2nd Ser. 12 (1959/60) 247–254.

89. Mann: *Wallenstein* (see Fn. 42), pp. 370 f.

90. D. Parrott: *The Administration of the French Army during the Ministry of Cardinal Richelieu*. Oxford, D. Phil. thesis 1985, pp. 161–223.

91. Paris-based financiers/entrepreneurs who were prepared to make large-scale contracts to supply the armies with the basic bread ration throughout a campaign or the winter months.

92. G. Parker: 'Mutiny and Discontent in Spanish Army of Flanders, 1572–1607.' In: *Spain and the Netherlands* (see Fn. 3), pp. 104–121, p. 108.

93. Richelieu, in his *Testament Politique*, made the despairing statement that: 'Il se trouve en l'histoire beaucoup plus d'armées periés faute de pain et de police que par l'effort des armes ennemies' (ed. André. Paris 1947, p. 280). In this, he was echoing the common experience of all his contemporaries.

94. A. Aubery: *Mémoires pour servir à l'histoire du Cardinal de Richelieu*. Vol. 1.2. Paris 1660/61, vol. 1, p. 481.

95. Richelieu: *Mémoires*. Vol. 8. (28). Paris 1824, p. 334: *Collections des Mémoires relatifs a l'Histoire de France* (2nd Ser., ed. Petitot, Monmerqué. Vol. 21–30); G. Avenel: *Lettres, Instructions Diplomatiques et Papiers d'Etat du Cardinal de Richelieu*. Vol. 1–8. Paris 1843–77, here vol. 5, p. 309, 16th Oct. 1635; vol. 5, p. 73, 28th June 1635.

96. Kroener: *Die Entwicklung der Truppenstärken in den französischen Armeen* (see Fn. 28); Parrott: *The Administration of the French Army during the Ministry of Cardinal Richelieu* (see Fn. 90), pp. 103–118, 142.

97. Parker: *The Thirty Years' War* (see Fn. 38), p. 131; Mahr: *Wallenstein vor Nürnberg* (see Fn. 52), p. 64.

98. For example, the French advance to Mainz in 1635, which collapsed through supply failure evident from the outset of the campaign—B. Kroener: *Les Routes et les Etapes. Die Versorgung der französischen Armeen in Nordostfrankreich (1635–61). Ein Beitrag zur Verwaltungsgeschichte des Ancien Régime*. Münster 1980 (= *Schriftenreihe der Vereinigung zur Erforschung der Neueren Geschichte* e. V. Bd 11.), pp. 83–94.

99. *Archives des Affaires Etrangères* (see Fn. 27), vol. 816, fo. 226, undated (1635).

100. Clausewitz: *On War* (see Fn. 49), p. 143.

101. The *Vernichtungsstrategie* held by Professor Roberts to have been the conscious aim of Gustavus Adolphus (id.: *Essays in Swedish History*—see Fn. 1—, pp. 71 f.).

102. M. van Creveld: *Supplying War: Logistics from Wallenstein to Patton*. Cambridge 1977, p. 14.

103. Parker: *The Thirty Years' War* (see Fn. 38), p. 131.

104. Roberts: *Essays in Swedish History* (see Fn. 1), p. 73.

105. G. Perjes: 'Army Provisioning, Logistics and Strategy in the Second Half of the Seventeenth Century.' In: *Acta Historica Academiae Scientiarum Hungaricae* 16 (1970).

10

Tactics or Politics? "The Military Revolution" and the Hapsburg Hegemony, 1525–1648

SIMON ADAMS

THE CAMPAIGNS INITIATED by the landing of Gustavus Adolphus at Peenemünde in June 1630 are among the best-known events of the Thirty Years' War. The Swedish victory at Breitenfeld was, S. R. Gardiner concluded a century ago, "no common victory." Like Naseby, it was "the victory of disciplined intelligence," the success of which "could not be confined to mere fighting. It would make its way in morals and politics, in literature and science."[1] If Gardiner's Protestant liberalism now has a distinctly dated ring, the Swedish intervention has not lost its wider significance. In his magisterial biography of Gustavus Adolphus, Michael Roberts discovered in the campaigns of 1630–32 the focal point of what he identified as the "military revolution" of the century 1560–1660. By the end of the sixteenth century, he argued, "tactics had withered, strategy had atrophied." Following the military reforms that underlay the Swedish victories, war became once more an effective instrument of policy.[2]

A decade ago Geoffrey Parker subjected the Roberts thesis to a searching critical reappraisal. Parker identified four main elements in Roberts's military revolution: a revolution in tactics, a revolution in strategy, a dramatic increase in the scale of armies, and a transformation of the state. He queried both the novelty and the success of Swedish tactics and strategy but accepted the growth of armies and their impact on the state, though for somewhat different reasons.[3] For Parker the military revolution was above all logistical; as he has most recently concluded, "The states of early modern Europe had discovered how to supply large armies but not how to lead them to victory."[4]

Other assessments of tactical evolution in the period have reinforced Parker's argument that they were both more diffuse and adopted earlier than Roberts allowed for. Deployment by battalions, for example, appears to have been widely accepted by the end of the 1590s.[5] On the other hand, one aspect of the orginal thesis has survived more or less intact: the argument that, to quote Martin van Creveld, the military revolution "was characterised above all by the immense growth in the size of Europe's armies."[6] Roberts argued that Philip II "had dominated Europe in his day with the aid of an army which probably did not exceed 40,000: a century later, 400,000 was esteemed necessary to maintain the ascendency of Louis XIV," though he also conceded that it "may perhaps be legitimately objected that the instances I have chosen to illustrate the growth of armies are hand-picked."[7] Parker came to the same conclusion: "Between 1530 and 1710 there was a ten-fold increase both in the total numbers of armed forces paid by the European states and in the total numbers involved in the major European battles. ..."[8] Creveld compares the 10,000 men the duke of Alba took to the Netherlands in 1567 with the armies "far in excess of 100,000 men" that Gustavus Adolphus and Wallenstein commanded in 1631–32 and with the French establishment of 400,000 in the 1690s. He also concludes: "More and better statistics could be adduced, but they would only serve to prove what is generally recognized: namely, that apart from a period of twenty-five years between 1635 and 1660, Europe's armies multiplied their size many times over between 1560 and 1715."[9]

That there was a particularly dramatic increase in numbers in the latter half of the seventeenth century is undeniable. But if attention is focused on the period 1525–1648, certain other trends in the size of armies can be detected that provide significant grounds for reexamining the context of the military revolution. The evidence must, however, be approached with caution, for the subject is fraught with technical difficulties. The first is the apparently simple question of the definition of an army. Here a distinction must be drawn between the total number of military forces an individual government, paymaster, or commander could raise in a given year, which might be spread over a wide geographical area, and a force that campaigned, maneuvered or gave battle as a unit—a camp, an *armée de campagne*, a *feldleger*, or (as Wallenstein described it) a *Hauptarmada*.[10] The difference is that between, for example, the total number of men Gustavus Adolphus and his allies had under arms in 1632 and the army that invaded Bavaria and later fought the battle of Lützen.

Accurate measurement of either type of army is not easy. The literary sources and contemporary narratives from which the numbers of combatants in major battles have generally been drawn are notoriously inaccurate, owing in part to the understandable desire of the participants to magnify the opposing army in order to glorify victory or justify defeat.[11] For many engagements (Pavia, for example) the size of the forces employed has been a matter of some debate.[12] Frequently, the best figures available are estimates that may be several thousands out.

There are, however, two further reasons for caution in the use of the numbers involved in any particular battle. First, there is the distortion caused by eve-of-battle diversions. An obvious example is the controversial detachment of 6,000 men from the army of Francis I during the siege of Pavia. Similarly, Wallenstein faced Gustavus Adolphus at Lützen with only part of a widely dispersed army. Bernard of Saxe-Weimar refused to wait for reinforcements at Nördlingen.[13] But the converse is also true—and has a particular relevance for this period. "Armies" assembled at one place to lay siege or give battle were frequently the result of a recent junction of allied forces, and thus no guide to "national armies." Charles V's army at Metz in 1552 included the 15,000 of Albert-Alcibiades of Brandenburg-Kulmbach. Both armies at Breitenfeld were composites: Gustavus Adolphus's consisted of both his own and that of the elector of Saxony, and Tilly's the army of the Catholic League and the Imperialists under Fürstenburg. At Nördlingen, three years later, a more complex concentration occurred that makes even the description of the opposing sides difficult. The "Catholic" army was composed of three separate armies (Spanish, Imperial, and League) while the "Protestant" was composed of four (the Swedish army and three provided by various German Protestant allies).[14] The largest battle of the English Civil War—Marston Moor—was fought by a combination of two Royalist armies (Prince Rupert's and the earl of Newcastle's) and three Parliamentarian ones (the Scottish, the Eastern Association, and Sir Thomas Fairfax's).

We are on no firmer ground with the statistics of total forces raised, for the projections of treasuries, accounts of paymasters, and rolls of mustermasters are not necessarily more accurate. Many projections were never realized, and the figures given in state papers are frequently mere paper strengths. The reliability of accounts varied widely from army to army. The Army of Flanders, Geoffrey Parker has argued, undertook musters rigorously, and therefore its records can be used with some confidence.[15] The same may also be true for the Dutch army of the early seventeenth century, though clearly not for the French in the 1630s, let alone the more entrepreneurial German armies.[16] Wastage—however the rate is estimated or computed—makes it extremely difficult to translate recruiting targets into effectives.[17]

Nevertheless, if these caveats are borne in mind, several important points emerge from an examination of field armies and battle strengths. First, there is no dramatic contrast between strengths in the sixteenth and seventeenth centuries. Second, the upper limit appears to have been in the region of 35,000 to 40,000. At Pavia, which will act as a base point, the Imperialists had between 20,000 and 25,000; the French, between 25,000 and 30,000, and possibly slightly more.[18] The French and Imperial armies in the Picardy campaigns of 1543–44 were both in the region of 30,000, though the English sent to aid Charles V may have raised the Imperial total. Henry VIII fielded an enormous army of over 40,000 for the siege of Boulogne in 1544–45. Similar numbers were reached in the 1550s. Henry II took nearly 38,000 (including the Household) on the *voyage de Metz* in 1552, and Charles V raised over 50,000 (15,000 of which formed the army of Brandenburg-Kulmbach) to recover the city later in the year. In the St. Quentin campaign of 1557, Philip had some 40,000 (including 7,000 provided by his English ally). What is also clear, however, is that the raising of armies was scraping the limits of the practical. Both Henry II in 1552 and Philip II in 1557 could afford to keep forces of this scale in the field for only a few months.[19] Even a rapid demobilization did not enable them to escape bankruptcy.

The forces involved in the battles of the French Wars of Religion and the early engagements of the Dutch Revolt were considerably lower, for these were civil wars in which the rebel side frequently had considerable difficulty in putting large forces into the field. Alba's 10,000 of 1567 was only a cadre; an army of 66,000 had been proposed originally as necessary for the pacification of the Netherlands.[20] For his two campaigns in France in 1590 and 1592, the duke of Parma took first 11,000, then 30,000.[21] The figures for the major battles of the Thirty Years' War see a return to those of the first half of the sixteenth century, but no dramatic increase. The White Mountain (1620) was fought between armies numbering 28,000 and 21,000. Breitenfeld, probably the largest, involved 42,000 in Gustavus Adolphus's combined army, and 35,000 in Tilly's. The next year Gustavus invaded Bavaria with 37,000, but Lützen was fought by much smaller numbers. Gustavus had 19,000 men, while Wallenstein could muster only 16,000, plus the 3,000 cavalry that Pappenheim brought to his aid after the battle had begun.[22] Nördlingen was slightly larger in scale than the White Mountain: the Catholic army numbered 33,000; the Protestant, only 25,000.[23] R. A. Stradling considers that the army of 40,000 Olivares was preparing in Germany for the invasion of France in the winter of 1634–35 was "more than twice the size of the average field army of the time."[24] Of the later battles, only Wittstock (October 1636) and Zusmarshausen (May 1648) approached the scale of Breitenfeld and Nördlingen. To conclude with two further examples, Rocroi (1643) was fought by 24,000 French and 17,000 Spaniards, and Marston Moor (1644), by 28,000 Parliamentarians and 18,000 Royalists.

The significance of these figures lies in their nearly static quality. Rarely did the numbers rise above 40,000, and even 30,000 to 40,000 was by no means usual. Occasionally there may have been temporarily greater combinations. The three separate armies campaigning for the king of Bohemia in the spring of 1622 (the count of Mansfeld's, Christian of Brunswick's, and the margrave of Baden-Durlach's) may have reached a total of 70,000.[25] So, too, may the combined forces of Tilly and Wallenstein in the invasion of Denmark in 1627–28. The French and Dutch planned to invade the Spanish Netherlands with a combined army of 60,000 in 1635. Jonathan Israel has described this as "one of the largest field armies ever seen in Europe," but David Parrott's research reveals that the French were unable to field more than half their contribution of 30,000 men.[26] It is difficult to avoid the conclusion that 30,000 may have been a natural effective limit for a field army throughout the period. There is some evidence to suggest that contemporaries considered 20,000 to 30,000 the right size for a manageable balanced force. In January 1621 an English council of war presented a detailed report on the size of a field army to be sent to defend the Palatinate: its conclusion was 25,000 foot and 5,000 horse.[27] Sir James Turner, the Scottish veteran of the Swedish service, wrote that an "army royal" should consist of 18,000 foot and 6,000 horse.[28] The New Model Army was first established at 25,000 (16,000 foot and 9,000 horse) but later reduced to 21,000. Its initial-establishment strength is strikingly close to Wallenstein's original commission of 1625.[29]

Total strengths present a more complex picture. The best-researched army of the period—the Army of Flanders—occupies an equivocal position, for it was somewhere between a field army and a full establishment. Geoffrey Parker's and Jonathan Israel's figures show it exceeding 80,000 men on three occasions: 1574, 1624, and 1639–40. It reached 60,000 during the Dutch Revolt. During the Thirty Years' War it initially rose to the old establishment of over 60,000, but was then reduced in the later 1620s by as much as a third, though it expanded again in the 1630s.[30] The overall strength reached by Spanish forces is a more difficult question. Charles V claimed on several occasions to have more than 100,000 under arms.[31] In 1627 Philip IV boasted he had 300,000, but J. H. Elliot observes that the figure "seems wildly implausible."[32] In the winter of 1634–35 Olivares planned a concentric invasion of France with 100,000 men. Upon the outbreak of war in 1635 the establishments in Germany, Italy, and Catalonia were to be 79,000, which together with the Army of Flanders would have produced a total of nearly 150,000; but there is no evidence this figure was reached.[33]

The experience of the lesser states was more varied. The Venetians raised totals of nearly 30,000 in 1509 and 1529, 35,000 in 1570, but only 26,000 in 1617.[34] The United Provinces possessed no standing forces at the beginning of the Revolt of the Netherlands. Up to 1609, their army reached 60,000 only once (1607); for most of the 1590s their total ranged between 30,000 and 35,000. In 1621 it rose to 48,000, and then to 58,000 in 1627, and to over 70,000 from 1629 to 1643.[35] A similar dramatic increase can be found among the Swedes; it reached its peak in the ambitious projections of Gustavus Adolphus. At the beginning of 1632 he planned to raise a combined allied army of 210,000 (including a Saxon contingent of 40,000). He appears to have obtained no more than 120,000 allied troops and 20,000 Saxons.[36]

Both the Swedes and the Spaniards projected overall establishments considerably in excess of 150,000 in the 1630s. They were not alone; similar claims have been made for both Wallenstein and Louis XIII. It has recently been argued that between 1625 and 1630 Wallenstein's army grew from 61,000 to 150,000.[37] The source for these figures, the annual Imperial army lists (*Lista Kayserlichen Kriegs-Armada*), should, however, be handled cautiously. They outline the deployment of the army, regiment by regiment and company by company, but the strengths (which are purely paper) appear to have been obtained by interpolation from the assumption that the infantry companies were the standard 300 men of the German establishment.[38] Although Wallenstein was appointed commander of the Imperial army in July 1625, these troops were not so much his own army as forces in garrisons throughout the empire, from the Hungarian frontier to Jutland. How many were actually employed directly under his command in the Danish war is another question. Wallenstein's initial commission was to raise 24,000 men, which included 12,500 already on hand. By the end of 1625 he was talking about employing 50,000 in the campaign of 1626.[39] He may have reached 60,000 by the spring, but he only had 20,000 at Dessau Bridge, and he conducted his pursuit of Mansfeld later in the year with the same number.[40] That November he is said to have proposed the raising of an Imperial standing army of 70,000. His contribution to the invasion of Denmark in 1627, on the other hand, may only have amounted to 40,000; a force which, interestingly enough, he regarded as too large to campaign as a unit.[41] Last, although the Imperial army of 1628–30 may have had a paper strength of 130,000 to 150,000, much of it had already been dispersed to Italy, the Netherlands, and Poland by the summer of 1629, a year before Wallenstein's dismissal.[42]

The French war effort of the 1630s was no more successful. The standing army at the beginning of the century numbered under 10,000, less than it had been in 1559.[43] For his intervention in the Cleves-Jülich crisis in 1610 Henry IV planned to mobilize 54,000, of which 30,000 was to form his main field army.[44] Until the early 1630s this figure appears to have been accepted by French ministers (including Richelieu) as the upper limit of the possible, a total not greatly in excess of the forces raised by Francis I and Henry II.[45] In 1635–38 really massive increases in strength were projected, averaging over 150,000 and reaching just under 200,000 in 1636. The research of David Parrott has shown, however, that this was also a massive overestimation of what was practical, and that the effective strengths of French armies in the later 1630s were little more than half the projections.[46] Throughout the "French intervention" French armies campaigned at levels no greater than those of their opponents.

II

The conclusion that suggests itself is an important one. Certain aspects of the increase of armies can be accepted. The greater number of combatant powers in the 1630s may have led to a larger overall number of men serving in one army or another than had previously been the case. For some states (the United Provinces or Sweden) there was undoubtedly a novel increase in their military forces in the period that may have had a revolutionary impact.[47] But it appears equally clear that while the size of field armies remained relatively static throughout the period, the Thirty Years' War saw a dramatic increase in projected overall establishments. Moreover, this new policy appears to have met with only limited success; the number of effectives rose but little, and the scale of battles and campaigns was unchanged. The disparity between the strategic ambitions of governments and their abilities to realize them reached a dramatic peak.

The question of whether there were indeed logistical and organizational imperatives that made 35,000 to 40,000 a natural rather than accidental upper limit for field armies in this period has been addressed elsewhere.[48] What will be examined here are the reasons for the increase in projections in overall strength. Despite the widespread acceptance of the expansion of armies, more attention has been devoted to its impact than to its causes. Only Geoffrey Parker has attempted an overall explanation; his thesis is both clever and sophisticated. The initial expansion in the first decades of the sixteenth century he attributes to a decrease "both absolutely and relatively" in the numbers of cavalry, and their replacement by cheaper pikemen. Thereafter the growth of infantry was the product of the development of the new artillery fortifications: "an increase necessitated by the vast number of men required to starve out a town defended by the *trace italienne*." The increases were not progressive. There was a dramatic expansion in the 1530s, but then a stagnation until the 1580s, when new administrative procedures and improvements in logistics enabled further growth in the following century.[49] David Parrott, on the other hand, finds the reasons for expansion "obscure" and suggests that "it probably owed most to the drastic expansion of war aims, and the imposition of new, unpopular regimes over entire states."[50]

The two key elements in the Parker thesis—the decline of cavalry and the growth of the *trace italienne*—are most clearly observable in the Netherlands campaigns. Except for the 1570s and 1640s, the cavalry complement of the Army of Flanders was well under a tenth of the strength of the foot. The proportion in the Dutch army was roughly similar.[51] Yet in the Thirty Years' War, as Roberts has observed, the proportion of horse was, on the other hand, on the increase.[52] At Lützen, half of Wallenstein's 16,000 and one-third of Gustavus's 19,000 were cavalry, while Pappenheim's reinforcement was entirely horse. Similar proportions are found at Nördlingen: 13,000 of the Catholic army's 33,000 and 9,000 of the Protestant army's 28,000. The establishments of both Wallenstein's 1625 army and the New Model Army consisted of one-third horse to two-thirds foot.

The reasons for the revival of cavalry in the armies of the 1630s and 1640s are not obscure. First, the more open circumstances of the Thirty Years' War and the English Civil War gave greater room for the use of cavalry; the fact that the proportion of horse was not higher was due to the difficulties in raising cavalry rather than a decision to dispense with it.[53] Second, the proportion of cavalry to infantry would be higher in field armies than in overall establishments. The question that needs to be addressed, therefore, is really that of the "excess" infantry. Here there are two related, if contradictory, theses. Roberts points to a general phenomenon of the "bleeding" of field armies by garrisons; Parker argues for the demands of sieges.[54]

What is at issue is the role of the *trace italienne* fortress, a role which was fundamentally ambiguous. Its spread throughout Europe in the century after 1500 was patchy, for the expense involved could bankrupt a small principality or a city-state (as it did Siena in the 1550s and Geneva in the 1580s), and no major city could afford a complete enceinte.[55] Such fortifications were undertaken only when necessary, and their strategic role was largely dependent on geography, both political and physical; the classic examples being Italy, Piedmont, and the Netherlands. Yet even in the Netherlands their expansion was limited. As late as the 1586 campaign towns like Doesburg or Deventer were devoid of modern fortifications.[56] Their relative absence in Germany on the eve of the Thirty Years' War, and in England on the eve of the Civil War, meant that sieges lacked the central strategic significance that they possessed in the Netherlands campaigns.

The stopping power of sieges can also be overestimated. Of the centrality of such sieges as Ostend (1601–4) and Breda (1625) to the Low Countries wars there can be little doubt, but, if our scope is extended, the impact of sieges is more diffuse. In some cases their significance was primarily political: the French occupation and the Imperialist siege of Metz in 1552, for example. The disastrous defeat of Charles V has been legitimately attributed to his own rashness in trying to mount a major siege in winter.[57] The same is true for fortresses in the later stages of the French Wars of Religion, particularly the 1620s phase, when the fortified Huguenot towns derived much of their importance from their status as *places de sûreté* under the Treaty of Nantes.[58] As with the examples of Haarlem, Alkmaar, and Leiden in 1573–74, the long defense of La Rochelle in 1627–28 owed as much to the intransigence of the civilian population as to the inherent strength of its fortifications. In several celebrated instances, political unwillingness to conclude the siege on the part of the besiegers accounted for the apparent success of the defense: Magdeburg in 1549–50, La Rochelle in 1573, or Stralsund in 1628–29.[59]

The popularity of the new fortifications in the middle decades of the sixteenth century owed much to the mistaken belief that they provided a cheaper means of defense than a field army. The belief was held particularly strongly by smaller states, Siena in the 1550s, or Venice, for example. The duke of Somerset's occupation of Scotland between 1547 and 1550 was a bold attempt to use garrisons offensively. However, both the Sienese Revolt and Somerset's defeat revealed the limitations of this strategy; and later campaigns, in the Netherlands in particular, confirmed the lesson. Without a field army to relieve them or provide diversions, immobilized and isolated garrisons were extremely vulnerable to being picked off one by one.[60] The "bleeding of field armies" was a consequence of the need to maintain both garrisons and the necessary mobile force.

The problem was more one of frontiers than communications. The long supply lines the Swedish army possessed in Germany in the 1630s and 1640s were the exception rather than the rule. The greatest line of communications of the period— the famous Spanish Road—was too large to garrison; its security depended on diplomacy. What further complicated the defense of frontiers was the other aspect of the new fortifications—the use of citadels for the intimidation of the local population. In some of the Italian cities this was a long-established practice, but its spread during the seventeenth century throughout Europe (as, for example, in the Hapsburg citadels in Siena in 1549 and Antwerp in 1568–69), and the similar use of garrisons in counterinsurgency warfare (as the English employed in Ireland), marked a major increase in the demands on existing military resources.[61]

The significance of garrisons in their twin roles of defense of territory and control of populations can be seen most clearly in the growth of standing armies in the sixteenth century. Although regiments or tercios could be either administrative or tactical units, the assigning of territorial designations to permanent formations reveals that their function was essentially that of static garrisons. The old Spanish tercios of Lombardy, Naples, or Sicily; the French legions, *bandes,* or regiments of Piedmont, Picardy or Champagne; and the Dutch provincial regiments of North Holland, Friesland, Utrecht, or Zeeland derived their names from the provinces they garrisoned, not from the ones where they were recruited.[62] In the French case they were frontier garrisons; in the Spanish, they were those of occupied provinces.[63] As I. A. A. Thompson has shown, apart from a skeletal royal guard, there were no standing forces in peninsular Spain in the sixteenth century.[64] Standing armies were essentially garrison armies. Even the French gendarmerie was employed as a police force in the sixteenth century, beginning a long and notorious tradition that culminated in the *dragonnades* of the 1680s.[65] The much more limited growth of an English standing army under the Tudors was also part of the same process. It involved the spread of the Pale system of a permanent garrison from Calais to Ireland in the 1530s, then to Boulogne between 1545 and 1550 and Berwick after 1551.[66]

III

If the growth of garrisons provides an explanation for the "excess infantry," the strategic context of this expansion demands further attention. The battles of the Italian wars (La Bicocca, Pavia, and Ceresole) demonstrated conclusively that firearms and field fortifications made offensive campaigns a dubious enterprise. Thereafter it is difficult to detect a major advance in tactics or technology that altered the balance.[67] It is to the peculiar political concerns of the period 1525 to 1648—and two major international questions in particular—that changes in strategy are to be attributed.[68] They were not questions to which there were immediate objective answers; but they raised issues upon which contemporaries held strong convictions, and which dominated political debate. The first (chronologically speaking) was that of the Hapsburg Imperium. Did the dynastic inheritance of Charles V mark the first stage of an expansion of the house of Austria toward a universal monarchy, *la monarquía?* If so, then its ambitions posed a threat to the liberty of Europe and justified defensive coalitions. From the point of view of Madrid or Vienna, however, such opposition was seen as attempts by the envious to deprive the house of Austria of its legitimate possessions. It, too, was waging an essentially defensive struggle.

The Hapsburg threat was primarily a secular question: the hegemony of the house of Austria affected all regardless of confessional allegiance. Thus although it might be deliberately confused in propaganda, it was essentially distinct from the second great question (which really only emerges after 1559, though there are some elements detectable in the 1530s and 1540s) of whether a major religious struggle was about to break out. If so, then it would divide Europe into two major confessional armed camps. But religious alliances, too, were ultimately defensive in purpose; they were designed to protect one side from the threat of extermination posed by the other. The coexistence of both questions and the debates they engendered (leaving out lesser and more specific issues) made diplomacy hideously complex, but their influence over strategy was a joint one. If they provided new justifications for war, they did so in essentially defensive terms.

There were other strategic implications as well. The emergence of the confessional issue meant that all major wars between 1559 and 1648 were to some extent religious civil wars. Political boundaries became of less relevance, popular participation (particularly in the sieges of major cities) was far more extensive than in previous conflicts, and to a far greater degree the role of armies was that of crushing dissidents and controlling hostile populations. To some extent these issues had in fact emerged during the first half of the sixteenth century. If the origins of the Italian wars lay in the dynastic struggle between Hapsburg and Valois over Naples and Milan, the Hapsburg victories saw the issues at stake change. Increased Hapsburg control over the Italian peninsula inspired fears that the Imperium was becoming a reality; the French in turn began to pose as the protectors of Italian liberty. If this trend did not fully emerge until the early 1550s, it can be detected initially in Francis I's response to his defeat at Pavia.[69]

For Charles V a major strategic problem was posed. However great his apparent resources, he was faced with the need to defend his possessions (initially in Italy, but in 1552 in the Empire as well) from a combination of external invasion and popular revolt. The solution was found in a new strategy that can be legitimately termed the Spanish school. As William Maltby has shown in his biography of the duke of Alba, this strategy can first be seen at work in Alba's campaigns against the Schmalkaldic League in 1546–47 and the duke of Guise in Italy in 1557. It involved an acceptance of the tactical power of the defense, which, given the essentially defensive aims of the House of Austria and its potentially superior resources, could enable it to exhaust its enemies. Hostile powers would be isolated diplomatically and swamped by overwhelming force. They would then be forced to give battle at a disadvantage. The harrying of the Elector of Saxony and the Schmalkaldic League prior to the battle of Mühlberg christened this strategy with a dramatic success.[70]

The outbreak of the Dutch Revolt saw Alba employ the same strategy against William of Orange between 1568 and 1573. The dispatch of most of the companies of the Italian tercios to the Netherlands in 1567 was on one level simply the shifting of the garrison of one part of the Spanish empire to another.[71] The Netherlands were to be dominated by garrisons and cut off from external commerce; the isolated pockets of rebellion were then to be crushed with superior force. Foreign invasions would be held off by well-manned fortifications. What has been less appreciated is how closely Alba's strategy was followed by his successors, the duke of

Parma and Ambrosio de Spínola. Parma's memorandum to Philip II of January 1581 repeated Alba's earlier proposals practically item by item.[72] The rebel provinces were to be surrounded by garrisons drawn from an enormous army and then cut off from external trade and support. The army was not to be wasted in unnecessary sieges and battles; the urban centers of resistance were to be isolated and starved into submission. The difficulty lay in providing the vast military establishment that this strategy demanded. Alba went to the Netherlands with less than the number of troops he regarded as sufficient.[73] The full-scale rebellion of 1572 created an emergency that forced him to raise the Army of Flanders to its peak of 86,000 men, but it was too great a burden even for the Spanish treasury.[74] Parma's attempt in the autumn of 1583 to persuade Philip II to exploit the political chaos in the Netherlands left by the duke of Anjou with a massive military effort ran into similar financial barriers.[75] His successful reconquest of the southern provinces between the siege of Maastricht in 1579 and the siege of Antwerp in 1584 was largely a political one. However large the Army of Flanders appeared on paper, it was not sufficient to carry out its strategic purpose.

From these limitations the peculiar rhythms of the Netherlands wars—"these defensive garrison wars" as the earl of Leicester called them in his frustration—were derived.[76] It was not simply physical geography that created the patchwork of garrisons; political and military imperatives also necessitated the holding of forts that were all but isolated and the construction of the rings of blockading posts that swallowed up troops. Ironically, the very loss of the southern Netherlands in 1582–85 probably improved the strategic position of the United Provinces, for it gave them a more compact territory to hold and better interior lines.[77] The retention of Ostend, on the other hand, however politically desirable (and to some degree the result of English pressure), was a major strategic liability. The central military problem on both sides lay in scraping together enough men from the garrisons to provide an adequate field army. Of the 93 foot companies left in Parma's army after the withdrawal of the Spanish troops in 1580, 56 were employed in garrisons, leaving only 37 for a field force.[78] In 1585 the States General informed Elizabeth I that while they had 200 companies in pay, if they were to form a field army, English troops would be necessary.[79] Many of the difficulties encountered by the earl of Leicester as governor-general arose from his efforts to find the money and men for such an army.

The disparity between total and deployable effectives shaped the course of the Netherlands campaigns. The actual campaigning was undertaken by field forces rarely numbering above 10,000 to 15,000 men. In the autumn of 1586 Leicester and Parma confronted each other at Zutphen with armies numbering between only 9,000 and 10,000.[80] Moreover, battles became even less important (Turnhout and Nieuwpoort were fought almost by accident) because the elimination of a few thousand men was a waste of resources when compared to the gaining of a strategic town. In this respect the reforms of Maurice of Nassau of the 1590s—the creation of an effective field force and the employment of major concentrations of artillery in sieges—were of less significance than the Spanish intervention in France between 1590 and 1598.[81] With the departure of the Spanish field army, the garrisons could be picked off individually with minimal interference. On the other hand, once the field army returned after the Treaty of Vervins, the balance was restored, and the campaigns of 1601-9, for all the skill employed by both sides, were a strategic stalemate.

Although the Low Countries wars made the "Spanish school" the model for Europe, it did have its critics, particularly in France, where an offensive tradition survived from the Italian wars. Here the most celebrated exponent was Henry IV, who alone of all the major commanders of the later sixteenth century actually sought battle.[82] However, his reasons were primarily psychological and political, and did not involve a counterstrategy. The weakness of his strategic thinking was notorious; even his closest advisors commented on it. Indeed, insofar as there was a military art in the sixteenth century, it has no better example than Parma's brilliant outmaneuvering of Henry IV in the campaigns of 1590 and 1592.[83] Despite his doubts about the overall strategy of intervention in France, Parma was able to carry out his immediate objectives and withdraw successfully, despite all Henry's attempts to force a battle on advantageous terms. The French offensive against the Spanish Netherlands between 1594 and 1598, despite the theoretical advantages of the English and Dutch alliance, was, by contrast, a disaster.

The success of the Spanish school remained intact until the outbreak of the Thirty Years' War. Paradoxically, its repudiation came a decade before the Swedish intervention and was inspired by what was apparently a military success: Spínola's invasion of the Palatinate in August and September 1620. The circumstances deserve attention. There were obvious political and military reasons for a major strike against the Palatinate following Frederick V's acceptance of the Bohemian throne in 1619. But there were also dangers: the truce with the Netherlands would expire in 1621, and an invasion of the Palatinate might trigger intervention from Britain or even France. The operation was therefore carefully planned. Spínola was provided with a field army of 25,000 men, but he was expected to conquer the Palatinate in a single campaign in 1620. The disparity in force was considerable. The Palatinate boasted only three modern fortresses: Heidelberg, Frankenthal, and the new town of Mannheim, which together provided a central defended complex. Local troops consisted of one garrison regiment and some citizen militia. Otherwise the defense of the Palatinate rested on the demoralized army of Frederick's allies, the Protestant Union (between and 10,000 and 16,000), and several thousand English and Dutch reinforcements, who arrived after the campaign had opened.

Spínola's progress was cautious in the extreme. Although he occupied a number of undefended towns on the left bank of the Rhine, he made no attempt to assault the major fortresses. Instead he confined himself to building a bridge of boats across the Rhine (in the course of which, according to one account, he delivered a suitably Caesarian oration) and then quickly placed his troops in winter quarters at Oppenheim. Bloodless the invasion might have been, but conquest it was not.[84] Even though the feared foreign intervention did not occur, it took another two years for the final reduction of the Palatinate. Simultaneously, a more dramatic military operation was taking place. In Bohemia the combined army of the Emperor and the Catholic League, commanded by the League's general, Tilly, not only shattered the new king's army at the White Mountain, but by the end of the year had occupied almost the entire kingdom. In the decade that followed Tilly went on to a number of dramatic offensive victories: Wimpfen and Höchst in 1622, Stadtlohn in 1623, and Lutter am Barenberg in 1626. Only at Breitenfeld was one of his attacks defeated decisively. Tilly's aggressive campaigning was accompanied by a barrage of complaints about the dilatoriness and caution of Spínola and the Spanish commanders.[85] Spínola's reputation never recovered from the campaign in the Palatinate.

Tilly's revival of the offensive and his repudiation of the Spanish school were inspired and supported by his patron, Maximilian, duke of Bavaria. The reasons lie in the economic demands of the Spanish strategy. Perhaps the most important aspect of the first decade of the Thirty Years' War was the abstention, neutrality, or half-hearted intervention of Britain and France. Moreover, two of the major powers involved, the United Provinces and Spain, were exceedingly cautious about the extent of their commitment. There was thus a vacuum at the international level into which a number of lesser powers stepped: the Elector Palatine, Bavaria, Denmark, and Sweden. All became involved in a war that was on rational grounds beyond their means. (Their reasons for doing so are not directly relevant here, though confessional fears and allegiances were probably decisive.) It was Maximilian who earliest and most clearly perceived the problem, not least because his father William V had more or less bankrupted Bavaria through his earlier participation in the war for Cologne of 1583–85.[86]

For smaller states with limited resources, large-scale attrition warfare of the Spanish style was not possible. A short, decisive campaign was all that could be afforded. But there were further political and economic reasons for a return to an offensive strategy in Germany: what might be termed offensive logistics. It was important at all costs to avoid the damage of campaigning on one's own territory or that of allies, thus every effort had to be made to exploit the enemy's to quarter and supply troops. The race for winter quarters became a constant feature of the war. Here the League armies possessed the major advantage of operating under Imperial commissions, which gave them the power to demand supplies from neutrals. However, there remained the problem of the considerable areas over which the war was fought, the limited numbers of troops, and the existence of a large body of Protestant neutrals (Brandenburg, Saxony, Hesse-Kassel, and the numerous Free Cities) whose abstention and cooperation could not be taken for granted. As a result the aggressive use of intimidation and terrorism, though not unknown before, now became established. The widespread use of such devices as *Brandschatzung,* or the threat of quartering troops on areas that refused to make contributions, were not merely the sporadic practices of mercenary freebooters, but a deliberate system.[87] It could even be used politically, as Tilly demonstrated in 1623 when he threatened to quarter his army in the Lower Saxon Circle unless they expelled Christian of Brunswick.[88]

The Bavarian use of such methods, first in Bohemia and then in the Palatinate, inspired retaliation, such as that carried out by Christian of Brunswick in the bishopric of Paderborn in 1622. The system became institutionalized. Wallenstein's employment of these devices, for all its notoriety, was simply a somewhat idiosyncratic variant of the Bavarian practice. If he employed the Bavarian system of logistics, his strategy was, if anything, a last example of the old Spanish school. Unlike Tilly's, his campaigns were characterized by cautious and defensive tactics (Dessau Bridge or the Alte Veste), and his effort to amass large numbers was very much a revival of the attrition and saturation strategy of Alba and Parma.[89] The Danish and Swedish interventions saw further variations on this theme.[90] Christian IV relied in the main on foreign subsidies, largely inspired by Britain, that never (or seldom) arrived. The Danish Rigsråd's opposition to the war meant that he could not support it by taxation. Instead he was forced to fall back on his private war chest, derived from the profits of the Sound Tolls. Since his army never advanced beyond the allied territories of the Lower Saxon Circle he was never able to employ more aggressive logistics. The Danish intervention remained a private war in the fullest sense of the word. Gustavus Adolphus, on the other hand, developed offensive logistics in perhaps their most ruthless form. Not only did his demands for *assecuratio* and *satisfactio* resemble the Bavarian agreements with the Emperor, but his use of contributions, threats of quartering, and employment of enemy territory for winter quarters (as with the Catholic bishoprics in the winter of 1631–32) was little different to Wallenstein's.[91]

Given its purpose, the Swedish intervention had no use for a defensive strategy. The limited forces and resources at Gustavus's disposal meant that a decisive victory by battle was essential. But the Swedish strategy was no more successful than its predecessors. The significance of Breitenfeld lay in Tilly's failure to inflict a defeat on the Swedes that would drive them out of Germany. The victory of Swedish firepower over Tilly's attacking columns simply reinforced a lesson taught in a number of sixteenth-century battles. When employed offensively (as the mixed results of Gustavus's earlier Polish campaigns had already revealed), neither Swedish tactics nor Swedish resources were sufficient. Lützen was all but a draw; Nördlingen was a clear defeat.

It is from this perspective that the dramatic increases in projected armies obtain their significance. Gustavus's plan for an army of 200,000 in 1632 was intended to provide the means to force a final decisive conclusion to the war. It was not seen as a level that could be maintained indefinitely. Similarly the Spanish and French mobilizations of 1634–35 were means to the same end. The recent work of R. A. Stradling and David Parrott has revealed that both Olivares and Richelieu were planning major offensives with overwhelming strength that would achieve victory in a single campaign.[92] Neither intended to wage a defensive or attritional war. But like Gustavus, both completely overestimated the financial and military resources at their command. Not only did both offensives fail, but both countries found themselves in a war that they could only wage with forces too limited to produce more than an extended stalemate, while the expanded number of combatant powers saw a further diversion of forces to more dispersed fronts. Given the relatively small numbers engaged in the majority of the later battles, the casualties suffered were not, in themselves, sufficient to have a major strategic impact, even Rocroi.[93]

The political inspiration for this return to the offensive underlay its failure. Neither side's administrations were able to fund military expenditure at this level; both were operating on a scale beyond their means. In this respect the "greater powers" were reduced to the financial level of the lesser. Yet the fiscal irresponsibility of the Thirty Years' War was not necessarily typical of the period as a whole. If Elizabeth I's attempt to wage war by budget, as in the Netherlands intervention in 1585–87, owed much to her general parsimony, it also reflected the response of the English political elite to the near-bankruptcy caused by the military overextension of the 1540s. Nor were the worries of Sir William Cecil in 1565 over "the uncertainty of the charge of the war, as at this day it is seen that all wars are treble more chargeable than they were wont to be," unique.[94] At the same time the Venetians also concluded that war was the quick way to economic suicide.[95] Only Spain could bear the burden of an attritional strategy, and even its success was limited. For lesser powers the temptation to risk all on a possibly decisive offensive is understandable.

The strategic significance of the political context of the Thirty Years' War is highlighted by the comparison with the later seventeenth century. Louis XIV revolutionized the international context: first, by replacing fears of a Hapsburg Imperium with fears of a French Imperium, and second, by almost single-handedly bringing the confessional wars to a close by attacking Spain and the United Provinces indiscriminately. This transformed the nature of the later seventeenth-century wars, for religious tension (though not completely eliminated) no longer inhibited the anti-French coalition in the way anti-Hapsburg coalitions had been. The real causes of the tragedy of the Thirty Years' War were diplomatic rather than military: the failure to obtain a settlement in its early years, and the failure to create a decisive anti-Hapsburg grand alliance. Both can be attributed ultimately to confessional hostility.

Any final conclusions about the military revolution must therefore take its political context into account. It was the Thirty Years' War that led to the expansion of armies, not the converse. The relatively minor advances in weaponry and tactics between the development of effective small arms fire in the early sixteenth century and the replacement of the pike by the bayonet at the end of the seventeenth meant that on the tactical level changes were largely variations on a theme. Similarly the relatively limited size of field armies gave to none of the combatants a decisive advantage. Even comparatively minor states could (temporarily) raise armies of 20,000 to 30,000. If the Spanish monarchy possessed greater resources than its rivals, it possessed greater liabilities and greater commitments. The essentially defensive strategy described here as the Spanish school was the product of the political concerns of the house of Austria. Yet the scale of resources it demanded when employed in the Netherlands (let alone the combination of the Netherlands and Germany) was too great even for Spain to provide, and effective concentration of force proved impossible. Political frustration on the part of the minor powers led to the repudiation of this strategy. The return to the offensive in the Thirty Years' War was a political rather than a military imperative. Yet even the victory of one minor power (like Bavaria) over another (the Palatinate) was insufficient to sway the wider balance. Nor did the adoption of an offensive strategy by the major powers produce a short decisive war. No state of the period possessed the ability to raise armies of the size it considered necessary. To Geoffrey Parker's observation that the states of early modern Europe had not discovered how to lead armies to victory, we can add the suggestion that behind the failure of armies in this period lay the fact that much more was expected of them than they could provide.

Notes

1. S. R. Gardiner, *The Thirty Years' War, 1618–1648* (London, 1881), 139–40.

2. Michael Roberts, *Gustavus Adolphus* (London, 1958), 2:182. The "Military Revolution" is explored more directly in his essays "The Military Revolution, 1560–1660," (above, ch. 1) and "Gustavus Adolphus and the Art of War," reprinted in *Essays in Swedish History* (London, 1967).

3. Geoffrey Parker, "The 'Military Revolution, 1560–1660'—A Myth?," *Journal of Modern History* 48 (1976): 195–214, reprinted above, ch. 2, from *Spain and the Netherlands, 1559–1659* (London, 1979), 86–103, with significant revisions from the 1976 version. All further references are made to the later version, in this volume.

4. Quoted from *The Military Revolution: Military Innovation and the Rise of the West, 1500–1800* (Cambridge, 1988), 80.

5. Robert Barret, *The Theorike and Practike of Moderne Warres* (London, 1598), 75, 77, recommends its use, though with experienced men. See also John A. Lynn, "Tactical Evolution in the French Army, 1550–1660," *French Historical Studies* 14 (1985), 179–80, and David Parrott, "Strategy and Tactics in the Thirty Years' War: The 'Military Revolution,'" *Militärgeschichtliche Mitteilungen* 18 (1985): 8–9 (reprinted above, Ch. 9, pp. 228–230). I am most grateful to Professor Lynn and Dr. Parrott for bringing these articles to my attention, and to Dr. Parrott for permission to use his excellent dissertation "The Administration of the French Army during the Ministry of Cardinal Richelieu," D.Phil. diss., Oxford University, 1985.

6. Martin van Creveld, *Supplying War: Logistics from Wallenstein to Patton* (Cambridge, 1977), 4.

7. Roberts, "The Military Revolution," p. 19.

8. Parker, "Military Revolution—A Myth?," pp. 43–44.

9. Creveld, 5–6.

10. The distinction is noted in Parker, "Military Revolution—A Myth?," p. 43, and Parrott, "Strategy and Tactics," 239, but overlooked in the table of army strengths in J. R. Hale's, *War and Society in Renaissance Europe, 1440–1620* (London, 1985), 62–63.

11. Ferdinand Lot, *Recherches sur les effectifs des armées françaises des Guerres d'Italie aux Guerres de Religion, 1494–1562* (Paris, 1962), the one sustained attempt to analyze sixteenth-century army strengths, takes an impressively skeptical approach toward literary sources. Cf. their uncritical employment in Charles Oman, *History of the Art of War in the XVIth Century* (London, 1937).

12. For Pavia, see R. J. Knecht, *Francis I* (Cambridge, 1982), 170–71.

13. Ibid., 164. Golo Mann, *Wallenstein: His Life Narrated* (London, 1976), 649; A. van der Essen, *Le Cardinal-Enfant et la politique européenne de l'Espagne, 1609–1641* (Brussels, 1944), 1:422.

14. See Essen, *Cardinal-Enfant,* 1:413, n. 3.

15. Geoffrey Parker, *The Army of Flanders and the Spanish Road, 1567–1659* (Cambridge, 1972), 3.

16. The Dutch *Staaten van Oorlog* are summarized in tabular form in F. T. G. Ten Raa and F. de Bas, *Het Staatsche Leger, 1598–1795* (Breda, 1911–18). For the period 1588–1609, see vol. 2 (1913), 344–69. For 1621–1648 see also Jonathon I. Israel, *The Dutch Republic and the Hispanic World, 1606–1661* (Oxford, 1982), 96, 167–68, 176–77, 317. For the French, see Parrott, "French Army," 88–89. Cf. also the comments of W. Brulez, "Het Gewicht van de Oorlog in de Nieuwe Tijden. Enkele Aspecten," *Tijdschrift voor Geschiednis* 91 (1978): 398, n. 46.

17. For examples, see Parker, *Army of Flanders,* 207–11, and Parrott, "Strategy and Tactics," 243, and "Administration of the French Army," 96.

18. Knecht, *Francis I,* 171, and Lot, *Recherches,* 56.

19. In general, see Lot, *Recherches,* 69–100, 129–61, 171, passim. C. S. L. Davies, "Provisions for Armies, 1509–50: A Study in the Effectiveness of Early Tudor Government," *Economic History Review,* 3d. ser., 17 (1964–65), 234, gives 48,000 as the size of the English army of 1544.

20. P. D. Lagomarsino, "Court Factions and the Formulation of Spanish Policy Towards the Netherlands (1559–1567)" Ph.D. diss., Cambridge University, 1973, 268, 278.

21. Léon van der Essen, *Alexandre Farnèse, Prince de Parme, Gouverneur Général des Pays-Bas (1559–1567)* (Brussels, 1933–37), 5:294–95, 333.

22. Roberts, *Gustavus Adolphus,* 2:766.

23. Essen, *Cardinal-Infant,* 1:413, n. 3.

24. R. A. Stradling, "Olivares and the Origins of the Franco-Spanish War, 1627–1635," *English Historical Review* 101 (1986): 83.

25. Hans Wertheim, *Der Tolle Halberstädter: Herzog Christian von Braunschweig im Pfälzischen Krieg, 1621–1622* (Berlin, 1929), 2:308–11, 371–72, 494–95 gives the composition of the three armies, though some skepticism is justified.

26. Israel, *Dutch Republic,* 252. Cf. Parrott, "Administration of the French Army," 25–29, "Strategy and Tactics," 243.

27. London, Public Record Office, SP 14/119/93. In 1542 Charles V warned his brother Ferdinand that the army of 40,000 foot and 8,000 horse he was proposing to raise for the Hungarian campaign was too large to manage. See P. S. Fichtner, *Ferdinand I of Austria: The Politics of Dynasticism in the Age of the Reformation* (New York, 1982), 128–29.

28. Quoted in Roberts, *Gustavus Adolphus,* 2:470.

29. Mark A. Kishlansky, *The Rise of the New Model Army* (Cambridge, 1979), 36–37. For Wallenstein's commission, see pages 257–58 of this essay.

30. Parker, *Army of Flanders,* 271–72. Israel, *Dutch Republic,* 162–65.

31. Parker, *Army of Flanders,* 6.

32. J. H. Elliott, *The Count–Duke of Olivares: The Statesman in an Age of Decline* (New Haven and London, 1986), 509.

33. Ibid., Stradling, "Origins," 90.

34. M. E. Mallett and J. R. Hale, *The Military Organization of a Renaissance State: Venice c. 1400 to 1617* (Cambridge, 1984), 213.

35. See n. 16 above.

36. Roberts, *Gustavus Adolphus,* 2:676–77.

37. Gerhard Benecke in Geoffrey Parker, *The Thirty Years' War* (London, 1984), 100.

38. The lists for the period 1621–34 are printed in tabular form as appendices to *Documenta Bohemica Bellum Tricennale Illustrantia,* ed. Josef Janék, et al. (Prague, 1971–77), vols. 3–5.

39. *Documenta Bohemica,* 4:51, 77.

40. Ibid., 11, 130, 137. Wallenstein did send 74 foot companies (20,000 men at full strength) to Tilly on the eve of Lutter am Barenberg. See also Mann, 289.

41. *Documenta Bohemica,* 4:204–5, 215. Wallenstein's conference with the Imperial councillor Eggenberg at Bruck an der Leitha in November 1626, in which he is said to have proposed the creation of an Imperial standing army, is discussed in Mann, 324–29.

42. Mann, 438.

43. John A. Lynn, "The Growth of the French Army during the Seventeenth Century," *Armed Forces and Society* 6 (1980): 569, 573. Parrott, "Administration of the French Army," 103.

44. Lynn, "Growth," 573. Cf. David Buissert, *Henry IV* (London, 1984), 174. The remaining 25,000 were diversionary forces deployed in Navarre and Italy.

45. Parrott, "Administration of the French Army," 103–4.

46. Ibid., 105–17 passim, and the table on page 142.

47. This point was made to me by Professor Parker in conversation.

48. See Parrott, "Strategy and Tactics," 239–45. This article draws the same distinction between the growth of field armies and overall establishments as that made above and sees logistical considerations as the central limiting factor on the size of field armies. Cf. the comments of Davies, "Provisions," 246.

49. Parker, "Military Revolution—A Myth?," 45.

50. Parrott, "Administration of the French Army," 81.

51. See the tables in Parker, *Army of Flanders,* 271–72, and *Het Staatsche Leger,* 2:344–69.

52. Roberts, *Gustavus Adolphus,* 2:203.

53. Robert Stradling, "Catastrophe and Recovery: the Defeat of Spain, 1639–43," *History* 64 (1979): 216, and, more specifically, "Spain's Military Failure and the Supply of Horses, 1600–1660," *History* 69 (1984): 211–15. Parrott, "Administration of the French Army," 81–82.

54. Roberts, *Gustavus Adolphus,* 2:444. Parker, "Military Revolution—A Myth?," 45.

55. Simon Pepper and Nicholas Adams, *Firearms and Fortifications. Military Architecture and Siege Warfare in Sixteenth-Century Siena* (Chicago, 1986), 27–28. Judith Hook, "Fortifications and the End of the Sienese State," *History* 62 (1977): 373–74.

56. Practically all of the towns listed by Brulez, "Het Gewicht," 394, as fortified between 1529 and 1572 are southern.

57. William S. Maltby, *Alba. A Biography of Fernando Alvarez de Toledo, Third Duke of Alba, 1507–1582* (Berkeley, Calif., 1983), 81.

58. Buisseret, *Henry IV,* 70–71.

59. For Wallenstein and Stalsund, see Mann, 412–15.

60. Pepper and Adams, *Firearms and Fortifications,* 31, 129–30; Mallett and Hale, *Military Organization,* 411–12; M. L. Bush, *The Government Policy of Protector Somerset* (London, 1975), 7–39 passim.

61. For Italy, see the comments of Pepper and Adams, *Firearms and Fortifications,* 27–28, 157, and Mallett and Hale, *Military Organization,* 421–3. Cf. the observations of the earl of Leicester on Ireland: "I have oft times noted in the service of that land, whensoever we have placed any garrisons to front the enemy… it hath fallen out to be the way to chasten and plague him." Oxford, Bodleian Library, Carte MS 56, fols. 103v–4, to Sir William Fitzwilliam, 5 Dec. 1572.

62. For the creation of the Dutch provincial regiments after 1572, see *Het Staatsche Leger,* 1:254–62. J. W. Wijn, "Het Noordhollandse Regiment in de Eerste Jaren van de Opstand tegen Spanje," *Tijdschrift voor Geschiednis* 62 (1949), 245–46, notes that only a third of the original complement of the regiment was comprised of natives of the province, though the proportion varied from company to company.

63. For the dispersal of the French *bandes* after 1559, see Lot, 188, 253 ff.

64. *War and Government in Habsburg Spain, 1560–1620* (London, 1976), 19.

65. See, for example, the instructions of Francis II to Marshal Tavannes, 12 April 1560, printed in *Négociations, lettres et pièces diverses … tirées du portefeuille de Sebastien de L'Aubespeine, Evêque de Limoges,* ed. Louis Paris (Paris, 1841), 341–42.

66. For the Irish stage of this process, see Brendan Bradshaw, *The Irish Constitutional Revolution of the Sixteenth Century* (Cambridge, 1979), 119–21.

67. Cf. Parrott, "Strategy and Tactics," 234–39.

68. The arguments outlined in the following paragraphs are developed more fully in my paper "'The Catholic League' and the Emergence of Protestant Alliance Politics, 1559–1572," delivered at the Anglo-American Conference of Historians in London in July 1987, and to be published in *Historical Research.*

69. Francis I justified his Turkish alliance against Charles V in 1532 as a means to "rassurer toutes autres gouvernements contre un ennemi si grand." J. Ursu, *La politique orientale de François I (1515–1547)* (Paris, 1908), 75. For the French claim to be protecting the Sienese liberty in 1552, see Pepper and Adams, *Firearms and Fortifications,* 62.

70. Maltby, esp. 60–62.

71. For the establishment of the system whereby the Italian tercios provided trained companies for use elsewhere, see Parker, *Army of Flanders,* 33.

72. Essen, *Alexandre Farnèse,* 3:53–54. Cf. Maltby, 151–52.

73. Maltby, 140.

74. Parker, *Army of Flanders,* 140–41, 233.

75. Essen, *Alexandre Farnèse,* 3:143–44.

76. *Calendar of States Papers, Foreign Series, Elizabeth I,* vol. xxi, pt. 3 (London, 1929), 316, to Sir Francis Walsingham, 16 Sept. 1587.

77. As the States General informed the English in 1585; see the report of the Dutch commissioners at the making of the treaty of Nonsuch. The Hague: Algemeen Rijksarchief, Eerste Afdeling, Staten Generaal 8299, fol. 19–v.

78. Essen, *Alexandre Farnèse*, 2:264.

79. Algemeen Rijksarchief, Eerste Afdeeling, Regeringsarchieven I–97, art. 4. Cf. Israel, *Dutch Republic*, 96–97, who claims that both the Dutch and the Spaniards were forced to deploy over 30,000 men in garrisons during the 1620s.

80. Essen, *Alexandre Farnèse*, 5:62, 65.

81. On Maurice's reforms, see B. H. Nickle, "The Military Reforms of Prince Maurice of Orange," Ph.D. diss., University of Delaware, 1975.

82. See the comments of Cardinal Bertivolio quoted in Christopher Duffy, *Siege Warfare: The Fortress in the Early Modern World, 1494–1660* (London, 1979), 63.

83. See Buisserert, *Henry IV*, 36–39.

84. The best account of the invasion of the Palatinate is Anna Egler, *Die Spanier in der linksrheinischen Pfalz 1620–1632: Invasion, Verwaltung, Rekatholisierung* (Mainz, 1971). See pp. 31–51 and pp. 183–87, Archduke Albert's letter to Philip III of 14 April 1620. A contemporary translation of Spínola's oration can be found in the Henry E. Huntington Library, San Marino, Calif., MS EL 6899.

85. See M. S. Junkelmann, "Feldherr Maximilians: Johann Tserclaes, Graf von Tilly," in *Wittelsbach und Bayern. II. Um Glauben und Reich: Kurfürst Maximilian I,* ed. H. Glaser (Munich and Zurich, 1980), 2/1: 377–80. Cf. Roberts, *Gustavus Adolphus,* 2:264, and Wertheim, *Toller Halberstädter,* 1:177.

86. Dieter Albrecht, *Die auswärtige Politik Maximilians von Bayern, 1618–1635* (Göttingen, 1962), 2–3, 91.

87. Creveld, *Supplying War,* 16, describes the process as a "flight forward." Cf. Roberts, "Gustavus Adolphus and the Art of War," 73, and Wertheim, *Tolle Halberstädter,* 1:157.

88. W. Brunick, *Der Graf von Mansfeld in Ostfriesland (1622–24)* (Aurich, W. Ger., 1957), 109–11.

89. On Wallenstein's strategy, see Mann, 327, 655, 667.

90. E. Ladewig Petersen, "Defence, War and Finance: Christian IV and the Council of the Realm, 1596–1629," *Scandinavian Journal of History* 7 (1982): 277–313, esp. 280, 301–4.

91. Roberts, *Gustavus Adolphus,* 2:650–53. Creveld, *Supplying War,* 13–17.

92. Stradling, "Origins," 90–91. Parrott, "The Causes of the Franco-Spanish War of 1635–59," in *The Origins of War in Early Modern Europe,* ed. Jeremy Black (Edinburgh, 1987), 72–111, and "Administration of the French Army," 19.

93. Stradling, "Defeat of Spain," 216–17.

94. London, British Library, Cottonian MS Caligula B X, fol. 353, "A consideration of the whole matter of Scotland" (12 Sept. 1565). For Elizabeth's attitude to the financing of the Netherlands intervention, see J. E. Neale, "Elizabeth and the Netherlands, 1586–7," in *Essays in Elizabethan History* (London, 1958), 170–201.

95. Mallett and Hale, *Military Organization,* 215–16.

11

"Money, Money, and Yet More Money!" Finance, the Fiscal-State, and the Military Revolution: Spain 1500–1650

I.A.A. THOMPSON

FOLLOWING MICHAEL ROBERTS, there has been general agreement among historians that one of the principal consequences of the Military Revolution was a great increase in the cost of war, leading to the growth of state taxation, bureaucratic administration, and centralized government. The scale, the costs and the organizational demands of the new style of warfare are seen to have been the driving forces of a coercion-extraction cycle of power and resources that led inexorably to the monopolization of military force by the central government and to the consolidation of the territorial control of the state. The crucial features of the Military Revolution that are said to have made war so much more expensive are the increased size of armies and navies, more sophisticated battle tactics requiring longer periods of training and more intensive leadership, the heavy capital costs of artillery and new fortification works, expensive gunpowder weaponry, the continuous nature and the continental scale of sixteenth and seventeenth century wars, necessitating permanent defences and standing forces, and large administrative and logistical support staffs.[1]

That war was overwhelmingly the most important item of expenditure for virtually every government in early-modern Europe can hardly be doubted. That is not in question. The more pertinent issues are whether war was costing relatively more in this period than in previous ages; in what ways were the costs of war related to the changes in the nature and conduct of war that have come to be known as the Military Revolution; and how did those costs affect the development of fiscality and the state? Is war=taxes=state a universally valid syllogism? Or is this an inversion of the proper syntax, state=taxes=war? Indeed, to what extent was war a state activity? And how much of it was financed by the state, rather than by society, or by the soldier, or by its victims?

Spain can be regarded in many ways as the touchstone of the problem of the connection between the Military Revolution and the early-modern state. Spain had a dominant role in the wars of sixteenth- and seventeenth-century Europe. Because of the nature, composition and extent of the Spanish Monarchy her forces were involved in every type of contemporary warfare, on land, at sea, in the Mediterranean, on the oceans; her wars were internal, external, defensive, hegemonic. As Kennedy writes, "The Spanish Empire's army probably provided the best example of the 'military revolution' in action."[2] At the same time, Spain had developed a precocious government bureaucracy and a complex and effective system of public finance and credit which, though too often overlooked by historians, was for a long time far more advanced than those of her major international rivals (the Dutch included), until it was undermined by the collapse of the economy in the seventeenth century.[3] If the Military Revolution did not promote the permanent establishment of a powerful, centralized state in Spain, then the whole argument linking war and state development must be fundamentally weakened.

*   *   *

The expenditure of the Spanish treasury multiplied at least twenty-fold between the start of the sixteenth and the middle of the seventeenth centuries, approximately four times faster than the general price level. The great bulk of that expenditure was on war. Of the roughly 400 million ducats spent between 1621 and 1640, 47 percent went to war and defence; almost the same amount on the servicing of the debt, most of which had been undertaken in order to finance war in the past; and the rest, some 8 percent, on government, justice, the royal court and the household. More than three-quarters of disposable, unmortgaged income was spent directly on war, a proportion that all our evidence suggests was little different than it had been 150 years before, or was to be fifty years later.[4]

The two centuries that followed the accession of the Catholic Kings, Ferdinand and Isabella, in 1474, witnessed an enormous increase in the sums devoted to defence and to debt charges. There were four main periods of explosive growth: the 1480s, when the size of the Christian armies of Ferdinand and Isabella fighting for the reconquest of Granada increased from 20,000 to 60,000 within ten years; the 1530s–50s, the culmination of the Emperor Charles V's hegemonic struggles against the French, the Ottoman Turks and the Protestant princes of Germany; the 1570s–90s, the crucial decades of Philip II's defence of his Monarchy against infidels, rebels and heretics in the Mediterranean, the Low Countries, Portugal, England and France; and the 1620s–40s, when Philip IV was sustaining the Catholic and Habsburg cause in Germany, Italy, France and the Netherlands, and resisting the secession of Catalonia and Portugal from the Spanish Crown.

Over the ten years 1495–1504, the equivalent of 2.73 million ducats had been spent by Spain on the war in Naples. By 1559 the Venetian ambassador Soriano was reporting an *annual* wartime expenditure of 10 million ducats. No doubt he exaggerated, though that exaggeration is itself not without meaning; but in 1574 at least 7 million ducats must have been allocated to defence; in 1588 the President of Finance was claiming that the king was spending at the rate of 8.4 million a year; and in 1596 the secretary of war was looking ahead to an expenditure of 10 million ducats. By the early 1640s, Philip IV's chief minister, the Count-Duke of Olivares, was talking of an average of 17 million ducats being spent annually during the current war. Even after Westphalia and the peace with the Dutch in 1648, the demands of war on the treasury remained high, and the budget for 1678 was still calling for 11 million ducats in silver and *vellón*.[5]

Spain's military expenditures were made up of three components: 1) the ordinary budget for the military and naval establishment within the Spanish theatre (the men-at-arms and light horse of the Guards, the fortress garrisons in North Africa and on the French and the western frontiers, the galleys and galleons in the Mediterranean and the Atlantic, fortifications, shipbuilding, armaments and munitions works). The allocations on this account rose from just over 1 million ducats in the 1560s and 1570s to more than 3 million ducats in the two decades after 1587, and, after a brief remission in Philip III's reign, remained close to the 3 million mark under Philip IV after 1621.[6]

2) extraordinary military expenditures within Spain, for such campaigns as those against the Peñón de los Vélez in 1564 and Portugal in 1579–83, or the repression of the revolt of the Alpujarran *moriscos* in 1569–70, the preparation of the Armada against England in 1586–88, and the almost continuous actions against the French, the Catalans and the Portuguese between 1637 and 1668, when warfare within Spain itself became a permanent element in the life of many parts of the country. These expenditures are in their very nature the most difficult to reconstruct. By 1582 the conquest of Portugal had cost a minimum of 2,600,000 ducats; the Armada, only a few years later, probably cost another 4 million for the fleet alone; and some 2 million ducats (13.6 percent of the total defence budget) was spent on the Portuguese front in 1643. Though irregular, such occasions were so frequent and so costly that they had a cumulative long-term impact on Spain's finances.[7]

3) remittances from Spain to help pay for the wars in the Low Countries, France, Italy and Germany, to which substantial contributions were also made by other parts of the Monarchy. During the 1520s and 1530s Charles V was raising about ½ million ducats a year from the bankers to pay for his wars; in the early 1550s he was raising nearly 2 million. With the outbreak of revolt in the Netherlands, the 800,000 ducats spent there in 1566 leapt to an annual average of 2,750,000 for the next ten years, of which 1,750,000 were sent from Spain. By the early seventeenth century, Spain was sending 3,750,000 of the more than 4 million the war was costing. In 1574 alone, 5.7 million ducats were sent to the military paymasters in Italy and Flanders, and in 1615 the armies in Flanders and Milan were consuming ½ million ducats a month. In 1636 it was reported that credits of 12 million ducats had been arranged for military expenses in Flanders, Germany, Italy and France. The economic pundit, Alberto Struzzi, calculated in 1624 that re-

mittances from Spain for overseas defence payments in the previous forty years amounted to 240 million ducats; this was much the greatest part of the financial burden of Spain's global military role.[8]

*   *   *

How much of this increase in military spending is attributable to the Military Revolution? In one sense the question is a tautology; a quantitative leap in the costs of war can itself be regarded as one dimension of the Military Revolution.[9] However, it is not simply the amount of money, but also specific features of the changing conditions of warfare, notably the supposedly high costs of gunpowder technology, with its siege cannon, bastioned fortifications, arms and munitions manufactures, as well as the organizational and logistical consequences of the initial replacement of heavy cavalry by massed infantry formations and the later linearization of battlefield tactics, which are at the heart of the argument for the coercion-monopoly state-building implications of the Military Revolution. It is important, therefore, to try to establish not only *whether* but also the precise mechanism of *how* the technological, technical and tactical changes that composed the Military Revolution affected the costs of war.

The cost of artillery-resistant fortifications has generally been considered a major item of new expenditure, especially when what was undertaken was the rebuilding or redesigning of entire systems of defences, such as the 43 kilometers of new defences built in Flanders in 1529–72 at a cost of 10 million florins. In Spain, however, a coherent account of re-fortification costs is more difficult to come by.[10] Throughout the 1520s–1580s the Cortes petitioned repeatedly for fortifications to be repaired or rebuilt, primarily to resist the incursions of raiders from North Africa, and after the English landings in Cadiz and Corunna in 1587 and 1589 there was a call in the 1590 Cortes for 1 million ducats to be allocated to the construction and repair of fortifications. But the military pressure was not sufficiently consistent for a wholesale reconstruction of old medieval fortresses in the new style, although the new constructions designed by the Italian schooled engineers, Antonelli and Fratini, in the 1560s and 70s, and Spanocchi, a little later, did incorporate essential modern features of the *trace italienne*. Not until a complete survey of Spain's defences was undertaken in 1569 by J.B. Antonelli was a full-scale programme of construction and upgrading contemplated, to be begun on the Pyrenean frontier and the Mediterranean coasts and islands in the 1570s, and on the Atlantic front in the 1580s. Available information about fortification works and costs is therefore spotty. Improvements and repairs were being carried out in fortresses along the French frontier and on the Mediterranean coastline in the 1520s and 1530s, and again in the 1550s; the rebuilding of the North African fortresses was begun in the 1560s, with 100,000 ducats sent for La Goleta-by-Tunis in 1566–68. However, the maintenance, repair and reconstruction of the frontier and coastal fortresses was an unending, if sporadic, charge which grew even more onerous in the last decades of the century. Indeed, the Atlantic war made it necessary to fortify a virtually new line of coastal defences—Bayona, Corunna, Viana, Peniche, Cascaes, Cabeza Seca, Setubal, San Vicente, Cadiz, Gibraltar, Alarache, La Mamora. By the beginning of Philip IV's reign nearly three-fifths of what was required for defence works was targeted on the Atlantic theatre.[11]

There is no doubt that the capital outlay on these projects could be very substantial. One proposed scheme for the re-fortification of Pamplona would have cost 700,000 ducats. It was subsequently revised to reduce the cost to 200,000, but the new citadel still required 140,000 ducats for completion in 1575; whilst at the same time, 185,000 ducats over two years was needed for the extensive building works in Fuenterrabía and San Sebastián, and 74,467 ducats over the next three for the main castle of Perpignan. One official claimed that Philip II had spent almost 2 million ducats on Perpignan during the course of his life, and the great re-fortification of Oran was reputed to have cost 3 million ducats over thirty years. More reliable is a statement presented to the Council of War in 1622, detailing the money needed to complete new works, improvements and repairs to all the defences of Spain, the Mediterranean and Atlantic islands, and the North African fortresses: the total requirement amounted to some $2^1/_2$ million ducats, and that excluded a contract for 432,000 ducats over six years for the fortification of La Mamora signed in 1618.[12]

Sums of this magnitude are by no means negligible, but they need to be put into context. The notional costs of projects are not to be taken as representing actual expenditure, nor is it proper to annualize momentary requirements or retrospective totals in which it is not possible to separate the capital costs of re-fortification associated with the Military Revolution from the normal costs of maintenance and repair which would have had to have been undertaken anyway. Furthermore, we have piecemeal figures because we have piecemeal re-fortification. The improvement of defence works was a long-drawn-out yet erratic process, and rarely a financial priority. Many of the works listed in the 1622 survey had been instituted long before and were still not completed, or in some cases even begun. Capital expenditure was the most readily deferred as soon as the immediate danger passed. On the Mediterranean coast, 106 new watchtowers, decided on in the 1570s, having cost 112,000 ducats by 1608, with another 53,000 ducats outstanding, were still not "en defensa" in 1621 after nearly fifty years.[13] Such delays did not necessarily make things cheaper—the allocation for La Mamora had been paid only once since 1618 and by 1623 part of the walls had collapsed and repairs alone needed 50–60,000 ducats a year[14]—but they did mean that their budgetary impact was reduced. Although there were years when substantially larger sums were called for, the standard allocation across the period for "obras de fortalezas" was 50,000 ducats; that was 2.8 percent of the total domestic military budget in 1617, a figure close to that for the outlay on fortification works in 1495–1503 (4.1 percent of total military expenditure, 2.5 percent of overall expenditure).[15] These sums pale in comparison with those devoted to civil building. The more than 200,000 ducats a year for the construction of the Escorial in 1583–90 was four times as much as was being set aside for fortifications.[16] The 5¹/₂ million in all spent by Philip II on the Escorial was probably not much less than the total outlay by the central government on all defence works during his reign. On the other hand, it should be remembered that the Crown bore only part of the expense of re-fortification, the full costs of which were, therefore, rather more than appear in government budgets. The 168,000-ducat bill for Mallorca in 1576 was shared 50/50 with the island; of the 44,000 ducats for the fortifying of Cadiz, the Crown paid only 12,000; and of the 23,914 projected cost of the twenty-three towers planned for the Andalusian coast, the Crown's share was only 4,593 (19 percent)—the rest was the responsibility of the local lords.[17]

Not only were the fiscal implications of fortification construction for the state in Spain fairly modest, but the sums involved were by no means outside the financial capacity of individual provinces, cities and lords. It may even be that sixteenth-century fortifications were no more expensive to build and maintain than the great medieval castles,[18] and it is not at all obvious from a financial perspective that the cost of building fortifications in the new style by itself shifted the economics of scale away from local nodes of military autonomy, or that those fortifications played any great part in the centralization of coercive power within the body politic.

Artillery costs have also conventionally been considered to be a major element in the increased cost of war in the gunpowder age. Fortress guns and field and siege trains clearly required considerable up-front capital investment. It was, of course, not only the Military Revolution that was a major source of demand. The Naval Revolution also created a substantial demand for guns, overwhelmingly of bronze, because iron was not much used for the main pieces on royal ships before the middle of the seventeenth century. The ideal armament for a great galleon at the end of the sixteenth century was approximately one ton of artillery for every 20 tons of ship, which meant that the new royal Armada of the Ocean Sea was frequently carrying in excess of 1,000 tons of artillery, its armament (guns, shot, and powder) worth just about as much as the vessels themselves.[19] Periodic large-scale castings or acquisitions were needed to replace losses or to meet new requirements. We know of some 1,500 tons of bronze guns cast in Malaga and Lisbon alone in the 100 years after 1530: 18,115 quintals (about 900 tons) costing 266,292 ducats in the mid 1570s; 347 guns weighing 11,075¹/₂ quintals and costing about 180,000 ducats after the Armada in 1590–92; another 100 weighing 2,771 quintals and costing 77,288 ducats in 1608; and 260 more in 1628. That is not an exhaustive list, and it does not include guns brought from abroad, like Remigy de Halut's cannon from Malines and the Loeffer pieces from Augsburg that were found on ships of the Great Armada. In the seventeenth century, a foundry was established in Liérganes, near Santander, for the manufacture of cheaper cast-iron artillery, with a productive capacity of 15,000 quintals a year in 1637. Between 1628 and 1640, it supplied the Crown with some 3,600 tons of ironware, 1,171 guns and

250,000 cannonballs, to a value approaching 500,000 ducats, but also a considerable saving over the cost of an equivalent quantity of bronze guns.[20]

Guns naturally needed gunpowder, match and shot in proportion, and gunpowder assignments increased from 27,650 ducats in 1582 to 72,000 ducats in the 1660s. Domestic gunpowder requirements reached a peak in the mid seventeenth century with a contract for 500,000 ducats to supply 41,000 quintals (2,000 tons) over the nine years 1640–48. The 3,000 tons of iron shot fired by that quantity of powder would have cost a further 270,000 ducats or so.[21]

We are fortunate in having an almost complete account, drawn up in November 1588, of all guns, weapons and munitions in Crown establishments in mainland Spain, together with what was needed to bring the stock up to scratch. This makes it possible to calculate the total capital tied up by the state in gunpowder technology in the immediate wake of the Armada to have been 622,758 ducats, including approximately 300,000 ducats of artillery; another 1,412,000 ducats was required to bring the reserve stock up to the desired level. The addition of an estimate for stocks in the North African fortresses and the Mediterranean and Atlantic islands, omitted from the review, would bring the notional desired stock up to total of about $2\frac{1}{2}$ million ducats.[22]

However, we should not be misled by this figure. It was perhaps no more than $3\frac{1}{2}$ percent of the total capital of the Crown debt at that time. Like all pre-industrial enterprises, the fixed capital invested in armaments and munitions was low compared with running-costs. Most munitions plant was small-scale and cheap—a shot factory in Navarre, thought sufficient for all Spain's needs in the 1580s, would have cost only 2,000 ducats to put into operation; it ran in the seventeenth century with not many more than forty workers and an annual wage and maintenance bill of 8,200 ducats.[23] Even the largest culverin at the time of the Armada cost no more than 1,000 ducats, the pay of twenty infantrymen for a year, and there were guns on the Armada fifty years old. The entire armament of the royal fleet in the early seventeenth century could not have reached 500,000 ducats, half its running-costs for one year.[24] Of course, from a certain perspective a naval broadside was a spectacularly expensive event; at 5 ducats in shot, powder and match, every 40 lb cannonball fired was the equivalent of the price of a musket, or almost two months' basic wages of an ordinary soldier; but the observation is specious. The total cost of powder, match, iron shot and lead provided for the entire Armada in 1588 came to only some 120,000 ducats, less than 50 percent of one month's expenditure (256,588 ducats). Even for as artillery-preponderant an arm as the navy, the ordinary expenditure of powder, match, shot and lead amounted to a good deal less than 10 percent of total running costs.[25] Consequently, although current account assignments for armaments and munitions rose substantially between the mid sixteenth and the early seventeenth centuries, the entire annual expenditure on the artillery account hardly ever represented more than about 4 or 5 percent of Castile's total domestic military budget (a figure that was again reasonably constant from the 1490s).[26]

If gunpowder technology added only marginally to the cost of war to the state, neither was it a monopoly of the state. Evidence survives of large aristocratic arsenals even in the seventeenth century. The marquis of Las Navas, for example, a title by no means in the top rank of the Spanish nobility, had twenty-five pieces of artillery which he donated to the king in lieu of taxes; they were worth 30,000 ducats, and must therefore have been quite substantial pieces, weighing in all some 50 tons, as much as the entire siege train on the Spanish Armada.[27] Though private arsenals of this size were a rarity, they were in decline clearly not because they could not be afforded, but because they were not needed.

Neither were the equipment costs of the soldiery of Spain's sixteenth-century armies and navies affected significantly by the development of gunpowder and handgun technology. Compared with pay, provision and outfitting, weaponry costs were marginal, and the new weapons were not necessarily more expensive than the weapons they replaced; a crossbow in 1523 cost more than twice as much as a handgun (escopeta), for example.[28] In England the complete equipment for a late medieval bowman cost anywhere between three and five months' pay,[29] yet the cost of equipping an arquebusier (38 reales) or a musketeer (55 reales) in Spain was less than a month's wages. It cost far more to clothe him; 116 reales for a complete outfit in 1591, 140 reales in 1663, nearly three months' wages for an arquebusier, but that was not a charge specific to the Military Revolution.[30] On average between 1610 and 1632 the Crown paid only 31,818 ducats a year for pikes, arquebuses and muskets supplied by the manufacturers of Biscay, a relatively small sum and no more than was being spent fifty years earlier.[31] Moreover, these were not in principle charges on government, for weapon, powder, match, ball and clothing were the responsibility of the soldier himself, from whose wages deductions were made to recoup the cost of outfitting as well as to pay for munitions and rations, though not, of course, always the exact cost, either way.[32] The corseleted pikeman (coselete), the arquebusier and the musketeer were therefore paid more to compensate for the cost, maintenance and physical burden of the armour, weapon and ammunition, an extra ducat per month for the coselete and the arquebusier, an extra 3 ducats for the musketeer.

Tactical changes and changes in the command structure also had financial implications. The first, and perhaps most important, of these changes was the marked fall in the proportion of cavalry in sixteenth-century armies, and within the cavalry the progressive reduction in the number of men-at-arms compared with light horse, with the introduction of horse-pistoleers (herreruelos) around 1560, mounted arquebusiers in the 1570s, and dragoons in the 1630s. The replacement of the lance meant lighter armour, fewer horses, cheaper horses, and less training. The retreat of the horseman in face of massed formations of infantry, and then of the heavily armed hombres de armas in face of the caballería ligera probably halved the average unit cost of an army, and made consequential savings in training, equipment and upkeep of men and horses. From the 1630s, however, that fall in the number of cavalry was reversed. Overall the proportion of cavalry in the armies of the mid seventeenth century was double that of the previous 150 years.[33] But horsemen were very expensive. An ordinary cavalry trooper's wages were from two to two-and-a-half times those of an infantryman. The unit cost of cavalry was clearly far greater than that of any other arm on both the current and the capital accounts. A captain of light horse in Naples in 1575 claimed he needed 1,000 ducats a year for himself and seven servants and grooms to support his four horses, each of them worth 50 ducats and costing a month's wages to sustain.[34] In 1663 a troop of eight companies of German cavalry in Extremadura, with 497 horse, was costing 119,734 ducats a year, three times the cost of a comparable number of infantry.[35]

The saving achieved by the declining proportion of cavalry to infantry at the start of the period contributed to making possible a considerable overall increase in army size, the high cost of which was also partly offset by a shift in the balance between pikemen and arquebusiers. The fully-armed pikeman was the most expensive of the infantry to fit out; the full kit for the *coselete* cost more than twice as much as that for the arquebusier and half as much again as that for the musketeer.[36] In the early sixteenth century, the standard ratio of pikemen to handgunners was three to one; but the proportion of pikemen declined steadily, to just over half by 1560, 35 percent in the 1630s, 25 percent by the end of the century.[37] The fall in the number of pikemen was matched after about 1570 by a rising proportion of highly-paid musketeers, from 10 percent initially to 20 percent by the 1630s, and over 30 percent in the 1690s.[38] This movement, magnified overall from the end of the sixteenth century by an even greater prominence of musketeers on the new high-board fleets, revised the cost of the infantry upwards, and together with the revival of the cavalry arm in the middle third of the seventeenth century substantially increased the cost of a standard military corps consisting of one-third cavalry and two-thirds infantry, of which 25 percent were musketeers and 25 percent *coseletes*. On such figures, these tactical changes during the Military Revolution would by themselves have increased the cost of an army of a given size by nearly a quarter.

Among the organizational changes implicit in the reduction of unit sizes in sixteenth-century armies and in the linearization of tactics in the seventeenth century, which also had an effect on overall costs, was an intensification of command structures. The number of officers in a force increased with the reduction of company size from a standard 300 in the mid sixteenth century to 100, and in practice often a good deal fewer, a generation later,[39] a reduction for which there were supply-side as well as tactical causes. At the same time the number of corporals (*cabos*) was increased from one for every twenty-five men, to one for every ten.[40] The total wage-bill for the *primeras planas* (the company command: captain, lieutenant, ensign, sergeant, drummer, fifemen, quartermaster, barber-surgeon, and chaplain) rose proportionately as company size fell. The reduction in company size from 250 or 300 men to just 100 increased the proportion of the wage bill allocated to the *primeras planas* from about 12 to 22 percent, adding some 15 percent

Table 11.1 Relationship between number of military personnel and
domestic military expenditure in Spain, 1560--1621

Year	Personnel	Index	Expenditure	Index	Deflated
1560	12,985	100	782,000	100	100
1579	17,789	137	1,164,000	149	123
1583	22,603	174	1,823,410	233	183
1596	49,402	380	3,798,000	486	348
1600	30,041	231	2,810,250	359	216
1612	27,989	216	2,174,775	278	183
1621	33,320	258	2,921,940	374	247

to the overall cost of 1,000 men. Taken together, these tactical changes alone (in-creased number of officers and *cabos,* and altered proportion of cavalry and mus-keteers) would have added over 40 percent per 1,000 men to the cost of an army between the mid sixteenth and the later seventeenth centuries.

The Military Revolution in its revolutionary, that is its qualitative dimension, as a change in the *nature* of warfare, was not therefore the main vector of financial revolution. Although it is not possible to follow all the ramifications of the revo-lution in military technology associated with the development of gunpowder warfare through to quantifiable financial conclusions, the effect of naval guns on ship size, for example, or on the destructiveness of naval warfare, it seems that the new-style fortifications, artillery and the handgun made only a marginal contri-bution to the increased costs of war in this period: under 10 percent at the out-side.[41] The tactical changes in the proportions of various arms, paid at different rates and equipped more or less expensively, and in the ratio of officers and NCOs were of rather greater significance. However, although some of the true costs of these changes are concealed by the fact that much of the equipment and the mili-tary training was provided at private expense or at low marginal cost, our calcula-tions suggest that the combined tactical and technological changes of the Military Revolution, at extreme points and on the most unfavourable comparison with late medieval warfare, increased unit costs by perhaps 50 percent and can hardly account for more than one sixth of the real growth of the military account in the sixteenth and seventeenth centuries.

*   *   *

For all intents and purposes, the size of the military budget was determined straightforwardly by the number of men on the payroll. [Table 11.1]

The burden of manpower in pay and provisions was overwhelming. Even in the fleets, the pay and rations of the personnel amounted to some 80 percent of total running costs, compared with $12^1/_2$ percent for the ship (freightage, rigging etc.), and $7^1/_2$ percent for munitions.[42] But pay and rations were not variables which in themselves contributed significantly to the overall increase in costs. Remarkably, pay rates for the ordinary soldier remained fairly static for 200 years from the early sixteenth to the end of the seventeenth century, at 1 *real* per day, 3 *escudos* or ducats a month, with 1 ducat a month bonus for the *coselete* and the arquebusier, and 3 ducats bonus for the musketeer. Pay rates for higher ranks did rise, the infantry captain's from 15 *escudos* in 1534, to 25 *escudos* by the 1560s, and 40 *escudos* from the 1570s through at least to the 1660s, but their impact was, naturally, correspondingly less. The price of rations also rose. On the fleet they were costing the Crown 1^1/$_2$ to 1.75 *reales* a day per man during the first half of the seventeenth century—rather more than twice as much as in 1564; but again it was a fluctuating rather than a steadily rising charge, and one that over the long term kept broadly in line with the general movement of food prices.[43] In 1596 the Spanish secretary of war, Esteban de Ibarra, noted that, "If a comparison is made between what the men serving in the armies and navies now are costing His Majesty, and what they cost the Emperor Don Carlos, you will find that for the same number of men three times as much money is needed at the present time than was spent then, and that is without the pay of the troops having gone up one *maravedí*."[44] His observation is often quoted in support of the link between the Military Revolution and the burgeoning cost of war, but without regard for Ibarra's own explanation, which highlighted, not the features of the Military Revolution to which historians are most wont to draw attention, but financial laxity, corruption and waste. If it is indeed true, as Parker claims, that it cost five times as much to put a soldier in the field in the 1630s as it had in the 1530s,[45] it seems that much the most important factor in that increase was not the Military Revolution but monetary inflation; between those decades the general level of prices in Spain had risen approximately threefold.

Inflation apart, two things were primarily responsible for the bulk of the increase in the cost of war in Spain: 1) a much larger number of men in the military forces, and the more continuous employment of those forces; 2) the formation and maintenance of large, permanent navies.

The number of men in the armies of Spain increased six or seven-fold between the 1480s and the 1640s. The principal reason for this increase was the intersection of Habsburg imperial interests with the internationalization of war in the sixteenth century. Simply, there were more men because there was more to defend, and more with which to defend it. There was, however, a double aspect to this growth. As Parker has pointed out, a numerical peak in the size of European military forces seems to have been reached by the mid sixteenth century which was not surpassed, or not substantially, before a new burst of expansion in the later seventeenth century.[46] In Spain, the Catholic armies of Ferdinand and Isabella tripled in numbers during the ten years of the war in Granada from 16,000–26,000 in 1482–4 to 60,000 in 1491. By the year of Metz Charles V was paying 150,000 men, but thereafter that figure was probably not exceeded until the reign of Philip IV, when for perhaps two decades from the later 1620s the number of soldiers in Spanish service may again have reached, and perhaps gone beyond, the levels of

1552.[47] These were, however, exceptional figures for campaign armies on multiple fronts.

It is far more relevant, as far as Spain is concerned, to talk of the creation of a standing navy in the early-modern period than a standing army. The only permanent troops in Spain were the 2,000–3,000 mounted Guards of Castile and Granada—a force whose effectives fell at times to as few as 1,000—and the semi-civilianized garrisons of the frontier fortresses. It was the navy that was the first area of spectacular growth in regular defence expenditure in the sixteenth century. The trigger was not the new high-board fleets in the Atlantic from the 1580s, but the galley fleets in the Mediterranean from the 1520s. At the beginning of Charles V's reign the cost of naval activity in the Mediterranean was insignificant; fifty years later the Spanish and Genoese galleys alone were costing the Spanish treasury 671,000 ducats a year. Although that was a peak figure, the galleys were still assigned nearly 450,000 ducats before a major strategic reform was instituted in 1620, and 272,000 thereafter.[48] However, that fall was counterbalanced by the new naval activity taking place in the Atlantic, which, if occasional before,[49] from the mid 1580s generated, if not a regular fleet, a regular charge that was rarely under 500,000 ducats a year, and sometimes over 1 million.[50] Much more than armies, which could live off the land, the maintenance of large regular fleets had a disproportionate financial and administrative impact and represented a massive displacement of the cost of war from society to the state. Fleets not only required a considerable capital outlay, they also had to be supplied with naval stores and victualled in advance by the Crown, either directly or by contract. Victualling costs accounted for about one-third of the budget of the high seas fleets and about two-fifths of that of the galleys, and although they were discounted against the pay of the troops, the rebate generally did not cover more than half the real costs of the rations, which amounted to almost as much as the daily wage bill.[51] Despite the decline in the number and cost of the galleys, therefore, the overall naval budget in the Mediterranean and the Atlantic from the later 1580s through the seventeenth century was never less than 1 million ducats a year more than it had been at accession of Charles V. On top of this there was a capital investment in the ships of over 30 ducats a ton, and approximately the same again for the ship's artillery; that is to say, about 1 million ducats altogether for a fleet of forty front-line vessels, which was what was usually projected in the early seventeenth century, though by no means always achieved. Annual running costs, therefore, at least equalled, if they did not actually exceed, the entire capital value of the fleet.[52]

The financial impact of all this was an initial increase in expenditure attributable to the increased size of the military forces and to the continuous wars of the first half of the sixteenth century, followed by a spectacular rise in spending on the fleets from the mid to late sixteenth century which alone roughly doubled the size of Castile's domestic military budget. However, just as was the case with total force numbers, the peak expenditures of the mid sixteenth century were not substantially surpassed until the 1630s, even in monetary terms; the 10 million ducats a year spent on the Netherlands, Italian, Catalan and Portuguese theatres in 1649–54 probably fell below the peak expenditures of the 1550s in real terms, and below those of the 1570s and 1590s not only in real terms, but perhaps also in nominal terms as well.[53] The key to the long-term growth of military spending was not the relatively brief and unsustainable peaks of military action, but the steadily rising background level of military commitment which pushed the base-line of expenditure higher and higher. Even in years without active war overseas, Philip II was supporting on a continuous basis a minimum of 50–60,000 men, made up of permanent garrison troops in Spain, North Africa, Italy, the Army of Flanders, and the personnel of the Mediterranean galley fleets. The formal complement of permanent garrison and marine troops on the Castilian account alone rose from about 13,000 in 1560, to 50,000 in 1596, and to 30,000 for the first three decades of the seventeenth century, tripling the ordinary domestic military budget by the late 1580s, and never allowing it to fall below twice its level of the 1560s and 1570s, even in the years of general peace in Philip III's reign.[54] This permanently high base-line meant that it was never possible to catch up with anticipated income pledged in advance to secure credit for the exceptional demands of the years of maximum military effort, and thus extraordinary expenditure peaks were locked into a permanent charge through an irredeemable debt.

*   *   *

The growth of Spain's military expenditure was concentrated, as has been said, on four key moments: the 1480s; the 1530s–50s; the 1570s–90s; and the 1620s–40s. In each, immediate needs were met ad hoc; consequential adjustments to the fiscal system followed in their wake. Fiscal development was dragged along behind military demand. The military spending peaks were periods of fiscal unpreparedness, necessitating resort to extraordinary expedients and unsustainable levels of credit. Debt financing and the alienation of resources thus froze the high costs of these spending peaks into glaciers which then dominated the financial landscape of the plateau below.

In the 1480s, the conquest of Granada, and after it the conquest of Naples, was financed not primarily from the increase in royal rents, but from the direct contributions of the cities and the nobility of Castile, and by extraordinary ecclesiastical aids granted by the Papacy. The basic long-term structures of Castilian royal finances had been established by the beginning of the fifteenth century, and the financial achievement of the Catholic Kings in restoring the ordinary revenues was in fact no more than a recuperation of the best levels of the earlier fifteenth century. What the Catholic Kings did was to procure a spectacular increase in the extraordinary revenues. Some 600 *cuentos* of the 800 *cuentos* Ladero estimates to be the monetary cost for the Crown of the war in Granada came from the Papal "graces" of the Cruzada and the Subsidio.[55] That enabled the war to be fought without long-term financial consequences; there was some borrowing, but the legacy of long-term debt was modest, and there was consequently no major development of state fiscality.

The explosion of military expenditure that took place in the 1530s–50s was also sustained largely by expedients and extraordinary measures, though of a different type from those employed in the 1480s and 1490s. An attempt to establish a more permanent basis for fiscal expansion in 1539 with the proposal to introduce a general excise duty failed, largely because the apparent inelasticity of the ordinary royal revenues (manifested in the willingness of the Crown to accept from the cities a composition of its main source of tax income, the *alcabalas* and *tercias,* fixed for twenty years) left the treasury dependent on the ad hoc "services" of a Cortes of Castile insistent on preventing what was in essence a system of periodic financial subsidies, determined and administered locally by the cities themselves, from being transformed into a system of regular taxation.[56] The Crown was thus forced into a dead-end exploitation of regalian rights, extensive sales of offices and rents and of jurisdictions of the Military Orders and the abbeys, the repeated sequestration of private bullion from the Indies, but also, and overwhelmingly, into massive short-term borrowing, engaged on these and other extraordinary revenues at progressively more punitive premiums. In the fourteen years 1543–56, 18 million ducats were borrowed at rates rising from 28 percent to 49 percent, requiring the repayment of over 25 million ducats.[57] The legacy of the financial exigencies of this phase of hegemonic warfare was therefore ambivalent. On the one hand, the sales and alienations of regalian rights and jurisdiction can be said to have run counter to the concept of state-formation; fiscal "penetration"[58] was declining throughout the reign of Charles V, with the real per capita tax burden falling from the 1520s to a low point in the late 1550s, and not regaining its earlier levels until the 1570s.[59] On the other hand, the huge accumulation of debt created a *damnosa hereditas* that was to burden the Castilian fisc and the Spanish economy for two and a half centuries, but that was also the principal long-term vector for the extension and consolidation of a permanent public revenue system of taxes and ordinary revenues assigned to the servicing of the massive issue of undated government bonds (*juros*), the function of which was to enable repayment of the short-term debt to be deferred *sine die* (the so-called "bankruptcies" of 1557, 1560, 1575, 1596, 1607, 1627, 1647, 1652, 1660, 1662). Interest owing on *juros* increased three-fold (from a very low base) in 1504–54, more than quintupled in 1554–98, and then doubled again in 1598–1667. The importance of the rocketing quantities of revenues committed to the servicing of *juros* is not so much as a measure of debt, but as a measure of public fiscality, of a shift from a fiscality of subsidy to a system of regular and permanent taxation that is the essence of the tax-state. That was made possible because, in the remission which followed the climactic warfare of the 1550s, Philip II was able to increase his "ordinary" revenues by some 50 percent between 1558 and 1562, and then by a further 1¹/₂ million ducats in 1575–77. This was achieved on the back of an expanding economy, both with the assent of the Cortes, by renegotiating the sales tax agreements, and (free for once in 1559 of the immediate pressures of war) in disregard of their protests, by increasing the rates on import and export dues that pertained to the Crown by regalian right.[60]

The vertiginous leap in defence spending from the late 1560s was funded initially by the same means as in the previous period: ad hoc expedients, Papal grants, and borrowing. And, in much the same way as in 1557 and 1560, the consequent nemesis of debt was held off by the third "bankruptcy" of the reign, underwritten by the *alcabala* increase of 1575–77. The financial peculiarity of this period lies in the fact that the huge mobilizations for the annexation of Portugal and the enterprise of England in the 1580s were funded without recourse to new measures by the spectacular increase in bullion imports from the Americas in the second half of the reign. By 1596 it was possible to budget in the expectation of receiving 3 million ducats a year, nearly four times as much as in 1577 and about 30 percent of the entire increase in the Crown's income since 1559. But, more than a military disaster, the Armada was a financial disaster, for its failure committed Spain not only to the intensification of its involvement in France and the Netherlands, but also to a new maritime war in the Atlantic. Military activity on such a scale, coming at the precise moment when the economy was on the downturn and incapable of sustaining further expedients or existing levels of ordinary revenues, could not be financed without innovation. The *millones,* the first increase in the services granted by the Cortes for fifty years and introduced in 1590, not to pay for the Armada but to pay for its consequences, was an enforced reversion to the finances of subsidy which had fundamental constitutional and political implications for the balance between king and kingdom and for the "penetrative" power of the state into Castilian society. For the next seventy-five years, Cortes and Crown manoeuvred respectively to retain the *millones* as a "service", controlled by the cities which periodically regranted it, and to transform it into a permanent state tax.[61]

During the reign of Philip IV (1621–65), extraordinary military expenditures reached peaks in nominal terms double those of the 1570s–1590s. They were met by an extreme combination of measures which pushed the authoritarianism of the state to the limits of arbitrariness (forced loans, sequestration of private bullion, prerogative levies of men and supplies, monetary manipulations, retentions of interest payments, revocations of grants and concessions). But at the same time, in the pursuit of quick expedients, operational economies, and covert credit, royal rights, jurisdiction, revenues, and direct administrative control over military recruiting, provision and procurement were alienated to an unprecedented degree. By 1665, more of the ordinary and extraordinary income had been perpetuated as permanent, public revenues than ever before, and yet a progressively smaller proportion was reaching the government's coffers. The state was eating its own tail. When that became too painful, the meal had to stop. The reign of Charles II (1665–1700) saw the collapse of internal authority, a tax-freeze, and the retreat of Spain from hegemonic conflict. The three were closely interrelated.[62]

*   *   *

The different components of Spain's military expenditure demanded different forms of financing, and did not, therefore, necessarily move in harmony; nor did they all have the same fiscal consequences. The ineluctable need—for monetary, strategic and political reasons—to provide hard cash upfront in erratic and extraordinary quantities for the support of hegemonic wars outside Spain, and to provide that cash elsewhere than at source in an acceptable medium (usually silver or gold), required the employment of exchange and credit transactions which, in the last resort, depended on the guarantees of a fiscality of state taxation. Ordinary, domestic military expenses, on the other hand, because of their very regularity, could in principle be funded directly by the fixed assignment of specific ordinary revenues (hypothecation), or, because of their immersion in the local economy and the lower political dangers of compulsory subsidization, be in practice regularly underfunded by under-hypothecation or default.[63] Extraordinary internal expenditures, for their part, were generally presented as community rather than dynastic enterprises and so could be devolved and funded locally by a natural, or barter, fiscality in which direct contributions in kind were offset against existing tax obligations.[64] That was not always accepted willingly, and, as in France, in Extremadura and Old Castile the armies operated their own internal "contribution system", although their brutality was never the officially condoned policy in Madrid that it was in Paris.[65]

These alternative fiscalities are the key to explaining the paradox that from a purely financial point of view, the cost of war should have increased a great deal more than actually seems to have been the case. Expenditure in some years in the 1570s was as high in real terms as it was in the 1640s, when Spain was fighting not only in the Netherlands, France and Italy, but also had armies in Catalonia, Extremadura, Galicia and Old Castile, and was maintaining one of the largest battle fleets it had ever put to sea. There seems to be a palpable gap between government expenditure and the true cost of war. That was partly because the entire cost was not fully covered by budgetary assignments, and when assigned was not fully honoured; and partly because the entire cost was not necessarily paid by government.

The emphasis on the state as a monopoly of coercive force and on the Military Revolution as part of the process of the etatization of war has diverted us from recognizing how much military activity before the later part of the seventeenth century was subsidized directly by the economy. The emphasis on the "standing army" as an instrument of state power has obscured the reality (very clear in mainland Spain) that the very permanence of military fortresses and garrisons enabled a good deal of the military establishment to be maintained in partial independence of state support. The social costs of war in the age of the Military Revolution fell differently than they had in the age of "feudal" warfare. Those social costs are very much less easily determinable than the direct and overt costs on the fiscal account, but they did not for that reason cease to be crucial both to the ability of states and societies to bear the cost of the Military Revolution and to the impact of the Military Revolution on those same states and societies. Two small local examples illustrate the point. Between 19 April 1627 and early June, the royal sulphur works in the town of Hellín in Murcia ceased operation because the workers had gone to their homes to harvest the silk which was the main source of their income.[66] For the workers of Hellín, just as for the arms manufacturers of Guipuzcoa, and many of the garrison troops in Navarre, Catalonia and Galicia, their military employment was a supplementary activity, or even a sideline. Their permanent nature, their "standing-army"-ness, was more apparent than real; they were in reality part-time soldiers, even if outsiders, immersed in the local economy. It was because their military functions were subsidised by their participation in the local economy that they could survive not only exiguous rates of remuneration, but also the enormous backlogs of debt, and staggeringly long periods without any financial support at all, which enabled the Crown to totter on from one financial crisis after another without total collapse.[67] A second form of subsidy to the Crown's military treasury was monopoly. The gunpowder contracts with Alonso Mathía de Bolaños of Seville and with Juan Jácome Semiño of Granada in 1620 gave them an absolute monopoly of the manufacture and sale of gunpowder in their respective provinces in return for providing the king with gunpowder completely free of charge. That was only the most blatant example of the way the contracting out of military supply functions not only enabled the state to wage war without the full administrative and procurement apparatus that otherwise would have been needed, but also shifted part of the true costs of the operation from the fisc to the community.[68]

*   *   *

The Military Revolution was from the financial point of view a redeployment of the costs of war between society and the state, a transfer between the social and the public accounts. The cost of "feudal" warfare of the sort that was still so important in the Conquest of Granada was a charge on the economy levied directly through the social system; the cost of war in the Military Revolution was a charge on the economy levied by the state through the fiscal system. Government budgets, therefore, inevitably exaggerate the costliness of war in the age of the Military Revolution compared with "feudal" war. Bean's estimate that 1 percent of national income was spent on defence in the Middle Ages, 2 percent or more in the sixteenth century, and between 6 and 12 percent in the eighteenth century—the figure in Spain was nearer 4–5 percent in the late sixteenth century—leaves the social invoice entirely aside.[69] But government budgets also *understate* the cost of war, for the unaccounted social costs of war in this period did not disappear; they were simply levied in a different way.

Different types of war employed, and to a degree necessitated, different methods of financing; they therefore had different implications for state development. In certain circumstances war could be self-supporting, living off contributions, plunder, requisition, prize, piracy, contraband, or even trade. In other circumstances, considerations of strategy, morale, logistics, and political expediency required the steady provision of centrally raised cash and supplies or inward remittances of funds into the war zone from other parts of the empire. Major hegemonic land wars, fought at a distance from their main resource base, because of their high borrowing requirements, tended to lead to the development of taxation and the fiscal-state; contrariwise, a permanent military establishment could in appropriate circumstances promote the privatization of military and administrative functions by means of the contracting out of funding, maintenance and supply; and protracted wars within the territory of the state could be sustained by a more primitive (from the statist point of view), local fiscality. Both private contracting and local devolution, as forms of credit as well as of provision, reduced the need for an extensive apparatus of state bureaucracy and finance. The development of the state as a fiscal entity was thus related to the type of military activity in which it was engaged. War, therefore, did not necessarily have a centralizing effect, and Schumpeter's "common exigency" may have inhibited the development of the state as much as it inspired it.[70]

Nowhere was that more the case than for Spain. The massive contributions of the kingdom of Naples to the needs of the Spanish Monarchy during the Thirty Years War do not seem to have contributed in any way to the consolidation of the power of the state there, but rather to a new feudalism of landed banking and commerce empowered through their financial services to the Crown.[71] In Catalonia, the attempt of Olivares's Union of Arms to promote a new framework for the political integration of the Monarchy was if anything counterproductive; despite Madrid's ability to end the secession of the Principality by force, the Catalans contributed far more to the common treasury when the threat of integration was removed in the new age of provincial liberties and weak central government, the *neo-foralismo* of the second half of the seventeenth century, than they ever had before. In neither instance is the notion of an ascending cycle of coercion and extraction a particularly useful explanatory model of state building. The effective extractive potential of coercion was not very high in early modern societies, nor was extraction in practice much applied to domestic coercion and tax-enforcement, at least in Spain.

For Spain itself, it was the strategic dimension of the Military Revolution, rather than its tactical or technological aspects, that was primarily responsible for the relentless growth of defence expenditure. Involvement in the global (or at least continental), hegemonic wars which accounted for the greater part of the financial burden of empire was important;[72] but equally important was the ratchet effect of the unremitting, long-run succession of major conflicts, which wrecked every attempt to amortize the debt and disencumber the revenues.[73] The massive recourse to credit is evidence that the needs of war had outrun the immediate resources of the state. However, the continued availability of credit was secured by the potential of the state for fiscal advance, and that was a function both of accepted political authority and of a favourable economic conjuncture. With the collapse of the economy, credit could only be raised by authoritarianism, as Olivares and Philip IV succeeded in doing. When, on the death of Philip IV, royal authority also collapsed, the Spanish financial system collapsed with it.

Spain, therefore, provides another and more fundamental qualification of Brian Downing's thesis that military exigency was incompatible with constitutional principle, that "constitutional countries confronted by a dangerous international situation mandating extensive, domestic resource mobilization suffered the destruction of constitutionalism and the rise of military-bureaucratic absolutism."[74] The Spanish case shows that "authoritarian political outcomes" could be avoided, not only where warfare though continuous was "only moderate in scope and intensity", as in England, or where resources were provided from abroad, as in the United Provinces and Sweden, but also where intense and protracted military pressures overloaded the political and administrative circuitry of central government. Authoritarian solutions were attempted in Spain but they failed in face of the collapse of trade and tax revenues and of the ruralization of the economy that militated against the centralist extraction of resources. The state in Spain, unable to develop a fiscal system capable of maintaining the necessary levels of military spending demanded by its strategic position, was driven to self-destructive financial expedients involving compromises with local power centers and the devolution and privatization of coercive-extractive and military-administrative functions which left the state with great theoretical authority but limited effective power.[75] Spain was thus incapable of responding to the new leap in the scale and global scope of warfare that occurred in the second half of the seventeenth century, generating revolutionary administrative and financial changes and the creation of national debts of an unprecedented magnitude that were now quite beyond the diminished capacities of the Spanish state.

Notes

1. For a good summary and full bibliography of these positions, see Frank Tallett, *War and Society in Early-Modern Europe, 1495–1715* (Routledge, 1992), 168–72.

2. Paul Kennedy, *The Rise and Fall of the Great Powers* (Fontana, 1989), 57.

3. For accounts that reveal the full complexity of the Castilian fiscal system and the sophisticated relationship between *asientos* and *juros,* see R. Carande, *Carlos Quinto y sus banqueros,* 3 vols. (Madrid, 1943–67); M. Ulloa, *La hacienda real de Castilla en el reinado de Felipe II,* 2nd. ed. (Madrid, 1977); H. Lapeyre, *Simón Ruiz et les asientos de Philippe II* (Paris, 1953); F. Ruiz Martín, *Pequeño capitalismo, Gran capitalismo. Simón Ruiz y sus negocios en Florencia* (Madrid, 1990); J.C. Boyajian, *Portuguese Bankers at the Court of Spain 1626–1650* (New Brunswick, NJ, 1983); A. Castillo, "Los juros de Castilla. Apogeo y fin de un instrumento de crédito", *Hispania* 23 (1963), 43–70, and "Dette flottante et dette consolidée en Espagne de 1557 à 1600", *Annales E.S.C.* 18 (1963), 745–59; M. Steele, "International Financial Crises during the Reign of Philip II, 1556–1598", unpublished Ph.D. dissertation, University of London, 1986.

4. A. Domínguez Ortiz, *Política y hacienda de Felipe IV* (Madrid, 1960), 333–42, for 1621–40; M.A. Ladero Quesada, *La Hacienda Real de Castilla en el siglo XV* (La Laguna, 1973), 58, expenditure of Alfonso de Morales, *tesorero de lo extraordinario*, 1495–1504, 1,731,000,000 *mrs* [maravedís], of which 61% on war and 13.5% on loan repayments; J. Aparici y García, *Informe sobre los adelantos de la Comisión de Historia en el Archivo de Simancas*, 2 vols. (Madrid, 1848), I 102, 1584 76%; *Actas de las Cortes de Castilla*, lv 390–92, 1632–38 88.6%; AGS [Archivo General de Simancas] Estado 1947 f.135, "Provisiones Generales para el año de 1678", 79.6%.

5. Ladero, *Hacienda Real de Castilla en el siglo XV*, 58; E. Alberi, *Le relazione degli ambasciatori veneti* (Florence, 1839–63), I, iii, 363, for Soriano; G. Parker, "Spain, her Enemies and the Revolt of the Netherlands, 1559–1648", *Spain and the Netherlands, 1559–1659* (Collins, 1979), 32, for 1574; *CSP Venetian*, viii 336, no.623, for 1588; A. Pellegrini, *Relazione inedite di ambasciatori lucchesi alla corte di Madrid (sec.XVI–XVII)* (Lucca, 1903), 71, Iacopo Arnolfini 29.1.1644; AGS Estado 1947, f.135 for 1678. In constant silver ducats: 1574 7 million; 1588 7,600,000; 1596 8,300,000; 1640 12 million; 1678 7 million.

6. For details, I.A.A. Thompson, *War and Government in Habsburg Spain, 1560–1620* (Athlone: London, 1976), Table B, p.289.

7. For these and other figures, see Thompson, *War and Government*, 70; Lorraine G. White, "War and Government in a Castilian Province: Extremadura 1640–1668", unpublished Ph.D. dissertation, University of East Anglia, 1986, 502.

8. Ramón Carande, *Carlos Quinto y sus banqueros*, vol.3, *Los caminos del oro y de la plata (Deuda exterior y tesoros ultramarinos)* (Madrid, 1967); Geoffrey Parker, *The Army of Flanders and the Spanish Road 1567–1659* (Cambridge U.P., 1972); Parker, "Spain, her Enemies and the Revolt of the Netherlands", 32; AGS GA [Guerra Antigua] 799, Council of War 15.5.1615, "con que en estas dos partidas se biene a consumir lo que renta cada año la Real hacienda"; Cartas de Jesuitas 18.3.1636, *Memorial Histórico Español*, xiii 384; for Struzzi, H.G. Hambleton, "The Economic Decline of Spain in the Seventeenth Century. Contemporary Spanish Views", unpublished Ph.D. dissertation, University of London, 1964, 205.

9. Kennedy, *Great Powers*, 56, who defines the Military Revolution as "the massive increase in the scale, costs and organisation of war" in the 150 years following the 1520s.

10. Geoffrey Parker, *The Military Revolution. Military innovation and the rise of the West, 1500–1800* (Cambridge U.P., 1988), 12; Carande, *Carlos Quinto y sus banqueros*, ii 202.

11. *Cortes de los Antiguos Reinos de León y Castilla*, iv 374, 578, v 310, 431, 627, 750, 858; *Actas de las Cortes de Castilla*, iii 57, 395, vi 835, x 378, xi 354 (12.5.1590); F. Braudel, *The Mediterranean and the Mediterranean World in the Age of Philip II* (Collins, 1972), ii 855, 858, for Africa and La Goleta; AGS GA 878, "Relacion del estado en que se allan las Fortificaciones de los presidios de España Islas y fronteras y lo que parece que costara el acavar las unas y los reparos de otras", 18.12.1622.

12. F. Idoate, *Esfuerzo bélico de Navarra en el siglo XVI* (Pamplona, 1981), 386 (for Pamplona); Braudel, *Mediterranean*, II 857 n.89 (for Oran); AGS GA 80 f.102, for Fuenterrabía, San Sebastián and Pamplona; AGS GA 78 f.43 and GA 644, anon. *relación*, c.1603, for Perpignan. AGS GA 878, "Relacion del estado en que se allan las Fortificaciones", 18.12.1622; for La Mamora, AGS GA 889, Council of War 30.5.1623.

13. As in Peñíscola in 1529–32, R. Pinilla Pérez de Tudela, "Noticias en torno a la fortificación de Peñíscola por Carlos I (1526–36)" in *Temas de Historia Militar (Comunicaciones del Primer Congreso de Historia Militar—Zaragoza 1982)* (Zaragoza 1985),

2, 248–57. The construction of the new citadel in Pamplona, begun in 1571, was barely complete in 1592, but once in place it was still militarily effective in the Carlist Wars in 1872. The fortification of Cartagena, begun by Philip II, was still ongoing in 1626, BL [British Library] Egerton Ms 319, f.35. For the turrets in Andalusia, AGS GA 81 ff.445, 449; AGS GA 689, Council of War 31.7.1608; A. González Palencia (ed.), *La Junta de Reformación 1618–1625, Archivo Histórico Español*, vol. 5 (Valladolid, 1932), 367.

14. AGS GA 889, Council of War 30.5.1623.

15. For example, *Relación* 23.9.1617, BL Egerton Ms 2084, f.157; AGS GA 1301, Junta of War and Finance, 22.3.1604, 100,000 (reduced to 50,000, Lerma to Secretary Aguilar, 4.11.1606); AGS GA 744, Council of War, 29.10.1611, 172,000 *escudos* of 1,031,875 land account (8–9% of total defence budget); 2.7.1622 132,204 *escudos* for fortifications out of 1,557,837 (8.5%); Ladero, *Hacienda siglo XV*, p.58, for 1495–1504; Carande, *Carlos V y sus banqueros*, ii 203, for 1544 (50,000), 1553 (52,000). Lest it should be thought that Spain was peculiar in this regard within the Spanish Monarchy, it is worth pointing out that the 10 million florins spent on re-fortification in the Netherlands in the forty-three years 1529–72 was little more than the 8,600,000 florins that was received by the military treasury of the Army of Flanders in the single year 1572, Parker, *Army of Flanders*, 293. Domenico Sella talks of the Spanish government spending on "a stupendous scale" for the construction or modernization of fortifications in Lombardy during the first sixty years of the seventeenth century, but clearly has no figures to enable that expenditure to be quantified, *Crisis and Continuity. The Economy of Spanish Lombardy in the Seventeenth Century* (Harvard U.P., 1979), 57 and 206 n.40.

16. 200,000 ducats a year and more for the "obras de San Lorenzo" in the 1580s, AGS Estado 163, "Relacion del dinero que ay y sera menester en los quatro meses que restan de este año de 1583"; Aparici y García, *Informe*, i, 102.

17. AGS GA 81 f.178 (Mallorca); *Actas de las Cortes* x, 533 (Cadiz); AGS GA 81 f.441, GA 689 Council of War 31.7.1608 (Andalusia).

18. See the information in Edward Cooper's *Castillos señoriales en la Corona de Castilla*, 4 vols. (Junta de Castilla y León, Salamanca, 1991).

19. In the 1590s it was estimated that the total cost of the ideal armament for a galleon of 1,100–1,300 *toneladas* was 19,319 ducats, inclusive of shot and powder; it would have cost about 20,000 ducats to build a galleon of that size, AGS GA 347, *relación* 1591; AGS GA 899, paper of Secretary of War, Martín de Aroztegui, 18.11.1624: construction costs of six *galeoncetes* with total of 1,600 *toneladas*, "puestos a la vela ... a toda costa", 51,200 ducats; cost of 100 bronze guns, averaging 20 quintals each, 56,000 ducats.

20. For details see "Aspects of Spanish Military and Naval Organization during the Ministry of Olivares" in I.A.A. Thompson, *War and Society in Habsburg Spain* (Variorum: Aldershot, 1992), ch.4, p.5. Iron guns cost about one-quarter the price of bronze guns, weight for weight, though they could stand less charge and had a much shorter life.

21. AGS CJH [Consejo y Juntas de Hacienda] 807 (1111), Council of Finance, 31.7.1660, and Thompson, *War and Society*, ch.4, p.5; AGS GA 136, f.280, for the allocation for 1582. In emergencies, particularly until the 1570s, gunpowder, shot and firearms were also imported from Italy and the Low Countries, adding somewhat (10–15 percent would be a guess) to the global costs for these materials; for some instances, Thompson, *War and Government*, 237.

22. AGS GA 365, "Relacion general de la artilleria que ay en España", 17.11.1588.

23. Idoate, *Esfuerzo bélico de Navarra*, 387, 60.

24. On the figures of Secretary Martín de Aroztegui, 18.11.1624, AGS GA 899.

25. AGS GA 659, "Relacion de lo que a poco mas o menos ymportara cada año el sueldo y gastos forzosos del Armada", 1606: 858,544 *escudos*, of which 63,200 (7.4%) for munitions (powder, shot, lead and match). The Secretary of the Navy, Martín de Aroztegui, allowed 8,000 ducats for munitions in the first year, and 4,000 in subsequent years, of 104,000 ducats for the six *galeoncetes*. Munitions costs of the Armada del Mar de Sur amounted to only 5%, B. Torres Rámirez, "Situación económica de las Armadas de Indias", *Temas de Historia Militar. 2° Congreso de Historia Militar, Zaragoza, 1988* (Madrid, 1988), vol. 1, *Ponencias*, 243–59, at 254.

26. AGS GA 552, "Relacion de lo que convendra proveer este año de 1598", 116,000 ducats; AGS GA 569, *relación* with Council of War 28.4.1600, 136,000 ducats; AGS GA 1301, Junta of War and Finance, 22.3.1604, 166,229 (reduced to 100,000, Lerma to Secretary Aguilar, 4.11.1606); Domínguez Ortiz, *Política y hacienda de Felipe IV*, 375, "Resumen del estado de la real hacienda", Sept. 1650. The largest recorded allocation for "artillería, fortificaciones y fábricas" is the 172,500 ducats out of a domestic defence budget for 1608 of 2,216,563 ducats (7.8%)—4,216,563 including the assignment for Flanders, AGS CJH 345 (474), *relación* of royal revenues to 21.10.1608, 22.12.1607.

27. Calculated from C.J.M. Martin, "A 16th century siege train: the battery ordnance of the 1588 Spanish Armada", *The International Journal of Nautical Archaeology and Underwater Exploration* 17.1 (1988), 57–73, and F.P. de Cambra, *Don Alvaro de Bazan, Almirante de España* (Madrid, 1943), 300–1. In 1639, the duke of Medina Sidonia had as many as forty-two pieces in his castle in Sanlúcar de Barrameda. For these and other examples, Thompson, *War and Government*, 155 and 329 n.34. M.A. Ladero Quesada, *Castilla y la Conquista del Reino de Granada* (Valladolid, 1967), 127 for guns held by the great nobility in the late 15th century. There were more than fifty titled nobles at the end of the sixteenth century with revenues larger than those of Las Navas.

28. 450 to 187.5 *mrs*, Carande, *Carlos Quinto y sus banqueros*, iii 55.

29. Clifford J. Rogers, "The Military Revolutions of the Hundred Years' War", *Journal of Military History* 57 (1993), 246 (above, p. 58).

30. René Quatrefages, *Los Tercios Españoles (1566–77)* (Madrid, 1979), 192–7; M. Gracia Rivas, *Los Tercios de la Gran Armada (1587–1588)* (Madrid, 1989), 47; BL Additional Ms 28273 f.41, Council of War 14.6.1590. The cost of the handguns included a powder-horn and a fork for the musket; the helmet cost a further 24 *reales*, if engraved. The corseleted pikeman was even more expensive to equip: 6 *reales* for the pike, 80 *reales* for a plain breastplate. A complete outfit of clothing for 116 *reales* included a jacket (30), breeches (30), two shirts (24), doublet (13), hose (6), shoes (4) and hat (9).

31. AGS CMC 2ª [Contaduría Mayor de Cuentas, segunda época] 760, "Libro de la quenta de Pedro Fernández de Çaraa Bolibar", 29.11.1632. AGS GA 136 f.279, Secretary Delgado c.27.11.1582, 40,000 ducats needed; AGS GA 552, "Relacion de lo que convendra proveer este año de 1598 para el ministerio del artilleria", 30,000; AGS GA 569, *relación* with Council of War 28.4.1600, 40,000.

32. Gracia Rivas, *Tercios de la Gran Armada*, 47.

33. In 1636 the Cardinal-Infante was reported to have had 18,000 horse, "something never before seen in Flanders", "Cartas de Jesuitas", *Memorial Histórico Español* (Madrid, 1861), xiii, 394. During the previous sixty years, the cavalry usually made up less than one-

eighth, and sometimes less than one-twentieth, of the Army of Flanders; by the late 1640s some one-fifth of the Army was cavalry, Parker, *Army of Flanders*, Appendix A, pp. 271–2. For Thomas Styward in 1581 horsemen were secondary actors in battle (*The Pathwaie to Martiall Discipline*, cited by H.J. Webb, *Elizabethan Military Science* [University of Wisconsin Press, 1965], p. 43); for Francisco Manuel de Melo in 1638 it was "the cavalry which usually wins or loses battles" (*Política Militar en Avisos de Generales*, aviso xxxvi).

34. S.M. de Sotto, Conde de Clonard, *Historia orgánica de las armas de infantería y caballería españolas*, 16 vols. (Madrid, 1851–62), iv 155.

35. AGS CJH 1069 (1462), 28.7.1683.

36. Gracia Rivas, *Tercios de la Gran Armada*, 47.

37. For Sancho de Londoño in 1568 the pikes were still "reinas de las armas"; by the end of the century, the Spanish infantry was in great part composed of handgunners; see Parker, *Army of Flanders*, p. 277; Clonard, *Historia orgánica*, iii 145 (1516), iv 269 (*ordenanzas* of 8.6.1603), v 24 (1694); *Actas de las Cortes de Castilla*, xv 608 (26.5.1598); A. Cánovas del Castillo, "Del principio y fin que tuvo la supremacia militar de los españoles en Europa", *Estudios Literarios*, vol. 2 (Madrid, 1868), 433 (*ordenanzas* of 28.6.1632).

38. Introduced as an infantry weapon by the duke of Alba in 1567, Quatrefages, *Los Tercios Españoles*, 74.

39. Clonard, *Historia orgánica*, iii, 332 (5.12.1536), 426 (24.12.1560)—Spanish infantry company in Lombardy fixed at 300 "y no más ni menos"; Thompson, *War and Government*, 105.

40. Clonard, *Historia orgánica*, iv 416, an increase recommended by the baron de Auchy in 1642.

41. One reason for this was that over the long-term, in contrast to the view often perpetrated that munitions costs rose disproportionately, the prices of guns, weaponry and munitions do not seem to have kept up with the general movement of prices, nor for that matter with the overall rate of government spending. A high labour input and more efficient private procurement procedures may have helped. More information is needed to establish adequate price series for war materials, but it looks as if supply-side deficiencies were being overcome in most commodities by the second half of the sixteenth century. Arquebuses rose in price more than threefold overall between the 1480s and 1630s, relatively fast up to the 1570s—by 150 percent—but by less than 30 percent in the next 60 years; between the 1570s and the 1630s the price of the corselet rose similarly by 28 percent; but that of the musket remained unaltered; and that of the pike was halved. Gunpowder costing 74 *reales* a quintal in the 1480s was costing 150 *reales* in 1523, but no more than 154 *reales* in the 1570s, and only 160 *reales vellón* in the 1640s; shot, costing 13 *reales* in the 1480s, had more than doubled in price to 30 *reales* in the 1590s and tripled to between 41 and 43 *reales* in the 1640s, yet that was still well below the increase in the general price level between those dates; copper rose sharply in price at the end of the sixteenth century (with demand for coinage as well as for guns), but in 1608 it was still only three times more expensive than it had been in the 1480s.

42. AGS CJH 206 (310), "Relacion del dinero que es menester por todo el año de 1591 para las cosas de la guerra en mar": 1,158,000 ducats, all but 165,000 (14.25%) of which was manpower related; AGS GA 659, "Relacion de lo que a poco mas o menos ymportara cada año el sueldo y gastos forzosos del Armada": 81.8%; but only 70% in the Armada del Mar de Sur, Torres Rámirez, "Situación económica de las Armadas de Indias", 254.

43. Contract rations on the Armada del Mar Océano were 51 *mrs* in 1606, 56¹/₂ in 1660, 50 in 1684, AGS GA 659, CJH 809 (1111), CJH 1079 (1476).

44. BL Additional Ms 28373, ff.129–34.

45. Parker, *Military Revolution*, 61.

46. Parker, *Military Revolution*, 45.

47. Ladero, *Castilla y la Conquista del Reino de Granada*, 159; Parker, *Military Revolution*, 45; Philip II may have been paying 130,000 men in 1574; 108,000 according to the President of Finance in November 1587, *CSP Venetian* viii 319, no.593. There were reputedly 133,000 Spaniards alone fighting in Spain, Italy and Flanders in 1639; "It is worth some note that not for more than a century have so many Spaniards been seen together on campaign", wrote Pellicer in his "Avisos", M. Camacho y de Ciria, *Desistimiento español de la empresa imperial reconstituído sobre "Avisos" de Pellicer* (Madrid, 1958), 28.

48. Thompson, *War and Government*, 294, *War and Society*, ch.4, p.4. For galley costs in the early decades of Charles V's reign, Carande, *Carlos Quinto y sus banqueros*, ii 210.

49. In 1574, over 400,000, and possibly 500,000 ducats were spent on the fleet of Pedro Menéndez de Avilés, AGS GA 77 f.208.

50. Between 1621 and 1623 the allocation for the Armada del Mar Océano was increased by 50 percent to 1,080,000 ducats; it was 800,000 in 1632–34, and rose to an average of 1,340,000 ducats for 75–80 vessels in 1635–38, plus a further 161,528 *escudos* for shipbuilding in 1637; from 1642 a contract was in operation to maintain 40 galleons for 1.2 million a year; Thompson, *War and Society*, ch.4, p.4; *Actas de las Cortes de Castilla*, xxxviii, 28.

51. In 1624 the soldiers on the *galeoncetes* of the Armada del Mar Océano were to have deducted 25 *reales* (850 *mrs*) of their 60 *reales* a month pay; rations were costed at 57 *mrs* a day (1,710 *mrs* a month); the total cost of victuals for the soldiers was 23,316 ducats, total deductions for rations and munitions came to 12,540 ducats of a wage bill of 27,360; AGS GA 899, Secretary Martín de Aroztegui, 18.11.1624. In the 1588 Armada, the soldier on basic rates had 19 3/4 of his 30 *reales* a month discounted for rations, and the soldier on double pay, 25 of his 40.

52. AGS GA 563, Bernave de Pedroso, 6.10.1598, "lo que sera menester para armar sesenta galeones": 1,161,000 ducats for men and provisions, and 1,130,000 to build and fit out (at 18,000 for each of 28 new galleons); AGS GA 899, Secretary Martín de Aroztegui, 18.11.1624: running costs of six *galeoncetes* 104,000 ducats, 51,200 to build, and 56,000 to gun. Each of Martín de Arana's six galleons, averaging 444.5 *toneladas,* built on contract in 1625–28, cost 15,696/16,696 ducats (excluding artillery), less than half the costs of provisioning and operating a galleon on one round trip to the Indies, C.R. Phillips, *Six Galleons for the King of Spain* (Johns Hopkins, Baltimore, 1986), 90, 234.

53. *Actas de las Cortes de Castilla,* lix¹, 28, averaging 10 million ducats a year for 1649–54.

54. Thompson, *War and Government*, 289.

55. Ladero, *Castilla y la Conquista de Granada*, 201 ff.

56. J.I. Fortea Pérez, *Monarquía y Cortes en la Corona de Castilla: Las ciudades ante la política fiscal de Felipe II* (Salamanca, 1990), 450–61.

57. Carande, *Carlos Quinto y sus banqueros*, iii, *passim*, especially the figures following p.26.

58. The expression is Michael Mann's, "The Autonomous Power of the State: Its Origins, Mechanisms and Results", in John A. Hall (ed.), *States in History* (Blackwell, Oxford, 1986), 109–36.

59. L.M. Bilbao, "Ensayo de reconstrucción histórica de la presión fiscal en Castilla durante el siglo XVI" in E. Fernández de Pinedo (ed.), *Haciendas Forales y Hacienda Real* (Bilbao, 1990), 37–62; I.A.A. Thompson, "Castile: Polity, Fiscality, and Fiscal Crisis" in P. Hoffman and K. Norberg (eds.), *Fiscal Crises, Liberty, and Representative Government, 1450–1789* (Stanford, 1994), 175.

60. Thompson, "Castile: Polity, Fiscality, and Fiscal Crisis", 160–69.

61. Charles Jago, "Parliament, Subsidies and Constitutional Change in Castile, 1601–1621", *Parliaments, Estates and Representation* 13 (1993), 123–37; Thompson, "Castile: Polity, Fiscality, and Fiscal Crisis", 169–72, and also my "Castile: Absolutism, Constitutionalism, and Liberty", in Hoffman and Norberg, *Fiscal Crises, Liberty, and Representative Government*, ch. 5, 189–95.

62. I.A.A. Thompson, "The Government of Spain in the Reign of Philip IV" in *Crown and Cortes. Government, Institutions and Representation in Early-Modern Castile* (Variorum: Aldershot, 1993), ch.4, pp.71–74; and my "Castile: Polity, Fiscality, and Fiscal Crisis", 172–75.

63. Thompson, *War and Government*, 96–7, 73; AGS GA 1303, duke of Lerma to Martín de Aroztegui, 27.5.1617, on the fitting-out of the Escuadra del Estrecho, needing 144,000 ducats a year to maintain, but can get by giving the men six pays a year, "siendo puntual lo que toca a la comida, y con esto se presupone que con 100,000 ducados al año se podran sustentar estos seis navios."

64. White, "War and Government in a Castilian Province", 310; Thompson, "Castile: Polity, Fiscality, and Fiscal Crisis", 173.

65. White, "War and Government in a Castilian Province", 311, 319, 321. In 1650, the Councils of Finance and War rejected a proposal of the commander of the Army of Extremadura to introduce forced contributions, fearing it would result in the depopulation of the province, C. Sanz Ayán, "La problemática del abastecimiento de los Ejércitos de Extremadura y Cataluña durante 1652" in *Temas de Historia Militar. 2° Congreso de Historia Militar, Zaragoza, 1988* (Madrid, 1988), vol.2, *Comunicaciones I*, 221–31, at 226; for France, J.A. Lynn, "How War Fed War: The Tax of Violence and Contributions during the *Grande Siècle*", *Journal of Modern History* 65 (1993), 286–310.

66. AGS Contadurías Generales, 854, Don Alonso de Cuéllar Carrasco, 26.5.1628.

67. Duke of Alba, 14.1.1581, "the soldiers who generally garrison the castles are low, wretched people who, because they have been there some time, are married and have jobs, some as weavers, others as cobblers or other trades, by which they earn their crust and keep themselves alive. Those who don't do that, don't stay long in the castles ...", Alba, duque de, *Epistolario del III Duque de Alba, Don Fernando Alvarez de Toledo*, 3 vols. (Madrid, 1952), iii, 750; Thompson, *War and Government*, 73–5. The Council of War accepted the usefulness of tolerating such practices, "because it is to Your Majesty's benefit, since as long as they do their guard duty on their days off, they earn a dozen *reales* which gets them by while they wait for their pay, even if it is somewhat late", AGS GA 876, 16.2.1622, with specific reference to the garrison in Cadiz.

68. Thompson, *War and Government*, 259, 231–33.

69. R. Bean, "War and the Birth of the Nation State", *Journal of Economic History* 33 (1973), 203–21, at 212.

70. William H. McNeill, *The Pursuit of Power. Technology, Armed Force, and Society since A.D. 1000* (Blackwell, Oxford, 1982), 95, 103–16; Joseph A. Schumpeter, "The Crisis of the

Tax State", *International Economic Papers* 4 (1954), 15, "Out of the 'common exigency' the state was born."

71. R. Villari, *La rivolta antispagnola a Napoli. Le origini (1585–1647)* (Bari, 1967), ch.5.

72. See K.A. Rasler and W.R. Thompson, "War Making and State Making: Governmental Expenditures, Tax Revenues, and Global Wars", *American Political Science Review* 79 (1985), 491–507.

73. For another argument on the importance of "permanent" war, see E. Ames and R.T. Rapp, "The Birth and Death of Taxes: A Hypothesis", *Journal of Economic History* 37 (1977), 161–78.

74. Brian M. Downing, "Constitutionalism, warfare, and political change in early modern Europe", *Theory and Society* 17 (1988), 7–56, the quotation at p. 8.

75. This is the argument of my two contributions to the collective volume in the Making of Modern Freedom series, *Fiscal Crises, Liberty, and Representative Government, 1450–1789*, cited in notes 59 and 61 above.

◀ 12 ▶

The Military Revolution:
Origins and First Tests Abroad

JOHN F. GUILMARTIN, JR.

THE ORIGINS OF THE Military Revolution, however defined, and the immediate consequences of its exportation abroad are clearly a matter of importance, not only to military historians but to social and political historians as well. In his seminal work, *The Military Revolution: Military Innovation and the Rise of the West, 1500–1800,*[1] Geoffrey Parker placed his topic in context by citing Daniel Hedrick to the effect that Europe controlled about 35% of the world's land surface by 1800, a share which increased to 84% by 1914. Parker went on to argue, correctly in my view, that however important post-1800 imperial expansion was, it was not the crux of the matter. What really counted was the way in which the first 35% was acquired, for it was there that Western Europe established its superiority.[2]

Parker began his inquiry at the turn of the sixteenth century, showing how European armies and navies learned to articulate more powerfully the new technologies at their disposal, notably gunpowder weapons and trans-oceanic sailing vessels, and bend them to the process of imperial expansion. Here, I will press the logic behind Parker's approach a step further. Using Clifford Rogers' analysis of developments in the Hundred Years War[3] as a point of departure, I will begin by examining the origins of the innovations in technology and tactics which manifested themselves so dramatically on a global scale after 1500. I will then turn to an assessment of the pivotal initial engagements which began around the turn of the sixteenth century between the beneficiaries of the Military Revolution and those beyond Western Europe upon whom they sought to impose their will by force of arms.

I decided to address the various cases in inverse order of the technological capabilities of the opponents of Western European arms. This not only produced the smoothest narrative flow, but—more important—generated more promising hypotheses. That, therefore, is the scheme I shall follow. To avoid becoming embroiled in definitional hair-splitting, I will use the term Military Revolution not as

299

a precise description of a discrete phenomenon, but as an accepted and useful label for a field of scholarly inquiry.[4]

There can be no doubt concerning the suddenness and importance of the
transformation in war with which we are concerned. Viewing the world at the
turn of the fourteenth century through the eyes of a widely traveled and well-informed contemporary—say a Genoese sea captain, a Papal envoy, an Arab merchant or an official of the Great Khan's court—Europe was a backwater, unremarkable in cultural vitality, economic development or military might. By the
turn of the sixteenth century that had changed dramatically or, more precisely
from the standpoint of the world beyond Western Europe, was about to.

European mariners had reached the Caribbean and the Indian Ocean in vessels
with serious commercial and military potential. Amerindian, Arab and Indian
were learning to their dismay that these ships and the men aboard them posed
military problems to which they had no effective solution. At the same time, the
invasion of Italy in 1494 by the forces of King Charles VIII of France had initiated
a series of developments which were to have momentous military consequences.
The Wars of Italy, 1494–1559, initiated by Charles' invasion and the Spanish intervention it prompted, ended in strategic stalemate, but along the way European
soldiers, smiths and military engineers developed methods of war on land far in
advance of those practiced elsewhere. Within four decades of Columbus' landfall
at San Salvador, Charles VIII's invasion of Italy and Vasco da Gama's arrival at
Calicut, these new methods of land warfare merged with European capabilities in
trans-oceanic navigation and warfare at sea to begin reshaping the political and
economic face of the globe.

But as the fifteenth century gave way to the sixteenth, the Western European
superiority at war was not yet apparent. This was in part because that superiority
was just emerging; in part because it had not yet been tested beyond its point of
origin; and in part because Western Europe's neighbor to the east, the Ottoman
Empire, had itself undergone a military transformation in the preceding half century, acquiring heavy siege guns, disciplined gunpowder-armed infantry and a
powerful fleet.[5] In 1500, the Ottomans were in the process of administering to
Venice a series of sharp defeats in a war of conquest, 1499–1503, which cost the island republic most of her bases in the Morea and showed that Venetian mastery of
the sea could no longer be taken for granted. Then, after turning east to contain
the growing Persian Savafid threat, the Ottomans turned south to defeat the
Egyptian Mamluks and absorb their empire in 1516–17, dramatically expanding
the geographic extent of their realm, their prestige and—far from least—their fiscal resources. The Osmanli sultans returned to the west in 1526, crushed the Hungarian monarchy at the battle of Mohács and were turned back from Vienna in
1529 by the narrowest of margins. With the exception of the Persian War, intended
only to hold the Safavids at bay,[6] these Ottoman wars of expansion were decisive,
short and, insofar as we can judge, cheap. They were the last of their kind.

The Ottomans posed a continuing threat to the West, but their failure to take Vienna in 1529 proved to be their high-water mark. Many decades would pass before Christendom ceased to fear the Turk, but expansion to the west and the attendant absorption of non-Muslim lands, the *raison d'être* of the Ottoman state and vital to its social and economic health,[7] to all practical intents and purposes ceased after Mohács. Conversely, Western expansion commenced with explosive suddenness at about the same time and proceeded with remarkable ease save in the Mediterranean and the Balkans. Despite their lack of demographic and economic resources, the Portuguese quickly established a rich maritime empire stretching from the Malabar Coast to Ormuz, the Straits of Malacca and the Spice Islands. After repelling local, Mamluk and Ottoman efforts to dislodge them, the Portuguese enjoyed a century of exclusionary dominance, yielding regional primacy to the Dutch and English only after another century of struggle. During the same period Spanish conquistadors, fighting winds and currents, treacherous seas, distance and terrain as well as Amerindian arms, carved out an empire of immense size and wealth in the Caribbean, Mexico, Central America and Peru.[8] As with the Portuguese in the east, the main threat to Spanish power in the New World came not from indigenous arms but European interlopers. In short, the turn of the sixteenth century can be viewed as the beginning of an extended era in which the dominant polities of Western Europe, after checking the expansion of Islam in Europe—just how abruptly was not apparent until after the fact—determined by trial of arms how much of the rest of the world each would control.

On the surface of it, the enormous technological disparities among the opponents of Western expansion with whom we are concerned would seem to render direct comparisons among case studies of questionable value. The Andean armies which Francisco Pizarro and his men faced were armed almost entirely with wood and stone and lacked even an effective slashing weapon while contemporary Ottoman forces fought at no great technological disadvantage, if any. In fact, this seemingly disqualifying consideration strengthens the analysis and works to our advantage. From the Western European standpoint, the case studies involve situations where the same basic technologies, tactics and institutions were applied within essentially similar cultural frameworks. Examining how this was done against dramatically different foes under sharply differing circumstances should enable us to better appreciate the fundamental strengths, weaknesses and limits of accommodation of those who first brought the Military Revolution to bear beyond its point of origin. Comparing our case studies should thus enable us to distinguish between what was important and what was incidental.

As it developed, this scheme also provided a useful measure of just what the Military Revolution accomplished in terms of concrete strategic, operational and tactical capabilities at a pivotal time and—of at least equal importance—of what factors limited its exportability.

By treating Amerindian, Indian, Arab Muslim, North African and Ottoman military capabilities and effectiveness as dependent variables we should gain a better understanding of how the Portuguese, the Austrian Habsburgs, the Spanish and their Mediterranean client states, and the Venetians applied the fruits of the Military Revolution. This approach should also highlight the key cultural, political and economic factors which shaped the application of military force and forces at the pivotal first stage of European expansion. By considering the Ottomans, it might even point toward a more comprehensive understanding of just what the Military Revolution was and why it took root, grew and prospered, or died after a period of initial growth, where and when it did.

It is important to note in this regard that the use of the phrase "similar cultural frameworks" three paragraphs above is more than a vague generalization. Portuguese military culture, institutions and methods and those of their Spanish neighbors were formed in the same crucible: the 700 year *Reconquista* in which militant Christendom drove Islam from the Iberian peninsula. Nor was the influence of the *Reconquista* confined to Iberia. After the election of Charles I of Spain as Holy Roman Emperor Charles V in 1519, the same Habsburg monarch controlled both Spain and Austria, causing exchanges of personnel and cross-fertilization of ideas. When Charles was elected, German *Landsknechts* and gunners, the mainstay of Austrian Habsburg armies, had already been exposed to Spanish methods in the Wars of Italy for two decades. Spanish soldiers fought the Ottomans in the Balkans as well as the Mediterranean and were prominent in the defense of Vienna in 1529. At Lepanto Spanish *infantes* fought side by side with *Landsknechts,* Italian mercenaries in Spanish and Papal service, and Venetian *scapoli,* and Lepanto was unusual only in scale. Habsburg emperors and Portuguese kings alike favored German gunfounders as purveyors of bronze ordnance.

Nor were exchanges of personnel and ideas within this community of arms confined to the land or to Europe. Among the men who sailed with Da Gama, Cabral and Albuquerque were men who had fought Moors and Turks in North Africa. The Portuguese Ferdinand Magellan fought under Alfonso de Albuquerque in the capture of Malacca and circumnavigated the globe for the King of Spain; among the survivors of his expedition was the gunner Hans of Lübeck. Francisco Pizarro traveled from Panama to Spain between his first and second expeditions to Peru to petition the Emperor Charles for rights to whatever conquests he might acquire. While in Spain he consulted with Hernán Cortés, conqueror of Mexico. Cortés was present in the Emperor's suite when the Imperial fleet met with disaster before Algiers in 1541 ... and offered Charles the soundest advice he was given on that unhappy occasion—to ignore the destruction of the fleet and attack the city—a circumstance which shows that lessons of war learned beyond the seas were considered relevant by some.

Before proceeding, it is worth noting that the increased communication among the various Western military communities noted above was a new phenomenon. More than half a century ago Sir Charles Oman observed that the wars of fifteenth century Europe were waged in relative isolation from one another. They could, he said, "be described, not inaccurately, as being shut up in many water-tight compartments": the wars of the English and French, the wars of Castile against her neighbors, the wars of the Italian city-states, the Hussite wars, the Ottoman-Hungarian struggle, the Swiss Confederation's wars of expansion, and so on.[9] Charles VIII's invasion of Italy and the Spanish response it evoked immediately and irrevocably ruptured the boundaries between three of these compartments and compromised the rest. The immediate result, addressed below, was that the premier military establishments of Western Europe learned an extraordinary amount from one another in a very short time. The emergence of the Iberian/Habsburg community of arms alluded to above, one in which Italian military professionals shared, was both a consequence of the rupturing of the boundaries and an important contributor to the accelerated learning process which it fostered.

The above schema has two defects: First, it emphasizes many points of detail which would not have seemed terribly important to contemporary observers; they are to us because we know who won. Second, as the perceptive reader will note, the Ottoman Turks do not fit easily into it. The frequent use of Western Europe rather than simply Europe in the preceding pages is evidence of the latter problem. The Military Revolution is generally understood as the product of a Europe to which the Ottomans were external, yet by the time they established their capital at Edirne (Adrianople) early in the fifteenth century the Ottoman Turks were arguably more a European power which happened to be Muslim than an "Eastern" (whatever that means) power which had gained a lodgment in Europe.[10] In fact, the Ottomans paralleled and at times anticipated the Military Revolution, notably in the early adoption of individual gunpowder weapons and in the creation of an elaborate, efficient and well-articulated bureaucracy dedicated to the prosecution of war. Moreover, there was a Muslim counterpart to the Christian community of arms outlined above: Ottoman soldiers and technicians seconded to the Mamluks were sent to the Red Sea to fight the Portuguese under an Ottoman commander, Salman Re'is, even before the Mamluks were overthrown; the famed North African corsair, Hayreddin Barbarossa, became Kapudan Pasha, Head Admiral of the Ottoman fleet; in the course of the sixteenth century, Janissaries were dispatched as far afield as Afghanistan and Algiers. But the Turks ultimately fell behind. Their failure to match the innovations which emerged from the Wars of Italy was pivotal, but that is apparent only with the wisdom of hindsight. It was not at all clear until late in the seventeenth century—if even then—that the Ottomans were following an unsuccessful trajectory.[11]

Knowing that the Turks lost in the long run, we tend to discount their successes, many of them quite remarkable. That the Ottomans would fail to anticipate the military challenges of the seventeenth century as well as they did those of the fifteenth and early sixteenth was by no means pre-ordained or—more to the point—evident until well after the fact. On learning of the Ottoman victory at Mohács, perceptive and well-informed observers might well have been inclined to dismiss Spanish victories in the New World and Italy and Portuguese successes in the Far East as peripheral and put their money on the Turk. They would have been wrong, of course, but, given the information at their disposal, why? I have no answer, only tentative hypotheses, but the question is an important one and the following examination pays particular attention to the Turks.

My analysis begins with developments in the technology and tactics of field warfare which began in certain regions of Western Europe around the turn of the fourteenth century and reached maturity in its last quarter. These developments merit the term Infantry Revolution. The pivotal actors were the English longbow-man and Swiss halberdier and pikeman. Clifford Rogers' formulation describing developments which came to fruition in the Hundred Years War[12] fits with minor modification: before this revolution field armies were dominated, in tactical importance if not in numbers, by chivalric elites, specialists in mounted shock action who supported themselves on the proceeds of feudal land holdings and fought primarily to capture for ransom rather than kill. In consequence, battles tended to be relatively bloodless. Although missile troops were important in sieges, their role in battle was peripheral. After the revolution had run its course, the reverse was true on all points: field warfare was dominated by foot soldiers, commoners who served for pay and fought to kill; battles were bloody; missile weapons played an important role in battle and were at times decisive.

Perhaps the most important element of the Infantry Revolution was the development by the Swiss of a combination of weapons and tactics which enabled infantry to deliver shock action with devastating impact and to maneuver in the field in the face of first-class cavalry. The Swiss methods were based on compact mutually-supporting bodies of infantry armed with pikes of twelve feet or more in length for the initial shock and halberds for counter-attack if the pike charge were halted. The Swiss achieved their speed and cohesion by marching in step.[13] Formations were normally square, but could be quickly altered to suit changing tactical circumstances, for example into an oval "hedgehog" to repel cavalry attacks from several directions. Though shock action was the essence of Swiss tactics, the pike squares were screened by crossbowmen, and later handgunners, to drive off enemy skirmishers and hold missile-armed enemies at bay.[14] Swiss methods, imitated by the German *Landsknechts* and refined by the Spanish, laid the foundations of the modern army.

Interestingly, the practices of the Ottoman Janissary Corps, the only Islamic infantry elite of consequence from Muhammad's day until modern times, paralleled the Infantry Revolution, but belatedly and only up to a point. We know little about the early history of the Janissaries, but there is evidence of an elite infantry component in Ottoman field armies as early as the Battle of Nicopolis in 1396.[15] The Janissaries were early users of individual firearms, to which they were exposed by ex-Hussite Bohemian mercenaries in Hungarian service at the Second Battle of Kossovo in 1449 if not before.[16] Janissary musketry was a major factor in Selim I's victories over the Safavids and Mamluks. Unlike Western infantry, however, the Janissaries never developed the ability to maneuver independently in the face of cavalry. Perhaps their system worked too well for too long and they became set in their ways.

The next precursor to European expansion was the development, between the last quarter of the fourteenth century and the last quarter of the fifteenth, of sailing vessels, navigational methods and systems of armament which made trans-oceanic navigation technically feasible and economically remunerative. This revolution in seafaring emerged from the fusion of Atlantic and Mediterranean technologies to produce the ancestors of the early modern full rigged sailing ship.[17] These developments extended to all the maritime nations of Europe, though the pace varied from region to region. The Iberians led the way and Portuguese and Spanish mariners reached Madeira and the Canaries early in the fourteenth century, but as a general proposition routine long-range deep-sea navigation was beyond the reach of Europeans prior to this revolution. After it had run its course the Iberians still led the way, but European mariners across the board possessed the wherewithal to traverse the oceans of the globe.

The details of this revolution need not detain us long. The caravels of the European voyages of exploration, with hulls of Atlantic design and Mediterranean construction driven by a mix of Mediterranean lateen sails and Atlantic square sails, were an early product of that revolution. The three-masted *naos,* of which Columbus' *Santa Maria* is the most famous example, were another. From the *nao* came the carrack, lineal ancestor of the galleons of the mid-sixteenth century and the ships-of-the-line of the seventeenth and eighteenth which played so large a role in European expansion abroad. Developments in ship design and construction were backed by advances in navigational theory and practice in which Portugal led the way. At the turn of the fifteenth century, the best nautical charts were sufficiently accurate only for use in the relatively benign conditions of the Mediterranean.[18] By the last decade of the century, the Portuguese possessed charts sufficiently accurate to support navigation between known points on the Atlantic coasts when used by a skilled navigator in combination with dead reckoning and daily latitude determinations by cross staff.[19] Of equal importance was the adoption and progressive development of gunpowder ordnance for use afloat: from this point on Chinese and Arab ships and mariners might rival their European counterparts in long range navigation, but they could not in fighting potential.

Guns were used on ships almost as soon as they appeared in Europe, but they were at first light pieces with little more power than bows. The first guns which had sufficient power to do serious structural damage to ships or seaside fortifications to be routinely mounted on ships were the main centerline bow guns of Mediterranean war galleys around the middle of the fifteenth century.[20] The weight and recoil of heavy ordnance taxed the structures of ships and forced innovation, first evident in the appearance of sliding carriages for main centerline bow guns about 1500 and in the appearance of the lidded, watertight gunport on sailing vessels shortly thereafter.[21] The latter development was of crucial importance in making it possible to permanently mount heavy guns low in the hulls of seagoing vessels where their weight would not compromise stability. The early 1500s were a period of transition and the chronology is uncertain, but the evidence suggests that the first ships built with a main battery of heavy guns mounted low in the hull behind lidded, watertight gunports were laid down no earlier than the first decade of the sixteenth century.[22] Change, however, was swift, at least in northern waters: based on iconographic evidence, lidded gunports were common by the 1520s and by the mid-1540s lower gundecks fitted with them were the norm, at least in England.[23]

Next came a revolution in heavy gunpowder ordnance on land which began in the 1420s, apparently in France, England and Flanders, spread from there, and was largely complete by mid-century. This series of developments, which Clifford Rogers has aptly termed the Artillery Revolution,[24] produced powerful siege trains which drove the English from Normandy and Guienne, enabled the Hohenzollerns to consolidate their power in Austria at the expense of the Quitzows and allowed Mehmed II to take Constantinople.[25] The Artillery Revolution was the product of connected developments in the techniques of positional warfare, gunfounding and powder manufacture, to name but a few. We do not fully understand how these developments played on one another, but the outlines are clear. The first indication was the progressive abandonment from about 1420 of high trajectory fire intended to damage structures inside fortress walls in favor of flat trajectory fire meant to bring down the wall itself.[26] This development was associated with improved methods of cannon construction in the form of larger and more powerful guns with tubular barrels long enough to harness gunpowder's propellant properties.[27] The earliest of these were wrought iron bombards, made up of hoops and staves, whence the term barrel.[28] The introduction of corned powder at about the same time was intimately bound up in the Artillery Revolution, for corned powder was more powerful—or at least more reliably powerful—than earlier "serpentine," or dry-compounded, gunpowder.[29] Bronzefounders soon imitated the wrought iron designs, and by the 1440s and -50s ordnance of cast bronze was edging out wrought iron as the premier European ordnance.[30]

The next major transformation in European warfare was a revolution in siegecraft and fortification sparked by the power and mobility of the siege train which Charles VIII brought to Italy in 1494. The French guns were products of evolutionary refinement in design, lineal descendants of those which blasted the English out of Normandy and Guienne a half century before.[31] That notwithstanding, they struck Italy with revolutionary impact: Guicciardini's lament that the new French artillery did as much damage to the walls of a fortress in a few hours as their predecessors had done in a like number of days was a sober statement of reality.[32] This was not a simple matter of destructive power: shot for shot, the huge bombards of the mid-fifteenth century were more powerful than the largest of Charles' guns.[33] What was new was the mobility of the French cannon, their numbers, the speed with which they fired and the skill of their gunners.[34]

The French ordnance was superior for many reasons: the guns were cast of high quality bronze and were therefore light for the weight of ball they fired;[35] the barrels were suspended in the carriages from integrally cast trunnions which made adjustments in elevation easy; the carriages were lighter and more efficient, with dished wheels for strength and stability and limbers for mobility; and the guns were pulled by teams of powerful, specially trained horses.[36]

In the event, the advantage which the French derived from the excellence of their artillery was short-lived; its main historical importance stems from the revolution in fortification design it unleashed. The hallmark of this revolution was the *trace italienne* fortress with its sunken profile. The key events were the siege of Pisa in 1500, which demonstrated the power of defensive flanking fire and the ability of a sloping rampart of earth to absorb cannon balls; the siege of Padua in 1509 which showed the power of enfilade fire in the ditch against assault; and the unsuccessful Ottoman attempt at Corfu in 1537 which showed that a fortress built according to the lessons of Pisa and Padua and competently defended by a small garrison could not be quickly reduced even by the most powerful of foes.[37] These examples contrast dramatically with the sack of Rome in 1527, where Charles V showed how easily a city devoid of the new fortifications could be taken. Rome was the last easy siege of consequence.

The developments just described amounted to a revolution in positional warfare although, as with the Artillery Revolution, it was preceded by an extended period of incremental development, a pattern which fits Rogers' concept of punctuated equilibrium evolution.[38] The revolution in positional warfare ended the expansion of gunpowder empires which the Artillery Revolution had sparked. It also provided an economical means of defense for European ports and factories overseas.

The revolution in positional warfare was paralleled by a revolution in tactics which I call the Combined Arms Revolution. A product of Spain's intervention in Italy, it picked up where the Infantry Revolution of the fourteenth century left off and, with regard to field artillery, where the Artillery Revolution of the fifteenth century ended. The outlines are too well known to merit detailed attention,[39] but the gist of it is that the Spanish army under Gonsalvo de Cordova learned from defeat at the hands of a French army well supplied with Swiss pikemen at the Seminara River in 1495. The Spanish transformed themselves in remarkably short order from a predominately light cavalry force adapted to the arid, rolling terrain of southern Spain into a balanced force of pikemen, arquebusiers and cavalry which could take on any army in the world.[40] Infantry was the key element. Gonsalvo increased the proportion of pikemen in his army and taught his infantry to maneuver in compact bodies, ready to repel cavalry or to charge home. Whether through his initiative or, more likely, through initiative from below, crossbows gave way to arquebuses, which grew in size and killing power in response to Swiss and French armor. These reforms bore fruit at Cerignola in 1503 where the Spanish defeated an army much like that which had beaten them seven

years earlier, though Gonsalvo's intelligent use of the ground and field fortifications were also important factors.[41] By Pavia in 1525 the concept of a balanced mix
of shock and shot infantry—pikemen and arquebusiers formed into compact
bodies—supported by enough cavalry to hold enemy skirmishers at bay and pursue a beaten foe was essentially in place. Tactical and administrative innovation
went hand in hand in the emergence of the *columna* and the tercio, the first modern permanent fighting organizations of mixed arms.

When armies using Spanish methods were pitted against one another in battle,
the results were frequently indecisive and invariably bloody, and in consequence
most observers tended to miss the global implications of the revolution in tactics.
In fact, where first-class Western armies were involved the logical response was to
avoid battle. The point was underlined by the outcome of Ceresole in 1544, where
the Marqués del Vasto lost his reputation and half his army in a day.[42] Far more
portentous, however, was the ability of Spanish infantry to defend itself against
cavalry on terrain favorable for mounted operations, a point grasped by perceptive soldiers. The contemporary French leader François La Noue noted with ad-
miration the behavior of a Spanish force of 4,000 men under Alvaro de Saude
which was compelled to retreat in the face of 18,000–20,000 Muslim cavalry during one of Charles V's North African campaigns, probably that of 1535. Saude's
men, he reported, beat off dozens of charges, killing some 700 Muslims for the
loss of only 80 men.[43]

Ironically, the larger implications of the Combined Arms Revolution can be
seen most clearly in a battle which never occurred. After the Ottoman failure to
take Vienna in 1529, Sultan Suleiman led his army west again in 1532. But Charles
V and Ferdinand of Austria had assembled a large force before Vienna and
Suleiman declined the gambit. Instead of following their traditional route up the
Danube toward Vienna, the Turks turned west along the Drava, which led to
nothing of importance, and ended the campaign with the reduction of the minor
fortress of Güns.[44] Suleiman's refusal to engage the Habsburg army in 1532
marked the maturation of European methods of land warfare. Many years would
pass before Ottoman imperial armies returned to the borders of Austria, and
when they did it was in much less threatening fashion than in 1529.[45] It was the
developments which culminated in the indecisive 1532 campaign which Sir
Charles Oman, writing over a century ago, termed the military revolution of the
sixteenth century.[46]

THE SPANISH IN MEXICO AND THE ANDES, 1519–39

The Caribbean cultures with which the Spanish first came into contact in the New
World were neither technologically advanced nor particularly warlike.[47] Armed
with simple bows, atl atls, and stone-tipped clubs and spears, they posed no real
threat to bands of well-armed Spaniards. The Spanish encountered their first serious Amerindian military opposition in 1517 when a Caribbean slaving expedition

under Hernández de Córdova was blown off course and landed on the coast of Yucatan. Finding a civilization more advanced and richer that anything previously encountered in the New World, the Spanish reconnoitered ashore and were assailed by large numbers of warriors wearing quilted cotton armor and bearing stone-tipped spears, bows and slings. Spanish swordplay, employed in concert with crossbow and arquebus fire, took heavy toll of the Amerindians but could not overcome the numerical odds.[48] Driven back to their boats with loss, the Spaniards coasted southward and tried again in Campeche, only to be driven back again. In this second encounter, the Amerindians focused their attention on Córdova, wounding him with arrows. Some of the warriors bore two-handed broadswords of wood edged with razor sharp flakes of flint or obsidian, the *macahuitl*.[49] After further misadventures and a clash with Amerindians in Florida the expedition returned to Cuba.[50]

A second expedition went out the next year under Juan de Grijalva and achieved similar results, save that the Spaniards were better prepared and suffered fewer losses. At one point, Grijalva was able to exploit the Spanish qualitative military advantage as an entering wedge for negotiations and obtained gold artifacts in barter.[51] It was a harbinger of things to come. Significantly, neither the Córdova nor the Grijalva expedition included horses. These initial encounters were preludes to the Cortés expedition of 1519.

We tend to approach the overthrow of the Aztec and Inca empires with a sense of inevitability, prompted by post-conquest Nahua chroniclers who reported that the destruction of the Aztec empire was foretold by strange portents and gloomy prophecies.[52] This perspective is essentially ahistorical. In fact, the Aztecs and Incas would have been overthrown by European arms sooner or later—the technological disparity was simply too great—but the success of the Cortés and Pizarro expeditions was anything but inevitable. The key question at issue is that of numerical odds. In certain instances, these were so overwhelming that victory, even in narrowly tactical terms, is difficult to explain in orthodox, military terms. A prime example is Cortés' success in breaking out of Tenochtitlan, a city with a population reasonably estimated at no less than 100,000–150,000,[53] with a force of only 1,300 Spaniards, many of them sick and wounded, and 96 horses.[54] Cortés' 5,000–6,000 Tlaxcalan allies no doubt played an important role in the breakout, but had no advantage over the Aztecs in weaponry or tactics.[55] The Spanish and Tlaxcalans were not only badly outnumbered, they had to fight their way out of the city across unbridged causeways and down narrow streets pelted with missiles from the roofs of houses on either side. Equally remarkable was the victory a week later at Otumba of the survivors of the catastrophic retreat, 425 Spanish, of whom 23 were mounted, and 3,000–3,500 Tlaxcalans, over an Aztec force which Cortés' historian, Francisco López de Gómara, estimated at 200,000 strong.[56] Even if Gómara exaggerated by an order of magnitude it was still a remarkable achievement. Francisco Pizarro's success at Cajamarca in overwhelming the bodyguard of the Emperor Atahualpa, reasonably estimated at 5,000–6,000 men, and capturing the Emperor himself with a force of only 62 mounted fighting men and 106 on foot is no less remarkable.[57] So too was the defeat before Quito of an Inca army estimated at 50,000 strong by some 200 Spaniards under Sebastián de Benalcázar, 62 of them mounted, and 3,000 Cañari allies.[58] Similarly, Cuzco was defended against the bulk of Manco Inca's army for nearly a year by a force of only 190 Spaniards, eighty of them mounted.[59] In light of these feats, the estimate by John Elliott that a combined Spanish force of as few as fifty infantry and cavalry could hold out against any number of Amerindians on level terrain unless overcome by sheer fatigue seems entirely reasonable.[60]

We must have some notion of the size the Amerindian forces to place such feats in context. Concerning the Aztecs, Spanish accounts assert that the conquistadors were hugely outnumbered except at the siege of Tenochtitlan—Gómara refers to "an infinity" of enemy dead at Otumba[61]—but that is what we would expect them to say. Assuming that ten percent of the inhabitants of Tenochtitlan were physically fit males of military age, a conservative estimate, and that all were armed and fought, Cortés' force fought its way out of the city against odds of between one and a half to one and three and a half to one. But warriors from other parts of the empire must have been present in at least equal numbers, raising the odds to between three and seven to one.

We are on firmer ground in the Andean case. The site of Cajamarca survives and John Hemming considers the estimate of the size of Atahualpa's bodyguard given above credible based on examination of the layout and size of the town square where the pivotal ambush occurred.[62] Though they lacked a written language, the Incas were numerate, and in the interval between Atahualpa's capture and the outbreak of war, Hernando Pizarro observed the army of the Inca general Calcuchima and watched as his scribes counted it, ticking numbers off on the knots of their *quipus,* or counting cords.[63] The Incas had two additional armies of the same approximate size in the field at the time, and it is reasonable to suppose that they had about 100,000 soldiers under arms.[64] Though the numbers are uncertain, for the Spaniards received significant reinforcements and sustained significant losses during the seven years that it took to overthrow the Incas and to fight for the booty among themselves, it is unlikely that the Spaniards ever had as many as 1,500 men under arms at one time to oppose the Inca armies.

It is hardly surprising that in attempting to explain victory in the face of such odds historians at first turned to non-military and even non-rational explanations.[65] A partial list includes the myth of returning white gods which presumably disarmed the Aztecs; terror of the unknown in the form of gunpowder weapons and horses which rendered warriors ineffective in battle; the ravages of European-introduced epidemic diseases, notably smallpox, which caused demographic collapse, shattering Amerindian faith in their gods and destroying their will to resist; and the prevalence of ritual forms of warfare revolving around the capture of prisoners among the Aztecs and their neighbors which left them tactically disarmed against the Spaniards, who fought to win.

Each of these explanations contains an element of truth, but none stands up under scrutiny. It is correct to point out that the Aztecs attached enormous religious importance to the sacrifice of captives taken in battle and that the desire to secure prisoners drove recruitment, promotion and tactics. This may have acted to the Aztecs' detriment in the initial encounters, but by the siege of Tenochtitlan if not before they knew they were fighting a no-holds-barred struggle for survival. More to the point, it is evident from close comparison of the Mexican and Andean cases that the Aztecs gave the Spaniards a harder run for their money than the Incas, who fought to kill and to win. To be sure, smallpox raged in Tenochtitlan during the siege, but recent scholarship indicates that the disease was less virulent than historians have supposed and that notions of demographic catastrophe owe more to the apocalyptic visions of Franciscan friars than to eyewitness accounts.[66] The defenders of Tenochtitlan continued fighting despite the epidemic and had to be rooted out, street by street and house by house, a task which taxed Spanish resources of endurance, weaponry and ingenuity. Beyond doubt, initial encounters with horses and firearms produced more than the usual quotient of fear among Amerindian warriors, but as I have said elsewhere even a cursory analysis shows that both Aztec and Inca adapted quickly and well to gunpowder and horses within the means available to them.[67] Those means were terribly deficient, but both Aztec and Inca at times showed an uncanny sensitivity to Spanish vulnerabilities and never lacked the will and courage to exploit them. The returning gods story applies only to the Mexican case, is essentially unprovable one way or the other, and need not be invoked to explain Amerindian defeat.

Latin Americanists, perceiving the shortfall between tactical reality and earlier hypotheses, have correctly pointed out the importance of Amerindian allies to the conquistadors.[68] Beyond doubt, neither Cortés nor Pizarro could have succeeded without the aid of numerous and well-motivated indigenous allies. But the ethnohistorians recognize that their explanation, though far more satisfying than previous hypotheses, is incomplete,[69] for the Spanish acquired allies willing to fight alongside them only after they had demonstrated their overwhelming tactical superiority in the field.[70] On what, then, did that superiority depend?

Sheer technological advantage was a crucial part of the answer. Probably the most important single Spanish advantage lay in the superiority of steel swords over hand-held Amerindian weapons. The *macahuitl* was a slashing weapon of awesome power, but to be effective required a time-consuming full swing, giving an alert Spanish swordsman or mounted lancer the opportunity to deliver a quick thrust and recover. Andean stone-headed clubs and spears were at an even greater disadvantage. Horses were essential to Spanish success, a fact reflected in the enormous value the conquistadors placed on the animals and the pains to which they went to care for them. Steel armor magnified the advantages of Spanish slashing and thrusting weapons and permitted greater aggressiveness in close combat. Except for helmets, however, the conquistadors mostly abandoned steel armor in favor of quilted protective garments of canvas or cotton in imitation of Amerindian practice and armor was not itself a major factor.

Spanish crossbows and arquebuses were superior to Amerindian missile weapons in range and lethality. Skilled Amerindian slingers could hurl stones with sufficient energy that a lucky hit could fracture a skull or snap a horse's leg and the sling was the one indigenous weapon the conquistadors feared. On the whole, however, sling stones wounded whereas crossbow bolts and arquebus balls killed; the advantage therefore lay with the conquistadors. That having been said, the superiority of Spanish missile weapons took effect in a supporting role. Arquebuses and artillery were essential to the blockade and destruction of Tenochtitlan as were the cannon-armed *bergantines*[71] that Cortés caused to be built and launched on Lake Texcoco, but the Spanish could probably have overthrown the Incas without gunpowder.

But we are concerned with the sources of Spanish tactical advantage only as a means to an end, to determine how the Military Revolution influenced the outcome and vice versa. Addressing the most obvious hypothesis first, the conquistadors were clearly beneficiaries of the Combined Arms Revolution. Cortés' and Pizarro's men surely knew of the dramatic changes in the art of war forged by Gonsalvo de Córdova and his successors; by the time of the battle of Ravenna in 1512, Spanish infantry were fighting in balanced formations of shock and shot.[72]

Few of Cortés' men and almost none of Pizarro's were military professionals.[73] They were, however, products of a society which had internalized military skills and values to a remarkable degree. Individualists to a fault, they understood the value of proper subordination and coordination in battle; factious in victory, they hung together in combat with instinctive cohesion. Though they were not organized in any formal military structure, in combat they were soldiers rather than warriors.[74] An observation concerning the division of booty makes the point: the owners of horses received a larger share than footmen, but rider and owner were not necessarily one and the same.[75] That the owner of a horse would yield his place in the saddle at the moment of combat to a better horseman who fought to receive a footman's share of the booty speaks volumes for Spanish priorities and Spanish competence.

Analysis of initial Spanish-Amerindian encounters suggests that the Military Revolution, however defined and broken down into subordinate revolutions, had deeper social and cultural roots than we have realized. On the most basic level, the terrible vulnerability of the bravest and most determined Amerindian infantry to mounted shock action shows dramatically by comparison how well European infantry had learned to cope with cavalry. Analysis of Spanish conduct in action against overwhelming odds in desperate and unanticipated circumstances yields a better appreciation of the tactical importance of shared and implicitly agreed upon standards of conduct and modes of behavior. These were an essential foundation for the Spanish techniques and tactical innovations which we associate with the Military Revolution. The point surely applies in some measure to other

European beneficiaries of the Military Revolution as well. One student of European military techniques has asserted that "Europeans have shown themselves able to think and act more effectively as members of a group than those of any other civilization."[76] The statement seems less extreme in light of the conquistador's behavior in battle than it otherwise would. We should add the remarkable ability of European fighting men to maintain cohesion in battle in the face of withering fire, with death and destruction falling around them.[77] We tend to associate that ability with the reforms of Maurice of Nassau and the linear warfare of the Age of Reason, but our examination of the Spanish experience in the New World suggests that it has deeper roots.

THE PORTUGUESE IN THE INDIAN OCEAN, 1498–1517

The Portuguese effort in the east differed from that of the Spanish in the Americas in that it was government-directed, underwritten by a sustained commitment of brain power, blood and treasure. That having been said, it is interesting to note that while Vasco da Gama's fleet departed Lisbon well prepared to face the sea and armed enemies, Portuguese knowledge of the cultural and economic geography of the Indian Ocean was deficient. The Zamorin of Calicut's scorn for the cheap cloth, hawks' bells and trinkets which the Portuguese proffered as gifts makes the point. So does the comment made—in Castillian!—by a Tunisian merchant to the first Portuguese ashore in India: "May the Devil take you! What brought you here?"[78] But the Portuguese recovered quickly and proved to be as good at diplomacy as they were at war, bearing in mind that their diplomacy was underwritten by successful coercion. It is fair to say that while the Portuguese could not have succeeded without important qualitative military advantages, those advantages were brought to bear with the aid of allies from the outset. The initial dealings between the Portuguese and the merchants and polities of the Malabar Coast were a reconnaissance. It was an important one in light of Portuguese ignorance. But once the Portuguese had a grasp of local realities they responded with a well-modulated combination of negotiation and force which secured at least interim bases.

Unlike the Spanish in the Americas, the Portuguese in Asia were opposed by foes who enjoyed rough technological parity. When Vasco da Gama's flotilla dropped anchor off Calicut in 1498, those who observed from the shore had weapons of steel, war horses and gunpowder; they also possessed ships and navigational methods capable of routine trans-oceanic navigation. Their knowledge of the sciences—astronomy, mathematics and so on—was in no way inferior to that of the Portuguese. These factors notwithstanding, the Portuguese in a remarkably short time imposed their will on the commerce of the Indian Ocean, crushing in the process those who sought to frustrate their designs by force of arms. I will focus on two pivotal engagements, one at sea and one on land: the defeat off the Malabar Coast in the winter of 1502 by Vasco da Gama's squadron of a combined Indian-Arab fleet led by an official of the Mamluk Sultanate of Egypt fighting at the behest of the Arab merchant community and the Zamorin of Calicut, and the capture of Malacca by Alfonso de Albuquerque in 1511. In both cases, the decisive military engagement was preceded by, and in the latter case accompanied by, negotiations, skirmishes and applications of terror.

In the initial sea engagement, the Portuguese were heavily outnumbered in manpower and vessels—da Gama's spies told him by ten to one—but employed ships which were at least equally seaworthy, more strongly built and far better armed with gunpowder ordnance.[79] We know little in detail about the Portuguese ships, caravels and *naos*, save that they were well provided with cannon. The caravels were low-lying, swift and exceptionally seaworthy, but were small and had limited carrying capacity. The *naos* were larger and more capacious, stood higher in the water and were therefore harder to board, but were slower and less maneuverable. The Portuguese allocated their ordnance according to the tactical implications of these differences. Da Gama put his caravels and *naos* in separate squadrons so as to take advantage of the caravels' greater speed and maneuverability without compromising formation integrity.

The Portuguese ordnance was probably mostly of wrought iron. From what we know of later developments, the largest Portuguese naval guns must have thrown stone balls of some thirty to forty pounds. These were apparently mounted on the caravels, whose upper decks were close enough to the water to confer most of the tactical advantages of a main gun deck as the term was later understood. The *naos* were armed with large numbers of lighter pieces in the upper works. All of the Portuguese vessels must have been well equipped with swivel-mounted *verços*, anti-personnel guns firing over railings and through openings in the bulwarks. The heaviest Portuguese ordnance was reserved for use ashore. Whatever the details, the Portuguese ordnance was far more powerful and more effective than that of the Arab and Indian vessels.

While we cannot categorically rule out the possibility that some of the Portuguese vessels mounted a small number of heavier guns behind lidded ports, the bulk of the Portuguese guns were surely light by the standards of European positional warfare, and the Muslim ordnance considerably lighter still.[80] These suppositions are supported by analysis of an incident which occurred during the Muslim siege of the fortress at Cannanore in 1507 which also illustrates Portuguese skill in positional warfare and Muslim resourcefulness. The Portuguese reinforced the fortress with 24 pieces of artillery in anticipation of the siege[81] and the place must have had a like number to begin with. Among them was a *serpe,* one of three such pieces brought from Portugal in Dom Francisco de Almeida's fleet in 1505.[82] We do not know what a *serpe* was, for terminology was in a period of transition and is frequently obscure, but it was clearly a large piece. Near-contemporary Spanish usage suggests that it was a full cannon or the equivalent, that is a piece throwing a cast iron ball of 30–50 pounds.[83] The hypothesis is supported by the piece's effect in action.

The Muslim ordnance was not heavy enough to threaten the fort's earthen rampart and the Portuguese guns initially kept the attackers at a safe distance, unable or unwilling to rush the ditch and the palisade behind it. Then, after weeks of stalemate, the Muslims adopted the expedient of advancing behind large bales of cotton, each big enough to shelter two men. The attack was mounted at night and the Portuguese guns were ineffective against the bales, which absorbed their projectiles.[84] By dawn the Muslims had established a continuous rampart of bales along the ditch behind which they mustered their guns and assault troops while filling the ditch with branches.

At this point, the Portuguese re-deployed the *serpe*, no doubt originally mounted to defend against attack from the sea, and brought it into action with horrendous effect. Each shot filled the air with ripped bales and shattered bodies and the Muslims were driven back with heavy loss. Pieces such as the *serpe* were few in number and were considered exceptional with good reason. The other Portuguese guns were plainly markedly smaller, the bulk of them probably *verços* and the like.[85]

In the pivotal sea engagement the vessels of the Muslim fleet, dhows and praus, were either unable to close with da Gama's caravels and *naos* for boarding or lay too low in the water for it to be feasible.[86] The Indian and Arab vessels carried gunpowder weapons, but even the largest dhows, built shell-first with flexible hulls, were too weakly constructed to mount heavy guns. The Portuguese seized the weather gauge at the start of the engagement, testimony to their ships' sailing qualities; this enabled them to engage or disengage at will. The Portuguese squadrons apparently fought in line ahead using broadside fire to systematically devastate the more lightly constructed, heavily manned Arab and Indian craft.[87] The victory was clearly decisive. Further resistance to the Portuguese at sea was either sporadic or dependent on external support.

The next serious challenge to the Portuguese came in 1508 in the form of an expeditionary force mounted from the Red Sea under Mamluk direction with Ragusan and Venetian technical assistance and based on a hard core of Mediterranean war galleys. Reinforced with a large number of local vessels provided by the Sultan of Gudjerat, the force, under Hussein Pasha, caught a Portuguese squadron at anchor in the River Chaul and attacked with overwhelming numerical superiority. The Portuguese held out for three days before being overwhelmed, eloquent testimony to the defensive power of their vessels and the effectiveness of their ordnance. Of three *naos* and five caravels engaged, only two caravels got away, a circumstance which suggests that the critical determinant of escape was handiness under sail and that the Portuguese could defend the low-lying caravels as well as the tall *naos*. Whether because of a lack of direction or heavy losses and the need for repairs, Hussein's squadron retired to Diu where it was caught in port and annihilated the following year by a Portuguese squadron under Almeida.

The capture of Malacca by an amphibious force under Alfonso de Albuquerque in 1511 was in some ways even more remarkable. The city was a major commercial entrepôt, desired by the Portuguese for its rich trade and geographic location commanding the straits which served as the main conduit for trade between east and west. The city had no masonry fortifications, but its ruler, Sultan Mohammed, commanded a force of some 20,000 mercenaries supported by considerable numbers of bronze cannon—Portuguese sources say 2,000 to 3,000, most of which must have been small. Against this, Albuquerque could put seventeen or eighteen ships, including three war galleys, carrying 900 Portuguese fighting men and 200 Indian mercenaries.[88] Albuquerque began his campaign with a mixture of intimidation and diplomacy, anchoring his fleet in the roadstead to the sound of cannon and proclaiming the Portuguese protectors of the shipping there. The alternation of military action and negotiations which followed was complex. The Portuguese began by exploiting the diversity of the merchant community, promising better treatment to those who were resentful of the Sultan's commercial exactions (the Chinese merchants had immediately approached Albuquerque for protection) and intimidating those who might be inclined to support him (several warehouses and Gujarati ships were burned). Albuquerque then attacked the bridge spanning the Malacca River which separated the two halves of the city by amphibious assault, briefly seized it—probably as a means of gauging Mohammed's strength and demonstrating Portuguese strength on land to the merchant community—and then withdrew. The Portuguese returned to the bridge several days later using a Chinese junk as an assault craft.

In the climactic assault, the Portuguese seized the bridge and overran the barricades which the Sultan's forces had erected on either end, brought up artillery to enfilade the streets and began fighting their way into the town. At this point, the Sultan threw in his war elephants, leading the counterattack in person. Relying as much on pikes as on shot, the Portuguese repelled the attack throwing the elephants back in disorder. The Portuguese then held their position for a week during which growing numbers of the city's merchants appealed to them for protection and were given flags to mark their houses to preserve them from looting. When the Portuguese renewed their attack, the Sultan had fled and the city was subjected to an orderly sack. Albuquerque followed up his victory by ordering a proper European-style fortress constructed.[89]

Military success in the face of seemingly overwhelming odds is a common theme in the Iberian conquests, no less in the Portuguese than the Spanish case. While the numerical odds confronted by Da Gama, Cabral, Almeida and Albuquerque may have been less than those faced by Cortés and Pizarro, the disparity was still overwhelming and the technological advantage considerably less. As in the Amerindian case, historians have correctly pointed to the key role played by local allies in Portuguese victories, but attempts to explain the tactical superiority on which those alliances were based have been unconvincing. It is tempting to turn to psychological factors: shock of the unknown in the form of gunpowder and horses in the American case and Portuguese fortitude and ferocity developed in the intolerant crucible of religious war with the Moors in the case at hand. In the words of historian George Winius, "Only their brutality, learned in Morocco, and their reckless disregard for personal injury can account for their regular— and baffling—successes."[90] To be fair to Winius, he is saying much the same thing as does Parker in emphasizing the relative lethality of European styles of warfare in comparison to Asian forms based on the use of slave soldiers.[91]

In truth, the Portuguese did make calculated use of what we would today consider atrocities to instill fear in their enemies; Vasco da Gama's capture and mutilation of Arab merchants on his first voyage, burning them alive and sending their severed ears and noses ashore with the tide, is the classic example. But the idea that they were uniquely ferocious by the standards of the day is suspect. The Spaniards used atrocities in Mexico and Peru and the Amerindians replied in kind. Indeed, in the Mexican case the conquistadors must have been hard pressed to rise to Aztec levels of frightfulness: ceremonially extracting a prisoner of war's living heart and eating it in view of his comrades, then tumbling his body down a temple staircase to be eaten sets a high standard even by modern norms. A veteran of the conquest of Peru explicitly compared the relative horrors of fighting Andeans and Muslims to the detriment of the latter: "I can bear witness," he wrote, "that this is the most dreadful and cruel war in the world. For between Christians and Moors there is some well-feeling, and it is in the interests of both sides to spare those they take alive because of their ransoms. But in this Indian war there is no such feeling on either side. They give each other the cruelest deaths they can imagine."[92] During the 1536–37 siege of Cuzco, Hernando Pizarro, noting the importance of women employed for porterage, food preparation and other logistically essential tasks, ordered all captured Indian women killed. He also ordered the right hands of several hundred captured male non-combatants cut off, then released them to spread fear and demoralization.[93] Nor were the Ottomans loath to indulge in demonstrative terror on occasion: the fate of Antonio Bragadino, the Venetian commander of Famagusta in 1570–71, who was flayed alive and his straw-stuffed skin paraded as a trophy, is a case in point.

Military analysis suggests that the Portuguese success in the pivotal early encounters sprung from a number of factors, none of which took effect or can be properly understood in isolation. The crucial factor was a decisive superiority in the technology of warfare afloat, notably ships capable of mounting effective gunpowder ordnance and sufficiently maneuverable to bring it to bear. Next in importance, though inseparable from the first factor, was the clear superiority of Portuguese ordnance. This encompasses not only the technical superiority of the guns and their greater numbers but also skill in employment. But none of these factors, essential as they were, would have counted for much had the Portuguese not had a clear vision of who they were and what they were about. They were notoriously fractious in victory and prone to pursue personal vendettas; but they worshipped the same God, obeyed the same monarch and stuck together in the face of adversity with impressive cohesion and solidity. That fixedness of purpose expressed itself not only in tactical cohesion, but in strategic design. The dispatch of an expeditionary force which, in 1541–43, saved the Christian kingdom of Ethiopia from an expansive Muslim enemy which was using acquired Ottoman gunpowder technology is perhaps the most dramatic case in point but hardly the only one.

Portuguese steadfastness of purpose and cohesion had an essential counterpart in intellectual flexibility and diplomatic skill, for da Gama, Cabral and Almeida secured their ports and the logistical wherewithal to engage their enemies as much by negotiation as by force. Finally, though we are prone to forget it, the Portuguese were thoroughly competent in positional and field operations on land though, to return to the previous two points, their numbers were so small that they could engage in field operations only with the support of local allies.

HABSBURG CONTAINMENT OF THE OTTOMANS IN THE BALKANS, 1529–1606

Not having participated in the Combined Arms Revolution, Ottoman field armies fought at a potentially enormous disadvantage against their Western foes from the 1530s on. Moreover, the Turks did not adopt the *trace italienne*, but remained attached to traditional notions of fortification. Logically, then, the Habsburgs should not only have contained the Turks, but rolled them back. In fact, the Ottomans clung tenaciously to their conquests and achieved a victory of sorts in the Long War of 1593–1606. They began to lose large chunks of territory irrevocably only with the Treaty of Karlowitz in 1699, timing which supports Jeremy Black's arguments for a later Military Revolution than that on which I have focused here.

Ottoman tenacity was aided by the strategic problems of their enemies to the west. Charles V's distractions with German Protestantism, of which the Schmalkald War of 1545–46 is the most prominent example, gave the Turk a measure of relief. So did Charles' wars with France, and his abdication in 1558 reinforced the westward shift in Habsburg concerns. Whatever assistance the Spanish Habsburgs might have given their Austrian brethren was almost entirely diverted by the demands of the Revolt of the Netherlands and the struggle to contain the Turk in the Mediterranean. That the Austrian Habsburgs accepted the partition of Hungary in 1568 and remained nominally at peace with the Ottomans until 1593 amounted to implicit recognition of changed priorities. Ironically, Suleiman's more or less simultaneous military engagement with the Persians which continued until the Treaty of Amasia in 1555 further reinforced the westward drift in Habsburg concerns by reducing the threat to Austria. These considerations, however, while of great underlying importance, do not explain the relative success of Ottoman arms.

In principle, a Western army should have been able to crush an Ottoman army in the field with major strategic gains ensuing, yet this did not happen until the relief of Vienna in 1683; Montecuccoli's victory of St. Gotthard in 1664 led only to a truce in place. In principle the Turks were at a disadvantage in positional warfare, but this took effect mostly on the defense, as at Güns in 1532 where a small fortress with a garrison of 700 men withstood the Ottoman imperial army for twenty days.[94] The reasons for Ottoman operational and tactical success were many, complex and interconnected. First, the Ottomans were favored by geography. The Danube and its major tributaries served as logistical highways, facilitating the movement of provender, materiel and manpower from base areas served by the Black Sea to campaign areas in the west. Each tributary served a discrete theater of operations: the Danube itself, central Hungary; the Thiess, Transylvania; the Maros, Moldavia; the Drava, Croatia; the Sava, Bosnia; and so on; yet all led back to the same source, convenient to Ottoman sources of supply.[95] This gave the Turks enormous operational flexibility, the more so as, in contrast to the Spanish Road which connected Flanders with Habsburg base areas in Italy and the Mediterranean, their military roads along the rivers traversed areas under their political control.[96] The advantages of access which the Danube system conferred were magnified by the richness of the Ottoman-controlled Hungarian plain, which provided a nearby source of livestock and grain. Of more fundamental importance, the Ottomans had an elaborate and remarkably efficient system of irregular taxes in kind to support their forces in the field.[97] Without going into detail, this system provided foodstuffs, other provisions, and the services of bakers, butchers, armorers, tailors, and so on, by means of a decentralized and largely self-sustaining bureaucracy,[98] and cavalrymen who supported themselves from the agricultural proceeds of their timar land grants were numerically the most important component of Ottoman field armies. The thrust of the system was to minimize cash payments from the center, an important consideration since the Ottomans lacked mechanisms of credit transfer and had to pay their troops with physical shipments of coinage.[99] In sharp contrast to contemporary Western practice, the Ottomans took care to minimize the adverse impact of the passage of armies on the peasantry in regions under their control, thus enhancing the long term viability of their system. They compensated for their lack of sophistication in fortress design with earthworks, active defenses and the profligate use of manpower. Fortress garrisons in times of peace increasingly supported themselves as tradesmen.[100]

The Habsburgs were not only less careful than the Ottomans to protect the peasantry on which their logistics depended, they lacked prosperous agricultural areas near the theater of operations and had much less political and fiscal control over their logistic base. Campaigns were fought in frontier areas which had been denuded of provender by irregular Ottoman *ghazi* horse based in frontier fortresses and advancing Habsburg forces had to stay close to major rivers to remain in supply. The result was a war of siege and counter-siege in which Ottoman numbers and logistical advantage were pitted against Austrian technique. Ottoman fortress architecture may not have been up to Western standards, but Ottoman soldiers were skilled in the minor tactics of positional warfare and the availability of water transport compensated for the unwieldiness of Ottoman siege guns.[101] Only rarely could sieges be maintained though the winter and under the circumstances the Ottoman field army could generally avoid battle. The only major field engagement of the Long War, Kerestres in 1596, was an Ottoman victory fought far from Habsburg bases, circumstances which suggest just how reluctant Ottoman commanders in the field must have been to commit their forces to battle.[102]

The revolution in positional warfare and the Combined Arms Revolution played a major role in halting Turkish expansion in the Balkans. The Ottomans, however, retained advantages derived from geography and the excellence of their logistical organization which were enough to induce stalemate. Western expansion at Ottoman expense had to await later developments: the flintlock musket, the socket bayonet, the perfection of linear tactics and the increased size of armies around the turn of the eighteenth century.

THE MEDITERRANEAN, 1510–CIRCA 1580

The first serious clashes between the beneficiaries of the Military Revolution and their Turkish foes in the Mediterranean were preceded by nearly a century of Spanish and Portuguese expansion along the North African Muslim coast and by a parallel process of Ottoman expansion in the Aegean. The Portuguese seizure of Ceuta in 1415 is generally taken as the starting point of Iberian expansion in the west; Ottoman expansion by sea in the Mediterranean began with the construction of the fleet which supported Mehmet II's attack on Constantinople in 1453.

The Portuguese and Spanish expanded into North Africa in the early 1400s at the expense of local Muslim dynasties which were unable to defend their cities against well-financed Iberian armies with their disciplined, salaried infantry and gunpowder artillery, paralleling the final stages of the *Reconquista* in Spain.[103] The inland topography, however, favored the lightly armed, highly mobile cavalry of the nomadic tribes of the Rif and Atlas and, as Andrew Hess has aptly put it, the terrain gobbled up armies.[104] In consequence, the Iberians, taking advantage of their superior ship and siege technology, established themselves in outpost cities along the coast, a clear antecedent for later developments in the Indian Ocean. The challenge to the Iberians came not by land but by sea and was a logical consequence of the integration of gunpowder technology into the Mediterranean system of maritime commerce and warfare. One of the early results of that integration was to convert the formerly marginal North African corsairs, who quickly mastered the new technology, into standard-bearers of Islam. The first clash of consequence was an attempt in 1510 by the Barbarossa brothers, Oruç and Hayreddin, to drive the Spanish from a newly-installed fortress blocking the port of the Muslim city of Bougie. The Muslims breached the wall with siege guns brought in by galley, but the ensuing assault was driven back with loss and the Barbarossas had to withdraw.[105] Though a Muslim failure, the action was a harbinger of things to come, for as the Iberians were expanding at the expense of weak sultanates in the west, the Ottomans were learning from their Venetian enemies in the east. The first clear indication that the Ottomans had mastered the use of gunpowder ordnance at sea as well as on land came in the Battle of Zonchio in 1499, where massive stone cannonballs inflicted heavy damage on some Venetian ships and induced others to withdraw.[106] This permitted the Turkish fleet to proceed with its cargo of siege guns, sappers and materiel to its objective, the Venetian fortress of Lepanto. The Venetian garrison surrendered on sighting the Turkish fleet.[107]

In the event, these initial clashes in the Mediterranean marked not the onset of new conquests, but the beginning of a new strategic balance. I have already noted the role of the *trace italienne* fortress in slowing Ottoman expansion; their pivotal repulse from Corfu in 1537 was symptomatic. The power of the new fortifications, however, was only part of the process. By the 1520s or 1530s, the Ottomans and their North African client states were as well adapted to the Mediterranean system of maritime commerce and warfare as were their Christian foes. That system, revolving around the symbiotic relationship between fortified port cities and squadrons of war galleys, was a highly efficient means of exploiting the available human and economic resources. It possessed, however, inherent characteristics which accommodated technological change in such a way as to produce strategic stasis. As late as the 1550s and -60s, fleets and squadrons of war galleys were a viable strategic means of projecting military power over long distances, and the Ottomans possessed important logistical advantages by virtue of their superior system of resource mobilization. The Ottomans also enjoyed the geographic advantage conferred by control of the northern coasts of the eastern Mediterranean,[108] an advantage magnified on occasion by French cooperation, as in 1543–44 when the Ottoman fleet wintered in Toulon. But from the 1550s, as I have written elsewhere, the accumulated weight of gunpowder ordnance which a war galley had to carry to be tactically viable combined with a geometric increase in the number of oarsmen needed to provide the dash speed under oars essential for survival in combat to sharply reduce the amount of water and provisions per man which a galley could carry.[109] The result was a progressive decline in the radius of action of galley fleets, accompanied by a sharp increase in operating costs accelerated by inflation.[110]

The unsuccessful siege of Malta in 1565 was the high-water mark of Ottoman expansion in the Mediterranean. Disastrous losses of experienced soldiers and seamen at Lepanto in 1571 followed. That the Ottomans were able to field a galley fleet in 1572 almost as large as the one they had lost the previous year was not a harbinger of Turkish resurgence at sea, for the human loss sustained at Lepanto could never be made good.[111] It was, however, clear evidence of the impressive

Ottoman ability to mobilize the resources needed to conduct galley warfare. The strategic relevance of that ability, however, was undermined by the declining strategic reach of galley fleets. The Turks and their Mediterranean enemies alike were overcome in the long run by progressive improvements in the commercial and military capabilities of North Atlantic sailing ships. Andrew Hess' argument that the Turks won the Mediterranean Wars, which ended in 1580 with a Habsburg-Ottoman truce in the wake of decisive Portuguese defeat at Al'cazar in 1578, is compelling.[112] Certainly, there can be no doubt concerning the decisiveness of Al'cazar, for the death of the Portuguese king there led to the absorption of Portugal by Habsburg Spain and the re-direction of Iberian efforts elsewhere, with momentous long-term consequences.

But Al'cazar also marked the beginning of the end for a dying system, for the Mediterranean was facing structural change imposed from without. This came in the 1580s in the form of broadside-armed northern sailing vessels which began to enter the Mediterranean in sufficient numbers to cause major distress to the nations whose commerce they displaced and on whose merchant ships they preyed. It was not a simple matter of northern broadside sailing ships rendering the war galley obsolete and driving their Mediterranean competitors from the seas,[113] for war galleys retained considerable military importance through the end of the seventeenth century. Moreover, certain of the Mediterranean states, notably Venice and the North African corsair principalities, showed considerable facility in the design and operation of sailing ships. In the final analysis Mediterranean power at sea was done in by exhaustion of timber reserves and a lack of economic strength and not by a lack of technological adaptability. If there is a useful hypothesis to be distilled from this, it is that the Ottomans adapted all too well to the Mediterranean system and in so doing irreversibly constrained their long-term options. They were not the only ones to do so. The last enduring Ottoman conquest, of Crete in 1645–1669, was won from Venice—which was following the same trajectory.

CONCLUSIONS

A number of common themes emerge from the above analysis. Perhaps most basic of these is the powerful influence of geography in shaping the development of institutions and technologies and influencing strategic and operational outcomes. Examples include the geographic peculiarities which fostered the development of an effective and highly specialized Mediterranean system of commerce and warfare at sea which, however, possessed inherent limitations which doomed it over the long run; the importance of Iberia's location in fostering the fusion of Mediterranean and North Atlantic methods of shipbuilding and navigation; and the logistical advantages to the Ottomans of the Danube river system. On a more superficial level, the ability of Spanish fighting men to deal effectively with strange and unexpected terrain, climates and comestibles in Mexico and the Andes provides a commentary on their logistical competence we would not otherwise have.

The second theme is the importance of social structures in fostering or inhibiting military innovation. If, as I have argued elsewhere, the causes of war are deeply imbedded in the social fabric,[114] the causes of victory are no less so. At first blush, this observation seems a statement of the obvious. But if the case studies have produced more questions than answers in this area, they have given that statement additional depth. We cannot say why, but it is evident from our examination of the Spanish in Italy, Mexico, and the Andes, and the Portuguese in the Indian Ocean, that the Christian societies of Iberia produced combatants with truly unusual capacities for technical and tactical innovation and for adaptability, cohesion and initiative in combat. Similarly, our examination of Ottoman military operations during their period of supposed decline points to a powerful underlying resilience and solidarity in their military institutions that few nonspecialists, at least, would have suspected. From the eve of the capture of Constantinople until their failure before Vienna in 1529, the Ottomans were highly receptive to military innovation, but then seem to have lost that capacity. The reasons for that failure are problematic, but, as with the reasons for Western success, were surely woven deeply into the social fabric.

The case studies highlight the importance of tactical and technological innovation, but in ways which emphasize the role of broad societal factors in fostering and adopting innovation. Why did it take root where it did and not elsewhere? The obvious hypothesis is the stimulus of defeat, a hypothesis given additional weight by the surprising capacity for tactical adjustment shown by Amerindians in fighting the conquistadors. That hypothesis fits English tactical innovations at the beginning of the Hundred Years War and the French development of siege artillery at its end; it clearly applies to the development of the *trace italienne* fortress and to Spanish developments in battlefield tactics in the Wars of Italy. But the Iberian Muslims showed neither tactical nor technological innovation in resisting their Christian neighbors; nor, initially, did their North African co-religionists. Indeed, the latter had to be shown the use of heavy ordnance by the Turks. I could go on, but these observations return us to the importance of the shaping role of the social fabric.

Finally, my analysis highlights the role of chance in shaping the Military Revolution. At any number of pivotal junctures the course of the Military Revolution was changed, in some cases dramatically so, by the decision of an individual or small group, by an unanticipated event, or by the outcome of a battle. I would argue that the outcomes in question were by no means pre-ordained and might have been very different. Consideration of "What ifs?" is fascinating and addresses my own objection that my schema is structured by knowledge of the outcome. But we need not consider only the "What ifs?" to make the point. The decisions by Charles VII of France and Sultan Mehmed II to commit resources to the development, construction and use of heavy siege guns heavily influenced the course of the Military Revolution. Charles VIII's decision to invade Italy and Ferdinand of Aragón's decision to intervene in response may have had inconclusive strategic results, but their impact on the Military Revolution was enormous. Indeed, if we were to pick a single motivating impulse which set the course of the Military Revolution during the period with which we are concerned here, it would be that which emerged from those two related decisions. But that invasion might have come a decade earlier, and from the southeast rather than the northwest. To be more precise, it did come, but was not sustained. In 1480 Mehmed II threw an invasion force into Apulia and seized the nominally Byzantine city of Otranto. Mehmed died unexpectedly the following year and in the turmoil of the succession struggle the garrison was abandoned and forced to surrender. The throne fell to Bayezid II, who was forced to adopt a non-aggressive policy in the Mediterranean until the death in 1495 of his brother Cem, who had fled to the west after being defeated.[115] Without going into the laws and customs governing the Ottoman succession, this outcome appeared to be among the least likely. In almost any other scenario, the Turks would have maintained themselves in strength at Otranto and moved to expand their foothold, though how aggressively we can only guess. The first serious encounters of Spanish armies beyond Iberia would thus have been with the Turk rather than the French and Swiss, and Italian engineers would have had to adjust their fortress designs to Turkish rather than French methods. I leave consideration of likely outcomes to the reader, but with the reminder that the Imperial troops who faced down Suleiman I's army before Vienna in 1532 did so on the basis of lessons which Gonsalvo de Córdova and his men had distilled from hard experience fighting the French and Swiss.

Notes

1. (Cambridge, 1988).

2. Parker, *Military Revolution*, 5.

3. "The Military Revolutions of the Hundred Years' War," *The Journal of Military History*, Vol. 57, No. 2 (April 1993), 241–278; reprinted with revisions above, chapter 3.

4. This approach was suggested to me by Theodore K. Rabb.

5. Andrew C. Hess, "The Ottoman Conquest of Egypt and the Beginning of the Sixteenth-Century World War," *International Journal of Middle East Studies*, Vol. 4 (1973), 62.

6. The Safavid alignment with the Shii sect of Islam, which enjoyed widespread support in eastern Anatolia, posed a serious internal threat to the Ottomans with which Selim I, The Grim, dealt in draconian fashion following his accession in 1512, Hess, "Ottoman Conquest," 67. The parallel with Charles V's later problems with German Protestantism is inescapable.

7. The link between territorial acquisitions in the west and the health of the empire was timar, a system of land allocation, taxation, local rule and military manpower mobilization which was a central pillar of the Ottoman state. Timar was based on the award of non-hereditary, feudatory land grants which gave the holder the right to collect agricultural taxes, normally in return for military service as an armored horse archer. Timar thus provided a

decentralized, self-supporting source of fighting manpower. In addition, timar holders performed important local governmental functions. The Ottomans, however, were perpetually short of cash and timar holdings were diverted to support administrative office holders, ladies of the harem and so on, particularly when the acquisition of booty from conquests began to fall off. A steady influx of new land was therefore necessary to sustain the numbers of timariot cavalry, who were numerically the most important element in imperial field armies. By 1529, potential timar lands in Anatolia, Syria and Egypt had long since been apportioned, and in the east the seizure of conquered lands from Muslim owners posed legal problems. The continued acquisition of Christian lands in the west was therefore necessary for the continuing health of the state. For a concise explanation of timar, Norman Itzkowitz, *Ottoman Empire and Islamic Tradition* (New York, 1972), 40–49; for the connection between the decay of the timar system and military decline, John F. Guilmartin, Jr., "Ideology and Conflict: the Wars of the Ottoman Empire, 1453–1606," *The Origin and Prevention of Major Wars*, Robert I. Rotberg and Theodore K. Rabb, eds. (Cambridge, 1989), 159–60. Ottoman gains at the expense of Venice, 1537–40 and 1570–73, and the seizure of Chios from Genoa in 1566 yielded military and economic advantages but little land.

8. The distances speak for themselves; for the wind and current patterns which made communications in the Caribbean difficult, Paul E. Hoffman, *The Spanish Crown and Defense of the Caribbean, 1535–1585* (Baton Rouge, Louisiana, 1980), 5–8. The Portuguese also faced enormous distances, but the extent of Spain's conquests on land was without precedent.

9. Charles W. C. Oman, *The Art of War in the XVIth Century* (London, 1937), 3.

10. Norman Itzkowitz introduced me to this argument in his Ottoman history seminars at Princeton University, 1967–68. Halil Inalcik states that "the center of gravity of the [Ottoman] state moved to Rumelia," that is from Asia Minor to Europe, when Edirne became the "main capital" of the divided empire after Tamerlane's capture of Bayezid I at Ankara in 1402, "The Rise of the Ottoman Empire," *The Cambridge History of Islam*, Vol. I, P. M. Holt, Ann K. S. Lambton and Bernard Lewis eds. (Cambridge, 1970), 278–79. After defeating his rival princes and reuniting the empire in 1413, Murad I made Edirne his seat of government.

11. When western Europeans became aware of a significant and permanent diminution of the Ottoman threat is unclear, and I know of no systematic study of the question. German Protestants invoked the Turkish threat to good advantage in their negotiations with the Emperor long after Suleiman I's repulse from Vienna. Stephen A. Fischer-Galati, *Ottoman Imperialism and German Protestantism 1521–1555* (Cambridge, Massachusetts, 1959).

12. Rogers, "Military Revolutions," 243–44; above, p. 56. I have used the term Infantry Revolution to describe the development of infantry in Europe, 1200–1500, "War, Technology of," *Encyclopædia Britannica* (1991), 539, too long a period to be described as a revolution in the usual sense, as noted by Rogers, "Military Revolutions," 244 (above, p. 79), n. 12. Here I have adopted Rogers' concept of a more tightly defined revolution beginning with the Battle of Courtrai, 1302, but place more emphasis on the Swiss.

13. Delbrück, *Medieval Warfare*, 588, notes that the Swiss undoubtedly marched to the cadence of a drum, but cautions that their notion of marching may have been quite different from modern ideas. Current orthodoxy holds that marching in step was abandoned in classical times and re-introduced by Maurice of Nassau from about 1590. There is, however, iconographic evidence to the contrary: "Army on the March," a woodcut by the Housebook Master, probably dating from the late 1470s, reproduced in John R. Hale, *Art-*

ists and Warfare in the Renaissance (New Haven, 1990), 8, shows six units of infantry, the first of which, though not in ordered ranks, is clearly marching in step to fife and drum while the rest are not (I disagree with Hale's interpretation that all are "strolling"). The 1529 painting *The Battle of Issus* by Albrecht Altdorfer in the Alte Pinakotheck, Munich, shows a column of *Landsknechts* with pikes shouldered running in perfect step. The 1533 Melchior Feselen battle piece *The Siege of Alesia*, also in the Alte Pinakotheck, depicts formations of *Landsknechts* in less detail, but in ways which clearly suggest marching in step. Turning to tactical evidence, from Sempach in 1386 until Ceresole in 1544 the Swiss had no equals in dismounted shock action. A telling datum is that among late medieval and early modern specialists in pike combat, only the Swiss could successfully disengage from a lost battle, Steven Stein, "Pike vs. Pike: An Analysis of the Battles Between the Swiss and *Landsknechts*," unpublished Ohio State University term paper, History 625.01, Professor Guilmartin, Spring 1993. There was something very different about the Swiss, and before others began to imitate them the only likely candidate is marching in step. For the positive effect of close order drill on unit cohesion and battlefield discipline, William H. McNeill, *The Pursuit of Power: Technology, Armed Force and Society since A.D. 1000* (Chicago, 1982), 132–35, esp. 132 n. 12.

14. This is a brutal abridgment of some three quarters of a century of interrelated developments in which the Swiss transformed themselves from predominately halberd-wielding infantry which required advantages of terrain and surprise to defeat armored chivalry to units armed predominately with the pike which could maneuver with confidence in the open field and run down any force in their path. For the rise of the Swiss, Delbrück, *Medieval Warfare*, 545–597, and Oman, *Middle Ages*, 233–280.

15. Oman, *Middle Ages*, 348–53; interestingly, the infantry in question were archers who fought in the center of the Ottoman array from behind a barrier of sharpened wooden stakes, much in the manner of contemporary English longbowmen.

16. Oman, *XVIth Century*, 356.

17. Björn Landström, *The Ship: An Illustrated History* (Garden City, New York, 1961), 78, terms this "the great revolution of the three masted ship." Though some details have been superseded by archaeological findings, *The Ship*, 78–99, gives a useful summation. Roger C. Smith, *Vanguard of Empire: Ships of Exploration in the Age of Columbus* (Oxford, 1993), is an exhaustive account of the final stages of the process from an Iberian perspective.

18. The principal problem lay in the way in which cartographers handled variation, the angular difference between true and magnetic north. Cartographers at first compensated for the difference by distorting shapes and bearings on their charts so that navigation could proceed on the assumption that true and magnetic north were the same. On a local, Mediterranean, scale, this was workable: there are no tides in the Mediterranean and most long range navigation was conducted between mid-March and mid-October when high seas and strong winds were rare. In contrast to Europe's Atlantic coasts, the bottom dropped off sharply in most areas, permitting safe navigation close to shore, and sheltered anchorages and beaches where ships could be dragged ashore were common. Under such conditions, the mariner could make landfall without knowing his precise location and determine his position from the contour of the coastline on his chart, then proceed on to his destination.

19. The chronology has not been established with precision, but it is clear that the Portuguese led the way and the Spanish were not far behind; J. H. Parry, *The Age of Reconnaissance* (New York, 1964), 113–14. By the time of Columbus' first voyage, skilled Iberian navigators clearly understood variation, the difference between true and magnetic north, and

had a growing appreciation of deviation, the difference between local and true magnetic north.

20. The date is an educated guess; see John F. Guilmartin, Jr., "The Early Provision of Artillery Armament on Mediterranean War Galleys," *The Mariner's Mirror,* Vol. 59, No. 3 (August 1973), 259–60: in 1481 the *Real* (Royal Galley) of Alfonso the Magnanimous of Aragon mounted "two bombards," by implication relatively large guns. Note, however, that in nautical usage "bombard" might designate a relatively small piece: Smith, *Vanguard of Empire,* 153 and 156–61, citing early sixteenth century references to caravels mounting as many as ten *lombardas* and of a *bombarda* used to arm a ship's boat. Kelly R. DeVries, "A 1445 Reference to Shipboard Artillery," *Technology and Culture,* Vol. 31, No. 4 (October 1990), 818–29, explicates the ordnance inventory of a Burgundian war galley which contains the earliest unequivocal references to shipboard artillery of known types of which I am aware, but the largest pieces are small breech loaders only four feet long which probably threw a stone ball of about three pounds.

21. The invention of the water-tight gunport is traditionally attributed to a French shipwright from Brest, one Descharges, Frank Howard, *Sailing Ships of War, 1400–1860* (New York, 1979), 53, and, for a useful discussion of the earliest naval gun carriages, 38–39.

22. The earliest example for which a strong case can be made is Henry VIII's warship *Mary Rose,* laid down in 1509, Margaret Rule, *The Mary Rose: The Excavation and Raising of Henry VIII's Flagship* (London, 1982), 152, though ships were no doubt fitted, or retrofitted, with small numbers of gunports earlier than this.

23. Howard, *Sailing Ships,* 45–46; the key datum is the 1546 Anthony Anthony Roll, depicting the King's ships in that year.

24. Rogers, "Military Revolutions," 258 (above, p. 64).

25. Christopher Duffy, *Siege Warfare: The Fortress in the Early Modern World, 1494–1660* (London, 1979), 2.

26. Rogers, "Military Revolutions," 264–272 (above, pp. 66–73). This is not to say that cannon were never used to bring down walls before 1420 or that cannon balls were never lofted over them thereafter; but, to cite the most prominent and probably most important example, the systematic use of battery to reduce English fortresses in the final stages of the Hundred Years War clearly *was* unprecedented in scope and pace.

27. Just how long that was is a matter of debate; suffice it to say that Rogers "Military Revolution," 267–68 (above, p. 68), is correct in stating that barrels with bores 1 to 1.5 times their diameter were too short and that very large guns with bores three times their diameter were long enough. The question revolves around the internal ballistics of black powder, which differ fundamentally from those of modern propellants and remain incompletely understood, see John F. Guilmartin, Jr., "Ballistics in the Black Powder Era," *British Naval Armaments,* Royal Armouries Conference Proceedings 1, Robert D. Smith, ed. (London, 1989), 73–98.

28. For the definitive examination and technical analysis of surviving large bombards, Robert D. Smith and Ruth Rhynas Brown, *Bombards:* Mons Meg *and her Sisters,* Royal Armouries Monograph 1 (London: Trustees of the Royal Armouries, 1989).

29. The amount of propulsive energy in a given mass of gunpowder was the same whether or not the powder was corned, that is formed into grains, but the ballistic properties of corned powder differed dramatically from those of earlier serpentine powder in which the ingredients were ground to a fine powder and mixed dry, Guilmartin, "Ballistics," 76.

30. Guns *de cupro*—presumably bronze—are recorded in European inventories from the mid-fourteenth century, but these were very small pieces. The thesis that wrought iron hooped bombards sparked the revolution with which we are concerned here is supported by the fact that the earliest heavy bronze pieces of modern proportions were cast with narrow raised hoops and reinforcing rings in obvious imitation of wrought iron construction. The hoops and rings of a wrought iron gun of composite construction, heated and shrunk into place to internally stress the barrel, were structurally essential. The equivalent rings on a monolithic bronze barrel added nothing to strength of the piece.

31. Oman, *XVIth Century,* 49; Duffy, *Siege Warfare,* 8.

32. Duffy, *Siege Warfare,* 8–9.

33. Although the difference was less than one might expect from the enormous disparity in projectile size. Impact energy, and therefore destructive effect, is a function of kinetic energy which increases with the square of the velocity, from $K_e = \frac{1}{2} mv^2$. Muzzle velocities higher than 250 m/sec are unlikely for the monster bombards and we know that the last muzzle-loading smoothbore cannon in British naval service obtained muzzle velocities of 488 m/sec (1600 ft/sec) from powder which was essentially the same as that used by Charles' gunners, Guilmartin, "Ballistics," 93. *Mons Meg,* the enormous bombard on display in Edinburgh, threw a stone ball weighing about 150 kg, Smith and Brown, *Bombards,* 49. Given the above velocities, *Mons Meg* would have imparted only twice as much energy to its projectile as would one of Charles' guns throwing a 20 kg ball and would have surpassed one firing a 12 kg ball by a factor of only 3.3:1. Reducing the velocity of the later guns to 425 m/sec would change the ratios to 2.6:1 and 4:1 respectively. These figures represent energy at the muzzle, and the cast iron balls would have lost less velocity to aerodynamic drag en route to the target than less dense projectiles of stone.

34. Frederick Lewis Taylor, *The Art of War in Italy, 1494–1529* (Cambridge, 1981), 83–89; quoting Guicciardini and Jovius Giovio, *Istoria del Suo Tempo* (Venice, 1581), states flatly that "in 1494 the Italians saw gun carriages for the first time;" see also Oman, *XVIth Century,* 49, and Duffy, *Siege Warfare,* 8.

35. In comparison with other iron-throwing guns. The barrels of stone-throwing guns weighed a half to a third less than those firing an iron ball of the same weight, but stone balls were far more expensive. In addition, the external diameters of the barrels of stone-throwing guns were two to three times larger, requiring heavier and more cumbersome carriages.

36. Duffy, *Siege Warfare,* 8–9. Hitherto, artillery in Italy had been pulled by hired teams contracted for the occasion and heavy guns were customarily drawn by oxen.

37. Duffy, *Siege Warfare,* 15–16, 192. For the Italian system of permanent fortifications, ibid., 25–34. Duffy's analytical accounts of the sieges of Pisa and Padua, 15–16, are particularly valuable. Italian engineers had experimented with all the essential elements of the *trace italienne* fortress before 1494, but did not apply them systematically and in combination until Charles' guns forced the issue. Note that the *trace italienne* and sunken profile were at first not necessarily applied in combination. The fortress of Nettuno, built in 1501, was the first fortification designed from the outset with a complete *trace italienne,* but had high walls and a decidedly medieval profile, Horst de la Croix, *Military Considerations in City Planning: Fortifications* (New York, 1972), 44–45, figs. 62, 63.

38. Rogers, "Military Revolutions," 277 (above, p. 77).

39. Oman, *XVIth Century,* 51–62 is the basic text.

40. The army with which Gonsalvo landed in Calabria in 1495 was composed of 500 *jinetes*, javelin-armed light cavalry; 100 men-at-arms; and 1,500 infantry, of whom "the majority" were Aragonese sword-and-buckler men, Oman, *XVIth Century,* 52.

41. The Spanish use of terrain and field fortifications was so competent as to obscure the growing power of their tactical formations. Spanish infantry might have been able to stand up to a Swiss charge on level ground—if so they would have been the only ones who could—but we will never know: they were too smart to try!

42. A point which the Duke of Alba grasped more clearly than other generals of his day, William S. Maltby, *Alba: A Biography of Fernando Alvarez de Toledo, Third Duke of Alba, 1507–1582* (Berkeley, 1983), 55–6.

43. Cited by Oman, *XVIth Century,* 44.

44. Oman, *XVIth Century,* 678–81, esp. 681 and 765, where the Imperial tactical dispositions before Vienna are described. Güns is roughly halfway between the Drava and Vienna and it might appear from a superficial look at the map that Suleiman was driving on Vienna from the south, but considerations of terrain, time, logistics and space made this impossible in a single season.

45. Duffy, *Siege Warfare,* 201; the Ottomans campaigned to the west with limited objectives in 1540 and 1566, Suleiman dying in the field during the latter campaign. In 1568, the Ottomans and Habsburgs concluded a peace treaty which lasted until 1593.

46. Charles W. C. Oman, *The Art of War in the Middle Ages A. D. 378–1515,* rev. and ed. by John Beeler (Ithaca, New York, 1953; first ed., Oxford, 1885), 162.

47. These were the Tainos. Generally pacific, their level of technology was roughly Neolithic. The neighboring Caribs were warlike, but were no more advanced technologically. See Irving Rouse, *The Tainos: Rise and Decline of the People Who Greeted Columbus* (New Haven, Connecticut, 1992), 17, 18–19, 22–23.

48. Bernal Díaz del Castillo, *The Discovery and Conquest of Mexico, 1517–1521,* A. P. Maudslay, tr. (New York, 1956), 7–9; Díaz was an eyewitness.

49. Díaz, *Conquest,* 11–18.

50. Díaz, *Conquest,* 14–16; interestingly, Díaz described the warriors as "very big men," suggesting that they benefited from a diet richer in protein than the Maya and Mexican warriors who were his standard for comparison.

51. Díaz, *Conquest,* 19–28.

52. Miguel Leon-Portilla, ed., *The Broken Spears: The Aztec Account of the Conquest of Mexico,* Angel Maria Garibay K. and Lysander Kemp, tr. (Boston, 1962), 3–12.

53. Charles E. Sharpe, *To Shake the Foundations of Heaven: A Military Analysis of the Spanish Overthrow of the Mexia-Aztec Empire,* unpublished MA thesis (The Ohio State University, 1992). The size of the population of pre-conquest Mexico is the subject of intense debate and Sharpe's estimate is in line with population figures based on agricultural technology and the carrying capacity of the land, cited in Francis J. Brooks, "Revising the Conquest of Mexico: Smallpox, Sources and Population," *Journal of Interdisciplinary History,* Vol. XXIV, No. 1 (Summer 1993), 6–7. Brooks' calculations support the lower estimates and his opinion, 29, that as many as 100,000 may have died of smallpox in Tenochtitlan during the siege suggests that Sharpe's figures are conservative. Francisco López de Gómara, *Cortés: The Life of the Conqueror by his Secretary [Istoria de la Conquista de Mexico (Zaragoza, 1552)],* Lesley Byrd Sympson, tr. and ed. (Berkeley, 1964), 156, states that Tenochtitlan had 60,000 houses "seldom containing fewer than two, three or ten inhabitants" each, suggesting a population of about 300,000.

54. Sharpe, *Foundations*, 177, 183–186.

55. Sharpe, *Foundations*, 196.

56. Sharpe, *Foundations*, 196–98; Gómara, *Cortés*, 225. The size of the Spanish force is subject to debate; for the losses in the breakout from Tenochtitlan, see Gómara, *Cortés*, 221.

57. John F. Guilmartin, Jr., "The Cutting Edge: An Analysis of the Spanish Invasion and Overthrow of the Inca Empire, 1532–1539," *Transatlantic Encounters: Europeans and Andeans in the Sixteenth Century*, Kenneth J. Andrien and Rolena Adorno, eds. (Berkeley: University of California Press, 1991), 46. The size of the Inca force is from John Hemming, *The Conquest of the Incas* (New York, 1983), 39, citing a letter written by Hernando Pizarro shortly after the fact.

58. Hemming, *Conquest*, 153, 156–58.

59. Hemming, *Conquest*, 191.

60. John H. Elliott, "The Spanish Conquest and Settlement of America," *Cambridge History of Latin America*, Vol. I, *Colonial Latin America* (Cambridge, 1984; henceforth *CHLA*), 175–76.

61. Gómara, *Cortés*, 225.

62. Hemming, *Conquest*, 39–555; Pizarro's estimate is the lowest cited or implied and, as Hemming notes, the numbers tended to increase with time.

63. Hemming, *Conquest*, 68.

64. Hemming, *Conquest*, 65. By comparison, the Tlaxcalans told Cortés that the Aztecs could put two to three hundred thousand men in the field, Gómara, *Cortés*, 122.

65. Sharpe, *Foundations*, 37–57, for the historiography of the Mexican case; Guilmartin, "Cutting Edge," 41–42, for early attempts to explain the Andean case.

66. Brooks, "Revising the Conquest," esp. 16–29.

67. Guilmartin, "Cutting Edge," 47.

68. Nathan Wachtel, "The Indian and the Spanish Conquest," *CHLA*, 210–211, for an ethnohistorical perspective; see also Elliott, "The Spanish Conquest," 174.

69. Wachtel, *loc. cit.*

70. The pivotal encounters were those between Cortés' force and the Tlaxcalans; Gómara, *Cortés*, 97–106 for the battle, and 114–116 for the negotiations by which the Tlaxcalans allied themselves with the Spaniards against the Aztecs.

71. The *bergantine* was a small oared fighting vessel about the size of a modern lifeboat, but slimmer and probably a bit longer, which was reasonably swift under sail. The main armament of those used to blockade Tenochtitlan was probably a swivel gun in the bow, most likely a *verso*.

72. Oman, *XVIth Century*, 130–149. The Imperialists lost the battle, but not because of any deficiency in the Spanish infantry: the outnumbered Imperial cavalry was provoked into a premature charge by artillery fire from the flank and driven off by the French cavalry.

73. James Lockhart, *The Men of Cajamarca: A Social and Biographical Study of the First Conquerors of Peru* (Austin, Texas, 1972), 22, makes the point explicitly with regard to the Pizarro expedition; he estimates that only three or four of the 168 Spaniards who fought at Cajamarca had European military experience and can be certain about only two.

74. Lockhart, *Men of Cajamarca*, 18, 18 n. 1, argues that the conquistadors were not "soldiers" as the term is commonly understood, and certainly not "troops," and that the application of these inaccurate labels has badly distorted our understanding of them and their

motivation. From the socio-economic perspective, Lockhart is clearly correct and his argument is a valuable corrective. My perspective, however, is military and tactical; my point is that whatever their social complexion and economic motivation, the conquistadors became soldiers in combat.

75. Guilmartin, "Cutting Edge," 54: in the division of Atahualpa's ransom, horsemen on the average received twice as much as footmen.

76. David B. Ralston, *Exporting the European Army: The Introduction of European Military Techniques and Institutions into the Extra-European World, 1600–1914* (Chicago, 1990), 2.

77. McNeill, *Pursuit of Power*, 133. McNeill notes that this ability was demonstrated so routinely in the eighteenth century that we tend to take it for granted.

78. Bailey W. Diffie and George D. Winius, *Foundations of the Portuguese Empire 1415–1580*, Vol. I of *Europe and the World in the Age of Expansion*, Boyd D. Schaefer, ed. (Minneapolis, Minnesota, 1977), 181.

79. I have depended on the account of the campaign by Peter Padfield, *Tide of Empires: Decisive Naval Campaigns and the Rise of the West*, Vol. 1, *1481–1654* (London, 1979), 48–52.

80. Artillery terminology was in flux and Portuguese usage was particularly complex, so I have used the generic term gun for anything larger than shoulder arms.

81. Geneviève Bouchon, 'Regent of the Sea': *Cannanore's Response to Portuguese Expansion, 1507–1528*, Louise Shackley, tr. (Oxford, 1988), 86–89.

82. Bouchon, *Regent of the Sea*, 93, 93 n. 163.

83. In 1536, a *cañon serpentino* was mounted as the main centerline bow gun on one of the 23 galleys in Don Alvaro de Bazan's squadron. The term *serpentino* served to differentiate the piece from other *cañones*, indicating that it was of a type no longer in general service, perhaps a wrought iron piece. All but two of the other galleys mounted a full cannon (*cañon*) or large culverin (*culebrina grueso*) in that position, so we may reasonably assume that the *cañon serpentino* was of equivalent size and power, the moreso since the galley in question was otherwise one of the more heavily armed, cf. Guilmartin, "The Early Provision of Artillery," Table II, 274–75.

84. Fabrics and fibrous materials are generally effective against low-velocity projectiles; however the events in question took place during the southwest monsoon, so the bales were probably water-soaked. What effect that would have had is unclear: on the one hand, soaking would have increased the mass of the bales; on the other it would have reduced the shock attenuation effects of the cotton fibers and lubricated them, allowing them to move aside more easily, Peter N. Jones, letter to the author, August 17 1993. My best guess, based on Jones' explanation of terminal ballistic considerations, is that soaked bales would probably have been a bit more effective against low velocity scatter shot and stone projectiles, but prone to shatter if hit by a sufficiently large, dense projectile at high velocity.

85. The matter is complicated by the fact that the Portuguese also had a *camelo*, a piece which fired a stone ball of 10–15 kg (22–33 lb.), Bouchon, *Regent of the Sea*, 94, 94 n. 166, and a 14.5 kg *camelo* in the Museu Militar, Lisbon, cast by Diogo Pires in 1518. It is hard to imagine that such a piece could not penetrate a bale of cotton, wet or dry, but that may have been the case; see the preceding note.

86. Dhow is a generic European term for the large, lateen rigged Arab sailing vessels of the Indian Ocean; at the time they were double enders and at least the smaller ones were of sewn construction. Prau, or prahu, from Malay for boat or vessel, is a similarly generic

term for relatively small local Indian and Indonesian sailing craft, generally fitted with a low lug sail; some had outriggers. Landström, *The Ship,* 212, 224.

87. Padfield, *Tide of Empires,* 48–52.

88. Diffie and Winius, *Foundations,* 255–56.

89. Diffie and Winius, *Foundations,* 257–59.

90. Diffie and Winius, *Foundations,* 214.

91. Parker, *Military Revolution,* 118–19.

92. Don Alonzo Enríquez de Guzmán, *Libro de la vida y costumbres de don Alonso Enríquez de Guzmán* (1543), C. R. Markham, trans., The Hakluyt Society, First Series, Vol. 29, 101, quoted in John Hemming, Conquest, 204.

93. Hemming, *Conquest,* 204.

94. Oman, *XVIth Century,* 680.

95. Caroline Finkel, *The Administration of Warfare: the Ottoman Military Campaigns in Hungary, 1593–1606,* Vol. 14 in *Beihefte zur Wiener Zeitschrift für die Kunde des Morgenlandes,* Arne A. Ambros and Anton Schaendlinger, eds. (Vienna, 1988), 64–65; map 325.

96. For the problems caused the Spanish by their lack of political control over their lines of communication, Geoffrey Parker, *The Army of Flanders and the Spanish Road, 1567–1659* (Cambridge, 1972), 50–79, cited in Finkel, *Administration of Warfare,* 64–65.

97. Finkel, *Administration of Warfare,* 119–208; see also G. Veinstein, "Some Views on Provisioning in the Hungarian Campaigns of Soleyman the Magnificent." *Osmanistische Studien Zur Wirtschaft-und Sozialgeschichte In memoriam Vanco Boskoi,* Hans Georg Majer, ed. (Wiesbaden, 1986), 177–83, and the characterization of Ottoman methods by Virginia Arkan, "The One-Eyed Fighting the Blind; Mobilization, Supply, and Command in the Russo-Turkish War of 1768–1774," *The International History Review,* Vol. XV, No. 2 (May 1993), 231.

98. Finkel, *Administration of Warfare,* 130 ff.

99. Finkel, *Administration of Warfare,* 91–93.

100. Duffy, *Siege Warfare,* 215–18.

101. Duffy, *Siege Warfare,* 199–204, 210–219.

102. Oman, *XVIth Century,* 747–52. The victory was also something of a fluke: after breaking the Muslim center and driving it back, the Imperial infantry became disordered looting the enemy camp and was taken in flank and destroyed by an uncommitted Turkish cavalry reserve.

103. Andrew C. Hess. *The Forgotten Frontier: A History of the Sixteenth-Century Ibero-African Frontier* (Chicago, 1978), 12, 19–20; Weston F. Cook, Jr., "The Cannon Conquest of Nāṣrid Spain and the End of the Reconquista," *Journal of Military History,* Vol. 57, No. 1 (January 1993), 50–54.

104. Hess, *Forgotten Frontier,* 54.

105. Hess, *Forgotten Frontier,* 61.

106. Frederic C. Lane, "Naval Actions and Fleet Organization, 1499–1502," *Renaissance Venice,* John R. Hale, ed. (London, 1973), 155, cites a letter by a Venetian commander exculpating himself for his ineffectiveness which "dwells on the impact, both physical and moral" of 150-pound stone cannonballs striking his ship; these were apparently fired by shipboard guns.

107. Lane, "Naval Actions," 149–54, for the campaign and battle.

108. See John H. Pryor, *Geography, Technology and War: Studies in the Maritime History of the Mediterranean 649–1571* (Cambridge, 1988), esp. Ch. 7, "The Turks," 165–196.

109. Guilmartin, *Gunpowder and Galleys*, 221–29.

110. Guilmartin, *Gunpowder and Galleys*, Fig. 11–14, 222–25.

111. Guilmartin, *Gunpowder and Galleys*, 251.

112. Hess, "The Battle of Lepanto and Its Place in Mediterranean History," *Past and Present*, no. 57 (November 1972), 72–73.

113. As Hess, *Forgotten Frontier*, 14, n. 12, points out, this is the implication of Carlo M. Cipolla's *Guns Sails and Empires: Technological Innovation and the Early Stages of European Expansion 1400–1700* (New York, 1965).

114. Guilmartin, "Ideology and Conflict," 174–75.

115. By Ottoman law and custom, each brother's claim to the throne was equally legitimate, and Cem, who enjoyed support among tribal groups, posed a political threat to Bayezid as long as he lived, particularly after he fell into Christian hands in 1482, Hess, "Conquest of Egypt," 63–64.

Rejoinder

◄ 13 ►

In Defense of *The Military Revolution*[1]

GEOFFREY PARKER

ALTHOUGH *The Military Revolution* is a relatively small book, it took twenty years to write. I had read and enjoyed Michael Roberts' seminal article before starting work on my dissertation and, while studying the Spanish Army of Flanders for my Ph.D. between 1965 and 1968, I looked for evidence that would support his model of a backward, benighted, ineffectual force. But I failed to find it. Instead at the battle of Nördlingen in 1634, Habsburg troops fighting in traditional fashion inflicted a crushing and decisive defeat on the masters of the new military science, forcing Sweden and her allies to abandon all their conquests in south Germany. It was most puzzling and the last chapter of my dissertation, entitled "A military revolution?", expressed my doubts. With that grim humor for which academics are famous, the History Faculty Board of Cambridge University appointed Michael Roberts to serve as my external examiner; I walked to my oral defence with heavy heart. Much to my surprise, however, that generous and gracious man told me that he found my critique convincing and advised me to publish it separately as an article, instead of tucking it away at the back of a book. In the event, I transferred some of the material to the front instead, to form the introductory chapter of *The Army of Flanders and the Spanish Road* (1972), and published the rest in 1976 as "The Military Revolution—a myth?" (see chapter 2 above.)

And there the matter rested until the summer of 1982 when, while beginning research at the archives of Simancas for a book on the Spanish Armada, I received an invitation from the Master and Fellows of Trinity College Cambridge to deliver four lectures on a topic—any topic—concerning Military History. Simon Adams, then also working at Simancas, suggested that I might take the opportunity to develop the theme advanced in that first chapter of *The Army of Flanders and the Spanish Road:* namely that early modern warfare involved far more sieges than battles, and that "actions" between men with firearms in and around the trenches proved far more common than full-scale encounters decided by saber and lance in the field.

It sounded so simple, but it turned into something that took me around the world in search of material. I decided to begin by arguing that the emergence around 1520 of new techniques of artillery-resistant fortification—the most successful of which was known in Italy as *alla moderna* (in the modern style) and elsewhere as the *trace italienne*—led not only to the predominance of protracted sieges in Western warfare, but also to substantial increases in the size and dramatic changes in the composition of armies. For to capture a town or city defended by bastions required large numbers of disciplined infantry, not an elite force of knightly cavalry; while to defend one's own expanding stock of new-style fortresses also called for unprecedented numbers of men and guns. These related developments presented the states of early modern Europe with two new sets of problems: how best to deploy the new infantry in action, and how to maintain them. Solutions to both came but slowly. The first problem gave rise to a succession of experiments to maximize the firepower of the troops and to increase the proportion of an army able to engage the enemy directly in action. The second produced a whole range of logistical challenges, for if armies now needed to be substantially larger and better armed, how could they be recruited and kept up to strength, clothed and fed, equipped and paid? And how were the expensive new defenses to be financed? Moreover the sixteenth century also saw a revolution in naval warfare, with the invention of the immensely expensive ship-of-the-line, which defeated its foes by artillery broadsides instead of by ramming or boarding. Over a century elapsed before the European states had expanded their administrative apparatus sufficiently to cope with all the logistical and financial consequences of the military revolution.

These innovations also proved highly significant for non-Europeans as well. On the one hand, the technique of gunnery bombardment at sea (and of building ships sturdy enough to deploy heavy cannon effectively) was unknown to most other societies, and so conferred an instant advantage on the Europeans as they sought to expand; on the other, thanks to the *trace italienne*, the small European enclaves perched around the coasts of Asia and Africa could defend themselves efficiently against their powerful neighbors until help arrived. The whole thrust of the enterprise therefore changed from a reconsideration of the military history of early modern Europe to an attempt to explain the rise of the West.

Researching all this took me to libraries, archives and museums not only in Europe, but also in India and Ceylon, in east and south Africa, and in east and southeast Asia. In Japan I found a remarkable parallel, for warfare there in the sixteenth century evolved in almost exactly the same sequence as in Europe: the introduction of firearms seemed to produce massive new artillery fortresses, huge armies, and rapid state-building, culminating in vigorous overseas expansion (the Korean campaigns of Toyotomi Hideyoshi in the 1590s).[2] Encouraged by this unexpected corroboration, I delivered the four Lees-Knowles lectures at Cambridge in 1984 and, after substantial revision and expansion, plus a visit to consult with Michael Roberts, published them in 1988.

On the whole, *The Military Revolution* received a good press. Translations appeared in Spanish, French, German, Italian, Greek, and Japanese; and a lively debate ensued.[3] Even Islamic fundamentalists welcomed it (at least until the Gulf War.) "The lessons for Muslims of today are obvious," claimed a long review in the journal *Crescent:* "To ensure freedom from and victory against the adversaries [i.e. the West], military adaptation and innovation are imperative".[4] So far, the only substantial critical notice remains a seven-page "essay review" by Bert S. Hall and Kelly R. DeVries, published in *Technology and Culture.* The scale, however, is deceptive for 90 per cent of their critique consisted of attacks on my dates,[5] my facts,[6] and my *apparatus criticus.*[7]

The sole substantive issue raised by Drs. Hall and DeVries was to deny the link I posited between technological innovation and military growth in early modern Europe: "Like a whole generation of economic historians," they announced, "Parker uses technology as a 'black box', a primary *explanans* whose nature is itself inexplicable" (p. 506). Although this important point unfortunately remained tucked away in the final paragraph of their "essay review," and remained undeveloped,[8] it nevertheless constitutes one of four general criticisms—conceptual, chronological and geographical as well as technological—leveled, both in the essays printed above and elsewhere, against my analysis of a military revolution in early modern Europe. Each deserves separate consideration.

1. CONCEPTUAL

The most fundamental criticism of the book concerns the use—or misuse—of the term "revolution" for a process that lasted three centuries. According to Clifford Rogers, "The length of time involved can range from a year to a century, depending on the scope of the revolution—depending on whether it is a government, a social structure, an idea or an economy which is overturned—but in none of these cases does the time-frame during which the reversal takes place exceed a single (maximum) human life span" (page 76 above.) Now clearly not all "revolutions" in History are alike. In the political sphere, one expects a "sharp, sudden change or attempted change in the location of political power which involved either the use or the threat of violence and, if successful, expressed itself in the manifest and perhaps radical transformation of the process of government, the accepted foundations of sovereignty or legitimacy, and the conception of the political and/or social order."[9] Dramatic changes in other spheres, however, take far longer and present more complexity because they affect, almost by definition, more than one country. One might disqualify the "agricultural revolution"—the deliberate alteration of natural systems to promote the abundance of exploited plant and animal species, which occurred independently in three or four different locations world-wide and took over a millennium in each of them—on the grounds that it occurred in prehistoric times. However both the scientific and the industrial revolutions lasted well over a century; and, in the case of the latter, no sooner had one aspect of the process (harnessing water and coal to provide energy) been mastered than other sources of power (electricity and petroleum) superseded it, creating the so-called "second industrial revolution."

Similar attempts have been made to divide the military revolution into discrete phases. Jeremy Black suggests that the "major changes" in the military emergence of the West occurred in the Renaissance, and again during the reign of Louis XIV, leaving "Roberts' century," 1560–1660, "in relative terms one of limited change between two periods of greater importance" (page 97 above). Others believe that many of the critical developments took place in the later Middle Ages.[10] Perhaps it is more fruitful to view the military revolution of early modern Europe as part of a cyclical process. One need not embrace crude determinism and assert the existence of either "concentrations of warfare ... in approximately fifty-year oscillations, each alternating period of concentration being more severe" (Quincy Wright), or the "definite tendency for a periodic increase in the level of violence about every twenty-five years" (Frank Denton and Warren Philips).[11] Instead Clifford Rogers proposes an elegant and convincing "punctuated equilibrium model," with early modern "punctuations" that include the birth of the capital ship, the spread of the artillery fortress and a major manpower increase between 1510 and 1560; the emergence of firepower as the dominant element in land warfare by both land and sea between 1580 and 1630; and a further rapid increase in the size of both armies and navies between 1690 and 1715.[12]

A consequential conceptual difficulty lies in the link between armies and navies, on the one hand, and "state formation" on the other, in each of these periods of change. In *A Military Revolution? Military Change and European Society, 1550–1800* (London, 1991), and again (although rather less forcefully) in chapter 4 above, Jeremy Black asserts that the rapid growth of the armed forces of early modern Europe stems from political rather than military factors. Basing his argument upon the dramatic expansion of Louis XIV's army and navy, he suggests that enhanced state power formed the critical precondition for military growth. Brian M. Downing, on the other hand, argued in *The Military Revolution and Political Change. Origins of Democracy and Autocracy in Early Modern Europe* (Princeton, 1992) that, in terms of state-building, the formative stage of the military revolution was in fact over by the reign of Louis XIV. By then, he claimed, it had already created the decisive political changes (such as the growth of a powerful bureaucracy) in several major states of continental Europe that eventually produced absolutism. So where Black saw political change leading to military revolution, Downing (like Colin Jones in chapter 6 above) perceived the reverse.

Perhaps both visions contain a measure of truth: clearly the two developments fed upon each other, and indeed required each other. The emergence of the "Renaissance State", with its more efficient bureaucratic structure and its improved methods of raising money, constituted an essential precondition for the important military changes of the late fifteenth and early sixteenth centuries; while, conversely, the need to mobilize resources for war could enhance governments' power over their subjects. The same pattern recurred in the later seventeenth century. But not all wars produced the same effects. The celebrated formula of Charles Tilly that "states made war but war also made states" is too simplistic.[13] As I. A. A. Thompson perceptively notes (page 290 above):

> Major hegemonic land wars, fought at a distance from their main resource base, because of their high borrowing requirements, tended to lead to the development of taxation and the fiscal-state; contrariwise, a permanent military establishment could in appropriate circumstances promote the privatization of military and administrative functions by means of the contracting out of funding, maintenance and supply; and protracted wars within the territory of the state could be sustained by a more primitive (from the statist point of view), local fiscality ... The development of the state as a fiscal entity was thus related to the type of military activity in which it was engaged.

In the broad sense, however, Tilly is right: military activity and state formation have always been inextricably linked, and periods of rapid military change have usually coincided with major political innovations. Rather than trying to establish a simple model of causation, we should perhaps envisage something like the "double helix" structure of the DNA molecule, with two complex spirals interacting at various discrete points over time.[14]

2. CHRONOLOGY

In spite of the doubts expressed by Black and others concerning the concept and the precise chronology of the military revolution, the sixteenth century still seems of central importance because it witnessed the emergence of three key innovations: the capital ship with its broadside; the development of gunpowder weapons as the arbiter of battles and sieges; and, in direct response to this, the "artillery fortress".

Even contemporaries could see the "revolutionary" nature of these changes. For example, Francesco Guicciardini—soldier, diplomat and historian—believed in 1509 that the mold of land war in his native Italy had been shattered for ever by the arrival in 1494 of modern siege trains. Previously,

> When war broke out, the sides were so evenly balanced, the military methods so slow and the artillery so primitive, that the capture of a castle took up almost a whole campaign. Wars lasted a very long time, and battles ended with very few or no deaths. But the French came upon all this like a sudden tempest which turns everything upside down ... Wars became sudden and violent, conquering and capturing a state in less time than it used to take to occupy a village; cities were reduced with great speed, in a matter of days and hours rather than months; battles became savage and bloody in the extreme. In fact states now began to be saved or ruined, lost and captured, not according to plans made in a study as formerly but by feats of arms in the field.[15]

Many other military writers believed that gunpowder weapons distinguished "Modern" from "Classical" warfare; Francis Bacon ranked them, together with printing and the compass, as one of the three critical discoveries in the history of humankind; while Campbell Dalrymple, writing in 1761, noted that "The effect of fire[arms] begins now to be disputed, at least, it is not believed so formidable, as it was; which in time may produce another military revolution, and send us back to the arms in use before the invention of gunpowder."[16] The same "revolutionary character" was ascribed by both contemporaries and subsequent generations to the broadside-firing warship and the artillery fortress. Each marked a turning-point after which warfare on sea and land (respectively) could never be the same again; each started an "arms race" in which states strove first to equal and then to surpass the innovations that had defeated them; each, finally, provided the crucial instruments that enabled the Europeans to acquire trade and territory in Asia, Africa and the Americas (see the pertinent remarks of John F. Guilmartin on this matter: chapter 12 above.)[17]

Admittedly not every part of these three developments occurred exclusively within this period. Writing in the first decade of the sixteenth century the Portuguese conquistador Duarte Pereira Pacheco could already boast that in "fortresses surrounded by walls ... Europe excels Asia and Africa; and she also excels them in her larger and better fleets, better equipped and armed than those of all other areas."[18] And, indeed, gunpowder weapons came into effective use in Europe far earlier and far more widely than many previously thought. They first appeared in the West in the 1320s, and about a century later the crucial invention of "corning" (turning the loose powder into granules) and improvements in manufacture transformed their power and efficiency.[19] However, their effective use on board ships took somewhat longer. Thus some Western vessels—Mediterranean galleys—carried heavy artillery from the 1440s, and pictorial evidence indicates the appearance of gunports as early as the 1470s; but the first vessel capable of firing a broadside, the hallmark of European naval warfare ever since, appears to have been the 1000-ton *Great Michael*, launched in Scotland in 1511, which carried 12 cannon on each side as well as three "grete basilisks" at the bow and stern. English and French capital ships of similar design soon followed.[20]

The use of hand-held firearms in battle likewise originated in the fifteenth century, and some of the battles fought by Charles the Bold in the 1470s, and by Castilian and Granadan troops in the 1480s, saw units equipped with firearms pitted against each other.[21] Given the technological limitations of the available weapons, however, optimum use of handguns in battle required a continuous barrage of fire; and that was only achieved in the later sixteenth century. The idea first appeared in a treatise written in 1579 by Thomas Digges which argued that, although untrained men should still be formed into squares, experienced soldiers armed with arquebus and musket should "after the old Romane manner make three or four several fronts, with convenient spaces for the first to retire and unite himselfe with the second, and both these if occasion so require, with the third.

The shot having their convenient lanes continually during the fight to discharge their peces."[22] Martín de Eguiluz, a Spanish veteran with 24 years' service, in 1586 likewise advocated forming three files of five soldiers each, in order to maintain a constant fire during a skirmish.[23] In the revised edition of his *Stratiotocos* (1590), Digges repeated that musketeers should be drawn up for action in "three or four rankes at the utmost", but now suggested that when the enemy approached "the first ranke shal give their volee, and presently deliver their peece to the second ranke to charge againe, taking theirs that are readie charged, with the which they may give another volee." But, Digges admitted, it was all hypothetical: "I know this opinion of mine, being different from common custome, will be of the common multitude of such men of warre as can brooke nothing but their owne customes, not onely disliked but derided and contemned."[24] The origin of continuous volley fire in European warfare therefore seems to originate, as claimed in *The Military Revolution*, pp. 18–19, with William Louis of Nassau in 1594, who made the critical link between the massed infantry firepower made available by sixteenth-century technology and the Roman close-order drill described by Aelian. It had become the standard tactic of the army of the Dutch Republic by 1610 at the latest.[25]

Discussion of the third sixteenth-century innovation, the evolution and impact of the artillery fortress, is complicated by its relationship to the contemporaneous rapid growth in army size. It is true that large—sometimes very large—forces had operated during the Middle Ages. For example during the First Crusade, 50,000 combatants may have marched eastwards in 1096–7 with some 35,000 men leaving Constantinople; and the force mustered for the Fourth Crusade in 1202 certainly exceeded 25,000 men, transported in a fleet of 200 Venetian ships.[26] On the eve of the Black Death, Philip VI of France maintained an army of almost 45,000 men in September 1340 while even Edward III of England, ruler of a far smaller state, commanded some 32,000 men at the siege of Calais in 1346–7 (with more in action in Brittany and Guienne and on the Scottish frontier.) But these concentrations all proved exceptional and short-lived; moreover in the century 1350–1450 both field armies and total military establishments declined dramatically. However, by the 1480s the French crown once more on occasion maintained an army of over 40,000, with some 24,000 in its campaign armies, while the Catholic Kings subdued Granada with forces that frequently exceeded 60,000 and in the final campaign (1491–2) may have reached 80,000 men.[27]

This upward trend continued and even accelerated during the sixteenth century. French expeditionary forces steadily increased in size—22,000–29,000 men marched to Italy under Charles VIII and Louis XII, but 36,000 went to Metz in 1552 and 40,000 mustered at Pierrepont in 1558 under Henry II—as did the total armed forces of the crown, at least on paper: 41,000 in 1515, 69,000 or more in 1544, and 80,000 by 1567–8.[28] Meanwhile the armies of France's great rival, the Habsburgs, grew even more: the Emperor Charles V led 42,000 men on his invasion of France in 1544, 56,000 to defeat the Schmalkaldic League in Germany in

1546, and 55,000 men to besiege Metz in 1552.[29] The total number of troops Charles commanded in 1552 approached 150,000—twice the size of the armies of his grandparents, the Catholic Kings—and his son, grandson and great-grandson all maintained forces of similar dimensions for much of the following century.

But why did the armies of France and the Habsburgs increase in size so rapidly in the mid-sixteenth century? Three possible explanations have been advanced. First, the rise of the "new monarchies" in the preceding half-century enabled several states to create military bureaucracies capable of raising and maintaining large armies. Events such as the "Tudor Revolution in Government" occurred at precisely the time when England's armed forces and military expenditure reached unprecedented levels; indeed the latter is inconceivable without the former. But that is not to say that the one caused the other; merely that when it became necessary to increase military establishments, several (but not all) European states proved able to respond. Second, army sizes may also have risen in response to inter-state competition. The coronation of Charles V as Holy Roman Emperor in 1519 brought together under a single scepter almost half the lands of Western Europe—Spain, much of Italy, the Netherlands, Franche-Comté, the Empire and even (from 1554 until 1558) England. France was encircled, and the contemporary Habsburg aphorism that "The heart of the Spanish empire is France" did little to reassure the government in Paris. Francis I and his successor Henry II therefore did everything they could to defeat their more powerful enemy, even if it meant allying with the Turks and with the German Protestants.

According to David Parrott (see chapter 9), the rapid increase in military manpower—however caused—produced strategic stagnation. "The overriding need to pay and supply armies inflated beyond the capacities of their states," he wrote, "reduced strategy to a crude concern with territorial occupation or its denial to the enemy" in this period (page 242 above.) But although examples of armies paralyzed by logistics abound, imperfect execution did not always imply absence of planning.[30] In the fall of 1552, for example, while the Emperor Charles V besieged the 6000 man garrison of Metz in Lorraine, France's field army hovered in Champagne, in case Metz needed to be relieved and, if not, to invade Flanders (and indeed, in December it seized the fortress of Hesdin, forcing the emperor to abandon the siege of Metz.)[31] Meanwhile another army operated in Italy, at first in defense of Parma and then to garrison the rebellious republic of Siena.[32] France thus fought on three fronts at once—four, if one counts the garrisons occupying Savoy and along the Pyrenees. Nor was this all: King Henry II had also arranged for both the German Protestants and the Turkish Sultan to attack Charles V at the same time, the former within the Empire and the latter in the Mediterranean.[33] The pressure of this Grand Alliance forced the Habsburgs to deploy armies on an unprecedented scale: in Germany and the Austro-Hungarian borderlands; around Metz; in the Netherlands; in Italy; along the coasts and frontiers of Spain; and in the isolated fortresses along the North African coast. According to the emperor's own advisors, a total of 148,000 men had been mobilized.[34]

So strategy and politics both enhanced the revolutionary growth in military manpower during the mid-sixteenth century, for no state had ever maintained armed forces in so many different theatres at the same time before—although many did so afterwards. However, a high proportion of the troops were required not for offense but for defense, and it is here that the third factor comes in: the creation, in the half-century before 1530, of what John Lynn has termed the "artillery fortress," which notably affected the military manpower requirements of most early modern states.

3. TECHNOLOGY

No one has yet cast doubt on the chronological coincidence of the diffusion of the artillery fortress and the rise in army size in France, Italy and the Netherlands in the first half of the sixteenth century. Nor has the intrinsic importance of the *trace italienne* been questioned. According to Lynn White in 1967:

> The early sixteenth century in Europe witnessed two revolutions, both of which altered habits of the previous thousand years and each of which, by the latter 1500's, had crystallized into patterns that remained nearly intact until the end of the nineteenth century. One was the Protestant Reformation and the defensive response to it in the regions still loyal to Rome. The other was a sudden and profound change in military technology, the chief element of which was the development of light, highly mobile cannon that shot iron balls in fairly flat trajectories. Since the older style of fortifications crumbled before such devices, an entirely new, and enormously costly, apparatus of defense was required. It would be hard to decide which of these simultaneous revolutions had the greater impact on European life, or the more lasting effects.[35]

The assessment of the doyen of historians of technology naturally carries enormous weight; but we must not fall into the trap of technological determinism. Once again we must study the medieval antecedents closely.[36] Cannon do not seem to have been used to batter down walls before the 1370s, and the practice remained rare until the 1420s.[37] Nevertheless, from the late fourteenth century onwards, a number of important innovations increased the capacity of fortifications to withstand gunpowder bombardment: first the addition of guns and gunports for offensive use as a counter-battery; then a variety of new structural designs, such as "countersinking" the fort, to minimize the damage done by incoming fire; and later the introduction of polygonal defensive designs to maximize the opportunities for outgoing fire. But such innovations proved the exception: in most areas the traditional "vertical system" remained the principal means of defense and, for a century after 1430, whenever good siege artillery bombarded vertical walls, the outcome was predictable.[38] The verdict of Andreas Bernaldez on the conquest of Granada in the 1480s—"Great towns, which once would have held out a year against all foes but hunger, now fell within a month"—was echoed by Niccolo

Machiavelli concerning the French invasion of Italy in the 1490s: "No wall exists, however thick, that artillery cannot destroy in a few days."[39] By 1530, however, this ceased to be true, thanks to the newly designed "artillery fortress" with its low, thick walls and its angled bastions.

In a report commissioned by the government of Florence in 1526, Machiavelli suggested three distinct ways of turning a town into an artillery fortress. Two involved starting from scratch: tearing down the existing walls and either building a new defensive system beyond them, so as to include all the suburbs and all points (such as neighboring high ground) from which an enemy might threaten; or else building a smaller circuit than before, abandoning (and leveling) all areas deemed indefensible. However both these methods involved colossal expense: on the one hand, the cost of building the fortress itself; on the other, high social costs, because the new-style fortifications covered far larger areas than before—including the suburbs lying just beyond the medieval walls, often the site of important buildings such as hospitals, religious houses and industrial plant (mills and furnaces).

Machiavelli's report of 1526 therefore considered a third technique of installing modern defenses which, although weaker than the others, proved both far quicker and far cheaper: a drastic modification of the existing fortifications, reducing the height and increasing the depth of the existing walls, redesigning the towers and gateways into bastions, and creating an escarpment to give a proper field of fire. Of course earthen ramparts, when unprotected by brick and stone, would not last for long (contemporary estimates ranged from four years, with minimal maintenance, up to ten) before the weather eroded them. But they proved relatively fast and cheap to erect; they could absorb incoming fire effectively; and, with enough determined defenders, they could defy even the largest armies of the day.[40] Thus in 1552 the city of Metz in Lorraine managed to resist for three months a siege mounted by 55,000 men despite its lack of a full "modern" defensive system. The French had captured the city in May, and the 5800-man French garrison worked day and night to strengthen the existing fortifications, erecting "boulevards" (sixteen feet thick in places) with "flancs" on either side of them at precisely the most vulnerable area, and backing all walls with ramparts constructed of earth and bales of wool. Metz had become an artillery fortress by September, when Charles V's forces arrived to recapture it. So when, on 27 November, having fired over 7000 rounds against a sector of the curtain wall, the besiegers finally brought some 70 feet of it crashing down, they dared not launch an assault because the defenders' guns on the flanks could not be silenced.[41]

Machiavelli's two other techniques of fortification, *alla moderna* large and small, of course maximized these strengths. In chapter 7 above, John Lynn provides an excellent account of all the novel aspects of the artillery fortress envisaged by Machiavelli, and of their remarkable constancy over time. However, some of his deductions seem open to question. First, it may be true that enlarging an artillery fortress three-fold would only increase the lines of circumvallation by 15 per cent, and that such a small increment seems insignificant (page 175 above.) But this misses the point: the critical development was not the "upgrade" from one *trace* to another but the switch from a system of vertical defence, which could be rapidly demolished by gunfire and taken by storm, to a *trace italienne* with bastions that bristled with guns—because even a relatively modest artillery fortress, in a good state of repair and sufficiently garrisoned, could seldom be taken by assault and therefore required a full-dress siege, a large army, time, and money to capture. Contemporaries seemed unanimous on this point. On the one hand, the French military expert Raymond de Beccarie, lord of Fourquevaux, held that only fortifications constructed since the year 1510 presented a serious threat to a well-armed aggressor:

> Because those fortified before that date cannot be called strong, seeing that the art of making bastions came to light only a short while ago. But those which have received ramparts since then, or in our own day, must (provided they were constructed at leisure and not in haste) be held extremely difficult to capture.

On the other hand, as the engineer Francesco Laparelli noted in the 1560s, "It is impossible to defend a place against an army with artillery without flanks." On the tactical level, size as such did not enter into it: either one had the new defensive system, however small, or one did not.[42]

This is not to say that new bastions remained impregnable for ever. In 1672, in the wake of Louis XIV's lightning conquest of much of the Dutch Republic, the king's chief engineer, Sébastien le Prestre de Vauban, noted the terrible state of neglect of the Dutch fortresses, most of which had fallen with scarcely a blow. Major expenditure, he warned, would be required to make them defensible.[43] Such an operation would take time, both because to build a new artillery fortress in the seventeenth century took at least twenty years, and because—as Thomas Arnold makes clear in chapter 8 above—for optimum effect each fortification needed to form part of an overall defensive system.

Although relatively small states such as Mantua, Montferrat, Lucca and Geneva could concentrate on a single "impregnable" superfortress, capable of holding out almost indefinitely, larger polities needed not one but many artillery fortresses in order to create a layered defence in depth.[44] Thus, soon after they gained control of the duchy of Lombardy in the 1530s, the Habsburgs began a comprehensive program of fortifications: Cremona and Lodi against Venice in the east, Alessandria and Novara against Savoy in the west, and Pavia and above all Milan itself as a strategic reserve. At the same time the Venetian Republic also embarked upon a program of defense in depth, constructing a network of refortified, mutually supporting cities both in the west and, slightly later, in the east—culminating with the magnificent stronghold of Palmanova in the 1590s.[45] Meanwhile, two similar systems were taking shape in the Low Countries. Already by 1572, when the Dutch Revolt began, twelve towns had been turned into artillery fortresses and the walls of eighteen more had been rebuilt in part—a total of 27 miles of new walls. By

1648, when the Revolt came to an end, the Spanish Netherlands alone boasted 28 artillery fortresses and a further 27 towns with partially modernized walls; and the provinces of Holland and Utrecht in the Dutch Republic, which in 1572 had possessed only one artillery fortress and three more towns with one or two bastions, by 1648 had 13 of the former and 14 of the latter.[46] An even more impressive "defense in depth" using artillery fortresses went up around the French frontier between 1670 and 1702, under the direction of Louis XIV's superintendent of fortifications, Vauban. It eventually included almost 300 fortified (and garrisoned) strongholds, and proved capable of halting every attempt by the king's enemies to reach the heart of the kingdom: between 1702 and 1711, in spite of a string of catastrophic defeats (Blenheim, Turin, Ramillies, Oudenaarde, Malplaquet) and the loss of innumerable towns through siege, Vauban's succession of "barriers" of artillery fortresses, each one arranged in a zig-zag of mutually supporting positions laid out like a giant *trace italienne* between the North Sea and the Meuse, kept France's enemies at bay until at the "Ne Plus Ultra" line the war came to an end. Not for nothing did Vauban term it "Le pré carré:" the dueling field.[47]

When constructed as part of an integrated system, fortifications *alla moderna* dominated the conduct of warfare. As John Cruso, an English military writer, observed in 1632: "The actions of the modern warres consist chiefly in sieges, assaults, sallies, skirmishes etc., and so affoard but few set battels." According to Roger Boyle, Lord Orrery, in 1677, "Battells do not now decide national quarrels, and expose countries to the pillage of conquerors, as formerly. For we make war more like foxes, than like lyons; and you will have twenty sieges for one battell;" while in exactly the same year Johann Behr stated that "Field battles are in comparison scarcely a topic of conversation ... Indeed at the present time the whole art of war seems to come down to shrewd attacks and artful fortification."[48] The point was expressed most cogently by Vauban himself in a tract of *circa* 1670:

> The attack on fortresses has with justice always been considered one of the most essential elements of the art of war. But since the number of strongholds has increased to the point where one can no longer enter enemy territory without encountering many fortified towns, its importance has increased to the point where one can say that today it alone offers the means of conquest and conservation. To be sure, winning a battle leaves the victor in control of the countryside for the time being, but only taking the fortresses will give him the entire country ... One might say that a war waged by sieges exposes the state less and secures conquests far better. It is therefore today the commonest form of warfare in the Low Countries, Spain, and Italy, where wars are without doubt conducted with more sophistication and discipline than anywhere else in the world. In Germany battles play a greater role because the country is more open and there are fewer fortresses.[49]

The Marshal was right. Outside the "dueling field", the destruction of a major field army did normally lead to the surrender of many if not all the fortresses that had depended upon it for relief: after Nördlingen (1634) during the Thirty Years' War almost all Protestant garrisons in south Germany surrendered; after Naseby

(1645) during the English Civil War almost all royalist garrisons in the Midlands came to terms. But in the Netherlands, where (as Vauban noted) few towns in his day lacked modern fortifications, in spite of "over 60 battles and 200 sieges" the country had never been totally subdued.

> The reason is obvious. A battle lost in the Low Countries normally has few consequences, for the pursuit of a defeated army continues for only two, three or four leagues, because the neighboring fortresses of the enemy halt the victors and provide a refuge for the vanquished, saving them from being totally ruined.[50]

As the construction of artillery fortresses continued, in one region of Europe after another sieges eclipsed battles in importance and wars eternalized themselves.[51]

The underlying explanation of this stagnation is clear. In the nineteenth century, the perceptive military theorist Carl von Clausewitz, in his influential treatise *On War,* borrowed from physics the concept of a "center of gravity" to explain what seemed to him the essential aim of strategy.

> A theater of war, be it large or small, and the forces stationed there, no matter what their size, represent the sort of unity in which a single center of gravity can be identified. That is the place where the decision should be reached.

Clausewitz drew upon his direct experience of the spectacular French victories of the period 1792–1812, and his extensive reading of military history, to conclude that: "For Alexander, Gustavus Adolphus, Charles XII, and Frederick the Great, the center of gravity was their army. If their army had been destroyed, they would all have gone down in history as failures."[52] But his analysis ignored the fact that the army of Gustavus Adolphus did in fact meet with a major defeat, at Nördlingen in 1634 (two years after the king's death at the indecisive battle of Lützen), and yet this did not lead Sweden to "fail." On the contrary, when the war eventually ended with the Peace of Westphalia in 1648, she achieved all her major war aims: extensive territorial gains, guarantees for future security, and a substantial war indemnity.

The contradiction between the defeat at Nördlingen and the gains at Westphalia stemmed from Sweden's control of numerous artillery fortresses which held steady even after the defeat of the main army. In 1648 the Swedish forces in Germany still numbered 70,000 troops, of whom almost half were dispersed as garrisons in 127 strategically located strongpoints: they thus presented no "center of gravity" that an adversary could destroy with a single blow. Other theaters of war dominated by the *trace italienne* in the sixteenth and seventeenth centuries proved equally resistant to the knock-out blows advocated by Clausewitz.[53] The problem was memorably summarized by the commander of the Spanish forces striving to suppress the Dutch Revolt, Don Luis de Requeséns. "There would not be time or money enough in the world," he warned Philip II in 1574, "to reduce by force the twenty-four towns which have rebelled in Holland if we are to spend as long in reducing each one of them as we have taken over similar ones so far." Or again, slightly later:

> Many towns and a battle have been won, each of them a success enough in itself to bring peace and even to win an entire new kingdom elsewhere; but here they have been to no avail ... I believe that God for my sins has chosen to show me so many times the Promised Land here, as he did to Moses, but that someone else is to be the Joshua who will enter therein.[54]

But no Spanish Joshua appeared: instead, the artillery fortresses of Holland and Zeeland defied all of Philip II's efforts at reconquest until his treasury declared bankruptcy in 1575 and his army mutinied and abandoned its posts in 1576.

Simon Adams (chapter 10 above) suggests that the Spanish Habsburgs—whose territories lay at the center of the Military Revolution—consciously decided to fight wars of sieges rather than of battles through political choice rather than through military necessity, but this flies in the face of the evidence. First, it takes two to tango: if the enemy cannot be brought to battle, as was normally the case in the Low Countries' Wars, no battle can be fought. Second, when an enemy offered to fight, the Spaniards usually accepted—and won: at Mühlberg (1547) against the German Protestants; at Pavia (1525), St Quentin (1557) and Gravelines (1558) against France; at Jemmingen (1568), at Mook (1574) and at Gembloux (1578) against the Dutch. Third, whenever possible, commanders sought to bypass bastions in favor of an old-style thrust to the enemy's heart, as Charles V did during his dramatic invasion of France in 1544.[55] But successes like these ultimately proved counter-productive, because they demonstrated—as little else could—the advantage of the new artillery fortress. Italian or Italian-trained military architects soon spread knowledge of their art all over Europe.[56]

How, then, did the artillery fortress influence army size? First, the advent of the *trace italienne* and the increased frequency of long sieges expedited the transition from cavalry to infantry as the backbone of armies. Whereas in 1494 Charles VIII of France invaded Italy with 12,000 cavalry, which represented two-thirds of his total strength, in 1525 Francis I invaded with only 6,000, which constituted but one-fifth of his army. The percentage of cavalry in Western field forces continued to fall for another century, and contemporaries saw a clear link between this development and the proliferation of artillery fortresses. In 1645 the English soldier George Monck suggested that:

> Where your service lieth in Campagnia [open country], the proportion of your army ought to be two footmen to one horseman ... But where the service of your army shall be most in sieges, there you ought to have three footmen unto one horseman; and sometimes four footmen to one horseman.

Eight years before, a senior commander of the Spanish Army of Flanders had made much the same point: "We need more infantry if we invade the rebel provinces and more cavalry if we campaign in France" he asserted, because the war on the northern frontier was almost entirely one of sieges, where horsemen could do little, whereas operations in the south afforded more opportunity for manoeuvre.[57]

The reduction of the mounted component of armies thus created a more "elastic" workforce—since infantry is far easier to increase than cavalry and much simpler to supply. Moreover the *trace italienne* actually forced up the number of footsoldiers in two distinct ways. To begin with, as already noted, an artillery fortress could, under normal circumstances, only be captured by a formal siege, often with elaborate walls of circum- and contravallation to guard against attacks from a relief army as well as sorties by the garrison. In these circumstances, success required very large concentrations of troops. John Lynn's denial of the correlation between fortification design and army size (pp. 175–178 above), although shedding much new light on the subject, rests upon some dubious data. A statistical table culled largely from entries in encyclopedias—in this case from those compiled by the Dupuys and by Bodart—may prove reliable concerning the duration of sieges, on which most sources agree; but it provides a perilous guide to numbers, whether of besiegers or defenders, which varied dramatically as the siege proceeded. Thus, to take a single example, at Metz in 1552 Lynn's table shows 60,000 attackers, 10,000 defenders and no relief army (in this case he cites as sources a biography of King Henry II published in 1910 and a general history of France published in 1904.) However, Gaston Zeller's meticulous study of the siege, published in 1943 and including many relevant documents, showed some 55,000 attackers but only 5800 defenders, together with a French relief army numbering 30,000 foot and 7000 horse.[58] Clearly errors on this scale render generalization about the changing size of armies and the fluctuating proportions of garrisons to besiegers extremely hazardous.[59]

Lynn uses the Metz example to suggest that "while modern fortifications claimed very real advantages over updated medieval walls, the effect on army size seems to have been the same;" and he butresses his case with the siege of St. Omer in 1638 where, he claims, the Habsburg garrison "kept at bay some 30,000 French for two months behind medieval walls." (A note informs us that "Saint-Omer's walls were still medieval in 1668.")[60] But this is incorrect. The detailed cityscape published by Jan Blaeu in 1649, which also describes the siege, clearly shows eleven bastions, nine ravelins, two hornworks and a crownwork surrounding St. Omer. Small wonder, then, that the French siege lasted two months—and in the end proved unsuccessful, because the Spaniards managed to relieve the town.[61]

Lynn's figures on the numbers involved in capturing towns in the later seventeenth and eighteenth centuries seem particularly misleading because he includes only the forces directly involved in the siegeworks and deliberately excludes "armies of observation" (see page 181). Admittedly, Vauban boasted that, before his time, a ratio of at least ten besiegers to one defender prevailed, which his "system" had cut back to six or seven to one; however that reduction made necessary the creation of large armies of observation. In a treatise written circa 1704 he asserted that:

> It is best to be stronger, and to have two armies whenever one can: that is to say one which besieges and one which observes. The siege army shuts itself off in its lines, as we shall later show; the army of observation simply covers and occupies the routes by which the enemy['s relief force] may arrive, or takes outlying positions.

"These two armies," he continued, "must always keep within range of one another, especially in the initial stages, in order to offer mutual support and keep the enemy at a distance."[62] The principal advantage of this division of forces, according to Vauban, lay in the fact that the troops manning the siegeworks no longer needed to face about when a relief army approached—and in many cases enemy troops lay in wait nearby, in a camp protected by its own bastions, ready to exploit any weakness.[63]

The available data thus flatly contradict Lynn's claim (page 181 above) that "Relief and observation forces were not involved in the actual defense or attack of fortresses. By definition they stood off miles, and often tens of miles, from the actual siege." On the contrary, according to Vauban himself, the "observation forces" formed an integral part of the siege process. Lynn's "Table of French sieges"—even if we admit his figures—should therefore show a rise in the "total attacking force" from a maximum of 50–60,000 in the mid-sixteenth century (Metz, Renty, St Quentin) to 90–110,000 in the late seventeenth and early eighteenth centuries (Mons and Namur in 1691–2; Lille and Mons in 1708–9—see appendix to Ch. 7 above.) This marked increase in the size of the armies engaged in sieges seems entirely compatible with the argument advanced in *The Military Revolution* that the development—and constant refinement—of defensive systems based upon the *trace italienne* helped to fuel an expansion in the armed forces of the major European states.

But of course attack represents only half the story, for the need to garrison artillery fortresses, especially when they formed part of a defense in depth, also drove up military establishments. Contemporary evidence suggests that garrisons tied down roughly half the armed forces of many Western states. In 1621 Cosimo del Monte, Venice's senior military advisor, neatly expressed the prevailing orthodoxy when he argued that the Republic would need a total of 25,000 infantry and 3500 cavalry to withstand any attack on its mainland possessions—half of them in garrisons and the rest "to serve on campaigns" and "to assist in the defence of the cities."[64] And the greater the number of fortresses, the greater the overall size of the garrisons. It may be true, as Mahinder S. Kingra has observed for the Dutch Republic, that individual "garrison sizes ... rarely exceeded one thousand soldiers, frequently hovering between two and five hundred, and sometimes totaling less than one hundred troops." However, although the size of individual garrisons may indeed have been small, the cumulative totals were enormous.[65] Unfortunately, because of the decentralized system of government within the Dutch Republic, no detailed figures can be advanced with confidence; however, in 1639, the opposing Spanish Army of Flanders numbered 77,000 men, of whom over 33,000 were distributed in 208 separate garrisons, the largest of which numbered scarcely 1000.[66] According to Vauban, the defense of France's fortresses already tied down 116,370 men in 1678, rising to 166,000 in 1688; while by 1705 no fewer than 173,000 men occupied 297 fortified positions. Each of these totals represented about 40 per cent of Louis XIV's army.[67] The rapid and sustained increase in French army size between 1670 and 1710 thus stemmed at least in part from Vauban's program of fortress building, which dramatically expanded the number of strongpoints requiring garrisons.[68]

I. A. A. Thompson's attempt (chapter 11 above) to diminish the impact of the new military architecture on the finances and the armed forces of early modern European states likewise seems unconvincing. He notes the small share of the central budget of the Spanish Habsburgs devoted to fortifications, and deduces that defenses therefore constituted a low priority. But this ignores two facts. First, protected by the Pyrenees until 1640 (when the revolts of Catalonia and Portugal opened up new theaters of operation within the peninsula), most of Spain had little need of artillery fortresses and therefore built few. Had Thompson included the money devoted by the Spanish Monarchy to constructing and maintaining fortifications in North Africa, Italy and the Netherlands, the picture would have been very different. Second, even when new fortifications became necessary, the local community was expected to fund much of the cost (especially labor costs, probably the most expensive component.) This had been the case in the Middle Ages—indeed in some states communities financed the entire operation.[69] Even in the sixteenth century a rich city like Antwerp could be forced to pay first for a full circuit of *trace italienne* defenses and then for a vast citadel (although the loans taken out to finance these projects remained outstanding in the 1790s!)[70] But Antwerp proved the exception: throughout early modern Europe, the cost of fortifying was normally shared between the state, the regional government and the community itself: in the Venetian Republic, for example, "central government funds contributed only one-third to the total cost of fortifications, the rest being borne by the cities concerned and by their surrounding territories."[71] This devolved system of finance makes it almost impossible to quantify the total costs, except by examining all the relevant sources for a particular area; it thus invalidates any attempt (such as those by Kingra and Thompson) to estimate total spending on fortifications—and thus the fiscal impact of the artillery fortress—based solely on the records of a state's central treasury.[72]

4. GEOGRAPHICAL

The fourth and final substantive criticism of *The Military Revolution* concerns the diffusion of the military innovations discussed above. To begin with, some questions have been raised concerning their spread both to the British Isles and to Poland. Admittedly, documenting the precise mechanics of diffusion of new military methods sometimes proves difficult. On the one hand, many manuals on training were published in London on the subject between 1590 and 1640, sometimes in more than one edition, which argues that a market existed (presumably among Militia officers); on the other hand, many young men served in Continental armies—some on a regular basis and others "swallowlike, for a summer or only for a siege"—and returned with some direct experience of the new ways in warfare.[73] The process of modernization began in Ireland and Scotland during the 1630s and accelerated in the 1640s with the return of many veterans from Continental armies.[74] In 1646, at the battle of Benburb in northeast Ireland, a commander trained in the Spanish Army of Flanders used the classic defensive tactics favored by Habsburg armies in order to defeat a Scottish force under a general who had fought for Gustavus Adolphus.[75] By then, in England, the "discontinuity in revenue totals, army and navy size, and the change in the nature of the armed forces" all reflected the profound military changes that had taken place; so did the fact that Gregory King's statistical profile of England in 1688 already recognized the "officer corps" as a distinct social group.[76]

If recent literature has confirmed the westward spread of the military revolution, its impact further east has been questioned. The case of Hungary seems clear enough: for example the 28-day resistance of the 800-man garrison behind the bastions of Günz in 1532 and the 34-day ordeal of the 1000-man garrison in the artillery fortress of Szigeth in 1566 both proved crucial in preventing the Ottoman army from breaking through into Austria. Not surprisingly, Italian architects always found a welcome in the Habsburg borderlands.[77]

Other areas, however, proved less receptive to the new military doctrines. A nephew of the Dutch statesman Johan de Witt, visiting eastern Europe in 1656, felt tempted to participate in the conflict then raging between Sweden and Poland. His uncle sternly discouraged any involvement since "in that war, which is so wild and savage, there is much less to learn than in others, where matters of fortification and siegecraft are practiced better." De Witt advised the young man to come home and acquire military experience more "relevant" to the West.[78] But such dismissal seems excessive. The armed forces of Russia and Poland needed to fight two distinct types of opponent: the infantry-based troops of their western enemies, and the cavalry hosts of their neighbors to the south and east. On the whole, they responded well to this dual challenge until the late seventeenth century. Thus Polish troops soundly defeated Gustavus Adolphus of Sweden in the 1620s; and although Charles X's Polish campaign of 1655 succeeded triumphantly, the following year his forces failed to take the artillery fortress of Zamość and his reinforcements met with defeat at Warka. By 1659 the Polish army of 54,000 regulars included almost 11,000 infantry serving in Western-style regiments. Charles X never came back. To the south, although the Turks invaded the Polish Commonwealth in 1621 and imposed a humiliating peace, King John Sobieski and a large Polish contingent spearheaded the spectacular defeat of the Ottoman army outside Vienna in 1683. The Russians, too, through a combination of "new forma-tion" (i.e. Western-style) infantry regiments and traditional cavalry, scored nu-merous successes against the Poles in the 1660s and also captured Azov from the Turks in the 1690s.[79]

The forces of Islam, however, did not always lose. The Turks conquered Crete from the Venetians in the 1660s, and soundly defeated Russia in 1711 and Austria in 1737–9; the Omanis captured Muscat in 1650 and Mombasa in 1698 from the Portuguese; Spanish attacks on Algiers failed in 1775, 1783 and 1784; even Napo-leon failed to take Acre in 1799. Strong and successful Muslim states possessed an extensive and sophisticated military tradition (both written and practical) of their own and rapidly adopted Western firearms into their military repertory—albeit often by a process of routine mimesis, of copying captured weapons and import-ing foreign specialists.[80]

Recent research has documented an interesting early transmission of the "Mili-tary Revolution" of early modern Europe to a Muslim society: the case of Sa'adian Morocco in the sixteenth century. As early as 1541, in the wake of the successful siege of a Portuguese outpost, King John III observed:

> We must recognize that warfare in Morocco has changed. The enemy is now very ad-ept in the arts of war and siegecraft, due in part to the aid of many Turks and rene-gades, numerous artillery weapons, and the important materials of war.

His son, Sebastian, demonstrated the truth of this in spectacular fashion in 1578 when he and his army met defeat and death at the hands of Sa'adian forces in the battle of Alcazarquivir. The subsequent conquest of the sub-Saharan Songhay empire by Moroccan troops in 1590–1 offers a "textbook gunpowder conquest," to rank with those of Cortés, Pizarro and Legazpi.[81]

But the process did not continue indefinitely. In most Islamic societies, the founding and management of artillery became the exclusive preserve of small cadres of foreign specialists, most of them renegades and adventurers with little training and less experience in their craft.[82] Once the Industrial Revolution began to transform the production of gunpowder weapons systems in Europe, the Mus-lim states' lack of the bureaucratic and financial institutions necessary to support capital-intensive and constantly changing military establishments, by land and sea, became critical. They could no longer meet and defeat the expanding reper-tory of innovations developed by their Christian adversaries, because the West-ernization of war also required replication of the economic and social structures and infrastructures, in particular the machinery of resource-mobilization and modern finance, on which the new techniques depended. But until the late eigh-teenth century, thanks to their ability to mobilize and maintain enormous armies, the major Islamic states—like the empires of East Asia—proved able to keep the West at bay. Although the Europeans managed to inflict great defeats on Muslim forces during the seventeenth century, such as the rout of the Turks outside Vienna in 1683, it must be remembered that it was the Turks at the gates of Vienna and not the Europeans at the gates of Istanbul.[83]

This perception brings us back to the true significance of the "Military Revolution" of early modern Europe. The sixteenth century saw a strong phase of Islamic expansion, with the Mughals gaining control of some 1.25 million square miles of India, and the Ottomans creating an empire of roughly 1 million square miles which stretched from Morocco, through Egypt and Iraq, to the Balkans and Hungary. So many states and societies were overwhelmed that the resistance of the West to this Islamic tide stands out as unusual. And it was a close-run thing: at Mohacs (1526) and Mezokeresztes (1596) in Hungary the Turks triumphed; and if they were routed at Lepanto in the Mediterranean in 1571, they nevertheless conquered Cyprus in 1570 and Tunis in 1574. Only military resilience and technological innovation—especially the capital ship, infantry firepower and the artillery fortress: the three vital components of the Military Revolution of the sixteenth century—allowed the West to make the most of its smaller resources in order to resist and, eventually, to expand to global dominance.

Notes

1. My thanks go to Paul Allen, Thomas Arnold, B. Cox, Paul Dover, Fernando González de León, John F. Guilmartin, John Lynn, Jane Ohlmeyer, Keith Roberts, Jon Sumida and, above all, Clifford J. Rogers for many helpful comments and references.

2. A good overview of the connection between fortifications, army size and state formation in Japan is offered by G. Moréchand, "'Taiko Kenchi': le cadastre de Hideyoshi Toyotomi," *Bulletin de l'Ecole française de l'Extrême Orient*, 53.1 (1966), 7–69. See also the revised edition of Hora Tomio, *Tanegashima-ju. Denrai to sono eikyo* (Tokyo, 1990).

3. See the useful review articles of J. A. Lynn, "Clio in arms: the role of the military variable in shaping history," *Journal of Military History*, 55 (1991): 83–95; D. A. Parrott, "The military revolution of early modern Europe," *History Today*, 42.12 (December 1992): 21–7; A. Espino López, "La historia militar entre la renovación y la tradición," *Manuscrits*, 11 (1993), 215–42; A. Roland, "Technology and war: the historiographical revolution of the 1980s," *Technology and culture*, 34 (1993): 117–34; and R. A. Stradling, "A 'Military Revolution': the fall-out from the fall-in," *European History Quarterly*, 24 (1994): 271–8.

4. Perwez Shafi in *Crescent*, March 1990.

5. B. S. Hall and K. R. DeVries, "Essay review—the 'military revolution' revisited," *Technology and culture*, 31 (1990): 500–7. They take 35 lines to show that an early reference to a ship carrying iron guns dated from 1410–12 and not 1338, even though "Parker's blunder is not, to be sure, fatal to his main line of argument" (page 503.)

6. "Parker can be rather cavalier with mere facts," Hall and DeVries announce on p. 503, having devoted 26 lines to refuting my statement that a musket "could throw a 2-ounce lead shot with sufficient force to penetrate even plate armour 100 meters away", an error that they claim "can be traced back (possibly through intermediaries) to Robert Held's *The Age of Firearms* (2d ed., Northfield, Ill., 1970)", a work they then dismiss ("Held's readers are unlikely to confuse his work with scholarship"). In fact, I have never read Held's book, in any edition; but I have perused several tracts from the 1590s which made strong claims

for the long-range hitting power of the musket. Thus Thomas Digges, a veteran of the Low Countries' Wars, believed that troops should be trained to hit their targets at "eight to ten score [paces: 133–166 yards]," but conceded that a ball would only carry that far when it fit the barrel tightly; otherwise effective range was more likely to be 100 paces (83 yards, assuming a "military pace" of around 2.5 feet.) See Thomas Digges, *An arithmetical warlike treatise named Stratiotocos,* 2nd edn., London, 1590, 108 and 122. Similarly, Humfrey Barwick, who had been a soldier for more than forty years, claimed in his *Breefe discourse concerning the force and effect of all manuall weapons of fire* (London, 1591), fo 10v, that "The musketes are weapons of great force, and at this day ... will kill the armed of proofe at ten skore paces [166 yards]." Recent test-firing of fourteen early modern firearms from the magnificent collection at the Graz Arsenal in Austria revealed that musket balls can indeed penetrate between 2 and 4 mm of plate armor at 100 meters—precisely the figure given in *The Military Revolution!* See P. Krenn, *Von alten Handfeuerwaffen: Entwicklung-Technik-Leistung* (Graz, 1989: Veröffentlichungen des Landeszeughaus Graz, nr 12), and Krenn, "Test-firing selected 16th–18th century weapons", *Military illustrated,* 33 (1991): 34–8.

7. On p. 504 Hall and DeVries claim that "some of Parker's notes in this chapter [chapter 3] play so loosely with book and journal titles that even experienced sleuths in a well-equipped library are going to have trouble tracking them." However in subsequent correspondence both authors admitted this charge to be unfounded: Hall conceded that all of the references that he believed to be mistaken were in fact correct (letter of January 16, 1991); DeVries did the same, adding "I found your notes to be elaborate and intelligent. In fact, I probably spent more time reading your notes and profiting from them than I did from any other part of the book" (letter of February 27, 1991).

8. This point was made by H. Dorn, "The 'Military Revolution': military history or history of Europe," *Technology and Culture,* 32 (1991): 656–8, criticizing the neo-antiquarianism of Hall and DeVries. The editor of *Technology and Culture* invited the authors to respond to Professor Dorn, but they declined: letter from Robert C. Post, March 17, 1992.

9. R. Forster and J. P. Greene, eds., *Preconditions of revolution in early modern Europe* (Baltimore, 1970), 1. Surprisingly, the authors of the essays in this collection could find only two sets of early modern events that fully justified the term "revolution": the Netherlands in the 1570s and England in the 1640s.

10. See Volker Smidtchen, *Kriegswesen im späten Mittelalter. Technik, Taktik, Theorie* (Weinheim, 1990), passim; and K. R. DeVries, *Medieval military technology* (Peterborough, Ontario, 1992), passim.

11. Q. Wright, *The study of war* (Chicago, 1942), 227; F. Denton and W. Philips, "Some patterns in the history of violence," *Journal of conflict resolution,* 12.2 (1968): 185. Many others have claimed to detect cyclical patterns in military history, from Arnold Toynbee's *Study of History* in 1954 to J. David Singer and Melvyn Small, *The wages of war 1815–1965* (New York, 1972), 215. But how much of this is mere coincidence: does some sort of Kondratieff cycle explain, for example, the curious fact that a naval arms race has occurred in the last decade of each of the past four centuries—1590s, 1690s, 1790s, and 1890s?

12. See Rogers, p. 77, and also Black, p. 98 above. Black's desire for "aggregate totals of European warships" (p. 97 above) has now been satisfied by the tables in Jan Glete, *Navies and nations. Warships, navies and state building in Europe and America 1500–1860* (2 vols., Stockholm, 1993.)

13. See the recent discussion of the views of Tilly and others in B. D. Porter, *War and the rise of the state. The military foundations of modern politics* (New York, 1994), 1–22.

14. On this complex issue see also G. Parker, ed., *The Cambridge Illustrated History of Warfare* (Cambridge, 1995), 14–15; M. Mann, *The sources of social power. I: A history of power from the beginning to AD 1760* (Cambridge, 1986), 433; and F. Tallett, *War and society in early modern Europe, 1495–1715* (London, 1992), 198–205.

15. G. Canestrini, ed., *Opere inedite di Francesco Guicciardini. III: Storia Fiorentina* (Florence, 1859), 105. Interestingly, this passage forms virtually the only analytical break in Guicciardini's detailed narrative of the years between 1494 and 1508, which heightens the impression of shock these events evinced. Twenty-five years later, however, the same Guicciardini recognized that times had changed again: by the 1530s, thanks to the artillery fortress, the balance between offense and defense had shifted back in favor of the latter. See the views cited by Arnold, pp. 212–13, 223 [n. 22], above, and by Parker, *Military Revolution,* 10.

16. This, the earliest known use of the term "military revolution" occurs in C. Dalrymple, *A military essay containing reflections on raising, arming, cloathing and discipline of the British infantry and cavalry* (London, 1761), 56. I thank Jeremy Black for bringing it to my attention. For exponents of the belief that gunpowder weapons distinguished Ancient from Modern warfare, see the quotations in Parker, *Military Revolution,* 6 (Williams) and 18 (Barret), both from the 1590s; and, rather earlier, Girolamo Garimberto, *Il capitano generale* (Venice, 1557), 125f.

17. An interesting example of the power conferred by Western naval technology even on vessels operating alone occurs in a report made to the English East India Company in 1647, claiming that now "Any man may trade with India, [and] with £200 worth of powder and shot in the Redd Sea by piracy may waste the Company's estate there and quickly cost them £100,000:" E. B. Sainsbury, ed., *A calendar of the Court minutes etc of the East India Company 1644–1649* (Oxford, 1912), 197. The threat to the assets of Asian merchants was similar, although their means of retaliation might prove superior: see Parker, *Military Revolution,* 108.

18. D. Pacheco Pereira, *Esmeraldo de situ orbis,* ed. J. Barradas de Carvalho (Lisbon, 1991), 190f. Pacheco, who had played a prominent role in the exploration of the West African coast in the 1480s and served in Portuguese Asia in 1500–5, wrote his treatise between 1505 and 1508.

19. See details on pp. 68–73 above; and also H. Dubled, "L'artillerie royale française à l'époque de Charles VII et au début du règne de Louis XI (1437–69). Les frères Bureau," *Mémorial de l'artillerie française,* 50 (1976): 555–637.

20. Besides the sources quoted in *Military Revolution,* 190 n. 24, see K. R. DeVries, "A 1445 reference to shipboard artillery", *Technology and culture,* 31 (1990): 818–29; and N. A. T. Macdougall, "'The greattest schipp that ewer saillit in Ingland or France': James IV's 'Great Michael'", in Macdougall, ed., *Scotland and War AD 79–1918* (Edinburgh, 1991), 36–60. On subsequent developments, see the magisterial survey of Glete, *Navies and nations.*

21. On the latter conflict, see the important article of Weston F. Cook, "The cannon conquest of Nāṣrid Spain and the end of the Reconquista," *Journal of Military History,* 57 (1993): 43–70—infantry outnumbered cavalry by three to one in the Christian army and the standard infantry company included one arquebusier and one crossbowman for every three other soldiers.

22. Thomas Digges, *An arithmeticall militare treatise named Stratioticos, compendiously teaching the science of numbers ... requisite for the profession of a soldiour. Together with the moderne militare discipline* (London, 1579), fo 103. On fo 105 Digges proposed a "ring

march" to be maintained by detachments of 25 men who would fire and retire in sequence "so as the Head shal be sure always to have charged, before the taile have discharged; and this in a circulare martch, the skirmish all day continued." Descriptions and diagrams of the "ring march," again always involving small formations, appear in Thomas Styward, *The pathwaie to martiall discipline* (London, 1581), and William Garrard, *The arte of warre* (London 1591, but completed before 1587). Sir Francis Walsingham, Elizabeth's Secretary of State, in 1588, ordered the musketeers of all county militia units to practice "in that order which the Frenche men call 'à la file,' or as we terme yt in ranke," coming forward to fire and then retiring to reload while others did the same. (See A. J. Kempe, ed., *The Loseley Manuscripts. Manuscripts and other rare documents illustrative of some of the more minute particulars of English history, biography and manners* [London, 1835], 296–7.) It is worth recalling that the Japanese had already adopted this technique in the 1560s: see Parker, *Military revolution*, 140.

23. Martín de Eguiluz, *Milicia, discurso y regla militar* (Madrid, 1592: but written in 1586), fos 126v–127v, noting that after four rounds an arquebus overheated and could no longer be used accurately.

24. Digges, *Stratioticos* (1590), pp. 122–4. Again on p. 122 Digges notes that he described how "I would have them trained", not how troops actually did train.

25. It is possible that volley fire was used at the battle of Nieuwpoort in 1600. J. J. Orlers and M. van Haesten, *Den Nassausche Lauren-crans* (Leiden, 1610), fo 156 and battle plan, show ranks of Dutch musketeers in the Dunes exchanging fire at almost point-blank range with ranks of Spanish musketeers. The accompanying text notes that the troops "began to fire very fast": "'t volck op de Duynen vast aende handt quamen ende met musketten en roers heel dicht begonnen te schieten, alsoo inde Caert gehesien werdt." Other first hand accounts of the battle—such as the eye-witness accounts of Francis Vere, *Commentaries* (Cambridge, 1657), 81–105 and Lord Grey in *Calendar of the Manuscripts of the … Marquis of Salisbury*, vol. 10 (London, 1904; Historical Manuscripts Commission), 197–9—shed no further light on whether this was simply a protracted fire fight, or the first use of the countermarch volley in Europe. However Vere did note (*op. cit.*, p. 87f) that "by the situation of the country, that skill and dexterity we presumed to excel our enemies in, which was the apt and agile motions of our battalions, was utterly taken from us."

26. Data kindly supplied by (respectively) Bernard S. Bachrach and Donald E. Queller.

27. See P. Contamine, *Guerre, état et société à la fin du moyen âge. Etudes sur les armées du roi de France, 1337–1494* (Paris, 1972), 70, 73, 317; John A. Lynn, "Recalculating French army growth", 121–122 above; and Cook, "Cannon conquest," 47, 68.

28. Figures from Lynn, "Recalculating French army growth", pp. 122–123 above. Professor Lynn stressed the stability of these figures ("less military growth than might be expected": p. 123); but some would consider an increase of 100 percent significant.

29. G. Zeller, *Le siège de Metz par Charles-Quint* (Nancy, 1943), 35–6.

30. Even France, whose military record during the Thirty Years' War was indeed abysmal, did not operate without a grand strategy: see the forthcoming thesis of Derek Croxton, "Perceptions of strength, realities of war: Cardinal Mazarin's changing negotiating position, 1643–1648" (University of Illinois), with very different conclusions from those of D. Parrott on Richelieu's war: "The administration of the French Army during the ministry of Cardinal Richelieu" (Oxford D. Phil. thesis, 1985).

31. Zeller, *Siège de Metz*, 155, Charles V to Marie, 22 December 1552.

32. See details in H. Lutz, *Christianitas Afflicta: Europa, das Reich und die päpstliche Politik im Niedergang der Hegemonie Kaiser Karls V. (1552–1556)* (Göttingen, 1964), 46–158; F. Lot, *Recherches sur les effectifs*, 132.

33. For details on this dimension see E. Charrière, *Négociations de la France dans le Levant*, vol. 2 (Paris, 1850), 178 n.1: M. de Aramon, French ambassador to the Sultan, 20 January 1552. Charles V's agents intercepted the letter, providing welcome intimation that the Turks would not attack Hungary and thus freeing forces for use elsewhere: see K. Lanz, *Correspondenz Kaisers Karl V.*, vol. 3 (Leipzig, 1846), 137, Instruction to sieur de Rye, 22 March 1552.

34. See Parker, *Military Revolution*, 45, quoting contemporary "Relaciones" of Charles V's forces.

35. Lynn White Jr., *Medieval religion and technology. Collected essays* (Berkeley, 1986), 149 (from "Jacopo Aconcio as an engineer," first published in *American Historical Review*, 62 [1967]: 425–4.)

36. See the important strictures of S. Pepper and N. Adams, *Firearms and fortifications. Military architecture and siege warfare in sixteenth-century Siena* (Chicago, 1986), xxii.

37. See H. Koller, "Die mittelalterliche Stadtmauer als Grundlage staatliche Selbstbewusstseins," in B. Kirchgässner and G. Scholz, eds., *Stadt und Krieg* (Sigmaringer, 1989: *Stadt in der Geschichte*, xv), 9–25. France soon took over as the European center of artillery warfare, but by the 1490s Spain had 180 large and medium pieces and five state-run gun and powder factories: see Cook, "Cannon conquest," 52.

38. See the important chronology of the increasing force of artillery in Rogers, "Military Revolutions," pp. 64–65 above.

39. Bernaldez, *Memorias*, quoted by Cook, "Cannon conquest," 43; Machiavelli, *Art of War*, quoted Parker *The Military Revolution*, 10. See also the similar views of the late fifteenth-century military engineer di Giorgio discussed in F. P. Fiore, "L'architettura militare di Francesco di Giorgio: realizzazioni e trattati," in C. Cresti, A. Fara and D. Lamberini, eds., *Architettura militare nell' Europa del XVI secolo* (Siena, 1988), 35–47, at p. 40.

40. Machiavelli's "Relazione di una visita fatta per fortificare Firenze" in S. Bertelli, ed., *Niccolo Macchiavelli: Arte della guerra e scritti politici minori* (Milan, 1961), 289–302, at p. 295. See also the perceptive discussion of D. Lamberini, "La politica del guasto. L'impatto del fronte bastionato sulle preesistenze urbane," in Cresti, *Architettura militare*, 223–4.

41. Zeller, *Siège de Metz*, 219: Guise to Cardinal of Lorraine, 5 Dec. 1552; and J. Rigault, "Une relation inédite du siège de Metz en 1552," *Annales de l'Est*, 5th series 3 (1952): 293–306, at p. 298. Metz had only been captured in May, and a few months only allowed time to back the existing walls with earth, bales of wool, and other makeshifts (Zeller, 230). The siege of Haarlem, which lasted for seven months in 1572–3 because the medieval walls were backed by huge earthen ramparts, offers another, later example of Machiavelli's "third technique:" see the contemporary sketches reproduced in G. Schwartz and M. J. Bok, *Pieter Saenredam: de schilder in zijn tijd* (Maarssen, 1989), especially plates 28, 30 and 31 on pp. 38–9.

42. Fourquevaux, *Instructions sur le faict de la guerre* (Paris, 1548), fo. 85; Laparelli quoted in R. J. Tuttle, "Against fortifications: the defence of Renaissance Bologna", *Journal of the society of architectural historians*, 42 (1982): 198. For an earlier expression of the superiority of "bastioni" over "muro" see G. della Valle, *Vallo libro continente appertinente a capitanii, retenere et fortificare una città con bastioni* (2nd edn., Venice, 1531), book 1 fo. 6. Examples could be multiplied almost endlessly.

43. See, for example, Archives Nationales, Paris, 261AP44 liasse 1/1, Vauban memorandum on the course of the campaign, 12 June 1672; 261AP45 liasse 1/26, Vauban to Luxembourg, 18 August 1672, minute, and liasse 5/1, Vauban to Turenne, 29 August 1672. My thanks for these references, from Vauban's own archive, go to Paul Sonnino.

44. See the interesting discussion in J. F. Pernot, "Guerre de siège et places-fortes," in V. Barrie-Curien, ed., *Guerre et pouvoir au XVIIe siècle* (Paris, 1991), 129–50; and in Arnold, pp. 220–222 above.

45. See A. S. Tosini, "Cittadelle lombarde di fine '500: il castello di Milano nella prima età spagnola," in Cresti, *Architettura militare*, 207–17; and M. E. Mallett and J. R. Hale, *The military organization of a Renaissance state. Venice c. 1400 to 1617* (Cambridge, 1984), 409–28.

46. Data taken from W. Brulez, "Het gewicht van de oorlog in de nieuwe tijden. Enkele aspecten," *Tijdschrift voor Gechiedenis*, 91 (1978): 386–406, based on (inter alia) a comparison of the town plans made by Jacob van Deventer in the 1560s and by Johan Blaeu in the 1640s. See M. van Hemelrijck, *De Vlaamse Krijgsbouwkunde* (Tielt, 1950), 131–307, still provides the best overall survey of fortifications constructed in Belgium and northern France by the Habsburgs.

47. I am most grateful to Ir. B. Cox for sharing with me his fascinating reconstruction of Louis XIV's Grand Strategy, partially deduced from *Le théâtre militaire du Roi Louis XIV de France* (Paris, 1690).

48. J. Cruso, *Militarie instructions for the cavallrie* (Cambridge, 1632), 105; Boyle quoted in Parker, *Military Revolution*, 16; Behr in C. Duffy, *The Fortress in the age of Vauban and Frederick the Great, 1660–1789* (London, 1985), 13f. See also the useful discussion in Tallett, *War and society*, 50–54.

49. Sébastien le Prestre de Vauban, *Mémoire pour servir d'instruction dans la conduite des sièges et dans la défense des places* (circa 1670, but misdated 1704: Leiden, 1740), 3–5, checked against the manuscript copy in the Anna S. K. Brown Military Collection at the Hay Library, Providence, R. I., fos. 1–1v.

50. Vauban, *Traité de l'attaque des places* (Manuscript in the Anna S. K. Brown Military Collection at the Hay Library, Providence, R.I.: in the same volume as the *Mémoire*, second pagination, pp. 1–2.) This passage does not appear in Sébastien le Prestre de Vauban, *De l'attaque et de la defense des places*, 2 vols. (The Hague, 1737–42, but written circa 1704), although in other respects the two works are almost identical. The Brown Manuscript appears to be an interim draft, written at some point between 1670 and 1704.

51. This ceased to be true only when various governments in the later eighteenth century chose to invest in roads rather than in walls. The cost was much the same, but the speed of movement permitted by the new road network finally rendered a defensive system based on heavily fortified strongpoints both ineffective and uneconomical. See Parker, *Military Revolution*, chap. 5; reinforced by H. Eichberg, "Zirkel der Vernichtung oder Kreislauf des Kriegsgewinns? Zur Ökonomie der Festung im 17. Jahrhundert," in Kirchgässner and Scholz, *Stadt und Krieg*, 105–24.

52. Carl von Clausewitz, *On war* (ed. M. Howard and P. Paret, 2nd edn., Princeton, 1984), 487 (book VI chap. 27) and 596 (book VIII chap. 4.) The most perceptive modern treatment of this question is A. Beyerchen, "Clausewitz, non-linearity and the unpredictability of war," *International Security* 17.3 (1992–3), 59–90.

53. A. Oschmann, *Der Nürnberger Executionstag 1649–50. Das Ende des dreissigjährigen Krieges in Deutschland* (Münster, 1991), 506–20 and 550–67. In fact Clausewitz did recog-

nize the problem presented by the *trace italienne* in another part of his work: "In theaters of war where there are plenty of fortresses, almost every movement turns on their possession. The attacker tries to approach them unexpectedly, using various feints, while the defender attempts to forestall this by means of well–planned movements. That was characteristic of almost all campaigns in the Low Countries between the days of Louis XIV and those of Marshal Saxe." (Clausewitz, *On War*, 505—book VI chap. 30.) Actually it remained "characteristic" from the 1570s, not just the 1670s.

54. *Nueva colección de documentos inéditos para la historia de España*, vol. 5 (Madrid, 1894), 368: Don Luis de Requeséns to Philip II, 6 October 1574; British Library, *Additional Ms* 28,388 fos 70v–71, Requeséns to Don Gaspar de Quiroga, August 1575.

55. Francis I, considering his bastion-studded northern frontier to be proof against attack, had sent an army to Italy, where a large part of its strength was immediately dissipated in garrisoning 16 towns and 28 forts. But the king overlooked the fact that his eastern frontier was less secure until the emperor brought this omission dramatically to his attention by leading an army of some 42,000 men through Lorraine and on towards Paris. The scale of Charles V's ambitions appears from his campaign map, which portrays France as his army would have seen it from Lorraine: Fontainebleau, Francis I's favorite residence, is shown at the upper right. (See D. Buisseret, ed., *Monarchs, ministers and maps. The emergence of cartography as a tool of government in early modern Europe* [Chicago, 1992], color plate 7.) One set of medieval walls after another fell before the Imperial siege train: Commercy, which Francis I had expected to hold out for 3 weeks, surrendered after 3 days; Ligny fell almost as swiftly. Only St Dizier, a mere 125 miles from Paris, resisted—because it was equipped with a *trace italienne*—but the garrison ran out of ammunition and surrendered after six weeks. The Imperial forces went on to capture Vitry, Joinville, Vaucouleurs, Châtillon-sur-Marne, Château-Thierry and on 10 September Soissons, while another army in the north besieged and took Boulogne. On 18 September Francis made peace. A better advertisement for the superiority of the *trace italienne* would be hard to find. See C. Paillard and G. Hérelle, *L'invasion allemande en 1544: fragments d'une histoire militaire et diplomatique de l'expédition de Charles V* (Paris, 1884); R. J. Knecht, *Francis I* (Cambridge 1982), 362–76; and F. Lot, *Recherches sur les effectifs des armées françaises des Guerres d'Italie aux Guerres de Religion, 1494–1562* (Paris, 1962), 83, 90–108.

56. On the diffusion, see the sources cited in Parker, *Military Revolution*, 159 n. 18; and the chapters by L. Zangheri, C. van den Heuvel, Z. Wazbinski, and A. M. Porciatti, in Cresti, *L'architettura militare*.

57. Quotations and data from Parker, *Military Revolution*, 69 and 183 n. 78.

58. See Zeller, *Siège de Metz*, 35, 73–7 and 82.

59. On page 177 above, Lynn admits that his "sample might invite the criticism that it is not based on first-hand archival research" but argues that this "is not a fatal flaw" because "those claiming to see a strong relationship between army size and fortification have not, to my knowledge, presented any such sample, archival or otherwise, in defense of their claims." True, such a series should be compiled; but the lack of alternatives does not of itself validate a misleading quasi-statistical exercise. Lynn's meticulous archival-based data assembled for his "French army size" project (chap. 5 above) is, by contrast, a model of its kind for which all military historians will be grateful, and it shows the way forward.

60. Above, pp. 178, 177, 198 n. 24.

61. J. Blaeu, *Toonneel der Steden van 's Konigs Nederlanded met hare Beschrijvingen* (Amsterdam, 1649), sig. iiij B; illustration, history and description of St. Omer. The fortifications also stand out clearly in the maps of A. Sanderns, *Flandria illustrata* (Cologne, 1641).

62. Sébastien le Prestre de Vauban, *De l'attaque et de la défense des places,* 2 vols. (The Hague, 1737–42, but written circa 1704), 1: 2–3, collated with one of the five surviving original manuscripts in the Anna S. K. Brown Military Collection at the Hay Library, Providence, Rhode Island, fos. 2v–3. Far more will become known about Vauban's views when his personal archive in the Collection Rosanbo, at present on deposit in the Archives Nationales series AP261 but accessible to few scholars, can be consulted.

63. See, for example, the print of the French siege of Breisach in 1638, which clearly shows an Imperial relief army waiting in its fortified camp, in Parker, *Military Revolution,* 15. For another example, this time from the Low Countries, see the heavily entrenched relief army lurking on the far left beyond the siegeworks around Breda in 1624–5 in the illustrations to S. Zurawski, "New sources for Jacques Callot's Map of the siege of Breda," *The Art Bulletin,* 70 (1988): 621–39.

64. Archivio di Stato, Venice, *Misc. Cod. Storia Veneta* 143 no 21, fos. 223ff. I owe this reference to the generosity of Sir John Hale.

65. See M. S. Kingra, "The *Trace Italienne* and the Military Revolution during the Eighty Years' War, 1567–1648," *Journal of Military History,* 57 (1993): 431–46, at p. 437.

66. Figures from G. Parker, *The Army of Flanders and the Spanish Road. The logistics of Spanish victory and defeat in the Low Countries' Wars 1567–1659* (Cambridge, 1972), 11–12. Two years earlier a senior officer of the Army of Flanders claimed that garrisons alone required 44,000 soldiers: Archivo General de Simancas, *Estado* 2051 fo 225, Don Miguel de Salamanca to Philip IV, 8 February, 1637. On the importance of garrisons in the Dutch army, see H. L. Zwitzer, *'De militie van den Staat.' Het leger van de Republiek der Verenigde Nederlanden* (Amsterdam, 1991), 36–37.

67. See Lynn, "The *trace italienne,*" page 183 above. See also the remarkable figures on the size and regional impact of French garrisons in C. Sturgill, "The French army in Roussillon," in J. M. Ultee, ed., *Adapting to conditions: war and society in the eighteenth century* (Tuscaloosa, AL, 1986), 16–25.

68. On page 178 above Lynn only partially reproduces Vauban's calculations concerning the size of garrison required to defend an artillery fort: 600 foot and 60 cavalry per bastion, making a total of 3960 for a stronghold of six bastions. But Vauban went on to note that where outworks exist, the garrison must be increased accordingly—a further 600–700 for each outlying fort capable of resisting artillery bombardment; 600 for each hornwork; 150 for any redoubt. So the total garrison needed for Vauban's new-style defenses could be very large indeed. See Vauban, *Mémoire pour servir d'instruction dans la conduite des sièges et dans la défense des places* (Leiden, 1740, but drawn up circa 1670), 194–5.

69. See, for example, P. Contamine, "Les fortifications urbaines en France à la fin du Moyen Age: aspects financiers et économiques," *Revue historique,* 260 (1978): 23–47.

70. See H. Soly, "Cités marchandes et besoins de sécurité: les fortifications d'Anvers au XVIe siècle: coûts économiques et sociaux" in A. Guarducci, ed., *Investimenti e civiltà urbana, secoli XIII–XVIII* (Florence, 1989), 183–97, at pp. 188f. Brulez, "Het gewicht van de oorlog," 395, calculates the cost of the 27 miles of *trace italienne* built in the Netherlands between 1529 and 1572 at 10 million florins, little of it paid from central funds.

71. Mallett and Hale, *Military organization*, 409; see also 468–72.

72. Kingra, "The *Trace italienne*," 440f, argues on the basis of the *Staten van Oorlog* of the States-General alone that "the Dutch were not building new bastionned fortresses at a rate to match, or bring about, so massive an increase in army size." This may be true, but his figures do not prove it. For some idea of the complex arrangements used to finance fortifications in the Dutch Republic, see M. C. 't Hart, *The making of a bourgeois state. War, politics and finance during the Dutch Republic* (Manchester, 1993), 81 (and passim); H. A. van Oerle, *Leiden binnen en buiten de Stadsvesten. De Geschiedenis van de stedebouwkundige ontwikkeling binnen het Leidse rechtsgebied tot het einde van de gouden eeuw*, 2 vols. (Leiden, 1975), 1: 251–349; and W. A. van Ham, *Merck toch hoe sterck. Bijdragen tot de geschiedenis van de vestingwerken van Bergen op Zoom* (Bergen op Zoom, 1982), 36–72.

73. See K. Roberts, "Musters and May Games: the effect of changing military theory on the English militia," *Cromwelliana*, (1991), 5–9; and J. Stoye, *English travellers abroad, 1604–67. Their influence in English society and politics* (revised edn., New Haven, 1989), 190.

74. See details in R. Loeber and G. Parker, "The military revolution in seventeenth century Ireland," in J. H. Ohlmeyer, ed., *Ireland from independence to occupation, 1641–60* (Cambridge, 1995), 66–88; and E. M. Furgol, "Scotland turned Sweden: the Scottish Covenanters and the Military Revolution" in J. Morrill, ed., *The Scottish National Covenant in its British Context, 1638–51* (Edinburgh, 1990), 134–54.

75. See R. A. Stradling, *The Spanish Monarchy and Irish mercenaries. The Wild Geese in Spain 1618–68* (Dublin, 1994), 91: the commanders were Owen Roe O'Neill, who had served Spain between 1605 and 1642, and Robert Monro, who had fought first for Denmark and then for Sweden in Germany from 1627 to 1634.

76. For England, see the review article of H. J. Braddick, "An English military revolution?" *Historical Journal*, 36 (1993): 965–75 (quotation from p. 975).

77. See L. Zangheri, "Gli architetti italiani e la difesa dei territori dell'Impero minacciati dai turchi" in Cresti, *Architettura militare*, 243–51; and R. Schäfer, "Festungsbau an der Türkengrenze. Die Pfandschaft Rann im 16. Jahrhundert," *Zeitschrift des historiches Vereins für Steiermark*, 75 (1984): 31–59.

78. R. Fruin and J. W. Kernkamp, eds., *Brieven van Johan de Witt*, vol 1. (Amsterdam, 1906: Werken uitgegeven door het historisch Genootschap, 3rd series 18), 326–7: de Witt to Jan van Sijpesteyn, 23 June 1656.

79. On Poland see R. I. Frost, "The Polish-Lithuanian Commonwealth and the 'Military Revolution'" in *Poland and Europe. Historical Dimensions* (forthcoming); and Z. Wazbinski, "Bernardo Morando e il suo contributo alla difesa dei confini orientali della Polonia," in Cresti, *Architettura militare*, 271–8. On Russia, see the forthcoming thesis of W. Reger, *In the service of the Tsar* (University of Illinois.) See also further references in the notes to Parker, *Military Revolution*, 37–9.

80. See the perceptive review by J. Aubin in *Bulletin critique des annales islamologiques*, 1990, no 6. pp. 153–5. D. Ralston, *Importing the European Army: the introduction of European military techniques and institutions into the extra-European world, 1600–1914* (Chicago, 1990), sheds little light on this; but see the interesting case studies of C. F. Finkel, "French mercenaries in the Habsburg-Ottoman war of 1593–1606: the desertion of the Papa garrison to the Ottomans in 1600," *Bulletin of the School of Oriental and African Studies*, 55 (1992): 451–71; R. Murphey, "The Ottoman attitude towards the adoption of Western technology: the role of the *Efrenci* technicians in civil and military applications," in J. L.

Bacqué-Grammont and P. Dumont, eds., *Contributions à l'histoire économique et sociale de l'empire ottoman* (Louvain, 1983), 287–98; and S. Christensen, "European-Ottoman military acculturation in the late Middle Ages," in B. P. McGuire, ed., *War and peace in the Middle Ages* (Copenhagen, 1987), 227–51.

81. See W. F. Cook, *The Hundred Years War for Morocco. Gunpowder and the Military Revolution in the early modern Muslim world* (Boulder, 1994), quotation from p. 193. On the spread of Western military techniques to the other Islamic states of North Africa see A. C. Hess, *The Forgotten Frontier. A history of the sixteenth-century Ibero-African frontier* (Chicago, 1978); on the changing pattern of war in the Muslim states of early modern Indonesia see A. R. Reid, *Southeast Asia in the age of commerce: expansion and crisis 1450–1680* (New Haven, 1993), 87–90, 224–33.

82. J. F. Richards, *The Mughal Empire* (Cambridge, 1993: The New Cambridge History of India, vol. I.5), 288–9. In Ch'ing China too, despite the keen interest of many government officials in military technology, most innovations involving firearms remained the work of foreigners of limited practical experience: see J. Waley-Cohen, "China and Western technology in the later eighteenth century," *American Historical Review*, 98 (1993): 1525–44.

83. W. J. Hamblin, "Gunpowder weapons and medieval Islamic military theory" (Paper graciously sent to me by Dr Hamblin in October 1989). See also chapters 4 and 12 above. On the remarkable logistical achievements of the Ottoman empire, see C. Finkel, *The administration of warfare: the Ottoman military campaigns in Hungary, 1593–1606* (Vienna, 1988: Beihefte zur Wiener Zeitschrift für die Kunde des Morgenlandes, XIV.) On the size of early modern East Asian armies, see *The Military Revolution*, 136–45.

About the Book and Editor

THE DEBATE ABOUT the "Military Revolution" has been one of the most controversial and exciting areas of discussion and research in the fields of early modern European history and military history. Scholars have long sought to explain the massive changes in European military techniques and technologies that took place between the end of the Middle Ages and the beginning of the industrial age—changes that transformed the armies and navies of the West into the most powerful war-making entities the world had ever known.

Historians have disagreed about and vigorously debated the importance of these changes for European politics, for the process of state formation, for the rise of the West, and for warfare itself. This book brings together, for the first time, the classic articles that began and have shaped this debate, adding important new essays by eminent historians of early modern Europe to further this important scholarly interchange. The contributors consider topics ranging from the battlefield to the gunmaker's workshop, from England to India, and from the fourteenth to the eighteenth centuries. *The Military Revolution Debate* will be required reading for anyone interested in what is undoubtedly one of the hottest areas in military history today.

Clifford J. Rogers is an Olin Fellow in Military and Strategic History at Yale University.

About the Contributors

Simon Adams is Senior Lecturer in History at the University of Strathclyde. His related work includes co-editorship of *England, Spain, and the* Gran Armada, *1585–1604* (1991) and the sixteenth-century entries in the English edition of André Corvisier (ed.), *A Dictionary of Military History* (revised and edited by John Childs, 1994).

Thomas F. Arnold is Assistant Professor of History at Yale University. He is currently working on two books: *Blood and Stone: Fortifications and Statecraft of the Gonzaga, 1530–1630*, a larger discussion of the issues sketched in his essay for this volume, and *The Geometry of Power*, an analysis of the relationship between the science of geometry and the practice and understanding of war in early modern Europe.

Jeremy Black is Professor of History at the University of Durham, where he has taught since 1980. A graduate of Queens' Cambridge, he is a member of the Councils of the Royal Historical Society and the British Records Association. His eighteen books include *Pitt the Elder, European Warfare 1660–1815, Culloden and the '45, War for America: The Fight for Independence, 1776–1783*, and *The Politics of Britain 1688–1800*.

John F. Guilmartin, Jr., is Associate Professor of History at The Ohio State University. His related publications include *Gunpowder and Galleys. Changing Technology and Mediterranean Warfare at Sea in the Sixteenth Century* (1974), "Ideology and Conflict: The Wars of the Ottoman Empire, 1453–1606," *Journal of Interdisciplinary History* 18 (1988), and "The Cutting Edge: An Analysis of the Spanish Invasion and Overthrow of the Inca Empire, 1532–1539," in K. J. Andrien and R. Adorno, eds., *Transatlantic Encounters* (1991).

Colin Jones is Professor of History at the University of Exeter. His books include *The Cambridge Illustrated History of France* (1994), *The Longman Companion to the French Revolution* (1990), and *The Charitable Imperative: Hospitals and nursing in the Ancien Régime and revolutionary France* (1989).

John A. Lynn is Professor of History at the University of Illinois at Urbana-Champaign and also holds the Brigadier General Harold L. Oppenheimer Chair of Warfighting Strategy at the Marine Corps University for 1994–1995. His publications include "How War Fed War: The Tax of Violence and Contributions During the *grand siècle,*" *Journal of Modern History* 65 (1993), *Bayonets of the Republic: Motivation and Tactics in the Army of Revolutionary France, 1791–94* (1984), and (ed.) *Feeding Mars: Logistics in Western Warfare from the Middle Ages to the Present* (Westview, 1993).

Geoffrey Parker holds the Robert A. Lovett chair in Military and Naval History at Yale University. He has authored, co-authored, or edited over twenty books, including *The Army of Flanders and the Spanish Road, 1567–1659* (1972), *The Dutch Revolt* (1977), *Philip II* (1978), *The Thirty Years War* (1984), and *The Military Revolution. Military innovation and the rise of the West* (1988). He is a Fellow of the British Academy and of the Spanish Royal Academy of History.

David A. Parrott is Fellow and Tutor in Modern History at New College, Oxford. Dr. Parrott is a member of the Editorial Board of the journal *War in History.*

Michael Roberts, currently at the Institute of Social and Economic Research of Rhodes University, was formerly Professor of History at the Queen's University of Belfast. His books include *Gustavus Adolphus. A history of Sweden, 1611–1631* (1953, 1958), *Essays in Swedish History* (1967), *The Early Vasas: A history of Sweden, 1523–1611* (1968), and *British Diplomacy and Swedish Politics, 1758–1773* (1980).

Clifford J. Rogers is an Olin Fellow in Military and Strategic History at Yale University. His publications include "Edward III and the Dialectics of Strategy, 1327–1360," in the *Transactions of the Royal Historical Society* (1994), and "By Fire and Sword: *Bellum Hostile* and 'Civilians' in the Hundred Years War," in Mark Grimsley (ed.), *Civilians in the Path of War* (forthcoming).

I.A.A. Thompson is currently a Fellow of the University of Keele. His publications include *War and Government in Habsburg Spain, 1560–1620* (1976), *War and Society in Habsburg Spain* (1992), and "Castile: Polity, Fiscality, and Fiscal Crisis," in P. Hoffman and K. Norberg (eds.), *Fiscal Crises, Liberty and Representative Government, 1450–1789* (1994). Until recently, he was Editor of *Parliaments, Estates and Representation.*

Index

LaVergne, TN USA
08 October 2010

200057LV00003B/1/A